# Ethical Dilemmas and Decisions in Criminal Justice

*Fifth Edition*

## Joycelyn M. Pollock

*Texas State University—San Marcos*

**WADSWORTH**
CENGAGE Learning™

Australia • Brazil • Japan • Korea • Mexico • Singapore • Spain • United Kingdom • United States

*To Eric and Gregory, as always.*

WADSWORTH
CENGAGE Learning™

**Ethical Dilemmas and Decisions in Criminal Justice, Fifth Edition**
**Joycelyn M. Pollock**

Acquistions Editor:
Carolyn Henderson Meier

Assistant Editor: Jana Davis

Editorial Assistant:
Rebecca Johnson

Technology Project Manager:
Amanda Kaufmann

Marketing Manager: Terra Schultz

Marketing Assistant: Jaren Boland

Marketing Communications
Manager: Linda Yip

Project Manager, Editorial
Production: Matt Ballantyne

Creative Director: Rob Hugel

Art Director: Vernon Boes

Print Buyer: Rebecca Cross

Permissions Editor: Bob Kauser

Production Service: Matrix
Productions, Inc.

Text Designer: Rebecca Evans

Photo Researcher: Cheri Throop

Copy Editor: Donald Pharr

Cover Designer: Yvo Riezebos
Design/Hatty Lee

Cover Image: Royalty-free/Corbis

Compositor: Integra

For product information and technology assistance, contact us at **Cengage Learning Customer & Sales Support, 1-800-354-9706**

For permission to use material from this text or product, submit all requests online at
**www.cengage.com/permissions**
Further permissions questions can be emailed to
**permissionrequest@cengage.com**

Library of Congress Control Number: 2005938713

ISBN-13: 978-0-495-09343-5
ISBN-10: 0-495-09343-2

**Wadsworth**
10 Davis Drive
Belmont, CA 94002-3098
USA

Cengage Learning is a leading provider of customized learning solutions with office locations around the globe, including Singapore, the United Kingdom, Australia, Mexico, Brazil, and Japan. Locate your local office at:
**international.cengage.com/region**

Cengage Learning products are represented in Canada by Nelson Education, Ltd.

For your course and learning solutions, visit
**academic.cengage.com**

Purchase any of our products at your local college store or at our preferred online store **www.ichapters.com**

Printed in Canada
3 4 5 6 7 8 11 10 09 08

# Contents

# Preface

The first edition of this book was published in 1986, when there were very few texts for a course covering criminal justice ethics. In each subsequent edition, there have been important events that have shaped the content. For instance, the Rodney King incident occurred between the second and third editions; the Ramparts scandal occurred between the third and fourth editions; and, of course, this edition includes the Abu Ghraib incident. Since the first edition, this text has provided the basic philosophical principles necessary to analyze ethical dilemmas, but it has also included current news events in criminal justice to show how these analytical tools can be used in real life. To be sure, there is never a shortage of ethical issues to be gleaned from current events.

The book identifies themes that run through the entire system so that, for instance, issues such as discretion and due process are discussed in chapters concerning practitioners in law enforcement, the courts, and corrections. Although there are many texts available today on law enforcement ethics, there are fewer that treat the system as a whole. Also, this text offers the reader an essential primer on the ethical systems before addressing the dilemmas of practitioners. The other feature that we believe is unique to this text is the expanded chapters on justice and the law. It is important to understand not just the dilemmas that criminal justice professionals may face but also how their experiences relate to larger questions, such as the definition of justice.

## New to This Edition

Since the first edition, each chapter has offered ethical dilemmas to be used to apply the principles of ethical decision making. Many of these dilemmas have been supplied by police officers, probation officers, and students or others who work in the field, or have been adapted from current events. In this edition we have expanded the learning tools at the front and back of the chapter to include glossaries, enhanced reading lists, discussion questions, and study review questions. Inside every chapter except for the last one is a Policy box that shows how policy issues in criminal justice always have ethical implications. We have kept and added to the quotations featured in each chapter, but have accompanied them with "queries" to aid the instructor in leading the discussion of the principles involved. There are also class exercises, where appropriate, for the instructor to use in classroom discussions.

The last edition was published close on the heels of the tragedy of the World Trade Center attack. That event forever destroyed this country's sense of invulnerability and created fear and disquiet that continue to affect people's lives. The world seems a more dangerous place. The result has been a reordering of the nation's priorities and a mammoth federalization of law enforcement. Before September 11, 2001, the issues that might have been at the forefront of a discussion of ethics in the criminal justice system would have been racial profiling, how to address the drug problem, corruption by public or private leaders, and how to treat juvenile offenders. These issues are still important, but we must add to them a discussion of what is acceptable in war and in our fight against terrorism. Do these "ends" justify torture? Do they justify curtailing the civil liberties of resident aliens? Of citizens? I have tried to address these questions either directly or indirectly in several chapters of this edition.

Changes in this edition are, to some degree, reflective of the concerns expressed by the book's reviewers. I have attempted to make the chapters more equal in length and have increased the number to fifteen. I have also reworked the chapters to improve the logic and flow of the material. Chapters 1 and 2 remain substantially the same, but Chapter 3 now includes material on analyzing moral dilemmas that will prepare students for thinking about public policy (this information appeared in a couple of sections in Chapter 14 of the previous edition). Chapter 3 also includes a discussion of how someone develops into a moral person. Chapter 4 has now been divided into two chapters so that Chapter 4 deals with justice and Chapter 5 provides an expanded discussion of the law and the individual, bringing forward some material from Chapter 6. Chapter 6 now is titled "Ethics and the Criminal Justice Professional" and has some new material, as well as material that had previously been in several other chapters. This chapter is a response to reviewers' comments that suggested a more direct treatment of how the material applies to criminal justice professionals. This chapter now sets the stage for the second section of the book, which deals with the three subsystems (police, courts, and corrections).

The chapters on professionals have new material taken from current news items, as well as some revisions of chapter organization. The police chapters have been reworked to some degree and retitled to more closely reflect their content. The law chapters have been reworked to provide an expanded discussion of judicial ethics. This allows for a discussion of judicial independence that is picked up again in the last chapter. The chapters on corrections remain mostly unchanged but have been updated with recent events. The last chapter presents an expanded discussion of the "means–end" argument as related to terrorism—i.e., the idea that it is acceptable to use any means to fight terrorism is similar to earlier arguments referring to crime control. The literature on "just-war" arguments has been added to the discussion on the government's response to terrorism. It is also noted that the "war on terror" is central to the criminal justice system today because we have seen a federalization of law enforcement since 9/11 and the response to the terror threat has become the responsibility of even municipal police agencies.

In every edition I must balance the desire of some reviewers to lengthen the discussion of ethical systems and the philosophy of ethics against the desire of users who teach the course with a more direct focus on criminal justice issues. I have come to the conclusion that it is impossible to continue to add or expand discussions of philosophical topics such as existentialism, the social contract theory, Rawls's conceptions of justice, and moral pluralism. I could, but the book would keep expanding, and I could never cover these topics as well as a philosophy text and still discuss current issues in criminal justice. I would encourage and expect that those who are dissatisfied with the treatment of the ethical systems will use a second book written by an ethicist who will more comprehensively cover these issues. I believe that the greater value of this text is its coverage of current issues that exist in the criminal justice system, supplemented by basic ethical theory that will give students a good introduction to important terms and concepts. In this text, I have covered the Abu Ghraib prison scandal, the controversy over the use of torture, the aftermath of the New Orleans flood, recent Supreme Court holdings, the controversy surrounding some legislators' public criticism of federal justices over their rulings, and many other current events.

# Supplements

The following supplemental aids have been developed to enhance the course and to assist instructors and students. They are available to qualified adopters. Please consult your local sales representative for details.

### Instructor's Resource Manual with Test Bank

I have authored this helpful manual, which includes resources that will maximize your time and effort in preparing for your course: Detailed Chapter Outlines, Learning Objectives, Key Terms, and Lecture Suggestions, as well as a Test Bank of more than 600 questions in multiple choice, true/false, fill-in-the-blank, and essay formats.

### eBank PowerPoint Presentations

These handy PowerPoint slides, which outline the chapters of the main text in a classroom-ready presentation, will help you in making your lectures engaging and in reaching your visually oriented students.

# Acknowledgments

It is impossible to remember all the people who contribute to one's thinking in a field of study as rich as ethics. I am continuously impressed with the work of others and enriched by their contributions. If I list some—e.g., John Crank, Michael Caldero, Mickey Braswell, Carl Klockars, Tim Prenzler, Sam Souryal, and Vic Kappeler—unfortunately, I will forget others unfairly. I also thank those who have contacted me after using the book in a college classroom or training course. Such feedback is always welcome. Some of these individuals have provided commentary or criticim that has been very helpful. I thank, for instance, Michael Geary, Tom Martinelli, and Jack Van Steenburg, who have shared with me their thoughts and experiences. The anonymous reviewers provided astute, comprehensive feedback that greatly assisted me in creating this new edition. They are: Dennis W. Catlin, Northern Arizona University; Carl Franklin, Southern Utah University; Stanley K. Shernock, Norwich University; and Billy J. Slaton, Mercer University.

Reviewers from the previous editions have also given valuable advice that continues to shape this text. They are: Cyndi Banks, Northern Arizona University; Thomas Barker, Jacksonville State University; John Broderick, Stonehill College; David Carter, Michigan State University; Dennis Catlin, Northern Arizona University; Bradley S. Chilton, The University of Toledo; Lee Colwell, The University of Arkansas, Little Rock; John Conley, University of Wisconsin, Milwaukee; Walt Copley, Metropolitan State College of Denver; Jane Foraker-Thompson, Boise State University; Carl Franklin, Southern Utah University; Tara Gray, New Mexico State University; James Houston, Appalachian State University; Mark Jones, East Carolina University; Richard Kania, University of North Carolina, Pembroke; John Kleinig, John Jay College of Criminal Justice; Lee Libby, Washington State Community College; Tom Mahoney, University of California Santa Barbara; Nicholas Meier, Kalamazoo Valley Community College; Thomas Reed, Eastern Kentucky State University; Roy Roberg, San Jose State University; Stanley Shernock, Norwich University; B. J. Slaton, Mercer University; Bud Stephenson, Weber State College; Emilio Viano, American University; Mihi Vohryzek-Bolden, California State University, Sacramento; and Julius Wachtel, California State University, Fullerton.

The staff members at Wadsworth have been integral to the development as well. They are: Carolyn Henderson Meier, Senior Acquisitions Editor; Jana Davis, Assistant Editor and Development Editor; Terra Schultz, Marketing Manager; Matt Ballantyne, Production Project Manager; Bob Kauser, Permissions Editor; and Rebecca Johnson, Editorial Assistant. Thanks also to Aaron Downey at Matrix Productions and my copyeditor Donald Pharr. As always, I thank my husband Eric and my son Greg. They are eternally patient and endure my long nights and lost weekends without complaint.

# Ethical Dilemmas and Decisions in Criminal Justice

"What is good?" and "what is evil?" are questions that have been asked by all the great philosophers, such as Plato and Aristotle.

# 1
# Morality, Ethics, and Human Behavior

*Why Study Ethics?*

*Defining Terms*

*Morality and the Law*

*Morality and Behavior*

*Analyzing Ethical Dilemmas*

*Conclusion*

## Key Terms

| | |
|---|---|
| *actus reus* | moral rules |
| age of reason | morals |
| applied ethics | negligence |
| discretion | normative ethics |
| duties | *parens patriae* |
| ethical dilemma | professional ethics |
| ethical issues | proximate cause |
| ethics | public servants |
| Good Samaritan laws | recklessness |
| guidelines | regulations |
| imperfect duties | standards |
| intent | superogatories |
| knowing | universalists |
| laws | values |
| *mens rea* | wholesight |
| meta-ethics | |

# Chapter Objectives

1. Become familiar with the major arguments supporting the importance of studying ethics in the criminal justice field.

2. Understand the vocabulary of ethics—that is, morals, ethics, values, ethical codes, ethical standards, and dilemmas.

3. Understand how to analyze an ethical dilemma.

4. Become sensitive to the types of ethical dilemmas faced in one's professional life.

Consider the following dilemma: You are a police officer patrolling late at night and see a car weaving back and forth across lanes of traffic. You turn on your siren, and the car pulls over. The driver stumbles out of the car, obviously intoxicated. There is no question that the driver meets the legal definition of intoxication. He also happens to be your father. What would you do?

Or decide what you would do in this case: You are a correctional officer working the late night shift. Your sergeant and another officer from the day shift come onto the tier where you are working and ask you to open up an inmate's cell. You do so, they enter the cell, and you hear a series of sounds, including grunts, cries, and moans. They exit, muttering about how the inmate has been taught a lesson. You believe that you have just been a party to an assault, but say nothing. The next night, you find out that the inmate never reported the incident, nor did any other inmates. You believe that if you come forward and report what you saw, you will be severely ostracized, that you may not even be believed (especially if the inmate doesn't back you up), and that you might lose your job. What would you do?

Finally, consider this: You are a student interning in a criminal defense lawyer's office. As part of your duties, you sit in court with the lawyer you are working with, help her with legal research, and assist in interviewing witnesses. During the course of the internship you conclude that the lawyer is, in your opinion, extremely negligent. She does not return client calls, she misses appeal deadlines, and she ignores or does not follow up on promising leads that might lead to exculpatory evidence. You are appalled that several of her clients are advised to plead guilty, even though you think that the evidence against them is weak. After bringing up these issues with her, she fires you on the spot and tells you that all her clients are guilty anyway and that she is just another "cog in the wheel" of the justice machine. What, if anything, would you do?

# Why Study Ethics?

How would you decide what to do in these situations? Learning how to determine the "right thing to do" is the central purpose of this book. We make ethical decisions all the time, whether we recognize them or not. Think about some ethical choices you have been faced with in the last couple weeks or months. Perhaps you have been faced with one of the following ethical choices:

1. At work you were asked to cover for a friend who wanted to go home early and not report the time lost.
2. A co-worker took something from the store where you both worked and expected you to say nothing.
3. A friend asked you to lie for him.
4. You felt compelled to tell a professor a "white lie" when asking for an extension on an assignment or for a different test time.

All of us make choices that can be judged under ethical standards. Furthermore, we frequently judge other people's behaviors as right or wrong. Criminal justice professionals, whether they work in law enforcement, the courts, or corrections, experience a multitude of situations where they must make choices that can be judged after the fact as right or wrong. A characteristic of every criminal justice profession is that the role entails a public trust that involves power over others. Those who have such power over others must be especially sensitive to the ethical issues that may arise in their professional lives.

The criminal justice system is often examined using political, organizational, or sociological approaches. Let us shift the lens somewhat and look at the system through an ethics perspective. Whether something is legal, for instance, is not necessarily asking the same question as whether something is right. Actors at every stage of the justice process make decisions that can be analyzed and judged as ethical or unethical. Although the decisions they face may be different, there are also similarities, especially in the use of **discretion** and the presence of authority and power.

Legislators have the power to define behavior as illegal and therefore punishable. They also have the power to set the amount of punishment. They do so usually from some rationale of public safety, but also employ moral definitions for deciding which behaviors should be legal and which should be illegal. For instance, there is obviously a public-safety rationale for laws against murder or armed robbery, but is there a public-safety rationale for laws that prohibit same-sex marriages? It seems that the only argument against same-sex marriages is a purely moral one. "Protection of public morality" is the rationale for a number of other laws, including sodomy between consenting adults, drug laws, gambling, and prostitution. How do legislators use their great discretion to balance the rights of *all* people? Further, how do criminal justice leaders guide their subordinates in implementing the laws in a fair and just manner? Chapters 4 and 5 explore these questions in more detail.

Police officers have a great deal of discretionary power:

1. The power to deprive people of their liberty (through arrest).
2. The power to decide which individuals to investigate and perhaps target for undercover operations.
3. The power to issue a ticket or provide "mercy" and let a driver off with a warning.

Police serve as the interface between the awesome power of the state and the citizenry governed. In some countries, police operate as a fearsome coercive force for a controlling political body. In this country, a very small number of people see police operating in a similar way; however, we enjoy constitutional protections against untrammeled police power, and police are guardians of the law, not enforcers of power holders. In Chapters 7, 8, and 9, the ethical use of police discretion will be discussed in more detail.

Prosecutors probably face the least public scrutiny of all criminal justice professionals, which is ironic since they possess a great deal of discretion in deciding who and how to prosecute:

1. They decide which charges to pursue and which to drop.
2. They decide which cases to take to a grand jury.
3. They decide how to prosecute a case and whether to pursue the death penalty in homicide cases.
4. They make decisions about the types of crimes to pursue, affecting police officers' enforcement decisions.

Prosecutors have ethical duties to pursue "justice" rather than conviction, but some argue that, at times, their decision making seems to be influenced by politics.

Judges also possess incredible power, typically employed through decision making in the following areas:

1. Denying or accepting plea bargains
2. Decisions regarding rules of evidence
3. Decisions about sentencing

Chapters 10 and 11 explore the ethical issues of legal professionals in the criminal justice system.

Finally, correctional officials also have immense powers over the lives of certain citizens:

1. Probation officers make recommendations in pre-sentence reports and violation reports that affect whether an individual goes to prison.
2. Prison officials decide to award and take away "good time," and they make decisions regarding placing inmates into segregation—in both types of decisions, the individual's liberty is affected.
3. Correctional officers make daily decisions that affect the life and health of the prisoners they supervise.
4. Parole officials decide when to file a violation report, as well as make less serious decisions regarding the parolee's life.

In short, all correctional professionals have a great deal of discretion over the lives of those they control. The ethical issues of correctional professionals are discussed in Chapters 12, 13, and 14.

All the professionals discussed have several elements in common:

1. *They each have discretion, that is, the power to make a decision.* Although the particular decisions are different, they all involve power over others and the potential deprivation of life, liberty, or property.
2. *They each have the duty of enforcement of the law.* Although this concept is obvious with police, it is also clear that each of the professionals mentioned has a basic duty to uphold and enforce all laws; they serve the law in their professional lives.

3. *They must accept that their duty is to protect the constitutional safeguards that are the cornerstone of our legal system—specifically, due process and equal protection.* Due process protects each of us from error in any governmental deprivation of life, liberty, or property. We recognize the right of government to control and even to punish, but we have certain protections against arbitrary or unlawful use of that power. Due process protects us against such abuses. We also expect that the power of our government will be used fairly and in an unbiased manner. Equal protection should ensure that what happens to us is not determined by the color of our skin, our gender, nationality, or the religion we practice. Laws are for everyone, and the protection of the law extends to all of us. Although there is a fair amount of evidence to indicate that different treatment does exist, the ideal of equal protection is an essential element of our legal system and should be an operating principle for everyone working in this system.

4. *They are **public servants**.* That is, their salaries come from the public purse. Public servants possess more than a job; they have taken on special duties involving the public trust. Individuals such as legislators, public officials, police officers, judges, and prosecutors are either elected or appointed guardians of the public's interests. Arguably, they must be held to *higher* standards than those they guard or govern. Temptations are many, and often it seems we find examples of *double* standards, where public servants take advantage of their positions for special favors, rather than *higher* standards of exemplary behavior.

Obviously, the law governs many of the decisions that public servants make, but because of the discretion that exists at every step of the criminal justice process, there is always the possibility of an unethical use of such discretion. Understanding the ethical issues involved in one's profession might help to guide such discretion and prevent abuse. Therefore, all professionals in the criminal justice field must be sensitive to ethical issues. These issues may involve their relationships with citizens and others over whom they have power, their relationships with their agency, or their relationships with one another. Box 1-1, "Principles of Public Service Ethics," considers the ethical duties of public servants.

## QUOTE and QUERY

Part of what is needed [for public servants] is a public sense of what Madison meant by wisdom and good character: balanced perception and integrity. Integrity means wholeness in public and private life consisting of habits of justice, temperance, courage, compassion, honesty, fortitude, and disdain for self-pity.

Source: Delattre (1989b: 78–83).

*How do you define integrity? Do you feel it is necessary that public servants be better than the rest of us?*

---

**BOX 1-1 Principles of Public Service Ethics**

1. *Public service.* Public servants should treat their office as a public trust, using the power and resources of public office only to advance public interests and not to attain personal benefit or pursue any other private interest incompatible with the public good.
2. *Objective judgment.* Public servants should employ independent objective judgment in performing their duties, deciding all matters on the merits, free from avoidable conflicts of interest and both real and apparent improper influences.
3. *Accountability.* Public servants should ensure that government is conducted openly, efficiently, equitably, and honorably in a manner that permits the citizenry to make informed judgments and hold government officials accountable.
4. *Democratic leadership.* Public servants should honor and respect the principles and spirit of representative democracy and set a positive example of good citizenship by scrupulously observing the letter and spirit of laws and rules.
5. *Respectability.* Public servants should safeguard public confidence in the integrity of government by being honest, fair, caring, and respectful, and by avoiding conduct creating the appearance of impropriety or which is otherwise unbefitting a public official.

SOURCE: Adapted from Josephson Institute of Ethics, *Preserving the Public Trust,* available through www.josephsoninstitute.org.

---

Felkenes (1987: 26) explained why the study of ethics is important for criminal justice professionals:

1. Professionals are recognized as such in part because [a] "profession" . . . normally includes a set of ethical requirements as part of its meaning. . . . Professionalism among all actors at all levels of the criminal justice system depends upon their ability to administer policy effectively in a morally and ethically responsible manner.
2. Training in critical ethics helps to develop analytical skills and reasoning abilities needed to understand the pragmatic and theoretical aspects of the criminal justice system.
3. Criminal justice professionals should be able to recognize quickly the ethical consequences of various actions, and the moral principles involved.
4. Ethical considerations are central to decisions involving discretion, force, and due process which require people to make enlightened moral judgments.
5. Ethics is germane to most management and policy decisions concerning such penal issues as rehabilitation, deterrence, and just deserts.
6. Ethical considerations are essential aspects of criminal justice research.

In answer to a similar question, Braswell (1996/2002: 8) explained the five goals of a study of ethics:

1. Become aware and open to ethical issues
2. Begin developing critical thinking skills
3. Become more personally responsible
4. Understand how the criminal justice system is engaged in a process of coercion
5. Develop **wholesight** (which roughly means exploring with one's heart as well as one's mind)

The comprehensive nature of these two lists requires no additions. We will simply reiterate some basic points:

1. First, we study ethics because criminal justice is uniquely involved in coercion, which means there are many and varied opportunities to abuse such power.
2. Second, almost all criminal justice professionals are public servants and, thus, owe special duties to the public they serve.
3. Finally, we study ethics to sensitize students to ethical issues and provide tools to help identify and resolve the ethical dilemmas that they may face in their professional lives.

# Defining Terms

The words *morals* and *ethics* are often used in daily conversations. For instance, when public officials use their offices for personal profit or when politicians accept bribes from special interest groups, they are described as unethical. When an individual does a good deed, engages in charitable activities or personal sacrifice, or takes a stand against wrongdoing, we might describe that individual as a moral person. Very often, *morals* and *ethics* are used interchangeably. This makes sense because they both come from similar root meanings. The Greek word *ethos* pertains to custom (behavioral practices) or character, and *morals* is a Latin-based word with a similar meaning.

## Morals and Ethics

*Morals* and *morality* refer to what is judged as good conduct. (*Immorality* refers to bad conduct.) The term *moral* is also used to describe someone who has the capacity to make value judgments and discern right from wrong (Souryal, 1992: 12). *Ethics* refers to the study and analysis of what constitutes good or bad conduct (Barry, 1985: 5; Sherman, 1981: 8).

There are several branches, or schools, of ethics:

1. **Meta-ethics** is "the highly technical discipline investigating the meaning of ethical terms including a critical study of how ethical statements can be verified" (Barry, 1985: 11).
2. **Normative ethics** determines what people ought to do and defines moral duties.
3. **Applied ethics** is the application of ethical principles to specific issues.
4. **Professional ethics** is an even more specific type of applied ethics relating to the behavior of certain professions or groups.

To many people, ethics has come to mean the definition of particular behaviors as right and wrong within a profession. Very often, in common usage, morality is used to speak of the total person, or the sum of a person's actions in every sphere of life, and ethics is used to refer to behaviors relating to a profession and is an analysis of behavior relevant to a certain profession. For instance, the medical profession follows the Hippocratic Oath, a declaration of rules and principles of conduct for doctors to follow in their daily practices; it dictates appropriate behavior and goals. In fact, most professions have their own set of ethical standards or canons of ethics.

Even though professional ethics typically restricts attention to areas of behavior relevant to the profession, these can be fairly inclusive and enter into what we might consider the private life of the individual. For instance, doctors are judged harshly if they engage in romantic relationships with their patients, as are professors if they become involved with students. These rules are usually included in codes of ethics for these professions. We are very much aware of how politicians' private behavior can affect their career in politics. When politicians are embroiled in controversial love affairs or are exposed as spouse abusers, these revelations have definite effects on their futures. It is clear that—in some professions, anyway, typically those involving public trust such as politics, education, and the clergy—there is a thin line between one's private life and one's public life.

It does not make a great deal of difference for our purposes whether we use the formal or colloquial definitions of *morals* and *ethics*. This text is an applied ethics text, in that we will be concerned with what is defined as right and wrong behavior in the professions relevant to the criminal justice system and how people in these professions make decisions in the course of their careers. It is also a professional ethics text, because we are primarily concerned with professional ethics in criminal justice.

## Making Moral Judgments

We make moral or ethical judgments all the time: "Abortion is wrong." "Capital punishment is just." "It is good to give to charity." "It is wrong to hit your spouse." These are all judgments of good and bad behavior. We also make choices that can be judged as right or wrong. Should you call in sick, even though you aren't, to get a day in the sun?

Should you give back extra change that a clerk gave you by mistake? Should you tell a friend that her husband is having an affair even though he asked you not to tell? Not all behaviors involve questions of ethics. In order to more specifically draw the boundaries of our ethical discussion, we need to know which behavioral decisions might be judged under ethical standards. Decisions that can be judged involve four elements: (1) acts that are (2) human, and (3) of free will (4) that affect others.

*Act.* First of all, we must have some act to judge. For instance, we are concerned with the *act* of stealing or the *act* of contributing to charity, rather than an idle thought that stealing a lot of money would enable us to buy a sailboat or a vague intention to be more generous. We are not necessarily concerned with how people feel or what they think about a particular action unless it has some bearing on what they do. The intention or motive behind a particular behavior is an important component of that behavior. For instance, in ethical formalism (which we will discuss in Chapter 2), one must know the intent of an action in order to be able to judge it as moral or immoral. However, one must have some action to examine before making a moral judgment.

*Only Human Acts.* Second, judgments of moral or ethical behavior are directed specifically to human behavior. A dog that bites is not considered immoral or evil, although we may criticize pet owners who allow their dogs the opportunity to bite. Nor do we consider drought, famine, floods, or other natural disasters immoral, even though they result in death, destruction, and misery. Behaviors of animals or events of nature cannot be judged in the same way as actions performed by human beings. It is a belief widely held by philosophers that only humans can be moral (or immoral) because of their capacity to reason. Because only humans have the capacity to be "good," which involves a voluntary, rational decision and subsequent action, only humans, of all members of the animal kingdom, have the capacity to be "bad."

*Free Will.* In addition to limiting discussions of morality to human behavior, we also usually further restrict our discussion to behavior that stems from free will and free action. Culpability is not assigned to persons who are not sufficiently aware of the world around them to be able to decide rationally what is good or bad. The two groups traditionally exempt from responsibility in this sense are the young and the insane. Arguably, we do not judge the morality of their behavior because we do not believe that they have the capacity to reason and therefore cannot choose to be moral or immoral. Although we may punish a two-year-old for hitting a baby, we do so to educate or socialize, not to punish, as we would an older child or adult. We incapacitate the mentally ill to protect ourselves against their violence and strange behavior, but we consider them sick, not evil. This is true even if their actual behavior is indistinguishable from that of other individuals we do punish. For example, a murder may result in a death sentence or a hospital commitment, depending on whether the person is judged to be sane or insane, responsible or not responsible. Admittedly, at times we have difficulty in deciding whether behavior originates with free will, or we do not care whether it does.

*Effects on Others.* Finally, we usually discuss moral or immoral behavior only in those cases where the behavior significantly affects others. For instance, throwing a rock off a bridge would be neither good nor bad unless you could possibly hit or were aiming at a person below. If no one is there, your behavior is neutral; if someone is below, however, you might endanger that person's life, so your behavior is judged as "bad." All the moral dilemmas we will discuss in this book involve at least two parties, and the decision to be made affects at least one other individual in every case. In reality, it is difficult to think of an action that does not affect others, however indirectly. Even self-destructive behavior is said to harm the people who love us and who would be hurt by such actions.

We sense that these elements are important in judging morality when we hear the common rationale of those who, when judged as doing something wrong, protest, "But nobody was hurt!" or "I didn't mean to." Indeed, even a hermit living alone on a desert island may engage in immoral or unethical actions. Whether he wants to be or not, the hermit is part of human society; therefore, some people would say that even he might engage in actions that could be judged immoral if they degrade or threaten the future of humankind, such as committing suicide or polluting the ocean.

One's actions toward nature might also be defined as immoral, so relevant actions include not only actions done to people, but also to animals and to nature. To abuse or exploit animals can be defined as immoral—judgments can be made against cockfighting, dog racing, laboratory experimentation on animals, and hunting. The growth of environmental ethics reflects increasing concern for the future of the planet. The rationale for environmental ethics may be that any actions that harm the environment affect all humans. It might also be justified by the belief that humankind is a part of nature—not superior to it—and part of natural law would be to protect, not exploit, our world.

Thus far, we know that morality and ethics concern the judgment of behavior as right or wrong. Furthermore, such judgments are directed only at voluntary human behavior that affects other people, the Earth, and living things. We can further restrict our inquiries regarding ethics to those behavioral decisions that are relevant to one's profession in the criminal justice system. Discussions regarding the ethics of police officers, for instance, would concern issues such as the following:

1. Whether to take gratuities
2. Whether to cover up the wrongdoing of a fellow officer
3. Whether to sleep on duty
4. Whether to call in sick when one wants to play golf or go fishing
5. Whether to lie on an expense sheet

Discussions regarding the ethics of defense attorneys might revolve around the following:

1. Devoting more effort to private cases than appointed cases
2. Whether or not to allow perjury

Of course, all of these actions affect other people, as do most actions taken as a professional. Review the "Inventory of Ethical Issues" (Box 1-2). Notice that the ethical issues fall into three major categories:

1. Effects on citizenry
2. Effects on other employees
3. Effects on the organization one works for

---

**BOX 1-2  Inventory of Ethical Issues**

**The Individual and the Organization**

work ethic (day's work for a day's pay)
petty theft of supplies or cash
overtime abuse
gifts and gratuities
falsifying reports
misuse of sick days
personal use of supplies or equipment

**The Organization and Employees**

sexual or racial harassment by supervisors
discouraging honest criticism or feedback
arbitrary or unfair decisions
inadequate compensation
inadequate training
unrealistic or inappropriate demands
putting employees in unnecessary danger

**The Individual and Other Employees**

backstabbing and lack of support
gossip
sexual or racial harassment
lying to cover up blame
taking credit for others' work
sexual or racial harassment

**The Individual and the Public**

misuse of authority
inadequate performance of duty
sexual, racial, ethnic harassment
special treatment
lack of expertise (not keeping up with training)
malfeasance or misfeasance of duties
rudeness or incivility

---

## *Duties*

Another comment we should make about behavior and morality is that philosophers distinguish between moral duties and superogatories. **Duties** refer to those actions that an individual must perform in order to be considered moral. For instance, everyone might agree that one has a duty to support one's parents if able to do so, one has a duty to obey the law (unless it is an immoral law), and a police officer has a moral and ethical duty to tell the truth on a police report. Duties are what you must do in order to be good.

Other actions, considered **superogatories**, are commendable but not required. A Good Samaritan who jumps into a river to save a drowning person, risking his or her own life to do so, has performed a superogatory action—there is no moral condemnation of those who stood on the bank, because risking one's life is above and beyond anyone's moral duty. Of course, if one can help save a life with no great risk to oneself, then a moral duty does exist in that situation.

Police officers may have an ethical duty to get involved when others do not. Consider the 2001 attack on the World Trade Center. One of the most moving images of that tragedy was of police officers and firefighters running toward danger while others ran away. This professional duty to put oneself in harm's way is why we revere and pay homage to these public servants. Many civilians also put themselves in harm's way, and because they had no professional duty to do so, they could be said to be performing superogatory actions.

There are also **imperfect duties.** These are general duties that one should uphold, but without specific application as to when or how. For instance, most ethical systems would support a general duty of generosity, but there is no specific duty demanding a certain type or manner of generosity. Another imperfect duty might be to be honest. It is unclear to what extent honesty is required for virtue. There is the rule of "if you can't say something nice, don't say anything at all" that counters "brutal honesty." In general, the duty to be honest may not allow lying, but it may very well allow for a "don't ask, don't tell" policy.

## *Values*

**Values** are defined as elements of desirability, worth, or importance. Values and judgments of worth are often equated with moral judgments of goodness. We see that both can be distinguished from factual judgments, which can be empirically verified. Note the difference between these factual judgments:

1. "He is lying."
2. "It is raining."

and these value judgments:

1. "She is a good woman."
2. "That was a wonderful day."

The last two judgments are more similar to moral judgments—"facts" are capable of scientific proof, but values and moral judgments are not.

Some writers think that value judgments and moral judgments are indistinguishable because neither can be verified (Mackie, 1977; Margolis, 1971). Some also think that values and morals are relativistic and individual. For these people, there are no universal values; all values are subjective. In other words, values are merely opinions (Mackie, 1977: 22–24). In this view, because they are only opinions, no value is more important than any other value.

However, others believe that not all values are equal. In this view, values such as honesty are always more important than values such as pleasure. **Universalists** would not hesitate to propose that valuing money over life, for instance, would be wrong, as would placing a higher value on pleasure than charity. Discussions concerning values imply a choice or judgment. If, for instance, you were confronted with an opportunity to cheat on an exam, your values of academic success and honesty would be directly at odds. Values and morals are similar, although values merely indicate *relative* importance, whereas morals prescribe or proscribe behavior. The value of honesty is conceptually distinct from the moral rule against lying.

Individual values form value systems. All people prioritize certain things that they consider important in life. Behavior is generally consistent with values. For instance, some individuals may believe that financial success is more important than family or health. In this case, we may assume that their behavior will reflect the importance of that value and that these persons will be workaholics, spending more time at work than with family and endangering their health with long hours, stress, and lack of exercise. Others may place a higher priority on religious faith, wisdom, honesty, and/or independence than financial success or status.

Most of us live our lives in rough accordance with our values. But it is also true that very often we live our lives without taking a close look at the value system that influences our behavior. See the "Value Exercise" in Box 1-3.

This concept of a value system is fairly explicit in Messner and Rosenfeld's (1994) theory of crime. In their explanation of why the United States experiences a higher rate of violent crime than other Western countries, they propose that the U.S. value system, which emphasizes consumerism over family and money over honesty, creates an environment where crime results. Success in the United States is defined almost exclusively

---

**BOX 1-3 Value Exercise**

Rank the following values in order of importance, with 1 representing the most important value to you, and so on. Now go through the list again and rank these values according to how you believe most people would rank them. Compare your answers with others as a class exercise.

| | |
|---|---|
| Achievement | Success |
| Friendship | Creativity |
| Power | Knowledge |
| Altruism | Wealth |
| Health | Duty |
| Recognition | Love |
| Autonomy | Wisdom |
| Honesty | Emotional well-being |
| Religion | Loyalty |
| Beauty | Family |
| Justice | Pleasure |

by the accumulation of material goods, not by doing "good." Because behavior is influenced by one's value system, individuals who place material success over any other value will behave dishonestly or even violently in the pursuit of such goods.

An explicit value system is a part of every ethical system, as we will see in Chapter 2. Certain values hold special relevance to the criminal justice system. Privacy, freedom, public order, justice, duty, and loyalty are all values that will come up again in later discussions. The values of life, respect for the person, and survival can be found in all ethical systems.

## Morality and the Law

Laws govern many aspects of our behavior. **Laws**, in the form of statutes and ordinances, tell us how to drive, how to operate our business, and what we can and cannot do in public and even in private. They are the formal, written rules of society. Yet they are not comprehensive in defining moral behavior. There is a law against hitting one's mother (assault) but no law against financially abandoning her, yet both are considered morally wrong. We have laws against "bad" behavior, such as burglarizing a house or embezzling from our employer, but we have very few laws prescribing "good" behavior, such as helping a victim or contributing to a charity. The exception to this would be the **"Good Samaritan laws"** that exist in some states and are quite common in Europe. These laws make it a crime to pass by an accident scene or witness a crime without rendering assistance.

Some actions prohibited by law are thought to be private decisions of the individual and not especially wrong or harmful. Many people object to sodomy laws and other laws regulating sexual behavior because they feel that this is private behavior and outside the parameters of social control. When laws prohibit behaviors that are not universally condemned, such as laws prohibiting alcohol, drugs, gambling and prostitution, enforcement is more subject to criticism and, not incidentally, more prone to corruption because there is a greater ability to rationalize underenforcement or preferential treatment. Consider, for instance, the argument that organized crime grew tremendously during Prohibition and that an unknown number of law enforcement officers accepted bribes or were involved in protection rackets. Some argue the same scenario is occurring again today in the war on drugs. The rationalization of the officers who are inclined to accept protection money or bribes is that the offenders are engaged in providing a commodity that the public desires.

We have had laws in the past that were or are now considered immoral:

1. The internment of Japanese Americans during World War II
2. "Jim Crow" laws before the civil rights era
3. Pre–Civil War laws that mandated the return of runaway slaves to their owners

More recently, we have had legal authorities authorizing forms of interrogation that many argue constitute torture and are morally and ethically wrong, even if lawful.

An important question in the study of ethics is whether one can be a good person while obeying a bad law. Civil disobedience occurs when people voluntarily disobey what they consider to be an unjust or immoral law. In Chapters 4 and 5 we discuss morality and immorality in relation to law and the concept of justice.

A crime is composed of the following three elements:

1. An *actus reus*
2. A *mens rea* (with concurrence between the two)
3. Causation

The *actus reus* is the physical act that is defined as the crime. Furthermore, the act must have been the result of the defendant's own volition. If, for instance, the act was performed while sleepwalking or when the person was not fully conscious, then there was no *actus reus*. The *mens rea* is the level of culpability required for each crime in order to find guilt. There are four levels of legal culpability:

1. Negligence
2. Recklessness
3. Knowing
4. Intentional (or purposive)

Causation is when the *actus reus* creates the result prohibited or described by the law. "**Proximate cause**" is the law's attempt to use common sense to limit a defendant's capability. For instance, if the dependant's assault puts the victim in the hospital and then the person is killed in an accidental fire, even though death ultimately resulted from the assault, the defendant is not guilty of homicide because the assault was not the "proximate cause" of the death.

## Criminal Culpability/Moral Culpability

The law recognizes different levels of responsibility by the different levels of *mens rea*. First-degree homicide, for instance, requires proof of **intent**, whereas second-degree homicide requires only evidence of **knowing** that one is performing the act. Crimes that require only evidence of **negligence** (should have known the danger of the act) or **recklessness** (did know the danger of the act) have less severe punishments attached to them because the level of culpability, fault, or blame is less severe. Careless actions, such as driving while intoxicated or killing someone while playing with a loaded weapon, are judged as less "bad" than those actions performed with deliberation and intent. An individual who has weighed the consequences and knows the outcome and all the ramifications of the action and then proceeds has greater legal culpability than someone who has proceeded without such deliberation, albeit with a negligent disregard for potential or probable consequences.

It might be that one's mental state prevents the prosecutor from considering any level of guilt. If one is found "incompetent to stand trial," it means that there has been a legal determination that the individual is incapable of understanding the proceedings and assisting in his or her own defense. We have a long legal tradition of requiring the defendant to be at least minimally competent and rational, and we recognize different levels of culpability.

Historically, two groups have been considered "excused" from criminal culpability: the insane and juveniles. This is because of a belief that individuals in these groups are not rational—in other words, they cannot weigh the consequences of their actions and

**IN THE NEWS** **Whose Fault Is It?**

Scott Waddle was the captain of the *U.S.S. Greenville* when it accidentally rammed and sank a Japanese trawler on February 9, 2001. The accident killed nine people and cost over $100 million in damages and compensation costs. Waddle, in an unusual display of contrition, gave up his right to silence, refused to shift responsibility to others, and accepted all blame for the accident. He even went to Japan to apologize to the victims' families personally. He was dismissed after a court-martial. Despite his admission that he considered suicide, he now gives speeches on the experience and advises others that it is important to deal with failure honestly. He has expressed his disgust with military leaders in the Abu Ghraib prison scandal, arguing that "They can claim ignorance, but that ignorance in itself defines incompetence. . . ."

Source: Hight (2005: A11).

*Why do you think corporate executives, military leaders, politicians, and others refuse to say "It's my fault, and I'm sorry"? How do you determine the degree of culpability for reckless but not deliberate acts?*

therefore should not be held accountable. Thus, even those found competent to stand trial may be acquitted by reason of insanity. Or they may not. We continue to imprison and even execute those who show obvious signs of mental illness, despite our legal tradition of holding only "rational" people legally culpable.

The other group that has traditionally been excused from criminal culpability is the young. Attitudes toward the **age of reason** and when a child is said to have reached it seem to be changing. In the early twentieth century, there was a concerted effort to remove juveniles from the adult legal system and to create a legal system for juveniles that would include protection as part of its mission. The system would adhere to a *parens patriae* **model** (standing in the stead of a parent), rather than act purely as punisher. This philosophy was based on the belief that the juvenile acted with less rationality than the adult. Today that trend seems to be reversing itself. States have reduced the age at which a child is considered an adult, have developed procedures allowing youngsters to be remanded to adult courts for trial and sentencing, and have allowed juveniles, even though sentenced in the juvenile system, to be held in facilities for adults.

The insane and juveniles have traditionally been excused because they lack the ability to weigh their actions. Some argue that there are other individuals who are also not fully responsible for their actions. For instance, the myriad "abuse excuses" dominate the legal landscape today. These defenses argue that the defendant might have committed the crime, but did so because of some compelling reason or excuse, such as those listed below:

1. They were battered or abused.
2. They suffered from post-traumatic stress syndrome.
3. They suffered harassment.
4. They were under the influence of alcohol or drugs.

5. They were unduly influenced by music, television, or movies.
6. They were affected by sugar or food additives.
7. They were driven to desperate acts by the actions of a spouse.

Dershowitz (1994) argues that we have gone too far in allowing a multitude of excuses for criminal behavior, a conclusion that is somewhat ironic because, as a criminal defense attorney, he has helped introduce some of these defenses.

The moral culpability of an actor is not necessarily equivalent to legal culpability, although we often use the legal terms in discussions concerning ethical judgments. These concepts are useful for us in moral judgments, yet we should not be misled that moral judgments and legal judgments are always the same. One might not be guilty of a crime and might still be considered morally culpable. Alternatively, one might be guilty of a crime and be considered morally blameless; the last dilemma at the back of this chapter involves a loving mother who killed her suffering sons. Is she legally culpable but morally blameless, both legally and morally culpable, or some other combination?

## IN THE NEWS  A Scorned Woman

In Houston, an upper-middle-class professional woman found her husband at a hotel with his mistress after he had sworn to her that he had broken off the affair. She was devastated because the couple had very young twins and she had attempted to save her marriage through changing her appearance and de-emphasizing her career. She fought with the mistress in the hotel lobby and was dragged off the woman and pushed down by her husband. Then, in the parking lot of the hotel where the confrontation occurred, in front of many witnesses and with his daughter in the car, she ran over her husband and killed him.

*Would you find her guilty of first-degree murder, second-degree murder, or some other crime? What punishment does she deserve?*

## QUOTE and QUERY

Laws are just like spider's webs, they will hold the weak and delicate who might be caught in their meshes, but will be torn to pieces by the rich and powerful.

Anacharsis, 600 B.C.E.

The more mandates and laws which are enacted, the more there will be thieves and robbers.

Lao-Tze, 600 B.C.E.

Source: Quoted in Roth and Roth (1989: 3).

*What do these statements mean? Is it true that laws are manipulated by the powerful and oppress the weak?*

There is an argument that some actions are caused by life circumstances and are therefore not completely voluntary. For instance, if someone came from an impoverished background and was exposed only to criminal role models, is this person responsible for his or her subsequent delinquency? Do all people truly have freedom of choice? It is illegal for a rich man or a poor man to steal a loaf of bread, but a rich man doesn't have to, nor does he have to engage in armed robbery to obtain goods. However, he might commit tax evasion, toxic waste dumping, or embezzlement.

We are all bound by limitations (or opportunities) of birth and circumstance. If we were to analyze moral culpability on the basis of life choices, it might be that, because of their respective life positions, some people who commit serious crimes are less blameworthy than others who come from better backgrounds and commit less serious crimes. Who is more culpable, the executives of a company such as Enron who made extremely high salaries but broke the law to make even more money, or the burglar who has no job and steals your television set? You might argue that both are equally culpable, but then why do they not serve the same punishment? Also remember that the idea of moral culpability may be quite different from legal responsibility. Is there ever a good enough excuse for committing a crime?

## Regulations, Standards, and Guidelines

In addition to laws, we have other examples of behavioral rules that lead to a judgment of wrong and, in most cases, some form of punishment:

1. **Regulations** govern the activities of occupations from physician to plumber and organizations from governmental agencies to private clubs. Regulations typically come from a governmental authority and often specify sanctions for noncompliance.
2. **Standards** may come from private or public bodies and are often used as a basis for some type of accreditation.
3. **Guidelines** may come from a professional group and are usually recommendations rather than directions.

Distinctions can be made among these terms, although they are often used interchangeably. These rules for behavior usually do not carry the formal sanctions of criminal law, but some may carry civil liabilities.

Most regulations are set by state and federal governments. For instance, consider the following:

1. The Food and Drug Administration prescribes certain procedures and rules for pharmaceutical companies to follow in developing, testing, and distributing drugs.
2. The Environmental Protection Agency watches over industry to make sure that safe methods for disposal of hazardous wastes are implemented.
3. The Occupational Safety and Health Agency sets safety standards for the workplace in order to avoid or reduce the number of workplace injuries.

Noncompliance with standards and regulations is not equated with immoral behavior as readily as is criminal lawbreaking. Although fines may be levied against the construction supervisor who ignores Occupational Safety and Health Agency standards

**QUOTE and QUERY**

Why do 26 dead miners amount to a "disaster," and six dead suburbanites a "mass murder"? "Murder" suggests a murderer, while "disaster" suggests the work of impersonal forces. But if over 1,000 safety violations had been found in the mine—three the day before the first explosion—was no one responsible for failing to eliminate those hazards? And if someone could have prevented the hazards and did not, does that person not bear responsibility for the deaths of 26 men? Is he less evil because he did not want them to die, although he chose to leave them in jeopardy? Is he not a murderer, perhaps even a mass murderer?

Source: Reiman, cited in Scheingold (1984: 23).

*Do you feel that employers who put their employees in harm's way should be prosecuted for manslaughter?*

or the automaker who violates standards of the Consumer Safety Board, ordinarily these people are not considered criminals, even when their actions result in injury or death.

When rules or standards are violated, other relevant criminal charges may be imposed as well. For instance, if a company blatantly violates safety regulations by forcing employees to work with toxic chemicals, company officials may be charged with negligent manslaughter if a worker dies. However, this situation is extremely rare, and there is usually a great deal of difference between the sanctions related to a violation of regulations and criminal lawbreaking. Examples of businesses or individuals in business routinely violating standards and/or regulations include the following:

1. The WorldCom, Enron, and Arthur Anderson scandals
2. Insider information trading on Wall Street
3. Toxic waste dumping
4. The marketing of unsafe products

Some of the individuals who are caught and punished are truly surprised that their actions could result in criminal punishment. They also typically do not consider themselves criminals, even after they put on a prison uniform.

In addition to guidelines and standards, professions usually have a code of ethics or set of professional rules to educate and encourage their members to perform in accordance with an ideal of behavior. These guidelines may be fairly general or fairly specific; for instance, lawyers have extensive written rules, but other professions may have only a one-page code of ethics. Laws, standards, regulations, guidelines, and codes of ethics are all designed to control and guide behavior.

It is interesting to observe that regulations and rules for behavior often seem to expand in inverse relation to the practiced ethics of a particular profession or organization. Frequently, when a breakdown in ethical behavior is detected, there is an attempt to bring people back in line by the use of rules. However, it seems that in any profession, the most effective ethical guides are not those that specify behavior but rather those that are consistent with and support an organizational ideal. People can find many ways of violating the spirit of an administrative rule while complying with its exact wording. There always seem to be politicians who engage in behavior involving conflicts of interest, but argue that they are not breaking any laws, and lawyers who get around their ethical responsibilities by complying with the letter but not the spirit of the rules. Decision makers in organizations often feel it is necessary to give employees extensive lists of rules. In an office these may include injunctions not to take supplies, not to make personal telephone calls, and not to spend more than fifteen minutes on breaks. Enforcing rules is very different from promoting an ethical standard of honesty and integrity in the workplace. Where ethical standards are nonexistent, it is doubtful that multitudinous rules of behavior will be able to eliminate wrongdoing.

## Morality and Behavior

One of the most difficult things to understand about human behavior is the disjunction between moral beliefs and behavior. We all can attest to the fact that believing something is wrong does not always prevent us from doing it. Very often, in fact, we engage in acts that we believe are bad, such as lying, stealing, and cheating. In any group of people (such as a college class), a majority will have engaged in some type of wrongful act at least once.

Why do people engage in behavior that they believe to be wrong? Criminology attempts to explain why people commit unlawful acts, but the larger question is this: Why do any of us engage in wrongful acts? Psychological experiments show that a large percentage of schoolchildren will cheat when given the opportunity to do so, even though they know it is wrong (Lickona, 1976). More-recent studies show that many people will keep wallets or purses that they find, or the money in them, before they give them back to their owner. Some looters in New Orleans after Hurricane Katrina may have been stealing food as a matter of necessity, but many others exploited the natural disaster to take what they knew wasn't theirs. Theories that endorse everything from learning and role modeling to biological predisposition abound, but we still haven't answered fundamental questions of causation. Even with all the scientific and philosophical attempts to explain human action, we are left with troubling questions when we read or hear about people who kill, steal, or otherwise offend our sense of morality. Evil is still one of the great mysteries of life.

In discussions concerning these questions, basic beliefs about the nature of humankind must be considered. Are people fundamentally bad and held in check only by rules and fear of punishment? Or are people fundamentally good and commit bad acts because of improper upbringing or events that subvert their natural goodness? Or are there fundamentally bad and fundamentally good people who are just "born that way" for no reason? Ironically, our society seems to define "goodness" in one way while glorifying just the opposite. Bonnie and Clyde and Jesse James are, in some ways, cultural heroes even though they were known criminals. We have also glorified business executives when their actions could be defined as exploitative, as in the movie *Wall Street*. Yet when real people engage in such behavior, we prefer to see them punished. We are dismayed by the amount of violence and crime in our society, yet the television programs that play on these themes are the most popular ones. We abhor lying, but politicians who tell the truth are rejected by voters. We profess to be a country that cherishes our Constitution and due-process rights, but we clap and cheer in movie theaters when "Dirty Harry" types kill the "bad guys." In other words, what we say we believe and value doesn't always match our actions.

Why do we idolize people who have done things that we know and believe to be wrong? Some say we sublimate our wish for excitement and our greed through their exploits. Many of the ideals of success in this society involve aspects of ruthlessness and aggression—traits hard to reconcile with an ideal conception of the good person. At least in Western culture, a "good" person who upholds the ideals of honesty, charity, and selflessness is considered somewhat of a weakling. The fact that our society has mixed values regarding what is considered good and desirable is reflected both in our popular culture and in individual action.

## Analyzing Ethical Dilemmas

Ethical discussions in criminal justice can be either issues or dilemmas. **Ethical issues** are broad social questions, often concerning the government's social control mechanisms and the impact on those governed—for example, what laws to pass, what sentences to attach to certain crimes, whether to abolish the death penalty, and whether to build more prisons or use community correctional alternatives. The typical individual does not have much control over these issues. The ethical issues that arise in relation to criminal justice are serious, difficult, and affect people's lives in fundamental ways. These are just a sample of some criminal justice issues that have ethical implications:

1. Decriminalization of soft drugs
2. Megan's Law and other sex-offender registry statutes
3. The death penalty (for juveniles, the mentally ill, and the mentally retarded)
4. Mandatory DNA registries
5. Three-strikes legislation
6. Racial profiling
7. Law enforcement corruption
8. Waiver of juveniles to adult courts
9. Citizen oversight committees for police departments
10. The Patriot Act and other challenges to civil liberties in the wake of terrorism

Periodically, we will highlight a criminal justice policy issue in this text to illustrate the relationships among law, policy, and ethics. In Policy Box 1-1, the issue of the medical use of marijuana is examined.

**Ethical dilemmas** are those situations in which one person must make a decision about what to do. Either the choice is unclear or the "right" choice will be difficult because of the costs involved. Ethical dilemmas involve the individual struggling with personal decision making, whereas ethical issues are those topics wherein one might have an opinion, but rarely a chance to take a stand that has much impact (unless one happens to be a Supreme Court judge or a state governor).

---

**POLICY BOX 1-1** **Medical Use of Marijuana**

There is periodic controversy over whether marijuana should be legalized for the limited use of pain relief and nausea control for seriously ill individuals, including cancer patients and those individuals suffering from AIDS. Many medical professionals have testified in state and federal hearings that they believe that marijuana is more effective and has fewer side effects than other forms of legal relief. Others dispute the findings.

**Law:** The federal government's drug laws do not make an exception for the medical use of marijuana. California passed a law allowing certain uses of marijuana to be regulated but decriminalized. The Supreme Court held that the federal laws "trumped" California law.

**Policy:** Federal drug officials made it clear that they would enforce the federal laws against doctors and medical co-ops that distributed the drugs. State officials were upset that the mandate of the people was overturned by the Supreme Court, but had no power to control federal law enforcement.

**Individual ethics:** Some people, including doctors, decided to continue their distribution and use of marijuana, thereby setting the scene for arrests. (See *Raich v. Ashcroft,* 248 F.Supp. 2d 918 [N.D. Cal. 2003].)

---

However, it should be noted that there are times when one's belief regarding an ethical issue gives rise to a personal dilemma. In 2000, George Ryan, then the governor of Illinois, declared a moratorium on the use of the death penalty in his state when at least five individuals on death row were exonerated through the use of DNA evidence. One of his last acts as he left office at the end of 2002 was to pardon the rest of those on death row and commute their sentences to life without parole. Governor Ryan faced a difficult personal dilemma because he was in a position to do something about his belief that the death penalty was implemented in a way that could never be just. The fact that there was strong support *and* strong opposition to his action indicates the depth of his dilemma and the seriousness of the issue. Although most of us do not have the power to commute death sentences, we can do something about our beliefs. Writing letters, petitioning our legislators, marching in demonstrations, and working to pass (or overturn) laws are all examples of acting on our moral beliefs.

Personal ethical dilemmas occur when the individual is forced to choose between two or more choices of behavior. In order to analyze such dilemmas, one must discover all relevant information. The following steps might be taken in order to clarify the dilemma:

1. Review all the facts. Make sure that one has all the facts that are known—not future predictions, not suppositions, not probabilities.
2. Identify all the potential values of each party that might be relevant; in addition, identify all concepts (things that cannot be empirically proven).

3. Identify all possible moral issues for each party involved. This is to help us see that sometimes one's own moral or ethical dilemma is caused by the actions of others. For instance, a police officer's ethical dilemma when faced with the wrongdoing of a fellow officer is a direct result of that other officer making a bad choice. It is helpful to see all the moral issues involved in order to address the central issue.

4. Decide what is the most immediate moral or ethical issue facing the individual. This is always a behavior choice, not an opinion. For example, the moral issue of whether abortion should be legalized is quite different from the moral dilemma of whether I should have an abortion if I find myself pregnant. Obviously, one affects the other, but they are conceptually very distinct.

5. Resolve the ethical or moral dilemma by using an ethical system or some other means of decision making (these ethical systems will be discussed in Chapter 2).

Let us use the dilemma at the beginning of this chapter of the correctional officer who must decide what to do about the possible beating he observed:

1. First, this officer needs to make sure that he has all the facts. Was the inmate hurt? Did his injuries occur during the time the two other officers were in his cell? Is the officer sure that no one reported it? Would the inmate come forward if he believed that someone would testify against the other two officers, or would he deny the assault (if there was one)? What other facts are important to know? Remember that facts are those things that can be proven; however, this does not necessarily mean that the individual facing the dilemma has the proof.

2. Second, the officer might examine the relevant values. In this situation, one can identify duty, legality, honesty, integrity, safety, protection, loyalty, self-preservation, and trust. Are there any other values important to resolve the dilemma? Concepts are also important. They are like values in that they are not susceptible to empirical proof, but they are not necessarily values. Although this dilemma may not have any relevant concepts, others do—for instance, the issue of abortion revolves around the value of life, but it is also a concept in that there is no proof of when life begins or ends (although there are facts regarding respiration, brain activity, etc.). Many arguments surrounding ethical issues are really arguments about concepts, not necessarily values or ethical judgments.

3. There are several ethical issues here. The first is whether or not the other officers should have entered the prisoner's cell. There is probably an earlier issue involving whatever the prisoner did to warrant the visit. There is obviously the issue of whether the officer should have let off-duty officers into the cell in the first place. Finally, there is the issue of what the officer should do now that he believes an injustice may have taken place.

4. The next step is to resolve the immediate dilemma, which is whether or not to come forward with the information. For this step, it is helpful to work through Chapter 2 first because the way to resolve ethical dilemmas is to decide on an ethical system. If the officer was a utilitarian, he would weigh the costs and benefits for all concerned in coming forward and in staying quiet. If he followed duty-based ethics (ethical formalism), he would find the answer once he determined his duty.

**Figure 1-1** Ethical Pyramid

In order to resolve any dilemma, think of ethical judgments as a pyramid, as indicated in Figure 1-1. The tip of the pyramid is the judgment itself. We make ethical judgments all the time. The moral rules that support such judgments make up the body of the pyramid. Suppose someone said, "Capital punishment is wrong." If one asked, "Why is capital punishment wrong?" the answer might take the form of **moral rules**, which are general rules of right and wrong, or value statements. For instance, in this case, the rules cited might include the following: One should never take a life. One should preserve life. One should abhor violence. Two wrongs don't make a right. And so on. These rules, in turn, must be supported by ethical systems, which will be covered in the next chapter. However, some rules are inconsistent with some ethical systems. For instance, "One must always follow the law" may be consistent with ethical formalism and inconsistent with ethics of care. These concepts will be clearer as we work through a number of ethical systems in the next chapter. Suffice to say for now that ethical judgments always have some rationale behind them. These rationales tend to be consistent with traditional and historical ethical systems. In Chapter 2 we will explore some of these traditional ethical systems.

## Conclusion

In this chapter we defined the terms *morals* and *ethics* as both relating to standards of behavior. It was noted that not all behaviors would be subject to ethical judgments—only those that are performed by humans who are acting with free will and that affect others. Professional ethics deals with only those behaviors relevant to one's profession. We also discussed the relationship between law and ethics and discovered that although there is an overlap, the two are not synonymous. Our ethical judgments (what we consider right and wrong) are made using rationales derived from historical and traditional ethical systems. These ethical systems will be described in the following chapter.

This chapter closes with some review questions to answer in class or in a journal. Discussion questions have also been provided. These have no right or wrong answers and can be the basis for classroom discussions. Ethical dilemmas are also presented to encourage the reader to practice ethical analysis. Throughout the text, ethical dilemmas will be presented that are relevant to the topics discussed in each chapter.

## Key Terms

*actus reus*  the physical act that is defined as the crime

**age of reason**  the legal age at which a person is said to have the capacity to reason and thus to understand the consequences of his or her action

**applied ethics**  the study of ethics applied to a specific profession or subject

**discretion**  the power to make a decision or choice

**duties**  required behaviors or actions

**ethical dilemmas**  decisions that are difficult to make either because the right course of action is not clear or the right course of action carries some negative consequences

**ethical issues**  difficult social questions

**ethics**  the discipline of determining good and evil and defining moral duties

**Good Samaritan laws**  these define as a crime passing by an accident scene or witnessing a crime without rendering assistance

**guidelines**  suggested or preferred rules of behavior

**imperfect duties**  moral duties that are not fully explicated or detailed

**intent**  the highest level of *mens rea:* to deliberate and plan for the act and the consequence

**knowing**  the second level of *mens rea:* to intend to do the act but not necessarily plan for the consequence

**laws**  formal, written rules of society

*mens rea*  the level of blameworthiness of an offender

**meta-ethics**  the discipline of investigating the meaning of ethical terms, including a critical study of how ethical statements can be verified

**moral rules**  prescriptions or proscriptions of behavior that are consistent with an ethical system

**morals**  principles of right and wrong

**negligence**  occurs when an individual should have known of a risk, but didn't and caused harm

**normative ethics**  determines what people ought to do and defines moral duties

*parens patriae*  model that allows for the state to stand in the stead of a parent

**professional ethics**  applied ethics relevant to a particular occupation or profession

**proximate cause**  legal cause (the natural and predictable cause of a harm)

**public servants**  those professionals who are paid by the public and whose job entails pursuing the public good

**recklessness**  occurs when an individual knew of the risk of an action but did it anyway

**regulations**  orders issued by the government that have the force of law

**standards**  rules or models to be followed
**superogatories**  actions that are commendable but not required in order for a person to be considered moral
**universalists**  those who believe in universal truths
**values**  judgments of desirability, worth, or importance
**wholesight**  exploring issues with one's heart as well as one's mind

# Review Questions

1. What are some decisions by criminal justice professionals that may be evaluated under ethical criteria? What do all professionals in the criminal justice system have in common?
2. Discuss Felkenes's reasons for why it is important for criminal justice professionals to study ethics.
3. Define *morals, ethics, values, duties,* and *ethical systems.*
4. What are the four elements that specify the types of behaviors that are judged under ethical criteria?
5. Which groups have been traditionally exempt from legal and moral culpability? Why?
6. What is the difference between duties and superogatories?
7. Do laws cover all moral rules? If your answer is no, explain why.
8. What are the elements of a crime? What are the levels of legal culpability? Do they match moral culpability?
9. Define regulations, standards, and guidelines. What is the difference in the punishments for a violation of these rules and the punishments for lawbreaking?
10. What is the difference between an ethical issue and an ethical dilemma? What are the steps in analyzing an ethical dilemma?

# Discussion Questions

1. Should we be concerned with a politician who has extramarital affairs? Drinks to excess? Gambles? Uses drugs? Abuses his or her spouse? What if the person was a police officer? A judge? Should a female police officer be sanctioned for posing naked in a men's magazine, using pieces of her uniform as "props"?
2. Should a probation officer socialize in bars that his or her probationers are likely to frequent?
3. Should a prosecutor be extremely active in a political party and then make decisions regarding targets of "public integrity" investigations of politicians?
4. Do you agree that a child before the legal age of reason is not morally culpable for his or her actions? Why or why not? What should the age of reason be?
5. What are some situations in which the individual cannot be considered rational or, alternatively, is not acting from free will? Can the behavior that results be defined as moral or immoral?
6. What about people who say that they "couldn't help themselves"? Do you think there is such a thing as an "irresistible impulse"?

7. Do you believe the state should regulate behavior that arguably doesn't hurt anyone else (such as laws regarding the wearing of motorcycle or bicycle helmets)? Prostitution? Gambling? Which, if any, laws do you believe legislate what should be private decisions of individuals?
8. Do you hold someone just as accountable for acts that are reckless and acts that are deliberate?
9. Which, if any, laws do you believe are themselves morally wrong (or support immoral behavior)?
10. If you followed all laws, would that make you a moral person?

# Ethical Dilemmas

## *Situation 1*

Patty was a rich businessman's daughter. She had the best of everything all her life. Her future would have been college, a good marriage to a successful young man, and a life of comparative luxury, except that she was kidnapped by a small band of radical extremists who sought to overthrow the government by terror, intimidation, and robbery. After being raped, beaten, and locked in a small, dark closet for many days, continually taunted and threatened, she was told she must participate with the terrorist gang in a bank robbery; otherwise, she and her family would be killed. During the course of the robbery, a bank guard was shot. Was her action immoral? What if she had killed the guard? What if the terrorists had kidnapped her mother or father, too, and told her if she didn't cooperate, they would kill her parents immediately?

What would you have done in her place? (Many readers might recognize this dilemma as the Patty Hearst case. In the 1970s the Symbionese Liberation Army, a terrorist group, kidnapped the daughter of Randolph Hearst, the tycoon of a large newspaper chain. Her subsequent capture, trial, conviction, and prison sentence have been portrayed in books and movies and provide ripe material for questions of free will and legal and moral culpability.)

## *Situation 2*

You are taking an essay exam in a college classroom. The test is closed book and closed notes, yet you look up and see that the person sitting next to you has hidden under his blue book a piece of paper filled with notes, which he is using to answer some questions. What would you do? Would your answer change if the test was graded on a curve? What if the student was a friend? What would you do if the student was flunking the course and was going to lose the scholarship he needed in order to stay in school?

## *Situation 3*

You are selected for a jury in a trial of a sixty-four-year-old mother who killed her two adult sons. The two men were institutionalized and suffered from Huntington's disease, a degenerative brain disease. They were certain to die and would endure much pain and suffering before they did. Her husband had also died from this same disease, and she had nursed him through his suffering. She took a gun into the nursing home, kissed her sons good-bye, and then shot them both through the head. She was arrested for first-degree murder. The prosecutor informs you that there is no "mercy killing" defense in the law as it is written. How would you decide this case if you were on the jury? What punishment does she deserve? (See K. Ellington, "Justice Tempered with Mercy," *Houston Chronicle*, January 30, 2003, 10A. The prosecutor accepted a plea of guilty to assisting suicide.)

## Situation 4

You are completing an internship with a juvenile probation agency and have truly enjoyed the experience. Although working with the kids is challenging, you also feel that there are many rewards in the job, especially when you sense that you are reaching a client and making a difference. Mr. Childers, the probation officer with whom you work, is less optimistic about the kids and operates in a strictly by-the-book legalistic manner. He is pretty burned out and basically does his job without getting too involved. Although you respect him, you know you would approach the clients differently if you got hired full time. One weekend you are out with friends and in a downtown bar frequented by college students. To your surprise, you look up and see Sarah, a sixteen-year-old probationer, dancing. You watch her and realize she is drunk and, in fact, is holding a beer and drinking it while she is dancing with a man who is obviously much older than she is. You go over to her, and she angrily tells you to mind your own business and immediately leaves with the guy. Later, though, she comes back into the bar and pleads with you to keep quiet. She is tearfully apologetic and tells you that she has already had several violations on her probation and at the last hearing was told that if she has one more, she will be sent to a juvenile detention center. You know Sarah has been doing much better in school and has plans to graduate and even go to college. On Monday morning you sit in Mr. Childers's office. What should you tell him?

## Situation 5

All your life you have played by the rules. Even after you went to college, you studied hard and never partied to the extent that it hurt your grades. During your senior year you began to make plans to graduate and begin your career. One Friday night you were in a car with four other students heading home from a bar. Before you knew what happened, the car was hit head on, and all of you were seriously injured—especially you. In fact, you are now paralyzed and facing the rest of your life in a wheelchair. The car that hit you was driven by a drunken student who, ironically, was in several of your classes. Several days after you return home from the hospital, he wants to see you. Despite your anger, you do see him, and he begs for your forgiveness. In fact, he totally breaks down and cries and tells you that he had never done anything like that before and wishes he were dead. Can you forgive him? When he is prosecuted, what would your sentence recommendation be? Would your answers be different if someone died? What if he had prior drunk-driving incidents? What if he had also committed other crimes and was not a fellow college student?

# Suggested Readings

Braswell, M., McCarthy, B., and McCarthy, B. (Eds.). 2002. *Justice, Crime and Ethics,* 3rd ed. Cincinnati: Anderson.

Dershowitz, A. 1994. *The Abuse Excuse and Other Cop-Outs, Sob Stories, and Evasions of Responsibility.* Boston: Little, Brown.

Leighton, P., and Reiman, J. 2001. *Criminal Justice Ethics.* Upper Saddle River, NJ: Prentice-Hall.

Miller, K., and Radelet, M. 1993. *Executing the Mentally Ill.* Newbury Park, CA: Sage.

Muraskin, R., and Muraskin, M. 2001. *Morality and the Law.* Upper Saddle River, NJ: Prentice-Hall.

Solomon, R. 2006. *The Big Questions: A Short Introduction to Philosophy.* Belmont, CA: Wadsworth.

One's ethics and morals, at times, may lead to expressing one's views and disagreeing with others, such as these conscientious objectors.

# 2
# Determining Moral Behavior

*Ethical Systems*

*Deontological and Teleological Ethical Systems*

*Other Ethical Systems*

*Other Methods of Ethical Decision Making*

*Relativism and Absolutism*

*Toward a Resolution: Situational Ethics*

*Resulting Concerns*

*Conclusion*

## Key Terms

act utilitarianism
cultural relativism
deontological ethical system
egoism
enlightened egoism
ethical formalism
ethical system
ethics of care
ethics of virtue
explication
generalization principle
hypothetical imperative
imperative principle

moral pluralism
natural law
principle of forfeiture
principle of the golden mean
psychological egoism
religious ethics
rule utilitarianism
situational ethics
social contract theory
teleological ethical system
utilitarian principle
utilitarianism

# Chapter Objectives

1. Become familiar with the major ethical systems and the criticisms leveled against each.

2. Become familiar with other ways to resolve ethical dilemmas in addition to the ethical systems.

3. Understand the controversy between relativism and absolutism.

4. Become familiar with how the major ethical systems have relevance to issues in criminal justice.

5. Learn how to apply the major ethical systems to ethical dilemmas.

Detective Russell Poole was a Robbery–Homicide Division investigator with the Los Angeles Police Department. In 1998 he was assigned an investigation regarding the alleged beating of Ismael Jimenez, a reputed gang member, by L.A.P.D. officers, and a suspected cover-up of the incident. In his investigation he uncovered a pattern of complaints of violence by the anti-gang task force in the Ramparts Division. Gang members told Poole and his partners that a number of officers harassed them, assaulted them, and pressured them to provide untraceable guns. The beating occurred because Jimenez would not provide the officers with a gun. In fact, in a search of the house of Rafael Perez, a member of the anti-gang task force, Poole found a box with a half-dozen very realistic replica toy guns. He concluded that a number of the officers in the division were "vigilante cops" and requested that the investigation proceed further.

Bernard Parks, the L.A.P.D. chief at the time, ordered him to limit his investigation solely to the Jimenez beating after Poole had informed his superiors of what his investigation had uncovered. Poole prepared a forty-page report on the Jimenez case for the district attorney's office, detailing the pattern of complaints, alleged assaults, and other allegations of serious wrongdoing on the part of the Rampart officers. Poole's report never reached the district attorney's office because his lieutenant, enforcing the chief's orders, replaced his detailed report with a two-page report written by the lieutenant and another supervisor. Poole knew that in not providing the district attorney's office with all the information he uncovered, he could be charged with obstruction of justice, and the report provided so little information that the officer probably would not even be charged. He was then asked by his lieutenant to put his name on the report (Golab, 2000). How did Sergeant Poole decide what was the right thing to do in this situation? He had conflicting duties and conflicting values. He knew that not signing the report might have serious consequences for his career. How would you determine the right thing to do if you were in a similar situation?

As discussed in the first chapter, if one is confronted with an ethical dilemma, there is a series of steps that can help one come to an ethical resolution:

1. *Identify the facts.* It is important to first identify all relevant facts.
2. *Identify relevant values and concepts.* One's values of duty, friendship, loyalty, honesty, and self-preservation are usually at the heart of professional ethical dilemmas. Concepts are like values in that neither is subject to empirical proof.
3. *Identify the possible choices one might make.* In order to resolve the dilemma, one must make a moral judgment about the right thing to do.
4. *Analyze the choices under an ethical system.* This judgment is made with the help of basic moral rules that are embedded in ethical systems. This chapter presents descriptions of a number of ethical systems.

# Ethical Systems

Our principles of right and wrong form a framework for the way we live our lives. But where do they come from? Before you read on, answer the following question: If you believe it is wrong to steal, why do you believe this to be so? You probably said it is because your parents taught you or because your religion forbids it—or maybe because society cannot tolerate people harming one another. Your answer is an indication of your **ethical system**. Ethical systems have a number of characteristics:

1. They are the source of moral beliefs.
2. They are the underlying premises from which you make judgments.
3. They are beyond argument. That is, although ethical decisions may become the basis of debate, the decisions are based on fundamental truths or propositions that are taken as a given by the individual employing the ethical system.

C. E. Harris (1986: 33) referred to such ethical systems as *moral theories* or *moral philosophies,* and defined them as a systematic ordering of moral principles. To be accepted as an ethical system, the system of principles must be internally consistent, must be consistent with generally held beliefs, and must possess a type of "moral common sense." Baelz (1977: 19) further described them as having the following characteristics:

1. *They are prescriptive.* Certain behavior is demanded or proscribed. They are not just abstract principles of good and bad but have substantial impact on what we do.
2. *They are authoritative.* They are not ordinarily subject to debate. Once an ethical framework has been developed, it is usually beyond question.

3. *They are logically impartial or universal.* Moral considerations arising from ethical systems are not based on favoritism: If something is considered wrong, it is wrong for everyone. Relativism has no place in an ethical framework.
4. *They are not self-serving.* They are directed toward others; what is good is good for everyone, not just the individual.

We don't consciously think of ethical systems, but we use them to make judgments. For instance, we might say that a woman who leaves her children alone to go out drinking has committed an immoral act. That would be a *moral judgment.* *Moral rules* that underlie this judgment might include the following:

"Children should be looked after."
"One shouldn't drink to excess."
"Mothers should be good role models for their children."

These basic moral rules are derived from an *ethical system.* The ethical judgment pyramid in Chapter 1 is a visual representation of this discussion. In this pyramid the ethical system is the base from which come moral rules or principles. In Figure 2-1, we revisit the ethical pyramid, but this time the moral judgment discussed above is displayed.

In this chapter we will not discuss all possible ethical systems, nor are the short descriptions here enough to fully explain each of the systems mentioned. A reader would be well advised to consult texts in philosophy and ethics for more detail. However, we will explore and provide brief summaries of the most often used ethical systems.

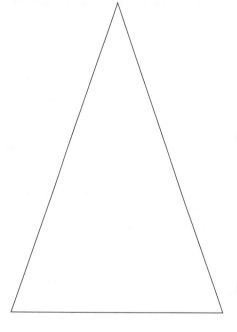

**Moral Judgment:**  A woman who goes out drinking leaving her children at home is bad.

**Moral Rules:**  Women should take care of their children. People should not drink to excess. Chilc should come before self. Drinking should be don moderation. One should do one's duty.

**Ethical System:**  This could be ethical formalism or utilitarianism or religion or ethics of care. The rules are logically inconsistent with egoism.

**Figure 2-1**  Ethical Pyramid

# Deontological and Teleological Ethical Systems
ᘜᗅᔆ

*Deontological* and *teleological* may be unfamiliar words, but the concepts that underlie them will be very familiar to you. There are two basic types of ethical systems:

1. Deontological systems
2. Teleological systems

A **deontological ethical system** is one that is concerned solely with the inherent nature of the act being judged. If an act or intent is inherently good (coming from a good will), then even if it results in bad consequences, it is still considered a good act. **Teleological systems** judge the consequences of an act. Even a bad act, if it results in good consequences, can be defined as good under a teleological system. The saying "the end justifies the means" is a teleological statement. The clearest examples of these two approaches are ethical formalism (a deontological or "nonconsequentialist" system) and utilitarianism (a teleological or "consequentialist" system).

## *Ethical Formalism*

**Ethical formalism** is a deontological system because the important determinant for judging whether an act is moral is not its consequence, but only the motive or intent of the actor. According to Kant, the only thing that is intrinsically good is a *good will*. If someone does an action from a good will, then even if it results in bad consequences, it can be considered a moral action. On the other hand, if someone performs some activity that looks on the surface to be altruistic but does it with an ulterior motive—for instance, to curry favor or gain benefit—then that act is not moral. For instance, Gold, Braswell, and McCarthy (1991) offer the example of a motorist stranded by the side of the road; another driver who comes along has a decision to help or pass by. If the decision is made to stop and help, this would seem to be a good act. Not so, according to ethical formalism, unless it is done from a good will. If the helper stops because he or she expects payment, wants a return favor, or for any reason other than a good will, then the act is only neutral—not moral. Only if the help springs from a good will can we say that it is truly good.

Immanuel Kant (1724–1804) believed that moral worth comes from doing one's duty (Kant, 1949). Just as there is the law of the family (father's rule), the law of the state and country, and the law of international relations, there is also a universal law of right and wrong. Morality, according to Kant, arises from the fact that humans, as rational beings, impose these laws and strictures of behavior upon themselves.

The following constitute the principles of Kant's ethical formalism (Bowie, 1985: 157):

1. *Act only on that maxim through which you can at the same time will that it should become a universal law.* In other words, for any decision of behavior to be made, examine whether that behavior would be acceptable if it were a universal law to be followed by everyone. For instance, a student might decide to cheat on a test, but for this action to be moral, the student would have to agree that everyone should be able to cheat on tests.

2. *Act in such a way that you always treat humanity, whether in your own person or that of any other, never simply as a means but always at the same time as an end.* In other words, one should not use people for one's own purposes. For instance, being friendly to someone so that you can use her car is using her as a means for one's own ends. Even otherwise moral actions, such as giving to charity or doing charitable acts for others, would be considered immoral if done for ulterior motives such as self-aggrandizement.

3. *Act as if you were, through your maxims, a lawmaking member of a kingdom of ends.* This principle directs that the individual's actions should contribute to and be consistent with universal law. Also, because we freely choose to abide by moral law and these laws are self-imposed rather than imposed from the outside, they are a reflection of the higher nature of humans.

These are absolute commands—together, they form the categorical imperative. According to Kant, **hypothetical imperatives** are commands that designate certain actions to attain certain ends. An example is, "*If* I want to be a success, *then* I must do well in college." By contrast, a categorical imperative commands action that is necessary without any reference to intended purposes or consequences (Kant, 1949: 76):

> This imperative is categorical. It concerns not the material of the action and its intended result but the form and the principle from which it results. What is essentially good in it consists in the intention, the result being what it may. This imperative may be called the imperative of morality.

A system such as ethical formalism is considered an absolutist system—if something is wrong, it is wrong all the time, such as murder or lying. To assassinate evil tyrants such as Adolf Hitler, Saddam Hussein, or Osama Bin Laden might be considered moral under a teleological system because of the action's consequence of ridding the world of dangerous people. However, in the deontological view, if the act and intent of killing are wrong, then killing is always wrong; thus, assassination must be considered immoral in all cases, regardless of the good consequences that might result. Even lying is deemed to be immoral in this system, despite some good arguments for the case that, at times, lying might be beneficial. For instance, Kant argued that if someone asked to be hidden from an attacker in close pursuit and then the attacker asked where the potential victim was hiding, it would be immoral to lie about the victim's location. This seems wrong to many and serves to dissuade people from seeing the value of ethical formalism. However, according to Kant, lying or not lying is not the determining factor in that scenario or in any other. An individual cannot control consequences—only actions—therefore, one must act in a moral fashion without regard to potential consequences. In the example, the attacker may not kill the potential victim; the victim may still be able to get away; the attacker may be justified—the point is that no one person can control anything in life, so the only thing that makes sense is to live by the categorical imperative.

Kant also defended his position with semantics—he distinguished untruths from lies with the explanation that a lie is a lie only when the recipient is led to believe or has a right to believe that he or she is being told the truth. The attacker in the previous scenario or an attacker who has one "by the throat" demanding one's money has no right to expect the truth; thus, it would not be immoral to not tell this person the truth. Only if one led the attacker to believe that one were going to tell the truth and then did not would one violate the categorical imperative. In other words, Kant distinguishes untruths from lies. To not tell the truth when the attacker doesn't deserve the truth is not a lie, but if one intentionally and deliberately sets out to deceive, then that is a lie—even if it is being told to a person who doesn't deserve the truth (Kant, 1981).

This ethical framework follows simply from the beliefs that an individual must follow a self-imposed moral law and that one is capable of using reason to determine right actions because any action can be evaluated by using the principles just listed. There are several criticisms of ethical formalism:

1. *It seems to be unresponsive to extreme circumstances.* If something is wrong in every circumstance regardless of the good that results or good reasons for the action, then otherwise good people might be judged immoral or unethical.
2. *Morality is limited to duty.* One might argue that duty is the baseline of morality, not the highest aspiration of it. Further, it is not always clear where one's duty lies. At times one might face a dilemma where two duties conflict with each other.
3. *The priority of motive and intent over result is problematic in some instances.* It may be seriously questioned whether the intention to do good, regardless of result or perhaps with negative result, is always moral. Many would argue that the consequences of an action and the actual result must be evaluated to determine morality. (Maestri, 1982: 910)

How would ethical formalism help resolve the dilemma faced by Sergeant Poole when he was asked to sign the "doctored" report for the district attorney's office? First, what was his duty? His duty was obviously to uphold the law. Did he also have a duty to obey his superiors? Did he have a duty to protect the police department from scandal? Did he have a duty to serve the public? Could he perform all these duties at the same time, or are they inconsistent with one another?

Applying the principles of ethical formalism to the dilemma, we can make the following observations:

1. *Act in such a way that the behavior could be universal.* Would covering up potential police misconduct be a rule that we would want to endorse universally? Probably not. It seems that if evidence is routinely held back from prosecutors, they would not be able to do their job.
2. *Do not treat others as a means to an end.* It seems clear that Poole's superiors were attempting to use him to further their own interest. Would he be using someone as a means to an end by signing the shortened report? Would he be using someone as a means to an end by not signing the shortened report?
3. *Behavior must be autonomous and freely chosen to be judged as moral.* If Poole was frightened or pressured into doing something, then the action would not be moral regardless of what it was. If, for instance, he believed that the district attorney would find out and come after him for falsifying a legal document, then he might not sign it, but it would not be because of a good will and therefore could not be considered a moral act.

Other writers present variations of deontological ethics that do not depend so heavily on Kant (Braswell, McCarthy, and McCarthy, 2002). The core elements of any deontological or duty-based ethical system are the importance placed on intention and the use of a predetermined set of principles to judge morality rather than looking at the consequences of an act.

## *Utilitarianism*

**Utilitarianism** is a teleological ethical system: What is good is determined by the consequences of the action. Jeremy Bentham (1748–1832), a major proponent of utilitarianism, believed that the morality of an action should be determined by how much it contributes to the good of the majority. According to Bentham, human nature seeks to maximize pleasure and avoid pain, and a moral system must be consistent with this natural fact.

The "utilitarian doctrine asserts that we should always act so as to produce the greatest possible ratio of good to evil for everyone concerned" (Barry, 1985: 65). That is, if you can show that an action significantly contributes to the general good, then it is good. In situations where one must decide between a good for an individual and a good for society, then society should prevail, despite the wrong being done to an individual. This is because the utility or good derived from that action generally outweighs the small amount of harm done (because the harm is done only to one, whereas the good is multiplied by the many). For instance, if it could be shown that using someone as an example would be an effective deterrent to crime, whether or not the person was actually guilty, the wrong done to that person by this unjust punishment might be outweighed by the good resulting for society. This assumes that citizens would not find out about the injustice and lose respect for the authority of the legal system, which would be a negative effect for all concerned.

### QUOTE and QUERY

Nature has placed mankind under the governance of two sovereign masters, pain and pleasure. It is for them alone to point out what we ought to do, as well as to determine what we shall do. On the one hand, the standard of right and wrong, on the other the chain of causes and effects, are fastened to their throne. They govern us in all we do, in all we say, in all we think; every effort we can make to throw off our subjection, will serve but to demonstrate and confirm it. In words, a man may pretend to abjure their empire: but in reality he will remain subject to it all the while. The principle of utility recognizes the subjection, and assumes it for the foundation of that system.

Source: Bentham, quoted in Borchert and Stewart (1986: 183).

*What is Bentham saying in this passage? Do you believe that all decisions are based fundamentally in seeking pleasure and avoiding pain?*

Bentham did not judge the relative weight of utility. He considered pleasure a good whether it derived from vice, such as avarice or greed, or from virtue, such as charity and kindness. Later utilitarians, primarily John Stuart Mill (1806–1873), believed that utilities (benefits) had different weights or values. In other words, some were better than others. For instance, art offers a different utility for society than alcohol, altruism carries more benefit than pleasure, and so on. On the other hand, who is to determine which is better? (Borchert and Stewart, 1986: 190). In fact, although the concept of weighing utilities to decide what action to take makes sense, the actual exercise is sometimes very difficult.

Another major difficulty related to utilitarianism is that the system presumes you can predict the consequences of your actions, but is that realistic? In the well-known "lifeboat" dilemma, five people are in a lifeboat with enough food and water only for four. It is certain that they will survive if there are only four; it is also certain that they will all perish if one does not go overboard. What should be done? Under ethical formalism, it would be unthinkable to sacrifice an innocent, even if it means that all will die. Under utilitarian ethics, it is conceivable that the murder of one might be justified to save the others. But this hypothetical situation points out the fallacy of the utilitarian argument. In reality, it is not known whether any will survive. The fifth might be murdered, and five minutes later, a rescue ship appears on the horizon. The fifth might be murdered, but then the remaining four are still eaten by sharks. Only in unrealistic hypothetical situations does one absolutely know the consequences of one's action. In real life, you never know if your action will result in a greater good or ultimate harm.

An important criticism of this ethical system is that there is little concern for individual rights in utilitarianism. Ethical formalism demands that each individual must be treated with respect and not be used as a means to an end. However, under utilitarianism, the rights of one individual may be sacrificed for the good of many. For instance, in World War II, Winston Churchill allowed Coventry to be bombed so the Germans would not know the Allies had cracked the Germans' secret military radio code. Several hundred English people were killed in the bombing raid of Coventry: Many might have been saved if they had been warned. It was a calculated loss for greater long-term gains: bringing the war to an end sooner. This could be justified under utilitarianism but perhaps not under ethical formalism. The Iraq war has been justified by the argument that it will save the lives of countless American citizens from some future terrorist acts and also protect Iraq citizens from a brutal dictator, but there is no question that in order to bring about this good end, innocent Iraq citizens have died, as have thousands of American soldiers. A utilitarian argument is used to justify these deaths.

Utilitarianism has two forms: act utilitarianism and rule utilitarianism. The basic difference between the two can be summarized as follows: In **act utilitarianism**, only the basic utility derived from an action is examined. We look at the consequences of any action for all involved and weigh the units of utility accordingly. In **rule utilitarianism**, one judges that action in reference to the precedent it sets and the long-term utility of the rule set by that action.

Act utilitarianism might support stealing food when one is hungry and has no other way to eat because the utility of survival would outweigh the loss to the store owner. On the other hand, rule utilitarianism would be concerned with the effect that the action would have if made into a rule for behavior: "Anytime an individual cannot afford food, he or she can steal it" would contribute to a state of lawlessness and a general disrespect for the law. Such a rule would probably not result in the greatest utility for the greatest number. With rule utilitarianism, then, we are not only concerned with the immediate utility of the action, but also with the long-term utility or harm if the action were to be a rule for all similar circumstances. Note the similarity between rule utilitarianism and the first principle of the categorical imperative. In both approaches, one must judge as good only those actions that can be universalized.

Applying utilitarianism to Detective Russell Poole's dilemma, it seems clear that his superiors were engaged in damage control. They did not want a scandal, especially considering that it had not been that long since the Rodney King incident. By suppressing evidence of further wrongdoing, they probably assumed that they could keep the information from the public and deal with it internally. In fact, Chief Parks fired more than 100 officers during his time as chief, but he did so in a way that the district attorney's office was unable to prosecute any of the officers for their alleged crimes. Internal Affairs routinely used a practice of compelling testimony without reading the officer his rights before questioning. This meant that the evidence obtained could be used to discipline the officer, but not to prosecute him or her. The result was that officers were fired, but their cases never ended up in court—or in the newspaper.

If Detective Poole used utilitarian reasoning, where did the greatest benefit lie? Was there greater benefit to all concerned in opposing his superiors' attempts to suppress the investigation, or with going along with the cover-up? Actually, the attempt to suppress the actions of the Ramparts Division officers was unsuccessful, anyway. A year after Poole refused to sign the report, Rafael Perez was prosecuted for stealing a large amount of cocaine from the evidence room. In a plea arrangement, he told investigators from the D.A.'s office the whole story of the Ramparts Division officers, leading to the biggest scandal in L.A.P.D.'s history (Golab, 2000; Boyer, 2001). This illustrates one of the problems with utilitarianism: If people sacrifice their integrity for what they consider is a good cause, it may result that they lose their integrity and still not achieve their good cause.

In summary, utilitarianism holds that morality must be determined by the consequences of an action. Society and the survival and benefit of all are more important than any individual. This is a functional theory of right and wrong—something is right when it benefits the continuance and good health of society. Rule utilitarianism may be closer to the principles of ethical formalism because it looks at general universal laws; the difference between the two is that the actions themselves are judged right or wrong depending on the motives behind them under ethical formalism, whereas utilitarianism looks to the long-term consequences of the behavior prescribed by the created rule to determine its morality.

# Other Ethical Systems

The following ethical systems can be described as deontological or teleological as well, although utilitarianism and ethical formalism are arguably the two best representatives of the contrast. As you read through these systems, apply the definitions of teleological systems and deontological systems to determine if you can categorize each. Some, such as egoism, are easy to categorize. It is clearly teleological. The others might not be so easy.

## *Religion*

Probably the most frequently used source of individual ethics is religion. Religion might be defined as a body of beliefs that addresses fundamental issues such as "What is life?" and "What is good and evil?" A religion also provides moral guidelines and directions on how to live one's life. For instance, Christians and Jews are taught the Ten Commandments, which prohibit certain behaviors defined as wrong. The authority of **religious ethics**, in particular Judeo-Christian ethics, stems from a willful and rational God. For believers, the authority of God's will is beyond question, and there is no need for further examination because of His perfection. The only possible controversy comes from human interpretation of God's commands. Indeed, these differences in interpretation are the source of most religious strife.

Religious ethics is, of course, much broader than simply Judeo-Christian ethics. Religions such as Buddhism, Confucianism, and Islam also provide a basis for ethics because they provide explanations of how to live the "good life" and also address other philosophical issues, such as "What is reality?" Pantheistic religions, those of primitive hunter–gatherer societies, promote the belief that there is a living spirit in all things. A basic principle follows from this belief that life is important and one must have respect for all things, including trees, rivers, and animals. However, there must be a willful and rational god or god figure before there can be a judgment of right and wrong, thus providing a basis for an ethical system. Those religions that do have a god figure consider that figure to be the source of principles of ethics and morality.

It is also true that of the religions we might discuss, many have similar basic moral principles. Many religions have their own version of the Ten Commandments; in this regard, Islam is not too different from Judaism, which is not too different from Christianity:

1. The Golden Rule: "Do unto others as you would have them do unto you."
2. Hinduism: "Do naught to others which, if done to thee, would cause thee pain: this is the sum of duty."
3. Buddhism: "In five ways should a clansman minister to his friends and familiars . . . by treating them as he treats himself."
4. Confucianism: "What you do not want done to yourself, do not do unto others."
5. Judaism: "Whatsoever thou wouldest that men should not do unto thee, do not do that to them." (Reiman, 1990: 147)

In Box 2-1, some other major world religions are described.

One issue in Western religious ethics is how to determine God's will. Some believe that God is inviolable and that positions on moral questions are absolute. This is a legalist position. Others believe that God's will varies according to time and place—the situationalist position. According to this position, situational factors are important in determining the rightness of a particular action. Something may be right or wrong depending on the circumstances (Borchert and Stewart, 1986: 157). For instance, lying may be wrong unless it is to protect an innocent, or stealing may be wrong unless it is to protest injustice and to help unfortunates. In fact, some would say it is impossible to have an *a priori* knowledge of God's will because that would put us above God's law: We ourselves cannot be "all-knowing." Thus, for any situation, if we are prepared to receive them, we can know God's divine commands through faith and conscience.

## BOX 2-1 Other Major World Religions

### Islam

One of the newest yet largest religions is Islam. Like Christianity, this religion recognizes one god, Allah. Jesus and other religious figures are recognized as prophets, as is Muhammed, who is considered the last and greatest prophet. Islam has the Koran, which is taken much more literally as the word of Allah than the Bible is taken by most Christians. There is a great deal of fatalism in Islam: *In Shallah,* meaning "If God wills it," is a prevalent theme in Muslim societies. On the other hand, there is recognition that if people choose evil, they do so freely. The five pillars of Islam are (1) repetition of the creed (*Shahada*), (2) daily prayer (*Salah*), (3) almsgiving (*Zakah*), (4) fasting (*Sawm*), and (5) pilgrimage (*Has*). One of the other features of Islam is the idea of the holy war. In this concept, the faithful who die defending Islam against infidels will be rewarded in the afterlife (Hopfe, 1983). However, this is not to say that Islam provides a legitimate justification for terroristic acts. Devout Muslims protest that terrorists have subverted the teachings of Islam and do not follow its precepts, one of which is to never harm innocents.

### Buddhism

Siddhartha Gautama (Buddha) attained enlightenment and preached to others how to do the same and achieve release from suffering. He taught that good behavior is that which follows the "middle path" between hedonistic pursuit of sensual pleasure and asceticism. Essentials of Buddhist teachings are ethical conduct, mental discipline, and wisdom. Ethical conduct is based on universal love and compassion for all living beings. Compassion and wisdom are needed in equal measures. Ethical conduct can be broken into right speech (refraining from lies, slander, enmity, and rude speech), right action (abstaining from destroying life, stealing, and dishonest dealings, and helping others lead peaceful and honorable lives), and right livelihood (abstaining from occupations that bring harm to others, such as arms dealing and killing animals). To follow the "middle path," one must abide by these guidelines (Kessler, 1992).

### Confucianism

Confucius taught a humanistic social philosophy that included central concepts such as *Ren,* which is human virtue and humanity at its best, as well as the source of moral principles; *Li,* which is traditional order, ritual, or custom; *Xiao,* which is familial love; and *Yi,* which is rightness, both a virtue and a principle of behavior—that is, one should do what is right because it is right. The doctrine of the mean exemplifies one aspect of Confucianism that emphasizes a cosmic or natural order. Humans are a part of nature and are included in the scheme of life. Practicing moderation in one's life is part of this natural order and reflects a "way to Heaven" (Kessler, 1992).

---

**Hinduism**

In Hinduism the central concept of *Karma* can be understood as consequence. Specifically, what one does in one's present life will determine what happens in a future life. The goal is to escape the eternal birth–rebirth cycle by living one's life in a moral manner so that no bad Karma will occur (Kessler, 1992). People start out life in the lowest caste, but if they live a good life, they will be reborn as members of a higher caste, until they reach the highest Brahman caste, and at that point the cycle can end. An early source for Hinduism was the Code of Manu. In this code are found the ethical ideals of Hinduism, which include pleasantness, patience, control of mind, nonstealing, purity, control of the senses, intelligence, knowledge, truthfulness, and nonirritability (Hopfe, 1983).

---

According to Barry (1985), human beings can "know" God's will in three ways:

1. *Individual conscience.* An individual's conscience is the best source for discovering what God wants one to do. If one feels uncomfortable about a certain action, it is probably wrong.
2. *Religious authorities.* They can interpret right and wrong for us and are our best source if we are confused about certain actions.
3. *Holy scriptures.* The third way is to go directly to the Bible, Koran, or Torah as the source of God's law. Some believe that the written word of God holds the answers to all moral dilemmas. (Barry, 1985: 51–54)

Strong doubts exist as to whether any of these methods are true indicators of divine command. Our consciences may be no more than the products of our psychological development, influenced by our environment. Religious authorities are, after all, only human, with human failings. Even the Bible seems to support contradictory principles.

The question of whether people can ever know God's will has been explored through the ages. Thomas Aquinas (1225–1274) believed that human reason was sufficient not only to prove the existence of God but also to discover God's divine commands (Borchert and Stewart, 1986: 159). Others feel that reason is not sufficient to know God and that it comes down to unquestioning belief, so reason and knowledge must always be separate from faith. These people believe that one can know whether an action is consistent with God's will only if it contributes to general happiness, because God intends for us to be happy, or when the action is done through the *holy spirit*—that is, when someone performs the action under the influence of true faith (Borchert and Stewart, 1986: 164–171).

To summarize, the religious ethics system is widely used and accepted. The authority of the god figure is the root of all morality; basic conceptions of good, evil, right, and wrong come from interpretations of the god figure's will. Many people throughout history have wrestled with the problem of determining what is right according to God, and current controversies within and between religious groups illustrate the unresolved difficulties that continue to exist.

**IN THE NEWS Conscientious Objectors**

Benjamin Hart Viges joined the army the day after September 11, 2001, in order to protect his country. It wasn't until he was in Iraq, however, before he realized that he couldn't kill. After freezing up instead of killing an Iraqi who had a rocket-propelled grenade aimed at his Humvee, he filed for a discharge under conscientious objector status. He said that his misgivings grew as he was being trained to kill, but his feelings regarding killing solidified after watching the movie, "The Passion of Christ." His religious beliefs, according to Viges, prohibit him from taking another's life—for any reason. He has encountered harassment from fellow soldiers and was assaulted by two masked men in his barracks before his final hearing. He didn't fight back. He was successful in proving his conscientious objector status and has received an honorable discharge from the army.

Source: A. Price, "Soldier's Path Winds from Front Lines to Protest Line," *Austin American Statesman,* September 19, 2005, A1, B9.

*Do you think that soldiers should be able to obtain discharges based on conscientious objector status? Why is it that Viges's Christian beliefs convince him that killing is wrong whereas other Christians who continue their army careers see no inconsistency between their profession and their faith?*

## *Natural Law*

The **natural law** ethical system holds that there is a universal set of rights and wrongs that is similar to many religious beliefs, but without reference to a specific supernatural figure. Originating with the Stoics, natural law is an ethical system wherein no difference is recognized between physical laws—such as the law of gravity—and moral laws. Morality is part of the natural order of the universe. Further, this morality is the same across cultures and times. In this view, Christians simply added God as a source of law (as other religions added their own prophets and gods), but there is no intrinsic need to resort to a supernatural figure because these universal laws exist quite apart from any religion (Maestri, 1982).

The natural law ethical system presupposes that what is good is what is natural and what is natural is what is good. The essence of morality is what conforms to the natural world; thus, there are basic inclinations that form the core of moral principles. For instance, the preservation of one's own being is a basic, natural inclination and thus is a basic principle of morality. Actions consistent with this natural inclination would be those that preserve one's own life, such as in self-defense, but also those that preserve or maintain the species, such as a prohibition against murder. Other inclinations are peculiar to one's species—for instance, humans are social animals; thus, sociability is a natural inclination that leads to altruism and generosity. These are natural and thus moral. The pursuit of knowledge or understanding of the universe might also be recognized as a natural inclination of humans; thus, actions that conform to this natural inclination are moral.

Souryal (1992) described natural law as the "steward" of natural rights. This country's founders might be described as natural law theorists. In the Constitution, "natural rights" endowed by the Creator are recognized. However, Fishman (1994) explained that Thomas Hobbes and John Locke transformed the original natural law theory that emphasized duties or obligations of humans in the natural order to one that emphasized "natural" human rights. In order to stay true to the internal consistency and historical legacy of natural rights theory, one must balance the emphasis on rights with an emphasis on obligations. For instance, the protection of individual freedoms as natural rights is an important component of any democracy, but that democracy can exist only when citizens accept and perform their obligations of citizenship. Citizens who are not vigilant in protecting their freedoms through the political process risk losing them. In this sense, natural law theory echoes the emphasis on duty found in ethical formalism.

Hobbes's claim that self-preservation (the law of the jungle) is paramount, and Locke's view that property is a natural right, created the foundation for the **social contract theory**. According to the social contract theory, members of society were originally engaged in a "war of all against all." The "contract" is one where individuals give up the freedom to aggress against others in return for their own safety. According to Hobbes, each individual has chosen to "lay down this right to all things; and be contented with so much liberty against other men, as he would allow other men against himself" (from Hobbes, *Leviathan,* 1651, quoted in Beauchamp, 1982: 264).

Natural law theory defines good as that which is natural. The difficulty of this system is identifying what is consistent and congruent with the natural inclinations of humankind. How do we know which acts are in accordance with the natural order of things? Who determines the natural laws? These are the fundamental problems with this ethical system.

## The Ethics of Virtue

Each of the foregoing ethical systems asks "What is a good action?" The **ethics of virtue** instead asks "What is a good person?" This ethical system rejects the approach that one might use reason to discover what is good. Instead, the principle is that to be good, one must do good. Virtues that a good person possesses include thriftiness, temperance, humility, industriousness, and honesty. It is a teleological system because it is concerned with acting in such a way as to achieve a good end (Prior, 1991). The specific "end" is happiness, or *eudaimonia.* However, the meaning of this word is not the same as the meaning given by utilitarians. This version of happiness does not mean simply having pleasure but also living a good life, reaching achievements, and attaining moral excellence.

The roots of this system are in the work of Aristotle, who defined virtues as "excellences." These qualities are what enable an individual to move toward the achievement of what it takes to be human. Aristotle distinguished intellectual virtues (wisdom, understanding) from moral virtues (generosity, self-control). The moral virtues are not sufficient for "the good life"; one must also have the intellectual virtues, primarily "practical reason." Evidently, Aristotle was a learning theorist—he believed that we are, by nature, neither good nor evil but become so through training and the acquisition of habits:

> [T]he virtues are implanted in us neither by nature nor contrary to nature: we are by nature equipped with the ability to receive them and habit brings this ability to completion and fulfillment. (Aristotle, quoted in Prior, 1991: 156–157)

Habits of moral virtue are obtained through following the example of a moral *exemplar.* They are also more easily instilled when "right" or just laws also exist. Moral virtue is a state of character in which choices are consistent with the **principle of the golden mean.** This principle states that virtue is always the median between two extremes of character. For instance, liberality is the mean between prodigality and meanness, proper pride is the mean between empty vanity and undue humility, and so on (Albert, Denise, and Peterfreund, 1984). The "Catalog of Virtues" (Box 2-2) lists others.

Moral virtue comes from habit, which is why this system emphasizes character. The idea here is that one does not do good because of reason; rather, one does good because of the patterns of a lifetime. If one has a good character, she or he will do the right thing, but if one has a bad character, she or he will usually choose the immoral path. In *Character and Cops: Ethics in Policing,* Edwin Delattre uses an excerpt from a police chief 's biography to illustrate an individual who represents the ethics of virtue:

> One Friday, just before Christmas in 1947, Seedman helped lug into the Safe and Loft office dozens of cartons of toys that had been recovered from a hijacking case. There were dolls, teddy bears, stuffed animals of all kinds. Ray McGuire, busy overseeing the operation, suddenly looked up and saw that it was close to three o'clock. "I'm never going to get to lunch," he said. "I was going to stop at Macy's to pick up some toys for my girls." One of the detectives mentioned he had to do the same at Macy's. McGuire handed him a twenty-dollar bill. "Pick up a pair of dolls for me, will ya?" (cited in Delattre, 1989a: 41)

It never even occurred to McGuire to take any of the dolls and toys surrounding him because that would be stealing. As Delattre writes, "The habit of not even considering

---

**BOX 2-2  Catalog of Virtues**

| Area | Defect | Mean | Excess |
|------|--------|------|--------|
| fear | cowardice | courage | recklessness |
| pleasure | insensitivity | self-control | self-indulgence |
| money | stinginess | generosity | extravagance |
| honor | small-mindedness | high-mindedness | vain |
| anger | apathy | gentleness | short temper |
| truth | self-depreciation | truthfulness | boastfulness |
| shame | shamelessness | modesty | self-hate |

SOURCE: Adapted from Prior (1991: 165).

greedy behavior, of not speculating about ways to profit from vice, prevents such conduct from ever occurring to us" (1989a: 41).

An ethical formalist might say that McGuire applied the categorical imperative to the situation and concluded that the action of taking a doll violated the categorical imperative of universalism. A utilitarian formulation would have McGuire weigh the relative utilities of taking the doll or not. However, in the ethics of virtue, as Delattre indicates, if one has developed a habit of integrity, taking advantage of the situation never even occurs to that person. Under this moral system, those individuals who possess the necessary virtue will act morally, and those who don't will act immorally.

It should also be noted that most of us have some virtues and not others. There are many other virtues besides those already mentioned, including compassion, courage, conscientiousness, and devotion. Some of us may be completely honest in all of our dealings but not generous. Some may be courageous but not compassionate. Therefore, we all are moral to the extent that we possess moral virtues, but some of us are more moral than others by having more virtues. One difficulty is in judging the primacy of moral virtues. For instance, in professional ethics there are often conflicts that involve honesty and loyalty. If both are virtues, how does one resolve a dilemma in which one virtue must be sacrificed?

The ethics of virtue probably explains more of individual behavior than other ethical systems because most of the time, if we have developed habits of virtue, we do not even think about the possible "bad" acts we might do. For instance, most of us do not have to analyze the "rightness" or "wrongness" of stealing every time we go into a store. We do not automatically consider lying every time a circumstance arises. Most of the time, we do the right thing without thinking about it a great deal. However, when faced with a true dilemma—that is, a choice where the "right" decision is unclear—the ethics of virtue may be less helpful as an ethical system.

Alasdair MacIntyre (1991: 204), a current philosopher, defines virtues as those dispositions that will sustain us in the relevant "quest for the good, by enabling us to overcome the harms, dangers, temptations and distractions which we encounter, and which will furnish us with increasing self-knowledge and increasing knowledge of the good." In recent works, MacIntyre (1999) seems to move closer to an ethics of care approach because he discusses the need for virtue as necessary in order to care for the next generation. He sees life as one of "reciprocal indebtedness" and emphasizes "networks of relationships" as the locale of giving and receiving the benefits of virtues. This language is very similar to the ethical system of the ethics of care, which will be discussed in the next section.

Detective Poole reported that he never considered putting his name on a report he knew was wrong. His superiors, co-workers, and colleagues describe him as "professional," "hard working," "loyal, productive, thorough and reliable," "diligent," "honest," and "extremely credible." He was known as a first-rate investigator and trusted by the D.A.'s office to provide thorough and credible testimony. In other words, his habits in his professional life were directly contrary to participating in a cover-up. Those who advocate the ethics of virtue would predict that Poole would not participate in a cover-up because of his character—and they would be right because he did not sign the report (Golab, 2000).

## The Ethics of Care

The **ethics of care** is another ethical system that does not depend on universal rules or formulas to determine morality. The emphasis is on human relationships and needs. The ethics of care has been described as a feminine morality because women in all societies are the childbearers and consequently seem to have a greater sensitivity to issues of care. Noddings (1986: 1) points out that the "mother's voice" has been silent in Western, masculine analysis: "One is tempted to say that ethics has so far been guided by Logos, the masculine spirit, whereas the more natural and perhaps stronger approach would be through Eros, the feminine spirit." The ethics of care is founded in the natural human response to care for a newborn child, the ill, and the hurt.

Carol Gilligan's work on moral development in psychology, discussed in more detail in Chapter 3, identified a feminine approach to ethical dilemmas that focuses on relationships and needs instead of rights and universal laws. She found that in their responses to ethical dilemmas, some women were resistant to solving the dilemmas given the restraints of the exercise. They wanted to know what would happen after the fact, they wanted to know what the person felt, and they wanted to know other elements that might be deemed irrelevant if one were applying a "rights-based" ethical system.

These women were ranked fairly low on the moral development scale, yet Gilligan proposed that theirs was not a less developed morality but rather a different morality. The most interesting feature of this approach is that while a relatively small number of women emphasized needs over rights, no men did. She attributed this to the fact that in Western society, both men and women are socialized to Western ethics, which are primarily concerned with issues of rights, laws, and universalism (Gilligan, 1982).

Applying the ethics of care leads not to different solutions necessarily, but perhaps to different questions. In an ethical system based on care, we would be concerned with issues of needs rather than rights. Other writers point to some Eastern religions, such as Taoism, as illustrations of the ethics of care (Gold et al., 1991). In these religions, a rigid, formal, rule-based ethics is rejected in favor of gently leading the individual to follow a path of caring for others. In criminal justice, the ethics of care is represented to some extent by the rehabilitative ethic rather than the just-deserts model. Certainly the "restorative justice" movement is consistent with the ethics of care because of its emphasis on the motives and needs of all concerned, rather than simply retribution. In personal relationships, the ethics of care would promote empathy and treating others in a way that does not hurt them. In this view, meeting needs is more important than securing rights.

Recently, there have been several writers who have exemplified the "ethics of care" operating in criminal justice. Whether it is called feminine justice, peacemaking justice, restorative justice, or some other term, various authors are discussing alternative concepts to retribution and punishment that are distinct from treatment goals that characterized an earlier era. For instance, in a recent text, Braswell and Gold (2002) discuss a concept called *peacemaking justice*. They show that the concept is derived from ancient principles, and it concerns care as well as other concepts: "Peacemaking, as evolved from ancient spiritual and wisdom traditions, has included the possibility of mercy and compassion within the framework of justice" (2002: 25). They propose that the peacemaking process is composed of three parts: connectedness, caring, and mindfulness.

1. "Connectness" has to do with the interrelationships we have with one another and all of us have with the Earth.
2. "Caring" is similar to Noddings's concept that the "natural" inclination of humans is to care for one another.
3. "Mindfulness" involves being aware of others and the world in all personal decision making (Braswell and Gold, 2002: 25–37). Policy Box 2-1 explores this approach as a policy decision.

To summarize, the ethics of care approach identifies the needs of all individuals in any ethical situation and attempts to maximize them. It is different from utilitarianism, however, in that one person cannot be sacrificed for others. Also, there is an attempt to resolve situations through human relationships and a sense that decisions should come from compassion rather than attention to rights or duties.

---

### POLICY BOX 2-1  Peacemaking Justice

Whether one calls the approach peacemaking justice, restorative justice, or some other term, there are many examples across the nation of a different approach to lawbreaking. It is more often used with juvenile offenders and involves an emphasis on the needs of both parties in the criminal event—the victim and the offender. Often, the offender and victim meet in some type of mediation setting. Very often, the offender is asked to agree to some form of restitution, in many cases specifically to the victim. It could be the case that the offender meets with not just the victim but also with family members, teachers, and neighbors in an intervention designed to identify the cause of the wrongdoing. Some people, particularly prosecutors and victims' rights advocates, are not in favor of the justice system moving in this direction.

**Law:** There may need to be enabling laws that allow for certain types of sentences developed under restorative justice programs. In general, the discretion of the judge would probably allow for any form of resolution that was arranged.

**Policy:** In general, prosecutors' offices have policies that require that the victim be involved and agree to any sentence. This is not contradictory to restorative justice. If the policy of the prosecutor's office was to pursue the harshest sentence possible for all offenders, then that policy would be counter to the restorative approach.

**Individual ethics:** District attorneys set the policy of the office. Their definitions of justice play an important role. They may create an environment where their jurisdiction is a model for restorative justice programs, or they may discourage or forbid such programs from being implemented.

## *Egoism*

Very simply, **egoism** postulates that what is good for one's survival and personal happiness is moral. The extreme of this position is that all people should operate on the assumption that they can do whatever benefits themselves. Others become the means to ensure happiness and have no meaning or rights as autonomous individuals. **Psychological egoism** is a descriptive principle rather than an ethical prescription. Psychological egoism refers to the idea that humans are naturally egoists and that it would be unnatural for them to be any other way. All species have instincts for survival, and self-preservation and self-interest are merely part of that instinct. Therefore, it is not only moral to be egoistic, but it is the only way we can be, and any other explanations of behavior are mere rationalizations.

**Enlightened egoism** is a slight revision of this basic principle, adding that the objective is long-term welfare. This may mean that we should treat others as we would want them to treat us to ensure cooperative relations. Even seemingly selfless and altruistic acts are consistent with egoism because these acts benefit the individual by giving self-satisfaction. Under egoism, it would be not only impossible but also immoral for someone to perform a completely selfless act. Even those who give their lives to save others do so perhaps with the expectation of rewards in the afterlife.

Egoism completely turns around the priorities of utilitarianism to put the individual first, before anyone else and before society as a whole. As Harris (1986: 47) puts it,

> Egoism as a moral philosophy originated in ancient Greece, but the modern emphasis on the individual in competition with other individuals has given it special prominence. The egoistic moral standard states that actions are right if and

---

**EXERCISE  The Prisoner's Dilemma**

This group exercise illustrates some of the issues that have been discussed in this section. The scenario is that there are two prisoners; they are told that if one confesses, that person will go free, but the partner will face the death penalty. If neither confesses, they will both get two years. If both confess, they will both get life. Of course, the decision has to be made *without knowing* what the other prisoner will choose. One sees that if a prisoner depends on the other's cooperation, he or she may suffer serious consequences. Assign two individuals to be the prisoners, and have the individuals make decisions in successive trials. Or do it as a group exercise, and have two groups be the prisoners. See what happens over six trials of the game.

***What would an egoist do? What would a utilitarian do? What would someone who followed the ethics of care do?***

only if they produce consequences that are at least as good for the self-interest of the egoist as the consequences of any alternative action. Each egoist must personally define self-interest and propose a hierarchy of goods within that definition. Most egoists will be concerned with the fullest realization of their self-interest over a lifetime rather than during only a short period of time.

Ayn Rand (1905–1982) is perhaps the best-known modern writer/philosopher associated with this system. She promoted both of the following:

1. psychological egoism (that humans are naturally selfish)
2. ethical egoism (that humans should be self-interested)

It should also be noted that our capitalistic economic system is, to some degree, premised upon egoism. Capitalism is based on the premise that everyone pursuing self-interest will create a healthy economy: Workers will work harder to get more pay; owners will not exploit workers too badly because they might quit; merchants will try to get the highest price for items whereas consumers will shop for the lowest price; and so on. It is only when government or liberal do-gooders manipulate the market, some argue, that it does not work optimally.

Egoism is rejected by most philosophers because it violates the basic tenets of an ethical system. Universalism is inconsistent with egoism, because to approve of all people acting in their own self-interest is not a logical or feasible position. It cannot be right for both me and you to maximize our own self-interests because it would inevitably lead to conflict. Egoism would support exploitative actions by the strong against the weak, which seems wrong under all other ethical systems. However, psychological egoism is a relevant concept in natural law (self-preservation is natural) and utilitarianism (hedonism is a natural inclination). But if it is true that humans are *naturally* selfish and self-serving, one can also point to examples that indicate that humans are also altruistic and self-sacrificing. What is the true nature of humankind?

## Other Methods of Ethical Decision Making

There are other approaches to ethical analysis in addition to the ethical systems discussed above. John Rawls (1957) presents a somewhat abstract procedure for deciding moral issues. He explains that moral principles can be developed through inductive logic. The method to discover these moral principles is through the considered moral judgments of a number of cases by a number of moral judges. These individuals would have the following characteristics:

1. They would possess common sense—they would not intellectualize the problem but apply common reason to arrive at a resolution.
2. They would have open minds.
3. They would know their own emotions.
4. They would have a sympathetic knowledge of humans.

The cases given them to decide would be such that the judges would not be harmed or benefited in any way by their decision in order to ensure neutrality.

The cases would present real conflicts of interest, but conflicts that were not too difficult and that were likely to present themselves in ordinary life. The judges would be presented with all relevant facts in the matter so that they could make a reasoned judgment. The judgments should be certain, and they should be stable; that is, other judges at other times should also arrive at the same judgments. Finally, the judgments should be intuitive. The reason for this is that ethical principles are to be derived from a series of judgments, and if judges were already using predetermined rules, there would be no way to derive general rules from the judgments.

Rawls (1957: 180) describes the procedure in the following way:

> Up to this point I have defined, first a class of competent judges, and, second, a class of considered judgments. If competent judges are those persons most likely to make correct decisions, then we should take care to abstract those judgments of theirs which, from the conditions and circumstances under which they are made, are most likely to be correct.

The next step is to formulate an explication of the total range of judgments. An **explication** is a set of principles described as follows (Rawls, 1957: 182):

> [I]f any competent man were to apply them intelligently and consistently to the same cases under review, his judgments, made systematically nonintuitive by the explicit and conscious use of the principles, would be, nevertheless identical, case by case, with the considered judgments of the group of competent judges.

These explications must be written in ordinary language, be written in the form of principles, and be comprehensive in solving the range of moral judgments. In other words, common principles are extrapolated from the decisions of the moral judges, and these common principles are then used by the rest of us in decision making (Rawls, 1957).

Obviously, Rawls's proposal is more a rhetorical device than a useful tool for deciding ethical issues. However, the basic premise of his approach is to discover common principles that can be used to decide moral questions. This is fundamental to any logical solution to moral dilemmas. The ethical systems present principles similar to the explications Rawls seeks through moral judges. Another principle that one can derive from Rawls' discussion is that only neutral judges can develop objective and fair moral principles.

The use of basic moral or ethical principles can also be found in more pragmatic guidelines for use in decision making. A method proposed by Laura Nash (1981) helps individuals make business decisions, and these same questions seem applicable to those situations faced by criminal justice professionals (see Box 2-3).

Although Nash's guidelines are obviously directed to business decisions, they have applicability to other fields. Basically, the questions are designed to lead individuals to analyze their behavior and its implications. There is an assumption that exposure of unethical conduct will make the individual feel uneasy. To some extent, there is an assumption that a commonly agreed-upon definition of right and wrong exists.

---

**BOX 2-3  How to Make an Ethical Decision**

1. Have you defined the problem accurately?
2. How would you define the problem if you stood on the other side of the fence?
3. How did the situation occur in the first place?
4. To whom and to what do you give your loyalty as a person and as a member of the corporation?
5. What is your intention in making this decision?
6. How does this intention compare with the probable result?
7. Whom could your decision or action injure?
8. Can you discuss the problem with the affected parties before you make your decision?
9. Are you confident that your position will be as valid over a long period of time as it seems now?
10. Could you disclose without qualms your decision or action to your boss, your CEO, the board of directors, your family, your society as a whole?
11. What is the symbolic potential of your action if understood? If misunderstood?
12. Under what conditions would you allow exceptions to your stand?

SOURCE: Nash (1981: 81).

---

The general principles that can be drawn from these questions are obvious:

1. First, we are interested in attaining all the facts of the situation; this includes the effects of the decision on oneself and others. It is important to understand hidden motivations and indirect effects.
2. Second, the concept of scrutiny works well to evaluate the decision taken; one must be comfortable with public disclosure. Along with this concept goes the notion that others should be able to make the same decision and have it judged acceptable.
3. Finally, the concept of rationale or reason implies that the individual decision is based on a larger set of moral or ethical principles.

Let us apply these guidelines to a criminal justice example. If a police officer were confronted with an opportunity to accept some type of gratuity, either a dinner or a more expensive present, the officer could go through these steps:

1. First, evaluate all facts. Is anything expected in return? Is the gift really a gift, or a payment for some service?
2. Would the officer be comfortable if others knew of the gift or gratuity? Would he feel comfortable if other officers or other citizens knew he received the gift or gratuity?
3. Could the officer reconcile the decision to take the gratuity with a larger set of moral principles, such as the Law Enforcement Code of Ethics? What is the "symbolic potential" of the gratuity?

Krogstand and Robertson (1979) describe three principles of ethical decision making:

1. The **imperative principle** directs a decision maker to act according to a specific, unbending rule.
2. The **utilitarian principle** determines the ethics of conduct by the good or bad consequences of the action.
3. The **generalization principle** is based on this question: "What would happen if all similar persons acted this way under similar circumstances?"

These should sound familiar because they are, respectively, religious or absolutist ethics, utilitarianism, and ethical formalism. If one is familiar with these ethical principles, then any specific dilemma can be analyzed using an ethical framework as a guideline. To question one's general ethical behavior, take the challenging self-survey in Box 2-4. The set of questions takes a general approach to evaluating one's ethics. It comes from the American

---

**BOX 2-4　Ethics Self-Survey**

1. Do I confront difficult ethical decisions directly and attempt to think through the alternatives and the principles involved? Am I inclined to make decisions on grounds of convenience, expediency, pressure, impulse, or inertia?
2. Do I systematically review my behavior and question whether what I do is consistent with my professional values?
3. If someone asked me to explain my professional ethics, what would I say?
4. Have my values and ethics changed since I began working? If so, why and how have they changed? What are the primary influences that have changed my thinking?
5. Looking ahead to the remainder of my career, are there particular areas of my ethical conduct to which I would like to pay closer attention?
6. Do I ever find myself in situations in which providing equitable treatment to clients, members of my organization, or members of other organizations creates ethical conflicts? How do I handle such dilemmas? Can I perceive any consistent pattern in my behavior?
7. Where do my professional loyalties ultimately lie? With the Constitution? The law? My organization? My superiors? My clients? The general public? Do I feel torn by these loyalties? How do I deal with the conflicts?
8. Do I ever confront situations in which I feel that it is unfair to treat everyone in the same way? How do I determine what to do in those cases? How do I decide what is fair?
9. When I am responsible for some activity that turns out to be inappropriate or undesirable, do I accept full responsibility for it? Why? How?
10. Do I ever dismiss criticism of my actions with the explanation that I am only "following orders"? Do I accept any responsibility for what happens in these circumstances?

SOURCE: Adapted from American Society for Public Administration (1979: 22–23).

Society for Public Administration (1979: 22–23) but has been adapted where necessary to apply to those who work in the criminal justice field.

Close and Meier (1995: 130) provide a set of questions more specific to criminal justice professionals and sensitive to the due-process protections that are often discarded in a decision to commit an unethical act. They propose that the individual decision maker should ask the following questions:

1. Does the action violate another person's constitutional rights, including the right of due process?
2. Does the action involve treating another person only as a means to an end?
3. Is the action illegal?
4. Do you predict that your action will produce more bad than good for all persons affected?
5. Does the action violate department procedure or professional duty?

Finally, the simplest formulation of questions on which to base an ethical decision is as follows:

1. Does it affect others?
2. Does it hurt others?
3. Would I want it done if I were on the other side?
4. Would I be proud of the decision?

These four simple questions may be sufficient to address most ethical dilemmas. In the end, most of us seek to make good decisions when confronted with moral or ethical dilemmas. Whichever decision-making method one chooses, the first step is to recognize that there is a choice to be made.

---

### QUOTE and QUERY

All I really need to know about how to live and what to do and how to be I learned in kindergarten. Wisdom was not at the top of the graduate-school mountain, but there in the sand pile at Sunday School. These are the things I learned:

Share everything.
Play fair.
Don't hit people.
Put things back where you found them.
Clean up your own mess.
Don't take things that aren't yours.
Say you're sorry when you hurt somebody. . . .

Robert Fulghum, *All I Really Needed to Know I Learned in Kindergarten* (New York: Villard Books, 1986): 6. Copyright © 1986, 1988 by Robert Fulghum. Reprinted by permission of Villard Books, a division of Random House, Inc.

**Would you add any basic rules to these that Fulghum, somewhat tongue-in-cheek, proposes as a code to live by?**

# Relativism and Absolutism

Ethical relativism describes those moral systems in which what is good or bad changes, depending on the individual or group. The generation of the 1960s encapsulated this belief in the saying "You do your thing, and I'll do mine." What is right is determined by culture and/or individual belief; there are no universal laws.

There are two main arguments for relativism:

1. There are many different moral standards of behavior. According to Stace (1995: 26), "We find that there is nothing, or next to nothing, which has always and everywhere been regarded as morally good by all men."
2. We do not know how to determine the absolute rules. Who is to say what is right and what is wrong?

One may look to anthropology and the rise of social science to explain the popularity of moral relativism. Over the course of studying different societies—past and present, primitive and sophisticated—anthropologists have found that there are very few universals across cultures. Even those behaviors often believed to be universally condemned, such as incest, have been institutionalized and encouraged in some societies (Kottak, 1974: 307). Basically, **cultural relativism** defines good as that which contributes to the health and survival of society. For instance, societies where women are in ample supply may endorse polygyny, and societies that have a shortage of women may accept polyandry; hunting and gathering societies that must contend with harsh environments may hold beliefs allowing for the euthanasia of burdensome elderly, whereas agricultural societies that depend on knowledge passed down through generations may revere their elderly and accord them an honored place in society.

In criminology, cultural differences in perceptions of right and wrong are important to the subcultural deviance theory of crime, wherein some deviant activity is explained by subcultural approval of that behavior. The example typically used to illustrate this is that of the Sicilian father who kills the man who raped his daughter, because to do otherwise would violate values of his subculture emphasizing personal honor and retaliation (Sellin, 1970: 187). A more recent case of subcultural differences involves a father who sold his fourteen-year-old daughter into marriage. Because he lived in Chicago, he was arrested; if he had lived in his homeland of India, he would have been conforming to accepted norms of behavior. We should also note how governments attempt to change culture through the criminal law. The cultural support in India for killing wives whose families do not provide the dowry is being slowly eroded by the current legal system that (albeit halfheartedly) investigates and punishes those responsible. Cultural relativists recognize the differences in cultures; absolutists argue that the mere existence of cultural norms does not make them moral.

Although cultural relativism accepts the fact that different societies may have different moral standards, it also dictates that individuals within a culture conform to the standards of their culture. Therein lays a fundamental flaw in the relativist approach: If there are no universal norms, why should individuals be required to conform to societal or cultural norms? If their actions are not accepted today, it might be argued, they could be accepted tomorrow—if not by their society, perhaps by some other. An additional inconsistency in cultural relativism is the corresponding prohibition against interfering in another culture's norms. The argument goes as follows: Because every culture is correct in its definitions of morality, another culture should not step in to change those definitions. However, if what is right is determined by which culture one happens to belong to, why then, if that culture happens to be imperialistic, would it be wrong to force cultural norms on other cultures? Cultural relativism attempts to combine an absolute (no interference) with a relativistic "truth" (there are no absolutes). This is logically inconsistent (Foot, 1982).

Cultural relativism usually concerns behaviors that are always right in one society and always wrong in another. Of course, what is more common is behavior that is judged to be wrong most of the time but acceptable in certain instances. For example, killing is wrong except possibly in self-defense and war; lying is wrong except when one lies to protect another. Occupational subcultures also support standards of behavior that are acceptable only for those within the occupation. For instance, some police officers believe that it is wrong to break the speed limit unless one happens to be a police officer—even an off-duty one. Some politicians believe that certain laws don't apply to them because they are the ones who create the laws or because they can substitute their own judgment about what is best for the country. Some of these occupational ethics may be justified, but others may not be by any of the ethical decision-making methods we have discussed in this chapter.

It must be noted that even absolutist systems may accept some exceptions. The **principle of forfeiture** associated with deontological ethical systems holds that people who treat others as means to an end or take away or inhibit their freedom and well-being forfeit the right to protection of their own freedom and well-being (Harris, 1986: 136). Therefore, people who aggress first forfeit their own right to be protected from harm. This could permit self-defense (despite the moral proscription against taking life) and possibly provide justification for lying to a person who threatens harm. Critics of an absolutist system see this exception as a rationalization and a fatal weakness to the approach; in effect, moral rules are absolute *except* for those exceptions allowed by some "back-door" argument.

Relativism allows for adaptation to specific circumstances, but universalists would argue that if moral absolutes are removed, subjective moral discretion leads to egoistic rationalizations. I might believe that lying for a good cause is acceptable, but how do I determine what is a "good enough" cause to lie for? And if I can justify it for one reason, why not another, and another?

## Toward a Resolution: Situational Ethics

**Situational ethics** is often used as a synonym for *relativism;* however, if we clarify the term to include certain fundamental absolute elements, it might serve as a resolution to the problems inherent in both an absolutist and a relativist approach to ethics. Recall that relativism, on one hand, is criticized because it must allow any practice to be considered "good" if it is considered good by some people; therefore, even human sacrifice and cannibalism would have to be considered moral, a thoroughly unpalatable consequence of accepting the doctrine. Absolutism, on the other hand, is also less than satisfactory because we all can think of some examples where the "rule" must be broken; even Kant declined to be purely absolutist in his argument that lying isn't really lying if told to a person who is trying to harm us. What is needed, then, is an approach that resolves both problems.

Hinman (1998) resolves this debate by defining the balance between absolutism and relativism as **moral pluralism.** In his elaboration of this approach, he stops short of an "anything goes" rationale but does recognize multicultural "truths" that affect moral perceptions. The solution offered here, whether one calls it situational ethics, or some other term, is as follows:

1. There are basic principles of right and wrong.
2. These can be applied to ethical dilemmas and moral issues.
3. These principles may call for different results in different situations, depending on the needs, concerns, relationships, resources, weaknesses, and strengths of the individual actors.

Situational ethics is different from relativism because absolute laws are recognized, whereas under relativism there are no laws. What are absolute laws? Natural law, the Golden Rule, and the ethics of care could help us fashion a set of moral absolutes that might be general enough to ensure universal agreement. For instance, we could start with the following propositions:

1. Treat each person with the utmost respect and care.
2. Do one's duty or duties in such a way that one does not violate the first principle.

These principles would not have anything to say about dancing (as immoral or moral), but they would definitely condemn human sacrifice, child molestation, slavery, and a host of other practices that have been part of human society. Practices could be good in one society and bad in another—for instance, if polygamy was necessary to ensure the survival of society, it might be acceptable; if it was to serve the pleasure of some by using and treating others as mere objects, it would be immoral. Selling daughters into marriage to enrich the family would never be acceptable because that is not treating them with respect and care; however, arranged marriages might be acceptable if all parties agree and the motives are consistent with care.

To resolve the dilemma from Chapter 1 of the police officer who stops his father for DWI, one might argue that he can do his duty and still respect and care for his father. He could help his father through the arrest process, treat him with care, and make sure that he received help, if he needed it, for his drinking. Although this might not be enough to placate his father, and his father might still be angry with him, as would others, their reaction could then be analyzed: Are they treating the officer with care and respect? Does his father respect him if he expects his son to ignore a lawful duty?

This system is not too different from a flexible interpretation of Kant's categorical imperative, a strict interpretation of rule-based utilitarianism, or an inclusive application of the Golden Rule. All ethical systems (except egoism) struggle with objectivity and subjectivity, along with respect for the individual and concern for society. Interestingly, situational ethics seems to be entirely consistent with the ethics of care, especially when

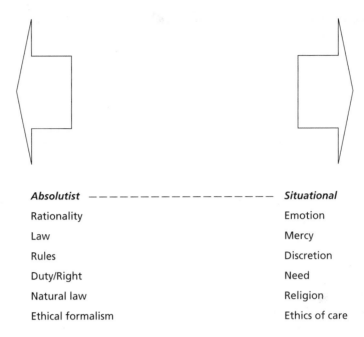

| Absolutist — — — — — — — — — — — — — — — — — | Situational |
|---|---|
| Rationality | Emotion |
| Law | Mercy |
| Rules | Discretion |
| Duty/Right | Need |
| Natural law | Religion |
| Ethical formalism | Ethics of care |

**Figure 2-2**  An Ethical Continuum

one contrasts this ethical system with a rule-based, absolutist system. In the ethics of care, you will recall, each individual is considered in the equation of what would be the "good." The schemata in Figure 2-2 may help to isolate the differences and similarities between these concepts.

Utilitarianism is arguably on the legal/rule side because the absolute rule of "the greatest utility for all" is often at the expense of the individual. Interestingly, the ethics of virtue, at least Aristotle's version, might be placed on the situational side, even though Aristotle believed that "practical reason" was more important than "moral virtues." This is because he recognized the concept of individuality in the "Golden Mean." In other words, one person's "mean" of courage might be different from another's, and this would have to be taken into account before judging behavior.

# Resulting Concerns

As mentioned previously, ethical systems are not moral decisions as such; rather, they provide the guidelines or principles to make moral decisions. Box 2-5 ("The Major Ethical Systems") summarizes the key principles for these ethical systems.

It can happen that moral questions are decided in different ways under the same ethical system—for instance, when facts are in dispute. When there is no agreement concerning the accepted facts in a certain case, it is confusing to bring in moral arguments before resolving the factual issues. Capital punishment is supported by some because of a belief that it is a deterrent to people who might commit murder. Others believe that

---

**BOX 2-5  The Major Ethical Systems**

**Ethical formalism:** *What is good is that which* conforms to the categorical imperative.

**Utilitarianism:** *What is good is that which* results in the greatest utility for the greatest number.

**Religion:** *What is good is that which* conforms to God's will.

**Natural law:** *What is good is that which* is natural.

**Ethics of virtue:** *What is good is that which* conforms to the Golden Mean.

**Ethics of care:** *What is good is that which* meets the needs of those concerned.

**Egoism:** *What is good is that which* benefits me.

---

capital punishment is wrong regardless of its efficacy in deterrence. Most arguments about capital punishment get confused during the factual argument about the effectiveness of deterrence. "Is capital punishment wrong or right?" is a different question from "Does capital punishment deter?" The second question might be answered through a study of facts; the former can be answered only by a moral judgment.

Another thing to consider is that none of us are perfect—we all have committed immoral or unethical acts that we know were wrong. Ethical systems help us to understand or analyze morality, but knowing what is right is no guarantee that we will always do the right thing. Very few people follow such strong moral codes that they *never* lie or *never* cause other people harm. One can condemn the act and not the person. The point is that just because some behaviors are understandable and perhaps even excusable does not make them moral or ethical. Very few people consistently use just one ethical system in making moral decisions. Some of us are fundamentally utilitarian and some predominantly religious, but we may make decisions using other ethical frameworks as well.

Most of us try to behave ethically most of the time. Dilemmas occur when we are confused about the right thing to do or when the right thing to do carries considerable cost. Detective Poole knew what the right course of action was. He also knew that he would pay a price for doing it. In fact, he was transferred to a less prestigious position and denied a promotion. He was vilified and treated as a traitor by some officers when he went public with his evidence of a cover-up. Ultimately, he resigned from the Los Angeles Police Department (Golab, 2000). This illustrates the sad fact that doing the right thing sometimes comes at a high cost.

## Conclusion

In this chapter we have explored some of the major ethical systems. Ethical systems are ordered principles that define what is right or good. Each of these ethical systems answers the question "What is good?" in a different way. Sometimes the same conclusion to an ethical dilemma can be reached using several different ethical systems, but sometimes using different ethical systems can result in contradictory answers to the determination of goodness. Ethical systems are more complex to apply than they are to explain. For instance, utilitarianism is fairly easy to understand, but the measurement of utility for any given act is often quite difficult. Ethical formalism says to "do one's duty," but it does not help us when there are conflicting duties. The ethics of care emphasizes relationships but is quite vague in providing the steps necessary to resolve ethical dilemmas. Relativism and absolutism are contrary principles but may be reconciled using the concept of situational ethics.

# Key Terms

**act utilitarianism**  the type of utilitarianism that determines goodness of a particular act by measuring the utility for all, but only for that specific act and without regard for future actions

**cultural relativism**  the idea that many values and behaviors differ from culture to culture and are functional in the culture that holds them

**deontological ethical system**  the study of duty or moral obligation emphasizing the intent of the actor as the element of morality

**egoism**  the ethical system that claims that good results from pursuing self-interest

**enlightened egoism**  the concept that egoism may look altruistic because it is in one's long-term best interest to help others in order to receive help in return

**ethical formalism**  the ethical system espoused by Kant that focuses on duty; it holds that the only thing truly good is a good will, and what is good is that which conforms to the categorical imperative

**ethical system**  a structured set of principles that defines what is moral

**ethics of care**  the ethical system that defines good as meeting the needs of others and preserving and enriching relationships

**ethics of virtue**  the ethical system that bases ethics largely upon character and possession of virtues

**explication**  a systematic set of principles that are extrapolated from a range of moral judgments that can be then used to resolve other ethical dilemmas

**generalization principle**  the principle that all decisions should be made assuming that the decision could be applied to everyone else in similar circumstances

**hypothetical imperative**  a statement of contingent demand (if I want something, then I must work for it), usually contrasted with the categorical imperative, which is a statement of "must" with no "ifs"

**imperative principle**  the principle that all decisions should be made according to absolute rules

**moral pluralism**  the concept that there are fundamental truths that may dictate different definitions of what is moral in different situations

**natural law**  the ethical system that bases ethics on natural laws; such laws are discovered by reason but exist apart from humankind

**principle of forfeiture** the idea that one gives up one's right to be treated under the principles of respect for persons to the extent that one has abrogated someone else's rights; for instance, self-defense is acceptable according to the principle of forfeiture

**principle of the golden mean** Aristotle's concept of moderation, in which one should not err toward excess or deficiency; this principle is associated with the ethics of virtue

**psychological egoism** the concept that humans naturally and inherently seek self-interest, and that they can do nothing else because it is their nature

**religious ethics** the ethical system that is based on religious beliefs of good and evil; what is good is that which is God's will

**rule utilitarianism** the type of utilitarianism that determines the goodness of an action by measuring the utility of that action when made into a rule for behavior

**situational ethics** the philosophical position that although there are a few universal truths, different situations call for different responses; therefore, some action can be right or wrong depending on situational factors

**social contract theory** the concept developed by Hobbes, Rousseau, and Locke in which the state of nature is a "war of all against all" and, thus, individuals give up their liberty to aggress against others in return for safety; the contract is between society, which promises protection, and the individual, who promises to abide by laws

**teleological ethical system** an ethical system that is concerned with the consequences or ends of an action to determine goodness

**utilitarian principle** the principle that all decisions should be made according to what is best for the greatest number

**utilitarianism** the ethical system that claims that the greatest good is that which results in the greatest happiness for the greatest number; major proponents are Bentham and Mill

# Review Questions

1. Discuss the differences between teleological systems and deontological systems.
2. Describe two teleological ethical systems, and describe two deontological systems.
3. What seems to be one similarity among all religious systems?
4. Contrast the ethics of care and utilitarianism. Compare the natural law system with religion.
5. If you had to choose one ethical system, which one most closely conforms to your own beliefs? Be explicit.
6. Describe another way of resolving ethical dilemmas that does not use the ethical systems.
7. Discuss the arguments against and supporting relativism. Do the same for absolutism.
8. Is there a universal truth relating to right and wrong, moral and immoral? If you answered yes, what are the principles of such a system?
9. Explain the differences between situational ethics and relativism.
10. Determine which ethical system(s) support the questions in Nash's "How to Make an Ethical Decision."

# Discussion Questions

1. Are there any situations in which lying is acceptable?
2. Can you think of any acts that result in bad consequences but should still be considered good acts? What about bad acts that result in good consequences?
3. Do people do things solely for altruistic reasons, or are there always hidden motives and egoistic agendas operating?
4. In the movie *Sophie's Choice,* a woman is forced to choose which one of her children to send to the gas chamber. If she does not decide, both will be killed. How would ethical formalism resolve this dilemma? How would utilitarianism?
5. There is a continuing debate over whether the United States needed to bomb Hiroshima and Nagasaki at the end of World War II. Present the arguments on both sides. Now consider this: Are they utilitarian arguments, ethical formalist arguments, or some other?
6. What are "natural rights"—rights that everyone has purely by virtue of being alive?
7. What are the "natural" inclinations of human beings?
8. Do you think most people do the right thing out of habit or reason?
9. Do you think that people who have the virtues discussed above never perceive moral dilemmas because they always do the right thing?
10. Do you believe that there are no absolute moral truths and that morality is simply an individual's definition of right and wrong? If you answered yes, then are you also saying that child molesters and cannibals have the right to decide which behaviors are acceptable for them?

# Ethical Dilemmas

## Situation 1

You are a manager of a retail store. You are given permission by the owner of the store to hire a fellow classmate to help out. One day you see the classmate take some clothing from the store. When confronted by you, the peer laughs it off and says the owner is insured, no one is hurt, and it was under $100. "Besides," says your acquaintance, "friends stick together, right?" What would you do?

## Situation 2

You are in a lifeboat along with four others. You have only enough food and water to keep four alive for the several weeks you expect to be adrift until you float into a shipping lane and can be discovered and rescued. You will definitely all perish if the five of you consume the food and water. There is the suggestion that one of you should die so that the other four can live. Would you volunteer to commit suicide? Would you vote to have one go overboard if you choose by straws? Would you vote to throw overboard the weakest and least healthy of the five? If you were on a jury judging the behavior of four who did murder a fifth in order to stay alive, would you acquit them or convict them of murder?

## Situation 3

You aspire to be a police officer and are about to graduate from a criminal justice department. Your best friend has just been hired by a local law enforcement agency, and you are applying as well. When you were both freshmen, you were caught with marijuana in your dorm room. Although you were arrested, the charges were dismissed because it turned out that the search was illegal. On the application form, there is a question that asks if you have ever been arrested. Your friend told you that he answered no because he knew this agency did not use polygraphs as part of the hiring process. You must now decide whether to also lie on the form. If you lie, you may be found out eventually, but there is a good chance that the long-ago arrest will never come to light. If you don't lie, you will be asked to explain the circumstances of the arrest, and your friend will be implicated as well. What should you do?

## Situation 4

You are a legislator about to vote on a bill that has been highly controversial. It basically strips those who have terminal illnesses of any health care. The extreme budget crisis that your state has been in for several years prompted the creation of the bill, and its proponents argue that scarce resources are being used in a way that hurts everyone. The state's social services budget is strained by providing medical services to indigents who have serious, terminal illnesses; consequently, others who have less serious problems cannot get treatment. It is like the triage system that wartime medics use, proponents argue: Those who can be cured should get the resources. How will you vote? What ethical system justifies your answer?

## Situation 5

You are working in internal affairs and through the course of another investigation discover disturbing evidence regarding the police chief's son, who is also an officer in the department. Several informants have confided in you that this individual has roughed them up and taken their drugs, yet you find no record of arrest or the drugs being logged in the evidence room. When you write your report, your sergeant tears it up and tells you that there is not enough evidence to justify an investigation and for you to stick to what you are told to do. What would you do? What would you do if the chief calls you into his office the next day and offers you a transfer to a high-status position that will definitely lead to a promotion?

# Suggested Readings

Braswell, M., McCarthy, B., and McCarthy, B. (Eds.). 2002. *Justice, Crime, and Ethics*, 3rd ed. Cincinnati: Anderson.

Foot, P. 1982. "Moral Relativism." Pp. 152–167 in Meiland, J., and Krausz, M. (Eds.), *Relativism: Cognitive and Moral*. Notre Dame, IN: University of Notre Dame Press.

Hinman, L. 1998. *Ethics: A Pluralistic Approach to Moral Theory,* 2d ed. Fort Worth, TX: Harcourt Brace.

Prior, W. (Ed.). 1991. *From Virtue and Knowledge: An Introduction to Ancient Greek Ethics.* New York: Routledge, Kegan Paul.

Stace, W. 1995. "Ethical Relativity and Ethical Absolutism." Pp. 25–32 in Close, D., and Meier, N. (Eds.), *Morality in Criminal Justice.* Belmont, CA: Wadsworth.

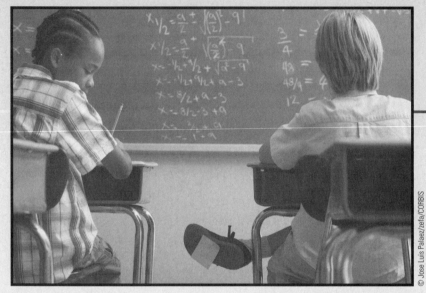

Even when students know cheating is wrong, some do it anyway.

# 3

# Making Ethical
# Decisions

*Theories of Moral Development*

*Ethics, Behavior, and Criminality*

*Why Be Ethical?*

*Conclusion*

## Key Terms

cognitive dissonance
developmental theories
inductive discipline
Kohlberg's moral stages
modeling
predeterminers

recognition measures
reinforcement
socio-moral reasoning
   programs
subcultural deviance
   theory

# Chapter Objectives

1. Become familiar with the major theories regarding the development of moral behavior, especially Kohlberg's moral development theory and learning theory.

2. Become familiar with Gilligan's research exploring gender differences in moral development.

3. Recognize the difficulty associated with the relationship between moral beliefs and behavior.

4. Become familiar with some of the applications of moral development theory to criminal offenders.

5. Become familiar with some issues regarding teaching ethics in criminal justice.

6. Understand the range of answers to the question "Why be ethical?"

In the previous chapter we explored the question "How does one determine what is good?" In this chapter we will discuss "How does one become a good person?" and "Why be ethical?" As we have seen, philosophers have looked to God, natural law, reason, intuition, and emotion to determine moral truths. The fundamental question about the nature of morality is whether it is subjective and of human construction, or whether it is apart from and only discoverable by humans, thus universal and objective. The fundamental question regarding the nature of humans is whether we are born good or evil, or whether we become that way through life circumstances. Philosophers and psychologists both address this question, and it is the central issue in the field of criminology. In fact, the premise of this chapter is that the study of moral development clearly overlaps the study of criminology.

## Theories of Moral Development

Psychology seeks to understand why people behave the way they do. If someone is a chronic liar, why is he that way? If someone is aggressive and takes what she wants regardless of other people's needs or desires, why does she behave that way? It should also be noted that *beliefs* and *actions* are related, but one does not necessarily predict the other. As stated before, just because we know something is wrong does not mean that we never do it. The most important contributions to this discussion involve biological approaches, learning theory, and moral development theories. Simple definitions of the approaches are listed below:

1. *Biological theories* propose that we are good or bad because of biological predispositions.

2. *Learning theory* argues that our behavior is based on the rewards we have received.

3. *Developmental theories* explain that people's behavior is influenced by their intellectual and emotional stage of development and that one reaches or doesn't reach higher stages of development based on one's environment.

## Biological Theories

The most controversial theories of human behavior point to biological **predeterminers**. Researchers who study the brain have discovered links between the brain and the predisposition to certain behaviors, as well as (potentially) the development of moral behavior. The frontal lobes seem to be the part of the brain implicated in feelings of empathy, shame, and moral reasoning. Individuals with frontal-lobe damage display the following characteristics (Ellis and Pontius, 1989: 6):

1. Increased impulsiveness
2. Decreased attention span
3. Difficulty in logical reasoning
4. Difficulty adjusting to new events
5. Tendency toward apathy and erratic mood shifts
6. Tendency toward rude, unrestrained, tactless behavior
7. Tendency to not be able to follow instructions, even after verbalizing what is required

Ellis and Pontius (1989) present a theory postulating the frontal lobe and limbic system's influence on the individual's capacity for moral reasoning. The authors discuss sex differences in brain activity and research presenting evidence that women are more inclined to empathy and sensitivity to human relationships.

### QUOTE and QUERY

Our model suggests that individuals who have frontal–limbic functioning which is lateralized toward the right hemisphere will be more antisocial than those who have lateralization toward the left hemisphere. Second, those with frontal–reticular functioning that is relatively insensitive to environmental input at a given intensity will be more antisocial than those with more sensitive frontal–reticular functioning. Third, individuals whose prefrontal lobes are disinclined to carefully devise long term goals and continuously monitor and fine-tune strategies for achieving those goals will be more antisocial than persons with opposite prefrontal lobe tendencies.

Source: Ellis and Pontius (1989: 19).

*Can you rephrase this highly technical language to be more understandable to laypeople? What does "lateralized" mean? What behaviors are likely in individuals who have the characteristics described?*

More than seventy studies examining sex differences in brain functioning found evidence that men

1. are more antisocial
2. commit more serious types of offenses
3. more often have serious childhood conduct disorders

There are also sex differences in

1. delinquency
2. school performance
3. hyperactivity
4. impulsivity
5. attention deficit disorders

Some analysts propose that these differences are due to sex-linked brain activity, specifically in the frontal lobes and limbic regions. Males' sex hormones influence brain development prenatally and during puberty. Although there is a great deal of overlap between male and female populations in brain development and activity, there are also distinct and measurable differences; specifically, these differences may influence the brain's ability to absorb "moral messages" or act upon them.

Wilson (1993) is one of the few criminologists who include biological elements in causation theory. He argues that values such as sympathy, fairness, self-control, and duty are moral "senses" that are inherent in humans and arise through a combination of genetics and socialization. A detailed explanation of how biology might be used to help us understand why people engage in bad behaviors is offered by Walsh (1995, 2001), who also postulates how bad behavior might be explained in evolutionary terms. The area of biological criminology is growing, but slowly. Many social scientists are unwilling to explore biological causation, even though there are excellent treatments of the subject available, such as Fishbein's (2000) review of bio-behavioral influences on criminality. The application of these issues to a discussion of moral development is obvious. It seems increasingly clear that the ability to understand moral principles and to apply them to behavioral decisions may be at least influenced by biological factors.

## *Learning Theory*

Learning theorists believe that children learn what they are taught, including morals and values as well as behavior. In other words, right or wrong is not discovered through reasoning; rather, all humans are shaped by the world around them, and they form completely subjective opinions about morality and ethics. This learning can take place through modeling or by reinforcement.

In **modeling,** values and moral beliefs come from those one admires and aspires to identify with. If that role model happens to be a priest, one will probably develop a religious ethical system; if it happens to be a pimp or a sociopath, an egoistic ethical system may develop. If the identification is broken, moral beliefs may change. It is no surprise that when asked who has been important in their moral development, most people say their parents, because parents are the most significant people in one's life during the important formative years. Although we may not hold exactly the same views and have exactly the same values as our parents, there is no doubt that they are influential in our value formation.

Another way that learning theorists explain moral development is through **reinforcement**. Behaviors and beliefs that are reinforced (either through material rewards or through more subjective rewards, such as praise) are repeated and eventually become permanent. Because behavior is more easily stabilized and tends to come before permanent attitude change, it is often the case that behavior leads to the development of consistent beliefs. For example, I am rewarded for sharing (by parental praise or a realization of reciprocity), and eventually I develop the belief that "sharing is good." Alternatively, I might be rewarded for being selfish and bullying others to gain what I want. On the playground, other children are afraid of me, and I use their fear to demand toys or extra turns. No adults reprimand me, or they do so inconsistently, so the rewards far outweigh the negative consequences of such behavior. Eventually I may develop a "me first" and "every person for herself is the way to live" philosophy of life.

When behavior is not consistent with beliefs, the discomfort that results is called **cognitive dissonance**. This leads to the development of attitudes to support one's behavior. The child who is constantly told to share toys and is disciplined upon refusal is learning not just the desired behavior but also the values of cooperativeness and charity. In an adult, these values may be manifested by lending one's lawn mower to a neighbor or contributing to charities. On the other hand, if a child is never punished for aggressive behavior and instead is rewarded—by always getting the desired object—then aggressiveness and the accompanying moral principle of "might makes right" develop. If we do acts that are contrary to the beliefs that we have been taught, we will either stop doing the acts or change our beliefs to reduce the dissonance.

Bandura (cited in Boyce and Jensen, 1978: 123–124) states that there is a developmental approach to teaching, keyed to what the child is capable of understanding:

> According to the social learning view, people vary in what they teach, model and reinforce with children of differing ages. At first, control is necessarily external. In attempting to discourage hazardous conduct in children who have not yet learned to talk, parents must resort to physical intervention. . . . Successful socialization requires gradual substitution of symbolic and internal controls for external sanctions and demands. . . .

According to learning theorists, even the most altruistic behaviors provide rewards for the individual. For instance, acts of charity provide rewards in the form of goodwill from others and self-satisfaction. Acts of sacrifice are rewarded in similar ways. Honesty, integrity, and fairness exist only because they have been rewarded in the past and present and are part of the behavioral repertoire of the individual. According to learning theorists, the moral principles of "honesty is right," "integrity is good," and "fairness is ethical" come after the behavior has been stabilized, not before. This theory is very different from the view that moral beliefs influence actions.

There is little room in this theory for universalism, absolutism, or the idea that a moral truth exists apart from humans that is not of their construction but that awaits their discovery. The theory is completely humanistic in that morality is considered a creation of humans that explains and provides a rationale for learned behavior. Behavior is completely neutral; an infant can be taught any behavior desired and the moral beliefs consistent with that belief. In one experiment, children were told a hypothetical story in which an adult punished a neutral act, such as a child practicing a musical instrument. The children later defined that act as bad, despite the intrinsic neutrality of the action. This indicates the power of adult definitions and punishment in the child's moral development (Boyce and Jensen, 1978: 133–170).

Quite a bit of research exists to support a learning theory of moral development. For instance, it was found that large gains in moral maturity (as measured by paper-and-pencil tests of expression of beliefs) could be achieved by direct manipulation of rewards for such beliefs. Contrary to the view that an individual comes to a realization of moral principles through cognitive development, this theory proposes that one can encourage or create moral beliefs simply by rewards (Boyce and Jensen, 1978: 143).

## *Developmental Theories*

**Developmental theories** propose that individuals mature physically, cognitively, and emotionally:

1. Normal *physical* development can be charted by a pediatrician. We discover at the pediatrician's office whether the height and weight of our child are in the "normal curve" of development.
2. *Intellectual* development is also measured by a variety of intelligence tests and charted against a normal curve of development. We do not expect the child to understand concepts before certain developmental markers.
3. *Emotional or social* development also progresses at a predictable and normal pace, although it may be more difficult to measure.

Social maturity is marked by the ability to empathize with others and a willingness to compromise one's desires with others' needs. An emotionally mature person neither abandons self for others nor puts oneself above others but rather balances individual needs with others' demands; however, that development might be stunted by negative environmental influences.

### Kohlberg's Moral Stages

The contributions of Jean Piaget and Lawrence Kohlberg have become essential to any discussion of moral development. Piaget believed that we all go through stages of cognitive, or intellectual, growth. These stages parallel moral stages of development, and together they describe a systematic way of perceiving the world. Piaget studied the rules that children develop in their play. These rules reflect the perceptions they hold of themselves and others and move from egocentrism to cooperativeness.

Kohlberg carried on with Piaget's work and more fully described the stages each individual passes through in moral and cognitive development (Kohlberg, 1984; Boyce and Jensen, 1978: 87–95). Two-year-olds do not understand the world in the same way as twenty-year-olds do. This lack of understanding also affects their moral reasoning ability. The infant lacks sensitivity toward others and has a supreme selfishness regarding his or her needs and wants. Infants are not concerned with others because they are only vaguely aware of their existence. An infant's world is confined to what is within reach of his or her hands and mouth. Even a mother is only important as the source of comfort and food. Very slowly the infant becomes aware that others also have feelings and needs.

---

**BOX 3-1  Kohlberg's Moral Stages**

**Level A: Preconventional**

Stage 1: "Right is blind obedience to rules and authority, avoiding punishment, and not doing physical harm."

Stage 2: "Right is serving one's own or others' needs and making fair deals in terms of concrete exchange."

**Level B: Conventional**

Stage 3: "Right is playing a good 'nice' role, being concerned about other people and their feelings, keeping loyalty and trust with partners, and being motivated to follow rules and expectations."

Stage 4: "Right is doing one's duty in society, upholding the social order, and the welfare of society or the group."

**Level C: Post-Conventional**

Stage 5: "Right is upholding the basic rights, values, and legal contracts of a society, even when they conflict with the concrete rules and laws of the group."

Stage 6: "Right is guided by self-chosen ethical principles of justice, equality, and respect. Laws and social agreements are usually consistent with these principles."

SOURCE: "The Six Stages of Moral Judgment," by Lawrence Kohlberg in "Moral Stages and Moralization: The Cognitive-Developmental Approach" in *Moral Development and Behavior* by Thomas Lickona, 1976. Used by permission.

---

This awareness leads to empathy and the recognition of right and wrong. At later stages, abstract reasoning develops, which leads to the ability to understand more difficult moral concepts. Kohlberg describes three levels of moral reasoning; included in each level are two stages (Barry, 1985: 14–16; Kohlberg, 1976). **Kohlberg's moral stages** are shown in Box 3-1.

Some characteristics of these cognitive and moral stages include the following (Hersh, 1979: 52):

1. *They involve qualitative differences in modes of thinking, as opposed to quantitative differences.* The child undergoes dramatic changes in perceptions; for instance, in an early stage the realization occurs that what one does has an impact on others. An infant realizes that when she pulls someone's hair, the person reacts; when she cries, someone comes; and when she performs certain behaviors, she is praised.

2. *Each stage forms a structured whole; cognitive development and moral growth are integrated.* Perceptions of the world and the corresponding moral framework are similar among all individuals at that particular stage. Simplistically, this means that a child cannot be sensitive to larger issues such as world hunger until he is able to grasp the reality of such conditions.

3. *Stages form an invariant sequence; no one bypasses any stage, and not all people develop to the higher stages.* In fact, according to Kohlberg, very few individuals

reach the postconventional level; the majority of people reach the conventional level and stay there.

4. *Stages are hierarchical integrations.* That is, each succeeding stage encompasses and is more comprehensive and complicated than the stage that precedes it.

At the *preconventional level*, the person approaches a moral issue motivated purely by personal interests. The major concern is the consequences of the action for the individual. For instance, young children do not share toys with others because they see no reason to do so. They derive pleasure from their toys, so to give them to others does not make sense. Even if the toys belong to others, there is a predisposition for children to appropriate them. Parents know the tears and tantrums associated with teaching a child that toys belonging to others must be given back. Young children at play first start sharing, in fact, when they perceive benefit to themselves, such as giving someone their doll in exchange for a game or a ball, or they grudgingly share because they fear punishment from an adult if they do not.

*Stage 1* has a punishment and obedience orientation. What is right is that which is praised; what is wrong is that which is punished. The child submits to an authority figure's definition and is concerned only with the consequences attached to certain behaviors, not with the behavior itself.

*Stage 2* has an instrument and relativity orientation. The child becomes aware of and is concerned with others' needs. What is right is still determined by self-interest, but the concept of self-interest is broadened to include those who are within the child's sphere of relationships. Relationships are important to the child, and he or she is attached to parents, siblings, and best friends, who are included in the ring of self-interest. There is also the emerging concept of fairness and a recognition that others deserve to have their needs met.

At the *conventional level*, people perceive themselves as members of society, and living up to role responsibilities is paramount in believing oneself to be good. Children enter this level when they are capable of playing with other children according to rules. In fact, games and play are training grounds for moral development because they teach the child that there are defined roles and rules of behavior. For instance, a game of softball becomes a microcosm of real life when a child realizes that he or she is not only acting as self, but also as a first baseman, a role that includes certain specific tasks. Before this stage, the child runs to the ball regardless of where it is hit. Thus, in a softball game with very young children playing, one may see all the players running after the ball and abandoning their bases because they have difficulty grasping the concept of role responsibilities. Furthermore, although it would be more expeditious to trip the runners as they leave the base so they can be tagged out, the child learns that such behavior is not "fair play" and is against the rules of the game. Thus, children learn to submerge individual interest to conform to rules and role expectations.

*Stage 3* has an interpersonal concordance orientation. The person performs conventionally determined good behavior to be considered a good person. The views of "significant others" are important to one's self-concept. Thus, individuals will control behavior so as to not hurt others' feelings or be thought of as bad.

*Stage 4* has a law-and-order orientation. The individual is concerned not just with interpersonal relationships but also with the rules set down by society. The law becomes all-important. Even if the laws themselves are wrong, one cannot disregard them, for that would invite social chaos.

At the *postconventional level*, a person moves beyond the norms and laws of a society to determine universal good—that is, what is good for all societies. Few people reach this level, and their actions are observably different from the majority. For instance, Mahatma Gandhi might be described as a person with postconventional morality. He did not subscribe to the idea that laws must be obeyed, and he carried out peaceful noncompliance against the established law to conform to his belief in a higher order of morality. At this level of moral development, the individual assumes the responsibility of judging laws and conventions.

*Stage 5* has a social contract orientation. The person recognizes larger interests than current laws. This individual is able to evaluate the morality of laws in a historical context and feels an obligation to the law because of its benefits to societal survival.

*Stage 6* centers on universal ethical principles. The person who has reached this stage bases moral judgments on the higher abstract laws of truth, justice, and morality.

*A seventh stage?* Kohlberg advanced the possibility of a seventh stage, which has been described as a "soft" stage of ethical awareness with an orientation of cosmic or religious thinking. It is not a higher level of reasoning, but qualitatively different. According to Kohlberg, in this highest stage individuals have come to terms with such questions as "Why be just in a universe that is largely unjust?" It is a different question from the definition of justice that forms the content of the other stages. In this stage, one sees oneself as part of a larger whole and humanity as only part of a larger cosmic structure. This stage focuses on *agape*—a nonexclusive love and acceptance of the cosmos and one's place in it (Kohlberg, 1983; Power and Kohlberg, 1980).

## Critics of Kohlberg

Some believe that Kohlberg's theory of moral development has several serious flaws. Some of the most prevalent criticisms are listed below:

1. The stages tend to center too much on the concept of justice, ignoring other aspects of morality.
2. The stages, especially 5 and 6, may be nothing more than culturally based beliefs regarding the highest level of morality: "Kohlberg assumes that the core of morality and moral development is deontological, that it is a matter of rights and duties as prescriptions" (Levine, Kohlberg, and Hewer, 1985: 95).
3. Justice, rules, and rights are emphasized as higher values than are caring and relationships.
4. Others say Kohlberg emphasizes reason in moral decisions and ignores emotional factors. In response, Kohlberg and his associates assert that the theory is a measurement of "justice reasoning," not an attempt to present the "total complexity of the moral domain" (Levine, Kohlberg, and Hewer, 1985: 99).
5. Studies have found significant cultural differences in the age at which children reach different stages of moral development. This does not necessarily negate the validity of a stage sequence theory; however, it does call into question the specifics of movement through the stages (Boyce and Jensen, 1978).
6. Some criticize the lack of connection between reasoning levels and moral action in particular situations. There does not seem to be a strong correlation between

one's moral stage, as measured by the interview format of Kohlberg's research or more recently devised paper-and-pencil tests of recognition, and how one will respond when faced with a situation that offers a choice to be honest or dishonest (Lutwak and Hennessy, 1985).

7. Kohlberg's research can also be described as sexually biased because he interviewed boys almost exclusively in early research. Subsequent studies have found that women tend to cluster in Stage 3 because of their greater sensitivity to and emphasis on human relationships. Stage 3 is lower than the law-and-order stage, where men tend to be clustered. Unless one believes that women are generally less moral or less intellectually developed than men, this is a troubling finding and one that calls into question the hierarchical nature of the theory.

## A Different Morality?

Carol Gilligan (1982, 1987), one of Kohlberg's students, researched the apparent sex difference in moral reasoning and proposed that women may possess a *different* morality from men. Most men, it seems, analyze moral decisions with a rules or justice orientation (Stage 4), whereas many women see the same moral dilemma with an orientation toward needs and relationships (Stage 3). Gilligan labels this a *care perspective*. A morality based on the care perspective would be more inclined to look at how a decision affects relationships and addresses needs, whereas the justice perspective is concerned with notions of equality, rights, and universality. (Ethics of care is described in Chapter 2 as one of the ethical frameworks.)

In Gilligan's study, although both men and women raised justice and care concerns in responses to moral dilemmas, among those who focused on one or the other, men exclusively focused on justice whereas half of the women who exhibited a focus did so on justice concerns and the other half focused on care concerns (Gilligan, 1987). It was also found that both male and female respondents were able to switch from a justice to a care perspective (or back again) when asked to do so; thus, their orientation was more a matter of perspective than inability to see the other side. What Gilligan points out in her research is that the care perspective completely drops out when one uses only male subjects—which is what Kohlberg did in his early research for the moral stage theory. The "In the News" box: "Are Women More Ethical?" examines this sex difference.

Another study of fifty college students (half men, half women) tested the subjects' orientation to three moral dilemmas, and the results were consistent with Gilligan's findings. However, the content of the dilemma evidently influenced whether care considerations would be found. The dilemmas involving interpersonal relationships were more likely to stimulate care considerations than those without (Rothbart, Hanley, and Albert, 1986; Flanagan and Jackson, 1987). It should also be noted that other studies failed to find any differences between men and women in their responses to moral dilemmas (see reviews in Walker, 1986, and Thoma, 1986).

## Teaching Moral Reasoning

The importance of Kohlberg's work is the link he makes between moral development and reason. This concept originated with Kant and even earlier philosophers, but Kohlberg provides a psychological analysis that sheds light on *how* reason influences moral judgments. Also important in Kohlberg's work is the guidance it provides to

**IN THE NEWS** **Are Women More Ethical?**

A Baylor University study found that there were significant differences between men and women when asked to respond to different hypothetical scenarios, with women more often taking the ethical "high road." The study included 1,831 women and men from all 50 states who worked in professional and managerial positions. Women responded with more ethical responses to hypothetical situations involving exceeding legal pollution limits, bribery, corporate espionage, promotion practices, product safety, and executive salaries versus workers' salaries. Men responded more ethically to situations involving collusion in construction bidding and copying computer software. Researchers suggest socialization differences between men and women as a possible explanation for such differences.

Source: M. A. Roser, "Business Study Finds Women More Ethical," *Austin American Statesman*, December 26, 1996, A1, A11.

*How would Carol Gilligan explain the differences that these researchers found?*

education. According to the theory of moral stages, one can encourage movement through the stages by exposing the individual to higher-stage reasoning. The procedures for encouraging moral growth include presenting moral dilemmas and allowing the individual to support his or her position. Through exposure to higher reasoning, one sees the weaknesses and inconsistencies of lower-level reasoning (Hersh, 1979) Kohlberg indicates clearly what is needed for moral growth. Even if one may have reservations about the specific descriptions of the moral stages, the proposed guidelines to encourage moral development seem valid and are supported by other authorities.

Kohlberg (1976) described the following as necessary for moral growth:

1. *Being in a situation where seeing things from other points of view is encouraged.* This is important because upward-stage movement is a process of getting better at reconciling conflicting perspectives on a moral problem.
2. *Engaging in logical thinking, such as reasoned argument and consideration of alternatives.* This is important because one cannot attain a given stage of moral reasoning before attaining the supporting Piagetian stage of logical reasoning.
3. *Having the responsibility to make moral decisions and to influence one's moral world.* This response is necessary for developing a sense of moral agency and for learning to apply one's moral reasoning to life's situations.
4. *Exposure to moral controversy and to conflict in moral reasoning that challenges the structure of one's present stage.* This is important for questioning one's moral beliefs and forcing a look at alternatives.
5. *Exposure to the reasoning of individuals whose thinking is one stage higher than one's own.* The importance here is in offering a new moral structure for resolving the disequilibrium caused by moral conflict.
6. *Participation in creating and maintaining a just community whose members pursue common goals and resolve conflict in accordance with the ideals of mutual respect and fairness.*

People may become stuck at a certain point in moral development for several reasons, including not having sufficiently developed cognitive skills and/or living in a social environment that does not allow for role-taking opportunities or personal growth. For instance, a child growing up in a family that repeats basic moral views with little attempt to explain or defend them will learn to be closed to other viewpoints. A child who is never given responsibility or never forced to take responsibility for his or her own actions will have difficulty developing moral reasoning skills and will not advance to higher stages. Such children will be, in a sense, stunted at the Kohlberg pre-conventional level of an infant, constantly fed and cared for, but not allowed to discover that other people exist and must be considered. As adults, if we surround ourselves only with people who think as we do, then it is very unlikely that we will ever develop our moral growth or even consider other positions.

# Ethics, Behavior, and Criminality

Can one predict behavior from moral beliefs? Psychologists who have studied "immoral" behavior, such as lying and cheating among adults and children, have found it hard to predict who will perform these behaviors. There is not a strong correlation between beliefs and behaviors.

## *Predicting Behavior*

However, some studies do find beliefs and actions to be correlated. In one study, "honesty scores" for people in three organizations were compiled from an attitudinal questionnaire about beliefs. It was found that the organization with the highest average honesty score had the least employee theft, and the organization with the lowest average honesty score had the most employee theft (Adams, 1981). In contrast, Kohlberg cites the Hartshone and May study, which found no correlation between different tests of honesty and behavior, and another study in which a group of female prisoners were found to have the same rank orderings of values as female college students. He uses these studies as support for the proposition that one cannot measure a trait in isolation and expect to find consistency between values and action (Kohlberg and Candel, 1984: 499–503).

Recall that learning theory proposes that behavior precedes moral beliefs. Good behavior is created by external rewards, and then one develops the beliefs that go along with such behavior. However, there is some evidence to indicate that compliance gained from external rewards is not stable until it becomes internalized, which involves adaptation to existing personality structures (Borchert and Stewart, 1986: 133–145). The question of when and why beliefs and values are internalized is not as easy to research. Even if ethical behavior could be ensured by providing rewards, this would not necessarily develop "moral character" or moral principles unless beliefs were somehow internalized.

Part of the problem is the difficulty in measuring moral beliefs and the validity of the instruments used. Kohlberg's work has been so influential in this field that it is difficult to find any measurement of morality that does not directly or indirectly use his

**EXERCISE**

Talk to a child (three to eight years old) about a variety of moral issues—e.g., what is bad? What is good? Give the child a moral dilemma relevant to his or her world (make the characters children, the issue a familiar one). How does the child respond? Can you identify any moral principles? Can you identify which of Kohlberg's stages seems to describe the child's reasoning?

stage definitions. If one attempts to examine whether bad behavior is associated with lower-stage scores, there is the assumption that lower-stage scores mean the person has less developed moral reasoning. We have previously discussed Carol Gilligan's challenge of this conception, yet practically all studies that examine the correlation between behavior and belief continue to use stage scores as a measure of moral development.

Measurement of moral stages was accomplished in Kohlberg's work by interviews with subjects who were questioned using hypothetical moral dilemmas, much as the exercise above illustrates. Their responses were then rated by interviewers, with emphasis placed not necessarily on the answer given but rather on the reasoning for the answer. The individual was given a stage score based on what factors were emphasized. This procedure is time-consuming and expensive, so paper-and-pencil tests have been devised, arguably measuring the same type of reasoning but through simpler, quicker means. Much criticism is directed at these so-called "recognition" tests, which require the subject merely to recognize and identify certain moral principles and agree with them, as opposed to "production" measures, which require the subject actually to reason through a dilemma and provide some rationale, which is then analyzed. It may be that **recognition measures** are less reliable in predicting behavior. For instance, Gavaghan, Arnold, and Gibbs (1983) reported that although production measures were able to distinguish between a group of delinquents and nondelinquents, recognition measures could not.

Those who subscribe to a stage theory of moral development would argue that inconsistent behavior merely means that the individual has not fully incorporated the higher-level reasoning. By contrast, learning theorists would propose that the rewards for good behavior are weak or not immediate. For instance, individuals who believe stealing is wrong may nevertheless be tempted because of the immediacy of the reward (the coveted item). If they have internalized a strict sense of morality regarding stealing that would result in unpleasant feelings of guilt, then that immediate punishment will counteract the immediate reward. If, however, they had not been punished enough in the past (either physically or emotionally) for such action, then the guilt feelings will not occur quickly enough to counteract the temptation. The "In the News" box reports on one unscientific study of what people do when faced with immediate temptation.

## Teaching Ethics

Many people believe that the general morality of this nation is declining. Others point to examples abroad. Transparency International (2003) is an organization that compiles evidence of corruption from across the world and rates countries on how much

---

**POLICY BOX 3-1** **Moral Education in the Schools?**

There is a growing trend among school districts to include character education or moral education in school curriculums. Among a number of packaged curriculums available for schools to distribute to teachers include those that concentrate on promoting honesty, diversity, and citizenship. "Anti-bullying" curriculums gained a new prominence after the Columbine shooting because of a perception that the schools were doing a very poor job of protecting children from their peers' bullying. Although most people believe that this is a good thing, there are those who resent schools taking on this role and believe that it should be a parent's prerogative. This argument grows in intensity when applied to such issues as tolerance for gay or alternative lifestyles.

**Law:** There are no laws that are at issue in this policy choice, unless the character education is faith based, in which case there might be a challenge to the constitutionality of the curriculum.

**Policy:** School districts should uphold the will of the parents. If parents overwhelmingly disapprove of such curriculums, one assumes that districts would remove them or not begin them. It is probably also true that many parents are not aware of what is being taught in schools.

**Individual ethics:** There may be individual dilemmas that arise on the part of teachers. For instance, if there is a teaching unit on diversity that promotes the idea that everyone should be treated with equal respect, including gays, and a teacher's religious belief is that gays should be condemned, how should he or she reconcile his or her individual beliefs with the teaching curriculum? If you said that the teacher should follow the curriculum and promote a tolerant viewpoint because that's part of the job, would you also agree that teachers in Nazi Germany were correct to promote a racist viewpoint in their teachings because that was "their job"? How do you distinguish between the two situations?

---

Ethics classes have gained new importance recently because of the business scandals that emerged in 2002. The perpetrators periodically appear in headlines as they are prosecuted and sentenced. Evidently, there is a growing new field of ethics instruction and "ethics officers" hired by businesses to ensure that their workers behave honestly and ethically. Whether such classes are successful will depend, in large part, on whether CEOs are good students. As the "In the News" box "Ethics Classes: Solution or Scam?" indicates, such courses may not do much to raise the ethical standards of employees if managers don't take them seriously.

Administrators and managers exert the strongest influence on the ethical climate of an agency, regardless of whether ethics classes are offered. If leaders are honest, ethical, and caring, there is a good chance that those who work for these managers are also ethical. If administrators and/or managers are hypocritical, untruthful, and use their positions for personal gain, then workers often march in these same footsteps. If the

**IN THE NEWS   Ethics Classes: Solution or Scam?**

In an editorial poking fun at the recent rise of ethics classes, Joan Ryan of the *San Francisco Chronicle* writes that Raytheon, a defense contractor, has produced a video where the company's vice president, along with Roger Ebert, the film critic, give thumbs up or down to a series of behaviors. Ryan wonders if Bert and Ernie of *Sesame Street* might have done a better job. An attempt to improve the ethics of a work force is laudable, but the approach may be patronizing or even cynical, depending on the company's motivation. She points out that businesses that have ethics programs in place are eligible for reduced fines if they are found guilty of corporate wrongdoing. The behavior of leaders and the values of the company are more important determiners of employees' behaviors than whether or not they sat through a class. Says Ryan, "[T]he post-Enron era is much like the pre-Enron. Companies were cooking the books, faking transactions, lying to shareholders. The problem was about perpetuating a sham. Now so, too, is the solution."

Source: J. Ryan, "The Appearance of Ethics," *Austin American Statesman,* November 16, 2002, A11.

*Do you think that ethics classes will help in reducing corporate wrongdoing? Why or why not?*

business itself is premised on misleading the consumer and perpetrating fraud to secure higher profits, then why should business leaders expect that workers would behave any differently?

## *Morality, Criminology, and Offender Populations*

Even though criminology is directly concerned with crime—behavior that is usually judged as immoral—it typically avoids moral definitions. Deviance is a sociological concept that simply means behavior outside the norm, and crime is defined simply as unlawful behavior. The social sciences have generally avoided using moral definitions for wrongdoing. Of course, it may not be true that criminal acts are always immoral behaviors. Radical criminologists raise important points in their discussion of how certain behaviors are defined as criminal and who is allowed to do the defining. However, most criminal behavior—stealing, killing, assaulting, bribing, and so on—can also be defined as immoral or unethical. The field of psychology offers theories of moral development, and the fields of sociology and criminology propose theories of deviance and criminality. Interestingly, only recently have there been attempts to merge the two.

Current criminologists seem to be moving back to developmental rather than social force theories of delinquency and crime. Tonry, Ohlin, and Farrington (1991) propose three major theoretical perspectives that address the origins of delinquency—temperament, attachment, and social learning. After exploring the relative merits of these approaches, the authors postulate that temperament and attachment are interrelated in that the personality of the child may affect parental interaction, which, in turn, affects attachment. Alternatively, parents themselves may be poor or inconsistent caregivers, in which case attachment will be weak. Not rejecting any of the three perspectives, the researchers state that although parental child-rearing methods (attachment) may affect age of onset of delinquency, peer influence (social learning) may affect continuation or intensity of delinquency.

Other criminological theorists point to parental discipline and influence as well. Parental practices, such as the use of affection and **inductive discipline** rather than power assertion or the withdrawal of affection, have been identified as important in the moral development of adolescents (Leahy, 1981). Whether the association of parental practices and moral development (as measured by paper-and-pencil tests) operates in the same way that parental practices influence delinquent behavior is a separate question. Some current approaches reject the **subcultural deviance theory** that delinquent or criminal behavior is learned in a subcultural group along with a different moral code that justifies such behavior. Rather, they view deviance as the absence of learning, or incomplete socialization. When the individual does not develop self-control or internal standards of behavior, he or she will not make correct decisions when faced with opportunities to indulge in immediate gratification. What this probably means is that people who commit crime do not have different moral codes; rather, they know what is right but are simply unwilling to conform their behavior to it because they were not taught to do so at a very early stage of development.

These theories are consistent with learning theory, although biological research sheds light on the interplay between family socialization and biological predispositions as well. One should note that such theories ignore the importance and influence of socioeconomic factors on crime causation. It may be that such factors determine not the existence of antisocial (immoral) behaviors but rather the form that such behaviors will take. Individuals who are born into poor families and experience the parenting styles that are associated with antisocial development may end up committing street crime, whereas children who are born into middle-class and upper-middle-class families and experience similar parenting styles will ultimately engage in "suite crime" (white-collar crime) because of the different opportunity structures between the two groups of children.

If the current science of criminology has avoided questions of morality, there was no such hesitation in early corrections. Historically, criminality and sin were associated, and correctional practitioners were primarily concerned with reformation in a religious sense. Hence, early prisons were built to help the individual achieve redemption. There was a heavy dose of moral instruction in corrections; those who were said to lead dissolute and immoral lives were also targeted for reform. Society approved of official attempts to intervene in individuals' lives to help them become moral and productive citizens. For instance, the juvenile court system was given the mission to reform and educate youth (primarily those from immigrant groups) in a manner consistent with societal beliefs (Platt, 1977).

The orientation of corrections in the latter part of the twentieth century (1950s–1970s) became more scientific than religious, and intervention adopted the aim of psychological readjustment rather than personal redemption. After the rehabilitative era (1960–1970s), however, the rationale for corrections and punishment seemed to return to a moral orientation. Interestingly, "faith-based" correctional programs are experiencing a resurgence, with the support of the White House. Religious instruction

IN THE NEWS **Florida Opens Faith-Based Prison for Women**

Hillsborough Correctional Institution in Florida began a faith-based program with 300 female prisoners who agreed to be transferred to the prison to participate. While most programs for male prisoners begin in an existing prison, this prison receives volunteers who will participate in counseling, vocational and religious instruction.

Source: "Florida Opens Faith-Based Prison for Women," *Los Angeles Times,* April 15, 2004, A27.

*Do you believe that faith-based correctional programs violate the First Amendment?*

and correctional programs that use a religious orientation have emerged as options for correctional administrators seeking programs. Critics argue that public finances should not be used for such programs because the First Amendment prohibits state endorsement of any religion, but President George W. Bush evidently disagrees and heartily supports such programs.

In the last twenty years or so, there have been various attempts to introduce offenders to "moral education." Hickey and Scharf (1980), who studied under Kohlberg, undertook an early attempt to apply moral development theory to corrections in their creation of a therapeutic community in a Connecticut prison. Eventually, they had "just communities" for both men and women that were run according to principles of fairness, justice, and rights. Prisoners were exposed to moral analysis in discussions and group meetings. Increases in stage scores were measured as averaging one-and-one-half stages after prisoners had lived in the just community.

It appears that simply offering moral discussion groups may also result in an increase in stage scores. Gibbs and his colleagues (1984) report on another intervention involving sixty incarcerated juvenile delinquents. Socio-moral reasoning improved significantly after eight weeks of discussion groups using moral dilemmas. Whereas 87.5 percent of the treatment group moved from Stage 2 to Stage 3, only 14.3 percent of the control group moved to Stage 3.

Wiley (1988) reported on a more modest application of moral development education in the Texas Department of Corrections. She reports that teacher style influenced gains in moral development scores. Specifically, inmate–students in prison classrooms where the teacher employed an interactive style (challenging and allowing active participation) showed significant gains in post-tests of moral development, unlike those inmate–students in classrooms where the teaching style was authoritarian and teacher-centered. Interestingly, the course content was less important. These were not moral development classes but standard social science classes.

Arbuthnot and Gordon (1988) reviewed findings from several studies that show that interventions with delinquents and adult offenders using socio-moral reasoning result in stage score improvement and also behavioral change. In one program for delinquents, for instance, subjects were monitored for one year, and significant differences in post-experimental problem behaviors existed between the experimental group and the control group. These authors also discussed some reasons that socio-moral reasoning development programs are not prevalent in corrections; specifically, they pointed to the following:

1. The need for organizational support
2. The need for consistent organizational goals
3. The continuing need for expert consultation
4. The need for an onsite champion of the program
5. The need for careful selection and training of staff

Arbuthnot (1984) also discussed the interplay of environment and **socio-moral reasoning programs**. He pointed out that some prisoners find no rewards for expressing higher-stage reasoning, much less acting upon such reasoning. Therefore, any gains made in reasoning through an intervention such as a moral analysis discussion group would be unlikely to result in changes in behavior unless the environment was more supportive of higher stages. It seems fairly clear that for such programs to work in prison, an isolated living situation must be created to insulate participants from the negative reward structure of the prison. Also, if the intervention is in the community, attention must be given to the social environment of the participants. If there are no social supports for stage improvements, the gains may not be expressed in behavioral choices. Arbuthnot's discussion, then, combined Kohlberg's stage theory with a type of reinforcement theory.

More recently, moral reasoning programs have been used with sex offenders (Buttell, 2002). It was found that sex offenders tested at significantly lower moral stage development than a control sample. Pearson (2002), in a recent review of cognitive programs, including moral reasoning programs, concluded that such programs did decrease recidivism when compared to control groups.

# Why Be Ethical?

So far, we have explored how to determine what is ethical and the various explanations of why people either choose ethical (and legal) behaviors or unethical (and/or illegal) behaviors. Regardless of which ethical system or set of principles the individual feels more comfortable with, everyone would do well to become more aware of the implications of day-to-day choices—sharpen his or her ethical antennae, so to speak. Small decisions become larger life positions in a slow, cumulative way.

When faced with a choice of behavior, one should at least perform the following steps:

1. *Examine all possible solutions to the problem and be aware of the direct and indirect effects of each response.* Often, ethical issues arise and are not recognized for what they are. The individual may limit analysis of a problem to finding a short-term solution or making a quick decision, in which case the larger issues or the situation's ethical implications are never addressed. It becomes easy to rationalize unethical behavior in this way by the explanation that it only happened once, or it was the easiest way, or there was no intention to do wrong.

2. *Determine whether any solutions would be viewed as unacceptable if made public, and for what reason.* If an individual would be uncomfortable with publicizing an action, then chances are it is questionable. Too often, unethical decisions are protected by a shroud of secrecy, and then the secrecy is defended by pleading institutional or agency confidentiality. On an individual level, unethical behavior is almost always hidden, and further unethical behavior may follow to cover up what has already been done. Probably the best signal that something is wrong is when a person hesitates to make it public knowledge.

3. *Reconcile the decision with one's personal set of values or ethical system.* When one has to make a difficult decision about a moral issue, although one has recourse to value systems passed on by family and advice and counsel from friends and colleagues, ultimately the decision made should be one for which the individual is willing to take responsibility.

After completing a class on ethics that involved detailed explanations and applications of the ethical systems discussed in this book, an individual responded with the question "Why should we?" The student was really asking why anyone should be ethical or moral. There is a long version and a short version of the answer to this question. The short answer was what was given by another class member: "So you can sleep at night."

The long version of the answer is that philosophers down through the ages have examined, debated, and analyzed this same question. The ethical systems can be seen as not only answering the question "What is good?" but also the question "Why be good?"

1. *Under ethical formalism,* the answer is that the world works better, and it is rational to do one's duty and live up to the categorical imperative.

2. *Under utilitarianism,* the answer is that it is better for everyone, including the individual, to do what benefits the majority.

3. *Under the ethics of care,* the answer is that we naturally and instinctively have the capacity to care and to be concerned about others.

Each of the other frameworks also provides answers. One dominant theme emerges from all the ethical systems—that we are connected to one another in fundamental and emotional ways. This connection is recognized in

1. the golden rule
2. the universalism principle under the categorical imperative
3. rule utilitarianism
4. enlightened egoism

The theme running through the ethical systems is empathy and caring for one another. The reason we should act ethically can be explained rationally (ethical formalism and utilitarianism) or intuitively (ethics of care and religion).

A similar question was asked by Tyler (1990) in a book titled *Why People Obey the Law.* The answers found in his research may shed light on this discussion. He found that people obey the law not because of fear of being punished but rather because of a fundamental belief in the goodness of law. If they believe that the system is fair, that their rights are protected, and that they are treated with dignity and respect, then they typically believe in and abide by the law. Arguably, the converse is that if people *do not* hold these beliefs, then they have no normative controls on their behavior, and the only thing left is deterrence. Tyler's findings present an interesting commentary on what effect the criminal justice system has on citizens. One obvious conclusion is that criminal justice professionals who display unethical behavior that ignores rights create the very criminality that they are trying to prevent.

Professional ethics is merely an application of moral systems to a particular set of questions or a specific environment. The basis of all professional ethical codes is the same: To be a good professional, one must be a good person. Many of the ethical choices one will make throughout the course of a career are easy: No one needs to tell a police officer that bribery is wrong, or correctional officers that hitting a shackled and helpless inmate is wrong. These actions occur because individuals have chosen to take the path of least resistance, pursue personal interests over organizational values, or succumb to emotions such as fear and anger. For those choices that are truly difficult, people of goodwill, using rationality and sensitivity, can apply any ethical system and come up with an ethical solution. It may not be one that everyone will agree upon, but it will allow the individual to make the decision public and will allow the person to be satisfied that his or her choice was based on ethics rather than egoism.

# Conclusion

Philosophers, religious scholars, biologists, psychologists, sociologists, and criminologists have all tried to explain why people do bad things. Three approaches were explored in this chapter:

1. Biological theorists do not propose biological determinism, only that certain traits or biological characteristics may influence one's behavior.
2. Learning theorists argue that people learn morals through rewards. This approach is relativistic in that it postulates human learning as neutral. There is no one true moral theory to discover; rather, the individual will adopt whatever moral theory has been rewarded.
3. Developmental theorists propose that morality comes only at an advanced stage of emotional and social development and is linked to cognitive development. Kohlberg's theory proposes a hierarchy of moral stages, with the highest stage holding the most perfect moral principles. However, not everyone has the cognitive capacity or the proper exposure to discover these principles. According to Kohlberg, in the higher stages of moral development, ethical relativism must give way to universalism, and all those who reach the highest stages have discovered the true moral principles that are absolute and exist apart from humanity.

If one believes that morals are simply what humans choose to define as such, then one might be more inclined to a learning theory perspective. If one believes that morals exist naturally and humans discover their existence only through reasoning ability, one might be more inclined to accept the developmental stage theory of moral development. However, the approaches to moral development presented in this chapter are not necessarily mutually exclusive. One can believe in biological influences along with learning theory or developmental theory. One might agree with stage theory with the understanding that at lower stages, rewards are necessary to elicit moral behaviors (e.g., rewarding young children for sharing). One might support learning theory but also accept the notion that when we are intellectually mature, our reasoning abilities mediate simple rewards. Thus, although small children might be fooled into thinking that practicing the piano is bad because someone was punished for it in a story, no older child or adult would be taken in by such a trick, and individuals in a totalitarian society may continue to believe in democratic ideals (through reasoning) regardless of punishments they may receive for such beliefs.

In this chapter we also explored the connection between immorality and criminality. There has been interesting research that indicates that some types of interventions can improve the moral reasoning abilities of some offenders. Whether moral reasoning will affect behavior is a different question.

# Key Terms

**cognitive dissonance** psychological term referring to the discomfort that is created when behavior and attitude or belief are inconsistent

**developmental theories** theories of behavior proposing that individuals have normal growth patterns in such areas as morality and emotional maturity

**inductive discipline** form of discipline that requires child/student to understand why what he or she did was wrong

**Kohlberg's moral stages** the idea that moral development is hierarchical; each developmental stage is described as moving from pure egoism to a higher moral stage leading to altruism

**modeling** learning theory concept that people learn behaviors, values, and attitudes through relationships; they identify with another person and want to be like that person and so pattern themselves after the "model"

**predeterminers** factors that predict a certain outcome

**recognition measures** "paper and pencil" tests that measure an individual's ability to recognize and/or agree with moral terms

**reinforcement** rewards

**socio-moral reasoning programs** programs that help the individual learn how to think better; the individual learns how to identify inappropriate thinking patterns and change them to pro-social patterns of thought

**subcultural deviance theory** criminological theory that identifies subcultural norms and values as the cause of crime

# Review Questions

1. Provide your own answer to the question "Why do people do bad things?"
2. What are the three basic approaches to explaining human behavior? Explain each.
3. Briefly explain how biological approaches might explain antisocial behavior.

4. What are some sex differences noted by biological researchers?
5. Discuss learning theory as it applies to moral development. Explain modeling and reinforcement. What problems do critics see with this theory?
6. Explain Kohlberg's moral development theory. What problems do critics see with his theory?
7. How does one measure moral beliefs? What are the problems with such measurements?
8. How did Carol Gilligan disagree with Kohlberg's stage theory?
9. What are the elements necessary for teaching ethics?
10. Describe some applications of moral training in corrections.

# Discussion Questions

1. Who has been the greatest influence on your moral development? Why? How?
2. Why do you think people behave in ways that hurt other people?
3. Have you ever done something you knew to be wrong? Why did you do it?
4. Do thieves have the same moral beliefs as others? Do they know that stealing is wrong?
5. Can we successfully predict which individuals will perform unethical or immoral actions?
6. Why do you think the United States doesn't rank higher on the Transparency International integrity survey?
7. How many students cheat? (In a survey of 1,139 students at 27 universities, 60 percent admitted cheating [Ryan, 2002: A11].)

# Ethical Dilemmas

### Situation 1

You are a rookie police officer and are riding with a field training officer (FTO). During your shift the FTO stops at a convenience store and quickly drinks four beers in the back room of the store. He is visibly affected by the beers, and the smell of alcohol is very noticeable. What should you do? What if the FTO had just written a favorable evaluation of you even though you should have received a reprimand for an improper disposition of a traffic accident?

### Situation 2

You are a criminal justice student interning at a police department. One of the tasks you learn at the department is how to look up individuals' criminal histories on the computer. You are telling your friends about your experiences, and they want you to look up their names to see what, if anything, is listed for them. You are pretty much left alone to do your work at the police department, and it would be an easy matter to look up anyone. What would you tell your friends?

### Situation 3

You are a senior getting close to graduation and have taken too many classes during your last semester. You find yourself getting behind in classes and not doing well on tests. One of the classes requires a thirty-page term paper, and you simply do not have the time to complete the paper by the due date. While you are on the Internet one day, you see that term papers can be purchased on any topic. You ordinarily would do your own work, but the time pressure of this last semester is such that you see no other way. Do you purchase the paper and turn it in as your own?

### Situation 4

Your fifteen-year-old brother is visiting you at college. You are surprised by how much he drinks, and by the second day you understand that he really has a problem. When you tell him that you have to tell your parents, he freaks out and tells you that he'll run away or do something crazy if they find out and that he will get it under control during the summer when he has time to "chill out." What do you do?

### Situation 5

You are working as a jail officer while working your way through college. You hate the job, partly because of the inmates, but partly because of the other officers. Many of them are redneck sadists who enjoy and abuse their power. You try to stay out of the way of the most vocal of these idiots, but one day you are on the floor when one of them proceeds to castigate a black inmate for not sweeping properly. He utters a number of racial epithets and pushes the inmate around. You can see that the inmate is tensed up and ready to fight. What should you do?

## Suggested Readings

Arbuthnot, J. 1984. "Moral Reasoning Development Programmes in Prison: Cognitive–Developmental and Critical Reasoning Approaches." *Journal of Moral Education* 13(2): 112–123.

Gavaghan, M., Arnold, K., and Gibbs, J. 1983. "Moral Judgment in Delinquents and Non-delinquents: Recognition Versus Production Measures." *Journal of Psychology* 114: 267–274.

Gilligan, C. 1982. *In a Different Voice: Psychological Theory and Women's Development.* Cambridge, MA: Harvard University Press.

Hickey, J., and Scharf, P. 1980. *Toward a Just Correctional System.* San Francisco: Jossey-Bass.

Kohlberg, L., and Power, C. 1984. "Moral Development, Religious Thinking and the Question of a 7th Stage." Pp. 311–372 in Kohlberg, L. (Ed.), *The Psychology of Moral Development.* New York: Harper & Row.

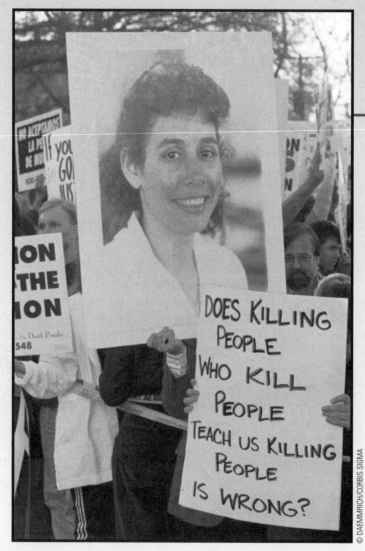

What is justice? Do some deserve mercy? There was a great debate about whether or not Karla Faye Tucker deserved mercy. The state of Texas executed her despite worldwide protests (including that of the Vatican).

# 4

# The Origins and Concept of Justice

## Key Terms

commutative justice
corrective justice
distributive justice
due process
exclusionary rule
justice

natural right
procedural justice
retributive justice
substantive justice
utilitarian justice

# Chapter Objectives

1. Understand the origins of justice.

2. Understand the components of justice, including distributive, corrective, and commutative.

3. Be able to define procedural and substantive justice.

4. Understand the difference between the utilitarian rationale and retributive rationale under corrective justice.


What is justice? How is justice related to law? Professionals in the criminal justice system serve and promote the interests of law and justice, and this chapter explores these concepts. An underlying theme will be that the ends of law and justice are different—perhaps even, at times, contradictory. Although *law* is often defined as "the administration of justice," it may very well be the case that law forces consequences that many might conclude are "unjust." Legal rights might be different than moral rights, rights might be different than needs, and needs may not be protected under either the law or justice.

Definitions of justice include the following concepts:

1. fairness
2. equality
3. impartiality
4. appropriate rewards or punishments

According to Lucas (1980: 3), justice "differs from benevolence, generosity, gratitude, friendship, and compassion." It is not something for which we should feel grateful but rather something upon which we have a right to insist. Justice should not be confused with "good." Some actions may be considered good but not necessarily just—for instance, the recipients of charity, benevolence, and forgiveness do not have a right to these things; therefore, it is not an injustice to withhold them. Justice concerns rights and interests more often than needs. Although the idea of need is important in some discussions of justice, it is not the only component or even the primary one. It is important to understand that what is just and what is good are not necessarily the same. See Box 4-1 ("Definitions of Justice") for the dictionary definitions of justice.

People can often be described as displaying unique combinations of generosity and selfishness, fairness and self-interest. Some writers insist that the need for justice arises from the nature of human beings and the fact that they are not naturally generous, open-hearted, or fair. On the one hand, if we behaved all the time in accordance with those virtues, we would have no need for justice. On the other hand, if humans were always to act in selfish, grasping, and unfair ways, then we would be unable to follow the rules and principles of justice. Therefore, we uphold and cherish the concept of justice in our society because it is the mediator between people's essential selfishness

---

**BOX 4-1 Definitions of Justice**

- "The maintenance or administration of what is just, especially by the impartial adjustment of conflicting claims or the assignment of merited rewards or punishments"
- "The administration of law; especially the establishment or determination of rights according to the rules of law or equity"
- "The quality of being just, impartial or fair"
- "The principle or ideal of just dealing or right action"

SOURCE: *Webster's Ninth New Collegiate Dictionary* (Springfield, MA: Merriam-Webster, 1984).

---

and generosity; in other words, it is the result of a logical and rational acceptance of the concept of fairness in human relations.

Anthony Walsh (2000) presents the interesting idea that justice is a biologically adaptive trait. He uses evolutionary psychology to argue that the sense of justice is emotional rather than rational and is the result of natural selection. His argument, simplified, is that humans, similar to other animal species, have "cheaters" and "suckers," with cheaters being those who do not engage in "reciprocal altruism" (basically, cooperation). Suckers would be those who are continually taken advantage of by cheaters. They are not optimally adapted for survival, and if they perish, then cheaters would perish as well because they need victims to take advantage of. Thus, "grudgers" evolve as a response— grudgers may be fooled once by cheaters, but they are outraged and demand punishment when victimized. This adaptation successfully ensures the continued existence of grudgers as well as cheaters. Our "moral outrage," in other words, is an evolutionary response, as is our emotional demand for justice.

David Hume, a philosopher, said that "Justice does not dictate a perfect world, but one in which people live up to agreements and are treated fairly" (cited in Feinberg and Gross, 1977: 75). Galston (1980: 282) described justice as follows:

> more than voluntary agreement, [but] . . . less than perfect community. It allows us to retain our separate existences and our self-regard; it does not ask us to share the pleasures, pains, and sentiments of others. Justice is intelligent self-regard, modified, by the requirements of rational consistency.

## Origins of the Concept of Justice

**Justice** originates in the Greek word *dike*, which is associated with the concept of everything staying in its assigned place or natural role (Feinberg and Gross, 1977: i). This idea is closely associated with the definitions of justice given by Plato and Aristotle. Even today, some writers describe justice as "the demand for order: everything in its proper place or relation" (Feibleman, 1985: 23).

According to Plato, justice consists of maintaining the societal status quo. Justice is one of four civic virtues, the others being wisdom, temperance, and courage (Feibleman, 1985: 173). In an ordered state, everyone performs his or her role and does not interfere with others. Each person's role is the one for which the individual is best fitted by nature; thus, *natural law* is upheld. Moreover, it is in everyone's self-interest to have this ordered existence continue because it provides the means to the good life—appropriate human happiness. Plato's society is a *class system,* based on innate abilities, rather than a *caste system,* which differentiates purely by accidents of birth.

Aristotle believed that justice exists in the law and that the law is "the unwritten custom of all or the majority of men which draws a distinction between what is honorable and what is base" (Feibleman, 1985: 174). Aristotle distinguished *distributive justice* from *rectificatory justice:*

1. *Rectificatory justice,* or *commutative justice,* concerns business deals where unfair advantage or undeserved harm has occurred. Justice demands remedies or compensations to the injured party.
2. *Distributive justice* concerns what measurement should be used to allocate society's resources. Aristotle believed in the idea of proportionality along with equality. In Aristotle's conception of justice, the lack of freedom and opportunity for some people—slaves and women, for instance—did not conflict with justice, as long as the individual was in the role in which, by nature, he or she belonged. In other words, unequal people should get unequal shares.

## Components of Justice

We still recognize these basic components of justice, and justice today can be separated into distributive, corrective, and commutative justice (Feinberg and Gross, 1977: 53):

1. **Distributive justice** is concerned with the allocation of the goods and burdens of society to its respective members. Rewards and benefits from society include wealth, education, entitlement programs, and health care. Because some people get less than others, it may be that these goods are not distributed fairly. Burdens and responsibilities must also be distributed among the members of society; for instance, decisions must be made about who should fight in war, who should take care of the elderly and infirm, who should pay taxes, and how much each should pay. The difficulties in deciding how to divide these goods and burdens and what each person deserves are the subject of any discussion of distributive justice.
2. **Corrective justice** concerns the determination and methods of punishments. Again, the concept of *desert* emerges. In corrective justice, we speak of offenders getting what they deserve, but this time the desert is punishment rather than goods. The difficulty, of course, is in determining the *just desert* for a specific crime.
3. **Commutative justice** is associated with transactions and interchanges where one person feels unfairly treated. The process of determining a fair resolution— for example, when one is cheated in a business deal or when a contract is not completed—calls into play the concepts of commutative justice. The method for determining a fair and just resolution to the conflict depends on particular concepts such as rights and interests.

There are at least three continuing themes in any discussion of justice: fairness, equality, and impartiality.

1. *Fairness.* Parents ordinarily give each child the same allowance unless differences between the children, such as age or duties, warrant different amounts. In fact, children are sensitive to issues of fairness long before they grasp more abstract ideas of justice. No doubt every parent has heard the plaintive cry "It's not fair—Johnny got more than I did" or "It's not fair—she always gets to sit in the front seat!" What children are sensing is unequal and therefore unfair treatment. The concept of fairness is inextricably tied to equality and impartiality.

2. *Equality.* Another theme of justice is the concept of *equality.* There is a predisposition to demand equity or equal shares for all. (In contrast to the concept of equal shares is the idea of needs or deserts; in other words, we should get what we need or, alternatively, what we deserve by status, merit, or other reasons.) The concept of equality is also present in retributive justice in the belief that similar cases should be treated equally—for instance, all individuals who commit a similar crime should be similarly punished. (Again, the alternative argument is that sometimes it serves the purpose of justice to treat similar crimes differently because of individual circumstances.) Are there ever any situations where people are truly equal? If we want to distribute opportunities equally to equals, how would we measure equality? Do we assume that everyone starts off with the same skills, backgrounds, and family circumstances, or must we not take into account individual differences, societal goals, and a host of other factors in decisions such as whether to employ affirmative action plans, individualized sentences, and receipt of social services?

3. *Impartiality.* This concept is at the core of our system of criminal justice. Our symbol of justice represents, with her blindfold, impartiality toward special groups and, with her scales, proportionally just punishments. Impartiality implies fair and equal treatment of all without discrimination and bias. It is hard to reconcile the ideal of "blind justice" with the individualized justice of the "treatment ethic" because one can hardly look at individual circumstance if one is blind toward the particulars of the case. Indeed, most would argue, individual differences and culpabilities should be taken into consideration—if not during a finding of guilt or innocence, then at least when sentencing occurs. The blindfold may signify no special treatment for the rich or the powerful, but then it must also signify no special consideration for the young, the misled, or extraordinary circumstances. These issues will be addressed again in the next chapter.

## Distributive Justice

The concept of the appropriate and just allocation of society's goods and interests is one of the central themes in all discussions of justice. According to one writer, justice always involves *rightful possession* (Galston, 1980: 117–119). The goods that one might possess include the following:

1. economic goods (income or property)
2. opportunities for development (education or citizenship)
3. recognition (honor or status)

**IN THE NEWS**   **After Cash Rains Down in Miami, Finders Remain Quiet Keepers**

MIAMI—Police went from door to door through one of Miami's poorest neighborhoods Thursday, asking people to admit they scooped up some of the half million dollars that spilled from a Brinks truck and, if they did, to give it back. Residents generally responded with a good laugh.

"Nobody's going to tell them," said Debbie, a resident of Overtown who, like most, would only give her first name.

"This is a once-in-a-lifetime thing," added another resident named George.

"This couldn't happen to a more *deserving* neighborhood."

Thousands of dollars in coins, bills and food stamps rained down on the street Wednesday morning after an armored Brinks truck carrying $3.7 million overturned on an Interstate 95 overpass. People swarmed over the area, digging money out of the dirt and scooping it off the street, stuffing bags, boxes and pockets before police took charge. An estimated $500,000 vanished. Thursday, police knocked on seventy-five doors urging people to turn in the money, no questions asked, before a two-day grace period ends at noon Saturday. Nobody did.

After the grace period expires, police plan to seek television news videotape to aid them in identifying money grabbers. Those caught with more than $1,000 could face grand theft charges.

Source: Associated Press. Reported in *Austin American-Statesman,* January 10, 1997, A7. Emphasis added. Reprinted with permission of the Associated Press.

*Which, if any, system supports the individual's justification that he or she "deserved" the stolen money? Did people "deserve" the material possessions that were looted in New Orleans after it was flooded? What about food? Gas?*

It is only in a condition of scarcity that a problem arises with the allocation of goods. Two valid claims to possession are *need* and *desert*. The principles of justice involve the application of these claims to specific entitlements. Different writers have presented various proposals for deciding issues of entitlement.

Lucas (1980: 164–165) lists several different distribution theories. They involve distributions based on

1. need
2. merit
3. performance
4. ability
5. rank
6. station
7. worth
8. work

9. agreements
10. requirements of the common good
11. valuation of services
12. legal entitlement

Despite differences, all schemes include some concept of need and merit (also see Raphael, 1980: 90). In the "In the News" box, "After the Cash Rains Down in Miami, Finders Remain Quiet Keepers," it is clear that some people's concept of what one *deserves* is related to need rather than merit.

The difficulty in distributing society's goods lies in deciding the weight of each of the criteria discussed above. The various theories can be categorized as egalitarian, Marxist, libertarian, or utilitarian, depending on the factors that are emphasized (Beauchamp, 1982):

1. *Egalitarian theories* start with the basic premise of equality or equal shares for all.
2. *Marxist theories* place need above desert or entitlement.
3. *Libertarian theories* promote freedom from interference by government in social and economic spheres; therefore, merit, entitlement, and productive contributions are given weight over need or equal shares.
4. *Utilitarian theories* attempt to maximize benefits for individuals and society in a mixed emphasis on entitlements and needs.

Sterba (1980) offers one system for distribution. It is displayed in Box 4-2, "Sterba's Distribution System."

---

**BOX 4-2  Sterba's Distribution System**

1. **Principle of Need.** Each person is guaranteed the primary social goods that are necessary to meet the normal costs of satisfying his or her basic needs in the society in which he or she lives.
2. **Principle of Appropriation and Exchange.** Additional primary goods are to be distributed on the basis of private appropriation and voluntary agreement and exchange.
3. **Principle of Minimal Contribution.** A minimal contribution to society is required of those who are capable of contributing when social and economic resources are insufficient to provide the guaranteed minimum to everyone in society without requiring that contribution or when the incentive to contribute to society would otherwise be adversely affected, so that persons would not maximize their contribution to society.
4. **Principle of Saving.** The rate of saving for each generation should represent its fair contribution toward realizing and maintaining a society in which all the members can fully enjoy the benefit of its just institution.

SOURCE: Adapted from Sterba (1980: 55).

How do the theories apply to the wide disparities in salaries found in this country? For instance, a professional athlete's salary is sometimes one hundred times greater than a police officer's salary. A few CEOs make $10 million per year. Which distribution principle justifies such extreme discrepancies? Libertarian theories would shrug at such disparity; Marxist theories would not. Obviously, few would agree that workers in all jobs and all professions should be paid the same amount of money. First, not many people would be willing to put up with the long hours and many years of schooling needed in some professions if there were no incentives. Second, some types of jobs demand a greater degree of responsibility and involve greater stress than others. However, we can readily see that some remuneration is entirely out of proportion to an analysis of worth. For instance, it is hard to see how any corporate executive could deserve $10 million for one year's work. The same argument applies to athletes, rock musicians, and actors. Compare your thoughts with your classmates on appropriate salaries, as suggested by the exercise "How Much Are They Worth?"

If we are primarily concerned with performance and ability, why do we not pay individual workers in the same job category differently if one works harder than the other? Although some production jobs pay according to how much is produced (the piecework payment method), most of us are paid according to a step-grade position, earning roughly what others in the same position earn. Which is the fairer system of payment? What about people who produce less in the piecework system because they are helping their co-workers or taking more time to produce higher-quality products?

### EXERCISE  How Much Are They Worth?

Determine the fair salary for these professions and occupations. Propose an average salary, balancing such factors as seniority and education.

Nurse:
Electrician:
Elementary schoolteacher:
Sanitation worker:
Police officer:
Prison guard:
Probation officer:
College professor:
Software engineer:
City council member:
Lawyer:
Secretary:
Judge:

Now compare your responses to those of others. Is there general consensus on salaries for these positions? Compare your responses to published figures (you can find this information in a library or at the career center of your university).

Is it fair for them to earn less? If all work were paid according to production, how would one pay secretaries, teachers, or customer service workers, whose production is more difficult to measure? How would one pay police officers—by the number of arrests?

Thus far, we have only discussed salaries, but even in the workplace there are other goods that are distributed, such as promotions, merit increases, job postings, desirable offices, and parking places. In the exercise "Who Should Be Promoted?" determine which of the distribution systems described above helped you decide whom to promote.

Marxist distribution systems propose that we pay people according to need. This sounds fair in one sense because people would get only what they needed to survive at some predetermined level. In that case, a person with two children would earn more than a person with no children. In the past, this was the argument used by employers to explain why they would favor men over women in hiring, promotions, and pay increases—because men had families to support and women did not. Two arguments were used against this type of discriminatory treatment:

1. The first was that women deserve as much as men if they are of equal ability and performance.
2. The second was that women also, more often than not, have to support families.

These two arguments emphasize different principles of justice. The first is based on an equal-deserts argument; the second rests on an equal-needs argument.

---

**EXERCISE  Who Should Be Promoted?**

You are on a promotion committee to recommend to the chief of police a candidate for a captain's position. All are lieutenants and have received similar scores on the objective tests available for the position. The candidates:

1. A thirty-nine-year-old woman who has been with the police department for nine years. She has obtained a college degree and a master's degree by going to school at night. She has spent relatively little time in her career on the street (moving quickly to juvenile, community service, and DARE positions).
2. A forty-six-year-old white male who has also had experience in command positions in the army before joining the police force. He has fifteen years of experience—all in patrol positions—and has a college degree.
3. A forty-year-old Hispanic male with ten years of experience. He has been very active with the community. Several community groups have endorsed him, and they demand that there be Hispanic representation on the command staff. He also has strong support among Hispanic officers, serving as their association president. He has a two-year college degree.

*Whom would you endorse? Why? If you need more information, what type of information would you want?*

Although race- and gender-based discrepancies in wages and hiring patterns are becoming a thing of the past, there are still continuing issues of fairness in employment rights. One such issue is family or pregnancy leave. The principle of justice that is used to support the right to take leave (whether it be the unpaid leave mandated by Congress or paid leave) is not worth, merit, ability, or performance; rather, it is need. Does justice dictate an employee's *right* to family leave? This is not equal treatment (because we're discriminating against people who do not fit any category of the family leave bill but desire leave for other reasons). In fact, this may be a question of *goodness* rather than *justice*. That is, it is a social good (good for society, good for the individual), but it is not a right. On the other hand, some people insist that there is a **natural right** to productive employment and also the ability to have a family; therefore, there is a state duty to provide adequate, affordable child care for workers and leave for pregnancy and sickness.

Just distribution of other goods in society is also problematic. Welfare is one example of this difficulty. The principle of need is the rationale we use to take from the financially solvent, through taxes, and give to those who have little or nothing. There is always some resentment over this redistribution because of the belief that some people choose not to work and take advantage of welfare. If there are such people, justice may dictate that they be dropped from welfare rolls, but what about their children? Do they also *deserve* to be punished? What do children deserve from the state? In Policy Box 4-1, the tragedy of the New Orleans flood created by Hurricane Katrina is used to illustrate these difficult issues of need and desert.

---

### POLICY BOX 4-1  What Do They Deserve?

As this book was being written, Hurricane Katrina displaced hundreds of thousands of people from their homes and livelihoods. It seems to be the case that many, perhaps hundreds, lost their lives after the city flooded because help did not arrive in time. Experts estimate that it will cost tens of billions of dollars to rebuild the damaged areas. There is much criticism of the federal response to the natural disaster, including earlier budget cuts for the Corps of Army Engineers (which predicted flooding in a Category 4 or higher hurricane), the lack of immediate response by the National Guard to prevent looting, and the inability of the Federal Emergency Management Agency (FEMA) to evacuate or provide needed medical services for hurricane and flood victims.

**Law:** There is no law that requires government to assist disaster victims unless Congress creates such a law. In this case, Congress has authorized the creation of disaster relief funds.

**Policy:** Much of the criticism directed at the administration has to do with policy. There has been a policy of reducing the budget of the Army Corps of Engineers, which creates and maintains the levee system, as well as reducing budgets for flood control and disaster response. The policy of allowing retail and residential development of tidelands and the reduction of barrier islands has been said to have contributed to the scope of the disaster. Others argue that the policy of refusing to acknowledge the findings regarding global warming has also contributed to the tragedy, although others point out that we are entering a natural cycle where hurricanes will be more frequent and more severe. Federal, state, and city policies all contributed to the disaster—all levels of government did not respond adequately to the obvious fact that a large city was below sea level without adequate protection from a Category 4 or 5 hurricane.

Policy is also at issue in response to the disaster. In the long term, there will need to be policy decisions regarding who is to pay for the housing and living expenses of those displaced. Further, how much do they deserve? Does a homeless person and someone who lost an expensive house deserve the same or different compensation from the government? Issues of entitlement and desert were also at issue after the 9/11 bombing. Family members of victims received federal compensation that was in addition to any private benefits they might have received (from life insurance). Family members of victims of the Oklahoma City bombing vocally wondered why they didn't deserve comparable compensation. Any assistance received by victims displaced by Hurricane Katrina will inevitably be compared to that provided to prior hurricane and flooding victims.

**Individual ethics:**  Individual ethics were most apparent during the aftermath of the flooding. A few individuals made the decision to loot, rape, assault, and perhaps even kill; however, many others shared scarce resources, including food, water, and gasoline. Others went to the site to help or assisted in refugee camps set up in their own cities in Texas, Mississippi, Arkansas, and other neighboring states. Many people gave generously to the Red Cross and other relief agencies. It is obvious that under any ethical system, helping those in need is the ethical and moral response. The more difficult question is how much? Should everyone open their homes to evacuated residents? What level of assistance is needed to satisfy justice?

Another "good" that society distributes to its members is opportunity. Many people would argue that education (at least at the university level) is a privilege that should be reserved for those few who have the ability and the drive to succeed. However, the educational system of this country is fundamentally democratic. Not only do we have guaranteed, in fact, compulsory, education at elementary and secondary levels; we also have open admission to some universities. Moreover, remedial courses are available to help those without the skills to meet college standards. In fact, massive amounts of time and money are devoted to helping some students improve their skills and ultimately graduate from college. Might some argue that this system wastes resources? Other countries "track" students very early and identify those who have natural skills, then allow only that selected group to take advantage of state-supported higher education. Is this a more efficient use of state resources?

There is also a compelling argument that although the *ideal* of education is demo-cratic, the *reality* is that because of unequal tax bases, school districts are incredibly unequal and distribute the opportunity of education unequally. Although some school districts have swimming pools, computers in every classroom, and teachers with spe-cialized education, other school districts make do with donated textbooks and build-ings that are poorly heated and ventilated. Likewise, there are vast differences in the quality and status of higher education, with degrees from some universities worth much more than others. Who deserves to go to these better universities? And, if you said those with better grades, then do you also agree with the process whereby high schools are ranked by admissions committees so that a 4.0 in one high school is ranked lower than a 4.0 from another high school?

Affirmative action attempts to provide opportunities to groups that historically have been discriminated against—blacks, women, Hispanics. Now those groups that have been favored in the past—white males—feel that they are the new victims of dis-crimination. Some feel that taking affirmative steps to increase opportunities for minority groups has simply transferred unfair treatment to another group. What is acceptable to overcome previous discrimination? Unfortunately, a promise to hire "the best person for the job" is not enough, because historical and institutionalized discrimination may take many years to overcome. For instance, some claim that underfunded schools produce students who are less qualified, and then these individuals are denied jobs based on their lack of abilities. To assume that one is eliminating discrimination by hiring on the basis of individual abilities does not solve the problem of blocked access; it merely perpetuates it in a more subtle way.

The Supreme Court has ruled against affirmative action attempts, such as race-based criteria in law school and university admissions. States are also passing legislation to bar hiring decisions, promotions, and admission to state schools based on race. The same "equal protection" argument used to pass civil rights legislation in the 1960s is now being used to dismantle these programs. What effect such decisions will have on access to the opportunity of education remains to be seen. Some predict that the progress we have seen in educational and economic success for historically blocked minority groups will be negated.

This controversy only points out the extreme difficulty of determining a just distri-bution of goods. The fact that everyone is not equal, in terms of ability, performance, motivation, need, or any other measure, is easy enough to agree on. Very few people would argue that everyone in every position should receive the same salary, get the same education, and achieve the same status in society. On the other hand, to acknowl-edge inequality puts us in the position of distributing goods and other benefits on the basis of other criteria, and it is here that problems arise. When injustice occurs, we sense it on the basis of fairness. We feel somehow that it is not fair that there are starv-ing children and conspicuous wealth in the same country or the same world. We sense unfairness when people work hard yet still struggle to get along on poverty wages, while star actors or athletes make millions of dollars largely through luck or for contri-butions to societal welfare that seem trivial.

John Rawls's theory of justice is perhaps the best-known current conception of justice. He elegantly combines utilitarian and rights-based concepts in his theory. Basically, he proposes an equal distribution unless a different distribution would benefit the disadvantaged. Rawls believes that any inequalities of society should be to the benefit of those who are least advantaged (Rawls, 1971: 15). He proposes the following (cited in Kaplan, 1976: 114):

1. Each person is to have an equal right to the most extensive total system of basic liberties compatible with a similar system of liberty for all.
2. Social and economic inequalities are to be arranged so that they are both reasonably expected to be to everyone's advantage; and attached to positions and offices open to all (except when inequality is to the advantage of those least well-off).

Rawls uses a heuristic device that he calls the *veil of ignorance* to explain the idea that people will develop fair principles of distribution only if they are ignorant of their position in society, for they may just as easily be "have-nots" as "haves" (Rawls, 1971: 12). Thus, justice and fairness are in everyone's rational self-interest because, under the veil of ignorance, one's own situation is unknown, and the best and most rational distribution is the one most equal to all.

The following criticisms of Rawls' theory of justice have been presented:

1. The veil of ignorance is not sufficient to counteract humanity's basic selfishness: given the chance, people would still seek to maximize their own gain, even if doing so involved a risk (Kaplan, 1976: 199).
2. Rawls's preference toward those least well-off is contrary to the good of society. Rawls states that "all social values—liberty and opportunity, income and wealth and the bases of self-respect—are to be distributed equally unless an unequal distribution of any, or all, of these values is to the advantage of the least favored" (quoted in Sterba, 1980: 32). This may be ultimately dysfunctional for society, for if those least well-off have the advantages of society preferentially, there will be no incentive for others to excel.
3. Some also argue that Rawls is wrong to ignore desert in his distribution of goods (Galston, 1980: 3).

Let us now turn to how these theories of distributive justice relate to the ethical systems discussed in Chapter 2. The ethics of care is consistent with a Marxist theory of justice, for both emphasize need. Utilitarian theories try to maximize societal good, so some balance of need and merit would be necessary to provide the incentive to produce. Ethical formalism is solely concerned with rights; thus, issues of societal good or others' needs may not be as important as the individual's rights (however those might be defined). Rawls's theory is both utilitarian and Kantian because it demands a basic level of individual rights but also attempts to establish a preference toward those who have less, for the good of all society.

How are these concepts of distributive justice relevant to criminal justice? First, the discussion illuminates the issues regarding the appropriateness of affirmative action in the hiring and promotion of police officers and other criminal justice professionals. Should your race give you special hiring privileges? What if the profession is one like policing, which has been historically closed to minorities? People's opinions regarding affirmative action can be traced to their ideas of distributive justice. Another issue that is related to distributive justice is how much to pay police officers compared to other professions. Most people believe that police are underpaid. If so, how much is a fair salary, and how does that salary compare to others, such as elementary school teachers? The criteria you used to determine these answers should have some basis in the distribution systems discussed above.

Finally, there is a connection between distributive justice and corrective justice, which will be discussed in the next section. If it is true that socioeconomic status predicts criminal predisposition, should we care? Is it fair that poor people tend to end up in prison and those with more resources usually receive a lesser form of punishment? Further, should we consider issues of distributive justice (i.e., what someone has by accident of birth) in any discussion of corrective justice (i.e., what people deserve when they commit a crime)? Reiman (2004), for instance, presents a comprehensive argument that places economic power as the center of lawmaking, lawbreaking, enforcement, and punishment practices. Clearly, distributive justice is an important concept in any discussion of the criminal justice system.

# Corrective Justice

As mentioned before, corrective justice is concerned with dispensing punishment. As with distributive justice, the concepts of equality and desert, fairness and impartiality are important. Two components of corrective justice should be differentiated. **Substantive justice** involves the concept of just deserts, or how one determines a fair punishment for a particular offense; **procedural justice** concerns the steps we must take before administering punishment.

## *Substantive Justice*

What is a fair punishment for the crime of murder? Many believe the only just punishment is death because that is the only punishment of a degree equal to the harm caused by the offender. Others might say life imprisonment is equitable and fair. One's beliefs about what is fair punishment are usually related to one's perception of the seriousness of the crime. More-serious crimes deserve more-serious punishments.

Since the beginning of codified law, just punishment has been perceived as punishment set in relation to the degree of harm incurred. This was a natural outcome of the early, remedial forms of justice, which provided remedies for wrongs. For instance, the response to a theft of a slave or the killing of a horse involved compensation. The only just solution was the return or replacement of the slave or horse. This remedial or compensatory system of justice contrasts with a punishment system: The first system forces the offender to provide compensation to the victim or the victim's family, and the second apportions punishment based on the degree of seriousness of the crime suffered by the victim. They both involve a measurement of the harm, but in the first case, measurement is taken to adequately compensate the victim, and in the second it is to punish the offender. In a punishment-based system, the victim is a peripheral figure. The state, rather than the victim, becomes the central figure—serving both as victim and as punisher (Karmen, 1984). In the exercise "Determining Severity," you are asked to decide what punishments should be given to each offender and then share your answers with others.

Two *philosophies* of corrective justice can be identified: retributive justice and utilitarian justice.

---

**EXERCISE Determining Severity**

Rank the following crimes in order of seriousness, with 1 being the most serious and 14 being the least serious. Compare your rank orderings with those of others.

sexual assault (with force)
death caused by drunken driving
embezzlement of $15,000
tax evasion of $15,000
shoplifting ($15,000)
assault (broken bones)
robbery of $15,000
sexual molestation (no penetration)
toxic waste dumping (unknown damage)
murder (during barroom brawl)
drug possession (marijuana)
perjury
murder in heat of passion
solicitation of murder

---

## Retributive Justice

The concept of **retributive justice** is one of balance. The criminal must suffer pain or loss proportional to what the victim was forced to suffer. In an extreme form, this retribution takes the form of *lex talionis,* a vengeance-oriented justice concerned with equal retaliation ("an eye for an eye; a tooth for a tooth"). A milder form is *lex salica,* which allows compensation; the harm can be repaired by payment or atonement (Allen and Simonsen, 1986: 4). A life for a life might be easy to measure, but most cases involve other forms of harm. In other types of victimizations, how does one determine the amount of physical or mental pain suffered by the victim, or financial loss such as lost income or future loss? And if the offender cannot pay back financial losses, how does one equate imprisonment with fines or restitution?

Historically, corporal and capital punishment were used for both property crime and violent crime. With the development of the penitentiary system in the early 1800s, punishment became equated with terms of imprisonment rather than amounts of physical pain. In fact, the greater ease of measuring out prison sentences probably contributed to the rapid acceptance of prison sentences. One might sentence an offender to one, two, or five years, depending on the seriousness of the crime. Imprisonment had several advantages over earlier forms of punishment:

1. It was considered more humane than corporal punishment.
2. It was incapacitating (preventing the offender from further crime).
3. It allowed the offender to reflect on his crime and repent.
4. It did not elicit sympathy for the offender from the populace.

However, a term of imprisonment is much harder to equate to a particular crime. Although one can intuitively understand the natural balance of a life for a life, $10 for $10, or even a beating for an assault, it is much harder to argue that a burglary of $100 is equal to a year in prison or that an assault is equal to a term of two years. A year in prison is hard to define. Research on prison adjustment indicates that a year means different things to different people. For some, it might be no more than mildly inconvenient; for others, it might lead to suicide or mental illness (Toch, 1977).

In addition to retribution, imprisonment was tied to the reform of the criminal offender. Reform or rehabilitation may be a laudable goal, but it has no place in a retributive scheme of justice. Retributive punishment is based on balancing the victim's harm with the offender's pain or suffering. Treatment involves no such balance; therefore, there is no retributive rationale for its existence. Philosophical support for rehabilitative treatment of criminal offenders is found in utilitarianism.

Retributive justice is not a simple equation because other factors are taken into account in addition to the seriousness of the crime. For instance, *mens rea* (intent) has long been considered a necessary element in determining culpability. Those who are incapable of rational thought—the insane, the very young—are said to be neither morally nor legally culpable; therefore, to punish them would be an injustice under a retributive framework. Other situations might prove to involve partial responsibility—for example, the presence of compulsion, coercion, or irresistible impulse. In these cases, most people feel that justice is not compromised by a lesser amount of punishment, even though the harm to the victim is obviously the same as if the offender had acted deliberately and intentionally. In this sense, we see that the amount of punishment is not solely measured by the amount of harm to the victim but involves characteristics of the offender as well.

Just punishment may also involve considering the participation of the victim. Victim precipitation may lessen the culpability of the offender. Other factors also play a part in determining punishment, some of which would not be consistent with retributive justice. In earlier systems of justice, the status of the victim was important in determining the level of harm and, thus, the punishment. Nobles were more important than freemen, who were more important than slaves. Men were more important than women. Punishment for offenders was weighted according to these designations of the worth of the victim. Although we have no formal system for weighting punishment in this way and have rejected the worth of the victim as a rationale for punishment (except in a few cases, such as assaulting a police officer), many feel that our justice system still follows this practice informally. People argue that harsher sentences are given when the victim is white than when the victim is black and when the victim is rich as opposed to poor. In a similar manner, many argue that the justice system discriminates unfairly and unjustly against characteristics of the offender. Many believe that offenders receive harsher sentences because of their race, background, or income.

Whether or not these charges are true, it is important to recognize that earlier systems of justice, including the Greek and Roman, approved of and rationalized such different treatment as perfectly fair and just. Our system of justice has rejected these discriminations even while holding on to others—specifically, intent, partial responsibility, and, to some extent, victim precipitation. It is difficult, if not impossible, for everyone to agree upon a fair and equitable measurement of punishment when one allows for exceptions, mediating factors, and partial responsibility. That is why there is so little agreement on what is fair punishment. Even when two defendants are involved in a single crime, our system of justice can support different punishments under a retributive rationale. These issues of culpability will be discussed in more detail in the next chapter.

In Rawls's theory of justice, retributive punishment is limited in the following way (quoted in Hickey and Scharf, 1980: 168):

> [T]he liberties of a person . . . may only be reduced, compared with the liberties of other people, when it is for the good of the least advantaged, considered from the "veil of ignorance" assumption of not knowing what role one will occupy.

This statement means that only when punishment can be shown to benefit the least advantaged (the victim) can it be justified; when the advantage changes (when the victim has been repaid), then punishment must cease. Hickey and Scharf (1980: 169) point out that this limitation is similar to that proposed by Norval Morris:

1. We must punish only to the extent that the loss of liberty would be agreeable were one not to know whether one were to be the criminal, the victim, or a member of the general public, and
2. The loss of liberty must be justified as the minimal loss consistent with the maintenance of the same liberty among others.

In both of these propositions, the moral limit of punishment is reached when what is done to the criminal equals the extent of his or her forfeiture, as determined by the crime.

One other issue that must be addressed here is the concept of *mercy*. Seemingly inconsistent with any definition of retributive justice, mercy is, nevertheless, always associated with the concept. From the very beginnings of law, there has also been the element of forgiveness. Even tribal societies had special allowances and clemencies for offenders, usually granted by the king or chief. For instance, the concept of *sanctuary* allowed a person respite from punishment as long as she or he was within the confines of church grounds. Benefit of clergy, dispensation, and even probation are examples of mercy by the court. However, it must be made clear that mercy is different from just deserts. If, on the one hand, because of circumstances of the crime, of the criminal, or of the victim, the offender deserves little or no punishment, then that is what he or she deserves, and it is not mercy to give a suspended sentence or probation. On the other hand, if an offender truly deserves the punishment and is instead forgiven, then the individual has been granted mercy. As the "In the News" box shows, sometimes mercy is not forthcoming.

Murphy (1985/1995) proposes that retributive emotions derive from self-respect, that it is a healthy response to an injury to feel angry, resentful, and, yes, even vengeful. However, it is also acceptable to forgive and extend mercy to one's assailant if the forgiveness extends not from a lack of self-respect but rather from a moral system. For instance, he points out that many religions include the concept of "turning the other cheek" and extending mercy to enemies. Mercy is appropriate when the offender is divorced in some way from her or his offense. One way to a separation is true repentance.

**IN THE NEWS  Karla Faye Tucker**

In 1998, Karla Faye Tucker received worldwide attention in her bid to receive a commutation of her death sentence. A legion of supporters, including international leaders and the pope, pleaded with Texas Governor George W. Bush to recommend that her death sentence be commuted and let her serve a life sentence instead. The major arguments were that she had changed from the drug-addled young woman who had embedded a pickaxe into her victim's chest. She was now thirty-five years old and had been a leader and calming influence upon the other women on death row. She had spent years engaged in charitable activities in the prison. She experienced real remorse for her crime and felt her lifetime was devoted to making up for it. Also, her childhood involved sexual and physical abuse; she was prostituted by her mother at a young age and was already addicted to alcohol by the time she was twelve. Further, she had become a true Christian. Her spirituality and, in all likelihood, true conversion to religion allowed her to face death with the attitude that it was part of a divine plan. Finally, similar murders by others did not result in the death sentence. Governor Bush refused to commute her sentence, and she was executed amid the cheers and tears of the opposing groups.

*Do you think that her death sentence should have been commuted? Why? Identify the rationales that underlie the above arguments. Are the arguments based on desert or mercy?*

Murphy (1985/1995: 10) summarizes the points of mercy as follows:

1. It is an autonomous moral virtue (separate from justice).
2. It is a virtue that tempers or "seasons" justice—something that one adds to justice in order to dilute it and to make it stronger.
3. It is never owed to anyone as a right or a matter of desert or justice.
4. As a moral virtue, it derives its value at least in part from the fact that it flows from love or compassion while not losing sight of the importance of justice.
5. It requires a generally retributive outlook on punishment and responsibility.

Therefore, mercy is related to justice but is not necessarily a part of it. It is connected with a change in the offender—typically, there must be repentance—and it is connected with a quality of the victim—some form of compassion, charity, or benevolence. Other questions of mercy remain, however. Who has the right to extend mercy? At times, victims or the families of victims are upset with a sentencing judge because of the lenient sentence administered to the offender. Should victims be the only ones who have the right to give the gift of mercy?

## Utilitarian Justice

We have been discussing retributive justice as a rationale for and means to determine punishment. However, other rationales also support punishment, such as **utilitarian justice.** Whereas the goal of a retributive framework of justice is to restore a natural balance by righting a wrong or neutralizing criminal gain with an equal amount of loss or pain, the goal of utilitarian justice is to benefit society by administering punishment to deter offenders from future crime.

Caesare Beccaria (1738–1794) and Jeremy Bentham (1748–1832) provided a utilitarian rationale for proportionality in punishment. Punishment should be based on the seriousness of the crime: The more serious the crime (or the greater the reward the crime offered the criminal), the more serious and severe the punishment should be in order to deter the individual from committing the crime. A utilitarian framework of justice would determine punishment on the basis of deterrence.

Bentham's *hedonistic calculus,* for instance, is concerned with measuring the potential rewards of the crime so that the amount of threatened pain could be set to deter people from committing that crime. The use of proportionality in this scheme is deterrence, not balance. In a retributive system, we measure to determine the proportional amount of punishment to right the wrong; in a utilitarian system, we measure to determine the amount of punishment needed to deter. We see that under the utilitarian framework, there is no necessity for perfect balance. In fact, one must threaten a slightly higher degree of pain or punishment than the gain or pleasure that comes from the criminal act; otherwise, there would be no deterrent value in the punishment.

In some cases, retributive notions of justice and utilitarian notions of justice may conflict. If a criminal is sure to commit more crime, the utilitarian could justify holding him in prison as a means of incapacitation, but to hold him past the time "equal" to his crime would be seen as an injustice under a retributive system. We might punish an offender more seriously than he "deserves" under a utilitarian system if it could be shown to deter many others. Deterrence is the primary determinant of justice under a utilitarian system, but desert is the only determinant of a retributive system of justice. Treatment is prevention, not deterrence *per se,* but it is also acceptable under a utilitarian justice system and irrelevant and unsupported by a retributive one.

## *Procedural Justice*

We turn now to the procedure of administering punishment—our legal system. *Justice* and *law* are not synonymous; most writers describe law as objective and justice as subjective. Law includes the procedures and rules used to determine punishment or resolve disputes. It is a system of rules for human relations—the "whole field of the principles laid down, the decisions reached in accordance with them, and the procedures whereby the principles are applied to individual cases" (Raphael, 1980: 74). There is, then, a differentiation between justice and law. Justice is the concept of fairness; law is a system of rules.

The law is an imperfect system. Fuller (1969: 39) explores the weaknesses of law and describes ways that the procedure of law may fail to achieve justice. Possible failures include the following:

1. a failure to achieve rules at all, so that every decision must be made on its own
2. a failure to publicize rules
3. retroactive application of law, which abuses the concept of justice
4. the existence of contradictory rules
5. too-frequent changes in rules
6. a lack of consistency between the rules and their actual administration

These failures weaken the law's ability to resolve disputes or control conflict in an objective and fair manner.

Some argue that because of the legal system's inability to determine what is just, justice derives not from the application of legal rules but from deciding each case on its merits without regard to rule or precedent. Early equity courts in England were developed because there was dissatisfaction with the King's (legal) courts' emphasis on rules and precedent that, in some cases, frustrated the ends of justice. Some argue that legal precedent is an unsatisfactory way of determining justice because the particularity of each case is important. However, individual, intuitive decisions are no better, for justice then becomes "unsteady" and "wavering" (Feinberg and Gross, 1977: 28–34). Some have argued that property and interest cases can be decided by legal rule but that cases involving conflicts of human conduct cannot. Even this bifurcation is criticized, however, because the most straightforward contract disagreements may involve human action, misinterpretation, and interest (Wasserman, cited in Feinberg and Gross, 1977: 34).

We are left to assume that although a system of law is necessary for the ordered existence of society, it is not necessarily helpful in determining what is just. In fact, "moral rights" may differ from "legal rights," and "legal interests" may not be moral. However, it should be noted that rules very often specify the procedures and steps necessary in judicial decision making. If these rules and procedures are broken, we believe

---

## QUOTE and QUERY

*The quality of mercy is not strained;*
*It droppeth as the gentle rain from heaven*
*Upon the place beneath. It is twice blest;*
*It blesseth him that gives and him that takes.*
*. . .*

*It is an attribute to God himself,*
*And earthly power doth then show likest God's*
*When mercy seasons justice. Therefore, Jew,*
*Though justice be thy plea, consider this,*
*That, in the course of justice, none of us*
*Should see salvation. We do pray for mercy,*
*And that same prayer doth teach us all to render*
*The deeds of mercy. I have spoke thus much*
*To mitigate the justice of thy plea,*
*Which if thou follow, this strict court of Venice*
*Must needs give sentence 'gainst the merchant there.*

Source: *The Merchant of Venice,* Act IV, Scene I, *William Shakespeare: The Complete Works* (Baltimore: Penguin, 1969).

**What is the magistrate in this passage asking Shylock to do? How do you believe mercy should "season" justice? What would be procedural justice in this case? What would be substantive justice?**

that an injustice has occurred. Shakespeare's *The Merchant of Venice* addresses many of the issues we discuss in this chapter. Here the plea for mercy emphasizes the relationship between justice and mercy. Shylock's demand for the court's enforcement of his legal right (his pound of flesh) and the unwillingness of the court to deny it, despite the clear implication that it would be a tragedy, illustrate how law sometimes has little to do with justice. Then Portia's surprise argument—that because Shylock's contract mentioned only flesh and not blood, so no blood could be spilled, and thus Shylock is denied his compensation—is a perfect illustration of the law's slavish devotion to technical rules over substance. As a legal trick, this interpretation of a contract has not been improved upon yet, in fiction or reality.

In our system of justice, **due process** exemplifies procedural justice. Our constitutional rights of due process require careful inquiry and investigation before punishment or forfeiture of any protected right can be carried out by the state. In Box 4-3,

---

### BOX 4-3  The Bill of Rights and Selected Amendments

**Article I.** Congress shall make no law respecting an establishment of religion, or prohibiting the free exercise thereof; or abridging the freedom of speech, or of the press; or the right of the people peaceably to assemble, and to petition the Government for a redress of grievance.

**Article II.** A well regulated militia, being necessary to the security of a free State, the right of the people to keep and bear arms, shall not be infringed.

**Article III.** No Soldier shall, in time of peace be quartered in any house, without the consent of the owner, nor in time of war, but in a manner to be prescribed by law.

**Article IV.** The right of the people to be secure in their persons, houses, papers, and effects, against unreasonable searches and seizures, shall not be violated, and no warrants shall issue, but upon probable cause, supported by oath or affirmation, and particularly describing the place to be searched, and the persons or things to be seized.

**Article V.** No person shall be held to answer for a capital, or otherwise infamous crime, unless on a presentment or indictment of a Grand Jury, except in cases arising in the land or naval forces, or in the militia, when in actual service in time of war or public danger; nor shall any person be subject for the same offense to be twice put in jeopardy of life or limb; nor shall be compelled in any criminal case to be a witness against himself, nor be deprived of life, liberty, or property, without due process of law; nor shall private property be taken for public use, without just compensation.

**Article VI.** In all criminal prosecutions, the accused shall enjoy the right to a speedy and public trial, by an impartial jury of the State and district wherein the crime shall have been committed, which district shall have been previously ascertained by law, and to be informed of the nature and cause of the accusation; to be confronted with the witnesses against him; to have compul-

*continued*

---

**BOX 4-3  Continued**

sory process for obtaining witnesses in his favor, and to have the assistance of counsel for his defense.

**Article VII.** In Suits at common law, where the value in controversy shall exceed twenty dollars, the right of trial by jury shall be preserved, and no fact tried by a jury, shall be otherwise reexamined in any Court of the United States, than according to the rules of the common law.

**Article VIII.** Excessive bail shall not be required, nor excessive fines imposed, nor cruel and unusual punishments inflicted.

**Article IX.** The enumeration in the Constitution, of certain rights, shall not be construed to deny or disparage others retained by the people.

**Article X.** The powers not delegated to the United States by the Constitution, nor prohibited by it to the States, are reserved to the States respectively, or to the people.

**Article XIII. Section 1.** Neither slavery nor involuntary servitude, except as a punishment for crime whereof the party shall have been duly convicted, shall exist within the United States, or any place subject to their jurisdiction. **Section 2.** Congress shall have power to enforce this article by appropriate legislation.

**Article XIV. Section 1.** All persons born or naturalized to the United States, and subject to the jurisdiction thereof, are citizens of the United States and of the State wherein they reside. No State shall make or enforce any law which shall abridge the privileges or immunities of citizens of the United States; nor shall any State deprive any person of life, liberty, or property, without due process of law; nor deny to any person within its jurisdiction the equal protection of the laws. . . .

**Article XV. Section 1.** The right of citizens of the United States to vote shall not be denied or abridged by the United States or by any State on account of race, color, or previous condition of servitude. . . .

**Article XIX.** The right of citizens of the United States to vote shall not be denied or abridged by the United States or by any State on account of sex. . . .

---

certain selected rights embodied in the Bill of Rights have been provided. Notice that the Fourteenth Amendment is specifically referred to as our "due process" amendment.

One has the right to due process whenever the state seeks to deprive an individual of protected rights of life, liberty, or property. Due process is the sequence of steps taken by the state that is designed to eliminate or at least minimize error. Procedural protections include the following:

1. notice of charges
2. neutral hearing body
3. right of cross-examination

4. right to present evidence
5. representation by counsel
6. statement of findings
7. appeal

These do not eliminate deprivation or punishment, but they do result in more accurate and just deprivations and punishments. Thus, if due process has been violated—by use of a coerced confession, tainted evidence, or improper police procedure—an injustice has occurred. The injustice does not arise because the offender does not deserve to be punished but because the state does not deserve to do the punishing, having relied on unfair procedures.

Some point out that procedural justice is recognized only for certain groups—specifically, "all persons born or naturalized in the United States. . . ." Many people believe that illegal aliens and noncitizens should have no rights recognized by the Constitution. This allows such practices as the incarceration of the Cuban "Marielitos" without any form of due process at all. Some of these refugees were imprisoned for more than a decade in federal prisons without any finding of guilt, harm, or reason. Jimmy Carter, in 1993, discussed their imprisonment (quoted in Hamm, 1995: 39):

> Every nation that grossly violates human rights justifies it by claiming they are acting within their laws. The way we are doing it now is the same kind of human rights violation that we'd vehemently condemn if it was perpetrated in another country.

Recently, the Supreme Court held that such detentions were illegal. In a 7–2 decision, the Court held in *Clark v. Martinez,* 125 S. Ct. 716 (2005), that the government may not "indefinitely" detain illegal immigrants, even if they have been found guilty of a crime. The Court said the government could not restrain individuals past a "reasonable" amount of time. The government argued that the ruling would affect counterterrorism efforts. In fact, recently there have been several important decisions about the right of the executive branch to fashion new rules regarding due process in the "war on terror."

After 9/11, several thousand individuals who were suspected of terrorist ties were held without charges and without any procedural protections that might allow them to prove in a fair and neutral hearing that those ties did not exist. Part of the reasons given for their detention was that they violated immigration laws—for instance, they overstayed their visas. Instead of deportation, however, more than one thousand individuals were incarcerated, sometimes without even notice to their families of where they were. The federal courts have had to wrestle with how to protect individual liberties balanced against the government's right to protect itself. The touchstone of this analysis is always and always has to be due process.

In *Hamdi v. Rumsfeld,* 542 U.S. 507, 124 S.Ct. 2633 (2004), the Supreme Court held that a U.S. citizen could not be held indefinitely as an "enemy combatant" without some form of due process. However, the decision was split between those who believed that U.S. citizens could be held and prosecuted as enemy combatants by a military court and those who distinguished U.S. citizens from noncitizens. In *Rasul v. Bush*, 542 U.S. 466, 124 S.Ct. 2686 (2004), the Supreme Court held that those being held in Guantanamo Bay were subject to the laws of the United States and deserved some form of due process. On the other hand, the Court, in *Hamdan v. Rumsfeld*, 125 S.Ct. 972, 160 L.Ed.2d 910 (2005), recently denied *certiorari* to another Guantanamo Bay detainee who lost at the court of appeals level in his bid to have the Court recognize various protections granted to the detainees by the Geneva Convention.

Is the right to be free from governmental deprivation of liberty without some finding of guilt a *natural* right that every government must recognize for all people, or a *legal* right that can be written into existence, written out of existence, and defined in whatever way a government chooses, depending on a perceived threat? These questions depend on one's beliefs regarding natural law, individual rights, and definitions of justice.

The **exclusionary rule** is supposed to ensure that the state follows the correct procedures before exacting punishment by excluding illegal evidence from the trial. There is debate as to whether the exclusionary rule is a mere legal protective device created by the Supreme Court or a natural inherent right embedded in the Constitution. The exclusionary rule has been subject to a great deal of criticism because it is perceived as a rule that lets criminals go free.

A utilitarian framework might support punishment even if the procedural rules were broken, for the net utility of punishment might outweigh the violation of due process. On the other hand, even a utilitarian may argue against punishment when the procedural protections have been broken if the damage to general respect for the law is greater than the deterrent utility of punishment. In fact, one of the rationales for the exclusionary rule is that it serves as a judicial "slap" to police departments and a deterrent against improper investigation procedures. This is clearly a utilitarian argument.

Under a retributive system of punishment, it would seem that justice is violated whether one is punished or not if procedural justice is violated. If we allow the offender to go free because of the error, then the crime has not been balanced by punishment. If we punish the offender, we violate our system of procedural justice and protection of individual rights.

Recent Supreme Court decisions have shown reduced support for the exclusionary rule. Exceptions have been created that some say threaten to undermine the rule itself. Three landmark cases illustrate some exceptions:

1. The *inevitable discovery exception* allows the tainted evidence if it would have been discovered without the improper procedure (*Nix v. Williams*, 104 S.Ct. 250 [1984]).

2. The *good faith exception* was recognized by the Court in a case where the law enforcement officers thought they had a legal warrant even though the warrant and therefore their search was actually unlawful (*United States v. Leon*, 104 S.Ct. 3405 [1984]).

3. The *pubic safety exception* was recognized in *New York v. Quarles* (104 S.Ct. 2626 [1984]). In this case, because the officer's goal was public safety and not collection of evidence, his failure to give Miranda warnings did not result in excluding the evidence he obtained by questioning a suspect without Miranda warnings.

The majority displayed distinctly utilitarian reasoning in their cost/benefit arguments to support the holdings of the previously mentioned cases. It may be that the Supreme Court will become reluctant to uphold sanctions against any but the most extreme misconduct by police and use a *shocking to the conscience test* rather than a test that measures the violation to procedural rights. In the "shocking to the conscience" test, police behavior is evaluated against substantive rights to be free from outrageous governmental action, such as torture, forced blood samples or surgery, or, in the case most closely associated with the test, forced regurgitation (*Rochin v. California*, 343 U.S. 165 [1952]).

We have been discussing legal procedures for determining punishment, but in some cases legal procedures may be strictly followed and injustice still occurs. For instance, it is unlikely that anyone would argue that Nelson Mandela, when he was imprisoned in South Africa, or Andre Sakharov, a Soviet dissident, received *just* punishment even though the legal procedures of their respective countries might have been scrupulously followed. These are clear examples that illustrate the difference between "procedural" justice and "substantive" justice.

# Conclusion

In this chapter we have explored the origins and components of justice. Whereas justice is a philosophical concept concerned with rights and needs, law is the administration of justice. Justice can be further differentiated into distributive justice and corrective justice. Corrective justice is the central concern of the criminal justice system and can be further divided into substantive and procedural issues. Substantive justice is concerned with the fairness of what we do to offenders; procedural justice is concerned with the procedures that must be undertaken before punishment occurs.

# Key Terms

**commutative justice**  the component of justice concerned with the fairness of contracts and business relations

**corrective justice**  the component of justice concerned with punishments and sanctions

**distributive justice**  the component of justice concerned with the allocation of the goods and burdens of society

**due process**  constitutionally mandated procedural steps designed to eliminate error in any governmental deprivation of protected liberty, life, or property

**exclusionary rule** court-created rule of evidence that excludes evidence obtained through illegal means

**justice** the quality of being impartial, fair, and just

**natural right** the concept that one has certain rights just by virtue of being born

**procedural justice** the component of justice that concerns the steps taken to reach a determination of guilt, punishment, or other conclusion of law

**retributive justice** the component of justice that concerns the determination and methods of punishment

**substantive justice** the concept of just deserts: the appropriate amount of punishment for a crime

**utilitarian justice** the type of justice that looks to the greatest good for all as the end

# Review Questions

1. Explain how Aristotle and Plato associated status with justice.
2. Define rectificatory justice.
3. Describe distributive, corrective, and commutative justice.
4. Describe the various types of distributive justice.
5. Describe Sterba's system of distribution.
6. Discuss the differences between substantive justice and procedural justice.
7. How do you define mercy?
8. Define due process.
9. What is the retributive argument for punishment?
10. What is the utilitarian argument for punishment?

# Discussion Questions

1. Explain why *reciprocal altruism* is similar to *psychological egoism*, a term from Chapter 2. Do you believe that humans have adapted such that reciprocal altruism is a trait that endures through natural selection?
2. Think about the symbol of U.S. justice—what does it represent to you? Do you believe that who you are makes a difference in today's system of justice? Give examples.
3. How would you answer the argument of a couple who did not believe they should have to pay school taxes because they have no children? What about the argument that rich school districts should share their wealth with poor districts (keeping in mind that those who pay higher taxes in that district might have moved there because of the reputation of the school)?
4. If you were being punished for a crime, would you rather receive a year in prison or fifty lashes?
5. Why do we not use corporal punishment for criminal offenders? Do you think we should?

6. Analyze this case under procedural and substantive justice: An eighty-seven-year-old man living in Chicago is exposed as a soldier who took part in killing hundreds of Jewish concentration camp victims. U.S. extradition procedures are followed to the letter, and he is extradited to Israel to stand trial. Israeli law determines that courts in Israel have jurisdiction over Nazi war crimes. Israeli legal procedure is followed without error, and he is convicted of war crimes and sentenced to death.

7. Analyze this case under procedural and substantive justice: Federal law enforcement agents determine that a citizen of another country participated in a drug cartel that sold drugs in the United States. A small group of agents goes to the foreign country, kidnaps the offender, drugs him, and brings him back to the United States to stand trial. Upon challenge, the government agents explain that although these actions would have been unconstitutional and illegal against a citizen of the United States in this country, since they were conducted on foreign soil against a non-U.S. citizen, they were not illegal.

8. Let's assume that in a civil dispute, one side has a very strong claim and would almost surely win in court, yet because the attorney missed a filing deadline, the judge throws out the case. Do you believe this is fair? In a death penalty case, new evidence emerged that supported the defendant's allegations of innocence, but the evidence was uncovered after the deadline for filing an appeal. Should the execution go forward?

9. Consider the case of an individual who befriends an elderly person, takes care of him, and provides him comfort in his old age even at the sacrifice of personal time and expense. When the elderly person dies, however, a distant relative who expressed the view that it wasn't her duty to take care of her relative inherits substantial assets. Is this fair? Is this just? If the law (which would typically uphold the inheritance absent any special elements such as contract or payment for personal services) does not support any recognition of the friend's nonlegal "rights" to any portion of the inheritance, what theory of justice might support it?

# Ethical Dilemmas

## Situation 1

Two individuals are being sentenced for the exact same crime of burglary. You are the judge. One of the individuals is a twenty-year-old who has not been in trouble before and participated only because the other individual was his friend. The second person has a history of juvenile delinquency and is now twenty-five. Would you sentence them differently? How would you justify your decision?

## Situation 2

In your apartment building there lives a young man who appears to be of Middle Eastern descent. You notice that other young men often visit him and that they come and go at odd hours of the day and night. You engage in a conversation with him one day, and during the course of the conversation he states that "The United States deserved what happened to them on September 11 because of their imperialistic actions across the world and their support for the oppression of the Palestinian people." You feel that it is your duty to report him to the local police, and they appear to be interested in your report. One day you observe him taken away in handcuffs, and you never see him again. Several weeks later, his apartment is vacant; you do not know what happened to his belongings. Would you attempt to find out what happened to him? Do you feel you should investigate further?

## Situation 3

You are serving on a jury for a murder trial. The evidence presented at trial was largely circumstantial and, in your mind, equivocal. During closing, the prosecutor argued that you must find the defendant guilty because he confessed to the crime. The defense attorney immediately objected, and the judge sternly instructed you to disregard the prosecutor's statement. Although you do not know exactly what happened, you suspect that the confession was excluded because of a some procedural error. Would you be able to ignore the prosecutor's statement in your deliberations? Should you? Would you tell the judge if the jury members discussed the statement and appeared to be influenced by it?

## Situation 4

You are a legislator who believes absolutely and strongly that abortion is a sin. You have polled your constituents and are surprised to find that the majority do not believe that the government should legislate the private decision of a woman to have an abortion. How do you vote—your conscience or the will of the majority of your constituents?

## Situation 5

You are a probation officer who must prepare sentencing recommendation reports for the judge. The juvenile defendant to be sentenced in one case grew up in a desperately poor family, according to school records. He had a part-time job in a local grocery store, stocking the shelves and providing general cleanup. The store owner caught him stealing meat. Actually, this is the second time he has been caught stealing food. The first time he shoplifted at the store, and the deferred adjudication included his commitment to work for the store owner. He explained that he was trying to help his mother, who could not provide enough food for his family. In general, failure to succeed at deferred adjudication results in a commitment to a juvenile facility. What would you recommend to the judge?

# Suggested Readings

Cole, D. 1999. *No Equal Justice*. New York: Free Press.

Hamm, M. 1995. *The Abandoned Ones*. Boston: Northeastern University Press.

Murphie, J. 1988. "Forgiveness, Mercy, and the Retributive Emotions." *Criminal Justice Ethics* 7(2): 3–15.

Rawls, J. 1971. *A Theory of Justice*. Cambridge, MA: Belknap.

Reiman, J. 2005. *The Rich Get Richer and the Poor Get Prison: Ideology, Class, and Criminal Justice*. Boston: Allyn & Bacon.

Walsh, A. 2000. "Evolutionary Psychology and the Origins of Justice." *Justice Quarterly* 17(4): 841–864.

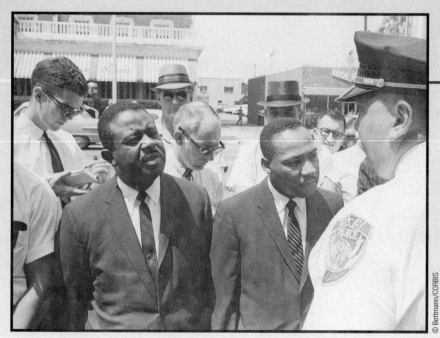

The great civil rights activist Martin Luther King, Jr., advocated civil disobedience when one is faced with immoral laws.

# 5

# Law and the Individual

*Paradigms of Law*

*Justifications for Law*

*Criminal and Moral Culpability*

*Immoral Laws and the Moral Person*

*Victims' Rights*

*Restorative Justice*

*Conclusion*

## Key Terms

civil disobedience
conflict paradigm
consensus paradigm
culpability
legal moralism
legal paternalism
McNaughten rule
mechanical solidarity
natural law
organic solidarity
paradigm

pluralist paradigm
positive law
repressive law
restitutive law
restorative justice
social contract theory
victim-compensation
    programs
victim precipitation
victimology

# Chapter Objectives

1. Understand the paradigms of law.

2. Understand the justifications for law, including legal paternalism and legal moralism.

3. Distinguish between moral culpability and legal culpability.

4. Be familiar with the issues of culpability for juveniles, the mentally ill, and the mentally handicapped and for white-collar criminals.

5. Understand the issues concerning victim rights and victim precipitation.

6. Be familiar with the concepts of restorative justice.

A s we discussed in the last chapter, justice and law are different. Law can be considered the administration of justice. It can also be viewed as a tool of behavior change (Hornum and Stavish, 1978: 148). In this theory, law is seen as a tool of social engineering and a way of changing behavior to a desired state (Aubert, 1969: 11). Law may influence behavior directly by prohibiting or mandating certain behavior, or indirectly by affecting social institutions such as family or education that, in turn, influence behavior (Dror, 1969: 93). Thus, law controls behavior by providing sanctions but also, perhaps even more importantly, by teaching people which behaviors are acceptable and which behaviors are not. Those people who commit crimes will be evaluated as to their culpability or responsibility, which will then determine the degree of punishment. There are some who may be less culpable, either because of certain characteristics they possess or because of actions of the victim.

# Paradigms of Law
〰️

The law serves as a written embodiment of society's ethics and morals. It is said to be declarative as well as active—it declares correct behavior and serves as a tool for enforcement. Law is both a prohibition and a promise. It cautions against certain types of behavior and warns of the consequences for ignoring the warning. **Natural law** refers to the belief that some law is inherent in the natural world and can be discovered by reason. A corollary of this thought is that some behavior is intrinsically wrong (*mala in se*). In contrast, **positive law** refers to those laws written and enforced by society. This type of law is of human construction and therefore fallible (Mackie, 1977: 232).

We can trace the history of law back to very early codes, such as the Code of Hammurabi (ca. 2000 B.C.E.), which mixed secular and religious proscriptions of behavior. These codes also standardized punishments and atonements for wrongdoing. Early codes of law did not differentiate between what we might call public wrongs and private wrongs. As mentioned before, two different areas of law can be distinguished today:

1. criminal law, which is punitive
2. civil law, which is is reparative

The first punishes whereas the second seeks to redress wrong or loss. Of the two, criminal law is more closely associated with the moral standards of society, yet it is by no means comprehensive in its coverage of behavior. Nor is there unanimous agreement about what it should or does cover.

Basic paradigms aid our understanding of the function of law in society. According to Rich (1978: 1), a **paradigm** is a "fundamental image of the subject matter within a science. . . . It subsumes, defines, and interrelates the exemplars, theories, and methods/tools that exist within it."

1. The **consensus paradigm** views society as a community consisting of like-minded individuals who agree on goals important for ultimate survival. This view is functionalist because it sees law as an aid to the growth and/or survival of society.
2. The **conflict paradigm** views society as being made up of competing and conflicting interests. According to this view, governance is based on power; if some win, others lose, and those who hold power in society promote self-interest, not a "greater good."
3. The **pluralist paradigm** shares the perception that society is made up of competing interests; however, pluralism describes more than two basic interest groups and also recognizes that the power balance may shift when interest groups form or coalitions emerge. These power shifts occur as part of the dynamics of societal change.

## The Consensus Paradigm

According to the consensus paradigm, law serves as a tool of unification. Emile Durkheim (1858–1917) wrote that there are two types of law: the *repressive*, criminal law, which enforces universal norms, and the *restitutive*, civil law, which developed because of the division of labor in society and resulting social interests. In Durkheim's view, criminal law exists as a manifestation of consensual norms: "We must not say that an action shocks the common conscience because it is criminal, but rather that it is criminal because it shocks the common conscience" (Durkheim, 1969: 21). What this statement means is that we define an action as criminal because the majority of the populace holds the opinion that it is wrong. This "common" or "collective" conscience is referred to as **mechanical solidarity.** Each individual's moral beliefs are indistinguishable from the whole. The function of **repressive law** is the maintenance of social cohesion. Law contributes to the collective conscience by providing an example of deviance.

Although Durkheim recognized individual differences, he believed that these differences, resulting from the division of labor in society, only made the individual more dependent on society as a part of a whole. His concept of **organic solidarity** draws the analogy of individuals in society as parts of an organism: all doing different things, but as parts of a whole. Individuals exist, but they are tied inextricably to society and its common conscience. **Restitutive law** is said to mediate those differences that may come about because of the division of labor. Even here the law serves an integrative function.

The consensus view would point to evidence that we all agree, for the most part, on what behaviors are wrong and the relative seriousness of different types of wrongful behavior. In criminology, the consensus view is represented by classical thinkers such as Bentham and Beccaria, who relied on the accepted definitions of crime in their day without questioning the validity of these definitions, only their implementation. Although the Positivist school of criminology, which looked for the cause of crime in the individual, virtually ignored societal definitions of crime, Garofalo (1852–1932), a legal anthropologist, believed in natural law. As defined earlier, natural law is the view that certain behaviors are so inherently heinous that they go against nature; therefore, there are natural proscriptions against such behavior that transcend individual societies or time periods (Kramer, 1982: 36).

We have recent evidence that there is at least some consensus in people's definitions of what constitutes criminal behavior; studies have shown that not only do individuals in Western culture tend to agree on the relative seriousness of different kinds of crime, but there is also substantial agreement cross-culturally as well (Nettler, 1978: 215). In the consensus paradigm,

1. *Law is representative.* It is a compilation of the do's and don'ts that we all agree on.
2. *Law reinforces social cohesion.* It emphasizes our "we-ness" by illustrating deviance.
3. *Law is value-neutral.* That is, it resolves conflicts in an objective and neutral manner.

## The Conflict Paradigm

A second paradigm of law and society is the conflict paradigm. Rather than perceiving law as representative, this perspective sees law as a tool of power holders that they use for their own purposes, which are to maintain and control the status quo. In the conflict paradigm, law is perceived as restrictive or repressive, rather than representative, and as an instrument of special interests.

Basically, there are three parts to the conflict paradigm:

1. Criminal definitions are relative.
2. Those who control major social institutions determine how crime is defined.
3. The definition of crime is fundamentally a tool of power. (Sheley, 1985: 1)

Quinney (1974: 15–16) outlines the following points as making up the conflict paradigm:

1. American society is based on an advanced capitalistic society.
2. The state is organized to serve the interests of the dominant economic class. . . .
3. Criminal law is an instrument of the state and ruling class to maintain and perpetuate the existing social and economic order.
4. Crime control in capitalist society is accomplished through a variety of institutions and agencies established and administered by a governmental elite. . . .

5. The contradictions of advanced capitalism . . . require that the subordinate classes remain oppressed by whatever means necessary. . . .
6. Only with the collapse of capitalist society and the creation of a new society . . . will there be a solution to the crime problem.

Advocates of the conflict paradigm would point to laws against only certain types of gambling or against the use of only certain types of drugs as evidence that the ruling class punishes the activities of other classes more severely than their own activities. In other words, cultural differences in behavior exist, but only the activities of certain groups (the powerless) are labeled deviant. For instance, numbers running is always illegal, yet some states have legalized horseracing, dog racing, and/or casinos. Heroin and cocaine are illegal; Valium and alcohol are not.

An even better example of differential definitions and enforcement is that federal drug laws impose more severe sanctions on crack cocaine than on powder cocaine. Many believe that it is not merely a coincidence that crack cocaine is more likely to be the drug of choice for minorities (crack is cheaper), whereas powder cocaine is associated with Caucasians and social elites. Policy Box 5-1 discusses this policy.

---

**POLICY BOX 5-1  Crack or Powder?**

There is continuing controversy over the federal sentencing guidelines that dictate a punishment for crack cocaine that is 100 times more severe than that for powder cocaine (in that one would have to have 100 grams of powder to equal the sentence for 1 gram of crack). Opponents argue that it is a clearly racist response to drug use patterns. Proponents argue that crack is more addictive, more criminogenic, and more easily accessible, thus warranting the more severe punishment.

**Law:** The Sentencing Commission is a body of appointed commissioners who set policy, but the power of federal sentencing ultimately comes from Congress. Thus, when the Sentencing Commission resolved to equalize the punishments between powder and crack cocaine, it could only make a recommendation to Congress. Congress refused to act on the recommendation; thus, the differential continues. However, the whole federal sentencing guideline structure is in legal limbo at this point because of a Supreme Court case that held that if such sentencing is decided without adequate due-process protections, it is unconstitutional.

**Policy:** Policy considerations generally relate to the war on drugs, and the emphasis of the federal and most state governments is to focus on interdiction and punishment rather than treatment and prevention. There is a great difference between viewing drugs as a public health problem and viewing drugs as a criminal problem, with concomitant choices made as to where public moneys are best spent and how to view those involved (as sick or criminal).

**Individual ethics:** Federal judges have taken individual stands against the perceived injustice of the differential sentencing by refusing to convict, or in some cases, judges have resigned rather than be forced to sentence a drug offender to what they felt were unfairly excessive sentences.

Recall Jeffrey Reiman's description of the difference between reporting a mining accident and a multiple murder. Despite the same result (dead victims), the mining company would probably not be prosecuted, or it would receive a very minor punishment for its role in the death of the miners. For the conflict theorist, this would be an example of how law has been written differentially to serve the interests of the power holders. The definition of what is criminal often excludes corporate behavior, such as price fixing, toxic waste dumping, and monopolistic trade practices, because these behaviors, although just as harmful to the public good as street crime, are engaged in by those who have the power to define criminality. The regulation of business, instead of the criminalization of harmful business practices, is seen as arising from the ability of those in powerful positions to redefine their activities to their own advantage.

Even though the Occupational Safety Board, the Food and Drug Administration, the Federal Aeronautics Administration, and other similar governmental agencies are charged with the task of enforcing regulations governing business activities in their respective areas, no one seriously believes that the level of enforcement or labeling is as serious as in criminal law. Relationships between the watchdog agencies and those they watch are frequently incestuous: Heads of business are often named to governmental agencies, and employees of these agencies may move to the business sector they previously regulated.

Some draw parallels between corporate crimes and organized crime, or at least describe them as occurring in the same spectrum of behavior (Krisberg, 1975: 35). Certainly, it is fairly well documented that large and small corporations engage in dishonest and even criminal practices. One study reported that from a sample of businesses, 60 percent reported enforcement activity in response to one of the following violations: restraint of trade, financial manipulation, misrepresentation in advertising, income tax evasion, unsafe working conditions, unsafe food or drug distribution, illegal rebates, foreign payoffs, unfair labor practices, illegal political contributions, and environmental pollution (Clinard, 1985: 205). Even the highly publicized indictments of a few Enron and Worldcom officials rapidly gave way to silence. How many of the officials involved in wrongdoing will ever be punished remains to be seen.

In criminology, the conflict view was represented by early theorists such as Bonger (1876–1940), a Marxist sociologist who explained that the cause of crime was the economic power differential and that power holders labeled only others' behavior as criminal. During the 1970s, a small number of criminologists attempted to redefine criminals as political prisoners, based on their views that the state used criminal definitions to control minority groups (Reasons, 1973). Labeling theorists also questioned the criminal justice system's definitions by pointing out that only some offenders are formally labeled and treated as deviant.

Conflict theory is represented by theorists such as Platt, the Schwendingers, Krisberg, Quinney, Taylor, Walton, and Young and Chambliss (Kramer, 1982: 41). The conflict theorists explain that the myth of justice and equality under the law serves to protect the interests of the ruling class, because as long as there is a perception of fairness, fundamental questions about the distribution of goods will not be raised (Krisberg, 1975). Law functions to depoliticize even the most obviously political actions of the oppressed by defining these actions as crime, but its greatest power is to hide the basic injustice of society itself. Reiman (2005) presents the conflict theorist's view that the definitions of law, as well as its enforcement, are fundamentally affected by power.

Definitions are shaped by our paradigms of law. The Los Angeles riots of 1992 were sparked by the acquittal of four police officers who were videotaped beating Rodney King, a motorist who had outstanding arrest warrants for traffic violations. The riots were described by some as political action. According to this view, minorities who were frustrated by economic hopelessness and angered by the criminal justice system's oppressive and brutal treatment retaliated in like form. In this view, the riots were political statements against oppression. Alternatively, others described the same actions as blatant and simple criminality. In this perspective, violent individuals merely took advantage of the incident to exhibit their individual deviance. Conflict theorists would support the first definition, and consensus theorists would support the second.

A more recent example of how paradigms shape perceptions is the looting and general lawlessness that resulted in the aftermath of the New Orleans flooding. Conflict theorists would see the looting and crimes of those left behind through the prism of economic hopelessness and desperation. Conflict theorists argue that the poor and African American citizens were left behind while those who had the means to do so escaped; as well, government bodies did not make any effort to evacuate the poor even after a general evacuation order was administered. Further, they would point to other forms of lawlessness, such as price gouging, as just as heinous as looting and assault. Consensus theorists would see the crimes as examples of individual deviance and point to the fact that most people who were trapped in the city did not resort to violence. Further, some later evidence emerged that deaths did not occur disproportionately among minorities and the poor, as some had claimed (Simerman, Ott, and Mellnik, 2005).

## The Pluralist Paradigm

Distinct from the conflict paradigm is the *pluralist paradigm*. In this view, law is seen as arising from interest groups, but power is more complicated than the bifurcated system described by the Marxist tradition. Roscoe Pound (as cited in Quinney, 1974) defines the following as interests protected by power holders:

1. security against actions that threaten the social group
2. security of social institutions
3. security of morals
4. conservation of national resources
5. general progress
6. individual life

Power is exercised in the political order, the economic order, the religious order, the kinship order, the educational order, and the public order. Law and social control constitute the public order, and powerful interests affect the law by influencing the writing of laws and the enforcement of written laws (Quinney, 1974).

Pluralism views law as influenced by interest groups that are in flux. Some interests may be at odds with other interests, or certainly the interpretation of them may be.

For instance, conservation of natural resources is a basic interest necessary to the survival of society, but it may be interpreted by lumber companies as allowing them to harvest trees in national forests as long as they replant trees or, alternatively, interpreted by conservation groups as mandating more wilderness areas. According to the pluralist paradigm, laws are written by the group whose voice is more powerful at any particular time.

Interest groups hold power, but their power may shrink or grow depending on various factors. Coalitions and shared interests may shift the balance of power. The definition of crime may change, depending on which interest groups have the power to define criminal behavior and what is currently perceived to be in the best interests of the most powerful groups.

# Justifications for Law

The major justification for corrective (criminal) law is prevention of harm. The **social contract theory** explains that law is a contract—each individual gives up some liberties and, in return, is protected from others who have their liberties restricted as well. But how much liberty should be restricted, and what behaviors should be prohibited? Rough formulas or guidelines indicate that the law should interfere as little as possible in natural liberties and should step in only when the liberty in question injures or impinges on the interests of another. There is an obvious need for law in those circumstances where one individual harms another; however, in the following sections we discuss in more detail two rationales for laws that do not necessarily involve direct harm to another—*legal paternalism* and *legal moralism*. Box 5-1 presents the major justifications for laws.

## *Legal Paternalism*

Many laws can be described as examples of **legal paternalism**—the state tries to protect people from their own behavior. Examples include seat belt laws, motorcycle helmet laws, speed limits, drug laws, licensing laws, alcohol consumption and sale laws,

---

**BOX 5-1 Justifications for Law**

1. *The harm principle:* to prevent harm to persons other than the actor when probably no other means are equally effective.
2. *The offense principle:* to prevent serious offense to persons other than the actor.
3. *Legal paternalism:* to prevent harm—physical, psychological, or economic—to the actor.
4. *Legal moralism:* to prohibit conduct that is inherently immoral.
5. *Benefit to others:* to provide, through prohibition of an action, some benefit to persons other than the actor.

SOURCE: Feinberg, cited in Feibleman (1985: xiii).

smoking prohibitions, and laws limiting certain types of sexual behavior. The strict libertarian view would hold that the government has no business interfering in a person's decisions about these behaviors as long as they don't negatively affect others. The opposing view is that as long as a person is a member of society (and everyone is), he or she has a value to that society, and society is therefore compelled to protect the person with or without his or her cooperation.

It may also be true that there are no harmful or potentially harmful behaviors to oneself that do not also hurt others, however indirectly, so society is protecting others when it controls each individual. Speeding drivers may crash into someone else, drug addicts may commit crimes to support their habit, gamblers may neglect their families and cause expense to the state, and so on. You may remember that in Chapter 1 we limited moral judgments to behavior that influences another. The justification of paternalistic laws depends on the view that very little of what we do does not affect others, however indirectly.

Some believe that government can justify paternalism only with certain restrictions. These rules try to create a balance between an individual's liberty and government control (Thompson, 1980):

1. The decision-making ability of the person may be somehow impaired, by lack of knowledge or competency. An example would be child labor laws or laws that restrict the sale and consumption of alcohol by children. In both cases, there is a presumption that children do not understand the dangers of such behavior and therefore need protection.
2. The restriction should be as limited as possible. For example, DUI laws define the point of legal intoxication as when one's ability to drive safely is impaired, not simply after any alcohol consumption at all. When mountain passes close, they are reopened as soon as it is relatively safe to cross them. Laws exist that ban the sale of cigarettes to minors, but cigarettes are still available to adults— who supposedly have reached a level of maturity to understand the dangers associated with smoking.
3. The laws should seek only to prevent a serious and irreversible error: a death from DUI, an accident on an icy road, and so on.

Paternalistic laws can be supported by an ethics of care. Remember that in this framework, morality is viewed as integral to a system of relationships. The individual is seen as having ties to society and to every other member of society. Relationships involve responsibilities as well as rights. We can expect the minimum level of care necessary for survival from society under the ethics of care. However, the corollary is that society can also care for us by restricting harmful behaviors. Rights are less important in this framework; therefore, to ask whether society has a right to intervene or an individual has a right to a liberty is not relevant to the discussion. Utilitarianism would also support paternalistic laws because of the net utility to society that results from protecting each of its members.

Other ethical systems may not so clearly support paternalistic laws. Individual rights are perhaps more important under ethical formalism than the other ethical systems; individuals must be treated with respect and as ends in themselves. This view results in recognizing the rights of individuals to engage in careless or even harmful behavior as long as it is consistent with the universalism principle of the categorical imperative. In other words, people may have the moral right to engage in self-destructive or careless behavior as long as they do not hurt others. Of course, the opposing argument would be that all behaviors prohibited by paternalistic laws have the potential to affect others indirectly.

## *Legal Moralism*

The law also acts as the moral agent of society, some say in areas where there is no moral agreement. This rationale is called **legal moralism.** Some sexual behaviors, gambling, drug use, pornography, and even suicide and euthanasia are defined as wrong and are prohibited. The laws against these behaviors may be based on principles of harm or paternalism, but they also exist to reinforce society's definitions of moral behavior. For example, consensual sexual behavior between adults arguably harms no one, yet the Georgia state law prohibiting sodomy was upheld by the U.S. Supreme Court in *Bowers v. Hardwick*, 106 S.Ct. 2841 (1986). What harm was the state preventing by prohibiting this consensual behavior? The answer may be harm to community standards of morality. However, in *Lawrence v. Texas*, 539 U.S. 558 (2003), the Supreme Court held that Texas's law criminalizing same-sex sodomy was unconstitutional, effectively overturning *Bowers*. More recently, there has been a great debate over whether the law ought to recognize and legitimize same-sex marriages. The underlying justification that both sides employ is legal moralism.

Pornography (at least that involving consenting adults) that is defined as obscene is prohibited arguably because of moral standards, not harmful effect. One governmental commission concluded that pornography contributed to sex crimes (Attorney General's Commission on Pornography, 1986), but this commission's findings contradicted an earlier commission's report created by President Lyndon Johnson, which found that pornography did not contribute substantially to sex crimes (Report of the Commission on Obscenity and Pornography, 1970). Hence, we have a factual issue as to whether pornography is harmful. Yet even if pornography does not prove to be harmful to others, legal moralism endorses the government's right to prohibit the sale and purchase of pornographic materials. Under legal moralism, pornography is prohibited simply because it is wrong. Recently, the issue became even more complicated with the increasing use of the Internet and the ease with which individuals may obtain pornographic materials from anywhere in the world. Privacy rights conflict with the government's right to enforce morality.

One's opinion regarding the rights of individuals versus the government is greatly influenced by whether one subscribes more to the consensus or conflict viewpoint. If we operate under the consensus view that laws represent the majority, then legal moralism as a justification for laws would be less controversial, but in our society, there is by no means agreement among all citizens that the government represents the people's view. Conflict theorists argue that the government has no moral authority because it does not represent the views of everyone.

It should also be noted that whether an action is moral or immoral is a different question from whether there should be laws and governmental sanctions regarding the behavior. In some cases, individuals may agree that a particular action is immoral but at the same time may not believe that the government should have any power to restrict an individual's choice. Some proponents of choice regarding abortion take great care to distinguish the difference between pro-choice and pro-abortion. To them, one does not have to approve of abortion to believe that it is wrong for government to interfere in the private decision of the individual to use the procedure. Similarly, some who advocate decriminalization of drugs do so because of cost effectiveness or libertarian reasons, not because they approve of drug use. As mentioned in the last chapter, we do not have a legal system that completely overlaps our moral code, and some would argue that it would be impossible in a society as heterogeneous as ours for this to occur.

Hate-crime legislation gives us another example of a law that might be rationalized under legal moralism, although it could also be supported by a harm principle. In challenges to hate-crime legislation, appellate courts have typically drawn a line between action and speech. That is, if a person commits an act that is already a crime, such as vandalism, assault, stalking, or harassment, and does so because of an expressed hatred for the victim's membership in a protected class, then the act can be punished as a "hate crime." However, if the only act prohibited by the hate-crime legislation is speech, then the law violates the First Amendment's protection of free speech. Even though we abhor the message, we must protect the right of the person to express it, unless he or she also engages in a "legal harm." However, the interesting question is why we feel it necessary to create a new law instead of using the existing act-based law (such as vandalism). The reason might be that the true rationale for hate crime is legal moralism—we believe it important to enforce our moral code that hating others because of their race or sexual orientation is wrong.

Evidence indicates that hate crimes are predominantly less serious instances of harassment or vandalism but that they are not rare (Wilson and Ruback, 2003). Even the federal statistics, which probably seriously underreport such crimes, indicate that the numbers are not inconsequential. Does this show that laws are not effective in changing behavior, or does it support the need for such laws?

Some propose that only those actions that violate some universal standard of morality, as opposed to merely a conventional standard, should be criminalized. This *limited legal moralism* would prevent the situation of some groups forcing their moral code on others. Of course, this begs the question of what behaviors would meet this universal standard. Even child pornographers argue that their behavior is unfairly condemned by a conventional, rather than a universal, morality. The vast profits that are made by producing and distributing child pornography indicate that large numbers of people buy such products; does this mean that it is simply a matter of choice and not morals that should influence whether children should be seen as objects of sexual gratification? What would Immanuel Kant say about child pornography? What would Jeremy Bentham say about it?

In conclusion, we must allow for the possibility that some laws that are justified under legal moralism may not necessarily conform to our personal views of good and bad. Many criminal justice professionals also feel that some of the so-called gray areas of crime are not very serious, so it is not surprising that one sees discretion operating in enforcement patterns. Police will ignore prostitution, for instance, until the public complains; police may routinely let petty drug offenders go, rather than take the trouble to arrest; and police may let gamblers go with a warning if no publicity is attached to the arrest. Police use discretion in this way partly because these behaviors are not universally condemned. One can see, for instance, that the state loses its moral authority to condemn gambling when there is a state lottery.

# Criminal and Moral Culpability

In Chapter 4 we discussed some **culpability** issues concerning corrective (retributive) justice. Culpability can be defined, for our purposes, as legal responsibility. Both terms have been analyzed in great detail in studies of law and morality. Cane (2002) takes great care, for instance, to distinguish between responsibility and liability. One might be responsible (causally) for a result but not be liable for it (under the law). Legal liability relates to the formal rules and decisions that have defined the limits of what a person will be held legally responsible for, whereas moral responsibility is a concept that derives from ethical analysis.

Positive law (human-made law) defines legal liability (or culpability), but many legal theorists subscribe to the concepts of "natural law." For instance, Hart (1961: 176) argues that morality is something "to be recognized," not made by "deliberate human choice." Human-made law derives from moral truths. Thus, according to this viewpoint, legal rules stem from natural law. One moral and legal truth is that we recognize different levels of mental blameworthiness in the concept of *mens rea*. Someone who intentionally or knowingly commits an act is more blameworthy than someone who recklessly or negligently commits an act. In the latter case, the individual is still responsible, but his or her culpability is moderated by a lack of intent.

In Chapter 1 we also discussed how moral culpability depends on rationality. One cannot be held accountable for one's actions morally if one is not rational, and the two groups that have historically been seen as irrational are the mentally ill and the young. We uphold this distinction in our legal system as well, but there are indications that the historical and traditional exceptions for these two groups are eroding.

## *Punishing the Mentally Ill*

Miller and Radelet (1993: 2–4) discuss the long history of excusing the mentally ill, a practice that dates back to medieval times. The supporting rationales for not punishing those judged insane are as follows:

1. Humanitarian reasons require mercy.
2. The mentally ill can't help themselves.
3. Retributive goals are not met because they don't appreciate their suffering.
4. They can't spiritually prepare for death, so it is cruel to execute them.
5. Deterrence is not served because others identify only with premeditated acts, not those borne of insanity.
6. They can't help in their own defense, calling into question the accuracy of guilt.

What would cause someone to kidnap an innocent woman, rape her, kill her, and mutilate her body by cutting out her vagina and eating it? For Arthur Shawcross, condemned to 250 years in prison in Rochester, New York, it may have been the sexual abuse by his mother that he endured as a child, or it may have been a cyst and scarring in the frontal lobes of his brain that was revealed in an MRI but never shared with the jury during his trial. He killed two children and served fifteen years for that crime; after his release he committed gruesome rapes and killings while serving in Vietnam, and he confessed to the grisly mutilation murders of eleven women in Rochester, New York, but the jury found him sane (Lewis, 1998). How is this possible? It seems that the murderers who commit the most bizarre acts are those who we are most likely to label as sane.

Probably the reason is that many believe such people must be punished for their crimes, and only by finding them sane will they be sure to be executed or serve life without parole. Or perhaps there is such a revulsion and fear over their acts that we experience a primitive urge to kill them. There are many examples of individuals who were not only prosecuted but convicted and executed, arguably because of the extreme nature of their crimes, rather than a belief that their actions stemmed from rational thought. Several states have passed laws that create a "guilty but insane" conviction rather than the previous acquittal "by reason of insanity." Thus, these states need no legal fiction of "sanity" in order to punish. Individuals are housed in forensic facilities until (or unless) they are "cured," at which time they are transferred to penal facilities for punishment.

Dorothy Lewis (1998) is a psychiatrist who has examined dozens of murderers on death rows across the country, including Arthur Shawcross, Ted Bundy, and Mark Chapman. She describes how the violent killers she has diagnosed were physically abused, deprived, and sexually brutalized as children; many had suffered severe head trauma and, in all likelihood, were brain injured. The neurological injuries and psychiatric illnesses of these killers are evidence that they were not in control, or in some cases not even aware of their own actions at the time they committed their crimes. Yet, time after time, despite expert testimony to the contrary, juries found them sane.

Holding the mentally ill responsible for their behavior runs contrary to our conception of rational culpability. In most states, in order to find a defendant insane, the jury must find that the person did not know what he or she was doing, or did not know it was wrong. This test, known as the **McNaughten rule**, was developed in the mid-nineteenth century. It forces psychiatrists to explain the defendant's behavior to the jury solely on the question of whether he or she knew right from wrong. Compulsion, or diminished capacity, is not recognized in this definition.

Andrea Yates was convicted in Houston, Texas, in 2002 and sentenced to forty years in prison. She was a thirty-six-year-old mother of five children, ranging in age from six months to seven years. One day when her husband was at work, she systematically took each child into the bathroom and drowned them. Her lawyers presented evidence that she was under psychiatric care for postpartum depression, that she most probably suffered from postpartum psychosis, that she had been institutionalized because of depression and suicide ideation, and that an earlier diagnosis by a doctor indicated that she should not have any more children because her syndrome seemed to be worsening with each pregnancy. In a deep depression after the birth of her last child, she came to believe that she was a terrible mother and that some great harm would befall the children if she did not commit them to God's care. After she killed them, she called the police. Many people argue that the death penalty surely must be for someone like Andrea Yates, who killed five helpless children. Yet is it possible to imagine that a mother who, by all accounts, was a loving mother when she wasn't suffering from depression or psychosis could commit such a horrible act rationally?

Does one rationally kill one's children and then call the police? A small number of people proposed the ridiculous argument that she was "tired of being a mother" and killed them because she was sure she would be acquitted; however, most people struggled to resolve concepts of culpability and justice in this case. The jury hedged their bets. They did not acquit her by reason of insanity. Therefore, they declared her sane, but they sentenced her to forty years instead of the death penalty. If she rationally and sanely killed her five children, why was she not executed? If she was not rational and insane, why did the jury not acquit her? In Texas, she would have been sent to a mental facility and could have lived the rest of her life in confinement if doctors diagnosed her as a continuing threat. Currently, she is in a community mental health facility pending the appeal of her conviction. Ironically, not too long after Yates was sent to prison, another Texas woman, also evidently suffering from postpartum psychosis, killed her infant. She was acquitted.

Other cases pose difficult questions concerning what we should do when individuals commit violent acts. We are only beginning to understand how brain functioning and life experiences are dynamically related to each other and how they influence behavior. Children who are raised in abusive homes and endure constant stress have reduced serotonin levels, a brain chemical that tends to inhibit aggressive impulses. Over time, chronic stress can literally change the brain; thus, it should come as no surprise when we discover that those on death row have almost always endured severe abuse as children. Ironically, the law does allow some reduction of culpability under a diminished-capacity argument for "passion" crimes (killing an unfaithful spouse), arguably because the "reasonable" person might also be tempted to commit the violent act. However, most of us are clearly unable to empathize with those who do the most horrific, "unreasonable" crimes. Thus, they are often found to be "sane" and receive our most severe punishments.

Related to the issue of punishing the mentally ill is the issue of punishing the mentally handicapped. In *Atkins v. Virginia*, 536 U.S. 304 (2002), the Supreme Court has determined that it is unconstitutional to execute the mentally handicapped. However, juries can ignore the evidence and sentence individuals to death who might not understand how they got there, or perhaps even what is happening to them. Lewis (1998) relates a case of a death row inmate whose mental impairment was so severe that it was unlikely he knew what was about to happen to him, and there was strong evidence to indicate that he had been incapable of even assisting in his own defense. He saved the pecan pie from his last meal so that he could have a midnight snack, evidently not understanding that after midnight he wouldn't be around to enjoy it. He was executed.

## *Punishing Juveniles*

Nathaniel Brazill brought a gun to school and shot a well-liked teacher in the face, killing him. Brazill was thirteen. The jury was asked to decide if he committed premeditated murder. Is a thirteen-year-old capable of "cold-blooded murder"? Throughout most of this country's history, we have excused juveniles from their crimes because of a belief that their immaturity prevented them from engaging in the calm, rational deliberation that is required for criminal (and moral) culpability. It is the same reasoning that supports laws preventing juveniles from drinking alcohol or buying cigarettes, voting, or serving in the military. Others argue that thirteen-year-olds know right from wrong and should be held accountable for their actions.

If you feel that a thirteen-year-old murderer is responsible enough for his or her own behavior to serve a life sentence or even be executed, would you also agree that a thirteen-year-old is mature enough to know whether to smoke or drink? Quit school if he feels like it? Serve in the military? If you answered yes to the life sentence, but no to the smoking or military, how do you explain the contradiction? Brazill's jury found him guilty of second-degree murder, and he was sentenced to serve twenty-eight years in prison. His earliest release date will be when he is forty-one.

Lionel Tate was twelve years old when he killed a six-year-old by breaking her neck, imitating what he saw while watching pro wrestlers. His attorneys argued that he had not meant to hurt her and was just playing. It seems very possible that he did not mean to hurt the girl, and prosecutors must have thought so too, since they offered him a sentence of three years in a juvenile facility, one year of house arrest, and ten years of probation. However, because he was a juvenile, his mother made the decision to refuse the plea bargain and go to trial. The jury found him guilty of first-degree murder, and he was sentenced to a mandatory term of life without parole (CNN.com, 2001). Lionel Tate has now become the poster child for a reexamination of how we treat juvenile offenders. Even the prosecutor in that case is now advocating a less harsh sentence for juveniles convicted of murder (Riddle, 2001). On January 29, 2004, after an appeal seeking a retrial, the prosecutor and defense reached a plea agreement whereby Tate pleaded guilty to second-degree murder with a sentence of three years in juvenile custody and one year of house arrest. Because he had already served that amount of time, he was released. Recently, he has been arrested for new crimes.

In the 1990s, many states enacted new laws or changed existing laws to increase the controls and sanctions over juveniles. Some of these laws included curfew laws, parental responsibility laws, anti-gang laws, juvenile boot camps, gun laws, removing laws that seal juvenile records, and laws that allow transfer of juveniles to adult court (Bartollas and Miller, 2001: 7). The move to treat juvenile criminals more harshly has been fueled by the Columbine and other school shootings, by the serious crimes committed by gang members, and by the pervasive view that juvenile crime is growing and that the juvenile justice system is too lenient. Juvenile offenders are increasingly being waived through and prosecuted in the adult court system, and sent to adult prisons. In 2001 Florida had 572 juveniles in adult prisons, Connecticut had 505, New York had 316, Texas had 272, and California had 163 (Riddle, 2001).

Part of the impetus for this harsher treatment of juveniles has been a public perception that juvenile crime is increasing and is becoming more violent. Because lawmakers respond to public pressure, public perceptions affect laws. For instance, the public perceives there is a growing risk of violence in schools; therefore, we have seen an incredible escalation of security procedures and zero-tolerance treatment of juveniles who express hostile feelings.

In some cases the zero-tolerance approach toward expressions of violence has reached extreme levels that many believe are counterproductive. A ten-year-old girl who whispered "I could kill her" after she wet her pants because her teacher refused to let her go to the bathroom was suspended; a ten-year-old who said "I oughtta murder his face" when a classmate messed up his desk was suspended; a classmate who uttered a threat after he was pushed was suspended. A nine-year-old boy who shot a wad of toilet paper and a youth in the school cafeteria line who warned his classmates if they ate all the potatoes he would "get them" were also suspended. Many of these children now have juvenile records for such acts. In all, fifty suspensions in six weeks occurred in one school district after the county prosecutor met with school officials and told them they had no discretion in reporting threats to authorities (Zernike, 2001). Some parents and other observers believe that the "cure" is worse than the problem if schools are attempting to prevent violence by such draconian policies. The American Bar Association has passed a resolution condemning zero-tolerance policies that allow no discretion in defining children's acts as criminal (Zernike, 2001).

Observers note that there have been cyclical periods of repressive and treatment-oriented movements for juveniles from the beginning of our nation's court systems. What distinguishes the juvenile system from the adult legal system is that it supposedly addresses the needs of those who are abused or neglected, as well as those who have committed acts that would be crimes if committed by adults. Many juveniles, of course, fit into both groups. Up until the 1970s, children who were taken into care for "their own good" were sometimes housed with adjudicated offenders. In the 1970s, this practice was ruled unconstitutional, and some due-process rights of juveniles were recognized in a series of court cases that forced the system to behave, in some ways, more like the adult system (Bartollas and Miller, 2001). However, differences were still recognized. Juveniles do not need all of the protections afforded adult criminals, supposedly, because the system's mission is to do what is best for them.

Before waiver to adult court, juveniles must be determined to be *competent.* This legal concept means that juveniles are mature enough to know what is happening, to be able to judge the consequences of the decisions they make, and be able to assist in their defense. This determination expects that juveniles understand right from wrong, but it does not require that juveniles understand why they did what they did, or that they be able to control their actions.

Although some states require that juveniles have counsel or parents present when being interrogated by police, other states have no such requirement, or the juvenile is allowed to waive that right (Bartollas and Miller, 2001: 74). Advocates for juveniles argue that they are simply unable to protect their own interests and are vulnerable to manipulation and intimidation by police officers. The danger can be illustrated by the 1989 Central Park jogger rape case. The juveniles who pled guilty have been exonerated by the confession of another serial rapist and by DNA evidence that linked him alone to the crime. Lawyers for the boys (now men) argue that their confessions were coerced by police through threats of the death penalty. Adults have been known to confess to crimes they did not commit, so it is not difficult to understand why fourteen-year-olds might be manipulated into confessing. Even though the prosecutor's office has declined to retry the case and they have won their freedom, they have all served prison time for this conviction (Schanberg, 2002).

There are many who believe that juvenile crime is becoming increasingly violent and that kids are literally "getting away with murder." This perception has been nurtured by the media's attention to a few notorious cases, the emphasis on gang activity in both fiction and news, and the idea that juvenile crime is increasing. According to 2002 crime figures, however, violent crime arrests of juveniles decreased 47 percent and property crime arrests decreased 43 percent from 1994 rates (Snyder, 2004).

There are also serious concerns by observers that the juvenile justice system discriminates on the basis of race. African American and other minority youth are much more likely to be formally processed and end up in juvenile or adult facilities than whites. Poor children are also more likely to be taken into the system. Part of this is because of lack of family support. Those juveniles who have families who are willing and able to work with justice officials are more likely to be referred to community programs rather than institutionalization.

There are no easy answers for what to do with intractable juveniles. In some cases, youths sent to juvenile institutions are raped and abused by other youths. They, in turn, become more violent and so are sent, after a more serious crime, to adult facilities, where they once again become prey for adult predators. It is highly doubtful that they will emerge as anything but bitter and damaged. Hate and rage are often the only emotions young offenders are familiar with.

Only recently has the United States joined the majority of nations in banning the execution of juveniles. In *Roper v. Simmons* (May 7, 2005), the Supreme Court, in a 5-4 decision, held that the Eighth and Fourteenth Amendments barred the execution of anyone who committed the crime before the age of eighteen. At the time, twenty states allowed the execution of offenders who committed their crimes when they were sixteen or seventeen. Texas had twenty-nine of these offenders on death row when the Court reached its holding in the *Roper* case. In 2004, fifty-nine individuals were executed who committed their crime before the age of eighteen (Lane, 2005: A1).

## Punishing White-Collar Criminals

In 2001 the public discovered that the Firestone tires installed on the Ford Explorer were vulnerable to blowing out in high temperatures at a high rate of speed, causing rollovers. More than 100 fatal accidents were tied to tire blowouts. When this fact came to light, the media also reported that both the tire company and Ford Motor Company knew about the tires' weakness and continued to use the tires on new Explorers. Angry consumers were even more enraged when they discovered that Ford had voluntarily replaced the tires and stopped using them on Ford vehicles sold overseas, but not in the United States. Ford eventually replaced 13 million tires at a reputed cost of $3 billion. A costly lesson, surely. But the financial loss was less costly than going to prison for knowingly exposing an unsuspecting public to a preventable risk.

Should Ford executives who knew of the test results have been held criminally culpable for their decision to continue to sell vehicles with the faulty tires? The case was similar to the infamous Ford Pinto case back in the 1970s, when it was discovered that there had been corporate knowledge that the gas tank would be more vulnerable to explosions, but a decision had been made that it was less costly to defend wrongful-death suits than it would be to reengineer the automobile. Ford executives were charged with negligent manslaughter, but they were ultimately acquitted of criminal wrongdoing.

The difficulty in attaching criminal culpability to corporate criminals is that it is usually unclear who has responsibility for the decision that might form the offense. Thus, in a decision to continue marketing an unsafe product, no one person emerges as the clear culprit and everyone has an excuse as to why it was not his or her responsibility to do anything. Obviously, such acts are not the same as taking a gun into a convenience store and shooting a clerk in the course of a robbery. On the other hand, if we accept as fact that some robbers end up killing their victim unintentionally, is the corporate criminal any less morally culpable when participating in actions where deaths are weighed against profits and factored into the bottom line?

Fraud and other forms of white-collar crime are easier to prosecute. The Enron executives who knew that their accounting practices were fraudulent and engaged in them to hide corporate losses and to obtain high bonuses for themselves were no different than criminals who use stolen credit cards or run a "scam" on an elderly victim. Other white-collar criminals have also been prosecuted, and some have received long sentences:

1. WorldCom—CEO Bernie Ebbers, convicted of masterminding an $11 billion accounting fraud scheme, received a twenty-five-year sentence.
2. Adelphia Communications—CEOs Jon Rigas and Tim Rigas, convicted of theft, received, respectively, fifteen and twenty years.
3. Tyco—CEO Dennis Kozlowski and CFO Mark Swartz were convicted of grand larceny.
4. ImClone Systems—CEO Sam Waksal, convicted of insider trading, received an eighty-seven-month sentence.
5. Martha Stewart—convicted of obstruction and perjury and received a three-month sentence and house arrest.

In other cases, white-collar defendants were either acquitted or the prosecution was dropped:

1. HealthSouth—CEO Richard Scrushy was acquitted of a $2.7 billion fraud even though the government had already received fifteen guilty pleas in the same case.
2. Kmart—two indictments against company executives for accounting fraud were withdrawn.
3. Arthur Andersen—a judge threw out the conviction against the company, holding that the jury instructions were faulty.
4. Qwest—two mid-level executives were acquitted of criminal charges in relation to accounting fraud even though the government had already secured guilty pleas from two other executives. (Farrell, 2005)

Some argue that white-collar criminals do not "deserve" prison. Why? What is a just sentence for someone who engages in price fixing, insider trading, gouging, or other forms of corporate crime? What is a fair punishment for someone who dumps toxic waste because it is too expensive to dispose of properly and a community suffers high rates of cancer because of it? It may be harder for prosecutors to secure convictions in these cases because there is a perception that the individual is less "guilty" than a so-called street criminal. We seem to be much less forgiving toward poor burglars than rich embezzlers. Further, a sentence of prison seems somehow more punitive for them, and, indeed, it may be. Should that make a difference in the determination of punishment? If we do take into consideration that prison is a harsher sentence for an upper-class executive, then is that not somehow punishing the poor burglar for being poor?

# Immoral Laws and the Moral Person

In the section discussing legal moralism, we discussed laws that prohibit behaviors that are judged as immoral, at least by some part of the population. In this section, we will look at laws and governmental edicts that are themselves immoral. Examples might include the laws of the Spanish Inquisition permitting large numbers of people to be tortured and killed for having dissenting religious beliefs, or the laws of Nazi Germany demanding that Jews give themselves up to be transported to concentration camps and often death. Examples in this country might include the internment laws during World War II that forced U.S. citizens of Japanese descent to give up land and property and be confined in internment camps until the end of the war, or the segregationist laws that once forced blacks to use different doors and water fountains.

These laws are now thought of as immoral, but they were not at the time. The most common example of immoral laws are those that deprive certain groups of liberty or treat some groups differently, either giving them more or fewer rights and privileges than other groups. Most ethical systems would condemn such laws, and an objective ethical analysis would probably prevent the passage of such laws in the first place. The example of Japanese American internment can be used to illustrate how one might use the ethical systems to judge a specific law. The religious ethical framework would probably not provide moral support for the action because it runs contrary to some basic Christian principles, such as "Do unto others as you would have them do unto you." Ethical formalism could not be used to support this particular law because it runs counter to the categorical imperative that each person must be treated as an end rather than as a means, and to the universalism principle. The principle of forfeiture could not justify the action because these were innocent individuals, many of whom were fiercely loyal to the United States. The only ethical framework that might be used to support the morality of this law is utilitarianism. We must be able to show that the total utility derived from internment outweighed the negative effect it had on the Japanese Americans who lost their land and liberty. Did it save the country from a Japanese invasion? Did it allow other Americans to sleep better at night? Did the benefits outweigh the harm to Japanese Americans?

Are there any laws today that might be considered immoral? After the World Trade Center attack, there was some discussion of deporting all those of Middle Eastern origin, regardless of their immigration status. This idea was rejected, perhaps partly because moral hindsight has shown that the Japanese internment was a flawed response to the fear created by World War II. However, we have rounded up thousands of illegal aliens and are holding them without due-process protections. How does this action compare with internment?

In other countries the legal climate has allowed torture and death squads to be used against political dissidents. If you lived in a South American country and knew of assassinations by government police and nighttime kidnappings and disappearances, would you follow a law that required you to turn in political subversives? If you lived in a troubled country in Europe, such as Bosnia, would you support a law that dispossessed members of a rival faction of their property? These issues are at the heart of our next discussion. Can one be a moral person while enforcing or obeying an immoral law?

Martin Luther King, Jr., Mahatma Gandhi, and Henry David Thoreau agreed with St. Augustine that "an unjust law is no law at all." There is a well-known story about Thoreau, jailed for nonpayment of what he considered unfair taxes. When asked by a friend "What are you doing in jail?" Thoreau responded with "What are you doing out of jail?" The point of the story is that if a law is wrong, a moral person is honor-bound to disobey that law (see Box 5-2, "Civil Disobedience"). If moral people disobeyed laws, what would happen to the stability of society? Another story concerns Socrates. About to be punished for the crime of teaching youth radical ideas, he had the opportunity to escape and in fact was begged by his friends to leave the country, yet he willingly accepted his death by hemlock because of a fundamental respect for the laws of his country.

If we agree with the proposition that an unjust law is no law at all, we may set up a situation in which all citizens follow or disobey laws at will, depending on their own conscience. If one held a relativist view of morality, specifically the belief that one can intuit morals or decide morality on an individual basis, then two people holding different moral positions could both be right even though one position might be inconsistent with the law. An absolutist view holds that there is only one universal truth, which would mean that if one knew a law to be wrong based on this universal truth, then that person would be morally obliged to disobey the law. Evidently, either position could support civil disobedience.

Civil disobedience is the voluntary disobedience of established laws based on one's moral beliefs. Rawls (1971) defines it as a public, nonviolent, conscientious, yet political act contrary to law and usually done with the aim of bringing about a change in the

---

**BOX 5-2  Civil Disobedience**

1. It must be nonviolent in form and actuality.
2. No other means of remedying the evil should be available.
3. Those who resort to civil disobedience must accept the legal sanctions and punishments imposed by law.
4. A major moral issue must be at stake.
5. When intelligent men [sic] of good will differ on complex moral issues, discussion is more appropriate than action.
6. There must be some reason for the time, place and target selected.
7. One should adhere to "historical time."

SOURCE: Hook, quoted in Fink (1977: 126–127).

**QUOTE and QUERY**

Under a government which imprisons any unjustly, the true place for a just man is also a prison. . . .

Thoreau, quoted in Fink (1977: 109).

[T]here are two types of laws[:] just and unjust. I would be the first to advocate obeying just laws. One has not only a legal but a moral responsibility to obey just laws. Conversely, one has a moral responsibility to disobey unjust laws.

Martin Luther King, Jr., quoted in Barry (1985: ii).

*Do you believe that a just person has a moral obligation to disobey an unjust law?*

law or policies of the government. Many great social thinkers and leaders have advocated breaking certain laws thought to be wrong. Philosophers believe that the moral person follows a higher law of behavior that usually, but not necessarily, conforms to human law. However, it is an exceptional person who willfully and publicly disobeys laws that he or she believes to be wrong. Psychological experiments show us that it is difficult for individuals to resist authority, even when they know that they are being asked to do something that is wrong.

The Milgram experiments are often used to show how easily one can command blind obedience to authority. In these experiments, subjects were told to administer shocks to individuals hooked up to electrical equipment as part of a learning experiment (Milgram, 1963). Unbeknownst to the subjects, the "victims" were really associates of the experimenter and only faked painful reactions when the subjects thought they were administering shocks. In one instance, the subject and "victim" were separated, and the subject heard only cries of pain and exclamations of distress, then silence, indicating that the "victim" was unconscious. Even when the subjects thought they were harming the "victims," they continued to administer shocks because the experimenter directed them to do so and reminded them of their duty (Milgram, 1963).

Although it is always with caution that one applies laboratory results to the real world, history shows that individual submission to authority, even immoral authority, is not uncommon. Those who turned in Jewish neighbors to Nazis or those who participated in massacres of Native Americans in this country were only following the law or instructions from a superior authority. To determine what laws are unjust, Martin Luther King, Jr. used the following guidelines: "A just law is one that is consistent with morality. An unjust law is any that degrades human personality or compels a minority to obey something the majority does not adhere to or is a law that the minority had no part in making" (quoted in Barry, 1985: 3).

To explore this issue further, one could refer to the two paradigms of conflict and consensus. The consensus view of society would probably provide a stronger argument for the position of following laws whether one agrees with them or not. However, the conflict and pluralist perspectives hold that laws may be tools of power and are not necessarily the embodiment of the will of the people; therefore, individuals may legitimately disagree with immoral laws and have a duty to disobey them. From another perspective, Kohlberg might propose that only individuals who have reached higher stages of morality would think to challenge conventional definitions of right and wrong.

There is a widespread belief that law is synonymous with morality and that as long as one remains inside the law, one can be considered a moral person. Callahan (1982: 64) points out the following: "We live in a society where the borderline between law and ethics often becomes blurred. For many, morality is simply doing that which the law requires; a fear of punishment is the only motivation for behavior in some minimally acceptable way." Obviously, Callahan is concerned with the false perception of law as a total representation of morals. Most of us struggle to achieve goodness using the definitions of the society we live in; very few reach beyond accepted definitions to meet a higher standard of morality. Luckily, most of us have little need to—or do we?

Remember that civil disobedience occurs when the individual truly believes the law to be wrong and therefore believes that the enforcement of it or obedience to it would also be wrong. We are not referring to chronic lawbreaking because of immediate rewards. Indeed, most criminals have a fairly conventional sense of morality. They agree with the laws, even though they break them. Even those gray-area laws that

---

### QUOTE and QUERY

What there was, from the start, was the great silence, which appears in every civilized country that passively accepts the inevitability of violence, and then the fear that suddenly befalls it. That silence which can transform any nation into an accomplice. The silence which existed in Germany, when even many well-intentioned individuals assumed that everything would return to normal once Hitler finished with the Communists and Jews. Or when the Russians assumed that everything would return to normal once Stalin eliminated the Trotskyites. Initially, this was the conviction in Argentina. Then came fear. And after the fear, indifference. "Nothing happens to someone who stays out of politics." Such silence begins in the channels of communication. Certain political leaders, institutions, and priests attempt to denounce what is happening, but are unable to establish contact with the population. The silence begins with a strong odor. People sniff the suicides, but it eludes them. The silence finds another ally: solitude. People fear suicides as they fear madmen. And the person who wants to fight senses his solitude and is frightened.

SOURCE: Jacobo Timerman, *Prisoner Without a Name, Cell Without a Number,* trans. Toby Talbot (New York: Knopf, 1981): 51. Reprinted with permission of Alfred A. Knopf, Inc.

*Why do people keep quiet when they see others being oppressed or mistreated?*

involve disagreement over the "wrongness" of the behavior are not proper grounds for disobedience unless one believes that the government is immorally oppressing certain people.

Thus far, we have been focusing on the culpability of the offender. Laws are written as proscriptions directed toward behaviors that are deemed to be harmful. Some people may be less culpable than others because of either their age or mental illness. Another situation entirely is one in which an individual may be morally culpable for obeying a law when that law is immoral. Now we will shift the focus to the victim.

## Victims' Rights

In ancient codes of law, the focus was on compensating the victim. This focus changed to the state and punishment in English common law around the time of the Magna Carta (1215). Eventually, two systems of law developed, one to deal with private wrongs (civil law) and one to deal with public wrongs (criminal law). The two may overlap—a rape victim may sue her attacker in civil court concomitantly with a state prosecution; for example, the family of Nicole Simpson sued O. J. Simpson for wrongful death after he was acquitted in a criminal trial of her murder. This does not create double jeopardy, and because rules of evidence and standards of proof are different, one may be acquitted in a criminal trial and still be held responsible civilly. The legal theory of the state as opponent is that the harm done in any crime is only incidentally to an individual. The more important harm is the crime against the state, even though it is the individual victim who is injured.

**Victimology** has emerged as a separate discipline in criminology, and this focus may help to provide a better balance between state harm and individual harm. For instance, victims' rights bills provide various protections and rights to victims of crime. Although it is popular for politicians to campaign with a pro-victim, crime-control agenda, their message usually panders to the voting public's fears rather than sheds light on a complex social problem where there are at times no distinct lines between victims and offenders. The media also contribute to public fear and to the stereotype of the white middle-class victim and the lower-class minority criminal.

Actually, minority groups and the poor are much more likely to be victimized than the middle class. Most victims and offenders come from the same neighborhood. Criminals are often victims themselves of past or current crimes. Moreover, there are many more victims than those defined as such by the system. Customers of inner-city supermarkets that charge higher prices because they know their customers do not have transportation to shop competitively are victims of economic exploitation. There are victims of retail credit schemes in which furniture rental stores rent and repossess a single piece of furniture several times for multiple profits. There are victims of employers who pay less than minimum wage or suddenly do not pay at all because they know the employees will not protest—either because they are illegal aliens or because they desperately need the job. Finally, there are victims of slum landlords, who must pay rent or be evicted even though the apartment has a multitude of health and safety hazards. These victims are rarely considered part of the "crime problem."

**IN THE NEWS**

In 1997 two news stories raised questions of media ethics: In one case, the terrible sexual abuse and murder of a child in a prominent family in Colorado created a media frenzy before police were able to identify any suspects. One tabloid published crime scene photos of the body, shocking even some hardened newspaper professionals by the insensitivity and gratuitousness of the graphic nature of the photos, not to mention the issue of how the photos were obtained. Should crime scene photos of murders be published?

*Should those who provided them be prosecuted?*

In a Dallas case, two prominent athletes were accused of raping a young woman at gunpoint. The police department immediately held a news conference, and papers across the country and world reported the allegations, along with the past legal troubles of one of the athletes. The woman then recanted, and police and prosecutors charged her with providing a false report. Now some members of the media propose that they were "victims" of her false allegations, also claiming that the police department was at fault for having a news conference that they were bound to report. The athletes and their lawyers demanded that the media report the recantation with the same enthusiasm that the initial allegations were reported.

*Should the police hold news conferences when their only evidence is a victim's allegation? Should the media withhold the accused party's name in a rape charge as they do the rape victim's, at least until they have probable cause?*

## Media's Portrayal of Victims

The media might be most responsible for creating a false perception of crime. Whereas violence occupies up to three-quarters of all television news time, it is a small percentage of actual crime (Elias, 1986: 43). The constant barrage of murders, rapes, and robberies in television drama contributes to the public's general fear of crime, as does the local news media's sensationalistic treatment of such crimes even while ignoring more pervasive social problems. In fact, an individual is more likely to die of pneumonia, cancer, heart disease, household fires, auto crashes, or suicide than of homicide (Elias, 1986: 43). See "In the News" above for a further look at the media's role.

This is not to say that violent crime is not a problem, but there is disproportionate emphasis on violence relative to other types of victimization, and there is a tendency to present every criminal event as a case of pure innocence versus pure evil. Recently, there has been recognition of the tendency of the news media to focus on disappearances of young, pretty white women. The story is carried by all major news sources as if it was a movie, with the original disappearance as a mystery, the search as the drama, and the resolution the climax—either in a successful return or with the arrest and conviction of an offender. Examples include the Laci Peterson case, Chandra Levy, and Lori Hacking. On the other hand, young black women such as Tamika Huston, who disappeared in Spartanburg, South Carolina, garner no interest at all from the national news agencies, even when families repeatedly ask for help in the search efforts. The trouble with this pattern of coverage is that other disappearances—of men, of minority women, of homeless people—are ignored. There is a perception that it is primarily racism that is responsible for the uneven coverage, and it is a charge that is hard to refute (Mankiewicz, 2005).

Most crime victims suffer relatively small losses but receive virtually no help from the system. Police do not respond at all to many burglary calls because there are so many calls and so little the police can do about them. Assault calls may be handled informally and cavalierly when the combatants are acquaintances or relatives. Victims rarely have much to do with the system unless a suspect is arrested, a rare occurrence in many categories of crime. When there is a prosecution, the victim might feel used by the system because the goal is to get a conviction, not to provide aid or compensation. The prosecutor is more interested in how the jury will perceive the victim than how much the victim lost or suffered from the crime.

In the last twenty years, there has been a "rediscovery" of victims' rights (see Box 5-3, the "Texas Crime Victims' Bill of Rights"). Many states have enacted victims' rights bills that enumerate various rights that victims have under the law. These rights may include the following:

- Being present at trial (circumventing procedural rules that exclude victim witnesses from the courtroom during other testimony)
- Being notified of any hearing dates and plea-bargain arrangements
- Submitting a victim-impact statement to be considered during the sentencing decision
- Being treated courteously and compassionately by all law enforcement and justice system personnel

Some of these bills have created victim-witness programs in police departments or prosecutors' offices that attend to the needs of victim witnesses. Duties of program personnel might include keeping victims informed of their case, providing information, accompanying victims to court, and helping them fill out victim-compensation forms.

**Victim-compensation programs** have been created in many states. These programs provide compensation for certain types of crime when the victim is without insurance or other means of reimbursement. Funding comes either through court costs paid into a general fund by all criminal offenders or through the state's general funds. Usually, only violent crimes and not property crimes are targeted by such programs. However, they can provide help with such expenses as lost wages, hospital and doctor bills, and even burial expenses, whether or not the offender is arrested. Restitution programs are much more common today than they have been, and these programs target property victims as well as victims of violent crime. However, restitution programs help only victims of criminals who are caught, and that, unfortunately, is not likely for crimes such as burglary or larceny.

Victims have a right to be treated fairly by the system. All people should be afforded the same level of service and treatment, regardless of who they are. The "bag lady"

**BOX 5-3 Texas Crime Victims' Bill of Rights**

A victim of a violent crime is (1) someone who has suffered bodily injury or death or who is the victim of sexual assault, kidnapping or aggravated robbery, (2) the close relative (spouse, parent, or adult brother, sister or child) of a deceased victim, or (3) the guardian of a victim. As a victim of violent crime, close relative of a deceased victim or guardian of a victim, you have the following rights:

1. The right to receive from law enforcement agencies adequate protection from harm and threats of harm arising from cooperation with prosecution efforts.
2. The right to have the magistrate take the safety of the victim or his family into consideration as an element in fixing the amount of bail for the accused.
3. The right, if requested, to be informed of relevant court proceedings and to be informed if those court proceedings have been canceled or rescheduled prior to the event.
4. The right to be informed, when requested by a peace officer concerning the defendant's right to bail and the procedures in criminal investigations and by the district attorney's office concerning the general procedures in the criminal justice system, including general procedures in guilty plea negotiations and arrangements, restitution, and the appeals and parole process.
5. The right to provide pertinent information to a probation department conducting a pre-sentencing investigation concerning the impact of the offense on the victim and his family by testimony, written statement, or any other manner prior to any sentencing of the offender.
6. The right to receive information regarding compensation to victims of crime as provided by Subchapter B, Chapter 56, including information related to the costs that may be compensated under the Act and the amounts of compensation, eligibility for compensation, and procedures for application for compensation under that Act, the payment for a medical examination under Article 56.06 of this code for a victim of a sexual assault, and when requested, to referral to available social service agencies that may offer additional assistance.
7. The right to be informed, upon request, of parole procedures, to participate in the parole process, to be notified, if requested, of parole proceedings concerning the defendant in the victim's case, to provide to the Board of Pardons and Paroles for inclusion in the defendant's file information to be considered by the Board prior to the parole of any defendant convicted of any crime subject to this Act, and to be notified, if requested, of the defendant's release.
8. The right to be provided with a waiting area, separate or secure from other witnesses, including the offender and relatives of the offender, before testifying in any proceeding concerning the offender, if a separate waiting area is not available, other safeguards should be taken to minimize the victim's contact with the offender and the offender's relatives and witnesses, before and during court proceedings.

9. The right to prompt return of any property of the victim that is held by a law enforcement agency or the attorney for the state as evidence when the property is no longer required for that purpose, and
10. The right to have the attorney for the state notify the employer of the victim, if requested, of the necessity of the victim's cooperation and testimony in a proceeding that may necessitate the absence of the victim from work for good cause, and
11. (a) The right to counseling, on request, regarding acquired immune deficiency syndrome (AIDS) and human immunodeficiency virus (HIV) infection and testing for acquired immune deficiency syndrome, human immunodeficiency virus (HIV) infection, antibodies to HIV, or infection with any other probably causative agent of AIDS, if the offense is an offense under Section 21.11(a)(1), 22.011, or 22.021, Penal Code.

    (b) A victim is entitled to the right to be present at all public court proceedings related to the offense, subject to the approval of the judge in the case.

    (c) The office of the attorney representing the state, and the sheriff, police, and other law enforcement agencies shall ensure to the extent practicable that a victim, guardian of a victim, or close relative of a deceased victim is afforded the rights granted by Subsection (a) of this article and, on request, an explanation of those rights.

    (d) A judge, attorney for the state, peace officer, or law enforcement agency is not liable for a failure or inability to provide a right enumerated in this article. The failure or inability of any person to provide a right or service enumerated in this article may not be used by a defendant in a criminal case as a ground for appeal, a ground to set aside the conviction or sentence, or a ground in a habeas corpus petition. A victim, guardian or a victim, or close relative of a deceased victim does not have standing to participate as a party in a criminal proceeding or to contest the disposition of any charge.

SOURCE: Texas Code of Criminal Procedure, Art. 56.02.

should receive the same care as the mayor if both are mugged. Victims should also receive equal treatment in any punishment decision. The amount of punishment inflicted on an offender should not be based on the economic or social status of the victim, any more than it should be based on the economic or social status of the offender.

Other issues are not so simple. For instance, should the victim have equal say in the amount of punishment? What if the prosecutor believes that a plea bargain of probation is sufficient punishment, considering the crime and the costs of a trial, but the victim demands imprisonment? Should a burglary victim have the right to veto a plea bargain? What about an assault victim? Some argue, in fact, that we have gone too far in catering to victims' rights and that the system is now oriented toward victim satisfaction, rather than justice (Stickels, 2003).

We spoke of mercy before; would not some argue that the state does not have the power to grant mercy, only the victim? These questions also relate to the decision to parole. Many states now have procedures whereby the victim or the victim's family has the right to address the parole board when the criminal's parole date comes up. Should these victims have the right to veto parole when the board would have otherwise paroled the criminal? We characterize the victim's feelings of vengeance as personal revenge and the state's as retribution or justice, with the implication that one is bad and the other is good.

In fact, victims who "take the law into their own hands" become criminals themselves. But why is the state's determination of sufficient punishment any better than the victim's? Supposedly, it is because the state has the power to objectively and rationally determine the correct measurement, but if there are other variables at work, such as goals of efficiency and convenience, then where is the objective measurement of punishment? Favoritism, bribery, and incompetence may also affect outcomes. Obviously, in these cases neither the victim nor the offender receives justice.

Some mistrust the current interest in victims' rights and believe that this movement is really a cynical manipulation of victim witnesses to advance the goal of making them better witnesses for the state. Also, because the definition of the victim continues to be narrow and limited to stereotypes, obfuscation about who are victims continues. This serves to blind those most at risk to the realities of their own victimization and to protect those who victimize in ways other than street crimes, such as white-collar and social crimes (Elias, 1986).

## Victim Precipitation

**Victim precipitation** refers to the victim's role in the criminal event. Some people fear that this examination has the potential to blame the victim for the crime rather than the offender. Nevertheless, some research indicates that the victim plays a significant part in some types of crime (Karmen, 1984: 78). Retributive justice would consider instances where the victim "caused" victimization by enraging or threatening the offender, or precipitated victimization by engaging in careless or dangerous behavior. This does not mean that individuals who go out late at night deserve to be robbed or that women who are out alone drinking deserve to be raped.

Victim precipitation refers to those situations where, for instance, batterers taunt their victims to shoot them—and they do. In this case, the batterer is ostensibly the victim because he has been shot, but an examination of his conduct would reveal that the so-called offender is also a victim and that the batterer's own behavior largely contributed to his victimization. In barroom brawls, pure luck often determines who becomes the injured and who becomes the offender. In these situations, the victim actually participates in the criminal event. We might allow for partial culpability, for the responsibility for the crime must be shared by both the offender and the victim.

The point is that the media and the justice system seem to conspire to paint a picture where there are perfectly innocent victims and purely evil offenders. The real world doesn't work that way. It may be the case with some crime, but more often, the offender may also be a victim, and the victim might not be purely innocent. It does not mean the justice cannot be served, but it does mean that there are often no simple answers.

# Restorative Justice

Our current system of law and justice is oriented completely to the offender. What would a system be like if the emphasis was on the victim's rights, needs, and compensation? In a system with a primary emphasis on the victim rather than the offender, money would be spent on victim services rather than prisons. It would be victims who received job skills training, not offenders. Some of the money that now goes to law enforcement and corrections would be channeled to compensation programs for victims of personal and property crimes. Victims would be helped even if their offenders were not caught. The major goal would not be punishment, but service. Offenders would be peripheral figures; they would be required to pay restitution to victims, and punishment would occur only if they did not fulfill their obligation to their victims. Could such a system work? Would such a system provide better justice?

Although the *restorative justice movement* does not propose quite this level of radical restructuring, it does dramatically redesign the justice system and offers a new alternative to retributive justice. **Restorative justice** is a term used to describe a number of programs that seek to move compensation back to center stage in the justice system, rather than retribution. A similar philosophy has been called "peacemaking justice" by Braswell and Gold (2002). Programs that require the offender to confront the victim and provide compensation, and programs that place the victim in the middle of the process of deciding what to do about the offender, can be categorized under the restorative justice rubric. The propositions of the movement are as follows:

1. Justice requires restoring victims, offenders, and communities who have been injured by crime.
2. Victims, offenders, and communities should have the opportunity to be a fully active part of the justice process.
3. Government should restore order, but the community should establish peace. (Van Ness and Strong, 1997)

The roots of restorative justice can be found as far back as Roman and Grecian law. Both were based on repayment to victims. Recall that Aristotle's "rectificatory justice" was concerned with ill-gotten gains in contract and business relationships that needed to be remedied. The idea was also part of justice related to crimes and injuries in that there was attention paid to the victim's injuries and an attempt for the victim to be made whole.

In the 1970s there was a trend toward "community justice" that was a part of the larger movement of community empowerment and development. Community justice boards or local justice committees were created as part of the justice system (Schweigert, 2002). This model actually comes from earlier examples of tribal justice, such as the Maori trial council of New Zealand, which involves members of the families of both victims and offenders. The model uses reintegrative shaming, and responsibility for the crime is shared by the offender's family. Another example is the Skokomish Community Peacemaking Panel. Tribal peacemakers are selected from community members, and an adversarial system is specifically rejected in favor of one that seeks to solve the issue rather than simply assess punishment (Schweigert, 2002).

**QUOTE and QUERY**

I have by degrees given up my faith in the rule of law. It is not only that the relatively absolute power we give lawgivers and law enforcers tends to corrupt these power holders absolutely. It is that imposing a pre-existing law or rule on someone literally amounts to letting one's prejudices override one's capacity to hear the many and various explanations and desires parties have.

Source: Pepinsky (1999: 64).

*Explain what Pepinsky means when he argues that the law allows people to let their prejudices override their capacity to hear explanations.*

Hallmarks of community justice models include the following:

1. The process of justice employs local leadership, is informal, and invites participation from community members.
2. The goal is to repair the harm done to a community member by another community member in a way that will restore the health of the community relationship.
3. The authority of the justice is through the customs and traditions accepted by all members. (Schweigert, 2002: 25)

In community or restorative justice models, crime is viewed as a natural human error that should be dealt with by the community. Offenders remain a part of the community. Some make distinctions between restorative justice and community justice models:

Restorative justice is a philosophical approach to correctional intervention, in which crime is seen as a conflict between individuals and their community whereby the party that causes the injury incurs an obligation to make things right—whenever and however possible. . . . Community justice is similar to restorative justice but with a stronger emphasis on prevention. Community justice involves a partnership between the justice system and community organizations to control crime and social disorder. (Carey, 2005: 5)

More generally, however, community and restorative justice can be distinguished from retributive justice in fundamental ways. Carey (2005: 25) details the differences between retributive justice and restorative justice:

1. In retributive justice, the question is "Who did it?" while in restorative justice the question is "What is the harm?"
2. In retributive justice, the question is "Which laws were broken?" while in restorative justice the question is "What needs to be done to repair the harm?"
3. In retributive justice, the question is "What should the punishment be? while in restorative justice, the question is "Who is responsible for this repair?"

Types of restorative justice programs include victim–offender mediation (or victim–offender reconciliation programs), whereby victims and offenders get together so that the victim can make it clear to the offender what harm has occurred and they can decide together how to make it right. Reparative boards have community members (rather than justice officials) decide what should happen after a crime has been committed and an offender identified. Family group conferencing and circle sentencing include family members and other interested parties in the decision on what should happen to an offender (Braithwaite, 2002). It has been found that victims are more satisfied in restorative justice programs than with traditional sentencing (79 percent compared to 57 percent). Offenders were also more likely to successfully satisfy their restitution orders in such programs (Braithwaite, 2002: 71).

"Community reparative boards" are more common with youthful offenders. They are also called youth panels, neighborhood boards, or community diversion boards, and they have been in use since the 1920s. These boards re-emerged in the mid-1990s, especially in Vermont. The goals are as follows:

1. promote citizen ownership of process
2. provide opportunity for victims and community members to confront offenders in a constructive manner
3. provide an opportunity for the offender to take personal responsibility
4. generate meaningful community based responses to crime and reduce dependence on formal justice processing (Braithwaite, 2002: 73)

"Family group conferencing" comes from the Maori tribal model and was made a part of national legislation in New Zealand in 1989. The Wagga Wagga model in Southern Australia employs police to set up family conferences of offenders, victims, families, and interested or involved others to resolve the problem. The goals of this type of program are as follows:

1. provide an opportunity for the victim to be directly involved in the decisions of sanctions
2. increase the offender's awareness of the human impact of his/her behavior and give an opportunity for the offender to take responsibility for it
3. engage the collective responsibility of the offender's support system
4. allow both offender and victim to reconnect to key community support systems (Braithwaite, 2002: 76)

"Circle sentencing" is a similar model and comes from North American tribal societies. Everyone involved directly in a criminal offense sits in a circle and gets a turn to speak. The entire circle decides what should be done. The goal is not to respond only to the current offense but also to heal the community. The goals of this type of sentencing are as follows:

1. promote healing
2. provide the offender an opportunity to make amends
3. empower victims, community members, families and offenders
4. address underlying causes of criminal behavior
5. build sense of community; promote and share community values (Braithwaite, 2002: 77)

There are potential problems with and some criticisms of these types of programs (Dzur and Wertheimer, 2002, Braithwaite, 2002). For instance, victims may feel pressured to forgive before they are ready. There may be less due process given to offenders because the goal is not to punish; thus, there may be issues of guilt or innocence that are unresolved. However, restorative justice seems to offer an alternative to retributive justice that might benefit both offender and victim.

## Conclusion

Paradigms of law help us understand that there are different perceptions regarding the function of law in society. Although some view law as enforcing the will of the majority, others see law as a tool of oppression by those in power. The justification for law is primarily prevention of harm, including paternalistic laws that seek to protect individuals from themselves, and laws that enforce society's morals. One's paradigm influences one's views on the moral authority of the government to enforce such laws.

Ultimately, law defines who is legally, if not morally, culpable. Certain groups have special issues of culpability, such as the mentally ill, juveniles, and white-collar criminals. We also discussed civil disobedience. There may be some instances where a moral person must disobey law. Finally, we explored the relationship between victims and offenders, and noted that the trend toward victims' rights could focus solely on retribution or could move toward a restorative justice approach that carries the potential of leaving the victim more fully compensated than retributive justice models.

## Key Terms

**civil disobedience** voluntary disobedience of established laws based on one's moral beliefs

**conflict paradigm** the idea that groups in society have fundamental differences and that those in power control societal elements, including law

**consensus paradigm** the idea that most people have similar beliefs, values, and goals and that societal laws reflect the majority view

**culpability** blameworthiness

**legal moralism** a justification for law that allows for protection and enforcement of societal morals

**legal paternalism** laws that protect individuals from hurting themselves

**McNaughten rule** a legal test of insanity

**mechanical solidarity** Durkheim's concept of societal solidarity as arising from similarities among a society's members

**natural law** principles of morals and rights that are inherent in nature and not human-made

**organic solidarity** Durkheim's concept of societal solidarity as arising from differences among people, as exemplified by the division of labor

**paradigm** the process of organizing knowledge; a way of seeing the world

**pluralist paradigm** the concept that there are many groups in society and that they form allegiances and coalitions in a dynamic exchange of power

**positive law** human-made law

**repressive law** Durkheim's view that law controls behavior that is different from the norm (related to mechanical solidarity)

**restitutive law** Durkheim's view that law resolves conflicts between equals, as in commutative justice (related to organic solidarity)

**restorative justice** an approach to corrective justice that focuses on meeting the needs of all concerned

**social contract theory** the idea that individuals give up the liberty to aggress against others in return for protection

**victim-compensation programs** programs in which state funds are used to compensate victims of crime for their medical and financial losses

**victim precipitation** the victim's part in a criminal transaction

**victimology** the study of victims

## Review Questions

1. Explain how people distinguish between law and justice.
2. Discuss the three paradigms of law. How is pluralism distinguished from conflict theory?
3. Discuss the major justifications for law.
4. Discuss some laws justified by legal paternalism—provide the rationale for such laws as well as opposing arguments.
5. Discuss some types of laws that are justified by legal moralism. What are the major arguments for and against such laws?
6. What is the McNaughten rule?
7. What are some recent laws passed to control crime by juveniles?
8. Define and give examples of civil disobedience. What are the principles?
9. What are victims' bills of rights? Explain victim precipitation.
10. Describe restorative justice.

## Discussion Questions

1. Discuss how the conflict and consensus paradigms would interpret the following: decriminalization of marijuana for medical purposes, stem cell research, passage of hate-crime legislation, prohibiting the use of race in admissions procedures in universities and in competitions for state scholarships, and laws prohibiting racial profiling in police stops.
2. Do you agree with laws that prohibit gambling? Drinking while driving? Underage drinking? Prostitution? Liquor violations? Drugs? Helmet laws for bicycles or motorcycles? Leash laws? Seat belts? Smoking in public places? Underage drinking or smoking laws? Can you think of any paternalistic laws not mentioned above?
3. Should offenders who vandalize, assault, or kill people purely based on the victim's identity as a member of a racial group be punished more severely than "garden-variety" criminals? What if the target victim was a homosexual? What if the target victim was visibly of Arab extraction?

4. Analyze pornography, gambling, homosexuality, and drug use under the ethical systems discussed in Chapter 2. What other laws have limited Americans' (or certain groups') freedoms? Can they be justified under any ethical rationale?

5. Analyze cases of civil disobedience such as the anti-abortion groups that picket abortion clinics or those who have been arrested for protesting the war at President Bush's campaign stops. What laws are at issue? Do they meet the definitions of civil disobedience?

6. Discuss the constitutional issues of punishing the mentally ill and juveniles. What are the legal arguments? What are the moral arguments?

7. Discuss some of the restorative justice programs described. Do any ethical issues arise from such programs?

# Ethical Dilemmas

## Situation 1

You ride a motorcycle, and you think it is much more enjoyable to ride without a helmet. You also believe your vision and hearing are better without one. Your state has just passed a helmet law, and you have already received two warnings. What will you do? What if your child was riding on the motorcycle? Do you think your position would be any different if you had any previous accidents and had been hurt?

## Situation 2

You are asked to enforce a law that you believe to be wrong. For instance, you are supposed to protect a member of the Ku Klux Klan during a speech when your feelings are directly contrary to the views expressed by this individual, and you don't believe that he should have the right to speak. What would you do? What would you do if you were told to deliberately perform your job in such a way as to ensure that the speaker will be injured by a hostile crowd?

## Situation 3

You are a D.A. and are prosecuting a burglary case. The defendant is willing to plead guilty in return for a sentence of probation, and you feel that this is a fair punishment because your evidence may not support a conviction. However, the victims are upset and want to see the offender receive prison time. They insist that you try the case. What should you do?

## Situation 4

You are a prosecutor and have the unwelcome task of prosecuting a twelve-year-old for a particularly brutal assault. You personally believe that the child basically went along with his older brother in the assault, and you think that he should have been left in the juvenile system. However, the juvenile court judge waived him to the adult system, and the media and victim's family are demanding that he be tried as an adult. You have to decide whether to try him for attempted murder, assault, or some lesser crime. You could deny the waiver and send the case back to juvenile court. What will you do? How do you determine your duty? Is it to the victims, to society, or to your own conscience?

## Situation 5

You are a juvenile prosecutor excited about the beginning of a new restorative justice program in your community. You truly believe that it will be a huge benefit for offenders and victims alike because it uses victim–offender mediation and circle sentencing in response to the juvenile's crime. The problem is that in the first case that has been referred to the program you believe that there is not enough evidence to justify prosecution. There is no eyewitness to the burglary, and the offender has confessed, retracted, and then confessed again. You believe that the evidence is equivocal and that he could be guilty or innocent—it is too close to call. You cringe at the possibility that an innocent person is going to be considered guilty without due process. On the other hand, you believe that circle sentencing may result in needed intervention for this youth, for if he didn't do this burglary, he certainly has been involved in other crimes. What would you do?

# Suggested Readings

Arrigo, B. 1999. *Social Justice/Criminal Justice*. Belmont, CA: Wadsworth.
Cane, P. 2002. *Responsibility in Law and Morality*. Portland, OR: Oxford Press.
Crank, J. 2003. *Imagining Justice*. Cincinnati: Anderson.
Lewis, D. 1998. *Guilty by Reason of Insanity*. New York: Ivy.
Perry, J. 2002. *Repairing Communities Through Restorative Justice*. Lanham, MD: American Correctional Association.
Van Ness, D., and Heetderks Strong, K. 1997. *Restoring Justice*. Cincinnati: Anderson.

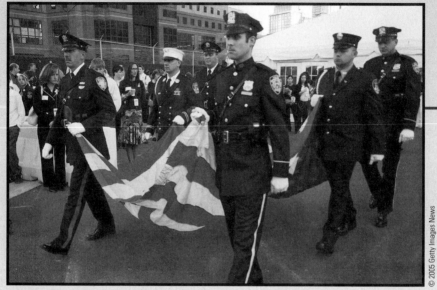

Criminal justice professionals are all public servants who safeguard the public and serve the law. This picture of the commemoration of those who died on 9/11 is a poignant reminder of this sacred duty.

# 6

# Ethics and the Criminal Justice Professional

*Policy Making in Criminal Justice*

*Balancing Law and Justice*

*The Criminal Justice Professional*

*Leadership and Training*

*Conclusion*

## Key Terms

burnout
gray areas of crimes
ideology
policies

street justice
whistleblower
wholesight

# Chapter Objectives

1. Become familiar with the ways that paradigms and ideologies shape our beliefs about crime and how to control criminals.

2. Understand how policy makers moderate the law and how criminal justice professionals implement policy.

3. Become familiar with some of the issues faced by criminal justice professionals.

4. Learn the elements of good, ethical leadership.

5. Become familiar with the reasons for and elements of ethics training.

In the preceding chapters we have discussed the concepts of morality, ethics, justice, and law. If law is the administration of justice, then policy making is the administration of law. The final and most important link in the chain of justice, of course, is the criminal justice professional.

# Policy Making in Criminal Justice

Professionals in criminal justice are called upon to enforce laws and also to implement policies. Policies can be formal or informal. Formal policy making is undertaken by the executive and legislative branches of the government, as well as by agencies in the criminal justice system. **Policies** can be considered the guidelines for action that dictate the priority of goals or objectives. They have tremendous influence on people's lives. For instance, the policy of *zero tolerance* in the war on drugs has meant that many individuals have become entangled in the criminal justice system who may not have been but for the policy. If one thinks of laws as the skeletal system of justice, then policies can be considered the muscular system—they influence the way that the laws are enforced.

There are also informal policies, which sometimes usurp or subvert formal policies. Although a mayor may preach crime control, a police department may informally instruct its members to ignore crimes in the red-light district. An informal policy may stem from management staff or develop among front-line workers and be related to their views of justice or their self-interest.

The development of policies sometimes has more to do with belief systems than with empirical reality. In the next section we present an extended discussion of liberalism and conservatism. Although these descriptions are stereotypical, they are so powerful in our thought processes that a great deal of meaning is transmitted by the use of the terms. The label of *liberal* or *conservative* communicates definitional elements that, if not universally agreed upon, at least provide the beginning of a dialogue.

## *Ideologies of Liberalism and Conservatism*

An **ideology** is "a set of general and abstract beliefs or assumptions about the correct or proper state of things, particularly with respect to the moral order and political arrangements, which serve to shape one's positions on specific issues" (Hornum and Stavish, 1978: 143). Two opposing ideologies regarding crime and criminals are the liberal view and the conservative view. Both the liberal perspective and the conservative perspective primarily operate under the consensus paradigm described in the last chapter in that they accept the basic definitions of crime as given by law.

### The Liberal Perspective

The liberal perspective explains criminal behavior and deviance through reference to psychological, social, or biological causation. Because individuals are seen as influenced by factors outside their control, they are not completely culpable for their crimes. Rather, explanations are developed to explain behavior, including psychological, sociological, and other definitions of "why" behavior occurs.

In policing, the liberal perspective is manifested by attempts of police departments to make themselves more accessible to the community. Innovations such as neighborhood or community policing, team policing, and youth groups attempt to help the police understand and empathize with certain groups with which they come into contact. The liberal ideology would endorse the use of police officers as a positive social control tool in their provision of services to the community that would, in turn, influence pro-social values. For instance, school safety officers not only teach bicycle safety tips but also give the message that the police officer is a friend and that the child should look up to him or her as a role model. "Storefront" police stations transmit the message that the police are a part of the community, and neighborhood policing allows the police officer to become involved in noncrime issues in the community, creating and cementing relational ties to the community that is being policed.

In courts, the liberal perspective is seen in *individualized justice*—the preference to consider the offender rather than the offense. This would involve the acceptance of reasons or rationales for unlawful behavior. For instance, the burglar who had lost his job and had bills to pay, the enraged wife who killed her husband because he left her for another woman, or the ghetto youth whose father turned him on to drugs would all have their individual backgrounds considered in decisions regarding responsibility and punishment. The liberal perspective perceives that law cannot easily label and set punishment for wrongdoing because human behavior is complex, not categorical. Thus, the courts, and their human representatives in the legal system, must use discretion to administer individual justice.

In corrections, the liberal ideology supports most correctional programming. Attempts to make criminals more like us, by vocational training, education, and social skills training, are based on the idea that the criminal could change given a different environment, different influences, or solutions to problems such as illiteracy or addiction. Correctional programs target the following:

1. biological problems (e.g., addiction)
2. social problems (e.g., negative role models)
3. psychological problems (e.g., weak ego state)

These programs are based on the assumption that if the problem is corrected, the criminal will no longer commit crime.

The liberal perspective may identify as unethical any treatment of the offender by the system that does not take into account individual factors. For instance, it would be considered unethical to

1. ignore the fact that an individual was coerced into an illegal action
2. ignore a prisoner's need for special attention or medical care
3. prosecute a very young offender in the same way that one would a more culpable older offender
4. ignore evidence that an individual was mentally ill when committing an offense

Basically, the liberal perspective is concerned when the law tries to uphold some unrealistic standard of objective justice, for that is not possible.

## The Conservative Perspective

The conservative perspective, in general, agrees with the liberal that the legal code is a true representation of society's morals and values, but differs in the perception of the offender. Rather than influenced by forces beyond their control, offenders are seen as persons who freely choose actions and must be held accountable for them. Public safety is paramount, and victims deserve more care and attention than offenders. Thus, if some technical rules are violated in order to get an offender off the street, then that is an acceptable cost for protecting innocent victims.

The conservative perspective views the police as enforcers of society's morality, and any attempts to weaken that role are to be resisted. Court restrictions against police power or police actions should be limited because criminals must be caught and punished in whatever way is most effective. Police are seen as becoming "soft" or bureaucratized in recent years, and there may be a wistful element in the popularity of such fictional characters as Dirty Harry, who bypass due process to get criminals off the streets.

In the conservative perspective, courts are the worst threat to society because they allow criminals to go free. Only the most punitively oriented judges achieve conservative approval, and the majority of judges are seen as do-gooders who do not give criminals the prison sentences they deserve. Conservatives believe the death penalty is justified and not used often enough. Criminals are believed to have too many rights and victims none.

Under the conservative perspective, correctional facilities have too many programs; these programs only coddle the criminals and teach them that they will be rewarded and excused for criminal behavior. Old-fashioned punishments, such as chain gangs and rock piles, are seen as appropriate and worthy. Although prisons should satisfy basic needs, anything beyond what is absolutely necessary for survival is considered a luxury and decreases the effectiveness of prison as a deterrent.

The conservative concern for ethics involves criminal justice practitioners who may use their powers of discretion too freely. For the conservative, the following steps would be considered unethical:

1. to let criminals off because of courtroom deals or because of some error in the proceedings

2. for police to ignore wrongdoing when it is done by informants, especially if it is someone who will continue the behavior
3. for criminal justice practitioners to give special privileges to criminals because of status or money—for instance, to give special favors to mobsters in prison

Whenever the system is less than objective in handing out punishment, the conservatives' concern for ethics is aroused, and that would also include disparate sentencing based on offender characteristics. For instance, if two defendants had committed the same crime, it would be considered unethical for one defendant to get fewer years in prison than the other due to different circumstances.

Smith (1982: 137) uses the terms *right* and *left* instead of our terms *conservative* and *liberal,* and presents additional definitional elements of the two ideologies. For the right, the paramount value is order—an ordered society based on a pervasive and binding morality. The paramount danger is disorder—social, moral, and political. For the left, the paramount value is justice—a just society based on a fair and equitable distribution of power, wealth, prestige, and privilege. The paramount evil is injustice. The left's concern for justice includes distributive justice, and that is why offenders' backgrounds are considered in the equation.

Smith (1982) and others associate the liberal (or left) viewpoint with due process. However, the liberal ideology does not necessarily or even logically imply a due-process position. Recall that due process is concerned with procedural justice; it is the procedural steps taken in order to ensure that individual liberty is protected against state power. The liberal support of treatment implies that one may go beyond what even conservative, retributive ends would dictate. Further, the liberal perspective does not distrust state power; in fact, it embraces the power of the state to do good. The liberal is ends-oriented; therefore, the means may be considered less important than due process requires. Thus, a due-process perspective may be a separate ideology, one that is more concerned with means than ends, and rights than results. A due-process advocate, as opposed to a liberal, would believe that a homeless alcoholic schizophrenic has a right to his or her affliction and lifestyle unless these pose a danger to self or others. A liberal would believe that the state could and should respond to the ills of the individual, even if the individual doesn't seem to know what is good for him or her.

Of course, these descriptions are fairly simplistic. Most people hate to be labeled as conservative or liberal, probably because it denies the presence of more complicated views of humanity and human relationships. Despite the obvious generalizations apparent in these characterizations, they can be detected in news coverage and political speeches, and are useful in order to understand the development of policy. The conservative position is obviously more popular today than the liberal perspective, which might explain the greater emphasis on accountability and punitiveness in discussions about crime and social control.

Braswell and Whitehead (1999) urge putting aside these two viewpoints in favor of a different approach. They point to dangerous practices when one presents research from one point of view or the other. Braswell and Whitehead show the liberal approach as represented by those who present prison research in a light that denies the possibility that prisons do have any effect on crime or that they might actually help offenders. The conservative approach is represented by those who view prisons as a management issue with no recognition or concern for the social, racial, and economic factors that so obviously play a part in the way prisons are used in society today. Conservatives point to research that shows the public favors incarceration and the death penalty; liberals point to research that shows that when the public is offered alternatives, the answers change. Both sides are dishonest, even if unconsciously, in presenting research that is less than the truth, unbalanced, and biased. Braswell and Whitehead (1999) argue for **wholesight**, meaning using one's heart as well as head to understand and present research findings.

## *Myths and Reality in Criminal Justice*

What we believe about crime and criminals is partially influenced by our ideology, as described above, but it also is influenced by what we know about crime—or what we think we know. Several excellent sources now debunk some of the more standard myths in criminal justice. Walker (1985/2000) was one of the first to address fundamental beliefs that influenced criminal justice policy—for example, the belief that more police patrols would reduce crime has little, if any, empirical support. He also addressed fundamental beliefs that support liberal ideology—for example, the belief that education reduces crime is refuted by studies that show no effect. Some of Walker's findings and use of empirical evidence may be criticized, but the approach of a skeptic is a necessary one if we want to avoid complacency and policy making influenced by unsupported truisms.

Others have continued this inquiry. For instance, Kappeler, Blumberg, and Potter (2000/2005) present in their work a series of myths that influence criminal justice policy:

1. the myth of crime waves
2. the myth of child abduction
3. the myth of the drug crisis
4. the myth of equal justice
5. the myth of the utility of punishment
6. the myth of a lenient criminal justice system

Bohm (1996) also discusses myths—crime is a bad social problem, the criminal justice system enforces all laws, crime is primarily violent, and crime is increasing—and their influence on criminal justice policy. He also explains their function:

1. They offer identities (good guy, bad guy).
2. They aid comprehension by creating order out of the bombardment of information we experience today.
3. They help to form common bonds and reinforce a sense of community.

These sources show us that what we think we know is not necessarily accurate. If our beliefs about what should be done with criminals are based on the myth that the system is lenient and/or the myth that crime is increasing, then we are operating under faulty assumptions. How do these myths develop? The media and government are obvious participants in creating and perpetuating false perceptions, but social science bears a great deal of responsibility as well.

## *Criminal Justice Researchers—Participants in Myth Making?*

The argument that social science can never be truly objective has been discussed in a variety of venues (Roberg, 1981). A social scientist is influenced by his or her value system, ideology, and perception of reality. Which questions to ask may be more important than the answers one finds. Individual perceptions will always somewhat influence the research process; however, if hypothesis construction and methodology are tainted by special interest groups or political agendas, then one must question any results that emerge from such research. For instance, the "In the News" box concerning the looting and violence that occurred in New Orleans after the flood illustrates how people's beliefs are affected by what they perceive as facts, but what we think we know may not necessarily be true. We tend to accept what we are told by the media and social or medical science research, but the veracity of such findings may be questionable.

In one study of criminal justice researchers' experiences with ethical dilemmas, it was found that the most common ethical dilemma was perceived pressure to study a certain topic, issue, or question, and/or pressure to influence the findings (Longmire, 1983). False research findings may occur because of laziness, incompetence, or political pressure. Recent exposés in the medical research field have called into question what we think we know about such things as heart disease and stem cell research; unethical researchers in criminal justice may also affect what we think we know about crime and criminals.

---

**IN THE NEWS   Looting as Fact or Fiction**

Many individuals were horrified by video of New Orleans residents looting businesses and residences. Some video even showed police officers carting away goods. Then some experts argued that stories of widespread looting were exaggerated. Several experts interviewed argued that there was no hard evidence and that it was "victim blaming" to focus on looting when there were only a few isolated cases; they said that widespread looting and violence do not happen and did not happen in New Orleans. They even argued that the rapes and murders that were said to have happened in the Superdome did not occur. These positions taken by experts were received with skepticism, but then later news stories indicated that it may be the case that the "bodies stacked up" in the Superdome were exaggerations and falsehoods that were then spread by the national news media. Evidently, there was one known homicide at the Convention Center and only one substantiated attempted rape. Of course, some argue that rapes may not be reported. The true number of incidents remains to be seen.

Sources: C. Shea, "Disaster Experts Rebut Tales of Looting," *Austin American Statesman*, September 18, 2005, H1, H4; B. Thevenot and G. Russell, "No Evidence Supports Tales of Murder, Rape," *Austin American Statesman*, September 28, 2005, A1, A7.

***Why do you think that stories of the looting and violence were exaggerated? What evidence exists that proves what actually did happen?***

In addition to outside pressures that influence the selection of a research question or prompt improper influence over, improper use of, or outright falsification of research findings, other dilemmas in research exist, including the following:

1. Protection of subject confidentiality
2. Negative effects of the research on the client (e.g., the Milgram experiment and the Zimbardo experiment are the two best-known examples of research that had tremendously negative effects on subjects) and issues of privacy for subjects
3. Deception of subjects in terms of what they will experience or the true focus of the research
4. Obtaining informed voluntary consent
5. Withholding benefits or services to subjects for the purpose of research
6. Use of research findings—either through misinterpretation or overreaching—to justify otherwise illegal or unethical treatment

There has been concern recently over the perceived influence exerted by government officials over scientific findings. The Bush Administration has been accused of attempting to influence or suppress scientific findings concerning global warming and the effects of oil exploration in the Alaska wilderness areas. In criminal justice, many saw an ominous trend when Congress planned to cut the budget of the Bureau of Justice Statistics (BJS). The BJS is a little-known division of the U.S. Department

---

**IN THE NEWS Government Cover-up?**

The ACLU and other advocacy groups are pressing the Bush Administration for the release of a Bureau of Justice Statistics report that showed highly disproportionate stops by police of black drivers. The BJS director was allegedly told to delete language that highlighted findings that supported the allegations that racial profiling was widespread. When he was refused, he was demoted and the report was posted, but with no news release, nor was an announcement made of the report's release. The report noted that blacks and Hispanics were three times more likely to experience police threat or use of force during interactions with police, almost three times as likely to be arrested after stops, and three times more likely to have their person or vehicle searched. According to the ACLU, the government's handling of the report is indicative of a pattern of concealment and attempts to control the flow of scientific information.

Source: ACLU news release, accessed on 9/1/05 from http://www.aclu.org/news/Newsprint.cfm?ID=18994&c=133.

*Why would anyone care whether the Bureau of Justice Statistics published such a report? Do you think that there is a greater degree of government control over scientific information in the Bush Administration or not? What are some other examples of such a practice?*

of Justice that compiles and distributes statistical reports on victims, offenders, and correctional populations. Criminal justice researchers use BJS reports almost exclusively when their research requires national statistics. Government officials made the decision to cut the budget in favor of awarding contracts to do statistical analysis to private/public contract vendors (such as private research foundations). Many criminal justice researchers were concerned that such vendors would be influenced by their desire to obtain more contracts and so would not be objective purveyors of facts. Further, because the contract vendors are a less stable source, the possibility of comparing longitudinal data would be compromised. If one believes the ACLU, the trend to influence criminal justice information has become even more direct, as indicated in the "In the News" box.

The interaction of ideology, knowledge acquisition, and policy formation is complicated. Policies may originate in ideology and then become supported by research, or research may influence a shift of ideology. The danger is that individual decision making may be subverted by myths and that individual ethics may be the victim of misguided ideologies. See Policy Box 6-1 for a discussion of how this might happen.

---

### POLICY BOX 6-1   Domestic Violence: Arrest or Not?

The widespread policy of mandatory arrest in domestic violence calls is directly related to the Minneapolis Study, which found that arrest was the only intervention that reduced future violence. The trouble with the policy is that when the research was replicated in several other cities, the findings were different. In fact, arrest made the situation worse in some circumstances and had no effect in some areas. The replication studies have earned much less press than the original studies, so law enforcement continues to justify the mandatory arrest policy by research findings that are in question.

**Law:** Although there are obviously laws against assault and domestic violence, as with all laws, there is a great deal of discretion in how and whether to implement such laws in every case.

**Policy:** The decision to have, in effect, a zero-tolerance policy for domestic violence and to make an arrest in almost all circumstances has resulted in what seems to be an unintended effect—that of greater arrests of women for domestic violence. Thus, a policy that was supposed to be put in place to assist victims of domestic violence (perceived to be largely women) has, in fact, created a situation where they are more likely to be arrested.

**Individual ethics:** Individual officers who might have ignored domestic violence can no longer do so, but officers who might have tried to intervene in alternative ways to arrest now have an ethical dilemma as to whether to ignore departmental policy or abide by it, even if they believe that arrest is unwarranted.

# Balancing Law and Justice

The passing of a law by legislators is only the first step in social control. In order for the law to be effective, it must be enforced by law enforcement, with violators prosecuted and punished. We know that policy making affects the passage of laws as well as their implementation. We also know that the discretion present in each step of the criminal justice system creates a situation in which written laws do not necessarily represent the reality of enforcement. Police departments create prostitution crackdowns, traffic ticket "blizzards," drug sweeps, and pornography raids with more or less cyclical patterns, sometimes in response to political pressure, sometimes not. The enforcement is, for the most part, independent of legislative intent. In this sense, police are *de facto* definers of the law because they are the agents of implementation.

If we see laws as an "ought" in societal definitions of misbehavior, then enforcement policies must be viewed as the "is" of what is tolerated and what is not. Many laws on the books are routinely ignored and forgotten, especially in the area of private behavior. One might ask why such laws are not thrown out as irrelevant to the times in which we live. The reason they continue to exist is that no politician is going to champion removal of "ought" laws because it would seem that he or she was in favor of the behavior that the law defines as immoral. Therefore, in some states there are still laws against private sexual behavior, "blue" laws restricting business activity or the sale of liquor, and so on. On the other hand, some argue that to have laws that are ignored endangers the credibility of the entire legal system.

Studies indicate that most corruption and graft come from those **gray areas of crimes** such as prostitution, gambling, and drugs. It is easy to explain the emergence of unethical behavior by criminal justice professionals in these areas because such crimes do not have the same moral sentiments behind them as do "serious crimes," such as murder and child molestation. Many police officers who would have no problem letting a prostitute go free will risk their lives to catch a child killer. Part of this discretionary enforcement comes from a personal perception of the immorality of the behavior and also a perception of society's tolerance or intolerance of such behavior.

Individual officers often administer what has been called **street justice**. For instance, when a store owner has a legal right to prosecute a shoplifter, but the shoplifter is eighty-seven years old, poor, and shoplifting food so she can eat, the police officer might try to convince the store owner not to prosecute in an attempt to soften the harshness of the law. Prosecutors may "lose" evidence in a subjective judgment that a criminal defendant doesn't need to be prosecuted. Alternatively, police may differentially enforce the law against those whom they consider jerks, and prosecutors may ask for continuances to keep a defendant in jail, knowing that the case will ultimately be dismissed. The trouble with street justice and *de facto* justice is that once law is ignored in favor of the application of subjective justice, individual definitions of what is "fair" and "just" may be arbitrary and capricious.

---

### BOX 6-1   Spader's Rule of Law Versus Rule of Man

| **Rule of Law** | **Rule of Man** |
|---|---|
| (Positives) | (Positives) |
| equal protection | individualization |
| evenhandedness | flexibility |
| due process | mercy |
| fairness | compassion |
| rationality | equity |
| notice | creativity |
| visibility | adaptability |
| predictability | informality |
| centralized limits on power | efficiency |
| universality | |
| | |
| (Negatives) | (Negatives) |
| inflexibility | disparity |
| harshness | inconsistency |
| rigidity | arbitrary and capricious abuse |
| mandatory legalism | uncertainty |
| technicalities | invisibility |
| red tape | uncontrolled provincialism |
| blind formalism | |
| inefficiency | |

SOURCE: Adapted from D. Spader, "Rule of Law v. Rule of Man: The Search for the Golden Zigzag Between Conflicting Fundamental Values." *Journal of Criminal Justice* 12 (1984): 379–394.

---

Spader (1984) discusses discretion and the rule of law as a *golden zigzag* between fundamental values (see Box 6-1, "Spader's Rule of Law Versus Rule of Man"). In this discussion, discretion has positive and negative elements, as does the rule of law. Of course, the ideal is to use discretion wisely in pursuit of ethical goals. Criminal justice professionals can be seen as mediating the harshness and inflexibility of law in the application of street justice; however, the same discretion that allows them to perform benevolent acts allows them to act in arbitrary and oppressive ways as well.

The moral commitment that professionals have toward the laws they are supposed to uphold influences their actions. Soldiers are more loyal when they believe in the morality of the war. Police are more determined when they believe in the laws they are enforcing. Prosecutors and defense attorneys are more committed to due process when they believe in it. Correctional officials are less likely to allow prisoners to corrupt them when they have a strong sense of their goals. And all criminal justice professionals are more likely to operate in an ethical manner when they believe in the validity and justness of the system that employs them.

# The Criminal Justice Professional

For the criminal justice professional who must uphold and enforce the law, this discussion of morality, justice, and law is not just academic. Line staff often face questions of individual morality versus obedience and loyalty. The My Lai incident has almost passed out of this nation's consciousness, but at the time there was a great debate over whether soldiers should follow their superiors' orders blindly or make an independent assessment of the morality of the action. In this case, several officers were prosecuted by a military court for killing women and children in a village during the Vietnam War without any evidence that they were a threat to the unit's safety. The officers' defense was that their superiors gave the orders to take the village without regard to whether the inhabitants were civilians or guerrillas. The rationale was that often there wasn't time to establish whether a civilian was friendly or not and that, in any event, civilians often carried grenades and otherwise harmed U.S. troops. There was heated public discussion in support of and against the soldiers' actions. Movies such as *Platoon* provide dramatic fictional accounts of other actions ordered by officers and the dilemmas of soldiers who knew that such actions were unethical and illegal. Is an individual excused from moral culpability when following orders, or should one disobey orders that one believes to be illegal or immoral? The Nuremburg war trials held individuals personally accountable when they committed war crimes (defined as actions that violated the Geneva Convention), whether they were following orders or not.

More recently, individual soldiers were responsible for the discovery and subsequent investigation of the brutal practices at the Abu Ghraib prison. At least one soldier was so distressed by what he observed that he sent camera phone pictures back home to relatives, who distributed the photos to the press. The resulting

## IN THE NEWS  Lynndie England and Abu Ghraib

Was Lynndie England a willing participant in the abuses that have been documented at Abu Ghraib or a mentally challenged young woman who was under the power of her lover, Charles Graner? It depends on whether you listen to the prosecutor or the defense attorney in her trial for conspiracy, maltreating detainees, and committing an indecent act. She had pled guilty in May 2005, but the judge refused to accept the plea, holding that it was inconsistent with the evidence because she and her witnesses argued that they did nothing wrong. She then pled not guilty but was convicted of numerous counts of mistreating prisoners and was sentenced to three years in prison.

Sources: M. Toohey, "Soldier a Willing Participant, Prosecutors Say," *Austin American Statesman*, September 23, 2005, B1, B3; D. Cloud, "Lynndie England Guilty of Abuses," *Austin American Statesman*, September 27, 2005, A1, A4.

*Whose responsibility is it when soldiers mistreat prisoners in a military prison? How far up in the command structure should the culpability lie?*

investigation has led to the courts-martial of many individuals and an inquiry into how high up the chain of authority blame could be directed. The photos were a damning indictment of the unethical and illegal interrogation practices of soldiers and private contractors. Interestingly, although some lauded the soldier who released the pictures as a hero, others condemned him as a traitor to his country, and he and his family received death threats.

A soldier's dilemma is not all that different from a police officer's. At times, police officers may receive orders that they know to be illegal and/or unethical. The hierarchical nature of police work is very similar to the military, which makes the analogy even more striking. Does the police officer (or any other criminal justice professional) have the duty to use personal moral judgment, or is obedience to superiors mandatory?

Each individual is faced with moral choices in the course of her or his career. Some of these choices are easy to make. However, some of the hardest decisions involve going against superiors or colleagues. Even if the behavior is obviously illegal, it is difficult to challenge authority, and when the accepted pattern of behavior has the law on its side, very few of us take an individual stand against the law or practice.

For criminal justice practitioners, ethical decisions often arise from the exercise of discretion and the use of power. In criminal justice we must wrestle with a number of important issues, including the following:

1. questions of responsibility and excuse
2. the limits of the state's right to control the individual
3. the ethical use of force
4. the appropriate use of discretion

Although professionals and practitioners may get bogged down with day-to-day problems and bureaucratic agendas may cause them to lose sight of larger goals, foremost in their minds should always be the true scope and meaning of the power inherent in the criminal justice system. It is people who make a *justice* system *just* or *corrupt.*

To protect citizenry from any misuse and abuse of power, personnel in the criminal justice system must have a strong professional identity. There is a continuing debate over whether police officers can be described as professionals; there is even more debate over whether correctional officers can be described as such. These arguments miss a central point. Whether one calls the men and women who wear these uniforms professionals, practitioners, or some other term, the fact is that they have immense power over other people's lives. This power must be recognized for what it is and held as a sacred trust. In the "In the News" box, an extreme example of the use of such power is portrayed.

Criminal justice professionals are public servants and, as such, should aspire to a higher standard of behavior. They have a duty to the citizenry they serve, but even more than that, they must possess the moral and ethical sense to prevent the power inherent in their positions from being used for tyranny. Education isn't enough. Learning a body of knowledge and acquiring essential skills do not give individuals the moral sense necessary to use those skills wisely. Witness the recurring scandals involving lawyers and business professionals—a highly educated group is not necessarily free from corruption.

**IN THE NEWS Eleven-Year-Old Assaulter?**

News stories followed the arrest of an eleven-year-old girl for assault after she threw a rock at a boy who had thrown a water balloon at her. In these days of zero tolerance for violence, the rock throwing incident between the children resulted in three police cars and a police helicopter hovering overhead. The eleven-year-old was charged with resisting arrest after she scratched a police officer's arm as well as felony assault for the rock throwing. News stories did not indicate whether or not the boy who threw the water balloon was also charged with assault. She escaped jail time with a plea agreement after spending five days in juvenile hall and a month under house arrest.

Source: L. Leff, "Girl, 11, Avoids Jail for Assault," *Austin American Statesman,* August 4, 2005, A18.

*Do you see something wrong with using the laws of felony assault and resisting arrest against children engaged in a water balloon/rock fight? How could this situation have been handled differently?*

Criminal justice practitioners find themselves faced with a wide spectrum of ethical choices:

1. Balancing friendship against institutional integrity—that is, when friends and colleagues engage in inappropriate or illegal behavior or rule breaking.
2. Balancing client (offender) needs against bureaucratic efficiency and institutional goals.
3. Balancing personal goals or biases that conflict with fair and impartial treatment of the public and the clients served. The inappropriate use of discretion occurs when the professional uses unethical criteria to resolve decisions.

Most people in the criminal justice field (or indeed any profession) have basically good characters. However, it can be argued that in some situations even those who have formed habits of honesty, truthfulness, and integrity are sincerely perplexed as to the correct course of behavior. These situations occur because the behavior choice seems so innocuous or trivial (e.g., whether to accept free coffee) or seems so difficult (e.g., a partner or friend wants you to cover up something he did wrong). In these instances where basically good people have trouble deciding what to do, the ethical systems might help them analyze their choices.

It must also be accepted that in some dilemmas, there are going to be costs involved when making the right decision. For instance, an officer who knows it is his duty to provide evidence against his brother-in-law who is a major drug dealer may lose his wife's love and, in the process, his children's. There is no assurance that "doing the right thing" will not come at a high cost. The ethical person may not necessarily be honored; some have been heavily sanctioned.

In any organization, there are those who will almost always make ethical choices, those who will usually make unethical ones, and those who can be influenced one way or the other. The best course of action is to identify those in the second group and encourage them to find other employment or at least remove them from temptation. Then organizational leaders must create an atmosphere for the third group that encourages ethical decision making. This can be done by promoting ethical administrators, rewarding morally courageous behavior, and providing clear and powerful organizational policies that emphasize worthwhile goals and honest means. Ethics training may also be helpful.

# Leadership and Training

An ethical organization must have ethical administrators and managers. They are responsible not only for their personal conduct but also for the actions of those they supervise. In other countries and cultures, this responsibility seems to be more pronounced than in the United States. For instance, when the Falkland War occurred, the foreign minister in Great Britain resigned. He did so because the situation happened on "his watch." Even though he did nothing personally blameworthy and was not negligent in his duties and in all respects performed his job competently, he held himself personally responsible because he failed to know of and therefore warn of or prepare for the threat that Argentina presented.

Contrast this with the attitude of the captain of the *Exxon Valdez,* responsible for the largest oil spill in history, who professed innocence because he wasn't the one on the bridge at the time of the incident, or Darryl Gates, the Los Angeles police chief who, even after the Christopher Commission described a widespread management lapse, insisted that the problem of brutal officers was an individual problem and not one for which he should be held responsible.

Of course, the explanation that one was unaware of wrongful behavior has been used by the highest leaders in the country; thus, it should not be surprising that it is frequently heard from administrators when faced with the wrongdoing of their subordinates. There seem to be so few of those who are willing to take responsibility for their actions that when someone does say, "I did it, I'm responsible, and I'm sorry," it comes as such a refreshing surprise. Recall the response of Scott Waddle, the commander of the submarine that killed several Japanese students. He did not attempt to displace or share the blame for the incident and, in fact, traveled to Japan to seek forgiveness. This response is, unfortunately, all too rare. After the New Orleans tragedy, the president and the Louisiana governor accepted blame, as indicated in the Quote and Query box on the next page. One would think that their statements would have been received with favor; however, the general response was lukewarm at best, perhaps because neither admission seemed very sincere.

What does it mean to be an ethical leader? Obviously, one first needs to be sure that one is not personally engaged in unethical and corrupt behaviors. Unfortunately, we have many recent examples where leaders cannot pass even this first test. In addition, one has to take responsibility for the larger role responsibilities of a leader position. Standards applied to public administrators can be helpful to this discussion. The American Society for Public Administration (1979) has promulgated standards

**QUOTE and QUERY**

"Katrina exposed serious problems in our response capability at all levels of the government, and to the extent that the federal government didn't fully do its job right, I take responsibility."

President George W. Bush.

"We all know that there were failures at every level of government: state, federal and local. At the state level, we must take a careful look at what went wrong and make sure it never happens again. The buck stops here, and as your governor, I take full responsibility."

Governor Kathleen Blanco.

Sources: "American Digest," *Austin American Statesman,* September 18, 2005, H1; Associated Press, "La. Governor Takes Blame for Response," *Washington Post,* retrieved on September 22, 2005 from www.washingtonpost.com/wpdyn/content/article/2005/09/14/AR2005091402254.html.

*Louisiana Governor Blanco and President Bush took responsibility for the perceived failures of the government in responding to disaster victims. Why, if these leaders took responsibility, did some people angrily label such statements as "empty" or "only public relations"? Is it their "fault" that the system didn't seem to work? Why has this natural disaster spurred discussions and debates regarding policy issues? Which policies are being debated?*

that can be applied to all administrators if they aspire to be good leaders. The standards include the following:

1. *Responsibility and accountability:* Measures of quality service delivery should be developed and implemented to enable the administrator to identify strengths and weaknesses.
2. *Commitment:* Leaders should be dedicated and enthusiastic about the role of the organization, as well as have a commitment to the law, codes, regulations, and professional standards of behavior.
3. *Responsiveness:* Leaders should be sensitive to changing circumstances and evolving demands and needs of the public. Good leadership exhibits flexibility in the face of social change.
4. *Knowledge and skills:* Technology is dynamic, and leadership must keep abreast of better ways of accomplishing its mission, as well as possess the understanding to interpret data that are relevant to the mission of the organization. Training—both upon entry and in-service—is a necessity in order to have an effective workforce.
5. *Conflicts of interest:* Since there will always be conflicts, the administrator should be sensitive to them, especially when personal needs conflict with organizational needs.
6. *Professional ethics:* Administrators should practice self-reflection and continually check their decision making against some ethical standard.

Administrators and managers do not necessarily ensure that an organization will be free from corruption merely by avoiding engaging in corrupt practices themselves; they must take affirmative steps to encourage ethical actions. Issues that could be examined in a discussion of ethical leadership include the practice of recruitment, training, discipline and reward structures, and evaluation of performance.

Souryal (1992: 307) offers advice to leaders who would like to advance ethical decision making and emphasizes the importance of organizational support for ethical actions. Ethical leaders should do the following:

1. Create an environment that is conducive to dignified treatment on the job.
2. Increase ethical awareness among the ranks through formal and informal socialization.
3. Avoid deception and manipulation in the way officers are assigned, rewarded, or promoted.
4. Allow for openness and the free flow of unclassified information.
5. Foster a sense of shared values and incorporate such values in the subculture of the agency.
6. Demonstrate an obligation to honesty, fairness, and decency by example.
7. Discuss the issue of corruption publicly, expose corrupt behavior, and reward ethical behavior.

Metz (1990) offers a similar set of advice. He proposes that ethical administrators follow these steps:

1. Establish realistic goals and objectives.
2. Provide ethical leadership (meaning set a moral tone by actions).
3. Establish formal written codes of ethics.
4. Provide a whistleblowing mechanism.
5. Discipline violators of ethical standards.
6. Train all personnel in ethics.

The common administrative reaction to unethical practices is to institute even more rules that cover a greater range of behavior. As discussed in previous chapters, extensive rules seem to be present in inverse proportion to high ethical standards; what often occurs is as more rules are written, more creative ways are found to get around them. Rules are not ethical standards, and without a commitment and belief in the legitimacy of the rules, there is no way that more rules will affect the ethics of an organization.

When top leaders take responsibility for their subordinates' behavior, they will lead and administer with greater awareness, interaction, and responsibility. Because of this responsibility, a supervisor or administrator must be concerned with how the workplace treats the worker, how the worker views the mission, and how the public views the organization. Concern for one's public image may be shared by ethical leaders and egoistic bureaucrats, but the first group has a sincere desire to understand the public's complaints and respond to them, and the second group is concerned solely with protecting the image of the organization—a stand that may mean **whistleblowers** are punished rather than appreciated for bringing problems out in the open.

A strong ethical leader would have a personal relationship with subordinates—without showing favoritism. This personal relationship is the building block of modeling, identification, and persuasive authority. Strong leadership involves caring and commitment to the organization. A strong leader is someone who is connected with others but also has a larger vision, if you will, of goals and mission.

Delattre (1989b) discusses a realistic idealist—it's possible he would also be content with the phrase an *idealistic realist.* What he is referring to is the capacity for good leaders to understand social realities but to avoid cynicism in the face of such social realities—for instance, in the use of force, a realistic idealist would understand that force is necessary at times but attempt every alternative means to protect all human life, including the offender's life. Leaders must never lose sight of the organizational mission; for public servants, this means public service.

Souryal also describes ethical leaders as those with "a mental state that is characterized by vision, enlightened reasoning, and moral responsibility" (1992: 186). Good leaders must recognize and relay the idea that public service applies to all, not just a favored few. Criminals are also part of the public that the criminal justice system serves. This means that they deserve the same civility, protections, and services as the rest of us unless such is prohibited by law or unless personal safety is threatened. When the protections represented by our Bill of Rights and democratic process become reserved for certain groups, the rights of all are threatened.

## *Teaching Ethics in Criminal Justice*

Many believe that it is much more effective to present moral or ethical questions to new members of a profession before these individuals are faced with "real-life" dilemmas. Of course, what often happens is that once students leave this setting they are usually told to forget what they've learned. This happens often in police academies, where cadets are taught "the book" and learn "the street" when they are paired with an older officer. This also happens when lawyers realize that the high ideals of justice they learned in law school have little to do with the bargaining and bureaucratic law of the courthouse.

People respond to the discrepancies between official and subcultural ethics in a number of ways. They may ignore, participate in, or confront activities of their peers that they feel are wrong. It is difficult to ignore actions that run contrary to one's own value system, but very often employees establish complicated rationalizations to explain why it is not their business that others around them steal, perform less than adequately, or conduct illicit business during working hours. People often do not feel it is right to confront the immoral behavior of others even when their own behavior is consistent with accepted standards of morality. Individuals are sometimes confronted with the choice of saying nothing and allowing corruption to continue or risk ostracism and censure from peers.

If one is interested in changing unethical behavior in an organization, the primary target might be new recruits, for those who have been engaging in unethical activities have built up comprehensive rationales for their behavior. Socio-moral reasoning opportunities could exist in classroom settings, such as academies. Learning theorists, on the other hand, might say that the most effective way to change the ethics of a profession is to make sure that behavior changes. According to learning theory principles, if one was sure to be punished for accepting bribes, lying, or performing other unethical behaviors, then the subcultural supports for such behavior and the moral apologia for it would disappear. However, only pure behaviorists would conclude that mere monitoring and application of consistent rewards and punishments would result in an ethical work force. Others believe that although monitoring might result in a work force that performed in an ethical manner, in order for ethical behavior to continue without monitoring, and for people to believe in principles of right and wrong, they must internalize an ethical system.

According to Sherman (1982: 17–18), the following elements are necessary for any ethics program relating to criminal justice:

1. Stimulating the "moral imagination" by posing difficult moral dilemmas.
2. Encouraging the recognition of ethical issues and larger questions instead of more immediate issues such as efficiency and goals.
3. Helping to develop analytical skills and the tools of ethical analysis.
4. Eliciting a sense of moral obligation and personal responsibility to show why ethics should be taken seriously.
5. Tolerating and resisting disagreement and ambiguity.
6. Understanding the morality of coercion, which is intrinsic to criminal justice.
7. Integrating technical and moral competence, especially recognizing the difference between what we are capable of doing and what we should do.
8. Becoming familiar with the full range of moral issues in criminology and criminal justice in the study of criminal justice ethics.

Issues include the following:

1. the definitions of justice and crime
2. the appropriate use of force
3. the relative importance of due process over efficiency
4. the ethical use of technology to control the populace
5. the variables used to determine responsibility and punishment
6. the right of society to treat (or punish)
7. the limits that should be placed on treatment (or punishment)

Furthermore, there has been a wealth of excellent material published in the last several years, so the student or interested reader should be able to find sources that explore the issues above, as well as others. Souryal and Potts (1996) propose that there is a standard body of knowledge available for those who want to become "literate" in the study of criminal justice ethics. In Box 6-2, "Cultural Literacy in Criminal Justice," Souryal and Potts's sources are presented.

## *Avoiding Cynicism and Burnout*

Two of the greatest dangers in criminal justice are cynicism and burnout. Cynical leadership, cynical instructors, and overwhelming evidence that we live in an imperfect world create the all-too-common occurrence of workers who are cynical, who are burned out, and who have abandoned the ideals that led them to the profession in the first place. As mentioned before, ethical leaders should be able to transmit a vision

---

**BOX 6-2 Cultural Literacy in Criminal Justice**

**The Philosophy of Ethics**

Adler, M. (1978). *Aristotle for Everybody: Difficult Thought Made Easy.*
Albert, E., Denise, T., and Peterfruend, S. (1988). *Great Traditions of Ethics.*
Bloom, A. (1987). *The Closing of the American Mind.*
Borchert, D., and Stewart, D. (1986). *Exploring Ethics.*
Campbell, K. (1986). *A Stoic Philosophy of Life.*
Keyes, C. D. (1978). *Four Types of Value Destruction: A Search for the Good Through Ethical Analysis of Everyday Experience.*
Lavine, T. Z. (1984). *From Socrates to Sartre: The Philosophic Quest.*
Porter, B. (1988). *Reasons for Living: A Basic Ethics.*
Thiroux, J. (1990). *Ethics: Theory and Practice.*
Warmington, E., and Rouse, P. (1984). *Great Dialogues of Plato.*

**Moral Rules and Moral Judgment**

Brink, D. (1989). *Moral Realism of the Foundations of Ethics.*
Carson, T. (1984). *The State of Morality.*
Cooper, N. (1981). *The Diversity of Moral Thinking.*
Fishkin, J. (1984). *Beyond Subjective Morality: Ethical Reasoning and Political Philosophy.*
Gert, B. (1970). *The Moral Rules.*
Goldman, A. (1988). *Moral Knowledge.*
Kekes, J. (1989). *Moral Tradition and Individuality.*
Lee, K. (1985). *A New Basis for Moral Philosophy.*
Singer, P. (1979). *Practical Ethics.*

**Justice Theories**

Cohen, R. (1986). *Justice: Views from the Social Sciences.*
Dworkin, R. (1977). *Taking Rights Seriously.*
Feinberg, J., and Cross, H. (1980). *Philosophy of Law.*
Hobbes, T. (1968). *Leviathan.*
Hochschild, J. (1981). *What Is Fair? American Beliefs About Distributive Justice.*
Lycos, K. (1987). *Plato on Justice and Power.*
MacIntyre, A. (1988). *Whose Justice? Which Rationality?*
Rawls, J. (1971). *A Theory of Justice.*
Reiman, J. (1990). *Justice and Modern Moral Philosophy.*

**Ethics of Public Service**

Beauchamp, T. (1975). *Ethics and Public Policy.*
Bok, S. (1978). *Lying: Moral Choice in Public and Private Life.*

Cleveland, H. (1985). *The Knowledge Executive: Leadership in an Information Society.*

Dubin, R. (1974). *Human Relations in Administration.*

Elliston, F., and Bowie, N. (1982). *Ethics, Public Policy and Criminal Justice.*

Herzberg, F. (1976). *The Managerial Choice: To Be Efficient and to Be Human.*

Nettler, G. (1982). *Lying, Cheating, Stealing.*

Regan, T., and Van DeVeer, D. (1982). *And Justice for All: New Introductory Essays in Ethics and Public Policy.*

Rohr, J. (1978). *Ethics for Bureaucrats: An Essay on Law and Values.*

Williams, J. D. (1980). *Public Administration: The People's Business.*

### Ethics of Criminal Justice Agencies

Braswell, M., McCarthy, B., and McCarthy, B. (1991). *Justice, Crime and Ethics.*

Delattre, E. (1989). *Character and Cops: Ethics in Policing.*

Fleisher, M. (1989). *Warehousing Violence.*

Heffernan, W., and Stroup, T. (1985). *Police Ethics: Hard Choices in Law Enforcement.*

Lozoff, B., and Braswell, M. (1989). *Inner Corrections: Finding Peace and Peace Making.*

Pollock-Byrne, J. (1989). *Ethics in Crime and Justice: Dilemmas and Decisions.*

Schmalleger, F. (1990). *Ethics in Criminal Justice.*

Souryal, S. (1992). *Ethics in Criminal Justice: In Search of the Truth.*

Travis, L., Schwartz, M., and Clear, T. (1983). *Corrections: An Issues Approach.*

Whitehead, J. (1989). *Burnout in Probation and Corrections.*

SOURCE: Souryal, S., and Potts, D. "What Am I Supposed to Fall Back On? Cultural Literacy in Criminal Justice Ethics." *Journal of Criminal Justice Education* 4 (1996): 15–41. Reprinted with permission of S. Souryal and the Academy of Criminal Justice Sciences.

and be committed to the mission of the organization, but many administrators and managers exhibit only pessimistic cynicism over the potential for change, the worth of humanity, and the importance of doing what is right.

How does one avoid cynicism and **burnout?**

1. First, adopt realistic goals before entering the profession. A police officer cannot expect to save the world, and a treatment professional should not expect to find success with every client. A more realistic career goal might be a resolution to do one's best and to always follow the law.

2. Second, find and nurture a network of mentors and colleagues that promotes ethical values. In every department that has a corruption scandal, there are also those who have managed to avoid participating in such activity. Cynical people are contagious, and cynicism breeds rationalizations for committing unethical behavior—from leaving work early or falsifying overtime records to violating the rights of suspects or defendants.

3. Third, seek self-fulfillment and personal enrichment. This could be higher education, reading self-help books, attending church, joining interest clubs, participating in charitable activities, volunteering to coach community sport teams, or becoming involved in the PTA. Note that such activities all have the element of communication and interaction with others. Such activities promote connectedness with the community at large and counteract the negativity that pervades the criminal justice field. Unfortunately, criminal justice professionals see humanity at its worst, and there is a great need to see the best of the human spirit as well.

## Conclusion

The last five chapters of this text have discussed issues such as morality, ethics, justice, and law in the abstract. This chapter focused on the criminal justice professional and how these concepts can be applied to them. Issues faced by the criminal justice professional involve a broad array of ethical questions, and it is important to recognize them for what they are. Further, what people do is sometimes influenced by what they think they know, so criminal justice researchers must also monitor their practices and be careful to avoid letting bias and political or financial pressure influence their research. Law and policy may be set by politicians and administrators, but informal policies are always the discretion of the line staff. How they perform their job determines whether justice is a reality or an illusion. The greatest protection against corruption of power is a belief in and commitment to the democratic process and all it entails. If one desires a career in criminal justice, one must ask these questions:

Do I love the Constitution?
Do I believe in the Bill of Rights?
Do I truly believe in the sanctity and natural right of due process?

If the individual views these as impediments, nuisances, or irrelevant, then that person should not be a public servant. In the chapters to follow, we examine in greater detail the issues that criminal justice professionals face.

## Key Terms

**burnout** the state in which a worker has abandoned the mission of the organization and is just "going through the motions"

**gray areas of crimes** crimes, such as prostitution, gambling, and drug use, that do not carry the moral opprobrium of other crimes

**ideology** a set of general and abstract beliefs or assumptions about the correct or proper state of things

**policies** guidelines for action that dictate the priority of goals or objectives

**street justice** individual discretion in applying the law

**whistleblower** an employee who exposes what he or she believes to be wrongdoing or illegality in the organization

**wholesight** using one's heart as well as head to understand and present research findings.

# Review Questions

1. Distinguish between the ideologies of conservatism and liberalism in such areas as rights of the accused and corrections.
2. Why is the liberal perspective not associated with due process?
3. How do social scientists contribute to the mythology of crime and criminal justice?
4. Explain Spader's rule of law versus rule of man.
5. What are some of the issues that criminal justice professionals face?
6. What are some standards that can be applied to good leadership?
7. What advice does Souryal offer to those who desire to be good leaders?
8. What advice does Metz offer for leaders?
9. What are the necessary elements that Sherman identified for teaching ethics in criminal justice?
10. How does one avoid cynicism and burnout?

# Discussion Questions

1. What policies can be identified in the federal government's approach to drugs? To crime? To poverty?
2. What connection, if any, do you see between the ideologies described and the major political parties? Why do some people argue that any attempt to categorize or typify is wrong?
3. Why are some conservatives opposed to drug control policies that emphasize interdiction and arrest?
4. Provide some examples of "crime myths."
5. If a police officer received orders to storm a hostage situation and there was certainty that many would be killed and there were other alternatives available, should he follow superiors' orders or refuse on the basis of his moral judgment?
6. Is it better for soldiers and police officers to follow orders without question or to evaluate the morality of their orders?
7. Do you think people can learn ethics in a class or training session? Why or why not?

# Ethical Dilemmas

### *Situation 1*

You are a prosecutor trying your first case. You are thrilled with how well it is going. Every objection you make is upheld, and every objection the defense makes is overruled. The judge shakes his head affirmatively every time you make a point and scowls and makes disparaging comments about and to the defense attorney. As the trial proceeds, you begin to see that it is going so well not because of your legal expertise, but because the judge is obviously and seriously biased against the defense. You do not know if he simply does not like the defense attorney or he does this in all the trials, but you do know that he is making it extremely difficult for the jury to ignore him and, thus, is violating the due process rights of the accused. Should you be grateful for your good luck and accept an easy conviction or make a stand against the judge's actions?

## Situation 2

You are a police officer assigned to the juvenile division. For the most part you enjoy your job and believe that you have even sometimes made a difference when the juvenile has listened to you and stayed out of trouble (at least as far as you knew). One day you are told repeatedly by your captain to pick up a juvenile, even though you don't think that there is any probable cause to do so. This is the third time you have been ordered to pick him up and bring him into the station. You discover that the detectives are trying to get the juvenile to become an informant because he is related to a suspected drug dealer. Should you participate in the attempt to intimidate him or refuse?

## Situation 3

You are an undercover officer involved in a drug sting at a local high school. You are told by your drug task force supervisor to get the evidence "at any cost" even if you have to use drugs or sex to gain the trust of dealers. You are told that if you don't bring in a conviction on this case, the task force will be disbanded, and you believe that it has been very effective in helping to get drugs off the street. What should you do?

## Situation 4

As a member of the mayor's task force on juvenile crime, you have the opportunity to set crime policy for the next decade. What principles, programs, or objectives would you emphasize and advocate for in the coming discussions?

## Situation 5

Your partner has twenty-five years on the force, and you value her opinion greatly. However, you have noticed that she has become progressively more lethargic and unenthusiastic about the job. When dispatch asks for available cars, she won't let you respond. When you see accidents on the highway, she instructs you to go around the block so that you won't have to stop. Even when you receive calls, she tells you to advise dispatch that you are otherwise occupied. You believe that she has just gotten burned out and isn't performing up to the standard that you know she is capable of. What, if anything, would you do about it?

# Suggested Readings

Braswell, M., McCarthy, B., and McCarthy, B. 2005. *Justice, Crime and Ethics.* Cincinnati: Anderson.

Kappeler, V., Blumberg, M., and Potter, G. 2005. *The Mythology of Crime and Justice.* Prospect Heights, IL: Waveland.

Souryal, S. 1992/2004. *Ethics in Criminal Justice: In Search of the Truth.* Cincinnati: Anderson.

Walker, S. 2000. *Sense and Nonsense About Crime and Drugs: A Policy Guide.* Belmont, CA: Wadsworth.

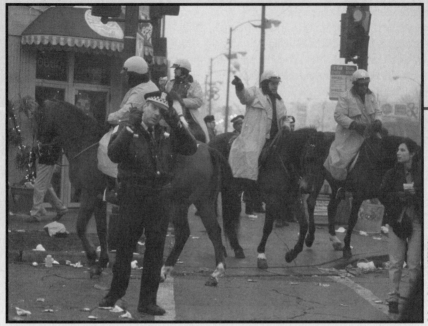

The formal code of police officers is exemplified by the International Chief of Police's Code of Ethics. The day-to-day activities and subculture of policing may not completely adhere to the formal code.

# 7

# The Police Role in Society: Crime Fighter or Public Servant?

## Key Terms

aspirational code
authority
community policing
discretion
discrimination
duty
force

group think
persuasion
power
public servants
social contract
zero-tolerance policy

# Chapter Objectives

1. Understand the role of law enforcement in a democracy, including the use of authority, power, force, and persuasion.

2. Become familiar with the differences between the formal ethics of law enforcement and the values of the police subculture.

3. Become familiar with the extent of discretion and its creation of opportunities for unethical decision making.

4. Become familiar with the issue of racial profiling, including the methodological problems present when attempting to establish its prevalence.

The images of the Rodney King beating are indelibly imprinted on the psyche of the American public. In this one violent encounter, many of the elements discussed in this chapter are reflected:

1. The "signification" of some citizens as criminal and deserving of greater police scrutiny

2. The P.O.P.O. ("pissing off a police officer") doctrine that describes how affronts to police authority (in the King case, refusing to stop) often end in unethical uses of force

3. The quick resort to violence in a department that encouraged aggressive "crime control" police performance

4. The subcultural and organizational support and/or tolerance for such violence (evidenced by the computer messages that joked about it afterward)

5. The initial easy acceptance of police and media definitions that justified such violence against some types of citizens (specifically, early reports indicating that Rodney King was a criminal and drug user, with the implication that he deserved what happened to him)

6. The presence of societal divisions based on race and socioeconomic circumstance that shaped the perception of the justice

Arguably, the Simi Valley jury acquitted the officers because white, middle-class citizens must (and do) see their police force as good; therefore, they couldn't believe that the "good guys" could be bad. The verdict for the plaintiff in the Los Angeles County civil trial was also predictable because in this world, doubt permeates public attitudes toward police—doubt that they tell the truth and doubt that they treat black and white citizens equally.

Other cases also indicate a crisis of credibility with at least some police departments in this country. The O. J. Simpson trial was as much a trial of police credibility as it was the guilt or innocence of the defendant. It indicated in a dramatic way what happens when doubt replaces trust in police performance, and when police testimony is received with suspicion rather than credence. The credibility of L.A.P.D. officers was under attack again after the Ramparts Division scandal. The highly publicized finding that some officers manufactured evidence, planted guns on suspects, and lied on the witness stand has inflicted a grievous harm to the credibility of all L.A.P.D. officers.

Other cities are not exempt. The Amadou Diallo case in New York City was moved to Albany, arguably so that the police officer defendants who shot an unarmed Diallo could obtain a fair trial. And perhaps it was fair, but African Americans in New York City, who have been subjected to what they perceive as a consistent pattern of oppression and brutality by some New York City police officers, will never be convinced of the fairness of the justice system.

# Crime Fighter or Public Servant?

We take a critical look at law enforcement in this and the next two chapters. It is important to keep in mind as we discuss issues of law enforcement ethics that the majority of officers are honest and ethical and spend their careers simply trying to do a good job. These men and women usually do not appear in newspapers or on the evening news, but they pay the price for the few who do through decreased public confidence and even public scorn. We are concerned with individual deviance in these chapters, but even more so with institutionalized tolerance of such deviance and with the perceptions, world views, and values that shape and influence such tolerance. Honest and ethical officers shirk their responsibility when they allow their fellow officers to act above the law. Even more troubling is when those officers who do expose wrongdoing are isolated and ridiculed, or receive even worse forms of peer sanctions. Why do some police—who supposedly are the law's agents—ignore and subvert the law when fellow officers are involved?

Harsh scrutiny is often directed at police actions; officers feel that they are treated unfairly by the public and the media. However, there is a very important reason for such scrutiny—the police represent the "thin blue line" between disorder and order, between the "war of all against all" and lawful order. No other criminal justice professional comes under so much constant and public scrutiny, but then no other criminal justice professional wields so much discretion in so many situations. The scrutiny is understandable when one realizes that the police are power personified. They often have the choice to arrest or not to arrest, to mediate or to charge, and in decisions to use deadly force, they even hold the power of life and death. In the Quote and Query box, the

## QUOTE and QUERY

[T]he police officer, in one split second, without the benefit of law school or judicial roles or legal appeals, acting as judge, jury and executioner may accomplish the same final result [as the death penalty].

Source: Murphy and Moran (1981: 91).

***Can you think of any other professional who holds the power of life and death?***

awesome power of police is described. Authority, force, and discretion are elements inherent in the role of a law enforcement officer.

We will approach law enforcement with an underlying premise that what drives individual decisions on the part of law enforcement officers and society's reactions to them derives from a perception of their mission. If one views police as a *crime control force*, certain presumptions follow:

1. Criminals are the "enemy" and fundamentally different from "good" people.
2. Police are the "army" that fights the enemy, using any means necessary to control, capture, and punish them.
3. "Good" people accept and understand that police are in a "war" and must be allowed deference in their decision making because they—not us—are the experts and only they "know the enemy."

If one views police as **public servants**, other presumptions follow:

1. Criminals are not a distinct group; they shop, pay taxes, have kids and parents, and often are one's next-door neighbor.
2. Police have limited ability to affect crime rates one way or the other because crime is a complex social phenomenon and, in fact, the history of law enforcement originates in order maintenance, not crime control.
3. Police as "public servants" serve *all* people, including criminals. In effect, there is no "enemy" or, if there is, then "the enemy is us."

Police perception of their role as crime fighters will lead to certain decisions in their use of force, their definition of duty, their use of deception and coercion, and other areas. Public perception of the police role as crime fighters leads to a willingness to accept certain definitions and justifications of behavior: that drug addicts are crazed, that individuals beaten must have deserved it, that all defendants must be guilty, and so on.

Typically, there is public outrage only when police accidentally violate the rights of the "good" guys instead of the "bad" guys: when a white person is the target of police brutality, when the victim of deadly force turns out to be a middle-class insurance agent, or when the evening news shows police officers beating someone. In these cases, the easy rationalization that people get what they deserve comes into question.

Alternatively, a perception of the police role as public servant implies a much more restrictive view of the use of force and the rejection of a utilitarian—"the ends (of crime control) justify the means"—decision-making approach in favor of an approach more protective of due process and equal protection. This would be a rights-based conception of social control. Law enforcement, above all, protects the rights of every citizen and—only in this way—escapes the taint of its historical role as a tool of oppression for the powerful.

This discussion is based on Herbert Packer's (1968) model of law enforcement. He described a crime control orientation as operating under the following principles:

1. Repression of criminal conduct is the most important function.
2. Failure of law enforcement means the breakdown of order.
3. Criminal process is the positive guarantor of social freedom.
4. Efficiency is a top priority.

5. Emphasis is on speed and finality.
6. A conveyor belt is the model for the system.
7. There is a presumption of guilt.

The due-process model, on the other hand, operates on these principles:

1. There is a possibility of error.
2. Finality is not a priority.
3. There is insistence on prevention and elimination of mistakes.
4. Efficiency is rejected if it involves shortcuts.
5. Protection of process is as important as protection of innocents.
6. The coercive power of the state is always subject to abuse.

The addition to Packer's original model that is proposed here is that, besides the emphasis on rights in the second model, law enforcement is also perceived as "owned" by all people, so the public servant role is foremost. These two models are better understood if we take a brief look at the history of law enforcement in this country.

Kappeler, Sluder, and Alpert (1984/1994: 41) discuss the early origins of law enforcement as a model of service. Police were involved in social service activities: They ran soup kitchens, provided lodging for indigents, and spurred moral reform movements against cigarettes and alcohol. Of course, early law enforcement personnel were also involved in social control and employed utilitarian violence—that is, they acted as the force for power holders in society and were union busters and political-machine enforcers. Such force was frequently used against immigrants and the poor.

There was also frequent graft and other forms of corruption in early police departments. Crank (2003: 70), for instance, discusses how police were involved in local political machines. They stuffed ballot boxes and coerced votes. Their graft was widely tolerated because of their meager salaries. In the 1940s the Kefauver Committee revealed that Philadelphia police overlooked prostitution, gambling, and other forms of vice in exchange for $3,000 to $4,000 a month per precinct (Fogelson, 1977: 172).

The move toward police "professionalism," starting in the 1920s, was spurred by several factors, one of which was to improve the image of police as *objective* enforcers of the law rather than enforcers for whoever happened to be in power. In effect, there was a real or perceived shift of police loyalty from political bosses to the law itself (Kappeler et al., 1994: 49; Fogelson, 1977). Part of this transformation involved the idea that police were crime fighters—professional soldiers in the war on crime—a concept that implies objectivity, professional expertise, and specialized training. This role deemphasized the social service role and ultimately led to policing characterized by detachment from the community being policed instead of integration in that community. In this new role, police were proactive, rather than simply reactive to public demands (Payne, 2002; Crank and Caldero, 2000).

Even though the professionalism (crime fighter) model has been well established for more than fifty years, we can see the legacy of both the early political enforcer role and the public service role. The political enforcer role is present when law enforcement is involved in responding to strikes or labor disputes. Its objectives today do not include strike busting; however, some might argue this point. The clearest recent example of the strike-busting image, perhaps, was in December 1999, when massive protests against the World Trade Organization set off the Seattle riots. Police were both praised for their restraint and criticized for excessive violence in their use of rubber bullets, tear gas, and concussion grenades to disperse large groups of protesters and bystanders. The handling of the protests was described as swings of underreaction, which allowed protesters to damage downtown businesses, and overreaction, which enveloped bystanders and office workers in the techniques of crowd dispersal. The other role—that of public service—is represented, of course, in the community policing trend.

## *Community Policing*

The early role of social service can be seen resurrected in the **community policing** movement, which involves having officers develop closer relationships with community leaders to help them solve some of the social problems that are believed to be associated with the development of disorder and lead to crime. Police officers may be involved in cleaning up parks, getting the city to raze abandoned houses, cleaning up graffiti, help-ing to start youth programs, and so on. The elements of community policing include the following:

1. A move away from a position of anonymity to direct engagement with the community, which will give officers greater information about neighborhood problems.
2. Freeing the officer from emergency response to engage in pro-active crime prevention.
3. More visible operations that increase police accountability.
4. Decentralized operations that lead to greater familiarity with specific neigh-borhoods.
5. Encouraging officers to see citizens as partners.
6. Moving decision-making and discretion downward to patrol officers who know the neighborhood best.
7. Encouraging citizens to take more initiative in preventing and solving crimes. (National Institute of Justice, 1992: 3)

Patrol officers' resistance to community policing models may make sense if one views neighborhood policing as trading in the "crime fighter" role for a much less esteemed "social worker" role. However, even those who resisted the community polic-ing model admitted that the role of law enforcement has always included community relations and community service, or what some have called "order maintenance."

Schafer (2002) describes the history and philosophy of community policing with a focus on its potential for corruption, although he notes that there is no evidence to indicate that community policing efforts are associated with more police corruption than traditional service delivery. He presents earlier inventories of what community policing involves (2002: 200):

1. A different philosophy and structure of policing
2. Problem-oriented approach to policing
3. Working with the community
4. Developing trust with the community

5. Creativity and innovation
6. A broader focus than just crime control
7. A geographic focus on one neighborhood or community

Schafer (2002) then presents some potential issues for community policing strategies as they relate to corruption. Gratuities may be more of an issue for officers who are expected to create and maintain close ties to the community. Gratuities then may create the slippery-slope slide into more serious forms of misconduct. Officers may be exposed to wider corruption among city employees, such as building inspectors, and, by such exposure, have a harder time withstanding minor transgressions themselves.

In addition to those issues, close relationships with the community blur the lines between good and bad people, and the police officer's discretion regarding when to enforce the law is compromised by personal relationships. Finally, increased freedom and autonomy and decreased supervision provide greater opportunity for misconduct.

Schafer also notes that because community policing seems to reduce cynicism and burnout, and reduces the anonymity of individual police officers, it may act as an insulator against misconduct. Further, because officers share a closer relationship with community members, the possibility of brutality may be reduced. However, there are no data to indicate that this is the case.

It is important to understand that both the crime fighter and public servant role have the potential and capacity for wrongdoing. The professional crime fighter may trample rights in the interest of efficiency in catching criminals, and community police officers may be too eager to do the bidding of community members in controlling those who upset the "order" of the community (by overenforcement of noise ordinances or loitering laws). The point cannot be overemphasized that police officers have a type of power that very few groups possess. In the next section we will more carefully examine police power.

# Authority and Power

Klockars (1984) describes police control as comprising the following elements: authority, power, persuasion, and force.

1. **Authority** is the unquestionable entitlement to be obeyed that comes from fulfilling a specific role. Neither persuasion nor force is needed to achieve domination when one possesses authority. Police officers are usually obeyed simply when they tell a citizen to do something. We do what they tell us because of their uniform. A teacher has a type of authority in the classroom, and parents have authority over their own children (but not over other people's children).

2. **Power** is similar to authority in that it is inherent in the role, and the individual merely draws upon it, but it is different from authority in that power implies that there might be resistance to overcome. It also implies that if there is resistance, then it will be crushed—power is the means to achieve domination. The baton, the handcuffs, and the power of arrest symbolize police power.

3. **Persuasion** may also be used in response to resistance but seeks to overcome it "by mobilizing signs, symbols, words, and arguments that induce in the mind of the person persuaded the belief that he or she ought to comply." Although those who have power don't need to use persuasion, they often do, in order to avoid the use of force.

4. **Force** is different from the previous three means of control in that it is physical, whereas the other three are exercised through mental domination and control. When force is used, "the will of the person coerced is irrelevant" (Klockars, 1984: 532). Police show their ability to use force when they use their arrest power, or when they physically restrain and subdue an individual. Force is ultimately behind every position of authority.

Police exercise four different types of domination, from unquestioned authority to physical force. Why does law enforcement have the right to employ these types of control? "We give it to them" is the easy answer. Police power is a governmental right invested in federal, state, and local law enforcement agencies. It means that these organizations, unlike almost any other except perhaps the military, have the right to control citizens' movements to the point of using physical and even deadly force to do so.

Cohen and Feldberg (1991) develop a careful analysis of and justification for police power and propose that it stems from the **social contract**. As discussed in an earlier chapter, Thomas Hobbes (1588–1679) and John Locke (1632–1704) created the concept of the social contract to explain why people have given up liberties in civilized societies. According to this theory, each citizen gives up complete liberty in return for societal protection against others. Complete freedom is given up in return for guaranteed protection. Police power is part of this *quid pro quo*—we give the police power to protect us, but we also recognize that this power can be used against us.

There are corollary principles to this general idea. First, each of us should be able to feel protected. If not, then we are not gaining anything from the social contract and may decide to renegotiate the contract by regaining some of the liberties given up. For instance, vigilante movements arise when the populace feels that formal agents of social control do not protect them.

Second, because the deprivations of freedoms are limited to those necessary to ensure protection against others, police power is circumscribed to what is necessary to meet the agreed-upon purpose. If police exceed this threshold, then the public rightly objects.

Third, police ethics are inextricably linked to their purpose. If the social contract is the basis of their power, it is also the basis of their ethics.

Cohen and Feldberg (1991) propose five ethical standards that can be derived from the social contract:

- fair access
- public trust
- safety and security
- teamwork
- objectivity

Delattre (1989b) approaches police authority and power from a slightly different point of view. Delattre asserts that police, as public servants, need those qualities one desires in any public servant. He quotes James Madison, who stated that essential to any public servant are these characteristics:

- wisdom
- good character
- balanced perception
- integrity

Only if the person entrusted with public power has these qualities can we be assured that there will be no abuse of such authority and power: "Granting authority without expecting public servants to live up to it would be unfair to everyone they are expected to serve" (Delattre, 1989b: 79). In this proposition, the right to authority lies in the character of the person—if one has those virtues necessary to be a public servant, one has the right to use the authority invested in the role; if one does not have those virtues, then one should not be in that position to begin with.

Is it simply a matter of individual character, or can the organization train officers to use their authority ethically and wisely? How can the organization maximize the possibility of ethical action and minimize any abuses in the exercise of the four types of control? Formal codes of ethics for police agencies attempt to provide such guidance.

## Formal Ethics for Police Officers

It is not uncommon to have a value system or a code of ethics to educate and guide the behavior of those who work within an organization; some organizations have both. An organizational value system identifies the mission and the important objectives of the organization. Just as individual values influence one's ethics, an organizational value system influences the ethics of the organization's members. For example, if a person's highest value is wealth, integrity may be sacrificed to achieve it; in a similar way, if the value system of an organization promotes profits over all else, customer satisfaction and quality may be sacrificed. A police department with a value system emphasizing crime control may allocate resources differently from one with a value system promoting community-oriented policing. Officers in these two departments may be rewarded differently, and the formal culture of the agency will encourage different behavior patterns.

A code of ethics is more specific to the behavior of the individual officer. A professional code of ethics addresses the unique issues and discretionary practices of that profession. Davis (1991) explains that there are three distinct kinds of codes:

1. an aspiration or ideal describing the perfect professional
2. principles or guidelines that relate to the value system of the organization
3. mandatory rules of conduct that can serve as the basis of discipline

The code of ethics promulgated by the International Association of Chiefs of Police, which will be discussed shortly, is the first kind of code. It is an aspiration or ideal that describes the perfect police officer. All police departments also have an oath of office that is a shorthand version of the value system or code of ethics. For instance, in a typical oath of office, duties are described that relate to service to the community and the sacred trust that it entails for the officer.

## The Law Enforcement Code of Ethics

The International Association of Chiefs of Police promulgated the Law Enforcement Code of Ethics and the Canons of Police Ethics (see the appendix to this chapter), and many departments have used these or adapted them to their own situations. Even though the code has been widely adopted, there is some question as to its relevance to individual police officers (Felkenes, 1984; Johnson and Copus, 1981: 59–65).

One argument is that the code specifies such perfect behavior that it is irrelevant to the realities of most officers. The wide disparity between the code and actual behavior is detrimental to the validity and credibility of the code. For instance, Davis, referring to the code provision "I will never act officiously or permit personal feelings, prejudices, animosities or friendships to influence my decisions," writes that "any officer who takes this mandatory language seriously will quickly learn that he cannot do what the code seems to require. He will then either have to quit the force or consign its mandates to Code Heaven" (Davis, 1991: 18). Others argue that the code is vague, confusing, and impractical (Felkenes, 1984: 212).

The opposing argument is that the code is valuable specifically because it provides an ideal for officers to aspire to. The code is a goal to work toward, not a descriptive average of existing behavior. It would be hard to be proud of a professional code that instructed an officer

- to be unbiased and objective *unless* there were extenuating personal reasons
- to be courageous *unless* personal danger were involved
- to be honest in thought and deed *unless* to do so went against personal interest

Because the code describes the highest standard of policing, all officers can improve because no officer is perfect. However, Davis (1991) contends that an **aspirational code** cannot be used to judge or discipline behavior that falls short of it. This comment is no doubt true; departmental policies and rulebooks, which are more objective and enforceable, better serve discipline systems. A code is far more valuable as a motivator than as a discipline device, a symbol rather than a stick. There are at least four major themes in the International Chiefs of Police code and many others:

1. The principle of justice or *fairness* is the single most dominant theme in the law enforcement code. Police officers must uphold the law regardless of the offender's identity. They must not single out special groups for different treatment. Police officers must not use their authority and power to take advantage, either for personal profit or professional goals. They must avoid gratuities because these give the appearance of special treatment.
2. A second theme is that of *service*. Police officers exist to serve the community, and their role appropriately and essentially concerns this idea. Public service involves checking on the elderly, helping victims, and, in the community service model, taking a broad approach to service by helping the community deal with problems such as broken street lights and dilapidated buildings.

3. Still another theme is the *importance of the law*. Police are protectors of the Constitution and must not go beyond it or substitute rules of their own. Because the law is so important, police not only must be concerned with lawbreakers, but also their own behavior must be totally within the bounds set for them by the law. In investigation, capture, and collection of evidence, their conduct must conform to the dictates of law.

4. The final theme is one of *personal conduct*. Police, at all times, must uphold a standard of behavior consistent with their public position. This involves a higher standard of behavior in their professional and personal lives than that expected from the general public. "Conduct unbecoming" is one of the most often cited discipline infractions and can include everything from committing a crime to having an affair or being drunk in public. (Bossard, 1981: 31)

The emphasis on service, justice for all groups, and higher standards for police behavior is consistent with the *public servant paradigm* more so than the *crime fighter paradigm*. In fact, this may be why the code is perceived as vague and confusing, for the code promotes a public servant ideal, but police are, for the most part, taught and rewarded for actions consistent with the crime fighter role.

Why is professional ethics important to law enforcement? First of all, ethics contributes to the image of law enforcement as a profession. Sykes (1989) writes that a profession includes the following:

- a body of specialized, internationally recognized knowledge
- a pre-professional education and continuing education
- legal autonomy to exercise discretionary judgment
- lateral movement
- authorized self-regulation

According to some authors, because law enforcement is missing certain of these elements, it cannot be defined as a profession.

Whether or not officers have "legal autonomy to exercise discretionary judgment" is perhaps the most important debate in this discussion. One argument is that officers have much less discretion to make decisions than is thought because they must abide by the law; however, others point out that officers are allowed the latitude to decide whether to write tickets and whether to handle neighbor disputes with formal arrest or informal threat. Sykes (1989) argues that because law enforcement is an example of a classic bureaucratic organization, with rules, supervisors, and many lines of authority, these reduce discretion, so the elements necessary to meet a definition of a profession are missing. An alternative argument is that the nature of law enforcement involves problem solving: Every situation is unique and must be handled differently, and "cookbook" approaches to law enforcement rarely work. These characteristics support the concept of the field as a profession.

One might also suspect that the discussion holds more interest for academics than for the officer on the street. Whatever one calls the job, it requires a certain set of skills and some amount of discretion. Officers make decisions regarding the calls they respond to in very different ways. Ideally, a set of ethics will help the officer make these decisions in a lawful, humane, and fair manner.

A code of ethics also helps engender self-respect in individual officers; pride comes from knowing that one has conducted oneself in a proper and appropriate manner. Further, a code of ethics contributes to mutual respect among police officers and helps in the development of an *esprit de corps* and common goals. Agreement on methods, means, and aims is important to these feelings. As with any profession, an agreed-upon code of ethics is a unifying element. A code can help define law enforcement as a profession, for it indicates a willingness to uphold certain standards of behavior and promotes the goal of public service, an essential element of any profession.

# The Police Subculture

Through a number of sources an image of the police and the police value system emerges that is very different from the value system prescribed by formal ethics. Research has found police officers to be generally cynical, isolated, alienated, defensive, distrustful, dogmatic, and authoritarian, and as having a poor self-image (Johnson and Copus, 1981: 52).

Scheingold (1984) describes the factors that lead to the extreme nature of the police subculture:

- Police typically form a homogenous social group.
- They have a uniquely stressful work environment.
- They participate in a basically closed social system.

Historically, police in the United States have come from the white middle and lower classes; they are similar racially, culturally, and economically. Because of these similarities, police feel themselves to be more similar to one another than to the public they encounter as a part of their job. Homogenous social groups lead to **group think**, the tendency for everyone to agree with the group values or beliefs, arguably because those that don't will be ostracized.

Police are further set apart by their work life. The job of a police officer entails a great deal of stress caused by danger and unpleasant experiences. This results in the feeling that police are special and different from everyone else. Police also have unusual working hours and experience some degree of social stigma; thus, their social life tends to be largely involved with other police officers. This leads to closed viewpoints and legitimization of subcultural values (Scheingold, 1984: 97–100).

## *Themes and Value Systems*

Van Maanen (1978), in an early exploration of the police culture, discussed how police operate under a typology of the people with whom they come into contact. The individual who does not recognize their authority is "the a\*\*hole." Other names for this type of person include creep, animal, mope, rough, jerk-off, clown, or wise-guy, but the idea is the same—that some individuals are troublemakers, not necessarily because they have broken the law, but rather because they do not recognize police authority (1978: 227). Others have also identified the same concept in terms such as bad guy, punk, idiot, knucklehead, terrorist, or predator (Herbert, 1996).

**QUOTE and QUERY**

Some guys need a beating. In the street or the back of the precinct, there's a guy who needs a beating. And you got to do it. If you don't do it, the next situation that a cop runs into this character, it's going to be bad. It's hard for people to understand or believe that. But the fact of the matter is, if this guy runs into a cop, gets into a fist-fight and really beats the shit out of him, he believes he can beat up all cops, if you arrest him without working him out. He's got to know that the next time he does this, he's going to get his ass kicked in. So I have no problem with that. Neither did any cop I've ever known have any problem with that. As long as you don't do it in public, as long as the guy really needs it, and as long as you don't carry it too far. . . .

Source: M. Baker, *Cops* (New York: Pocket Books, 1985): 286. Reprinted with permission of Simon & Schuster from *Cops: Their Lives in Their Own Words* by Mark Baker. Copyright © 1985 by Mark Baker.

*What part of the formal code justifies this principle? Which element of the "informal code" justifies it? Do you believe "some guys need a beating"?*

Herbert further points out the problem whereby officers are so quick to identify these types of individuals as threats to safety that they may overgeneralize and identify, for instance, everyone living in a neighborhood in the same way.

Van Maanen (1978: 226) observed that "certain classes in society—for example, the young, the black, the militant, the homosexual—are . . . 'fixed' by the police as a sort of permanent a\*\*hole grouping." He argued that the professionalism movement of law enforcement might widen the distance between the police and the community they served, and further allow them to be "moral entrepreneurs" who were even more likely to define some groups as "bad" simply because they did not conform to some preconceived standards of behavior (1978: 236).

Sherman (1982: 10–19) also has described some common themes running through police attitudes. First, loyalty to colleagues is essential; second, the public, or most of it, is the enemy (echoing, to some extent, van Maanen's research). Further, he explains that the values of police officers include the use of force, discretion, and a protective use of the truth. Sherman's description of the police subculture is more fully described in Box 7-1, "Police Values."

Scheingold (1984) has emphasized three dominant characteristics of the police subculture:

1. *Cynicism.* Police view all citizens with suspicion. Everyone is a possible problem, but especially those who fit a type, specifically van Maanen's "a\*\*hole." Recruits learn this way of looking at others from older officers. Cynicism spills over to their relations with everyone, for they have found that friends expect favors and special treatment, and police routinely witness negative behavior from almost all citizens. Their work life leads them to the conclusion that all people are weak, corrupt, and/or dangerous.

**BOX 7-1  Police Values**

1. **Discretion A:** Decisions about whether to enforce the law, in any but the most serious cases, should be guided by both what the law says and who the suspect is. Attitude, demeanor, cooperativeness, and even race, age and social class are all important considerations in deciding how to treat people generally, and whether or not to arrest suspects in particular.

2. **Discretion B:** Disrespect for police authority is a serious offense that should always be punished with an arrest or the use of force. The offense known as "contempt of cop" or P.O.P.O. (pissing off a police officer) cannot be ignored. Even when the party has committed no violation of the law, a police officer should find a safe way to impose punishment, including an arrest on fake charges.

3. **Force:** Police officers should never hesitate to use physical or deadly force against people who "deserve it," or where it can be an effective way of solving a crime. Only the potential punishments by superior officers, civil litigation, citizen complaints, and so forth should limit the use of force when the situation calls for it. When you can get away with it, use all the force that society should use on people like that—force and punishment which bleeding-heart judges are too soft to impose.

4. **Due Process:** Due process is only a means of protecting criminals at the expense of the law abiding and should be ignored whenever it is safe to do so. Illegal searches and wiretaps, interrogation without advising suspects of their Miranda rights, and if need be (as in the much admired movie, *Dirty Harry*), even physical pain to coerce a confession are all acceptable methods for accomplishing the goal the public wants the police to accomplish: fighting crime. The rules against doing those things merely handcuff the police, making it more difficult for them to do their job.

5. **Truth:** Lying and deception are an essential part of the police job, and even perjury should be used if it is necessary to protect yourself or get a conviction on a "bad guy." Violations of due process cannot be admitted to prosecutors or in court, so perjury (in the serious five per cent of cases that ever go to trial) is necessary and therefore proper. Lying to drug pushers about wanting to buy drugs, to prostitutes about wanting to buy sex, or to congressmen about wanting to buy influence is the only way, and therefore a proper way, to investigate these crimes without victims. Deceiving muggers into thinking you are an easy mark and deceiving burglars into thinking you are a fence are proper because there are not many other ways of catching predatory criminals in the act.

6. **Time:** You cannot go fast enough to chase a car thief or traffic violator, nor slow enough to get to a "garbage" call; and when there are no calls for service, your time is your own. Hot pursuits are necessary because anyone who tries to escape from the police is challenging police authority, no matter how trivial the initial offense. But calls to nonserious or social-work problems like domestic

disputes or kids making noise are unimportant, so you can stop to get coffee on the way or even stop at the cleaner's if you like. And when there are no calls, you can sleep, visit friends, study, or do anything else you can get away with, especially on the midnight shift, when you can get away with a lot.

7. **Rewards:** Police do very dangerous work for low wages, so it is proper to take any extra rewards the public want to give them, like free meals, Christmas gifts, or even regular monthly payments (in some cities) for special treatment. The general rule is: Take any reward that doesn't change what you would do anyway, such as eating a meal, but don't take money that would affect your job, like not giving traffic tickets. In many cities, however, especially in the recent past, the rule has been to take even those rewards that do affect your decisions, as long as they are related only to minor offenses—traffic, gambling, prostitution, but not murder.

8. **Loyalty:** The paramount duty is to protect your fellow officers at all costs, as they would protect you, even though you may have to risk your own career or your own life to do it. If your colleagues make a mistake, take a bribe, seriously hurt somebody illegally, or get into other kinds of trouble, you should do everything you can to protect them in the ensuing investigation. If your colleagues are routinely breaking rules, you should never tell supervisors, reporters, or outside investigators about it. If you don't like it, quit—or get transferred to the police academy. But never, ever, blow the whistle.

SOURCE: From L. Sherman, "Learning Police Ethics." *Criminal Justice Ethics* 1(1) (1982): 10–19. Copyright 1982 by the John Jay College of Criminal Justice. Reprinted by permission.

2. *Use of force.* The police subculture embraces force for all situations wherein a threat is perceived. Threats may be interpreted as threats against the officer's authority rather than the physical person, so anyone with an "attitude problem" is thought to deserve a lesson in humility. Force is both expressive and instrumental. It is a clear symbol of the police officer's authority and legitimate dominance in any interaction with the public, and it is also believed to be the most effective method of control. It cuts across all social and economic barriers and is the most effective tool for keeping people in line and getting them to do what is required without argument.

3. *Police as victims.* This refers to the perception that police are victims of public misunderstanding and scorn, of low wages and vindictive administrators. This feeling of victimization sets police apart from others and rationalizes a different set of rules for them. (Scheingold, 1984: 100–104)

Herbert (1996) discusses six "normative orders" of policing:

- law
- bureaucratic control
- adventure/machismo

- safety
- competence
- morality

The last concept, morality, is related to the idea that police draw on moral definitions to justify their actions. Herbert's observational study allowed him to draw on field experiences to present examples whereby officers would continually be told and express the view that they were the "good guys" against the "evil out there." This "overarching moralism" identifies a goal of crime prevention that is unattainable. What happens is an uneasy tension between their idea that they are the good guys and the need to use coercion. He describes a situation where police officers made the comment that "we are the police . . . the people you call when you need help and protection" and then, very soon after that, threatened to "thump [the girlfriend of a suspect they were searching for] so hard it will hurt to sit down." The idea here is that the use of coercion is fundamentally inconsistent with their role as good guys unless they can label the target as fundamentally evil.

Crank (1998) discusses a number of "themes" of policing. These themes are not values *per se* but rather elements of police work and/or shared perceptions of police officers:

- coercive territorial control
- force
- illicit coercion
- importance of guns
- suspicion
- danger
- uncertainty
- "maintaining the edge"
- solidarity
- masculinity
- excitement and crime

Crank argues that police learn how to be criminals from expertise gained through policing.

Zhao, He, and Lovrich (1998) examined police officers' values compared to those of the general population. They describe a value as an "enduring belief that a specific mode of conduct or end-state of existence is personally or socially preferable" (1998: 23), and they report that individuals' values (specifically freedom and equality) have been shown to affect their political preferences. They found that police exhibited similar value preferences across time (comparing 1961 to 1997) and across place (comparing Tacoma, Washington, to Spokane, Washington). In their study, they found police rated equality significantly lower than the general public and, in general, were more conservative in their viewpoint than the general public. Among police, the only significant associations were age and "mature love" (older officers rated this value higher), education and freedom (more educated officers rated freedom higher), education and national security and pleasure (more educated officers rated these values lower), and gender and happiness (women rated this value higher than their male counterparts did).

Crank and Caldero (2000) also discuss the values of police. They report on other research which shows that police officers place less emphasis on independence and more emphasis on obedience.

## The Cop Code

Many authors present versions of the informal "code of conduct" that new officers are taught through informal socialization. Muir (1977: 191) described some elements of the informal police code:

"You cover your men: don't let any officer take a job alone."
"Keep a cool head."
"Don't backdoor it" (a prohibition against certain gratuities).

Reuss-Ianni (1983: 14) presents a very inclusive list:

Watch out for your partner first and then the rest of the guys working that tour.
Don't give up another cop.
Show balls.
Be aggressive when you have to, but don't be too eager.
Don't get involved in anything in another guy's sector.
Hold up your end of the work.
If you get caught off base, don't implicate anybody else.
Make sure the other guys know if another cop is dangerous or "crazy."
Don't trust a new guy until you have checked him out.
Don't tell anybody else more than they have to know.
Don't talk too much or too little.
Don't leave work for the next tour.

Code rules specific toward management include these:

Protect your ass.
Don't make waves.
Don't give them too much activity.
Keep out of the way of any boss from outside your precinct.
Don't look for favors just for yourself.
Don't take on the patrol sergeant by yourself.
Know your bosses.
Don't do the bosses' work for them.
Don't trust bosses to look out for your interest.

## A Different Culture?

What is obvious is that the informal code is different from the formal code of policing. Officers seem to uphold an oppositional subculture to management and share an informal code that directly contradicts some of the principles of the formal code as presented by the International Chiefs of Police.

Scheingold (1984: 97) describes the police subculture as no more than an extreme of the dominant U.S. culture; it closely resembles a conservative political perspective:

> If the police subculture is ultimately shaped by American cultural values, does it really make sense to talk about a separate subculture among American police officers? My answer is that the police subculture is not so much separate as an *in extremis* version of the underlying American culture. When Americans in general become preoccupied with crime, we also move in punitive directions, but our preoccupation with crime tends to be abstract and episodic. . . . The real difference between police officers and the rest of us is that coping with crime is their full-time job.

In other words, we all agree with certain elements of the police value system; if the general public is less extreme in its views, it is only because we have not had a steady diet of dealing with crime and criminal behavior as have the police. Furthermore, citizens are not too upset when the civil rights of "criminal types" are violated, only when police misbehavior is directed at "good" people.

The subculture and the values described above may be breaking down among police departments today. Several factors contribute to the possible weakening of the subculture:

1. *Increasing diversity* of police recruits has eliminated the social homogeneity of the work force. Many diverse groups are now represented in police departments, including African Americans, Hispanics, women, and the college-educated, even if only in token numbers. These different groups bring elements of their own cultural backgrounds and value systems into the police environment.
2. *Police unions* with their increasing power formalize relationships between the line staff and the administration, and subcultural methods for coping with perceived administrative unfairness are becoming more formal rather than informal.
3. *Civil litigation* has increased the risk of covering for another officer. Although police officers may lie to Internal Affairs or even on a witness stand to save a fellow officer from sanctions, they may be less likely to do so when large monetary damages may be leveled against them because of negligence and perjury.

It is also no doubt the case that the subculture of police varies from department to department. Size, regional differences, and management may influence the strength of the subculture.

In a more recent but incomplete measurement of police subculture, Paoline, Myers, and Worden (2000) found that the police subculture is by no means monolithic. Using responses from officers in a survey research project, they were able to measure seven outlooks that they believed were associated with the informal subculture described in the literature:

- orientation to law enforcement
- orientation to order maintenance
- orientation to community policing
- aggressiveness

- selectivity
- distrust of citizens
- perceptions of citizen cooperation

They found that there was substantial variation among the officers and differences in their cultural views. Further, there were no factors that emerged as strong predictors of officers' values. There were very weak and inconsistent associations between sex and cultural values. There were some expected associations found between race and cultural values, with minority officers having more positive orientations toward order mainte- nance and community policing concepts than white officers; however, the associations were not strong. The association between aggressive patrol and race was stronger, with minority officers displaying less support for aggressive patrol than white officers. In gen- eral, most of the associations were of small magnitude. The authors conclude that the police culture may be less uniform and powerful than other researchers have portrayed. On the other hand, they admit that their measures did not directly or comprehensively measure the aspects of the police culture as described.

It is still safe to say that the police, like any occupational group, maintain some type of informal subterranean value system that guides and provides a rationale for decision making. This value system may be more influential than the police rulebook or code of ethics.

# Discretion, Duty, and Discrimination

**Discretion** can be defined as the ability to choose between two or more courses of behavior. Law enforcement professionals have a great deal of discretion regarding when to enforce a law, how to enforce it, how to handle disputes, when to use force, and so on. Every day is filled with decisions—some minor, some major. **Duty** can be defined as the responsibilities that are attached to a specific role. In the case of police officers, there are a myriad of duties, both minor and major, that are attached to their role. However, there is a great deal of individual variation in how officers perceive their duty. Discretion allows officers to choose different courses of action, depending on how they perceive their duty. **Discrimination** occurs when discretion allows a decision maker to treat a group or individual differently from others for no justifi- able reason.

## *Discretion*

Discretion is by no means limited to law enforcement. In the subsequent chapters, we will see that discretion is an important element in the role of other criminal justice practitioners and plays a part in the creation of ethical dilemmas for them as well. Dis- cretion in criminal justice has been attacked as contributing to injustice. McAnany (1981) chronicles disillusionment with discretion, citing such works as Davis's *Discre- tionary Justice* (1973) and the American Friends Service Committee's *Struggle for Justice* (1971). An argument might be made that solutions that attempt to establish guidelines for discretion are unsatisfactory because the suggested rules and standards either limit decision making to mechanistic applications of given rules or provide only rhetorical ideals with little or no enforcement capability.

Discretion is a necessary element in law enforcement, but the need for discretion also leads to a greater dependence on individual ethical codes in place of rules and laws. Patrol officers are the most visible members of the police force and have a duty to patrol, monitor, and intervene in matters of crime, conflict, accident, and welfare. Investigators are primarily concerned with collecting evidence to be used in court. The ethical decisions that these two groups encounter are sometimes different. Patrol officers may have to make decisions relevant to defining crime and initiating the formal legal process. Undercover officers must make decisions regarding informants, deception, and target selection. Managers and administrators have discretion in their decision-making role over their subordinates (Bossard, 1981: 25; Cohen, 1985). We should also note that because most police departments in this country are small, many officers fulfill two or more functions, so their discretion crosses the boundaries designated above.

Patrol officers possess a great deal of discretion in defining criminal behavior and deciding what to do about it. When police stop people for minor traffic violations, they can write tickets or give warnings. When they pick up teenagers for drinking or other delinquent acts, they can bring them in for formal processing or take them home. After stopping a fight on the street, they can arrest both parties or allow the combatants to work out their problems. In many day-to-day decisions, police hold a great deal of decision-making power over people's lives because of their power to decide when to enforce the law.

One study found that police do not make arrests in 43 percent of all felony cases and 52 percent of all misdemeanor cases (Williams, 1984: 4). The amount of discretion and how it is used depend on the style of policing characteristic of a certain area. For instance,

1. The *legalistic* style of policing is described as the least amenable to discretionary enforcement.
2. The *watchman* style describes police who define situations as threatening or serious depending on the groups or individuals involved, and act accordingly.
3. The *caretaker* style treats citizens differently, depending on their relative power and position in society. (Wilson, 1976)

Brown (1981: 224) describes four types of police officers, each with a different application of discretion:

1. *Old style crime fighters* are concerned only with action that might be considered crime control.
2. *Clean beat officers* seek to control all behavior in their jurisdiction.
3. *Service style officers* emphasize public order and peace officer tasks.
4. *Professional style officers* are the epitome of bureaucratic, by-the-book policing.

Muir describes these four types:

1. the *professional*, who balances coercion with compassion
2. the *reciprocating officer*, who allows citizens to solve problems and may engage in deals to keep the peace

3. the *enforcer*, who uses coercion exclusively
4. the *avoider*, who either cannot handle the power he or she must use or fears it and so avoids situations where he or she may be challenged (Muir, 1977: 145)

Each of these descriptions is obviously more detailed than our binary description of the crime control versus public servant model. However, all of these descriptions illustrate that different beliefs about their mission and their role in society will affect officers' decisions. The nature of policing necessarily involves some amount of discretion.

Cohen (1985, 1983) describes discretion as balancing justice for the individual against justice for the group and points out that full enforcement would be unfair at times to individuals. Even courts have seemed to support police discretion over full enforcement (Williams, 1984: 26). However, this opens the door for unethical decisions. The power to make a decision regarding arrest creates the power to make that decision using unethical criteria, such as not arresting someone in return for a bribe (Brown, 1981: 160).

The Commission on Accreditation for Law Enforcement Agencies promulgates standards, and one of the standards states that law enforcement agencies should have "A written directive [that] defines the authority, guidelines, and circumstances where sworn personnel may exercise alternatives to arrest . . ." (CALEA, 1994). Besides standard directives, perhaps another effective way to encourage using discretion in an ethical manner is to delineate ethical versus unethical criteria for decision making. For example, the decision to ticket a motorist stopped for speeding or to let him or her go with a warning can be made using ethical or unethical criteria. Ethical criteria might include the number of miles over the speed limit, the amount of danger posed by the speeding (school zone or open road?), the excuse used (emergency or late to work?), and probably others. Unethical criteria might include sexual attraction (or not), the identity of the motorist (fellow police officer, political figure, entertainment figure), the race of the motorist, the offer of a bribe, and so on. Other factors are less clear: Is the fact of a quota an ethical or unethical criterion? What about attitude? Many officers explain that a person might get a ticket, even for a minor violation, if she or he displays a hostile or unrepentant attitude. Is this merely an egoistic use of power on the part of an officer or a utilitarian use of the ticket as a tool for social learning? After all, if the individual does not display any remorse, there is no assurance that the person won't commit the same violation as soon as the officer is out of sight.

## Above the Law?

Many officers defend the use of professional courtesy to other officers stopped for speeding. Justifications for different treatment are diverse and creative. For instance, some honest justifications are purely egoistic: "If I do it for him, he will do it for me one day." Other justifications are under the guise of utilitarianism: "It's best for all of us not to get tickets, and the public isn't hurt because we are trained to drive faster." If the officer would let another person go with a warning in the same situation, it is not an unethical use of discretion. However, if *every other person* would have received a ticket, but the officer did not issue one only because the motorist was a fellow officer, then that is a violation of the code of ethics ("enforce the law . . . without fear or favor"). It is a violation of deontological universalism as well as utilitarianism: Under

**IN THE NEWS** **"Sorry, No Breaks!"**

According to the *New York Times* (December 8, 1995), Game Warden Joseph Dedrick of Caroline County, Virginia, is not the type of person to let someone go with a simple warning. Dedrick, on his day off (November 21), apparently went quail hunting and was lucky enough to bag one bird. Upon telling a friend about it, though, he was informed that quail season did not open until November 27, and the friend produced a game department brochure as proof. Mr. Dedrick, who has been a game warden for twenty-seven years, immediately called his lieutenant and said, "We're going to have to get a warrant on me." Dedrick charged himself with a misdemeanor (hunting out of season), for which a judge could fine him $25 to $1,000.

Source: "Sorry, No Breaks!" *The Ethics Roll Call* 3(1) (1996): 2. Used by permission of the Southwestern Law Enforcement Institute.

*Do you think that Dedrick was "overly technical" in issuing himself a ticket? What should his punishment be?*

deontological ethics, it is the officer's duty to enforce the law; under utilitarianism, the fact that the speeding officer can cause an accident just as easily as a civilian motorist means that the utility for society is greater if the ticket is issued, for it might make the officer slow down. (See In the News: "Sorry, No Breaks!" for a unique example of zero favoritism.)

## Discretion and Dilemmas

Discretion also comes into play when the officer is faced with situations with no good solutions. Many officers agonize over family disturbance calls where there are allegations of abuse, or when one family member wants the police to remove another family member; other calls involve elderly persons who want police to do something about the "hoodlums" in the neighborhood, homeless people with small children who are turned away from full shelters, and victims of crime who are left without sufficient resources with which to survive. In response to all of these calls, officers must decide what course of action to take and can decide to do nothing at all.

Most ethical dilemmas that police officers face derive from their powers of discretion. These ethical dilemmas are part and parcel of the job. Muir describes moral dilemmas of the police officer as frequent and unavoidable, not academic, always unpopular with some groups, usually resolved quickly, dealt with alone, and involving complex criteria (Muir, 1977: 211).

## *Discretion and Duty*

How would one characterize the duties of a police officer? Is enforcing the law the only duty of an officer? It is now clearly established that most of police work is *order maintenance*. Police are called into situations that do not involve crime control and are often termed social-work calls. Many police officers do not feel that these are legitimate calls for their time and either give them superficial attention or do not respond at all. Brown calls the skill that police develop in avoiding these calls *engineering* (Brown, 1981: 142).

Police may respond to a domestic dispute and find a wife not seriously injured, but bruised, upset, and without money or resources to help herself or her children. The officer may ascertain that departmental policy or law does not dictate any action and that the woman is afraid to press charges, so the officer can leave with a clear conscience that official duties have been completed. However, the officer could take the woman to a shelter or otherwise help her get out of a bad situation. What is the ethical choice? It is difficult to determine the extent of the officer's responsibility in cases where there is no offender to arrest or law to enforce.

Law enforcement's response to domestic violence calls has historically been noninterference, with the perception that domestic violence was not a crime control matter unless it involved injury amounting to felony assault, so women who were battered received different treatment depending on whether their batterer was their intimate partner or a stranger and whether the crime was determined to be a felony or a misdemeanor. This situation is personified most dramatically by *Thurman v. City of Torrington*, 595 F. Supp. 1521 (D. Conn. 1984), which involved a woman who was beaten, stomped, and stabbed by her ex-husband on the front steps of her mother's house while a police officer sat in a car and watched.

Obviously, there are few cases that are as dramatic as *Thurman*. Also, there are many other complicating factors in domestic violence, so how to intervene is not always a simple matter. Nevertheless, it must be recognized that part of the problem was a perception on the part of police that domestic violence was somehow different from stranger violence, and deserving of less intervention. A crime control approach supports such discrimination; a public service model probably would not. Mandatory arrest policies were supposed to protect victims of domestic violence by forcing police to take action by arresting the perpetrator. However, what seems to have happened is a greater likelihood that both victim and offender will be arrested when there is evidence that both exchanged blows. Police officers may simply refuse to sort out what happened. Thus, a crime control response may have resulted in unintended consequences for those who had attempted to force the system to respond to domestic violence victims.

The formal code of ethics gives no clear guidelines on how much consideration police should give a citizen in distress. The caretaker style of policing found in small cities and suburbs, where police departments are community oriented, emphasizes service and encourages police assistance to victims or citizens who need it. However, Matthews and Marshall (1981) discuss the lack of departmental support for any action beyond the minimal obligations of duty. Those officers who become personally involved or commit the resources of the department beyond the necessary requirements are not rewarded, but viewed as troublemakers. Structural support for this ethical action does not exist. Officers who attempt to do what they believe is right are often on their own, risking formal or informal censure.

Referring again to our two paradigms of police as crime fighters or public servants, it is apparent that the deemphasis on service and, indeed, sanctions for performing some service functions are due to the police and public's view of police as crime fighters first and foremost.

The approach of neighborhood or community policing changes these parameters considerably and renews the historical emphasis on peacekeeping and community integration functions, yet community policing never caught the imagination of a majority of officers, even while enjoying support and promotion from national organizations such as the Department of Justice. Today, because federal support seems to be waning, we suspect that it is a model that will continue to decline in popularity.

In situations involving questions of duty, there are three questions to ask:

1. What must police do under the law?
2. What does departmental policy dictate?
3. What do individual ethics dictate?

A very altruistic, involved style of interaction in which the police officer would be compelled to help the victims in any way possible is supported by the ethics of care, the ethics of virtue, utilitarianism, religious ethics, and ethical formalism. But a more self-protective standard, in which the actions mandated would be only those necessary to maintain a self-image consistent with the police role as crime fighter, might also be justified using utilitarianism or ethical formalism.

If police became personally involved in every case and went out of their way to help all victims, they would probably exhaust their emotional reserves in a very short time. As a matter of survival, police develop an emotional barrier between themselves and the victims they encounter. It is virtually impossible to observe suffering on a consistent basis if one does not protect oneself in such a way. Unfortunately, the result is often perceived as callousness, and because of the extreme personal resources needed to remain sensitive to individual pain, emotional deadening may result in unethical behavior toward individual victims.

### Duty and Dilemmas

When asked to share ethical dilemmas, police officers often raise the concept of duty. Officers are faced with the choice of responding to certain situations or not, leading to tempting opportunities to ignore duty. In the cases portrayed in the exercise box on page 211, the officer's duty is to serve the public, but shirking that duty does not seem to be an egregious lapse of ethics. On the other hand, these mundane, some might say trivial, decisions are faced by all officers, and their repeated decisions in such situations form the fabric of their moral character.

Officers must decide how much to get involved in any particular incident. Their legal duty is usually to take a report, and many officers feel that taking a report is also the extent of their moral duty, even when the victim or citizen is in need. Some officers do not consider "social work" their problem, but other officers do. These instances show clear differences between role conceptions of crime fighter or public servant.

Another issue of duty is raised by the nature of police work and how easy it is for officers to abuse their freedoms. Officers may report they are on a call, when in reality they are doing nothing or performing personal tasks such as shopping or standing in line at the post office. Some officers have been known to attend college classes during duty hours by informing the dispatcher that they are out on a call. Officers may turn in overtime slips for surveillance when, in fact, they were at home. They may misrepresent the times they started and finished the day. Finally, the way that

**EXERCISE**

Discuss how you might resolve these situations if you were an officer:

1. It is ten minutes to off-duty time. You see an accident. Do you work the accident even though you want to go home, or do you avoid the accident by sneaking around it?
2. You have received the same 911 call at the same location at least twenty times. Each time, it has been unfounded. You have just been dispatched to that 911 again. Should you check it or just clear it as unfounded without driving by?
3. If a young boy, upset over a lost bicycle, approaches you during your dinner, what do the strict guidelines of your job dictate? What is the ethical thing to do? Should you immediately interrupt your dinner and go search for the missing bicycle? Should you take a report to make the boy feel better, knowing you won't or can't do anything about it? Should you tell the boy to go away because you've had a hard night and are looking forward to a hot meal?
4. If you encounter travelers who have been robbed during their passage through the city, should you simply take a report and leave such victims on the street to fend for themselves? Should you transport them to a mission? Should you take up a collection to help them on their way?
5. You respond to a burglary and find that the victim is desperately poor and the theft has left her without the resources to pay rent, buy food, or keep the electricity on. What is your ethical duty?

court appearances can be used to increase one's monthly salary is part of the socialization of every rookie.

That these actions are wrong is not in question, and it is also true that they are not qualitatively different from the minor and not-so-minor egoistic actions of those in other occupations and professions: Office workers leave early or call in sick to go to a ball game; salespeople call in to say that they are out making sales calls when, in fact, they are heading home for a quiet afternoon nap; businesspeople declare imaginary expenses on travel vouchers. Police officers, like all employees, rationalize these behaviors in a variety of ways, such as by pointing out their low pay or the fact that they sometimes do "police work" when off duty. The general acceptance of such behavior leads to an environment where each individual sets personal limits on the extent to which he or she will deviate from formal ethics. Even those who stop at minor transgressions must cover their actions by lying, which is another layer of deception added to the first.

Another issue to consider is how an officer should resolve the dilemma when his or her own values conflict with a direct order. We have previously discussed the concept of civil disobedience—the act of resisting an immoral law. Do police have a duty to enforce laws they do not agree with, or do they have a larger duty to perform in a way that is consistent with their own moral code? The "In the News: Arresting the Homeless" box illustrates a situation where an officer took a moral stand and paid a price.

**IN THE NEWS  Arresting the Homeless**

A New York City police officer refused a direct order to arrest a homeless man who was found sleeping in a private garage. He disagreed with the "zero-tolerance" policy that has been enforced against the homeless, involving sealing off all the places they might find shelter and arresting those who are left on the street. The officer was suspended for thirty days, and his career doesn't look promising since Raymond Kelley, the police commissioner, had this to say about the officer's decision: "You have to be able to follow the directions of a supervisor. Being a police officer is not for everybody. And perhaps this officer feels he's not suited for the job."

Source: J. Getlin, "Officer Refuses to Arrest Homeless," *Austin American Statesman,* November 30, 2002, A8.

***Do you think the officer should have obeyed the order he disagreed with? Do you believe he should have been punished?***

How officers use their discretion—to file a report or not, to answer a call or not, to stop and investigate or not—is just as relevant to an evaluation of ethics as racial profiling, discussed below, or the decision to accept a gratuity or report the use of excessive force, issues that will be dealt with in the next chapter.

## Discretion and Discrimination

When individuals have discretion, it is possible that individual prejudices and perceptions of groups such as women, minorities, and homosexuals influence their decision making. Officers' views of the world affect the way they do their job. If this view includes prejudicial attitudes toward groups, it may be that action is affected and those groups may not receive the same protections as "good" citizens. The point is not that police officers are more prejudiced than the rest of us; it is that their special position creates the possibility that their prejudices could cause a citizen to receive less protection from the law than other citizens would: Essentially, when police act on personal prejudices while performing their jobs, they discriminate in the allocation of either services or enforcement of the law. Discrimination often takes the form of either enforcing the law differentially or withholding the protections and benefits of the law (Kappeler, Sluder, and Alpert, 1984/1994: 175).

As has been discussed before, officers form viewpoints regarding certain groups of people, and these viewpoints affect officers' behaviors and decision making. The "a**holes" in Van Maneen's typology, by whatever name, are one group that may be the target of discrimination because police may behave differently once a citizen is labeled as such. Other groups that may be treated differently are gays and the poor, and obviously there is the long-standing, pervasive—some may say endemic—issue of discrimination toward minorities, especially African Americans.

## Sexual Orientation

Kappeler, Sluder, and Alpert (1984/1994: 176–184) discuss the case of Konerak Sintha-somphone—one of Jeffrey Dahmer's victims—as an example of police bias and discriminatory treatment of homosexuals and racial minorities. Sinthasomphone was the Laotian boy who was found wandering the street, incoherent, naked, and bleeding from the rectum. He had escaped from Dahmer's apartment after he had been drugged, tortured, and sexually abused. Two African American women called the police; when the police arrived, the women tried to tell them that Sinthasomphone was an injured boy and that Dahmer was the one who hurt him. Despite the women's attempts, police officers on the scene helped Dahmer take Sinthasomphone back to his apartment and waved away emergency medical technicians who were starting to examine him. If they had examined him, they would have discovered the holes that Dahmer had already drilled into his skull and the acid that he had poured into the holes. Dismissing the incident as a "homosexual thing," the officers left Sinthasomphone with Dahmer, who strangled him shortly after they left.

This case is not about a mistake in judgment on the part of police officers. Their conduct represents a pattern of enforcement that allots police protection based on membership in certain categorical groups. If the Laotian boy had been white, if he had been a she, if Dahmer had been a minority member instead of a Caucasian, if the two women who requested assistance had not been African American, we might have seen a different response. Even more telling was the fact that even though the police chief suspended the officers involved, they were supported by the police union and were ultimately reinstated with back pay. No further sanctions were taken against them. See Box 7-2, "Dimensions of Police Discrimination," for other examples.

---

**BOX 7-2  Dimensions of Police Discrimination**

**Administrators/Managers**

*Internal*

Refusing to place female officers in "dangerous" assignments

Placing minority employees in undesirable assignments

Making promotion decisions on the basis of race/ethnicity or other factors not related to the ability to perform the job

Refusing to commend officers for exceptional performance on the basis of such factors as race/ethnicity, gender, age

Segregating in assignments by assigning only African American officers to work together as partners or Caucasian officers to work together as partners

Failing to take corrective action when subordinates discriminate against co-workers

*External*

Making selection decisions on the basis of such factors as race/ethnicity, gender, political, or religious affiliation

Refusing to respond to complaints by minority citizens or neighborhoods predominantly populated by minorities

*continued*

---

---

### BOX 7-2  **Continued**

Using police resources and personnel to harass certain segments of the community (e.g., businesses, community groups)

By practice or custom, failing to provide police services to minority segments of
the community (e.g., homosexuals, ethnic groups, religious groups)

Failing to take corrective action when officers discriminate against citizens

**Officers**

*Internal*

Intimidating minority officers by threatening not to back them up on calls

Making racist or sexist comments in the presence of minority officers

Writing graffiti or posting offensive pictures on lockers belonging to minority officers

Engaging in sexual harassment

*External*

Not trying to solve crimes where minorities are victims

Harassing youths, college students, or other groups

Hassling businesses frequented by minorities

Not responding to, or purposefully delaying responding to, calls in minority
neighborhoods

Using racial slurs or derogatory language when dealing with Hispanic citizens

SOURCE: Reprinted by permission of Waveland Press, Inc. From V. Kappeler, R. Sluder, and
G. Alpert, *Forces of Deviance: Understanding the Dark Side of Policing* (Long Grove, IL: Waveland,
1994): 173. All rights reserved.

---

## Race

There is a pervasive sense among minority groups in this country that law enforcement is fundamentally racist (Cole, 1999; Walker, Spohn, and DeLone, 2000). Some
argue that this perception is based in reality. Crank (1998) is one researcher who argues
that racial bias is "endemic" in police departments. However, it should be strongly
emphasized that the charge of racism is not limited to law enforcement but rather has
been leveled against the whole legal system. The system of laws and punishment, the
courts that administer the laws, and the corrections system that makes decisions
regarding the liberties of those convicted have all been described as agencies that systematically and pervasively discriminate against minority groups. Police, in this view,
are just one element in systematic, even institutional, racism.

Studies show that civil rights complaints against police are positively correlated to
the percentage of minorities in the population, as well as the income differential of the
jurisdiction (Holmes, 2000). Some studies report that lower-class African Americans
have significantly more negative interactions with police. More than twice as many
report in surveys disrespectful language or swearing by police officers (Weitzer,
1999). Interestingly, some studies indicate that middle-class African Americans

express more negative attitudes toward police behaviors such as racial profiling than do lower-class African Americans. One speculation for this finding is that those who live in bad neighborhoods and experience the danger and inconvenience of prevalent criminality allow police more latitude to control those who "have it coming to them" (Weitzer, 1999: 838). Weitzer and Tuch (2002), in their review of satisfaction studies, find that there is no consensus and that although some studies report that disadvantaged blacks have more negative views of police, others report that high-status blacks express more dissatisfaction, and other studies report that class is not a factor. In their study using a telephone survey of more than 2,000 respondents, they found that age, income, sex, and education all influenced attitudes toward police.

Studies have indicated that blacks and Hispanics are most supportive of police reforms such as racial diversification of police departments, enhanced mechanisms of accountability, and community policing. Not surprisingly, minorities who lived in metropolitan areas, had less education, had less income, were younger, and reported more bad experiences with the police perceived more police misconduct and exhibited the highest endorsement of police reforms (Weitzer and Tuch, 2000). Reisig and Parks (2000) found that areas of concentrated disadvantage showed the least satisfaction with police, but race was still a predictor, even when controlling for neighborhood. Kane (2002), in a retrospective longitudinal research design using information from 1975 to 1996 in New York City, examined whether or not race affected police satisfaction and misconduct rates. He found that although police misconduct rates seemed to be associated with a rise in Latino population, they did not seem to be affected by the population shifts in the black population.

The Project on Policing studies used 240 hours of observations of encounters with 3,130 suspects in Indianapolis and St. Petersburg in 1996–1997. In this study, trained observers noted characteristics of these encounters, and the results were used to examine such things as police officers' use of force and disrespect. The authors provide a careful review of prior studies and note that police behavior toward citizens is influenced by disrespectful or resistant behavior, intoxication, or mental illness. In other words, the results tend to point to aspects of demeanor rather than race or class. On the other hand, recall that studies that ask people about their experiences with police tend to show significant differences between blacks and whites in their perceptions about whether or not they feel they have experienced disrespect from police officers (Mastrofski, Reisig, and McCluskey, 2002, citing Wesley Skogan; but see also Weitzer, 1999).

The authors point to Donald Black's theory that individuals will treat people worse if there is great social distance and the recipient is of lower status. According to this idea, the actor engages in moralism, whereby the lower-status target can become even more vulnerable by resisting, in some way, the authority of the actor. In these cases, the authority figures may feel "morally justified" in their aggression toward the target (Mastrofski, Reisig, and McCluskey, 2002). Arguably, this explains why there may be more police violence in socially disadvantaged neighborhoods.

Observers noted that suspects were disrespectful toward police in 15 percent of encounters, while police were *initially* disrespectful toward suspects in 5 percent of encounters (this percentage does not include police disrespect after a suspect initiated disrespect). The elements that were related to suspect disrespect toward police included heightened emotion, size of the audience, intoxicants, being mentally impaired, and being in a disadvantaged neighborhood. However, the researchers noted that police disrespect toward the suspect was not a factor associated with suspect disrespect; in fact, suspects were less likely to be disrespectful toward police when police exhibited an initial show of force or disrespect.

On the other hand, citizen disrespect toward the officer did influence officer disrespect. Although only 5 percent of the citizens who did not initiate disrespect received it from the officers, 35 percent of those who did initiate disrespect received it in turn (Reisig, McCluskey, Mastrofski, and Terrill, 2004; Mastrofski, Reisig, and McCluskey, 2002: 534).

Noting other studies that indicated minorities consistently rated police respect and civility at lower rates than whites, and that satisfaction with police is rated lower among minorities, the researchers examined the relationship between race and police civility. Contrary to other studies and popular opinion, these researchers found that minority suspects experienced less "disrespect" than white citizens. The difference was more pronounced in St. Petersburg, arguably because a new police chief made race relations a priority in his administration (Mastrofski, Reisig, and McCluskey, 2002).

Note that this research controlled for other factors such as resistance. Only in the presence of large crowds when the minority suspects were disrespectful did they have a greater risk than whites of being shown disrespect. Other findings indicated that age, sex, and wealth influenced whether or not the citizen would experience disrespect, controlling for their behavior (Mastrofski, Reisig, and McCluskey, 2002). The authors point out that although the presence of observers may have affected the officers' treatment of citizens, it seems unlikely because the observers saw extreme cases where officers used excessive force. Further, race did seem to be a predictor in the use of verbal and physical coercion by officers observed in the encounters (Terrill, 2001; Terrill, Paoline, and Manning, 2003).

The authors also suggest the possibility that minority members may still experience more disrespect if the frequency of encounters for them is greater than for whites. In fact, that is what happened, because blacks in both cities appeared in the pool of encounters at roughly one-and-one-half times their percentage of the general population. In other words, even though when stopped, blacks were no more likely to receive disrespect than whites, they were stopped one-and-one-half times as often as their population percentage would have predicted. Thus, the rate of blacks receiving disrespect was higher than that of whites (Mastrofski, Reisig, and McCluskey, 2002: 543).

The "In the News" box on page 217 offers an egregious case of police misconduct. Although one officer is largely responsible for this travesty of justice, it should not be forgotten that the system itself failed those who were innocent of wrongdoing.

### Racial Profiling

Racial profiling occurs when a police officer uses a "profile" to stop a driver (although it can also be used to refer to stops of pedestrians). The so-called profile is based on race. When a young, black man is seen, for instance, driving a newer-model, expensive car, police officers suspect that the vehicle is stolen and/or that the man is holding drugs. A "pretext stop" refers to the practice of police officers to use some minor traffic offense to stop the individual and, in the course of the traffic stop, look for other evidence of wrongdoing, specifically by a search, usually a consent search.

Profiling began when federal agents developed a profile of drug smugglers to assist border patrol and custom agents in airports. The list of indicators included behavior

**IN THE NEWS**   **The Shame of Tulia, Texas**

Tulia, Texas, has gained an international reputation, but it is not a cause for pride for Texans. In this small Texas town, the local police department hired an investigator to gather evidence for arresting drug dealers. This investigator, who, it turned out, had been fired by other law enforcement agencies and had outstanding misdemeanor warrants against him in another county, collected his evidence, which resulted in 46 indictments. In 1999, 43 people were arrested.

No drugs or weapons were found during the surprise arrests, but all charged were found guilty, and the sentences of those convicted exceeded 431 years. What makes this an issue? The reason is that almost all 43 persons arrested were African American, and the few whites who were arrested were married or dating African Americans. In fact, the arrests were a substantial percentage (about 10 percent) of the small total of African Americans in the town. White juries who accepted the investigator's word that those arrested had sold him drugs, even though there was little evidence beyond his word, handed down the convictions. In some cases, he could not even recognize the person charged as the one who sold drugs to him. In at least one case, defense witnesses placed the accused in another state when the so-called sale was supposed to have occurred. Even though the charges were all sales worth less than $200, the sentences averaged 90 years.

The NAACP and out-of-state lawyers mounted a campaign to overturn these convictions, without much help from the Texas Attorney General's office or the Department of Justice. They have been successful in getting a district court judge to recommend to the Texas Court of Criminal Appeals that all convictions be overturned. Because it may take up to two years for the cases to reach the Court of Criminal Appeals, legislation was written and signed by Governor Perry that resulted in the immediate release of those incarcerated on the perjured testimony of this undercover officer. Tom Coleman, the undercover officer who is at the center of this scandal, was convicted of perjury, and the prosecutor is one of the few prosecutors ever to be formally sanctioned by the Bar Association.

Sources: Talvi, 2002; Herbert, 2002; Robinson, 2003; Hockstader, 2003; Herbert, 2003.

*Why do you think it took out-of-state journalists and lawyers to take up the cause of those wrongly accused in Tulia?*

as well as demographic indices, including race. The concept was developed for highway drivers by state patrol officers who were attempting to stem the flow of drugs up through the interstates in Florida, Georgia, Texas, and other southern states. Bob Vogel, a Florida Highway Patrol officer, became famous nationally for his profile-based stops and their supposed success in uncovering drug smugglers (Harris, 2004). Crank (2003: 242) reported that in Volusia County, Florida, 70 percent of stops and 80 percent of searches after stops were directed toward African Americans or Latinos, though these groups made up only 5 percent of drivers.

In 1999 President Clinton condemned the practice, and congressional hearings were held to investigate how widespread the practice was. Most people object to racial profiling. In their telephone attitude survey of 2,006 respondents in 1999, Weitzer and Tuch (2002: 441) discovered that only 6 percent of blacks were in favor of stops based on race, and only 16 percent of whites were. The result of federal attention was that many states passed legislation that required police departments to collect demographic information on police stops in order to determine whether racial profiling was an issue.

One way to discover the prevalence of racial profiling is to ask individuals about their experiences with police officers. In a 1999 police public contact survey, it was found that blacks reported more stops (12.3 percent) than Hispanics (10.44 percent) or whites (8.8 percent) (reported in Weitzer and Tuch, 2002: 436). Weitzer and Tuch's (2002) survey uncovered the fact that 40 percent of blacks felt they had been stopped because of their race. Also, 81 percent of blacks but only 60 percent of whites felt the practice was widespread. Further, blacks were about three times as likely to have unfavorable opinions of their local police and four times more likely to have unfavorable opinions of their state police. The authors found that race and personal experience with racial profiling were the strongest predictors of attitudes toward the police (2002: 443).

Lundman and Kaufman (2003) used the National Crime Victimization Survey's findings on "contacts between police and public" to analyze citizen reports of police stops. They argue that citizens are an important source of such data since police officers can affect the validity of police stop data simply by not reporting who they stop. Although the authors acknowledge that there are also problems with the citizen data (for instance, citizens may not tell the truth as to whether or not there was a legitimate reason for the stop), it is still an important source to compare with data generated by law enforcement. They found that factors significantly related to police stops included other police contacts (which led to more police stops), income (affluent drivers were stopped more often), age (younger drivers were stopped more often), sex (men were stopped more often), and race (black drivers reported more stops, but Hispanics did not). African American men were the least likely to believe that the stops were legitimate (Lundman and Kaufman, 2003: 207).

Smith and Alpert (2002) review the methodological problems involved in analyzing the extent of racial profiling, especially as it relates to the use of social science in courtrooms. They point out that about half of the available studies were done by law enforcement agencies using their own data and personnel. The other half were by outside researchers using the agencies' data. For instance, one study by the New York Attorney General's office found that although blacks represent only about 26 percent of the New York City population, 51 percent of all stops by N.Y.P.D. officers are of blacks (as represented by "field interrogation cards") (Smith and Alpert, 2002: 675).

Other studies reported on by Smith and Alpert (2002) included the following:

1. A New Jersey Attorney General's study reported that 77 percent of the searches of autos after traffic stops involved black drivers even though only 34 percent of all stops were of black drivers in New Jersey during a time period studied covering 1996 through 1999.

2. A Maryland study used a visual survey of traffic violators on state highways to estimate that about 18 percent of violators were black and 75 percent were white, yet 73 percent of all police stops were of blacks.
3. An Ohio study estimated the number of violators by using court records to find that blacks were twice as likely as whites to be ticketed.
4. A California study found that blacks and Hispanics were overrepresented in those who were stopped, searched, and arrested.
5. A North Carolina study learned that blacks were slightly more likely to be ticketed than whites compared to their percentages among licensed drivers. They were significantly more likely than whites to be searched. They were also less likely to be found with contraband than whites.
6. A Virginia study found that blacks were more likely to be stopped than their proportion of the population but that they were no more likely to be searched than whites and were less likely than whites to be arrested or ticketed.

A more recent study focuses on Texas law enforcement practices. Texas law enforcement agencies are mandated by law to collect information on the race of drivers, and such information has been analyzed by an independent group. The latest report revealed that over 60 percent of police agencies continue to stop and search blacks and Hispanics at a disproportionately higher rate than their population. The majority of searches were "consent" searches, meaning that officers had no legal right to search and simply asked to search, hence the title of the report: "Don't Mind If I Take a Look, Do Ya?" It also indicated that Anglos were either equally or more likely to be found with contraband during searches (Stewart and Totman, 2005).

Smith and Alpert (2002) review the court cases that dealt with police practices that use race in decision making. In such cases as *United States v. Martinez-Fuerte*, 425 U.S. 931 (1976), the U.S. Supreme Court has basically legitimated the use of race as a criteria in profiles (although lower courts are not in agreement when it appears that race is the sole or primary reason for the stop). Further, pretext stops have been accepted by the court in *Wren v. United States*, 517 U.S. 806 (1996), in effect allowing the police to use their discretion to enforce minor laws as a tool to implement race-based stops.

Bannister and Carter (2004) point out that there are great difficulties with measuring racial profiling. Difficulties of data collection revolve largely around how to arrive at the baseline number—that is, the number of black drivers versus white drivers to use as a basis for determining whether the number of stops is proportional to the baseline number of drivers who commit traffic offenses. The reasons why the baseline population is hard to determine include the following:

1. Population percentages are the least accurate method because the likelihood of driving may be differentially distributed (also, if one is measuring street stops of walkers, the likelihood of walking is also probably differentially distributed).
2. Even population numbers may be inaccurate if old census numbers are used; further, census numbers cannot capture transient populations or recent population shifts.
3. There may be differential patterns of who is driving at different times or in different areas of the city that may have different patrol patterns.

4. Simple percentage-of-population figures don't take into account calls for service, complaints received, the location of open-air drug markets that would attract more frequent patrols, the presence of prostitution (for the same reason), reported crime, or the accuracy of the information reported by officers.

Engel, Calnon, and Bernard (2002) reviewed all of the racial profiling studies conducted up to the time of their study and examined the various methods used by researchers. As with Bannister and Carter, they point out the problems identifying the base rate, but also mention other issues:

1. Determining the base rate is difficult because one might use the percentage of nonwhites in the population, the percentage of nonwhite drivers, the percentage of nonwhite drivers who engage in traffic offenses, or some other denominator. Most of the earlier studies used percentage-of-population figures, but other researchers are highly critical of this rough approximation of the base rate. Although some argue that perhaps young black drivers engage in traffic offenses differentially to other population groups and that is why they appear disproportionately in police stops, others point out that blacks are less likely to be automobile drivers than whites, which would make the disproportional stops even more disproportional to the true population that was driving.

2. Interpreting the data is also mentioned as a problem. Numbers are typically collected without any theoretical framework, and they are often collected by the agencies themselves. Newspapers have published results of their analysis of department-collected numbers (obtained via freedom-of-information acts) using questionable methodology and then reach the conclusion that the police department is racist without exploring any race-neutral alternative hypothesis.

3. No exploration of the connection between attitudes and behavior accompanies most racial profiling studies. Researchers have not asked the question of why officers stop black drivers or pedestrians differentially. Do police officers who stop blacks exhibit more racist attitudes than the general population or not?

4. Although it may not explain the initial stop, suspects' demeanor may explain why blacks are more likely to be searched. Racial profiling studies typically do not include measures of the suspects' demeanor even though there is another body of research concerning police–citizen stops and interactions (including use of force) that has identified the important role of a suspect's demeanor in police decision making.

5. Police departments may be implicitly encouraging racial profiling or not by reward structures and training. Most studies place the decision making solely within the purview of the individual officer, but it is important to note organizational influences on such behavior, especially because studies show that black officers are just as likely as white officers to stop blacks in disproportionate numbers.

In their study of stops in both predominantly white and predominantly black neighborhoods, Meehan and Ponder (2002) found that police were much more likely to stop blacks when they were driving in predominantly white neighborhoods. These decisions to stop were inconsistent with the actual "hit" rates of suspects or contraband found because blacks stopped in white neighborhoods were less likely to result in arrests than those stopped in predominantly black neighborhoods. The researchers

---

**IN THE NEWS  A Case of Profiling?**

In Austin, Texas, in 2002, an off-duty officer observed a very new truck being driven by two young, African American boys. He stopped the truck for a broken taillight, and the boys ran. He caught them and found cocaine in the truck, which was stolen. In an investigation of his actions, he stated that he "didn't think black kids would be driving that kind of truck." He was fired. The officer took his case to arbitration, and the departmental explanation was that he was not fired for racial profiling but for lying and insubordination.

Source: T. Plohetski, "Hearing Resumes Today for Fired Austin Officer," *Austin American States-man,* November 18, 2002, B3.

*Do you think that the officer should have been fired if he did stop them because they were black and driving a new truck?*

---

found that officers used their in-car computers to check license plates much more often than they actually effected stops and that such surveillance also reflected disproportional queries of black drivers. They explain such behavior by pointing out that "place" was just as important as "race"—it was when blacks entered white areas that they encountered the greatest degree of police scrutiny, and the researchers proposed that it was because officers tended to act out residents' demands for proactive patrolling. In other words, their "typification" of drivers was that if there were black drivers in white neighborhoods, they must be doing something wrong, although they didn't carry over that typification to white drivers in black neighborhoods.

A utilitarian argument for racial profiling would be that the "end" of drug interdiction justifies the "means" of harassing and inconveniencing the group. However, it appears that the end is not very well served. The "hit rate" for finding drugs is lower for African Americans than it is for other racial groups (Cole and Lamberth, 2001). Harris (2004) criticizes the argument that it is ethical to use statistical generalizations about a group of people even if the generalization is wrong in individual cases. This is the argument that supports stops based on race because of the statistical probability that blacks are more likely to be associated with drugs. As mentioned, the problem with this argument is that the facts do not support such an assumption to begin with. Harris (2004) proposes the idea that when officers use race in decision making, they become less effective, not more, because they do not concentrate on what is important for investigation—behavior, not demographics.

An ethical formalist system would probably not support profile searches because this approach is treating those individuals as a means, and it is probably contrary to the universalism principle unless everyone would agree that they should be stopped in the same manner. Because most of us would object to numerous stops every week by police who have no reason to be suspicious other than the color of our skin, it violates the first part of the categorical imperative. Policy Box 7-1 discusses this issue.

African Americans are not the only minorities who suffer from differential enforcement patterns. Perhaps some of the most egregious cases of discriminatory law enforcement occur on this nation's borders. Crank (2003) and Huspek, Martinez,

---

**POLICY BOX 7-1   Racial Profiling**

There is widespread public opinion condemning racial profiling, and departmental policies have seen some changes over the last several years in their endorsement of such practices.

**Law:** Many states now have laws mandating that police collect demographic information on stops. Case law is somewhat contradictory, but it seems clear that the courts will not allow police stops based solely on race, except perhaps in border areas. Searches must be based on probable cause unless consent is given.

**Policy:** After federal and public scrutiny, most police departments created formal policies that discourage and/or prohibit stops based solely on race. However, informal policies in departments must still support such stops because recent studies continue to show disproportionate stops of minorities. But it seems to be the case that such policies vary by city; thus, some departments are more successful in effecting formal policies.

**Ethics:** An individual officer has a duty to prevent crime. If he or she feels that an individual is very likely a criminal, based on race, then formal policies are going to conflict with individual ethics and the perception of duty. Some argue that police officers' informal policies will not change until they are educated as to the evidence that stops and searches of blacks are less likely to result in a discovery of contraband than stops based on more sophisticated, behavioral-based criteria. As long as police officers believe that racial profiling is effective policing, formal policies that prohibit it will be contrary to their individual ethics and perception of duty.

---

and Jiminez (2001) discuss the excessive force that is used against Latinos in controlling the flow of illegal aliens across the border. It was reported to researchers that Immigration and Naturalization Officers routinely violated the human rights of aliens and deported them before they could report actions of officers.

According to Huspek, Martinez, and Jiminez (2001: 185), there are a "substantial number" of brutal or harassing incidents on the border by INS officers toward legal and illegal residents. In their study of incidents over a three-year period, they found that such abuses are a routine occurrence and that there is a pattern to them and an identifiable logic. Of the 204 persons who participated in their study, 43 percent reported seeing physical brutality, and 12 percent reported being victimized by sexual or physical abuse (2001: 187). For example, in January 1996, Roman Gonzalez Garcia, after being stopped and handcuffed near the San Ysidro port of entry, was pulled up by the handcuffs while at the same time an agent stomped on his ankle with his entire weight, breaking the ankle. Near Campo in August 1995, after Rogelio Hernandez was stopped by Border Patrol agents, his head, hip, and testicles were injured as he was pulled out of his car window by the hair and arm. Agents then threw him to the ground, jumped on his back with their knees, beat him with batons, and held his face in the dirt, almost smothering him (2001: 187).

Many of those reporting incidents were legal residents of the United States though of Mexican origin. They had passports thrown away, official documents torn up, and told they should go back to Mexico. They then had to wait in Mexico until family members could replace documents and help them get back across the border. White citizens have been threatened when they questioned the actions of INS agents (2001: 193). Huspek, Martinez, and Jiminez (2001: 185) argue that agents act this way because they are encouraged by the "rhetoric of fear" and tacit acceptance of any means necessary to reduce or discourage illegal immigration.

After 9/11, those who looked like they were Middle Eastern were subject to increased scrutiny before they boarded airliners. In some cases, individuals were denied entry to airplanes when other passengers complained that they would not fly with the men who looked like they might be suicide bombers. In general, airline security now conducts random searches (along with more targeted searches), and many people object that it is wasteful to search "a little old lady from Kansas" in an effort to be "politically correct." Others argue that everyone should be subject to the same scrutiny because the risk is so high and people might have something slipped into their luggage without their knowledge. Applying a utilitarian argument again for this type of racial profiling, does the end (preventing terrorist bombings) justify actions that a less serious end (drug interdiction) would not? Is it acceptable to more thoroughly search all Middle Eastern individuals because the risk is higher and the number of them smaller than the number of black Americans (thus, reducing the "disutility" of the actions)? Many people who objected to racial profiling when the targets were African Americans and the "end" was drug interdiction do not object when the targets are Middle Eastern and the "end" is to prevent a terrorist attack. Has the argument changed, requiring different answers, or would the same arguments apply?

## Crime Fighter *and* Public Servant?

Police hear mixed messages from the public regarding certain types of crime. They are asked to enforce laws against gambling, pornography, and prostitution, but not too stringently. They are expected to enforce laws against drunk driving but also to be tolerant of individuals who aren't really "criminal." They are expected to uphold laws regarding assault, unless it is a family or interpersonal dispute that the disputants want to settle privately. In other words, we want the police to enforce the law unless they enforce it against us.

We also ask the police to take care of social problems such as the homeless, even if they have to step outside the law to do so. Extralegal means are acceptable as long as they are not used against us. Citizens who want police to move the transients out of a park or get the crack dealers off the corner aren't concerned with the fact that the police might not have the legal authority to do so. If a little "informal" justice is needed to accomplish the task, then that is fine with some people, as long as it is used against those we don't like.

When we accept and encourage such extralegal power in some situations, then we shouldn't be surprised when it is used in other situations as well. The police role as enforcer in a pluralistic society is problematic. The justification for police power is that police represent the public: "The police officer can only validly use coercive force when he or she in fact represents the body politic" (Malloy, 1982: 12). But if the police do not represent all groups, then their authority is seen as oppressive. It should be no surprise that police were seen as an invading army in the ghettos of the 1960s. They were not seen as representing the interests of the people who were the target of their force. The Los Angeles riots after the acquittal of the officers who were charged with beating Rodney King illustrate the tension between minority communities and police departments. More recent disturbances have occurred in other cities, sparked by perceived police abuses.

Police take their cue from the community they serve. If they serve a community that emphasizes "crime control" over individual rights or other public service, then we will see the results of that message in the way laws are enforced. A recent example of a crime control approach is William Bratton's **zero-tolerance policy**, implemented when he was police chief of New York City. Police officers were instructed to take an aggressive stance against street people and minor criminals, especially those who roamed the downtown Manhattan business area and subway system.

The dramatic decline in crime enjoyed by New York City was touted as the result of the zero-tolerance policy. When you arrest the little criminals, so goes the theory, the big crimes don't happen. It was true that arrests of minor offenses were often of those who had outstanding warrants for more serious crimes. From 1993 to 1997, felony complaints dropped by 44.3 percent. Murder and nonnegligent homicide dropped 62 percent, forcible rape dropped 12.4 percent, robbery dropped 48 percent, and burglary rates dropped 45 percent (Greene, 1999: 176). Critics argue that New York's success might have something to do with the 40-percent increase in sworn officers that also occurred during this time. Further, the decline of crime was felt all over the country, not just in New York City. San Diego, without an increase in sworn officers, had a crime rate that declined by almost as much as New York's (Greene, 1999).

The problematic issue regarding zero tolerance is the effect it has on police–community relations. Citizen complaints against New York City police went up 75 percent in the four-year period between 1995 and 1999 (Greene, 1999: 176). Even downtown merchants, who were thrilled with the effects of the crackdown when the Times Square area was described as "safe for tourists" again, were now feeling the effects of the pervasive police influence. Some complained that police were harassing them by enforcing trivial ordinances (such as placement and size of window signs or sidewalk sales). Some New Yorkers complained that the crackdown had altered what made New York what it was, such as sidewalk vendors hawking everything from hot dogs to sunglasses.

The most serious charge is that the policy and approach have led to some police officers employing an "anything goes" philosophy, leading to such extreme cases as the Abner Louima assault and the Amadou Diallo shooting. Interestingly, William Bratton is now the chief of Los Angeles, a city where there has already been serious tension between the minority community and the police department (LeDuff, 2002).

Whereas the formal code of ethics emphasizes the public servant role of law enforcement, the informal subculture emphasizes the crime fighter role. The public, too, probably expects the police to live up to the crime fighter role, but they also expect more. They expect the police to be problem solvers and supermen (and women). From noisy neighbors to incest, we expect the police to have the answers to our problems: to be the one-stop shop for solving problems.

The surprising thing is that the police do so well at this impossible task. At least one study shows that a majority of respondents hold favorable attitudes toward police:

- 79 percent agreed that police were responsive.
- 75 percent agreed that they do a good job maintaining order.
- 84 percent agreed that they care about the safety of residents.
- 82 percent agreed that they do a good job protecting people from crime.

Interestingly, although confidence ratings were higher among whites than minorities in this study, the difference was not significant. In fact, the difference in community attitude toward police had more to do with where one lived. Those who lived in disorganized (and most likely crime-ridden) communities held less positive attitudes toward police (Cao, Frank, and Cullen, 1996).

This is not a surprising finding, and it offers an interesting question: Do the individuals in the disorganized communities have more negative attitudes toward police because they experience greater fear of crime, or do they hold more negative attitudes because they are more likely to be the recipients of extralegal force on the part of police who are challenged to control such crime?

## Conclusion

In this chapter we have explored the formal and informal culture of law enforcement officers. We looked at how the police subculture is, in some respects, opposed to formal ethical standards. We explored reasons for the lack of consistency between the formal code and the informal subculture. The mission and role of police as crime control fighters or as public servants is a pervasive theme when discussing a range of issues, including how police use their discretion, the types of dilemmas they face, and the inconsistency between the formal code and the informal subculture.

Another very recent example illustrating the dual legacy of policing (protection and law enforcement) came in the aftermath of the New Orleans flood. Police swung between law enforcers (against looting) and service providers (when they broke into stores and distributed the goods to desperate citizens). At different times during the flooding and immediately afterward, politicians ordered police to concentrate on lawbreakers; then they switched to demanding that police prioritize lifesaving and ignore lawbreaking. Finally, when the public attitudes toward looting became very negative, the politicians ordered police (and the National Guard soldiers who had arrived) to emphasize law enforcement again. However, individual police officers in the flooded streets were the ones who had to choose between those sometimes conflicting role responsibilities in immediate decisions. Further, the event illustrates the fact that police are definitely a very "thin" blue line and that any major break in social order is beyond their control to contain. Of course, the most shocking news footage showed police officers "shopping" from stores, not to distribute to desperate people, but for their own benefit. When police ignore the law and join the lawbreakers, not for necessity, but for personal greed, it is truly a breakdown in the social order.

In the next chapter we discuss the different forms of graft and corruption. However, we continue to emphasize the fact that very few officers engage in any of these types of corruption.

# Key Terms

**aspirational code**  a code that sets a high standard of behavior with the knowledge that many employees will not live up to it at all times

**authority**  unquestionable entitlement to be obeyed that comes from fulfilling a specific role

**community policing**  a model of law enforcement that creates partnerships with the community and addresses underlying problems rather than simply enforcing the law

**discretion**  the power to make a decision between two or more choices

**discrimination**  the process by which a decision maker treats a group or individual differently from others for no justifiable reason

**duty**  the responsibilities that are attached to a specific role

**force**  the power to use physical coercion to overcome the will of the individual

**group think**  the tendency for similar people in a group to agree with the group's values or beliefs

**persuasion**  the use of signs, symbols, words, and arguments to induce compliance

**power**  the right, inherent in a role, to use any means to overcome resistance

**public servants**  those who are paid from the public purse and are expected to serve the public good

**social contract**  Hobbes's and Locke's idea that individuals give up liberties in return for societal protection

**zero-tolerance policy**  the law enforcement approach whereby small violations and ordinances are enforced to the maximum with the expectation that this will reduce more serious crime

# Review Questions

1. Explain the public servant role and the crime fighter role and why the two may be inconsistent.
2. Discuss what potential ethical issues arise with community policing. Why might community policing act as an "insulator" against unethical behavior?
3. Describe Klockars's descriptions of police authority, power, persuasion, and force.
4. Explain how the social contract is the source of police power, and explain the elements or characteristics of policing that logically flow from such power.
5. Describe the elements of the formal code of ethics, and contrast them with the values of the police subculture.
6. Present the criticisms leveled against the use of any code of ethics for police officers.
7. Describe Sherman's police "values."
8. Explain why some people think the police subculture is breaking down.
9. Describe Wilson and Brown's typologies of police, and explain how each might use discretion.
10. Evaluate the research on racial profiling. What methodological problems exist? What do most studies show?

# Discussion Questions

1. Define *discretion*, give examples of discretion, and discuss unethical and ethical criteria for the use of discretion.
2. Discuss community policing and whether it is likely to reduce or encourage unethical actions by police officers.
3. Evaluate the charge that police departments enforce the law in a discriminatory manner.
4. Discuss the parameters of police duty, especially as duty relates to situations where no crime has occurred but citizens are in distress for some reason.
5. Create a formal "code" for police—establish what you think are the most important elements of good policing, and incorporate these ideas into a code.
6. Discuss whether racial profiling to deter or prevent terrorism is justified.
7. Discuss the two perceptions of the police officer—crime fighter or public servant. Consider various police practices and innovations as supporting one or the other role.

# Ethical Dilemmas

### Situation 1

As a patrol officer, you are only doing your job when you stop a car for running a red light. Unfortunately, the driver of the car happens to be the mayor. You give her a ticket anyway, but the next morning you get called into the captain's office and told in no uncertain terms that you screwed up, for there is an informal policy extending "courtesy" to city politicians. Several nights later, you observe the mayor's car weaving erratically across lanes and speeding. What would you do? What if the driver were a fellow police officer? What if it were a high school friend?

### Situation 2

There is a well-known minor criminal in your district. Everyone is aware that he is engaged in a variety of crimes, including burglary, fencing, and drug dealing. However, you have been unable to make a case against him. Now he is the victim of a crime—he has been assaulted and robbed at gunpoint. How would you treat his case?

### Situation 3

You are completing an internship with a local police agency. The officers you ride with are great and let you come along on everything they do. One day, the officer you are riding with takes you along on a drug raid. You are invited to come in when the house is secure, and you observe six young men sitting on two sofas in the living room. The officers are ransacking the house and asking the young men where they have hidden the drugs. Four of the youth are African American, and two are white. One of the officers walks behind the sofa where the African Americans are sitting and slaps each one hard on the side of the head as he walks past. He ignores the two white boys sitting on the other sofa. You are shocked by his actions, but know that if you say anything, your chance of being hired by this agency will be very small. You desperately want a good recommendation from the officers you ride with. What would you do?

### Situation 4

You are a police officer in New Orleans. During the flood you are ordered to patrol a section of the downtown area to prevent looting. The water is waist high in some places, and the stores and shops in this section of blocks are, for the most part, inundated with floodwater. You come upon one shop where the plate-glass window has been broken, and there are about a dozen people coming out of the shop with clothing in their arms. You suspect that the shop's contents will be written off anyway by the owners and covered by insurance. Should that make a difference in your decision? What if the store was in an area of the city that wasn't flooded and the contents were not ruined? What if the people said they were desperate and didn't have any clothes because their belongings were under water? What if it were televisions and other electronics that were being taken?

### Situation 5

You are a rookie on traffic patrol. You watch as a young black man drives past you in a brand-new silver Porsche. You estimate the car's value at around $40,000, yet the neighborhood you are patrolling in is characterized by low-income housing, cheap apartments, and tiny houses on the lowest end of the housing spectrum. You follow him and observe that he forgets to signal when he changes lanes. Ordinarily, you wouldn't waste your time on something so minor. What would you do?

## Suggested Readings

Barker, T., and Carter, D. 1991. *Police Deviance.* Cincinnati: Anderson.

Cole, D. 1999. *No Equal Justice.* New York: Free Press.

Dunham, R., and Alpert, G. 2005. *Critical Issues in Policing,* 4th ed. Prospect Heights, IL: Waveland.

Heffernan, W., and Stroup, T. 1985. *Police Ethics: Hard Choices in Law Enforcement.* New York: John Jay Press.

Kappeler, V., Sluder, R., and Alpert, G. 1994. *Forces of Deviance: Understanding the Dark Side of Policing.* Prospect Heights, IL: Waveland.

Kleinig, J. (Ed.). 1996. *Handled with Discretion.* Lanham, MD: Rowman & Littlefield.

Lersch, K. 2002. *Policing and Misconduct.* Upper Saddle River, NJ: Prentice-Hall.

Manning, P. 1997. *Policework,* 2d ed. Prospect Heights, IL: Waveland.

Mastrofski, S., Reisig, M., and McCluskey, J. 2002. "Police Disrespect Toward the Public: An Encounter-Based Analysis." *Criminology* 40(3): 519–551.

Perez, D., and Moore, J. 2002. *Police Ethics: A Matter of Character.* Cincinnati: Copperhouse/ Atomic Dog Publishing.

Terrill, W., Paoline, E., and Manning. P. 2003. "Police Culture and Coercion." *Criminology* 41(4): 1003–1034.

Walker, S., Spohn, C., and DeLone, M. 2000. *The Color of Justice*. Belmont, CA: Wadsworth.

Weitzer, R., and Tuch, S. 2002. "Perceptions of Racial Profiling: Race, Class, and Personal Experience." *Criminology* 40(2): 435–456.

Weitzer, R., and Tuch, S. 2000. "Reforming the Police: Racial Differences in Public Support for Change." *Criminology* 38(2): 391–416.

# Appendix

## *Law Enforcement Code of Ethics*

As a Law Enforcement Officer my fundamental duty is to serve mankind; to safeguard lives and property; to protect the innocent against deception, the weak against oppression or intimidation, and the peaceful against violence or disorder; and to respect the Constitutional Rights of all men to liberty, equality, and justice.

I will keep my private life unsullied as an example to all; maintain courageous calm in the face of danger, scorn, or ridicule; develop self-restraint; and be constantly mindful of the welfare of others. Honest in thought and deed in both my personal and official life, I will be exemplary in obeying the laws of the land and the regulations of my department. Whatever I see or hear of a confidential nature or that is confided to me in my official capacity will be kept ever secret unless revelation is necessary in the performance of my duty.

I will never act officiously or permit personal feelings, prejudices, animosities or friendships to influence my decisions. With no compromise for crime and with relentless prosecution of criminals, I will enforce the law courteously and appropriately without fear or favor, malice or ill will, never employing unnecessary force or violence and never accepting gratuities.

I recognize the badge of my office as a symbol of public faith, and I accept it as a public trust to be held so long as I am true to the ethics of the police service. I will constantly strive to achieve these objectives and ideals, dedicating myself before God to my chosen profession . . . law enforcement.

## *Canons of Police Ethics*

### Article 1. Primary Responsibility of Job

The primary responsibility of the police service, and of the individual officer, is the protection of the people of the United States through the upholding of their laws; chief among these is the Constitution of the United States and its amendments. The law enforcement officer always respects the whole of the community and its legally expressed will and is never the arm of any political party and clique.

### Article 2. Limitations of Authority

The first duty of a law enforcement officer, as upholder of the law, is to know its bounds upon him in enforcing it. Because he represents the legal will of the community, be it local, state, or federal, he must be aware of the limitations and proscriptions which the people, through law, have placed upon him. He must recognize the genius of the

American system of government which gives no man, groups of men or institution absolute power, and he must insure that he, as a prime defender of the system, does not pervert its character.

### Article 3. Duty to Be Familiar with the Law and with Responsibilities of Self and Other Public Officials

The law enforcement officer shall assiduously apply himself to the study of the principles of the laws which he is sworn to uphold. He will make certain of his responsibilities in the particulars of their enforcement, seeking aid from his superiors in matters of technicality or principles when these are not clear to him; he will make special effort to fully understand his relationship to other public officials, including other law enforcement agencies, particularly on matters of jurisdiction, both geographically and substantively.

### Article 4. Utilization of Proper Means to Gain Proper Ends

The law enforcement officer shall be mindful of his responsibility to pay strict heed to the selection of means in discharging the duties of his office. Violations of laws or disregard for public safety and property on the part of the officer are intrinsically wrong; they are self-defeating in that they instill in the public mind a like disposition. The employment of illegal means, no matter how worthy the end, is certain to encourage disrespect for the law and its officer. If the law is to be honored, it must first be honored by those who enforce it.

### Article 5. Cooperation with Public Officials in the Discharge of Their Authorized Duties

The law enforcement officer shall cooperate fully with other public officials in the discharge of authorized duties, regardless of party affiliation or personal prejudice. He shall be meticulous in assuring himself of the propriety, under the law, of such actions and shall guard against the use of his office or person, whether knowingly, or unknowingly, in any improper or illegal action. In any situation open to question, he shall seek authority from his superior officer, giving him a full report of the proposed service or action.

### Article 6. Private Conduct

The law enforcement officer shall be mindful of his special identification by the public as an upholder of the law. Laxity of conduct or manner in private life, expressing either disrespect for the law or seeking to gain special privilege, cannot but reflect upon the police officer and the police service. The community and the service require that the law enforcement officer lead the life of a decent and honorable man. Following the career of a policeman gives no man special perquisites. It does give the satisfaction of safeguarding the American republic. The officer who reflects upon this tradition will not degrade it. Rather, he will so conduct his private life that the public will regard him as an example of stability, fidelity, and morality.

## Article 7. Conduct Toward the Public

The law enforcement officer, mindful of his responsibility to the whole community, shall deal with individuals of the community in a manner such as will inspire confidence and trust. Thus, he will be neither overbearing nor subservient, as the individual citizen has neither an obligation to stand in awe of him nor a right to command him. The officer will give service where he can, and require compliance with the law. He will do neither from personal preference or prejudice but only as a duly appointed officer of the law discharging his sworn obligation.

## Article 8. Conduct in Arresting and Dealing with Violators

The law enforcement officer shall use his powers of arrest in accordance with the law and with due regard to the right of the citizen concerned. His office gives him no right to prosecute the violator nor to mete out punishment for the offense. He shall, at all times, have a clear appreciation of his responsibilities and limitations regarding detention of the violator; he shall conduct himself in such a manner as will minimize the possibility of having to use force. To this end he shall cultivate a dedication to the service of the people and the equitable upholding of their laws whether in the handling of law violators or in dealing with the law abiding.

## Article 9. Gifts and Favors

The law enforcement officer, representing government, bears the heavy responsibility of maintaining, in his own conduct, the honor and integrity of all governmental institutions. He shall, therefore, guard against placing himself in a position which any person can reasonably assume that special consideration is being given. Thus, he should be firm in refusing gifts, favors, or gratuities, large or small, which can, in the public mind, be interpreted as capable of influencing his judgment in the discharge of his duties.

## Article 10. Presentation of Evidence

The law enforcement officer shall be concerned equally in the prosecution of the wrong doer and the defense of the innocent. He shall ascertain what constitutes evidence and shall present such evidence impartially and without malice. In so doing, he will ignore social, political, and other distinctions among the persons involved, strengthening the tradition of the reliability and integrity of an officer's word.

## Article 11. Attitude Toward Profession

The law enforcement officer shall regard the discharge of his duties as a public trust and recognize his responsibility as a public servant. By diligent study and sincere attention to self-improvement he shall strive to make the best possible application of science to the solution of crime and, in the field of human relationships, strive for effective leadership and public influence in matters affecting public safety. He shall appreciate the importance and responsibility of his office, hold police work to be an honorable profession rendering valuable service to his community and the country.

SOURCE: Reprinted by permission of the International Association of Chiefs of Police.

The three defendants convicted in the Abner Louima assault represent the dark side of policing. Justin Volpe (second from right), assisted by two other officers, brutally assaulted Louima. Volpe was convicted and sentenced to prison.

# 8

# Corruption and the "Code"

## Key Terms

# Chapter Objectives

1. Become aware of the range of law enforcement deviance.

2. Understand the arguments that support and criticize the practice of gratuities.

3. Become familiar with the prevalence of and explanations for the use of excessive force by police officers.

4. Become familiar with the types and range of law enforcement deviance in other countries.

5. Understand the various explanations offered for law enforcement deviance.

Although the vast majority of police officers are honest and strive to be ethical in all they do, it is a sad fact that examples of corruption and graft in law enforcement agencies are not difficult to find. Examples of widespread corruption have been uncovered by various committees and investigative bodies since the very beginnings of organized police departments (Barker and Carter, 1994; Murphy and Moran, 1981: 87). One study reported that by officers' own accounts, 39 percent of their number engaged in brutality, 22 percent perjured themselves, 31 percent had sex on duty, 8 percent drank on duty, and 39 percent slept on duty (Barker and Carter, 1994). Barker (1983) reported that between 9 and 31 percent of officers who had been employed for eleven months or less reported observing corrupt practices.

Unfortunately, the perception that police are corrupt is widespread in some cities. In a New York City poll, 93 percent of those polled believed that police were "corrupt" (Kraus, 1994). Moore (1997) reports, interestingly, that the public still has a high opinion of police, even though the majority also believe they are dishonest. Souryal also chronicles the extent of police deviance (1992: 300), as do many other authors who will be cited in this chapter.

Most misdeeds of police officers are only marginally different from the unethical behaviors of other professions—for instance, doctors may prescribe unneeded surgery or experiment with unknown drugs, businesspeople may cheat on their expense accounts, lawyers sometimes overcharge clients, and contract bidders and purchase agents might offer and accept bribes. It is an unfortunate fact of life that people in any profession or occupation will find ways to exploit their position for personal gain. This is not to excuse these actions but rather to show that police are no more deviant than other professional groups. In all of these occupational areas, most people attempt to uphold the profession's code of ethics and their own personal moral code. However, there are those who violate the ethical code in medium to minor ways, and then a very few who exploit their position blatantly and exhibit extremely unethical behaviors.

One way to identify and categorize police corruption is offered by Barker and Carter (1994), who propose that police abuse of authority comes in three different areas:

1. Physical abuse—excessive force, physical harassment
2. Psychological abuse—disrespect, harassment, ridicule, excessive stops, intimidation
3. Legal abuse—unlawful searches or seizures, manufacturing evidence

In this chapter we will examine deviant behavior. Why do some police officers abuse their position? Deviant behavior is largely a matter of abuse of authority or of discretionary power.

# Types of Corruption

Corruption, graft, theft, and accepting bribes and gratuities are all examples of unethical law enforcement practices. Cohen refers to these behaviors as exploitation, defined as "acting on opportunities, created by virtue of one's authority, for personal gain at the expense of the public one is authorized to serve" (1986: 23).

In 1973 the Knapp Commission detailed its findings of corruption within the New York City Police Department. The terms **grass eaters** and **meat eaters** were used to describe New York City police officers who used their position to engage in corrupt practices. Taking bribes, gratuities, and unsolicited protection money was the extent of the corruption engaged in by *grass eaters*, who were fairly passive in their deviant practices. *Meat eaters*, on the other hand, participated in shakedowns, "shopped" at burglary scenes, and engaged in more active deviant practices. The Mollen Commission, investigating New York City Police Department corruption twenty years later (1993), concluded that meat eaters were engaged in a qualitatively different kind of corruption in more recent times. More than just cooperating with criminals, the corrupt cops were active criminals themselves, selling drugs, robbing drug dealers, and operating burglary rings.

The distinction between passive and active corruption is a helpful one. However, another distinction that should be made is between crime and ethical transgressions. It is an insult to law enforcement officers when such actions described above are discussed as if they were ethical dilemmas in the same category as whether to avoid responding to a fender-bender call or whether to call in sick so you can go fishing. Stealing, robbing, and selling drugs are crimes. Officers who engage in such acts are criminals who happen to wear uniforms. The "In the News" box on page 236 describes this type of officer (if the allegations are true).

## *Gratuities*

**Gratuities** are items of value received by an individual because of his or her role or position, rather than because of a personal relationship with the giver. The widespread practices of free coffee in convenience stores, half-price or free meals in restaurants, half-price dry cleaning, and so on, are all examples of gratuities. Frequently, businesspeople offer gratuities, such as half-price meals, as a token of sincere appreciation

**IN THE NEWS  Mafia Cops**

Louis Eppolito and Stephen Caracappa were New York City police officers. They were indicted in September of 2005 for a range of crimes, including murder, said to have been committed while they were police officers on the payroll of the Luchese crime family. Prosecutors allege that the two officers received thousands of dollars a month for being "hit men" for the mob. They both had retired from N.Y.P.D. to Las Vegas where they were arrested. Ironically, Eppolito has written a book called *Mafia Cop: The Story of an Honest Cop Whose Family Was the Mob*, detailing his upbringing in the Gambino crime family and subsequent career as a police officer. The two were identified as mob informants as far back as 1994 by a mafia member who turned state's evidence, yet the two retired without ever having come up on charges.

Source: A. Feurer and W. Rashbaum, "Blood Ties: Two Officers' Long Path to Mob Murder Indictments." *New York Times Online.* Retrieved September 29, 2005, from http://www.ipsn.org/indictments/caracappa_indictment/blodd_ties_2_officers.htm.

*How could these two engage in acts of kidnapping, murder, and informing on drug raids and other police investigations without ever drawing the attention of internal affairs?*

for the police officers' work. Although the formal code of ethics prohibits accepting gratuities, many officers feel that there is nothing wrong with businesses giving "freebies" to a police officer. Many officers believe that these are small rewards indeed for the difficulties they endure in police work.

What do others think? Prenzler (1995: 21) collected 398 responses from patrons of sporting clubs in Brisbane, Queensland (Australia), concerning their attitude toward police gratuities. Only 4 percent of this group expressed unqualified support, 55 percent believed that police should not accept them, and 35 percent said that doing so was acceptable only under certain circumstances. However, when presented with hypothetical examples, two-thirds of respondents agreed it was acceptable for police to take coffee, and about one-quarter approved of Christmas gifts. The majority were still opposed to large gifts and regular gifts. Seventy-six percent were opposed to regular free coffee, cold drinks, or discounted meals when on duty.

Very few of Prenzler's respondents agreed with the commonly used arguments for acceptance of gratuities:

- that they build community relations (15 percent)
- that they give businesses police protection (8 percent)
- that every occupation has its perks (6 percent)
- that they compensate police for poor pay (6 percent)

It is unknown whether these responses from Australia are similar to what would be gathered here. In criminal justice classrooms, it is common to find fairly strong support for minor gratuities, but this may not be true if one polled other groups. Lord and Bjerregaard (2003) found that students initially ranked gratuities as a minor ethical issue but, after a criminal justice ethics class, ranked accepting gratuities as a more serious ethical transgression.

One author writes that gratuities "erode public confidence in law enforcement and undermine our quest for professionalism" (Stefanic, 1981: 63). How do gratuities undermine public confidence? Cohen believes that gratuities are dangerous because what might start without intent on the part of the officer may become a patterned expectation. It is the taking in an official capacity that is wrong, for the social contract is violated when citizens give up their liberty to exploit only to be exploited, in turn, by the enforcement agency that prevents them from engaging in similar behavior (Cohen, 1986: 26). To push this argument to the extreme, some might argue that there are similarities between someone coming into an inner-city store and demanding "protection money" (to avoid torching and vandalism) and a police officer coming in expecting liquor or other goods (if the store owner believes that he will receive a lower level of protection if he doesn't provide them). How does the store owner know that his silent alarm will receive the same response speed if he is not grateful and generous to police officers?

Kania, on the other hand, writes that police "should be encouraged to accept freely offered minor gratuities and . . . such gratuities should be perceived as the building blocks of positive social relationships between our police and the public" (1988: 37). He rejects the two major arguments against gratuities:

1. the slippery slope argument—that taking gratuities leads to future, more serious, deviance
2. the unjust enrichment argument—that the only honest remuneration for police officers is the paycheck

Kania proposes that gratuities actually help cement relations between the police department and the public. Officers who stay and drink coffee with store owners and businesspeople are better informed than those officers who don't, according to Kania. A gift, freely given, ties the giver and receiver together in a bond of social reciprocity. This should not be viewed negatively but rather as part of a community-oriented policing concept. He also points out that those who offer gratuities tend to be more frequent users of police services, justifying more payment than the average citizen. The only problem, according to Kania, is when the intent of the giver is to give in exchange for some future service, and not as reward for past services rendered. Another problematic situation would be when the intent of the taker is not to receive unsolicited but appreciated gifts, but rather to use the position of police officer to extort goods from business owners. Finally, if the giver expected special treatment, and the officer has the intent to perform the special service, then that would be an unethical exchange as well. See Box 8-1 on page 238 for a more detailed explanation of Kania's description.

Another issue that Kania alludes to but doesn't clearly articulate is that a pattern of gratuities changes what would have been a formal relationship into a personal, informal one. This moves the storekeeper–giver into a role more similar to a friend, relative, or fellow officer, in which case there are personal loyalty issues involved when the law

---

**BOX 8-1    Relationship of Giver and Police**

| Name | Giver's Perception | Police Perception |
|---|---|---|
| *Ethical* | | |
| True reward | gratitude for contribution or heroic deed | accepted with acknowledgment of significance |
| True gift | expression of gratitude for pattern of police service | accepted without further obligation |
| True gratuity | expression of wish that legitimate police services will be continued | accepted in spirit of continuing reciprocal obligation |
| *Unethical Only for Police* | | |
| Uncalled debt | expression of wish that legitimate police services will be continued | accepted in credit for future legal, quasilegal, or illegal favors |
| *Ethical Only for Police* | | |
| Bad investment | offered to receive future legal advantages, secure favors, gain special status | accepted in spirit of continuing reciprocal obligation |
| *Unethical and Illegal* | | |
| An understanding | offered to receive future legal advantages, secure favors, gain special status | accepted in credit for future legal, quasilegal, or illegal favors |
| A bribe | offered to exempt illegal actions or omissions from police action | accepted to overlook or ignore ongoing illegal activities |
| An arrangement | offered to exempt ongoing illegal actions or omissions from police action | accepted to overlook or ignore ongoing illegal activities |
| A shakedown | paid unwillingly to secure protection from police enforcement action | demanded to overlook or ignore present or future illegal activities |

SOURCE: Adapted from R. Kania, 1988, "Should We Tell the Police to Say 'Yes' to Gratuities?" *Criminal Justice Ethics*, 7(2): 37–49. Used with permission of the publisher.

---

needs to be administered. In the same way that an officer encounters an ethical dilemma when a best friend is stopped for speeding, the officer who stops a store owner who has been providing him or her with free coffee for the past year may also experience divided loyalties. They have become, if not friends, at least personally involved with each other to the extent that one's formal duty becomes complicated by the personal relationship.

Recently, Kania revisited this issue when he was asked to respond to two critics of his fifteen-year-old article. The critics (Ruiz and Bono 2004; Coleman 2004a, 2004b) argue against gratuities for the following reasons:

1. Police are professionals, and professionals don't take gratuities.
2. Gratuities are incipient corruptors because people expect different treatment.
3. Gratuities are an abuse of authority and create a sense of entitlement.
4. Gratuities add up to substantial amounts of money and can constitute as high as 30 percent of an officer's income.
5. Gratuities can be the beginning of more serious forms of corruption.
6. It is contrary to democratic ideals because it is a type of fee-for-service of public functions.
7. It creates a public perception that police are corrupt.

Kania (2004) continues to argue that gratuities, if freely offered and received with no strings attached, are ethical. He argues that

1. other professionals accept gratuities
2. there is nothing wrong with more frequent users of police services "paying" extra
3. "no gratuity" rules are tools of playing "gotcha" that erode morale
4. educators and academics tend to distort the seriousness of gratuities

Where should one draw the line between harmless rewards and inappropriate gifts? Is a discount on a meal OK, but not a free meal? Is a meal OK, but not any other item, such as groceries or tires or car stereos? Do the store or restaurant owners expect anything for their money, such as more frequent patrols or overlooking sales of alcohol to underage juveniles? Should they expect different treatment from officers than the treatment given to those who do not offer gratuities? For instance, suppose that an officer is told by a convenience store owner that he can help himself to anything in the store—free coffee, candy, cigarettes, chips, magazines, and such. In the same conversation, the store owner asks the officer for his personal pager number "in case something happens and I need to get in contact with you." Is this a gift or an exchange? Should the officer accept the free merchandise?

Many merchants give free or discount food to officers because they like to have police around, especially late at night. The question then becomes the one asked frequently by citizens: Why are two or three police cars always at a certain restaurant? Police argue that they deserve to take their breaks wherever they want within their patrol area. If it happens that they choose the same place, that shouldn't be a concern of the public. However, an impression of unequal protection occurs when officers make a habit of eating at certain restaurants or congregating at certain convenience stores. Free meals or even coffee may influence the pattern of police patrol and thus may be wrong because some citizens are not receiving equal protection.

What happens when all surrounding businesses give gratuities to officers and a new business moves in? Do officers come to expect special favors? Do merchants feel pressured to offer them? Many nightclubs allow off-duty officers to enter without paying cover charges. Does this lead to resentment and a feeling of discrimination by paying customers? Does it lead to the officers thinking that they are special and different from everyone else? Other examples of gratuities are when police accept movie tickets, tickets to ball games and other events, free dry cleaning, and free or discounted merchandise.

The extent of gratuities varies from city to city. In cities where rules against gratuities are loosely enforced, "dragging the sack" may be developed to an art form by some police officers, who go out of their way to collect free meals and other gifts. One story is told of a large midwestern city where officers from various divisions were upset because the merchants from some areas provided Christmas gifts, such as liquor, food, cigarettes, and other merchandise, whereas merchants in other divisions either gave nothing or gave less attractive gifts. The commander, finally tired of the bickering, ordered that no individual officer could receive any gifts and instead sent a patrol car to all the merchants in every district. Laden with all the things the merchants would have given to individual officers, the patrol car returned; the commander then parceled out the gifts to the whole department based on rank and seniority.

Ruiz and Bono (2004) present other instances of gratuities in a southern city. One example concerned a restaurant owner who had been giving free meals to officers and then stopped. Officers then engaged in a ticket-writing campaign, targeting his customers who double-parked. After several weeks of this, the restaurant owner changed his mind and began giving free meals to officers again. The authors also mention a type of contest whereby officers competed to see how many free bottles of liquor they could collect; the winning team collected fifty bottles from the bars and businesses in one district on a single shift. "The blue discount suit," according to the authors, was a term that indicated how officers felt about gratuities. Some other terms described businesses that offered free or discounted goods; these establishments were said to "show love" or give "pop"—hence the saying "If you got no pop, you got no cop."

Officers in some departments are known for their skill in soliciting free food and liquor for after-hours parties. In the same vein, officers also solicit merchants for free food and beverages for charity events sponsored by police such as youth softball leagues. The first situation is similar to individual officers receiving gratuities, but the second situation is harder to criticize. Officers bring up the seeming hypocrisy of a departmental prohibition against individual officers accepting gratuities, yet at the same time an administrative policy may exist of actively soliciting and receiving donations from merchants for departmental events, such as pastries, coffee, or more expensive catering items.

It might be instructive to look at other occupations. Do judges or college professors receive any types of gratuities? Obviously, any attempt to give these professionals gifts would be perceived as an attempt to influence their decisions in matters involving the gift giver. Professional ethics always discourages gifts or gratuities when the profession involves discretionary judgments about a clientele. Professors cannot receive gifts from students and expect to maintain the appearance of neutrality. Judges are usually very careful to avoid the appearance that they have received anything of value from the participants in any proceeding. If there is any chance of a conflict of interest, if the judge is compromised by a relationship with or knowledge of the participants, then he or she is supposed to pass the case on to a neutral colleague. A revelation that a gift from either side was accepted by the judge would probably result in a mistrial, successful appeal, and the judge being removed by the commission on judicial conduct. The system of electing judges is heavily criticized with the use of such terms as "justice for sale," for judges typically rely on attorneys for campaign contributions, and these same attorneys practice

**EXERCISE**

Indicate which of the following—if offered freely with no apparent exchange expected—are ethically acceptable. Then compare your answers with others.

| | | |
|---|---|---|
| free coffee | only on duty | on or off duty |
| free gum or candy | only on duty | on or off duty |
| half-price meal | only on duty | on or off duty |
| free meal | only on duty | on or off duty |
| free dry cleaning | only for uniform | unrestricted |
| free admission to clubs | n/a | off duty |
| free lottery tickets | only on duty | on or off duty |
| expensive merchandise | only on duty | on or off duty |
| any of the above to department as a whole? | | |

*If you decided that free coffee, meals, and other items are acceptable because they don't cost much, how do you explain the fact that, over time, the cost of the coffee or meals consumed by police officers would equal that of the more expensive items?*

in the judges' courts. The receipt of gifts or campaign contributions by politicians is a frequent news item because of the belief that such gifts are buying votes or influence.

When members of Congress receive large amounts of money from special interest groups, when companies routinely distribute complimentary gifts to members of Congress, or when a lobbyist takes politicians on an expensive fact-finding junket, there is the appearance of impropriety. Although politicians would argue that these gifts do no harm and are only tokens of esteem, there is a strong suspicion that such practices are not in the public interest because the politicians who receive gifts will be influenced.

On the other hand, it does not seem unusual or particularly unethical for a doctor, a lawyer, a mechanic, or a mail carrier to receive gifts from grateful clients. Whether gifts are unethical relates to whether one's occupation or profession involves judgments that affect the gift givers. The police obviously have discretionary authority and make judgments that affect store owners and other gift givers. This may explain why some feel that it is wrong for police to accept gifts or favors. It also explains why so many people do not see anything wrong with some types of gratuities, for police officers in most situations are not making decisions affecting the giver and, instead, are simply providing a service, such as responding to a burglary or disturbance call.

An important distinction that might help the discussion is the difference between a *gift* and a *gratuity*. A gift is something that is clearly given with no strings attached. An example might be when a citizen pays for a police officer's meal without telling the officer—when the officer gets ready to pay, the bill is already taken care of. Many officers have had this experience. In this case, because the police officer did not know of the reward (because the gift giver did not make the gift known), no judgment can be affected.

The ethical systems from Chapter 2 can be used to examine the ethics of gratuities. Religious ethics is not much help; no clear guidelines can be gleaned from religious proscriptions of behavior. Ethical formalism is more useful because the categorical imperative, when applied to gratuities, would indicate that we must be comfortable with a universal law allowing all businesses to give all police officers certain favors or gratuities, such as free meals, free merchandise, or special consideration. However, such a blanket endorsement of this behavior would probably not be desirable. The second principle of ethical formalism indicates that each should treat every other with respect as an individual and not as a means to an end. In this regard, we would have to condemn gratuities in those cases where the giver or receiver had improper motives according to Kania's typology. If the business owner was expecting anything in return, then he would be using the police officer as a means to his own end and would thus be violating the second principle of ethical formalism. This also explains why some gifts seem acceptable. When something is given freely and accepted without strings, there is no "using" of others; therefore, it might be considered an innocent, honorable act by both parties.

If utilitarian ethics were used, one would have to weigh the relative good or utility of the interaction. On one hand, harmless gratuities may create good feelings in the community toward the officers and among the officers toward the community (Kania's "cementing the bonds" argument). On the other hand, gratuities often lead to perceptions of unfairness by shopkeepers who feel discriminated against, by police who feel that they deserve rewards and don't get them, and so on. In fact, the overall negative results of gratuities, even "harmless" ones, might lead a utilitarian to conclude that gratuities are unethical.

There would be some differences in the argument if one used act utilitarianism versus rule utilitarianism. Act utilitarianism would be more likely to allow some gratuities and not others. Each individual act would be judged on its own merits—a cup of coffee or a meal from a well-meaning citizen or a store owner to a police officer who was unlikely to take advantage of the generosity would be acceptable, but gratuities given with the intent to elicit special favors would not. Rule utilitarianism would look to the long-term utility of the rule created by the precedent of the action. In this perspective, even the most innocuous of gratuities may be deemed unethical because of the precedent set by the rule and the long-term disutility for society of that type of behavior.

An ethics of care approach would be concerned with the content of the relationship. If the relationship between the giver and the receiver was already established, an exchange between the two would not be seen as harmful. If there was no relationship—that is, if the store owner gave the gratuity to anyone in a blue uniform—then there may be cause for concern. A preexisting relationship would create ties between the two parties so that one would want to help the other with or without the exchange. Kania's theory of social networking is appropriate to apply here. If there is no existing relationship, then the gratuity may indicate an exchange relationship that is based on rights and duties, not care. Does the gift or gratuity turn it into an exchange relationship? Officers can usually recite stories of store owners who gave gifts with an expressed purpose of goodwill, only to remind the officers of their generosity at the point where a judgment was made against them, such as a traffic ticket or parking violation. In this situation, the type of relationship isn't clear until "the bill is due."

Macintyre and Prenzler (1999) conducted a survey of officers to see if they would be influenced by gratuities. They asked officers what they would do if a café owner who gave them free coffee and meals was stopped for a traffic violation. The researchers found that supervisory officers were more likely to give a ticket than rookies. Although only 15 percent would not write the ticket and would continue to go back for meals, an additional 41 percent would also not write the ticket but would give him a warning and not go back for free meals. The remaining officers would write the owner a ticket.

The ethics of virtue would be concerned with the individual qualities or virtues of the officer. A virtuous officer could take free coffee and not let it affect his or her judgment. According to this perspective, no gift or gratuity would affect the judgment of the virtuous officer. On the other hand, if the officer does not possess those qualities of virtue, such as honesty, integrity, and fairness, then even free coffee may lead to special treatment. Further, these officers would seek out gifts and gratuities and abuse their authority by pursuing them.

An egoistic framework provides easy justification for the taking or giving of gratuities. It obviously makes police officers feel good to receive such favors, especially if they feel that they deserve them or that the favors are a measure of esteem or appreciation. Even if the person giving the gift had ulterior motives, the police officer could accept and be ethically justified in doing so under the egoistic ethical framework if the officer gained more from the transaction than he or she lost. In other words, if one could keep a positive self-image intact and obtain the gratuity at the same time, then one would be justified in doing so, and it would be a moral action. However, let us not forget that the egoistic ethical system is discounted by a majority of philosophers.

## On-Duty Use of Drugs and Alcohol

Carter (1999) discusses the extent of on-duty drug use; he cites previous research that found up to 20 percent of officers in one city used marijuana and other drugs while on duty. That seems to be a high figure because in other surveys, about 8 percent of employees reported drug use, and only 3 percent of all workers in a "protective services" category reported drug use. In fact, in a recent survey, protective service employees were the least likely to report any drug use (Mieczkowski, 2002: 168). It could also be that the decrease seen in the use of drugs by the general population is reflected in police officer samples. As well, the sources are not exactly comparable, and it is impossible to determine which source is more accurate. However, there are certain circumstances present in law enforcement that, perhaps, create more opportunities for drug use. Elements of police work (especially undercover work) that can lead to drug use include the following:

- the exposure to a criminal element
- relative freedom from supervision
- the uncontrolled availability of contraband

Carter (1999: 316) also discussed the phenomenon of police officers who go undercover and become socialized to the drug culture. They may adapt norms conducive to drug taking. Further, they may feel they need to use drugs in order to maintain their cover.

They are also able to rationalize stealing drugs from sellers in that it should not be a crime to steal something that is contraband in the first place. Drug use by officers creates the potential for even more serious misbehavior, such as stealing evidence, being blackmailed to perform other unethical or illegal actions, and being tempted to steal from drug users instead of arresting them. This, of course, is in addition to the obvious problem of being under the influence of any drug while on duty and compromising one's decision-making abilities.

The use of drug tests during the hiring process is long-standing; however, periodic and/or random drug tests of employed officers are a more recent phenomenon. Many police officers, as is true of many other types of employees, are now subject to drug testing. Although about 60 percent of protective service workers say that their workplace engages in random drug testing, only 14 percent of other professionals have the same experience (reported in Mieczkowski, 2002: 172). Employees in the protective services sector are the most likely to experience drug testing in the workplace. Generally, courts have upheld the right of law enforcement agencies to employ drug testing, applying the balancing test between a compelling governmental interest and individual privacy rights. The list of compelling-interest elements served by drug testing includes the following:

1. public safety
2. public trust
3. potential for official corruption
4. official credibility
5. worker morale
6. worker safety (reported in Mieczkowski, 2002: 179)

Officers have some due process rights, however, and they must be notified of the policies and procedures involved in the agency's drug testing, have access to the findings, and have some sort of appeal process before sanctions are taken (Mieczkowski, 2002: 179).

Alcohol use is more socially acceptable than drug use, and it has also been cited as a problem. In one survey it was found that about 8 percent of those in protective services occupations (which would include police officers) reported heavy alcohol use. This compared to 12 percent of construction workers and 4 percent of sales workers. Barker and Carter (1994) reported that 8 percent of officers reported drinking alcohol on duty. The problems of drinking on duty do not involve the vulnerability to corruption that drug use does, but there are obvious problems, and officers who are aware of another's on-duty intoxication are faced with an ethical dilemma of whether or not to take official action. Officers may choose to informally isolate themselves from drinking officers by refusing to partner with them or avoid working calls with them.

## Graft

**Graft** refers to exploitation of one's role by accepting bribes or protection money. Graft also occurs when officers receive kickbacks from tow truck drivers, defense attorneys, or bail bond companies for recommending them.

Muir (1977) described a small-town police department as relatively free from corruption, but widespread patronage and petty bribery occurred because of the functional and beneficial aspects of this type of graft. For instance, a "security" firm was more or less given carte blanche to operate in legal and illegal ways to control burglaries in particular areas of the city. The police also overlooked gambling, after-hours liquor violations, and other minor infractions in exchange for information and cooperation. This behavior was seen as useful; in fact, it would be very difficult to convince the involved police officers that the behavior was at all wrong or unethical. In larger cities, such corruption may be more prevalent.

The Knapp Commission documented examples of a wide range of graft, including taking bribes for changing testimony or "forgetting," or phrasing answers in a way that would aid the defense (Manning and Redlinger, 1991). Although there are some regional differences, bribery is considered one of the more serious forms of corruption by police officers. In Klockars, Ivković, and Haberfeld's (2004) international comparison of officers' views regarding hypotheticals drawn to illustrate various forms of corruption, officers in the United States rated bribery as the second most serious offense. Only theft from a crime scene was rated as more serious. On the other hand, officers in Austria, Finland, Japan, the Netherlands, Sweden, and the United Kingdom rated bribery as more serious than did U.S. officers.

## Sexual Harassment and Assault

It is a sad reality that a few police officers use their position of authority to extort sex from female citizens (there doesn't seem to be the parallel situation of female police officers extorting sex from male victims). The other category of sexual misconduct is sexual harassment of female police officers.

Amnesty International has documented widespread mistreatment of women by police across the world. Egregious cases in the United States include rapes by officers on duty and by jailers in police lock-ups, and a few instances where the sexual misconduct of police officers was widespread and protected by departmental supervisors, such as in Walkill, New York. In that town, the twenty-five-member police department evidently engaged in numerous instances of sexual intimidation of citizens before being investigated by the state police and sued in a federal civil rights lawsuit (reported in McGurrin and Kappeler, 2002: 133).

Kraska and Kappeler (1995) looked at a sample of 124 cases of police sexual misconduct, including 37 sexual assaults by on-duty officers. These authors challenged earlier studies that indicated sexual misconduct of officers occurred most often when women traded sexual favors for lenient treatment and that it was the victim that initiated the trade. This study's authors concluded that norms in a police department that ignored or condoned the exchange of sex for favored treatment opened the door to officers who used more aggressive tactics to coerce sex from citizens.

Kraska and Kappeler (1995: 93) propose a continuum of sexual invasion that ranges from some type of invasion of privacy to sexual assault. This range of behavior includes the following:

1. viewing a victim's photos or videos for prurient purposes
2. field strip searches
3. custodial strip searches

4. illegal detentions
5. deception to gain sex
6. provision of services for sex
7. sexual harassment
8. sexual contact
9. sexual assault
10. rape

Sapp's (1994) inventory of sexual misconduct includes the following:

1. nonsexual contacts that are sexually motivated (nonvalid traffic stops)
2. voyeurism (i.e., patrolling lovers' lanes to watch sexual activity)
3. contact with crime victims (excessive call-backs that are not necessary for investigative purposes)
4. contact with offenders (sexual demands or inappropriate frisks)
5. contacts with juvenile offenders (sexual harassment and sexual contact)
6. sexual shakedowns (demanding sex from prostitutes or the homeless)
7. citizen-initiated sexual contact (an officer is approached by a citizen because of his officer status)

Even the most innocuous of contacts between female citizens and officers—whereby an officer might ask a woman he has stopped for a date—involve issues of power and coercion. The authors report that police in their study described how they routinely went "bimbo hunting," which involved sexual harassment of women out drinking (Kraska and Kappeler, 1995: 104). Prostitutes and homeless women are extremely vulnerable populations to sexual extortion by police officers, but studies indicate that middle-class citizens have also been subject to intimidation and outright assault. Most victims are under thirty (McGurrin and Kappeler, 2002). The defense of officers is usually that if sex occurred, it was consensual. The problem is that when officers acting in their official capacity meet women (as victims, witnesses, defendants, or suspects), the power differential makes consent extremely problematic.

McGurrin and Kappeler (2002) reported on an investigation of official reports of sexual misconduct by police officers that uncovered hundreds of instances of sexual assault, rape, and even murder by police officers in and out of uniform. It was not uncommon for rape charges to be downgraded to a conviction of "official oppression" in a plea agreement. It was also discovered that some officers who had criminal records for sexual offenses simply moved and obtained law enforcement positions in other jurisdictions.

In their own study of newspaper articles concerning sexual misconduct, McGurrin and Kappeler uncovered over two dozen cases where the officers had been previously disciplined for sexual misconduct before the case that was reported in the news article (McGurrin and Kappeler, 2002: 134). They also found that of the cases that were taken up by the justice system, about half of the alleged offenders did not receive any punishment. Only a third received jail or prison time (McGurrin and Kappeler, 2002: 134). A department is often aware of an officer's pattern of sexual harassment and does nothing about it. This is an obvious lapse of supervision that is unfair to the public and also costs money. Kraska and Kappeler (1995) report that police lost 69 percent of the civil rights suits brought by the victim of sexual misconduct.

**IN THE NEWS   Guilty or Not?**

In one year, four Dallas police were accused of rape. All of the cases were taken to a grand jury for rape indictments, but were reduced to "official oppression" because they were missing the element of "use of force."

Source: Reported in Kraska and Kappeler (1995: 105).

*Do you feel that officers must use physical force to coerce sex from victims before a charge of sexual assault is warranted? Do you think that official oppression is an appropriate charge when the incident involved sexual coercion?*

Sexual harassment of fellow officers is also a problem. One research study found that 70 percent of female officers reported being sexually harassed by other police officers (Kraska and Kappeler, 1995: 92). The "macho" culture of policing exists despite the fact that women have been integrated into patrol since the early 1970s. This "locker room" culture supports the devaluation and objectification of women. Although female officers do not encounter the virulent harassment and hostility that was present in the 1970s, when patrol forces were first integrated, it is fair to say that there are some remnants of that culture still in force today. Sexual harassment is a violation of policy and against the law; it is also unethical. None of the ethical systems from Chapter 2 would support coercing co-workers for sex or creating a hostile work environment. Perpetrators' defense may be that it is innocent "kidding" or honest infatuation, but universalism is a good check on this type of behavior. Would the perpetrator want his daughter or sister subjected to the behavior?

## Criminal Cops

There are instances where the transgressions that officers engage in go beyond ethics and enter the realm of crime and criminal conspiracies. The "Buddy Boys" in New York were able to operate almost openly in a precinct rife with lesser forms of corruption. Ultimately, 13 officers in a precinct of only a little over 200 were indicted for crimes ranging from drug use to drug sales and armed robbery. The Buddy Boys graduated from stealing cash and drugs from drug dealers during official arrests to planned thefts where they would, sometimes on duty, target crack houses or apartments and break in and steal drugs, cash, and other valuables. In at least one such instance, customers came to buy drugs, and the officers obliged by selling drugs through the door. They had relatively nothing to fear from their victims because the individuals targeted were minority drug dealers. Their victims could hardly report a robbery, and if other police in the precinct had any idea about what was going on, they evidently did little to investigate. The situation was finally exposed when internal affairs investigators caught two of the individual officers accepting protection money and forced them to wear "wires" to help gather evidence on the others. Ultimately, the police commissioner transferred all officers in the precinct to other divisions (Kappeler, Sluder, and Alpert, 1984/1994).

Michael Dowd, another New York City police officer, testified to the Mollen Commission in 1993 that he and other officers accepted money for protecting illegal drug operations, used drugs and alcohol while on duty, robbed crime victims and drug dealers of money and drugs, and even robbed corpses of their valuables (Kappeler, Sluder, and Alpert, 1984/1994: 201–202). An NBC *Turning Point* special titled "The Tarnished Badge" described how the internal affairs officer who attempted to investigate Dowd was first given no assistance or encouragement and was then sanctioned by his superiors for his dogged persistence in exposing Dowd's criminal behavior. Dowd was exposed and, ultimately, indicted and prosecuted only after police officers in a suburban city videotaped Dowd buying drugs (in uniform and in a police car).

New York City has experienced police scandals with depressing regularity, with widescale investigations and exposés occurring in 1894, 1913, 1932 (the Wickersham Commission), 1949 (the Kefauver Commission), 1972 (the Knapp Commission), and 1993 (the Mollen Commission). The most recent scandal was the Abner Louima case in 1998 (Rothlein, 1999). But New York City is definitely not alone. The "Miami River Rats" also committed armed robberies of drug deals, collecting cash and drugs. These robberies by a small group of police officers eventually led to at least one homicide (Dorschner, 1989; see also Rothlein, 1999; Crank and Caldero, 2000: 162). A New Orleans police officer is in a federal prison today because he used a police radio to order a hit on a woman who was going to testify against him and others in a corruption trial. He was being monitored by federal agents, who decoded the thinly disguised assassination attempt (Human Rights Watch, 1998).

Many other large cities have their own historical cycles of corruption and exposure (Kappeler, Sluder, and Alpert, 1984/1994: 197). In 1998, forty-four Cleveland cops were indicted for providing protection for cocaine shipments. Chicago has also had its share of corruption scandals. In 1996, seven Chicago cops were indicted for conspiracy to commit robbery and extortion for shaking down undercover agents they thought were drug dealers (Crank and Caldero, 2000). In 2001, a former chief of detectives pled guilty to running a jewel-theft ring for more than a decade. This detective used police computers to follow the path of traveling jewelry sales representatives in order to target them (Fountain, 2001). Other Chicago police officers have been accused of shaking down Polish immigrants and robbing suspected drug dealers (who turned out to be F.B.I. agents). This group of officers evidently joined forces with a street gang in order to control the cocaine trade. Brutality charges and other corruption charges have also been recently leveled against Chicago officers (Babwin, 2001).

Drugs are the root of several different kinds of deviance. The range of behaviors where drugs are involved include using drugs on duty, buying drugs, selling drugs, providing protection to drug dealers, robbing drug dealers, stealing from drug dealers, and using drugs to pay informants. The large amounts of money present in the drug trade and the perception that it is "just drug money" lead to some officers stealing evidence or robbing drug dealers. In 1998 the General Accounting Office conducted a study for U.S. Representative Charles Rangel that collected academic and other findings to explore the extent and range of corruption in law enforcement that was due to drugs. It was clear that the large amount of money present in the drug trade was a powerful corruptor (General Accounting Office, 1998).

Carter (1999: 321) concludes that there are some mechanisms that can be used to control drug corruption:

- leadership by the chief
- management and supervision
- supervisory training
- organizational control and information management
- internal auditing of the use of informants
- internal affairs
- drug enforcement units having audit controls
- periodic turnover of staff
- better evidence handling
- early warning systems
- better training and discipline

Several books, such as *Serpico* (Maas, 1973) and *Prince of the City* (Daley, 1984), detail the pervasiveness of corruption and criminality in some departments and the relative ease with which individual officers may develop rationales to justify greater and greater infractions. For instance, the main character in *Prince of the City* progresses from relatively minor rule breaking to fairly serious infractions and unethical conduct, such as supplying drugs to an addicted informant, without having to make major decisions regarding his morality. It is only when the totality of his actions becomes apparent that he realizes the extent of his deviance.

We have examined a range of corruption, from the arguably trivial (gratuities) to criminal acts that include murder. There is a legitimate argument that the officers who engage in minor rule breaking or some types of unethical behaviors that are not criminal should not be discussed in the same manner as those "criminal cops" whose pattern of wrongdoing and criminality is much more serious. The opposing argument is that it is the minor transgressions that lead to an environment in which the truly rogue cops feel free to engage in criminality.

## Excessive Force

Police have an uncontested right to use force when necessary to apprehend and/or subdue a suspect of a crime. When their use of force exceeds that which is necessary to accomplish their lawful purpose, or when their purpose is not lawful apprehension or self-defense, but rather personal retaliation or coercion, then it is defined as **excessive force** and is unethical and illegal. The ultimate example of excessive force is when an unjustified use of lethal force occurs. We discuss this type of corruption separately partly because of its serious nature, but also because it has drawn the most attention of all the forms of unethical and/or illegal actions by police officers described in this chapter, as indicated by the Quote and Query box on the next page.

## QUOTE and QUERY

Police brutality is one of the most serious, enduring, and divisive human rights violations in the United States. The problem is nationwide, and its nature is institutionalized. For these reasons, the U.S. government—as well as state and city governments, which have an obligation to respect the international human rights standards by which the United States is bound—deserve to be held accountable by international human rights bodies and international public opinion.

Source: Human Rights Watch (1998: 1).

*Do you think that the perception that there is a pervasive use of excessive force and/or brutality by police officers who are sworn to uphold the law is accurate or not?*

The use of force by Los Angeles police against Rodney King is an example of force used for instrumental or expressive ends, depending on whom you believe. This case represents a situation in which policy, law, and ethics present different answers to this question: "Did the officers do anything wrong?" The legal question of unlawful use of force is contingent on whether the Los Angeles Police Department's use-of-force policy was legal and whether the officers conformed to departmental policy. The policy stated that the officers could use escalating and proportional force to a suspect's "offensive" behavior.

The reason that two use-of-force experts—one for the prosecution and one for the defense—disagreed was that the policy, like many other policies in policing, depends on the ethical use of discretion. The defense use-of-force expert analyzed the video and identified offensive movements in every attempt to rise and in every arm movement. The prosecution expert (who wrote the departmental policy) testified that a suspect lying on the ground is not in a position to present offensive movements to officers. If an officer perceives offensiveness in every movement of every suspect, the policy justifies his or her use of force.

One can see that the policy leaves a great deal of room for choice and that, in most cases, an officer's perceptions of the ethical use of force will become as powerful, if not more so, than the policy itself. If an officer gets shot at, the policy obviously would justify use of force, but if the officer decides that he or she is safe enough behind his or her patrol car to talk the suspect out of shooting again and into giving up the weapon, then the use-of-force policy would support that nonviolent response as well. If an officer is hit in the face by a drunk, the policy would support use of force because the drunk obviously performed an offensive action; however, the officer who accepts the fact that the drunk is irrational, allows for it, and simply puts the person in the back of the patrol car (in effect, giving him a "free punch") is also supported by the policy. In other words, the policy can be used to justify all but the most blatant abuse of police power, or not, depending on the interpretation of the individual officer.

Thus, in the Rodney King incident, an initial act of passing a police vehicle and leading officers in a high-speed chase (although the actual speed of such chase was subject to dispute) led to the involvement of twelve police cars, one helicopter, and up to twenty-seven officers. The incident resulted in King being struck at least fifty-six times, with eleven skull fractures, a broken cheekbone, a fractured eye socket, a broken ankle, missing teeth, kidney damage, external burns, and permanent brain damage (Kappeler, Sluder, and Alpert, 1984/1994: 146).

After the incident, officers justified their actions by the explanation that King was on PCP (he was not, and in fact his alcohol level was .075), impervious to pain, and wild. These claims were repeated in the newspapers and can be interpreted as the attempt to fit the use of force into a pattern that the public could understand and accept. In fact, police use of force probably became an incident in this case only because of the existence and widespread dissemination of a videotape. In other circumstances, it would hardly have rated a small newspaper article. The media typically become interested in police use of force when the victim cannot be fit into the stereotype of the "dangerous criminal": when he is a middle-class insurance agent (as in the Miami case that sparked riots), Andrew Young's son (in an incident involving the Washington, D.C., police), or a high-school athlete who would have been on his way to Yale on an academic/athletic scholarship. More examples are in the "In the News" box "Use of Force."

---

**IN THE NEWS**   **Use of Force**

A police officer pointed a gun at a nine-year-old's head and threatened to pull the trigger. The child was not a suspect trying to evade the officers or posing any other threat.

Source: *McDonald v. Haskins*, 966 F.2d 292 (7th Cir. 1992).

Two men on a motorcycle accidentally brushed the bumper of a DEA car. One DEA agent got out and began a physical altercation with the driver of the motorcycle. When the passenger intervened, both agents beat him and yelled anti-homosexual epithets. When the driver asked why they were beating the other man, he was beaten as well.

Source: *Anderson v. Branen*, 17 F.3d 552, rehearing denied 27 F.3d 29 (2nd Dis. 1994).

An individual was met by police officers in the hallway of his apartment building who were there looking for a person who was making fraudulent calls. They shoved him against the wall, threatened him, struck him, and dragged him down the stairs.

Source: *Goetz v. Cappelen*, 946 F.2d 511 (7th Cir. 1991).

*Why do these obviously inappropriate uses of force by police officers happen?*

The most common explanations for police officer use of force are similar to those used to explain correctional officer use of excessive force—that force is the only thing "these people" understand or that "officers are only human" and consequently get mad or frightened or angry, just like anyone else would in that situation. The weakness of such arguments is obvious. If other people get mad and use force, it is called assault and battery, and they are arrested and prosecuted. Even if the only thing "these people" understand is force, it removes the differences that we like to think exist between us and "them."

The most gruesome recent example of excessive force was the assault on Abner Louima by Justin Volpe of the New York City Police Department. The incident shocked the nation and led to a prison sentence for Volpe. The truly amazing thing about this criminal act is that it occurred in a police station with at least one officer reportedly assisting, but with a whole squad room right outside the door. According to Volpe's testimony, Louima was brought up to the squad room and taken into the bathroom for the purpose of beating him; in fact, the broken broom handle was put in the bathroom for that purpose. This evidently didn't raise any red flags to officers at the booking desk or other officers. How could this have happened in a police station? The fact that Louima was a minority, the fact that Volpe believed he had been hit in the head by Louima, and the fact that the blue curtain of secrecy is still intact in many police departments seem to be insufficient answers to this question.

How do victims of excessive force come to the attention of police? Often it is by challenging police authority—passing a patrol car, asking questions, challenging the stop, or intervening in the arrest of another (Kappeler, Sluder, and Alpert, 1984/1994: 159). In Klockars's description of types of police power (authority, power, persuasion, and force), force is brought into play when one's authority

---

**QUOTE and QUERY**

I saw one guy arrested once for speeding and the police officer lost his temper. Of course, this highway patrolman brought it on himself, because he was bad-mouthing the guy. Finally—he's a man, too—the guy lost his temper and spit on the highway patrolman. Right on the side of a U.S. highway on a Sunday afternoon, the highway patrolman wrestled the guy down, took a handful of hair and held his head down in the dirt and started packing the guy's mouth full of sand. The guy was choking and spitting and this patrolman was shoving sand in his mouth. "I'll teach you to spit at a trooper, boy." Those were his exact words. I'm standing in the background, watching the cars go by, slowing down to stare at this event. It looked bad.

Source: Mark Baker, *Cops* (New York: Pocket Books, 1985): 139–140. Reprinted with the permission of Simon & Schuster from *Cops: Their Lives in Their Own Words* by Mark Baker. Copyright © 1985 by Mark Baker.

*Do you think anyone "deserves" to be beaten by police officers?*

is challenged. Thus, individuals who question or refuse to recognize police authority become vulnerable to the use of force. Such use of force may be perfectly legal—officers have the right to tackle a fleeing suspect or hit back when they are defending themselves. Illegal or excessive force occurs when the officer goes beyond what is necessary to effect a lawful arrest or has no lawful reason to use force at all. For instance, gratuitous violence in response to verbal insults is excessive force, as is beating a suspect who is handcuffed and helpless.

## *Culture of Force*

The use of force in response to perceived challenges to police authority is highly resistant to change, even in the presence of public scrutiny and management pressure. Even with the notoriety of the Rodney King episode and the extreme public reaction to the spectacle of police use of force, several incidents involving other officers' abusive behavior toward motorists occurred shortly afterward. It might be that this pattern is so ingrained in some police department cultures that it remains relatively unaffected.

The Los Angeles Police Department (L.A.P.D.) seems to have had the type of culture that tolerates, perhaps even encourages, a high level of violence. Rothlein (1999) writes that the Christopher Commission reported that L.A.P.D. management was responsible, to some extent, for the brutality exhibited by the Rodney King incident in that there was an apparent failure to punish or control those who had repeated citizen complaints of violence. Further, there was a culture that encouraged the use of force, and there was an ineffective citizen complaint system, with no civilian oversight. In other words, leadership did not exist that actively discouraged the excessive use of force.

Skolnick and Fyfe (1993) also discuss the culture of L.A.P.D. as one where the use of violence was tolerated, even encouraged. The result has been civil rights cases—in 1990, for instance, Los Angeles paid out more than $11 million in civil rights cases for excessive force violations (Skolnick and Fyfe, 1993: 3). Breaking up departments into elite units seems to encourage "swashbuckling behavior." Skolnick and Fyfe (1993: 191) describe one case where an L.A.P.D. elite squad, acting on a tip, totally destroyed a citizen's home, including breaking toilets, ripping sofas, and spray-painting "L.A.P.D. Rules!" on the wall of the house. These specialized units create their own culture, even within the subculture of the larger department, and sometimes this subculture may promote violence.

Los Angeles is not the only city that has been in the news because of allegations of excessive force. Kappeler, Sluder, and Alpert (1984/1994: 222) report that Washington, D.C., has been widely known for incidents of brutality, including the one against Andrew Young's eighteen-year-old son. Yet of twenty-one cases in which the Civilian Complaint Review Board recommended adverse actions against officers for use of force, the police chief took action in only five.

The Human Rights Watch (1998) identified serious problems in Atlanta, Boston, Chicago, Detroit, Indianapolis, Los Angeles, Minneapolis, New Orleans, New York, Philadelphia, Portland, Providence, San Francisco, and Washington, D.C. The report cited police leadership and the "blue wall of secrecy" as serious barriers to reducing police violence. According to this report, the mechanisms for handling police offenders

**IN THE NEWS   Tasers as Torture?**

Amnesty International alleges that police use Taser or stun guns in hundreds of cases in which their use is unjustified and "routinely" inflict injury, pain, and death. Its investigation uncovered the fact that the Tasers were used on unarmed suspects 80 percent of the time and for verbal noncompliance in 36 percent of the cases. They have allegedly been used on "unruly schoolchildren," the "mentally disturbed or intoxicated," and those who do not comply immediately with police commands. There have been seventy Taser-related deaths in four years.

Source: B. Dart, "Police Use Taser Guns 'Excessively,' Rights Group Asserts," *Austin American Statesman*, November 30, 2004, A14.

**Should Taser use be curtailed considering its potential as a tool intended to inflict gratuitous injury?**

ensure that violence will continue. In most cases where a citizen alleges excessive force, there is no discipline, and the case is closed as unfounded. If there is a civil suit and the plaintiff wins, the city pays, and, again, the officer may not even be disciplined. One study is cited concerning the fate of police officers named in 100 civil lawsuits between 1986 and 1991 in 22 states in which juries ordered $100,000 or more. It was found that only 8 of these officers were disciplined (Human Rights Watch, 1998: 82; see also Payne, 2002).

Of course, Human Rights Watch has been criticized for focusing on unusual or extreme cases. Amnesty International is another human rights organization that looks at official oppression all around the world and has long been a critic of the U.S. justice and corrections system. Recently, this organization has alleged that police officers use Taser guns inappropriately and that their use constitutes excessive force in many cases. See the "In the News" box above for a description of this allegation. However, it should also be noted that Tasers seem to be associated with a decrease in the number of deaths of suspects, a decrease in the number of injuries to suspects, and a decrease in the number of injuries to officers (Dart, 2004: A14). Further, manufacturers allege that Tasers are safe in the vast majority of cases and are potentially lethal only when there is some underlying medical condition.

## Research on Excessive Force

All information regarding police use of force is controlled by police, including the number of incidents, the taking of reports, and the amount of information recorded. The ability to access this information is limited, even in cases dealing with a challenge to the officer's use of force. The official version of any event is that force was necessary because of dangerous, offensive actions. This interpretation is often supported by other police, and there is usually little evidence to the contrary (unless there is a videotape). The victim is often an unsavory character who would be a poor choice for sympathy, and supporting witnesses may have their credibility questioned. Thus, it is difficult to determine the true number of excessive force incidents. There are four ways researchers address the questions:

1. Use official documents, such as police incident reports
2. Ask police officers about their actions or the actions of their peers regarding excessive force
3. Use Civil Rights Complaints or public opinion surveys to ask people what their experiences have been
4. Use observers in police cars to record interactions between police and citizens, including instances of excessive force

In general, there is quite a lot of research, but it is on use of force, rather than specifically excessive force. One can perhaps assume that those officers who are identified as using force, or those factors that are associated with the use of force, are also related to the use of excessive force, but research usually does not specifically prove that connection. Further, some findings are inconsistent, but it seems to be the case that there are a few generalizations that can be made:

1. Force is present in a small percentage of the total encounters between police and citizens.
2. A small percentage of officers seem to be responsible for a disproportionate percentage of the force incidents.
3. Some studies do find an association between force and race or socioeconomic status, but other factors, such as demeanor, seem to be even more influential.

## Number of Incidents

Research seems to indicate that very few encounters actually end in the use of any force, much less excessive force. Worden and Catlin (2002) offer studies that show that use of force is present in between 1.3 to 2.5 percent of all encounters. Holmes (2000) also reviews a number of studies to reach the conclusion that the use of physical force by police is rare.

On the other hand, Weisburd and Greenspan (2000) asked officers about use of force, and they discovered that 22 percent of respondents said that police officers in their department "sometimes," "often," or "always" used more force than necessary when making an arrest. Further, 15 percent of respondents indicated that their fellow officers "sometimes," "often," or "always" responded to verbal abuse with physical force. Recall that in Barker and Carter's (1994) study, officers reported that 39 percent of their peers engaged in brutality. Garner, Maxwell, and Heraux (2002) found in their study that use of force ranged from 12.7 percent of encounters in one city to 22.9 percent of encounters in another city. Of course, the varying percentages reported are caused, to some extent, by different definitions of force.

## Disproportional Use by Small Number

Some officers seem to get involved in use-of-force situations repeatedly, whereas others, even with similar patrol neighborhoods, rarely get involved in such altercations. Thus, even if every use of force meets the guidelines of departmental policy, there are lingering questions as to why some officers seem to need to resort to force more often than others and why some interpret actions more often as offensive.

According to Souryal (1992: 242), the report by the Independent Commission of the Los Angeles Police Department (1991) reveals that the top 5 percent of officers ranked by number of reports of the use of force accounted for more than 20 percent of all reports, and that of approximately 1,800 officers who had been reported for excessive use of force from 1986 to 1990, most had only one or two allegations, but forty-four had six or more, sixteen had eight or more, and one had sixteen allegations.

Worden and Catlin (2002) report on a number of studies that document the presence of differential use of force by officers in police departments. Research indicates that there seems to be a small number of officers who are disproportionately involved in use-of-force incidents and, arguably, engaged in a greater degree than average of excessive force. Further, there is some evidence that seems to indicate that these officers may be identifiable by certain psychological traits:

- a lack of empathy
- antisocial and paranoid tendencies
- a proclivity toward abusive behavior
- an inability to learn from experience
- a tendency to not take responsibility for their actions
- cynicism
- a strong identification with the police subculture

Other risk factors include the age of the officer (being young and impressionable may increase the risk of using improper force) and being involved in a traumatic event (thus, use of force would be a type of post-traumatic stress behavior) (reported in Worden and Catlin, 2002: 101). Terrill, Paoline, and Manning (2003) found that those officers who more strongly identified with the police culture were more likely to use force and that differences between individuals were more predictive than differences in departments' management strategies or formal cultures of departments.

## Race

Nelson (2000) chronicles a long list of personal stories of harassment, brutality, illegal arrests, and coerced confessions by police toward minority members, especially African Americans. Her conclusion is that in the minority community, at least, there are reasons to fear police. Holmes (2000) found that the number of civil rights complaints filed (which were mostly claims of excessive force) was only weakly affected by the percentage of blacks in the population in small cities. However, there was a significant association in cities of over 150,000 in population, and there was also a stronger association between the number of complaints filed and the percentage of Hispanics in the city's population.

Garner, Maxwell, and Heraux (2002) reported on studies that found that minority status was associated with the likelihood of use of force. Smith and Holmes (2003) also found that the percentage of Hispanics in the population was positively correlated with the number of civil rights complaints.

Race seems to be associated with use of force. However, only a few studies have controlled for other factors, such as those in the next section, to determine if race continues to be a significant factor. The other issue, of course, is that most studies (except for those that use civil rights complaints) are measuring use of force, not excessive force.

## Other Factors

Garner, Maxwell, and Heraux (2002) review a number of studies to determine what factors are associated with police use of force. They conclude, through their literature review as well as their own study, that the following (not in order of rank) have been associated with a greater likelihood that the police officer will use force:

- suspect's race
- suspect's manner toward police (disrespectful demeanor)
- general agitation or emotionality of suspect
- intoxication of suspect
- number of citizens present (positive association)
- number of police officers present (positive association)
- possession of a weapon by the suspect (or belief there is a weapon)
- knowledge that suspect had committed other crimes (especially, violent crimes)
- suspect's use of force
- gang involvement
- suspect being male
- officer being male
- age of officer (younger)
- officer having prior injuries
- encounter involving a car chase
- race of officer (but the association is for Hispanics, not African Americans)
- socioeconomic status of suspect

However, these factors are not found to be significant by all researchers. For instance, Alpert and MacDonald (2001) did not find any relationship between officer gender or ethnicity and use of force. They did find a relationship between use of force and age, as well as the presence of alcohol and mental illness. They also noted that agency characteristics seemed to affect the use of force: Those agencies that required supervisors to fill out use-of-force forms had lower levels of use of force than did agencies that allowed officers to fill out their own forms. It should be noted that these factors are associated with the use of force, not necessarily excessive force. Terrill and Mastrofsky (2002) found in their analysis of encounters that the suspect's demeanor was not correlated with the use of force but that the age and education of the officer and the gender, socioeconomic status, and race of the suspect were correlated with the use of force.

## *Deadly Force*

There is nothing more divisive in a minority community than a police shooting that appears to be unjustified. Cities are quite different in their shooting policies and in their rates of civilian deaths. There can also be quite a change within one city. The District of Columbia, for instance, went from thirty-two police shootings (with twelve deaths) in 1998 to only seventeen in 2001 (with three deaths) (C. Murphy, 2002). The fact that the D.C. police department was under a court monitor might have had something to do with the fairly dramatic decline in shootings.

Skolnick and Fyfe (1993: 235) describe New York City's shooting policy and argue that the policy may be instrumental in why the N.Y.P.D. has such a low shooting rate. There is an automatic investigation every time shots are fired, the investigation is conducted by the Firearms Discharge Review Board, and there are multiple layers of report writing and investigation before the officer is cleared. The authors also note that N.Y.P.D. officers also experience a lower rate of being shot than other cities, so the stringent policy has not seemed to affect their safety.

Chevigny (1995) also discusses New York's shooting policy and compares it to the situation in Los Angeles. In L.A., police shoot more people in proportion to the size of their force than any other major U.S. police department. Between 1965 and 1993, one squad (the Special Investigations Section) shot fifty-five people, killing twenty-eight, yet only one officer was shot during that time, and he was shot by a police gun. Skolnick and Fyfe (1993) and Chevigny (1995) discuss how L.A.P.D. officers in this major crimes task force allowed criminals under surveillance to carry out robberies, and then the officers engaged in shootouts after the fact (see also Payne, 2002: 31).

In a couple of incidents, there was some evidence to indicate that the offenders were shot unnecessarily, although no charges against police were ever filed (Skolnick and Fyfe, 1993). For instance, one group of suspects was followed to a McDonald's, and police watched while they prepared themselves and carried guns inside after closing hours. The terrified clerk called in a robbery, and patrol officers responded to the 911 call but were waved away. The squad then allowed the robbers to come out of the drive-in and get in their cars, where they were surrounded. Three out of the four were shot to death. Evidence indicated that the robbers' guns were locked in the trunk of another car (Chevigny, 1995; Payne, 2002).

Even New York, however, has had its share of deaths that have raised tensions. Amadou Diallo allegedly resembled a rapist, and when he ignored police orders to show his hands and continued to unlock an apartment building door to go inside, he was shot at forty-one times by officers in the Special Crimes Unit of N.Y.P.D. The case threatened to spark riots in the city, especially when the police officers' trial was moved to Albany and the officers were acquitted. A wrongful-death suit by the family is pending. New York City paid $40 million in 1999 alone for civil rights claims. That year the number of complaints increased by 10 percent and was the largest in a decade. Policy Box 8-1 examines the use of shooting-review boards.

## Summary

The use of excessive force is probably not as pervasive in this country today as it was even twenty years ago. However, a concern is that it is hard to know what occurs because the data are not readily available and individual victims often do not come forward or, if they do, are not taken seriously. It seems that there are always a few officers in every department who are truly abusers of power, but the other officers and an organizational culture protect these officers from sanctions. The more common ethical issue concerning the use of force is that of the officer who observes an unlawful use of force by another officer. This issue is addressed in the next chapter.

---

**POLICY BOX 8-1**   **Shooting-Review Board**

All departments have some mechanism for reviewing an officer's use of a firearm. A shooting-review board would require the officer to appear before a hearing made up of fellow officers and supervisors. The review board would not only evaluate whether the case was justified but also review elements of the shooting to see if there were any improvements that could be made in training to assist officers.

**Law:** It is unlawful to shoot unless the officer is in fear of his life or the offender poses a threat to others. However, that law covers a wide spectrum of situations. If it is found that the officer's shooting was unjustified, he or she could be held on a range of charges, up to murder but usually some form of voluntary manslaughter. The department may be legally liable if it is found that training is insufficient.

**Policy:** No police department wants to endanger citizens' lives with police officers who shoot unnecessarily; therefore, policies are in place and officers are trained to use their weapon as a last resort. On the other hand, informal policies regarding shooting evidently vary quite a bit from department to department, as evidenced by the number of shootings that take place.

**Ethics:** Officers who would be asked to participate in this review board may have an ethical dilemma in that they might think that it is showing some form of disloyalty to their fellow police officer to appear as a board member. The individual who used his or her weapon has an ethical duty to tell the truth. The board members have a duty to decide against the officer if, in their collective judgment, they decide that it was not a "good" shooting.

---

# A Worldwide Problem

Police corruption does not just occur in the United States. Across the world there are instances of many different types of corruption. *Baksheesh* is a euphemism for graft and is endemic in many developing countries. Officials, including law enforcement officers, expect *baksheesh* to do the job they are supposed to do; alternatively, they extort money in exchange for not doing their job. "It is just the way it is" is the explanation for why such corruption exists. In all countries, corruption includes the following:

- corruption of authority
- kickbacks
- opportunistic theft
- shakedowns
- protection of illegal activity
- internal payoffs
- excessive force

Tim Prenzler and his colleagues have tracked and analyzed police corruption in Australia. In Queensland, the Fitzgerald Inquiry (1989) found a network of vertical corruption reaching to the commissioner and widespread misconduct, including fabrication of evidence and assaults on suspects. Ultimately, the police commissioner was jailed for fourteen years on charges of accepting payments from gambling and prostitution rackets. It was a huge scandal and eventually resulted in legislation pertaining to freedom of information and whistleblower protection. In addition, an independent watchdog agency—the Criminal Justice Commission—was created (Prenzler, Harrison, and Ede, 1996: 5; Prenzler and Ransley, 2002; Fitzgerald, 1989).

A similar investigation was conducted of the New South Wales Police Department in 1997. The Wood Commission Report (Wood, 1997) described instances of fabrication of evidence, theft, armed robberies, sale of drug evidence, sale of information, and a protection racket. An informant, Detective Trevor Haken, eventually named more than 200 police and civilians as involved in corrupt activities (Prenzler, Harrison, and Ede, 1996).

There have been notable scandals in every country, although some countries' police enjoy high degrees of public trust.

*Austria.* Austria's police enjoy the position of being ranked highest for public trust of all institutions. The number of complaints average around 100–200 for all federal police, with only about 10 being for corruption. There is a Council for Human Rights within the Ministry of the Interior. The most notable scandal occurred in the late 1970s, when police were suspected in the death of an illegal immigrant in police custody (Edelbacher and Ivković, 2004).

*Belgium.* In Belgium, the Marc Dutroux case led to a crisis in public confidence of police. Dutroux was convicted of raping five young girls, but served only three years of a thirteen-year sentence. Shortly after his release in 1996, young girls started disappearing in Belgium. What was discovered later was that he would kidnap them or pay an associate to kidnap them and then hold the girl in a basement cell or in one of his several houses. The evidence indicates that some of the girls were sold into the sex trade in Poland, but several bodies were dug up—buried in the backyard of his house. Two eight-year-olds evidently starved to death during a four-month period when he was in jail on theft charges. Officers, following informants' tips, were in Dutroux's house several times, even when there were captives in the basement. Finally, the basement cells were discovered, and two young girls were saved. At best, police showed incredible incompetence, at worst collusion, because there were allegations that high officials in the police department were involved in Dutroux's child pornography ring. The case led to mass demonstrations and the resignation of the minister of justice (Neyroud and Beckley, 2001: 12).

*Canada.* There have been a few instances where Canadian police were investigated for suspicious deaths, such as when two Quebec officers were accused of beating a vagrant to death. The Keable Commission was established in 1981 in response to police reactions to the activities of a terroristic group (Front de Libération du Québec) in the early 1970s. Police arrested more than 400 people and held many without charges. It came to light that they also committed crimes and then blamed them on the FLQ (Alain, 2004).

**China.** The Chinese vice minister of public security, Li Jizou, was arrested on charges of illegally importing thousands of cars. More than 11,000 Chinese police were punished for corruption in 1998 (Mores, 2002).

**France.** In 1998, twenty-three police officers went on trial in Perpignan, France, on charges of corruption. The alleged activities included bribes, pocketing traffic fines, selling confiscated alcohol, and stealing from stolen vehicles (Mores, 2002).

**Great Britain.** The Brixton disorders refer to a series of riots in the United Kingdom arising from tension between police and the minority community. They led to the Scarman Inquiry in 1981. Also, police were accused of mishandling the investigation of the racial killing of Stephen Lawrence in 1993. This situation elevated racial tensions and resulted in an inquiry that severely criticized the London police force, which was called "institutionally racist" (Neyroud and Beckley, 2001: 9). Barker (2002: 14) described the British police subculture as condoning some types of unethical practices, such as "verbals" (statements invented by officers in order to effect an arrest) and "working the oracle" (the belief of officers that they "know" the offender is guilty regardless of the lack of evidence).

Westmarland (2004) describes a series of scandals in Great Britain, including those concerning the Guildford Four, the Maguire Seven, and the Birmingham Six. These incidents concerned police interrogation methods and the investigations that led to convictions of innocent people. Others report that the cost of settling civil suits rose 500 percent for the Metropolitan (London) Police between 1991 and 1998 and that the British police will be paying over 300 million pounds a year in damages by 2005 (Fielding, 2003: 74).

**The Netherlands.** In the Netherlands, the VanTraa Commission (1996–1998) looked into how covert drug operations led to corrupt conspiracies between police and drug informants (Neyroud and Beckley, 2001: 12).

**Japan.** Although Japanese police seem to answer ethics surveys in a way that indicates the level of corruption is low, some wonder whether such surveys reflect the true nature of corruption in Japan. There has evidently been a long-standing tradition of slush funds, improper relations with the Yakuza (Japanese organized-crime gangs), and a variety of cover-ups of sexual and other misbehavior by Japanese police (Johnson, 2004).

**Mexico.** Mexico has a reputation for corruption within its national and local police forces. In 1996, 4,400 officers were dismissed allegedly for drug smuggling/corruption (Mores, 2002). More recently, police have been implicated in a range of crimes, including the notorious killings of literally hundreds of women in Juarez. In at least one border town, the police were so corrupt that the federal government was compelled to send in the *federales*, a police unit that has not escaped its own corruption scandals.

*Pakistan.* In Pakistan, police have used torture to extract confessions, and there have been allegations of anti-terrorist death squads. There are also reports of protection rackets, bribes in order to get police to investigate crimes, and other forms of corruption (Chattha and Ivković, 2004).

*Russia.* In a unique sting operation in 1997, the minister of the interior of Russia rented a Mercedes-Benz and drove across the country. He was stopped twenty-two times by traffic officers, and he offered each a bribe. Twenty-one of the twenty-two times the bribe was offered, the officers accepted. In 1997, 1,000 police officers in St. Petersburg were fired for corruption (Mores, 2002: 25).

*South Africa.* Police have been known to use extreme means to extract confessions. Police have been videotaped beating car thieves, and Johannesburg officers have been videotaped kicking suspects in the face and putting out a lit cigarette on the face of one of the suspects. There have also been allegations that police dogs have been used to attack suspects (Mores, 2002).

## *Measures of Corruption*

Transparency International charts corruption worldwide, ranking ninety-one countries. This agency defines corruption as abuse of public office (including police) for private gain (e.g., bribe taking). The countries with the highest scores for honesty included Finland, Denmark, New Zealand, and Sweden. Some of the poorest countries had very low scores, such as Azerbaijan, Bolivia, Kenya, Uganda, and Bangladesh. The United States, to many people's surprise, perhaps, does not rate as highly as a number of other countries.

Finland is a country that evidently has a very low level of police corruption (Puonti, Vuorinen, and Ivković, 2004). It has received the highest or one of the highest rankings by Transparency International for the last several years. According to official records, there have been only twenty-three cases of official corruption in the country in the 1990s, and only one of these cases involved a police officer (Laitinen, 2004). It is reported that only about 10 percent of all citizen complaints about officials are about law enforcement officers (Laitinen, 2002).

Surveys indicate that Finnish people trust their police more than any other professional group, including court officials and church officials (Laitinen, 2004). This phenomenon may be attributed to the culture of open and accountable government. Finland's police force is highly educated as well, and can be described as endorsing a public service model of policing. There are strong proscriptions against most of the types of corruption that have been described in this chapter, even gratuities. Laitinen (2004) illustrates the fact that gratuities are, in general, frowned upon by a joke in which gratuities are described as the difference between a "cold sandwich and a warm beer," which is acceptable, and a "warm sandwich and a cold beer," which is a gratuity. Although there are obviously cases of corrupt police officers in Finland, it seems that their police have a strong ethical code that minimizes the level of corruption.

Croatia, on the other hand, has been known as having fairly corrupt police. In 1999 Transparency International rated it seventy-fourth out of the ninety-nine countries participating in the study. In 2000, only 46 percent of the respondents had confidence in the police, according to public opinion polls. However, it appears that Croatia's police may be becoming less corrupt, or at least the perception is that they are. In 2000, their ranking in the Transparency International survey went up to fifty-first place, and in 2001 it went up to forty-seventh place (Ivković and Klockars, 2004). It would be instructive to examine countries that seem to have minimal levels of corruption and then contrast them with other countries to see what elements contribute to the relative higher levels of ethics.

One interesting study that has compared the police of different countries was conducted by Klockars, Ivković, and Haberfeld (2004). In this study, samples of police officers from fourteen countries rated the seriousness of eleven hypothetical situations that ranged from gratuities to "shopping" at a crime scene. They also indicated what level of discipline would be administered to the transgressions. This second measure reflected the officers' perception of the degree of seriousness that management staff would feel toward the incidents.

There were great differences in the rankings of some of the hypotheticals. For instance, the excessive force situation was ranked as the third most serious in Hungary but the least serious in Pakistan, and ranked seventh in seriousness by police in the United States. Although most countries ranked bribery very high, Croatia and Hungary did not. Theft from a found wallet was ranked high in all countries except South Africa.

Police in the United States ranked the following as the five most serious:

theft from a crime scene
bribery
theft from a found wallet
free drinks to ignore an open bar
kickback from an auto repair shop

Finland, on the other hand, ranked these five:

theft from a crime scene and bribery (tied)
theft from a found wallet
cover-up of a DUI by a police officer
free drinks to ignore an open bar
kickback from an auto repair shop and
supervisor granting holiday in exchange for a car tune-up (tied).

Interestingly, the cover-up was ranked eighth in seriousness by U.S. police, indicating either that drunken driving is considered more serious in Finland or that there is less of the "blue curtain of secrecy" there.

Countries were also different in the pattern of rankings. Some countries ranked all situations relatively high whereas other countries ranked all or almost all relatively low. For instance, Finland ranked all but three situations in the 4+ range (the scores went up to 5), but South African police ranked only one situation in the 4+ range. On the other hand, Pakistani police also ranked all but two situations highly, indicating perhaps that they answered the survey in the way they thought they were supposed to.

An important finding of the research was that the officers' beliefs seemed to be influenced by what discipline they perceived would be forthcoming for each incident. Thus, management has an opportunity to shape officers' beliefs by its responses to deviant behavior. Whether beliefs, in turn, influence behavior is another question. In the last section of this chapter, we will look at some explanations of deviance.

# Explanations of Deviance

Explanations of corruption can be described as

- individual
- institutional (or organizational)
- systemic (or societal)

Individual explanations, such as the *rotten apple* argument, assume that the individual officer has deviant inclinations before he or she even enters the police department and merely exploits the position. Sloppy recruiting and the development of a police personality are also individual explanations of deviance. Institutional (or organizational) explanations point to organizational problems (low managerial visibility, low public visibility, and peer group secrecy, among others). Institutional explanations also include looking at the police role in the criminal justice system (as the front-line interface with criminals), the tension between the use of discretion and bureaucraticism, and the role of commanders in spreading corruption. A systemic (or societal) explanation of police deviance focuses on the relationship between the police and the public (Johnston, 1995).

## *Individual Explanations*

The most common explanation of police officer corruption is the **rotten-apple argument**—that the officer alone is deviant and that it was simply a mistake to hire him or her. This argument has been extended to describe *rotten bushels*—groups of officers banding together to commit deviant acts. The point of this argument is that there is nothing wrong with the barrel—deviance is individual, not endemic.

Sherman (1982) explained that deviant officers go through what he called a "moral career" as they pass through various stages of rationalization to more serious misdeeds in a graduated and systematic way. Once an individual is able to get past the first "moral crisis," it becomes less difficult to rationalize new and more unethical behaviors. The previous behaviors serve as an underpinning to a different ethical standard, for one must explain and justify one's own behaviors to preserve psychological well-being (Sherman, 1982).

When one accepts gradations of behavior, the line between right and wrong can more easily be moved further and further away from an absolute standard of morality. Many believe, for instance, that gratuities are only the first step in a spiral downward: "For police, the passage from free coffee at the all night diner and Christmas gifts to participation in drug-dealing and organized burglary is normally a slow if steady one" (Malloy, 1982: 33). Malloy describes a passage from "perks" to "shopping" to premeditated theft (1982: 36).

Others dispute the view that after the first cup of coffee, every police officer inevitably ends up performing more serious ethical violations. Many police officers have clear personal guidelines on what is acceptable and not acceptable. Whereas many, perhaps even the majority, of police see nothing wrong with accepting minor gratuities, few police would accept outright cash, and fewer still would condone thefts and bribes. The problematic element is that the gradations between what is acceptable or not can vary from officer to officer and department to department.

Sherman also believes in the importance of a signification factor, or labeling an individual action acceptable under a personal rationale (Sherman, 1985a: 253). Police routinely deal with the seamier side of society—not only drug addicts and muggers, but middle-class people who are involved in dishonesty and corruption. The constant displays of lying, hiding, cheating, and theft create cynicism, and this, in turn, may develop into a vulnerability to temptation.

The following are some rationales that might easily be used by police to justify unethical behavior (Murphy and Moran, 1981: 93):

1. The public thinks every cop is a crook—so why try to be honest?
2. The money is out there—if I don't take it, someone else will.
3. I'm only taking what's rightfully mine; if the city paid me a decent wage, I wouldn't have to get it on my own.
4. I can use it—it's for a good cause—my son needs an operation, or dental work, or tuition for medical school, or a new bicycle. . . .

Given constant exposure to others' misdeeds, peer pressure, and vague ideas of right and wrong in these situations, the question is not why some officers engage in corrupt practices but rather why more don't. Although research indicates the lack of evidence for an affinity argument to explain police corruption—that is, deviant individuals being attracted to police work—an affiliation theory is persuasive, arguing that police learn from one another.

## *Organizational Explanations*

The Miami River scandal involved officers committing armed robberies of drug dealers. Some argue that it was caused by the rapid hiring of minorities during an affirmative action drive without proper background checks; disaffection by white, mid-level supervisors who basically did not do their job of supervision; who were, instead, merely counting the days to retirement; ethnic divisions in the department; and the pervasive influence of politics in the department, which disrupted internal discipline mechanisms (Dorschner, 1989). These concepts are largely organizational explanations of police corruption.

Another example of the effects of rapid hiring is the finding that of the 1,000 new officers hired by Washington, D.C., in the early 1990s as a result of political pressure, nearly a quarter have been fired due to their involvement in various acts of misconduct or crime (reported in Lersch, 2002: 77).

Murphy and Caplan (1989) argue that there are situational elements that "breed corruption," including lax community standards over certain types of behavior (gambling, prostitution), hesitation of the chief to enforce rules and discipline officers, tolerance by fellow officers, unguided police discretion and incompetence, and a lack of support from prosecutors and the courts (or corruption at that stage of the system as well). Most of these explanations fall into an organizational category as well.

Crank and Caldero's (2000) "noble-cause" explanation of some types of deviance (described more fully in the next chapter), whereby officers lie or commit other unethical acts to catch criminals, is an organizational explanation, as is any description of deviance that includes the aspect of subcultural support. Whenever one explains deviance as being supported by the organizational culture—whether that be the "formal culture" or the "informal culture"—it falls into this category.

## Societal Explanations

Rationalizations used by some police when they take bribes or protection money from prostitutes or drug dealers are made easier by the public's tolerant stance toward certain areas of vice—e.g., to accept protection money from a prostitute may be rationalized by the relative lack of concern that the public shows for this type of law-breaking. The same argument could be made about gambling or even drugs. We often formally expect the police to enforce laws while we informally encourage them to ignore the same laws. Signification occurs here as well. Although gambling carries connotations of the mob and organized crime, or numbers runners in the ghettos of our big cities, we typically don't think of church bingo or the friendly football pool down at Joe's Bar. If police were to enforce gambling laws against the stereotypical criminal, the public would support the action, but if the enforcement took place against upstanding citizens, there would be an outraged response. "Police Arrest Grandma Bingo Players!" would be the headline.

The solution is a choice: Either accept police discretion to enforce, which in most cases will be used against the poor, minorities, and the stereotypically criminal among us, or change the law and make it perfectly clear by statute that some gambling is acceptable and other types of gambling are not. Since the political feasibility of the latter solution is fairly limited—most politicians would not be eager to champion decriminalization of prostitution, drugs, or other types of vice—police are expected to make the distinction between "good" people and "bad." Good people should be excused, ignored, or, at worst, scolded for their involvement, and bad people should be investigated, caught, and punished—for example, the practice until recently of arresting prostitutes and letting "johns" go home, or ignoring campus crime while enforcement efforts target inner-city neighborhoods. The other possibility, of course, is that some police decide that a hypocritical public won't mind a few gambling operations, or a certain number of prostitutes plying their trade, or even a few drug dealers, so they might as well accept protection money. As long as the public supports certain types of illegal activities by patronage, it is no surprise that some police officers are able to rationalize nonenforcement. Also, as long as the public relays a message that crime control is more important than individual liberties and rights, then we should not be surprised when police act on that message.

# Conclusion

In this chapter we reviewed the range of deviant behaviors in law enforcement. There are types of deviance that are purely for self-interest, and then there is deviance that stems from "noble-cause" corruption—that type will be discussed in the next chapter. One of the most serious forms of deviance is the use of excessive force. An important factor that seems to be associated with excessive force is a challenge to police authority. Race also seems to be a factor. It was also noted that police scandals have occurred in all countries around the world but that there are apparent differences in the relative levels of corruption among police in different countries. Reasons for law enforcement deviance can be categorized into individual explanations, organizational explanations, and societal explanations.

# Key Terms

*baksheesh* graft

**excessive force** use of force that exceeds what is necessary to accomplish a lawful purpose, or when the purpose is not lawful apprehension or self-defense but rather personal retaliation or coercion

**graft** any exploitation of one's role, such as accepting bribes, protection money, or kickbacks

**grass eaters** when taking bribes, gratuities, and unsolicited protection money, those who are fairly passive in their deviant practices

**gratuities** items of value received by an individual because of his or her role or position, rather than because of a personal relationship with the giver

**meat eaters** deviant officers who engage in shakedowns, "shop" at burglary scenes, and engage in more deviant practices

**rotten-apple argument** that the officer alone is deviant and that it was simply a mistake to hire him or her

# Review Questions

1. List and describe various forms of law enforcement deviance.
2. What are Barker and Carter's types of abuse?
3. What are grass eaters and meat eaters?
4. What are the arguments for the acceptance of gratuities?
5. What are the arguments against gratuities?
6. What does research show concerning the number of officers who use drugs on duty?
7. What is the continuum of sexual misconduct?
8. Discuss the research concerning use of force. What factors seem to be associated with it?
9. Provide examples of law enforcement corruption in other countries.
10. What are the individual, organizational, and societal explanations for police officer deviance?

# Discussion Questions

1. Do you think gratuities are acceptable? If so, what limits would you put on them?
2. What should be done if a police department has a rule against gratuities but the majority of officers ignore the rule and have for a long period of time?
3. What should be done with an officer who has a drinking problem? Would your answer be different if the addiction was to drugs?
4. Should an officer be fired for taking a bribe? Stealing from a crime scene? Being drunk on duty? Hitting a handcuffed suspect? Having checks bounce? Being disrespectful to a member of a minority group? Sexually harassing a co-worker?
5. Should the age of hiring be raised to twenty-eight because some studies indicate that younger officers are more prone to use force?
6. What explanation of police deviance seems to make the most sense to you? What would explain excessive force?

# Ethical Dilemmas

### *Situation 1*

You are a rookie police officer on your first patrol. The older, experienced officer tells you that the restaurant on the corner likes to have you guys around, so it always gives free meals. Your partner orders steak, potatoes, and all the trimmings. What are you going to do? What if it were just coffee at a convenience store? What if the owner refused to take your money at the cash register?

## Situation 2

You are a rookie police officer who responds to a call for officer assistance. Arriving at the scene, you see a ring of officers surrounding a suspect who is down on his knees. You don't know what happened before you arrived, but you see a sergeant use a Taser on the suspect, and you see two or three officers step in and take turns hitting the suspect with their nightsticks about the head and shoulders. This goes on for several minutes as you stand in the back of the circle. No one says anything that would indicate that this is not appropriate behavior. What would you do? What would you do later when asked to testify that you observed the suspect make "threatening" gestures to the officers involved?

## Situation 3

You (a female police officer) have been working in a small-town police department for about six months. During that time you have been dealing with a fellow police officer who persists in making comments about how pretty you are, how you don't look like a police officer, how you shouldn't be dealing with the "garbage" out on the streets, and so on. He has asked you out over a dozen times even though you have told him every time that you are not interested and that you want him to stop asking you out and stop making comments. Although he hasn't made any derogatory or offensive comments, his constant attention is beginning to make you not want to go to work. You have a romantic partner, and you are definitely not interested in your fellow officer. You have mentioned it to your field training officer, who is a type of father figure, but he likes the guy and tells you that you should be flattered. You want to file a sexual harassment charge against him but hesitate because although you do feel harassed, you don't feel especially threatened; further, you know that you would encounter negative reactions from the other officers in the department who like the guy. What should you do?

## Situation 4

You and your partner have been working together for over five years. He has seen you through the serious illness of your small child, and you have been there for him during his divorce. After the divorce, though, you have become increasingly anxious about him. He is obviously not taking care of his health, he drinks too much, and he has been consistently late to roll call. Now you can smell alcohol on his breath during the day and suspect that the ever-present cup of coffee he carries has more than a little whiskey in it. You've tried talking to him several times, but he just gets angry and tells you to mind your own business. Today, when you both responded to an accident scene, a witness drew you aside and said "Aren't you going to do something about him?" pointing to your partner. Unfortunately, you knew what she meant, for he was literally swaying, trying to keep his balance in the hot sun. To make matters worse, he insists on driving. What would you do?

### Situation 5

You are a waitress (or waiter) in an all-night diner and are not too happy about pulling the midnight shift. Every evening, luckily, police officers drift in for their coffee breaks. You have been told that the diner does not offer gratuities and that you are not to give free coffee or meals to anyone, including police officers. On the other hand, it's 2:00 A.M., and there are a lot of scary people out there. You figure that the pot of coffee might cost a couple bucks, and so it's worth it to keep officers coming in. You suspect that the owner of the diner wouldn't be happy (because he doesn't like police), but he's not here, so you fall into the habit of giving all the officers free coffee. Then it kind of escalates to free pie (it was going to be thrown out anyway), and now when no one is around, you'll let the officers go without paying for their meal. Do you see a problem with your actions? Who should make the decision, the owner or the employee who is on site? If you stopped giving free coffee and pie, do you think the officers would stop coming in?

# Suggested Readings

Barker, T., and Carter, D. 1991. *Police Deviance.* Cincinnati: Anderson.

Dunham, R., and Alpert, G. 2004. *Critical Issues in Policing,* 2nd ed. Prospect Heights, IL: Waveland.

Bouza, A. 2001. *Police Unbound: Corruption, Abuse, and Heroism by the Boys in Blue.* Amherst, NY: Prometheus.

Einstein, S., and Amir, M. 2003. *Police Corruption: Paradigms, Models and Concepts: Challenges for Developing Countries.* Huntsville, TX: Office of International Criminal Justice (OICJ), Sam Houston State University.

Einstein, S., and Amir, M. 2004. *Police Corruption: Challenges for Developed Countries: Comparative Issues and Commissions of Inquiry.* Huntsville, TX: Office of International Criminal Justice (OICJ), Sam Houston State University.

Heffernan, W., and Stroup, T. 1985. *Police Ethics: Hard Choices in Law Enforcement.* New York: John Jay Press.

Holmes, M. 2000. "Minority Threat and Police Brutality: Determinants of Civil Rights Criminal Complaints in U.S. Municipalities." *Criminology* 38(2): 343–367.

Human Rights Watch. 1998. *Shielded from Justice: Police Brutality and Accountability in the United States.* Available from http://www.hrw.org.

Ivković, S., and Klockars, C. 2004. "Police Integrity in Croatia." In Klockars, C., Ivković, S., and Haberfeld, M. (Eds.), *The Contours of Police Integrity,* pp. 56–74. Thousand Oaks, CA: Sage.

Kappeler, V., Sluder, R., and Alpert, G. 1994. *Forces of Deviance: Understanding the Dark Side of Policing*. Prospect Heights, IL: Waveland.

Klockars, C., Ivković, S. and Haberfeld, M. (Eds.). *The Contours of Police Integrity*, pp. 130–160. Thousand Oaks, CA: Sage.

Lersch, K. 2002. *Policing and Misconduct*. Upper Saddle River, NJ: Prentice-Hall.

Nelson, J. (Ed.). 2000. *Police Brutality*. New York: Norton.

Prenzler, T., and Ransley, J. 2002. *Police Reform: Building Integrity*. Sydney, Australia: Hawkins.

Clint Eastwood's Dirty Harry personifies utilitarian ("the end justifies the means")
thinking as a police officer who seeks a good end by employing bad means.
That's why he was called dirty.

# 9

# Noble-Cause Corruption

*Introduction*

*Investigation*

*Interrogation*

*Loyalty and Whistleblowing*

*Reducing Corruption*

*Conclusion*

## Key Terms

blue curtain of secrecy
civilian review/
   complaint model
code of silence
Dirty Harry problem

informants
integrity testing
internal affairs model
noble-cause corruption
principle of double effect

# Chapter Objectives

1. Understand the concept of noble-cause corruption.

2. Understand the ethical issues involved in investigation and interrogation.

3. Distinguish between physical and mental coercion, and understand the arguments for and against these methods of interrogation.

4. Become familiar with the ethical justifications for and arguments against whistleblowing versus loyalty to co-workers.

5. Be able to describe an effective, ethical leader.

6. Understand the methods employed to reduce or minimize corruption among police officers.

The last chapter discussed a range of corrupt practices by some law enforcement officers. It is important to note that only a small percentage of officers in most police departments ever engage in any of the practices we discussed except, perhaps, the acceptance of gratuities. In this chapter we discuss other practices of law enforcement, specifically those activities engaged in during the investigation and interrogation of crimes. The central question of this chapter is "What means are acceptable in order to catch a criminal?" The answer will depend on whether you subscribe to a crime control or a public servant model of law enforcement, and whether you subscribe to utilitarianism or ethical formalism.

# Introduction

In 1983 Klockars presented us with the question of whether one could still be a good person if bad means were used to arrive at a good end. In the "Dirty Harry problem," he asked whether it was ethically acceptable for a police officer to inflict pain on a suspect in order to acquire information that would save an innocent victim (with due credit to Clint Eastwood). We will explore that question more carefully in the interrogation section later, but use it now to begin our discussion of what has been termed **noble-cause corruption**. The argument of those who discuss noble-cause corruption is that officers sometimes (maybe even frequently) employ unethical means to catch criminals because they believe it is right to do so. This is an example of the utilitarian viewpoint—"the end justifies the means." Crank and Caldero (2000), for instance, argue that such practices as testilying and coercion are not caused by selfishness but by *ends-oriented thinking*.

The noble cause of police officers is "a profound moral commitment to make the world a safer place to live" (Crank and Caldero, 2000: 9). Officers will do what it takes to get an offender off the street, even if it is a "magic pencil" (2000: 71), that is, making up facts on affidavits to justify illegal searches or to establish probable cause for arrests. They behave this way because we hire those who have values that support such actions and train and socialize them to internalize these values even more deeply, and then put them in situations where their values dictate doing whatever it takes to "make the world safe" (2000: 88).

Further, police are not the only actors who subscribe to noble-cause values. Crime lab investigators and prosecutors also engage in shortcuts and magic pencils in order to convict the perceived guilty. Prosecutors have been known to suppress evidence and allow perjured testimony, so it is not only police officers who feel compelled to break the law in order to further the noble cause of crime control (Crank and Caldero, 2000: 134).

How pervasive is this tendency? Studies show that about 60 percent of rookies support mild lies to achieve a conviction (Crank and Caldero, 2000: 157). Recall that Barker and Carter (1991) reported that officers surveyed reported that about a quarter of officers perjured themselves. *Dropsy* testimony occurs when officers report that a drug suspect dropped the drugs and ran. This is convenient because it puts the drugs in plain sight and justifies the subsequent arrest. The trouble is that *dropsy* testimony rose exponentially after the Supreme Court ruled that street pat-downs for evidence required probable cause. In reality, we simply do not know the extent of the type and pervasiveness of noble-cause actions.

Other authors argue vehemently that noble-cause corruption is a dangerous concept because it gives credence to illegal behavior on the part of officers. Alderson (1998: 68), for instance, protests that

> noble-cause corruption . . . is a euphemism for perjury, which is a serious crime. . . . In ethical police terms justice is not divisible in this way into means and ends, and the peddlers of this perversion of justice are guilty of the immorality of the totalitarian police state, and their views stand to be roundly condemned.

However, it may be that he misunderstands those who present the noble-cause concepts. Crank and Caldero (2000), for instance, do not seem to be supporting the rationale; rather, they argue that "noble cause" is the underlying reason for much of officers' unethical behaviors, so efforts to control corruption must take cognizance of this reason in order to be effective. If selfishness and personal gain are not the motives for misdeeds, then monitoring and punishments may not work. The culture of police is not supportive of egoistic criminality, but it is supportive of "catching the criminal—whatever it takes." If we want to change this attitude, then we need to address it directly. Further, they seem to argue that such an attitude must change because we are increasingly living in a world where pluralism is the reality and the values of the police organization may not be reflective of the citizenry they police. The following sections explore some of the law enforcement practices used to investigate and prosecute criminals. The underlying questions are always the same:

1. Can these practices be considered good acts?
2. Does the good end of crime control justify what are otherwise bad acts?

# Investigation

The goal of investigative law enforcement is to collect evidence in order to identify and successfully prosecute the criminal. There are different issues involved in reactive investigations versus proactive investigations. In reactive investigations, a crime has already occurred, and the police sift through clues to determine the perpetrator. When police and other investigators develop an early prejudice concerning who they believe is the guilty party, evidence is looked at less objectively, and there is a temptation to engage in noble-cause corruption in order to convict. This can take the form of ignoring witnesses or evidence or even manufacturing evidence to shore up a case against an individual. One example of this was the scandal concerning the FBI crime lab. Several news reports reported charges that FBI lab examiners had compromised cases by completing shoddy work and misrepresenting their findings. The description of the motivation of examiners was that they were not objective scientists, but rather co-conspirators with police, who were motivated and even pressured to find support for police theories regarding the guilty party. This led to overstating their findings on the witness stand and covering up tests that were done improperly. A whistleblower exposed these practices and was suspended for his efforts (Sniffen, 1997). Ultimately, thirteen examiners were implicated, although only two were even formally censured (Serrano and Ostrow, 2000).

Recently, the Houston crime lab has been the target of investigation. Lab practices and possible perjury by examiners have forced the district attorney's office to reexamine over one hundred cases. Similar charges have been leveled at the Fort Worth crime lab (Axtman, 2003). In the Houston case, the police lab was eventually shut down in 2002 because of shoddy practices. An independent investigation by the Justice Department discovered that untrained workers were conducting DNA analysis, there was evidence of contamination from a leaky roof, "drylabbing" (making up scientific results) was being done, and there was no quality control, among other problems. More than 2,000 cases required review because of potentially tainted testimony from the police lab. Two men have had their sentences overturned or been granted new trials because of the findings concerning the lab (Hays, 2005). The investigation of the lab was stalled after the first findings were released, however, when the city council would not release the money to continue the investigation (Associated Press, 2005).

Other labs across the country have also been the subject of news reports. Sometimes the criticism has been simple incompetence and shoddy work practices, but in other allegations, it appears that the lab examiners are engaged in "noble-cause" corruption by working with police departments to arrive at desired results.

The problem is that once investigators decide who the guilty party is, they may ignore evidence that doesn't fit with their idea of who did it and how it was done. It is human nature to "complete the puzzle"—to see things that conform to one's way of looking at the world. Good police work doesn't close the door to contrary evidence, but human nature does. Utilitarian ends-oriented thinkers would be more likely to ignore contrary evidence or overstate existing evidence if they believed they had the "guilty" party, but ethical formalists would be less likely to because their decision making is based on duty, not solely on results.

# *Proactive Investigations*

In proactive police investigations, there is a more active role on the part of police. Drug distribution networks, pornography rings, and fences of stolen property all tend to be investigated through methods that involve undercover work and informants. This is because such crimes often do not result in victims coming forward or crimes being reported. It may be that deception is a necessary element in this type of investigation.

According to one author, "Deception is considered by police—and courts as well— to be as natural to detecting as pouncing is to a cat" (Skolnick, 1982: 40). Offenses involving drugs, vice, and stolen property are covert activities that are not easily detected. Klockars (1984) discusses "blue lies and police placebos." In his description of the types of lies that police routinely use, he differentiates *placebos* as being in the best interest of those being lied to—for example, lying to the mentally ill that police will take care of laser beams from Mars, lying to people that police will keep an eye out for them, or not telling a person how a loved one was killed. The motive is benign, the effect relatively harmless. *Blue lies* are those used to control the person or make the job easier in situations where force could be used—for example, to make an arrest easier, an officer will lie about where the suspect is being taken, or to get someone out on the street to be arrested, the officer will say that she only wants to talk.

Barker and Carter (1991, 1994) also propose a typology of lies, including accepted lies, tolerated lies, and deviant lies. *Accepted lies* are those used during undercover investigations, sting operations, and so on. These lies must meet the following standards:

1. They must be in furtherance of a legitimate organizational purpose.
2. There must be a clear relationship between the need to deceive and the accomplishment of an organizational purpose.
3. The nature of the deception must be one wherein officers and the management structure acknowledge that deception will better serve the public interest than the truth.

The ethical standing of the deception and the issues of law appear to be collateral concerns.

*Tolerated lies,* according to Barker and Carter, are those that are "necessary evils," such as lying about selective enforcement. Police may routinely profess to enforce certain laws (such as prostitution) while, in reality, they use a selective manner of enforcement. Lies during interrogation or threats to troublemakers that they will be arrested if they don't cease their troublemaking are also tolerated lies.

*Deviant lies* are those used in the courtroom to make a case or to cover up wrongdoing. However, one might argue with Barker and Carter that there is some evidence to indicate that for some police organizations or certain isolated examples of rogue divisions, lies to make a case are so prevalent that they must be categorized as tolerated lies rather than deviant lies.

## Targets of Investigation

In proactive investigations, the central question is whom do police target and why? Selection of targets on any other basis than reasonable suspicion is a questionable use of discretion. Members of Congress convicted of bribery in the Abscam operation in 1980 alleged improper conduct in the FBI's selection of targets, and Marion Barry, the ex-mayor of the District of Columbia, alleged he was "set up" because of his race after he was video-taped using drugs with a girlfriend in a hotel room in 1990. How targets are selected is a serious question; arguably, the selection should be based on reasonable suspicion. However, Sherman (1985b) reports that "tips" are notoriously inaccurate as a reason to focus on a certain person.

Police operations that provide opportunities for crime change the police role from discovering who has committed a crime to one of discovering who might commit a crime if given a chance (Elliston and Feldberg, 1985: 137). For instance,

- A fake deer placed by the side of the road is used to entice overeager hunters, who are then arrested for violating hunting laws.
- Police officer decoys are dressed as drunks and pretend to pass out on sidewalks with money sticking out of their pockets.
- Undercover officers, posing as criminals, entice doctors to prescribe unneeded medications that are controlled substances, such as Percoset and Oxycontin.
- Police undertake various stings in which they set up fencing operations to buy stolen goods.

Are only bad people tempted? This role expansion is arguably dangerous, undesirable, and inconsistent with the social contract basis of policing.

The opposing argument is that burglaries would occur regardless of whether police set up a fencing operation and that the good of catching criminals outweighs the negative possibility that some burglars steal because they know the fence (police) will take their goods. Both of these arguments exist under a utilitarian framework. So even when using the same ethical system, a particular action may be judged as ethical or unethical.

Other stings are even more creative, such as sending party invitations to those with outstanding warrants, or staging a murder in a high-crime neighborhood and then arresting those (with outstanding warrants) who come out to see what is happening. The utility of such stings is undeniable. The only argument against them is that the government deception appears unseemly; it is also possible that such actions may undermine public confidence in the police when they are telling the truth.

### Entrapment

In legal terms, entrapment occurs when an otherwise innocent person commits an illegal act because of police encouragement or enticement. Two approaches have been used to determine whether entrapment has occurred. The subjective approach looks at the defendant's background, character, and predisposition toward crime. The objective approach examines the government's participation and whether it has exceeded accepted legal standards. For instance, if the state provided an "essential element" that made the crime possible, or if there was extensive and coercive pressure on the defendant to engage in the actions, then a court might rule that entrapment had occurred (Kamisar, LeFave, and Israel, 1980: 510). See the "In the News" box on the next page for a description of one such case.

**IN THE NEWS  A Case of Entrapment?**

When police raided an X-rated mail-order house, they found Keith Jacobsen's name and address, as well as the information that he had ordered two magazines, *Bare Boys I* and *Bare Boys II*, neither of which had been determined to be obscene material by any court. They created a fictitious company called "The American Hedonist Society" and sent Jacobson a membership application and questionnaire. He joined and indicated an interest in preteen sexual material. In other mailings over the course of three years, the government represented itself as "Midlands Data Research," "Hartland Institute for a New Tomorrow," and Carl Long, an individual interested in erotic material. Finally, a mailing from the government posing as the "Far Eastern Trading Company, Ltd." resulted in an order from Jacobson for *Boys Who Love*. He was arrested by federal agents after he accepted receipt.

Source: G. Dix, "When Government Deception Goes Too Far," *Texas Lawyer* 7(31) (1991): 12–13.

*Do you think federal law enforcement should be soliciting people to buy pornography?*

Stitt and James (1985) criticize the subjective test for the following reasons:

1. It allows the police to entrap people with criminal records who might not otherwise have been tempted.
2. It allows hearsay and rumor to establish predisposition.
3. It forces the individual charged to admit factual guilt, which may stigmatize him or her.
4. It provides a free rein for police discretion in choice of targets.
5. It degrades the criminal justice system by allowing the police to use misrepresentation and deceit.

On the other hand, supporters say that the subjective test allows police to go after those most likely to harm society. The objective test would punish the police and let the criminal go free, forcing police to perjure themselves to save a case (Stitt and James, 1985: 133–136).

Legal standards, as we have discussed earlier, are very often useful guidelines for determining ethical standards, but they are not the same thing as ethical standards. For instance, one might disagree with legal standards as being too restrictive if one believed that police should be able to do anything necessary to trap criminals. Alternatively, legal guidelines may not be sufficient to eliminate what some consider unethical behavior. For example, do you agree that an undercover officer should pose as a client in a methadone clinic and pretend to befriend other clients, then ask them to "hook him up" with a drug dealer? If they do it, they will be guilty of a crime. What if the undercover officer targeted someone for eleven months, continually begging and pleading with the target to sell him drugs, until finally, simply to get rid of him, the target did so and was promptly arrested? Does this violate the subjective test of entrapment? (Remember that a methadone client would be considered predisposed to drug crimes.) Is it ethical?

## Police and the Media

Journalists who unwittingly assist police by believing and publishing a false story criticize the use of deception by police. There are a number of ethical issues in the relationship between the police and the media. Should the police intentionally lie to the media for a valuable end? An example might be lying about the stage of an investigation or about the travel path of a public figure for security reasons. In the 2002 Washington, D.C., sniper case, the media and the police had an extremely close relationship, and the police were especially sensitive to media issues (e.g., how the media could be used to encourage tips), but also how the story might create public panic. There were some who believed the media were fed "red herrings," such as the importance of the white van, in order to divert the snipers' suspicions regarding how the police investigation was going.

On the other hand, should the media have complete power to publish or report crime activities regardless of the negative effect on the level of public fear or the possibility of receiving an unbiased trial? Should the media become so involved in hostage situations that they become the news rather than just the reporters of it? The situation involving David Koresh and his cult of Branch Davidians in Waco, Texas, in the spring of 1993 raised a number of questions concerning the relationship between the police and the media. For instance, the media were banished to a distance far away from the cult compound. Is this an acceptable use of police power, or does it infringe upon the public's right to know? Could police have ethically used the media to deceive Koresh into giving up by feeding the media false information in response to his stated wish for a sign? Should the media have been better informed during the course of the final assault?

These questions can all be analyzed using the ethical systems already described. Regarding the bombing at the 1996 Summer Olympics in Atlanta, should the FBI have disclosed to the public that Richard Jewell was its prime suspect and given the press background information that led to the massive publicity and exposure of his life? The FBI's statements indicated a level of certainty regarding his guilt that turned out to be unsubstantiated. Jewell's experience resulted in a public letter of apology from the FBI and a lawsuit against the FBI and the television networks and the newspapers that violated his privacy, illustrating one reason that law enforcement might not want to be so forthcoming on the progress of investigations ("FBI," 1996).

## The Use of Undercover Officers

Undercover officers may play drug dealers, prostitutes, johns, crime bosses, friends, and—perhaps—lovers in order to collect evidence of crime. They have to observe or even participate in illegal activities to protect their cover. Undercover work is said to be a difficult role for the individual officer, who may play the part so well that he or she loses his or her previous identity. If the cover involves illegal or immoral action, the individual may have to sacrifice personal integrity to get an arrest. Marx (1985a: 109) cites examples of officers who have become addicted to drugs or alcohol and destroyed their marriages or careers because of undercover assignments. He notes that there is a disturbing belief system among undercover officers that the laws don't apply to them or that they are exempt from the law because of their assignment. It has been found that undercover officers possess high levels of neuroticism and low levels of impulse control, and that there are adverse psychological effects from the experience of being undercover (Mieczkowski, 2002: 162).

Kim Wozencraft employed her background as an undercover narcotics officer in her novel *Rush* (1990). In the novel, two undercover officers use drugs and become friends with some of the pushers they are collecting evidence against. Although officials in the federal Drug Enforcement Agency (DEA), as well as local law enforcement, know that undercover officers sometimes use and even become addicted to drugs during the course of an investigation, they ignore or cover it up in order to get successful convictions. Although the work is fiction, one suspects that at least some of the experiences that Wozencraft portrays are taken from reality.

Conlon (2004), a Harvard-educated New York City police officer, described how undercover officers entered a no-man's land in the department where they were treated almost more like informants than fellow cops. Those who were successful at setting up buys were treated like "star performers," and some developed "prima donna" attitudes. In general, they were treated and they behaved in a way that made it hard for them to maintain relationships with other police, not to mention probable issues with their families.

Policemen routinely pretend they are johns, and policewomen dress up as prostitutes. Those community members who live in neighborhoods plagued with street prostitution may applaud any police efforts to clean up their streets. But do we want our police officers to engage in this type of activity? One important element of this debate is the type of relationship involved in the police deception. The two extremes of intimacy are, on one hand, a brief buy–bust incident where the officer pretends to be a drug pusher and buys from a street dealer, and moments later an arrest is made. At the other extreme would be a situation in which an undercover officer pretends to be romantically involved with a target of an investigation to maintain his or her cover.

The second situation violates our sense of privacy to a much greater degree, yet there have been instances of detectives engaging in such relationships to gain confessions or other information. In one particular case, a private detective (not a police detective) engaged in this type of relationship over a period of months and even agreed to an engagement of marriage with the suspect in order to get a confession on tape (Schoeman, 1986: 21). In another case, an officer acted as a friend to a target of an investigation, to the extent of looking after his child and living in his house for six months. The purpose of the investigation was to get evidence on the man so that the topless bar he owned could be shut down. Eventually, the officer found some white powder on a desk in the home that tested positive for cocaine, and a conviction was secured. The Supreme Court denied a writ of certiorari in this case (*United States v. Baldwin*, 621 F.2d 251 [1980]), letting the decision stand.

Many people do not see anything wrong with deceiving a criminal who is ultimately convicted, but what about others involved? In the above case, what does one say to the child who found out that a trusted friend had been living a lie? One of the reasons that some disagree with deceptive practices involving personal relationships is that they betray trust, an essential element of social life.

As Schoeman (1985: 144) explains, intimate relationships are different from public exchanges and should be protected:

> Intimacy involves bringing another person within one's soul or being, not for any independently personal or instrumental objective, but for the sake of the other person or for the sake of the bond and attachment between the persons. . . . There is an expression of vulnerability and unenforceable trust within intimate relationships not present in business or social relationships. . . . Exploitation of trust and intimacy is also degrading to all persons who have respect for intimate relationships. Intimate relationships involve potential transformations of moral duties. Morally, an intimate relationship may take precedence over a concern for social well-being generally.

Note that Schoeman is probably arguing from an ethics of care position. In this ethical system, the relationship of two people is more important than rights, duties, or laws. There is no forfeiture of rights in the ethics of care position; thus, one can't say the suspect deserves to be deceived. The harm to the relationship goes in both directions. In cases where a personal relationship has developed, if the target is hurt

---

**QUOTE and QUERY**

They were just looking at me. I couldn't even look these guys in the eyes. Here's guys I hung out with, guys I broke bread with. I really came to like some of them. And they liked me, trusted me. One guy comes up to me and says, "How could you do this, Ben? You're my friend. How could you do this?" He was sixty some years old. He was like anybody's grandfather, a nice guy, but he dealt in stolen securities. That's what we locked him up for. He put a heavy guilt trip on me. I couldn't look at him. I had to put my head down. . . .

Undercover is a very strange way to do police work, because you identify with them, the bad guys. It's a strange feeling to be trusted by someone and then betray them.

Source: Mark Baker, *Cops* (New York: Pocket Books, 1985): 139–140. Reprinted with the permission of Simon & Schuster from *Cops: Their Lives in Their Own Words* by Mark Baker. Copyright © 1985 by Mark Baker.

*Do you think you would be able to befriend suspects and become close to them in order to obtain incriminating evidence? Do you think that doing so is wrong? What if your target was another police officer?*

by the deception, so too is the deceiver. In the Quote and Query box on the previous page, it is clear that the experience was painful for the officer, regardless of the fact that the people he would testify against were criminals.

Schoeman goes on to suggest some guidelines to be used when police interact with others in a deceptive manner. First, he believes that no interaction should go on longer than twenty-four hours without a warrant with probable cause. During this twenty-four-hour period, the officer may not enter any private area, even if invited, unless it is specifically to undertake some illegal activity. Second, although an undercover officer may deceptively engage in business and social relationships during the course of an investigation, he or she may not engage in intimate relationships. Finally, any evidence obtained in violation of the first two principles should be excluded from criminal trials against the targets (1985: 140).

Police would obviously criticize these suggestions by raising the following objections:

1. If there is probable cause, an arrest is possible, so why engage in a dangerous undercover operation?
2. Almost all undercover operations last more than twenty-four hours.
3. Requiring a warrant is often unworkable, given how undercover operations develop.

The question remains: How can police best minimize the harm yet still obtain some utility from the action? This balancing is characteristic of utilitarian ethics. Do police engage in investigative deception because it is the best way to investigate drug sales, prostitution, organized crime, or illegal alien smuggling, or because it is simply the easiest way? Is it necessary in undercover work, especially in the area of vice, to employ deception and techniques that might be considered entrapment? If the goal of police is crime control, then there is a clear inclination to use utilitarian rationales to justify deception as a means to an end. If the goal of police is public service, such activities are arguably harder to justify.

Marx (1985a: 106–107) proposes that before engaging in undercover operations, police investigators should ask the following questions:

1. How serious is the crime being investigated?
2. How clear is the definition of the crime—that is, would the target know that what he or she is doing is clearly illegal?
3. Are there any alternatives to deceptive practices?
4. Is the undercover operation consistent with the spirit as well as the letter of the law?
5. Is it public knowledge that the police may engage in such practices, and is the decision to do so a result of democratic decision making?
6. Is the goal prosecution, as opposed to general intelligence gathering or harassment?
7. Is there a likelihood that the crime would occur regardless of the government's involvement?
8. Are there reasonable grounds to suspect the target?
9. Will the practice prevent a serious crime from occurring?

## *The Use of Informants*

**Informants** are individuals who are not police officers but assist police by providing information about criminal activity, acting as the part of buyer in drug sales, or otherwise "setting up" a criminal act so that police may gather evidence against the target. Informants perform such services for some reward: for money, to get charges dropped or reduced, or—in some documented cases—for drugs supplied by an officer. They may do it for retaliatory purposes. Informants typically are not middle-class, upstanding-citizen types. South (2001) lists the reasons why informants cooperate: money, revenge, dementia, kicks, attention, repentance, and coercion.

Informants have been or are probably engaged in criminal activities themselves. Police use informants who often continue to commit crime while helping police. The following describes an informant who had police protection withdrawn (Scheingold, 1984: 122):

> The problem is that by the time Detective Tumulty decided to bury Carranza, the informant had already committed, by his own count, two hundred crimes, and he had confessed over one hundred of them to the police. It is not surprising that business persons victimized by Carranza were not particularly pleased when they learned the police had failed to prosecute him.

It has come to light that the FBI has protected informers even after they have committed murders. John Connolly, an FBI agent, was convicted of obstruction of justice and is now serving a ten-year prison sentence for protecting two organized crime figures, now implicated in eighteen murders, during the time they worked for the FBI. Other agents have admitted that they "bend the rules" in order to keep information sources. Critics argue that FBI agents should not make decisions regarding which crimes are more or less important: "Is a federal official entitled to make that decision—that one person's life is more valuable than another's?" (Donn, 2003: A16).

The federal witness protection plan has provided new identities for some witnesses *after* they have accumulated bad debts or otherwise victimized an unwary public. The rationale for informant protection is that greater benefit is derived from using them to catch other criminals than their punishment would bring. This also extends to overlooking any minor crime that they engage in during the period of time they provide information, or afterward if that is part of the deal (Marx, 1985a: 109). However, the ethical soundness of this judgment may be seriously questioned.

Police use informants partly to avoid problems that undercover police officers would encounter if they attempted to accomplish the task, but also because informants are under fewer restrictions. As Marx reports, informers and—to an even greater extent, middlemen—are much less formally accountable than are sworn law officers and are not as constrained by legal or departmental restrictions. As an experienced undercover agent candidly put it, "[U]nwitting informers are desirable precisely because they can do what we can't—legally entrap."

An incident in Houston where an informant was killed in a drug buy brought to light the many ethical issues raised by using informants. This individual came to the police to help them identify pushers. He was married and had small children. He engaged in drug deals, and after they occurred, the police would arrest the drug sellers. In one such incident, the informant was in a motel room with the pushers and was evidently identified as an informant and killed before police could enter the room. The informant was not wearing a wire, and he had no weapon or means of protecting himself. Unlike the families of undercover police officers killed in the line of duty, his family did not receive compensation for his death ("Informant," 1993: A20).

Some observers question the use of civilians in such dangerous operations. However, one might point out the fact that this informant freely volunteered his services, unlike some informants, who are threatened with prosecution if they do not cooperate. Another problem with informants is that sometimes their reliability is highly questionable. Their rewards, whatever those might be, are contingent upon delivering some evidence of crime to law enforcement. In some cases, this evidence may be purely manufactured. In Dallas an informant was used to buy drugs from suspected drug dealers, who were then arrested and convicted using his testimony. When the supposed cocaine that he allegedly bought from those arrested was tested, it turned out to be powdered plasterboard. In fact, in several cases involving the same informant, there were no drugs. Defendants, in the meantime, had spent months in jail protesting their innocence before charges were dropped. It was concluded by police and prosecutors that this informant had planted the cocaine substitute on innocent men who had no relationship to drug use. Why? He had been paid $200,000 since 2000 for helping Dallas police make drug arrests (Curry, 2002).

Sometimes officers are tempted to manufacture informants. When writing affidavits for search warrants, officers may use information supplied by a "confidential informant" without having to name the informant. All the officer need do is state that the informant has given good information in the past and that it would be dangerous to reveal his or her identity. This boilerplate language is routinely accepted, so information is used to establish probable cause that cannot be verified or challenged. Sutton (1991) argues that some officers are tempted to use imaginary confidential informants to allow the use of otherwise illegally obtained or simply manufactured evidence. Barker and Carter (1999) report on a tragic case of this occurring in which an officer made up evidence from a so-called informant in order to get a search warrant. In the search, an officer was killed and the lie was exposed.

Some officers openly admit that they could not do their job without informants. However, there are other arguments that the perceived value of informants is overstated. In a British study, the Home Office concluded that informants were cost effective. But other analysts argued that the study did not factor in other issues, such as tolerating continued crime (by informants) and informants who create crime in order to report it (Dunningham and Norris, 1999).

Some police officers develop close working relationships with informants, whereas others maintain that you can't trust them no matter how long you've known them. Another issue is when informants are drug users and police officers supply them with drugs as payment in lieu of cash (Lersch, 2002: 71). South (2001) summarizes the ethical issues with using informants as follows:

1. Getting too close and/or engaging in love affairs with informants
2. Overestimating the veracity of the information
3. Being a pawn of the informant who is taking advantage of the system for money or other reasons
4. Creating crimes by letting the informant entrap people who would not otherwise have committed the crime
5. Engaging in unethical or illegal behaviors for the informant, such as providing drugs
6. Letting the informant invade one's personal life
7. Using coercion and intimidation to get the informant to cooperate

Interestingly, officers seem to have a pervasive disdain for informants because the informant is perceived as untrustworthy; after all, they are "ratting" on friends and acquaintances. At the same time, officers may be coercing such behavior, and they depend on the information. In many ways, officers share criminals' subcultural values against snitches.

There are disturbing questions one might ask about using private citizens in dangerous operations. It may be true that narcotics investigations are difficult, if not impossible, without the use of informants. If so, then guidelines and standards are needed to govern the use of informants. The Commission on Accreditation for Law Enforcement Agencies (CALEA) has developed such standards.

## Justifications for Undercover Operations

There are arguments both for and against the use of undercover operations and informants (see Box 9-1). Marx (1985b, 1991) argues that they might actually create more crime. They may also lead to unintended crime and danger. For instance, he mentioned situations where decoys have been attacked, undercover officers have been robbed, undercover officers have been killed by other officers who mistook them for criminals, and policewomen acting as prostitutes have been attacked. The use of informants sometimes leads to retaliatory assaults against them. There have even been scenarios where agents from one law enforcement agency pretended to buy drugs from drug dealers who turned out to be undercover police from another agency (Marx, 1991). Although these futile charades are rare, one wonders how many resources have been expended for them.

Undercover operations have been criticized for the following reasons (Marx, 1992: 17–18):

1. They may generate a market for the purchase or sale of illegal goods and services.
2. They may generate the idea for the crime.
3. They may generate the motive.
4. They may provide a missing resource.
5. They may entail coercion or intimidation of a person otherwise not predisposed to commit the offense.

6. They may generate a covert opportunity structure for illegal actions on the part of the undercover agent or informant.
7. They may lead to retaliatory violence against informers.
8. They may stimulate a variety of crimes on the part of those who are not targets of the undercover operation (for example, impersonation of a police officer, crimes committed against undercover officers).

---

**BOX 9-1  Justifications for and Arguments Against Undercover Work**

**For:**

1. Citizens grant to government the right to use means which they individually forsake.
2. Undercover work is ethical when its targets are persons who freely choose to commit crimes which they know may call forth deceptive police practices.
3. Undercover work is ethical when used for a good and important end.
4. Undercover work is ethical when there are reasonably specific grounds to suspect that a serious crime is planned or has been carried out.
5. Undercover work is ethical when it is directed against persons whom there are reasonable grounds to suspect.
6. When citizens use questionable means, government agents are justified in using equivalent means.
7. Special risks justify special precautions.
8. Undercover work is ethical when it is the best means.
9. Enforce the law equally.

**Against:**

1. Truth telling is moral; lying is immoral.
2. The government should not make deals with criminals.
3. The government should neither participate in, nor be a party to crime, nor break laws in order to enforce them.
4. The government through its actions should reduce, not increase crime.
5. The government should not create an intention to commit a crime which is impossible to carry out.
6. The government should neither tempt the weak, nor offer temptation indiscriminately, nor offer unrealistically attractive temptations.
7. Do no harm to the innocent.
8. Respect the sanctity of private places.
9. Respect the sanctity of intimate relations.
10. Respect the right to freedom of expression and action.
11. The government should not do by stealth what it is prohibited from doing openly.

*continued*

---

**BOX 9-1   Continued**

10. Convict the guilty.
11. An investigation should be as nonintrusive and noncoercive as possible.
12. Undercover work is ethical when it is undertaken with the intention of eventually being made public and literally judged in court.
13. Undercover work is ethical when it is carried out by persons of upright character in accountable organizations.

SOURCE: G. Marx, "Police Undercover Work: Ethical Deception or Deceptive Ethics." In *Police Ethics: Hard Choices in Law Enforcement*, ed. W. Heffernan and T. Stroup (New York: John Jay Press, 1985). All rights reserved. Reprinted by permission.

---

Ethical systems may or may not support undercover operations. The **principle of double effect** holds that when one does an action to achieve a good end and an inevitable but unintended effect is negative, then the action might be justified. We might justify police action in this way if the unethical consequence, such as the deception of an innocent, was not the intended consequence of the action and the goal was an ethical one. However, deceiving the suspect could not be justified under the principle of double effect because that is an intended effect, not an unintended effect.

Religious ethics would probably condemn many kinds of police actions because of the deceptions involved. Ethical formalism would probably also condemn such actions because one could not justify them under the categorical imperative. Further, innocent family members being used as a means to a conviction of an offender would also violate the categorical imperative. Egoism might or might not justify such actions depending on the particular officer involved and what his or her maximum gain and loss was determined to be.

Utilitarian ethics would justify police deception and deceptive techniques if one could make the argument that catching criminals provides greater benefit to society than allowing them to go free by refusing to engage in such practices. Act utilitarianism would probably support deceptive practices, but rule utilitarianism might not because the actions, although beneficial under certain circumstances, might in the long run undermine and threaten our system of law. Under act utilitarianism, one would measure the harm of the criminal activity against the methods used to control it. Deceptive practices, then, might be justified in the case of drug offenses but not for business misdeeds, or for finding a murderer but not for trapping a prostitute, and so on. The difficulty of this line of reasoning, of course, is agreeing on a standard of seriousness. I might decide that drugs are serious enough to justify otherwise unethical practices, but you might not. Pornography and prostitution may be serious enough to some to justify unethical practices, but to others only murder or violent crime would justify the practices.

Cohen (1991) proposes a test to determine the ethical justification for police practices. His focus is the use of coercive power to stop and search, but we might apply the same test to analyze undercover or other deceptive practices:

1. The end must be justified as a good—for instance, conviction of a serious criminal rather than general intelligence gathering.
2. The means must be a plausible way to achieve the end—for example, choosing a target with no reasonable suspicion is not a plausible way to reduce any type of crime.
3. There must be no better alternative means to achieve the same end: No less intrusive means or methods of collecting evidence exist.
4. The means must not undermine some other equal or greater end; that is, if the method results in loss of trust or faith in the legal system, it fails the test.

Many people see nothing wrong—certainly nothing illegal—in using any methods necessary to catch criminals. But we are concerned with methods in use before individuals are found guilty. Can an innocent person, such as you, be entrapped into crime? Perhaps not, but are we comfortable in a society where the person who offers you drugs or sex or a cheap way to hook into cable television turns out to be an undercover police officer? Are we content to assume that our telephone may be tapped or our best friend could be reporting our conversations to someone else? When we encounter police behavior in these areas, very often the practices have been used to catch a person who we realize, after the fact, had engaged in wrongdoing, so we feel that police are justified in performing in slightly unethical ways. What protectors of due process and critics of police investigation practices help us to remember is that those practices, if not curbed, may just as easily be used on the innocent as well as on the guilty.

It is clear that norms support police deception during the investigative phase. If their norms support deception during investigation, it is not surprising that some officers may protect themselves with deception when their methods are legally questioned. In fact, one of the problems with deceptive practices is that they may lead to more deception to cover up illegal methods. For instance, Skolnick (1982) argues that weak or nonexistent standards during the investigation phase of policing lead directly to lying on the witness stand because that is sometimes the only way an officer can save his or her case.

It is unlikely that these investigative techniques will ever be eliminated; perhaps they should not be, since they are effective in catching a number of people who should be punished. Even if one has doubts about the ethics of these practices, it is entirely possible that there is no other way to accomplish the goal of crime control. However one decides these difficult questions, there are no easy answers. Also, it is important to realize that although for us these questions are academic, for thousands of police officers they are very real.

# Interrogation

Deception often takes a different form in the interrogation phase of a case. Several court cases document the use of mental coercion, either through threat or promise. The use of the *father confessor approach* (a sympathetic paternal figure for the defendant to confide to) or *Mutt and Jeff partners* (a "nice guy" and a seemingly brutal, threatening officer) are other ways to induce confessions and/or obtain information (Kamisar, LeFave, and Israel, 1980: 54).

Skolnick and Leo (1992) present a typology of deceptive interrogation techniques. The following is a brief summary of their descriptions of these practices:

* Calling the questioning an interview rather than an interrogation by questioning in a noncustodial setting and telling the suspect that he is free to leave, thus eliminating the need for Miranda warnings
* Presenting Miranda warnings in a way designed to negate their effect, by mumbling or by using a tone suggesting that the offender better not exercise the rights delineated or that they are unnecessary
* Misrepresenting the nature or seriousness of the offense by, for instance, not telling the suspect that the victim has died
* Using manipulative appeals to conscience through role playing or other means
* Misrepresenting the moral seriousness of the offense—for instance, by pretending that the rape victim "deserved" to be raped in order to get a confession
* Using promises of lesser sentences or nonprosecution beyond the power of the police to offer
* Misrepresenting identity by pretending to be lawyers or priests
* Using fabricated evidence such as polygraph results or fingerprint findings that don't really exist

Skolnick (1982) writes that because physical means of coercion are no longer used—the infamous third degree—mental deception is the only means left for police officers to gain information or confessions from suspects. How does one get a killer to admit to where she left the murder weapon? If police are imaginative, they may be able to get the defendant to confess by encouraging her to think about what would happen if children found the gun. Or police might discover the location of a body by convincing the killer after he had refused to talk to police that the victim deserves a Christian burial (see *Brewer v. Williams*, 430 U.S. 387 [1977]). Courts have ruled that police who use these methods are unconstitutionally infringing on the defendant's right to counsel because the conversations, even if not direct questioning, constitute an interrogation. However, other cases that involve deception and vigorous attempts to obtain information before counsel has been appointed have been approved by the Supreme Court.

Whether police have a legal right to deceive a suspect is not the same question as whether it is ethical, and, if so, what are the limits of such deception? Skolnick's argument is that deception is used because physical coercion cannot be. It is true, of course, that the use of physical force to obtain a conviction is illegal. Most countries, in fact, have eliminated torture and formally condemn the practice. Unfortunately, some countries still endorse physical coercion as acceptable police practice. Amnesty

International documents abuses in Chile, Argentina, and many other countries around the world. It is important to note that very often in these situations, police are used as the means of control by the dominant political power. Therefore, they operate not under the law, as the code of ethics dictates, but above the law. Codes of ethics, adopted by many police departments that have recognized the danger of police power being misused, are very clear in directing police to abide by the law and not allow themselves to be used by people or political parties (Bossard, 1981).

In the last edition of this text, the interrogation practice of the U.S. military in Afghanistan was noted, including the allegations that U.S. forces had handed over captives to countries where torture was legal, and then participated in the interrogations in order to acquire information about Osama Bin Laden and future operations. It was also reported that U.S. officials admitted to the use of such techniques as withholding medical attention, depriving detainees of food and water, engaging in sleep and light deprivation, and using other means short of physical torture against Al Qaeda leaders (Van Natta, 2003). Several readers personally objected to the passage and argued that there was no credible evidence that the United States was engaged in such practices.

Unfortunately, later events proved that even worse practices emerged in Iraq and are documented by pictures smuggled out on soldiers' camera phones. Iraqi prisoners who were not being held because of suspected insurgent action were brutalized, including being stripped naked, stacked in human pyramids, dog collared, made to stand on a box for long periods of time and beaten when they fell off, had what they were told were electrical cords tied to their genitals, had their pictures taken in sexually suggestive poses with other men, were handcuffed in physically awkward or painful positions and left for long periods of time, were either threatened with or actually attacked by guard dogs, and, in a few documented cases, were literally beaten to death by military guards, interrogators, and soldiers.

Legal proscriptions against torture come not from an ethical rationale but from a legal rationale based on the fact that torture renders a confession unreliable. Tortured victims might confess to stop their suffering; thus, the court would not get truthful information. Many would argue that whatever information is gained from an individual who is physically coerced into confessing or giving information is not worth the sacrifice of moral standards even if the information is truthful. Human rights treaties signed by the majority of free countries condemn such practices, regardless of the reason for the interrogation.

One other point to be made is that when such techniques of torture are approved of in certain instances (e.g., for those who have important information about terrorism or insurgent action), some individuals then find it easier to extend the rationale to others (prisoners who have no information and are tortured for other reasons—e.g., they are combative). As far as can be determined, those who were tortured in Abu Ghraib were not insurgents and had no information to offer. Soldiers evidently felt comfortable engaging in the same behaviors that they knew military interrogators had used for other prisoners. Once human rights are discarded for one group, it is hard to reserve them for others.

Recall that at the time, emotion ran high against Iraqi insurgents because some U.S. soldiers and contractors had been killed in gruesome ways, including beheadings. Some Americans responded to the torture in the prison with the response that "they deserve it because 'they' were killing Americans." This form of simplistic retribution is the worst kind of illogical rationalization:

1. First, there was no evidence that the prisoners being tortured were involved in the killings.
2. Second, there was no evidence that they were even insurgents because the prison was being used to house those who had committed typical crimes such as looting. Thus, the only thing they had in common with the insurgents was that they were Iraqi.
3. Third, if one commits the same atrocities as one's enemies, how can you argue that you are any more moral or right?
4. Fourth, such thinking ends up in a cyclical chain of retribution (blood feuds) whereby individuals are killed or injured simply because of their membership in the other group, thereby justifying the next attack by the injured group.

Klockars (1983) describes the inevitability of certain unethical or immoral police behaviors as the **Dirty Harry problem**, after the movie character who did not let the law get in his way when pursuing criminals. In Klockars's view, using immoral means to reach a desired moral end is an irresolvable problem because there are situations where one knows the "dirty act" will result in a good end, there are no other means to achieve the good end, and the "dirty act" will not be in vain. Klockars's example of this type of problem, taken from a movie, is a situation where a captured criminal refuses to tell the location of a kidnapped victim. Because the victim is sure to die without help, the police officer (played by Clint Eastwood) tortures the criminal by stepping on his injured leg until he admits the location.

Obviously, this is an immoral act, but Klockars's point is that there is no solution to the situation. If the police officer behaved in a professional manner, the victim was sure to die; if he behaved in an immoral manner, there was a chance he could save a life. This is a dominant theme in detective and police fiction. Klockars's conclusion is that by engaging in "dirty" means for good ends, the officer has tainted his innocence and must be punished, for there is always a danger that dirty means will be redefined as neutral or even good by those who use them. Police may lose their sense of moral proportion if the action is not punished, even though the individual police officer involved may have no other way out of the moral dilemma.

Delattre (1989a) also discusses the use of coercive power. He disagrees with Klockars that the officer must inevitably be tainted in the Dirty Harry situation. Delattre points out that if one chooses physical coercion, regardless of temptation, this leads to perjury and lying about the activity and perhaps other tactics to ensure that the offender does not go free due to the illegal behavior of the police officer. However, he also excuses the actions of those who succumb to temptation in extreme situations and perform an illegal act (Delattre, 1989a: 211):

> Police officials are not tainted by refusing to step onto the slope of illegal action, neither are officials of demonstrated probity necessarily tainted by a last-ditch illegal step. Such an act may be unjustifiable by an unconditional principle, but it also may be excusable. . . . Still less does it follow that those who commit such acts are bad, that their character is besmirched, or that their honor is tainted.

However, one might argue that if officers commit an illegal and unethical act, it is hard for their character not to be affected or their honor tainted. To understand an action (in this case an act that results from anger or frustration) is not to excuse it. Delattre presents a virtue-based ethical system and evidently believes that an officer can have all the virtues of a good officer and still commit a bad action—in this case, the illegal use of force. His point that one act of violence does not necessarily mean that the officer is unethical in other ways is well taken. In fact, we usually reserve the terms *ethical* and *unethical* for actions rather than persons. The reaction of the officer to his or her mistake is the true test of character. Does the officer cover up and/or ask his or her partner to cover up the action? Does the officer lie to protect himself or herself? Or does the officer admit wrongdoing and accept the consequences?

Klockars's underlying point is more subtle: We all are guilty in a sense by expecting certain ones among us to do the dirty work and then condemning them for their actions. In times of war or other threats, the populace often wants results without wanting to know tactics. What percentage of the population cared that the CIA attempted to assassinate Fidel Castro or that the attorney general's office during the Kennedy years used questionable tactics and violated the due-process rights of Cosa Nostra members targeted in the campaign against organized crime? How many of us truly want to know about the clandestine operations of Special Forces in Afghanistan or Iraq?

Klockars points out the position of those who perform despicable acts that benefit the rest of us; we are comfortable in our ignorance and comfortable in our judgments as long as we don't have to look too closely at our own role in the events. In effect, police (and other law enforcement) become our *sin eaters* of early folklore; they are the shady characters on the fringe of society who absorb evil so that the rest of us may remain pure—shunned and avoided, these persons and their value are taken for granted.

It is certainly much easier to justify mental coercion than physical coercion and intimidation, but their justifications are the same—that is, they are an effective and perhaps necessary means to get needed information from a resisting subject. The criticism against them is also the same. Mental coercion may also result in untruths. Recently, several convictions have been overturned because new evidence proves that those convicted were innocent, yet they confessed. Why would someone confess to a crime he didn't commit?

A suspect might confess because he is a fourteen-year-old juvenile who was mentally overpowered by police using pressure and feeding him information from the crime. This is alleged to have happened in the Central Park jogger "wilding" case. In 1990, five black and Hispanic youths were convicted of the beating and rape of a female stockbroker. It appears that they may have been innocent. Matias Reyes confessed, stating that he acted alone in the crime. DNA evidence supports his contention that he raped the victim (Tanner, 2002; Getlin, 2002b). Evidently, the youths were intimidated into "confessing."

Suspects may confess because police use intimidation and fear tactics to extract a confession. This is allegedly what happened in an Austin case where two men were found guilty and sentenced to death for a robbery/murder. One of them confessed and implicated the other. Then, twelve years later, it appeared that the crime was actually committed by another man who wrote the district attorney offering his confession. DNA evidence has also confirmed his guilt. The convicted man who confessed alleges that he did so because the police officer who interrogated him threatened that if he did not confess, Mexican police would arrest his mother and they could not guarantee her safety. They told him he would receive the death penalty if he didn't confess (Hafetz, 2002).

Although such events sound like something from television drama rather than reality, they evidently do happen. In 2001, Illinois Governor Ryan commuted the death sentences of everyone on death row because of suspicion that there may be more innocent men in danger of being executed. Thirteen death penalty cases were overturned when evidence indicated the convicted might be innocent or, at the very least, did not receive due process. Five of those thirteen were from Chicago, and evidence indicated that the convictions were obtained through coerced confessions and manufactured evidence by the Chicago police investigators (Babwin, 2001).

Muir discusses the necessity for the use of coercion: A good police officer, he writes, "has to resolve the contradiction of achieving just ends with coercive means" (Muir, 1977: 3). According to Muir, the successful police officer is able to balance willingness to use coercion with an understanding of humankind, which includes such traits as empathy and sympathy toward the weaknesses of human nature. If officers overemphasize coercion, they become cynical and brutal; if they overemphasize understanding, they become ineffectual:

> Under certain conditions, a youthful policeman was likely to come upon solutions to the paradoxes of coercive power which enabled him to accept the use of coercion as legitimate. However, if his solution to his moral problems required him to blind himself to the tragedy of the human condition, then he became an enforcer. Under other circumstances, a young policeman's choice of responses to paradox left him in conflict about the morality of coercion. Then he would be transfixed by feelings of guilt, would tend to evade situations which aroused those feelings, and would develop a perspective to justify his evasions. This kind of officer became either a reciprocator or an avoider. Finally, some young officers found ways to exercise coercion legitimately without having to deny their "common sense of the oneness of the human condition." These men became professionals. (Muir, 1977: 24)

## Loyalty and Whistleblowing

One of the most difficult ethical dilemmas that officers confront is when faced with the wrongdoing of another officer. Informing or testifying against one's peers has always been negatively perceived by any group, whether that group be lawyers, doctors, students, prisoners, or police officers. The **code of silence** in police work is present in other occupations and groups as well; however, in policing it can be understood as a type of noble-cause corruption.

The books *Serpico* (Maas, 1973) and *Prince of the City* (Daley, 1984) describe two examples of police officers who chose to challenge the "blue curtain" of secrecy

## QUOTE and QUERY

The problem is that the atmosphere does not yet exist in which honest police officers can act without fear of ridicule or reprisal from fellow officers. . . .

Source: Frank Serpico, Knapp Commission, 1971, as reported in Hentoff (1999).

Cops don't tell on cops. . . . [I]f a cop decided to tell on me, his career's ruined. . . . [H]e's going to be labeled as a rat.

Source: Police officer witness, Mollen Commission, 1994, as reported in Walker (2001).

*How would you create an atmosphere in a police department wherein officers would feel more comfortable reporting the misdoings/criminality of other officers? Or would you even want to?*

and testify against their fellow officers in corruption hearings. In *Prince of the City*, the officer agreed to testify only if he could protect his partners. Ultimately, he was unable to do so and had to live with the hatred, betrayal, and even suicide of past friends. In *Serpico*, the author presents the real-life events of Frank Serpico, a New York City police officer who exposed a widespread scandal of bribery and corruption. Evidence of how little the blue curtain changes is the fact that even today, some officers use "Serpico" as a derogatory term for an officer who is not to be trusted.

The police subculture described in Chapter 7 has been identified as the source for the particularly strong pattern of protecting co-workers who commit unethical acts in law enforcement. This practice in policing has been called the **blue curtain of secrecy**. It should be noted that recent research indicates that it may be breaking down. Barker (2002), for instance, reports on some research indicating that minorities and women have torn the solidarity that once existed, and this can be seen by the proliferation of complaints against fellow officers. For instance, he notes that there were more than thirty cases in Los Angeles where officers were the primary witnesses against other officers. In their police attitude survey, Weisburd and Greenspan (2000) discovered that although 80 percent of police officers did not feel that the "code of silence" was essential for police trust and good policing, fully two-thirds reported that a "whistleblower" would encounter sanctions. Further, more than half agreed that it was not unusual for police to ignore improper conduct on the part of other officers.

There are special problems involved when police officers protect one another. One of the greatest harms of cover-ups is the harm that is inflicted upon a police officer's credibility. Sykes (1996) describes a civil case wherein a jury awarded $15.9 million in damages after a case of police brutality. Jurors simply did not believe the police version of the events, and a videotape supported the plaintiff 's allegations that excessive force was used. The "cost" of police cover-ups eventually becomes public distrust of police testimony.

**QUOTE and QUERY**

At the trial, it just really angered me that deputies could identify suspects from booking photos, people they never knew, and describe in detail what actions people did that night, people they hardly ever saw. And yet throughout the entire trial I don't think there was ever one deputy who was able to identify their fellow deputies or any of the actions that their fellow deputies did that night.

Source: Reported in G. Sykes, "How Much Is Our Credibility Worth?" *Ethics Roll Call* 3(1) (1996): 5.

*Explain why someone might use this statement as evidence that utilitarianism would not support "testilying" even in order to catch criminals.*

As mentioned previously, perhaps the O. J. Simpson trial has become the classic example of what happens when a jury loses confidence in police testimony. Prosecutors can ordinarily rely on a jury to take police testimony as fact and even believe police testimony over nonpolice witnesses. When police testimony is given no greater weight than any other witness—indeed, when jury members believe that police are prone to lie on the stand—then the justice system itself is at risk.

## Teleological Arguments

Recall that teleological rationales are those that argue the end justifies the means. Egoism may support not coming forward because it may not be in one's best interest. We don't want to get involved, we don't want to face the scorn of others, we feel it's not our job to come forward when there are others who are supposed to look out for and punish wrongdoing, or we don't want to alienate the peer who committed the wrong by reporting him or her. These are all egoistic reasons for not coming forward.

There are also utilitarian reasons to keep quiet about observed wrongdoing. For instance, it may be that some activities labeled corrupt may actually further the ends of justice and that complete adherence to regulations would undermine detection and enforcement. Also, the loss of a skilled police officer, even though that officer may be moderately corrupt, is a loss to society. One may believe that the harm to the police department in exposing the deviance of one officer is greater than the harm to society created by what that officer is doing, or that there is greater utility in stopping the officer without making the issue public.

However, there are also teleological arguments for coming forward. Egoism may dictate that an individual needs to come forward to protect himself from being accused of wrongdoing. The police officer may also endure such a crisis of conscience or fear of being punished that she can only attain peace of mind by "coming clean." Utilitarian arguments for coming forward exist as well. The harm that occurs from letting the individual carry on his misdeeds or not forcing the individual to a public punishment may be greater than the harm that would occur from the scandal of public exposure. This is especially true if one is forced to either tell the truth or lie; in this case, the harm to police credibility must be taken into account.

## Deontological Arguments

Deontological arguments can also be used to support not exposing other officers, or for coming forward. Arguments against exposing other officers include the idea that discretion and secrecy are obligations that one assumes by joining a police force, and that it would be unjust to subject an otherwise good and heroic police officer to the punishment of exposure. Arguments for coming forward include the fact that a police officer has a sworn duty to uphold the law. Also, one cannot remain silent in one situation unless one could approve of silence in all situations (Kant's categorical imperative), and one must do one's duty, which involves telling the truth when under an oath (Wren, 1985: 32–33).

It should be noted that, in general, deontological ethics support whistleblowing because it is a higher duty to uphold the law than it is to defend one's fellow officers. Of course, this argument also depends on whether the primary role is one of crime fighter or public servant. If one perceives oneself as primarily a crime fighter, then one's duties are perceived differently from those of a public servant.

## Loyalty

The previous arguments are what Wren (1985) calls external moral arguments, which he contrasts with internal arguments, such as loyalty. When one considers whether to come forward about the wrongdoing of others, external moral philosophies, such as the utilitarian "it is best for everyone" rationale, are rarely articulated. What often is the prime motivator for truth telling is personal integrity. Yet the individual often feels great anguish and self-doubt over turning in or testifying against friends and colleagues, and that is understandable because "a person's character is defined by his commitments, the more basic of which reveal to a person what his life is all about and give him a reason for going on" (Wren, 1985: 35). Loyalty is a difficult concept that others have written about extensively; it can be a vehicle of both ethical and unethical behavior (Fletcher, 1993).

Loyalty in police work is explained by the fact that police depend on one another, sometimes in life-or-death situations. Loyalty to one's fellows is part of the *esprit de corps* of policing and is an absolutely essential element of a healthy department. Ewin (1990) writes that something is wrong if a police officer doesn't feel loyalty to fellow officers. Loyalty is a personal relationship, not a judgment. Therefore, loyalty is uncalculating—we do not extend loyalty in a rational way or based on contingencies. Loyalty to groups or persons is emotional, grounded in affection rather than reflection.

Ewin (1990: 13) also points out that loyalty always refers to a preference for one group over another. Loyalty always involves some exclusion: One is loyal to X rather than to Y, with Y thus being excluded. At times, the reverse can also be true: That a group of people is excluded (whether or not they are properly excluded) can make them feel a common cause in response to what they see as oppression and can result in the growth of loyalty among them. That loyalty, provoked by a dislike and perhaps distrust of the other group, is likely to be marked by behavior that ignores legitimate interests and concerns of the other group.

The application to policing is obvious. If police feel isolated from the community, their loyalty is to other police officers and not to the community at large. If they feel oppressed by and distrust the police administration, they would draw together against the "common enemy." To address abuses of loyalty, one would not want to attack the loyalty itself because it is necessary for the health of the organization. Rather, one would want to extend the loyalty beyond other officers to the department and to the community. Permeability rather than isolation promotes community loyalty, just as the movement toward professionalism promotes loyalty to the principles of ethical policing as opposed to individuals in a particular department.

Wren believes that police departments can resolve the dilemma of the individual officer who knows of wrongdoing by making the consequences more palatable—that is, by having a fair system of investigation and punishment, by instituting helping programs for those with alcohol and drug problems, and by using more moderate punishments than dismissal or public exposure for other sorts of misbehavior. This is consistent with the ethics of care, which is concerned with needs and relationships. If the relationship can be saved and the need for honesty and change met, then that is the best alternative to the dilemma of exposing wrongdoing or not.

Delattre (1989a) handles the problem differently but comes to somewhat similar conclusions. He turns to Aristotle to support the idea that when a friend becomes a scoundrel, the moral individual cannot stand by and do nothing. Rather, one has a moral duty to bring the wrongdoing to the friend's attention and urge her or him to change. If the friend will not, then she or he is more scoundrel than friend, and the individual's duty shifts to those who might be victimized by the officer's behavior. One sees here not the ethics of care but a combination of virtue-based and deontological duty-based ethics.

Souryal (1996b, 1999b) discusses loyalty to superiors or to fellow police as misplaced. He argues that there are several kinds of loyalty: personal loyalty, institutional loyalty, and integrated loyalty (which relates to the ideal values of the profession). Loyalty to superiors is traced back to *divine right*—the idea that persons were indistinguishable from their office (1996b: 48). Today, however, we are governed by laws, not kings, and such loyalty should be properly placed in our laws and our values rather than an individual. Souryal (1996b) notes that personal loyalties often lead to unethical actions and that loyalty to values or organizations is more appropriate. One might argue that even loyalty to a police organization may be misplaced if it leads to lying to protect the organization against scandal.

## Sanctions Against Whistleblowers

The informal practice of punishing individuals who come forward is an especially distressing aspect of loyalty. For the individual who tears the blue curtain of secrecy, sanctions can be extreme. This is not just true of law enforcement agencies. In fact, sanctions against whistleblowers are so common that most states and the federal government now have laws designed to protect whistleblowers. See Box 9-2 for an example of one of these statutes.

---

**BOX 9-2  Texas Whistleblower Act**

Texas Whistleblower Act, 1983 (a) A state or local governmental entity may not suspend or terminate the employment of, or take other adverse personnel action against, a public employee who in good faith reports a violation of law by the employing governmental entity or another public employee to an appropriate law enforcement authority.

(b) In this section, a report is made to an appropriate law enforcement authority if the authority is a part of a state or local governmental entity or of the federal government that the employee in good faith believes is authorized to: regulate under or enforce the law alleged to be violated in the report; or (2) investigate or prosecute a violation of criminal law.

---

A typical example of retaliation was reported in a San Antonio newspaper concerning an officer in the San Antonio Police Department who arrested a sergeant for driving while intoxicated. Even though the officer had averaged fewer than two complaints a year during his eleven years at the police department, after he arrested the sergeant, he received nine complaints resulting in a total of eighty-six days of suspension. He also encountered hang-up calls on his unlisted home telephone, his belongings were stolen, his car was towed away from the police parking lot twice, officers refused to sit next to him, and officers did not respond to his requests for back-up. Witnesses also reported that they overheard officers discussing what other forms of retaliation to take against him. The sergeant who was arrested for drunken driving was released before being taken to a magistrate, contrary to departmental policy, and received no disciplinary sanctions (Casey, 1996).

Daisy Boria was a N.Y.P.D. cop who testified in a way that contradicted others in the death of Anthony Baez. In this case, a police officer allegedly used excessive force by applying a chokehold, which killed Baez, a young African American man. Boria testified that Baez was motionless on the ground when she and her partner arrived, which contradicted the testimony of her partner and the officer who killed Baez; both of them said that he was struggling. She reported that after she testified, she received death threats, she did not receive back-up when she called for it, and her supervisors routinely checked her locker for bombs. She quit the N.Y.P.D. and is now living in the Midwest (Hentoff, 1999).

Those who terrorize their fellow officers evidently believe that a violation of trust has occurred that justifies the harassment. Skolnick and Fyfe (1993: 110) argue that the danger to officers who violate the blue curtain is overstated and that the more common reason that officers have difficulty coming forward is that everyone is doing something wrong and risks exposure (Skolnick and Fyfe, 1993: 132). Daisy Boria and the officer in San Antonio might not agree. However often it happens, there are no ethical justifications for such actions, except for perhaps egoism.

Unfortunately, in many cases, such as the one described above, administrators participate in and thereby encourage a continuation of the practice. When

**IN THE NEWS FBI Suspends Agent Whose Charges Led to Critical Report**

Newspaper articles covered the story of the FBI suspending a scientist agent whose charges led to a still-secret Justice Department report critical of some FBI crime lab workers. A Republican senator was quoted as saying, "[The suspension] appears to be a reprisal." Evidently, the inspector general hired a panel of outside scientists to evaluate the work the lab after Whitehurst (the lab scientist) alleged in late 1995 that the lab mishandled evidence and testified with "a pro-prosecution bias." He alleged that misconduct may have tainted crime lab work or testimony on several high-profile federal cases.

Source: M. Sniffen, "FBI Suspends Agent Whose Charges Led to Critical Report," *Austin American-Statesman*, January, 28, 1997, A5.

*Why do you think the scientist was suspended after exposing the wrong doing in the lab?*

administrators and managers encourage or promote cover-ups, then the individual officer who exposes wrongdoing is truly alone. Such administrative support tends to be misguided utilitarianism: Scandal is so harmful to the organization that it must be avoided, even if one has to cover it up to do so. Of course, there may also be egoistic reasons for administrators' cover-ups: They may be implicated or blamed. The "In the News" box above describes a case where administrators allegedly sanctioned a whistleblower.

# Reducing Corruption

Malloy (1982: 37–40) offers some possible solutions to police corruption:

- increase the salary of police
- eliminate unenforceable laws
- establish civilian review boards
- improve training

One might add this solution: improve leadership.

Metz (1990) suggests several ways that police administrators can encourage ethical conduct among officers:

- setting realistic goals and objectives for the department
- providing ethical leadership
- providing a written code of ethics
- providing a whistleblowing procedure that ensures fair treatment of all parties
- providing training in law enforcement ethics

In this last section, we will explore some of the approaches that have been taken to nurture and encourage ethical behavior among police officers.

How does one minimize or eliminate existing corruption in a police department? Because so much of police work is unpredictable and encounters such a wide range of situations, it is impossible to fashion rules for all possible occurrences. What should take the place of extensive rules are strong ethical standards. However, the internalization of these standards by individual police officers is at best tenuous; the informal police subculture is the most obvious threat to the internalization of ethical standards.

It does seem to be the case, though, that the particular organizational values do influence the individual officer. As discussed in the last chapter, Klockars and associates (2000) used surveys to ask 3,235 officers in 30 U.S. police agencies to rank the corruptness of 11 hypotheticals. They ranked some as fairly nonserious: covering up a DUI accident and taking free meals. Others were ranked as more serious: excessive force, taking free drinks, and taking kickbacks. The most serious rankings were reserved for stealing from a found wallet, taking a money bribe, and stealing a watch from a crime scene. There was quite a degree of variability among agencies. Agencies where officers had belief systems that ranked all behaviors as more serious also reported that their agency would inflict harsher discipline on all misconduct (Klockars et al., 2000: 8). One might conclude from this that law enforcement administrators can affect the value systems of officers through appropriate discipline.

Crank and Caldero (2000: 159; see also Crank, 1998: 230) argue that even formal organizational values impose pressures that may lead to noble-cause corruption. Aspirations for promotion, "implicit quotas for arrests, directives from administrators, self-esteem, [and] moral ideological commitments" all put pressure on the individual officer to lie or otherwise subvert the formal values of law enforcement, and lead to violation of suspects' rights or other unethical behaviors. Thus, if management does not want officers engaging in noble-cause corruption, then it has to stop providing organizational incentives for doing so.

## Education and Training

Education has been promoted as necessary if police are to continue to be professional. However, education itself is certainly not a panacea, and, in fact, some of the officers with the worst examples of unethical behavior either had college degrees or scored above average on the academic tests to qualify for hiring. Although lack of education has been linked to a greater use of force, it is by no means clear that education, by itself, increases the ethics of police officers. It may be that educated officers believe that they can depart from standard operating procedures, which makes them harder to supervise and more likely to substitute individualistic definitions of justice.

Ethics training in the academy, as well as offering in-service courses, is common and recommended for all police departments today. Barker (2002: 21) reports on 1993 findings that only 1.6 percent of academy training in one state involved ethics.

However, some question what these courses might be able to accomplish. Reuss-Ianni (1983) describes how, after the Knapp Commission uncovered wide-ranging corruption in the N.Y.P.D., ethical awareness workshops were begun. Unfortunately, they have not stopped the periodic corruption scandals that have occurred since.

Many ethics courses use a moral reasoning approach, much as this book does, whereby various scenarios are examined in light of ethical perspectives, such as utilitarianism, to determine the right course of behavior. Implicit in this approach is the assumption that once officers know what is right, they will make the right decision. This may or may not be true.

Delattre (1989a) and Delaney (1990) offer a different perspective, one that emphasizes the importance of character. In Chapter 2 we discussed the ethics of virtue, which answers the question "How does one live a good life?" with "Developing and forming good habits of character." This is the approach that Delattre and Delaney apply to police ethics. If one has a bad character, ethical analysis is irrelevant because that individual will continue to behave in conformance to his or her traits of avarice, deceptiveness, cowardice, and so on. An individual who has good character possesses those virtues that are necessary for moral and ethical decision making. Training may help one by reinforcing appropriate values, but one's character is already formed. What are the virtues necessary for a good police officer? Delattre discusses justice, courage, temperance, and compassion. Delaney discusses sagacity, sincerity, and persistence.

This approach would seem to negate the relevance of any attempts to improve the ethics of officers, for character is fairly well formed by the time one is an adult. Yet we might say that ethics training at this point serves to delineate those situations that might not be recognized as questions of ethics. Also, discussions of such dilemmas point out egoistic rationalizations for unethical behavior, making them harder to use by those who would try. Other training options may concentrate on only one ethical system, such as utilitarianism, or involve a more balanced treatment of other ethical systems. All must resolve the issues of relativism versus absolutism, duty versus personal needs, and minor transgressions versus major transgressions.

Martinelli (2000) offers a different rationale for having an ethics training course. He proposes a course that is grounded in the actual discipline cases of each law enforcement agency. He argues that some of the law enforcement code provisions are ambiguous to officers and need explanations—such as keeping one's private life "unsullied." Officers may not realize that they can receive departmental sanctions for their behavior in their private life. Further, case law indicates that if some attempts are not made to instruct officers in appropriate behaviors, and if agencies and city councils continue to rubber-stamp the violation of civil rights that some officers commit, then the agencies themselves will be held responsible. For instance, if there is a pattern of abuse in a discipline record and the officer then commits another violation, the city and police department will probably lose a resulting civil suit.

There have also been instances where a "failure to train" argument has successfully established liability. "Police watch" law firms in major cities have a proven track record in winning multi-million-dollar lawsuits against departments and cities. Thus, if for no other reason than to avoid financial liability, administrators should institute training in this area.

## *Integrity Testing*

New York City has used **integrity testing** since the late 1970s, after the Knapp Commission exposed widespread corruption. *Field associates* were recruited straight from academies to investigate suspected officers (Reuss-Ianni, 1983: 80). This attempt to "police the police" involves setting up a situation where the officer might commit a wrongful act. For instance, an officer responds to a report of an open door to an apartment, and when he checks it out, he sees money in plain sight. However, the scene is being monitored to see if he takes the cash. There are also tests whereby a wallet is turned in to see if officers would take money (Marx, 1991). It is reported that almost 30 percent of officers have failed to turn in the wallet in this type of situation (Prenzler and Ronken, 2001a: 322). After the Mollen Commission in the mid-1990s, the integrity testing program was expanded. Prenzler and Ronken (2001a: 322) report that such

---

**POLICY BOX 9-1 Use of Integrity Testing**

As indicated in the chapter, New York City and some other cities have used integrity testing of officers. Most police officers are strongly against such a practice.

**Law:** There is no law that prevents a police department from setting up "stings" of its own officers. Case law that defines entrapment would apply to police as well as far as criminal charges but would be irrelevant to administrative sanctions. On the other hand, civil service and police unions may create contractual rights for officers.

**Policy:** Some police departments have a range of policies that make it clear that unethical behavior will not be tolerated. There is a difference between formal and informal policies, however, in that some police officers feel that investigation and sanctions are directed only to those officers without "juice" and that some officers who have friends in high places are immune from being targeted or from being punished. If true, that situation leads to informal policies in internal affairs where certain officers are protected from scrutiny. Management is distrusted, and behavioral practices of officers are adjusted to avoid detection rather than to avoid unethical behavior.

**Ethics:** The officers who are used in integrity test "stings" may have an ethical dilemma in that they feel they are lying to a fellow officer. Usually, new recruits are used for this reason so that officers do not know them by sight. The undercover officer may eventually have to testify against the targeted officer, and that may lead to ostracism and other sanctions by peers. It may be an ethical issue for members of management to use young officers in this manner because they probably can do little to protect such an officer from peer sanctions. If management targets certain officers unfairly for stings or ignores the wrongdoing of some officers, then that, of course, is an issue as well. The major ethical dilemma is that of the officer who is caught doing something wrong.

"integrity tests" may be getting better results today. Of 355 tests involving 762 officers, no criminal failures were reported, and only 45 procedural failures were reported. See the Policy Box on the previous page for a discussion of the policy of integrity testing.

Prenzler and Ronken (2001a) discuss integrity testing in police departments in Australia and around the world. They discuss how the London Metropolitan Police instituted random integrity testing in 1998. In their study of Australia, they discovered that only two reporting police agencies used *targeted* integrity testing, and none used random integrity testing. In New South Wales, integrity testing resulted in 37 percent failing. Only 27 percent passed, and the rest were referred for further investigation or discontinued (2001a: 327).

Needless to say, most police officers have very negative attitudes about integrity testing. Spokesmen argue that "testing raises serious issues regarding privacy, deception, entrapment, provocation and the legal rights of individuals" (Prenzler and Ronken, 2001a: 323–324). There is a widespread belief that testing is unfair, overly intrusive, and detrimental to morale. It is interesting to compare integrity testing with undercover operations. The planted wallet is similar to the buy–bust operation, and the use of field associates is similar to undercover operations. Officers hate the idea that an officer who pretends to be a friend may, instead, be someone who is trying to obtain evidence that they are doing wrong. The argument for undercover work is that if someone isn't doing anything wrong, there is nothing to fear. However, field associates create a sense of betrayal and lack of trust, regardless of whether someone is involved in wrongdoing. It is the same argument, of course, that is used to criticize undercover operations. Specifically, critics argue that the use of undercover operations may undermine the fabric of social relations by reducing the level of trust. After reading the "In the News" box, think about whether you believe that these efforts are a good or bad idea.

---

**IN THE NEWS   Integrity Tests for Police**

Baltimore police engage in random sting operations. New Orleans police stage car wrecks, leave money in abandoned cars, and set up fake drug buys. New York has undercover operators ask police officers for directions to see how polite they are. These are all integrity tests of officers. Some departments use such tests only when an officer is already under suspicion, but others engage in random testing. A Baltimore police officer was caught in a sting where a bag of cocaine was left on a park bench and then an anonymous tip was placed with the police dispatcher. The officer who responded did bring the bag in, but he lied when he stated that he saw a burglary suspect place it on the bench, and then falsely arrested the suspect. He was suspended and is facing charges of perjury.

Source: M. O'Hagan, "Putting Police to Honesty Test," *Washington Post*, October 6, 2000, B1.

***Is this a type of noble-cause corruption? Explain why or why not.***

## *Internal Affairs and Civilian Review/Complaint Boards*

There seems to be a growing belief that some police departments have proven themselves to be incapable of policing themselves and that what is needed is some outside oversight. Civilian review boards have been created in several cities to monitor and review the investigation and discipline of officers who have complaints filed against them. There are many models that exist for the idea of civilian review, and no one model has been reported to be more effective or better than any other. Prenzler and Ronken (2001b) argue that it is difficult to analyze the success of such bodies because a high level of complaints may mean that there is greater trust in the process rather than a spike in misconduct. The two models of misconduct review are described as follows:

1. In the **internal affairs model,** the police investigate themselves and use an internal discipline system. This is widely seen as ineffective. Citizens are discouraged from reporting, police are seen as ineffective, and the approach seems to be not to bring out corruption or misconduct but rather to hide it. In one Toronto study, 70 percent of people who filed complaints were not confident with the process, and only 14 percent felt their complaint was handled fairly (Prenzler and Ronken, 2001b: 180).
2. In the **civilian review/complaint model,** an independent civilian agency audits complaints and investigations. The board may also respond to appeals and act in an advisory role in investigations. Police still investigate and conduct the discipline proceeding. The Police Complaints Authority in the United Kingdom is one example of this model. *Compromise models* also exist that may have an external board, for instance, but without any powers of subpoena or oversight (Prenzler and Ronken, 2001b). Walker (2001) reviews the range of civilian review models but does not find that any one model seems to be better than any other. Worrall (2002) found that cities with civilian review procedures received more citizen complaints. This was a consequence of having a process that made it easier for citizens to complain rather than more incidents of police misconduct.

Prenzler and Ronken (2001b) report that external review models have about the same substantiation rate as do internal affairs models—about 10 percent of all complaints filed. The major criticism of such models centers on the idea that they are not truly independent, for police still conduct the investigations and sometimes even sit on the board. Prenzler (2000) argues the "capture" theory is operative in civilian review models. This occurs when the regulatory or investigative body is "co-opted" by the investigated agency through informal relationships.

## *Early Warning or Audit Systems*

Barker (2002) describes the evidence that indicates that a small percentage of officers often account for a disproportionate number of abuse or corruption complaints. This problem was first recognized as far back as the 1970s (Walker and Alpert, 2002). Therefore, the practice of identifying these officers through some form of early warning system seems logical. The officers who were prone to use force were the first targets of such early warning systems. It seemed clear that a small percentage of officers were responsible for a disproportionate share of excessive-force complaints. Then the practice spread to officers who garnered a disproportionate share of any type of citizen complaint.

Early warning systems have been used by New Orleans, Portland (Oregon), and Pittsburgh (Barker, 2002). The early warning systems look at number of complaints, use-of-force reports, use-of-weapon reports, reprimands, or other indicators to identify officers. Intervention may include greater supervision, additional training, and/or counseling. In one city's program, the officer's supervisor is alerted to the fact that the system has tagged the officer; then the supervisor may counsel the officer, engage in other responses, or do nothing (Walker and Alpert, 2002: 225). Walker and Alpert (2002: 223) describe Miami's early warning system and point out that officers identified by such systems may be subject to the following:

1. reassignment
2. retraining
3. transfer
4. referral to an employee assistance program
5. fitness for duty evaluation
6. dismissal (Walker and Alpert, 2002: 224)

Walker and Alpert (2002) note that these programs have been endorsed by the National Institute of Justice and have been incorporated into several consent decrees between cities and federal courts to avert civil rights litigation. By 1999, about 27 percent of all police agencies had early warning systems in place (reported in Walker and Alpert, 2002: 220). The "In the News" box describes a computer-assisted early warning system.

---

### IN THE NEWS  Computers Identify Rogue Cops

The Los Angeles police department has begun using a 35-million-dollar computer system that tracks citizen complaints and other indicators to alert supervisors to officers who may be engaging in misconduct. The system is in response to a consent decree with the U.S. Justice Department in which the department promised to improve oversight of rogue officers. The system tracks complaints, pursuits, lawsuits, uses of force, and other indicators to identify patterns of misconduct. Those who exhibit unusual patterns of action are flagged and supervisors are notified. Police union leaders argue that the system could create a situation where "good cops" hesitate to take action, creating the potential for harm.

Source: J. Marquez, "In Los Angeles, Computers Sniff Out Rogue Cops," *Austin American States-man*, July 24, 2005, A15.

*Do you think that the union leaders have a legitimate complaint against the system? Why or why not?*

These authors caution that one cannot simply count the number of incidents or complaints because the officer's shift and duty, length of service, types of calls responded to, and other factors will affect the number of complaints (Walker and Alpert, 2002: 223). Further, the programs are only as effective as the interventions that are triggered by the identification of a problem. They note that such systems are as much of a reflection of management as of individual officers. Supervisors are put on notice that they may have a problem officer and, thus, are more responsible if nothing is done and the officer engages in serious forms of misconduct.

## *Other Methods*

Hunter (1999) proposed several means to minimize or reduce misconduct among police:

- decertification of officers who commit serious misconduct
- community policing programs
- college
- enhanced discipline
- civilian review
- better training

In his survey of police officers in Florida, Hunter found that officers believed that strict and fair discipline was the best response and deterrent to misconduct. They also identified

- clear policies
- superior performance of supervisors
- peer review boards

It was clear that, according to officers, leadership had everything to do with an ethical police force—95 percent felt that supervisors should be moral examples, and 70 percent felt that unethical supervisors contributed to the problem. However, less than half (42 percent) agreed with the idea of a citizen review board.

Mores (2002) also discusses a range of methods to deter corruption, including the following:

- proper recruitment
- economic incentives
- community-oriented policing
- greater accountability
- rotation of assignments
- the use of informants
- the use of surveillance techniques
- prosecution of offenders

Prenzler and Ransley (2002) present the most exhaustive list, also found in the 1997 Wood Report, written after an investigation of widespread corruption in the New South Wales (Australia) police department. Their list of "Methods to Reduce Police Corruption" is reproduced in Box 9-3 on page 308.

---

**BOX 9-3   Methods to Reduce Police Corruption**

Internal affairs units
Independent civilian oversight agencies
Overt recording devices (videocameras in cars)
Covert high technology surveillance
Targeted integrity testing
Randomized integrity testing
Drug and alcohol testing
Quality assurance test (customer service monitors)
Internal informants
Complaints profiling
Supervisor accountability
Integrity reviews
Mandatory reporting
Whistleblower protection
Compulsory rotation in corruption-prone sections
Asset and financial reviews
Surveys of police
Surveys of public
Personnel diversification
Comprehensive ethics training
Inquisitorial methods (fact-finding rather than due-process emphasis)
Complaint resolution
Monitoring and regulation of police procedures (of informants)
Decriminalizing vice
Risk analysis (to see what areas are vulnerable to corruption)

SOURCE: J. Wood, *Royal Commission into the New South Wales Police Service: Final Report* (Government Printer, 1997).

---

## Ethical Leadership

Crank (1998: 187) and others note that there is a pervasive sense among rank-and-file police that administrators are not to be trusted: "Officers protect each other, not only against the public, but against police administrators frequently seen to be capricious and out of touch." The classic work in this regard is Reuss-Ianni's (1983) study of a New York City precinct in the late 1970s.

Reuss-Ianni described the "two cultures" of policing—street cops and management cops. She observed that law enforcement managers were classic bureaucrats who made decisions based on modern management principles. This contrasted with the street cop subculture, which still had remnants of quasi-familial relationships in which "loyalties and commitments took precedence over the rule book" (1983: 4). The result of this conflict between the two value systems was alienation of the street cop.

Despite the gulf between management and line staff, most people agree that employee behavior is influenced more directly by the behavior of superiors rather than by the stated directives or ethics of the organization. Executives engaged in price fixing and overcharging should not be surprised that their employees steal company supplies or time. Managers cannot espouse ethical ideals, act unethically, and then expect employees to act ethically. Thus, regardless of formal ethical codes, police are influenced by the standards of behavior they observe in their superiors. One might note that most large-scale police corruption that has been exposed has implicated very-high-level officials. Alternatively, police departments that have remained relatively free of corruption have administrators who practice ethical behavior on a day-to-day basis.

Administrators have their own unique ethical dilemmas to face. Budget allocations, the use of drug testing, affirmative action, sexual harassment, and decisions about corrupt officers all present ethical dilemmas for administrators and supervisors. For instance, some supervisors face problems when they are promoted from the ranks and have friends who now become their subordinates. Such friends may expect special consideration, leaving the supervisor to decide how to respond to such expectations. Supervisors also report ethical dilemmas over how they should allocate resources, such as a new patrol car or overtime. Should seniority take precedence over competence? Should friendship take precedence over seniority?

Another issue is what should be done with officers who have drug or alcohol problems. If the administrator decides to counsel or suggest treatment without any change in duty status and the officer endangers the life of someone or actually harms a citizen or other officer due to the problem, is the administrator to blame? In many situations where police leaders must make decisions, lives, property, or liberty can be at stake. It is extremely important for supervisors and administrators to understand the impact that their decisions and their behavior have on everyone in the organization.

Even if leaders are not directly involved in corruption, encouraging or participating in the harassment and ostracism that are directed at those who expose wrongdoers supports an organizational culture that punishes whistleblowers. In some departments there is a perception that favored cliques are not punished for behaviors for which others would receive punishment. This climate destroys the trust in police leadership that is essential to ensure good communication from the rank and file.

Reuss-Ianni (1983: 51) describes a trial of a cop who killed a prisoner in custody and the code of silence that was eventually broken down when other cops testified that they had lied in their reports and to the grand jury. The officers felt victimized by the press and betrayed by a management culture that, they felt, "threw them to the wolves." What is interesting about this event is that it occurred in 1976. Now, over thirty years later, one suspects that the same dynamics apply. For instance, in the Abner Louima case a couple of officers committed a brutal crime, other cops covered it up until outside pressure became too great, and then the code of silence broke down and officers were forced to testify against one another. The general effect was perhaps similar to what Reuss-Ianni described—the rank and file perceived lack of support from management when they were forced to testify against one another. What is important is that even after thirty years, the police officer who violated the law is still protected, and those who expose him (or her) are still perceived as the enemy.

However, it seems that management is just as likely as peer officers to cover up wrongdoing of officers. Only when the scandal cannot be contained does management "throw officers to the wolves." Unless there is a scandal, corruption is swept under the rug, and individual officers may receive little or no discipline. For instance, Crank and Caldero (2000: 114) report that in 100 civil lawsuits in 22 states between 1986 and 1991, the awards paid out by cities and police departments totaled $92 million, but of the 185 officers involved, only 8 were disciplined. In fact, 17 were promoted. It may be that noble-cause corruption is ignored by management and self-interest corruption is identified and sanctioned, but that does not seem to be the case when exploring case studies such as New York and Los Angeles. In fact, it seems that what starts out, perhaps, as noble-cause corruption leads to a perception that one is above the law, and self-interest corruption soon follows. See Box 9-4, "A Tale of Two Cities."

---

### BOX 9-4  A Tale of Two Cities

**New York**

*The Investigator:*

Sgt. John Tromboli was stymied in his attempt to investigate and expose the actions of Michael Dowd, an obviously crooked cop whose lifestyle far exceeded a cop's pay. For five years Tromboli had been trying to get enough evidence on Dowd to file charges but was routinely turned down by his superiors for extra resources and for permission for wiretaps and other means of investigation. He believed that his superiors were trying to shut down his investigation. Dowd was finally arrested by Suffolk County police when he was videotaped conducting narcotics transactions in uniform and in a police car. Internal Affairs routinely did not share information with the prosecutor's office on crooked cops. Instead, information on corrupt officers would be hidden in a "tickler file" that was never made public.

*The Scandal:*

The Mollen Commission in New York was formed in 1992 by Mayor David Dinkins to investigate the allegations of corruption. The practices of Dowd and a number of other officers were exposed. They included drug dealing, theft from corpses, robberies of drug dealers, setting up rival drug dealers for arrest and prosecution, protection rackets, and other misconduct. In the highly publicized hearings, officers were pressured to testify against others, and indictments and punishments were handed down. The hearings prompted Judge Mollen to comment that the Knapp Commission found that officers were in league with criminals but that today, officers have become the criminals themselves.

**Los Angeles**

*The Investigator:*

Detective Russell Poole, a Robbery–Homicide Division investigator, uncovered a pattern of complaints of violence by the anti-gang task force in the Ramparts Division when investigating an alleged beating of a gang member in a police squad room. He concluded that a number of the officers in the division were "vigilante cops" and requested that the investigation proceed further, but Chief Parks ordered him to limit his investigation solely to the Jimenez beating.

His superiors replaced a forty-page report he had prepared for the prosecutor's office with a two-page report that did not give any information about the possibility that there might be a pattern of corruption on the part of Ramparts officers. A year later, the Ramparts scandal exploded. Poole quit the force.

*The Scandal:*

The Ramparts scandal refers to the pubic disclosure of a wide range of corrupt activities by an anti-gang unit task force in the Ramparts Division of the L.A.P.D. (C.R.A.S.H.—Community Resources Against Street Hoodlums). Investigators from the prosecutor's office discovered the pattern of corruption when they made a deal with Rafael Perez, a Ramparts officer who had stolen cocaine from the evidence room. The scandal eventually led to dozens of criminal cases being voided because the prosecutor's office could not depend on the truthfulness of officers' testimony. Evidence indicated that the officers lied, planted evidence, beat suspects, and shot unarmed suspects between 1995 and 1998. They also evidently held parties to celebrate shooting, gave out plaques when one killed a gang member, and spread ketchup at a crime scene to imitate blood.

Hundreds of cases had to be reviewed by staff in the prosecutor's office to evaluate whether there was a possibility of manufactured evidence. At least one gang member's conviction was overturned when Rafael Perez, the officer who implicated all the others, confessed under oath that they had shot the man and then planted a gun on him and testified that he had shot at them first. The suspect has been released from prison, but is paralyzed and in a wheelchair.

Some evidence indicates at least ninety-nine people were framed by Ramparts officers. Prosecutors were also quoted in the paper as saying, "You can't trust the L.A.P.D. anymore." Mayor Richard Riordan reported to the press that the city would have to use $100 million of tobacco settlements to cover anticipated lawsuits. Eleven officers were fired, and forty convictions were overturned.

The L.A.P.D. responded with an internal management audit that admitted that there was a lapse of supervision and oversight. The report concludes that the corruption was caused by a few individuals whose wrongdoing had a "contagion effect." This report (conducted just eight years after the Christopher Commission presented a scathing commentary concerning the management and ethos of L.A.P.D.) recommended an outside civilian oversight committee. However, the issue might be out of the department's hands at this point because the L.A.P.D. is now under a court monitor.

SOURCES: Rothlein, 1999; Glover and Lait, 2000; Lait and Glover, 2000; Jablon, 2000; Sterngold, 2000; Deutsch, 2001; Golab, 2000.

***Why were police investigators blocked in their effort to uncover corruption? In what ways is the pattern of corruption similar in New York and Los Angeles? Do you see any differences?***

# Conclusion

We began these three chapters on law enforcement and will also close them with the images of the use of force by the Los Angeles police. Some of us remember earlier images from the 1960s, wherein law enforcement officers appeared on newscasts beating and using attack dogs against peaceful civil rights demonstrators. One might argue that those negative images of the 1960s led to greater professionalism, better training, and racial and sexual integration of police departments in the 1970s and 1980s. The Rodney King incident and the scrutiny that resulted have led to positive results in that they have fostered a groundswell of attention on "police ethics," including a national outcry against racial profiling and discriminatory enforcement. Today, we face the greatest challenge to law enforcement in recent memory with the threat of terrorism. The enemy is more fearsome, the stakes are higher, and the fear is stronger. Thus, noble-cause corruption has a new cause, even more noble than drug interdiction or simple crime fighting. The drug war has been eclipsed by the war on terrorism, but the question of whether it is ethical to achieve a good end through bad acts is still with us. Some argue that the question has changed; others argue that the answer is still the same. It seems clear that how one resolves the dilemmas has everything to do with whether law enforcement officers are seen fundamentally as crime fighters or public servants. We will revisit this important issue in the last chapter of this book.

# Key Terms

**blue curtain of secrecy**  another name for the code of silence

**civilian review/complaint model**  an outside agency or board that includes citizens and monitors and/or investigates misconduct complaints against police

**code of silence**  the practice of officers to not come forward when they are aware of the ethical transgressions of other officers

**Dirty Harry problem**  the question of whether police should use immoral means to reach a desired moral end

**informants**  civilians who are used to obtain information about criminal activity and/or participate in it so that evidence can be obtained for an arrest

**integrity testing**  "sting" operations to test whether or not police officers will make honest choices

**internal affairs model**  a review procedure in which police investigators receive and investigate complaints and resolve the investigations internally

**noble-cause corruption**  bad acts that are done for a good end: crime control

**principle of double effect**  a means taken for a good end results in the good end but also in an inevitable but unintended bad result

# Review Questions

1. Explain the term *noble-cause corruption*.
2. Describe Barker and Carter's typology of lies.

3. Define entrapment using the legal test. Discuss whether you believe that the legal test is the same as an ethical test of entrapment.
4. List the questions posed by Marx that police should use before engaging in undercover operations.
5. List and describe the ethical problems of using informants.
6. Discuss the justifications and criticisms of undercover operations as offered by Marx.
7. Explain the Dirty Harry problem.
8. Discuss the teleological and deontological arguments for and against whistleblowing.
9. Discuss all the possible efforts to reduce or eliminate various forms of police misbehavior.
10. Discuss the rights-based concept of policing versus a utilitarian crime control model, and explain how each would resolve questions of the use of deception and invasive investigative techniques.

## Discussion Questions

1. Discuss if you feel it is ever right for a police officer to do any of the following: lie on the witness stand, plant evidence, hide lab evidence, or ignore witnesses who want to give exculpatory evidence.
2. Discuss if you feel it is ever right for an undercover police officer to do any of the following to maintain his or her cover: lie to an innocent, engage in a sexual relationship, use drugs, injure someone, or allow a crime to take place.
3. Discuss if you feel it is ever right for a police officer to do any of the following: overlook crimes (distinguish between misdemeanors and felonies) by an informant, give drugs to an informant, let an informant perform a dangerous operation, or coerce the informant by threatening to arrest him or her or arrest a loved one.
4. Discuss if you feel it is ever right for police interrogators to do any of the following: lie about who they are, lie about what evidence they have (e.g., tell the suspect that they have forensic evidence that places him at the scene), lie about what their crime partners are saying, or lie about what deal can be made if the suspect confesses.
5. Do any of the acts in questions 1–4 deserve suspension? Firing? Prosecution?
6. What do you think about integrity testing of officers?
7. What do you think could be done to reduce corruption in police departments?

## Ethical Dilemmas

### *Situation 1*

You are a police officer testifying about a particular crime. It is a case where you honestly don't know whether or not the suspect is guilty. While on the witness stand, you answer all the prosecutor's and defense attorney's questions. You complete your testimony and exit the courtroom, knowing that you have specific knowledge that may help the defense attorney's case. You have answered all questions truthfully, but the specific question needed to help the defense was not asked. What should you do?

## Situation 2

You are an undercover officer, and during training your instructors have taught you how to avoid using drugs while maintaining your cover. Once out on the street, you are told by co-workers that such training is unrealistic and that if you want to stay undercover, you will eventually have to use drugs. What would you do?

## Situation 3

You are a male suspect in a murder case. You were drunk the night of the homicide and did meet and dance with the victim, a young college girl. You admit you had a lot to drink, but are 99-percent sure that you didn't see her except in the bar. The trouble is you drank way too much and passed out in someone's apartment close to the bar rather than drive home. The girl was found in an apartment in the same complex. Police are telling you that they have forensic evidence that ties you to the murder. They say that they have her blood on your clothes and that it is your DNA in the sperm found in her body. They have been interrogating you now for several hours, and you are beginning to doubt your memory. You are also told that if you plead guilty, you would probably get voluntary manslaughter and might get probation, but if you insist on your innocence, you will be charged with first-degree murder and face the death penalty. What would you do?

Obviously, this situation shifts our focus from the criminal justice professional's dilemma. If you decided earlier that the police tactic of lying about forensic evidence is ethical, this hypothetical illustrates what might happen when innocent suspects are lied to (assuming you are innocent!).

## Situation 4

There is an officer in your division who is known as a "rat" because he testified against his partner in a criminal trial and a civil suit. The partner evidently hit a handcuffed suspect in the head several times in anger, and the man sustained brain injuries and is now a paraplegic. Although none of the officers you know support the excessive use of force, they are also appalled that this officer did not back up his partner's story. After all, punishing the officer wasn't going to make the victim any better. Now no one will ride with this guy, and no one responds to his calls for back-ups. There have been incidents such as a dead rat being found in his locker, and the extra uniform in his locker was set on fire. One day you are parking your car and see your buddies in the employee parking lot moving away from his car—they admit they just slashed his tires. Each officer is being called into the captain's office to state whether he or she knows anything about this latest incident. Your turn is coming. What are you going to do?

## Situation 5

You are a police officer testifying in a drug case. You have already testified that you engaged in a buy–bust operation, and the defendant was identified by an undercover officer as the one who sold him a small quantity of drugs. You testified that you chased the suspect down an alley and apprehended him. Immediately before you caught up with him, he threw down a number of glassine envelopes filled with what turned out to be cocaine. The prosecutor finished his direct examination, and now the defense attorney has begun cross-examining you. He asked if you had the suspect in your sight the entire time between when you identified him as the one who sold to the undercover officer and when you put the handcuffs on him. Your arrest report didn't mention it, but there were a couple of seconds where you slipped as you went around the corner of the alley and fell down. During that short time the suspect had proceeded a considerable distance down the alley. You do not think there was anyone else around, and you are as sure as you possibly can be that it was your suspect who dropped the bags, but you know that if you testify to this incident truthfully, the defense attorney might be able to argue successfully that the bags were not dropped by the suspect and get him acquitted of the much more serious possession-with-intent-to-distribute charge. What should you do?

### *Situation 6*

You are a federal agent and have been investigating a major drug ring for a long time. One of your informants is fairly highly placed within this ring and has been providing you with good information. You were able to "turn" him because he faces a murder charge—there is probable cause that he shot and killed a co-worker during an argument about five years ago, before he became involved in the drug ring. You have been holding the murder charge over his head to get him to cooperate and have been able, with the help of the U.S. District Attorney's office, to keep the local prosecutor from filing charges and arresting him. The local prosecutor is upset because the family wants some resolution in the case. You believe that the information he is able to provide you will result in charges of major drug sales and racketeering against several of the top smugglers, putting a dent in the drug trade for your region. At the same time, you understand that you are constantly risking the possibility that he may escape prosecution by leaving the country and that you are blocking the justice that the family of the murdered victim deserves. What would you do?

# Suggested Readings

Alderson, J. 1998. *Principled Policing: Protecting the Public with Integrity*. Winchester, MA: Waterside.

Conlon, E. 2004. *Blue Blood*. New York: Riverhead.

Crank, J. 2004. *Understanding Police Culture*. Cincinnati: Anderson.

Crank, J., and Caldero, M. 2004. *Police Ethics: The Corruption of Noble Cause*. Cincinnati: Anderson.

Einstein, S., and Amir, M. 2001. *Policing, Security and Democracy: Special Aspects of Democratic Policing*. Huntsville, TX: Office of International Criminal Justice (OICJ), Sam Houston State University.

Haberfeld, M. 2006. *Police Leadership*. Upper Saddle River, NJ: Prentice-Hall.

Klockars, C., and Mastrofski, S. 1991. *Thinking About Police*. New York: McGraw-Hill.

Lynch, G. (Ed.). 1999. *Human Dignity and the Police: Ethics and Integrity in Police Work*. Springfield, IL: Charles C. Thomas.

Prenzler, T., and Ransley, J. 2002. *Police Reform: Building Integrity*. Sydney, Australia: Hawkins.

Walker, S. 2001. *Police Accountability: The Role of Citizen Oversight*. Belmont, CA: Wadsworth.

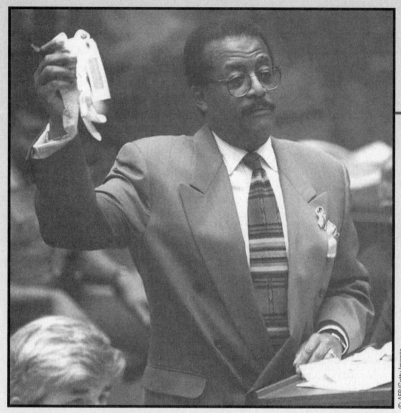

Johnny Cochrane exemplified the epitome of the defense lawyer: criticized for employing any and all means to get a client off, but in high demand among those who face the awesome power of the state.

# 10
# Ethics and Legal Professionals

*First, Let's Kill All the Lawyers . . .*

*Ethical Issues for Legal Professionals*

*Ethical Issues for Defense Attorneys*

*Ethical Issues for Prosecutors*

*Conclusion*

## Key Terms

asset forfeiture
attorney–client privilege
criminalistics
halo effect
plea bargain

shadow jury
situational model
systems model
tort reform

# Chapter Objectives

1. Become familiar with the source of legal ethics.

2. Understand the concept of attorney as a moral agent or as a legal agent.

3. Learn the variety of ethical issues faced by defense attorneys.

4. Learn the variety of ethical issues faced by prosecutors.

Just as the Rodney King incident directed public scrutiny toward the ethics of law enforcement, the O. J. Simpson trial acted as a catalyst for scrutiny of the criminal court system in this country. And in the same way that the King incident has been used to illustrate how racial prejudice, distrust, and class conflict affect law enforcement procedures, the Simpson case illustrates how these same issues carry over to judicial processing and influence the administration of justice.

# First, Let's Kill All the Lawyers . . .

Public perceptions of lawyers indicate that the public has little confidence in their ability to live up to ideals of equity, fairness, and justice. In a 2001 Gallup survey, lawyers were rated as "less ethical" and "less honest" than police officers, doctors, auto mechanics, and stockbrokers. Only labor union leaders, insurance salespeople, and car salespeople (among a few others) had lower ratings than did lawyers. Just 18 percent of those polled agreed that lawyers' ethics and honesty were high or very high (Gallup, 2001).

In the 1980s, the law scandal was the savings and loan fiasco, in which the greed and corruption of those in the banking industry were ably assisted by the industry's attorneys, and the taxpayers picked up the bill for the bankrupt institutions and outstanding loans. The scandal in the 1990s was the William Clinton–Monica Lewinsky investigation, with opinions mixed as to which set of lawyers was more embarrassing—those who could coach the president that oral sex wasn't technically "sexual relations" or the special prosecutor, Kenneth Starr, and his assistants, who spent millions of dollars in an investigation that centered on semen stains and the definition of sex. This new century brought us the debacle of WorldCom and Enron, and, again, lawyers have played a central role, along with business executives and accountants. Most recently, we have the situation of the White House counsel parsing the definition of torture.

Apparently, even lawyers don't think much of their profession. In a 1992 California bar poll, 70 percent of lawyers would choose another career if they could, and 75 percent would not want their children to be lawyers (Glendon, 1994: 85). The perception of the lawyer as an amoral "hired gun" is in sharp contrast to the ideal of the lawyer as an officer of the court, sworn to uphold the ideals of justice declared sacrosanct under our system of law. Interestingly, or perhaps not surprisingly, our government is made up largely of lawyers: A large percentage of elected officials are lawyers, twenty-three out of forty-one presidents have been lawyers, and thirteen out of the eighteen members of President Clinton's cabinet were lawyers (Glendon, 1994: 12). Our nation's leaders and historical heroes have just as likely been lawyers (Abraham Lincoln, for example) as generals, and our nation's consciousness is permeated with the belief in law and legal vindication.

On the one hand, the public tends to agree with a stereotype of lawyers as amoral, motivated by money, and with no conscience or concern for morality. On the other hand, the first response to any perception of wrong is to find a legal advocate and sue, with the belief that a lawyer will right any wrong and solve any problem. Continuing attempts for **tort reform**, legislation that limits the nature of personal injury lawsuits, either by restricting the type of suit, who can be sued, or the amount of damages, illustrate these two views: Those who advocate tort reform argue that lawyers are making millions by harassing businesses and medical professionals with needless lawsuits; those against tort reform argue that without lawyers to guard the interests of consumers, businesses, including HMOs, would continue to foist unsafe products upon and provide poor service to an unsuspecting and powerless public.

History indicates that the ethics of those associated with the legal process has always been suspect. Plato and Aristotle condemned the advocate because of his ability to make the truth appear false and the guilty appear innocent. This early distrust continued throughout history; early colonial lawyers were distrusted and even punished for practicing law. For many years, lawyers could not charge a fee for their services because the mercenary aspect of the profession was condemned (Papke, 1986: 32). Gradually, lawyers and the profession itself were accepted, but suspicion and controversy continued in the area of fees and qualifications. Partly to counteract public antipathy, lawyers formed their own organization, the American Bar Association (ABA), in 1878. Shortly afterward, this professional organization established the first ethical guidelines for lawyers.

---

### QUOTE and QUERY

Lawyers are upset. They have discovered what they believe to be an alarming new trend: people don't like them. The American Bar Association recently appointed a special panel to investigate the legal profession's bad image. The California State Bar has commissioned a survey to find out why so many people dislike lawyers. . . . We wish to reassure lawyers. This wave of anti-lawyer feeling is nothing new. People have always hated you.

Source: A. Roth and J. Roth, *Devil's Advocates: The Unnatural History of Lawyers* (Berkeley, CA: Nolo, 1989): i.

*The passage is humorous, but the underlying fact is not. Why do people have such low opinions of lawyers?*

Perhaps the best explanation for the long-standing distrust of lawyers is that they typically represent trouble. People don't require a lawyer unless they feel that a wrong has been done to them or that they need to be defended. The ability of lawyers to argue either side raises a level of distrust. We would prefer a passionate advocate rather than a paid advocate. In the next section, we explore basic perceptions that influence a lawyer's advocacy in our criminal justice system.

Finally, let us not forget the full context of "First, let's kill all the lawyers . . .," widely used as a stab at attorneys. In Shakespeare's *Henry IV, Part II,* the statement is from a despot who, before making a grab for power, argues that the first thing he must do is kill all the lawyers, for it is lawyers who are the guardians of law. However, it should also be pointed out that the reason the existing power holders in the play are attacked is because they use the law to oppress the powerless. And so it is today. The law can be either a tool of oppression or a sword of justice, but lawyers and judges are always the ones who wield its power.

# Ethical Issues for Legal Professionals

A profession, as defined in Chapter 6, involves a specialized body of knowledge, commitment to the social good, the ability to regulate itself, and high social status (Davis and Elliston, 1986: 13). The presence of ethical standards is essential to the definition of a profession. More importantly, membership in a profession implies a special set of rules, different from those applied to everyone else. Very often these rules may involve a higher standard of behavior, but they may also involve greater privileges or the right to act in a different way from everyone else by virtue of that membership.

Formal ethical standards for lawyers and judges were originally promulgated by the American Bar Association in the Model Code of Professional Responsibility. The original Canons, adapted from the Alabama Bar Association Code of 1887, were adopted by the ABA in 1908 and have been revised frequently since then. Several years ago, the ABA switched its endorsement of the Model Code as the general guide for ethical behavior to the Model Rules of Professional Responsibility. The Model Rules continue to be revised periodically, responding to changing sensibilities and emerging issues. The latest two revisions were in 2002 and 2003.

Today's Model Rules cover many aspects of the lawyer's profession, including such areas as client–lawyer relationships, the lawyer as counselor, the lawyer as advocate, transactions with others, public service, and maintaining the integrity of the profession. Ethical issues in criminal law may involve courtroom behavior, perjury, conflicts of interest, use of the media, investigation efforts, use of immunity, discovery and the sharing of evidence, relationships with opposing attorneys, and plea bargaining.

To enforce these ethical rules, the ABA has a standing committee on ethical responsibility to offer formal and informal opinions when charges of impropriety have been made. Also, each state bar association has the power to sanction offending attorneys by private or public censure or to recommend to the court suspension of their privilege to practice law. Thus, the rules promulgated by the state bar have essentially the power of law behind them. The bar associations also have the power to grant entry into the profession because one must ordinarily belong to the bar association of a particular state to practice law there. Bar associations judge competence by testing the applicant's knowledge, but they also judge moral worthiness by background checks of individuals. The purpose of these restrictive admission procedures is to protect the public image of the legal profession by rejecting unscrupulous or dishonest individuals or those unfit to practice for other reasons. However, many feel that if bar associations were serious about protecting the profession, they would also continue to monitor the behavior and moral standing of current members with the same care they seem to take in the initial decision regarding entry (Elliston, 1986: 53).

A practicing attorney is investigated only when complaints have been lodged against him or her. The investigative bodies have been described as decentralized, informal, and secret. They do little for dissatisfied clients because most client complaints involve incompetence—a vague and ill-defined term (Marks, Raymond, and Cathcart, 1986: 72). One study of client satisfaction found that the most frequent complaints against attorneys were that too little time was given the client by the lawyer, and that the lawyer were inaccessible (Arafat and McCahery, 1978: 205). Neither of these complaints is likely to prompt a disciplinary ruling by an ethics committee.

Many bar disciplinary committees are hopelessly understaffed and overburdened with complaints. Complaints may take years to investigate, and, in the meantime, if prospective clients call, they will be told only that the attorney is in good standing and has no substantiated complaints. A recent study of attorney discipline by an organization for legal reform reported that only 3 percent of investigations by state disciplinary committees result in public sanctions; only 1 percent end in disbarment (*San Antonio Express News,* 2002).

Individuals with complaints against their lawyers in the civil arena receive little enough satisfaction; however, criminal defendants are arguably even less likely to have anyone care or rectify incompetence or unethical behavior on the part of their attorney. "You get what you pay for" may be true to an extent, but even that phrase does not truly represent the possibility of a family mortgaging its home, signing over cars, and emptying its bank account for an attorney who promises to represent a family member against a criminal charge and then finding that the attorney will not answer calls, doesn't appear in court, or is unprepared and forgets to file necessary motions.

Law schools have been criticized for being singularly uninterested in fostering any type of moral conscience in graduating students. Law schools purport to be in the practice of reshaping law students so that when they emerge "thinking like a lawyer," they have mastered a type of thinking that is concerned with detail and logical analysis. Others, like Gerry Spence in the Quote and Query box, argue this is done at the expense of being sensitive to morality and larger social issues.

## QUOTE and QUERY

[L]aw school is no place for human beings who care about other human beings. . . .

Source: G. Spence, *With Justice for None* (New York: Penguin, 1989): 45.

***Why do you think an attorney would say this about law school?***

Gerry Spence, the flamboyant defense attorney who made the above-mentioned statement, boasts of receiving low grades in law school—an indication, he believes, that he did not "sell out" to the mindset of bottom-line winning and profit above all else that is representative of law school indoctrination (Spence, 1989). Stover (1989) writes how public interest values decline during law school. The reason for this decline seemingly has to do with the low value placed on public interest issues by the law school curriculum, which also treats ethical and normative concerns as irrelevant or trivial compared to the "bar courses" such as contract law and torts.

Even though all law schools today require professional-responsibility courses, morality and ethics are often made light of, even in those courses where there are stories (humorous and otherwise) of how to get around the ethical and legal mandates. For instance, law students are taught that in the discovery phase of a lawsuit, the legal rule that requires an attorney to turn over documents requested by the other side (that are not otherwise privileged) can be circumvented by burying important documents in 600 boxes of paperwork.

There has been greater attention to ethics in recent years. Bar exams have a special section devoted to the Model Rules and the state's own professional responsibility code, but these tests are often hyper-technical, testing the minutiae of the rules rather than the spirit of practicing law ethically and honestly. Most states also require continuing-legal-education-credit hours in the area of ethics. However, similar to our earlier discussion of police officers, classroom ethics training that encourages one set of behaviors is often contradicted and disparaged by the professional subculture. If this is the case, then such training might not be very effective.

## The Attorney–Client Relationship

Many of the Model Rules involve the special relationship the attorney has with the client. The separation of professional and personal responsibility poses difficult issues. Many lawyers feel that loyalty to the client is paramount to their duties as a professional. This loyalty surpasses and eclipses individual and private decision making, and the special relationship said to exist between lawyer and client justifies decisions that might otherwise be deemed unacceptable. The various relationships proposed between lawyers and clients are described below:

1. *Legal agent.* An extreme position is that the attorney is no more than the *legal agent* of the client. The lawyer is neither immoral nor moral, but merely a legal tool. This position is represented by the statement "I am a lawyer, first and foremost."

2. *Special relationship.* A more moderate position is that the loyalty to the client presents a *special relationship* between client and lawyer, similar to that between mother and child or with trusted friend. This protected relationship justifies fewer actions than the one described above. The lawyer is expected to dissuade the client from taking unethical or immoral actions, but loyalty would preclude putting anyone's interests above the client's.

3. *Moral agent.* The third position is that the lawyer is a *moral agent* who has to adhere to his or her own moral code. The client's interests come first only as long as they do not conflict with the lawyer's morality and ethical code. If there is a conflict, then the lawyer follows his or her conscience. Some reject perspectives that discount the lawyer's responsibility as an individual to make his or her own moral decisions. Lawyers are perceived as the legal *and* moral agents of their clients, rather than merely legal agents. Their personal responsibility to avoid wrongdoing precludes involving themselves in their clients' wrongdoing (Postema, 1986: 168). This position is represented by the statement "I am a person first, lawyer second."

## Legal Agent Versus Moral Agent?

Elliott Cohen (1991), an advocate of the moral agent position, believes that to be purely a legal advocate is inconsistent with being a morally good person in several ways. For instance, the virtue of justice would be inconsistent with a zealous advocate who would maximize the chance of his or her client's winning, regardless of the fairness of the outcome.

A pure legal agent would sacrifice values of truthfulness, moral courage, benevolence, trustworthiness, and moral autonomy. Only if the attorney is a moral agent, as well as a legal advocate, can there be any possibility of the attorney's maintaining individual morality. Cohen (1991: 135–136) suggests some principles that attorneys must follow to be considered moral:

1. Treat others as ends in themselves and not as mere means to winning cases.
2. Treat clients and other professional relations who are relatively similar in a similar fashion.
3. Do not deliberately engage in behavior apt to deceive the court as to the truth.
4. Be willing, if necessary, to make reasonable personal sacrifices—of time, money, popularity, and so on—for what you justifiably believe to be a morally good cause.
5. Do not give money to, or accept money from, clients for wrongful purposes or in wrongful amounts.
6. Avoid harming others in the process of representing your client.
7. Be loyal to your client and do not betray his confidences.
8. Make your own moral decisions to the best of your ability and act consistently upon them.

The rationale for these principles seems to be an amalgamation of ethical formalism, utilitarianism, and other ethical frameworks. Some of these principles may seem impossible to uphold and may be subject to bitter criticism on the part of practicing attorneys. For instance, how does one avoid harming others when one is an advocate for one side in a contest? There are losers and winners in civil contests as well as in criminal law, and lawyers must take responsibility for the fact that sometimes the loser is harmed in financial or emotional ways.

Recently, Cohen's position has been attacked as naïve and wrong on several counts. Memory and Rose (2002: 29) argue against Cohen's proposed principle that a lawyer "may refuse to aid or participate in conduct that he sincerely believes, after careful reflection on the relevant facts, to be unjust or otherwise morally wrong notwithstanding his obligation to seek the lawful objectives of his client." They believe that lawyers can be effective and morally good at the same time and argue that rules in place already prevent unscrupulous acts. For instance, Model Rule 3.3 prohibits lying. It states that lawyers may not make false statements of material facts or law, cannot fail to disclose a material fact to a tribunal when disclosure is necessary to avoid assisting a criminal or fraudulent act by the client, cannot fail to disclose legal authority that is directly adverse to one's client's interest, or cannot offer evidence that one knows to be false. According to the authors, this rule and others prevent attorneys from sacrificing truth even when zealously pursuing clients' interests.

Memory and Rose (2002) argue that decisions regarding justice and morality are so subjective that it is impossible for them to be judged and that rules are developing in ways that will avoid cases of abuse by lawyers using personal moral judgments. If lawyers acted as moral agents, the result would be the loss of the clients' trust in lawyers, for the lawyer would be able to substitute his or her individual morality for the clients.

Cohen (2002: 39), in a rebuttal article, uses the ethics of care as underpinning for his continued defense of the moral agent idea:

> [M]orality concerns concrete interpersonal relationships that can be understood only by people who have compassion and empathy for the predicaments of other people. . . . Morally virtuous lawyers (moral agents) possess such affective aspects of emotional development, but it is precisely such a dimension that must be lacking from the pure legal advocate who must get used to working injury upon others without having any strong feelings of guilt, sorrow, or regret.

In general, Cohen and Memory and Rose seem to be in agreement on the most egregious misconduct of lawyers; their disagreement comes from the value they place on rules versus individual responsibility for moral judgments.

An earlier chapter made the point that rules have never been able to substitute for moral decision making on the part of individual actors. This is more consistent with Cohen's position than that of Memory and Rose. Cohen's argument is essentially that training and socialization into the "culture of law" create the legal agent role and encourage a type of "noble-cause corruption" similar to that discussed in Chapter 9. In this profession, the "noble cause" is winning a case. In a culture that supports "ends" thinking (winning) over "means," rules are no more likely to control misconduct by lawyers than they do police officers.

In general, rules of ethics provide guidance that lawyers should consult with clients in the objectives and means and tactics of legal representation. One example of what happens when lawyers' and clients' beliefs diverge was in the Unabomber case. Ted Kaczynski's lawyers had medical reports that he was mentally ill, a fact that would have probably helped to avert a death penalty. Kaczynski reportedly refused to plead insanity. The lawyers and the defendant were at an impasse. Should they follow their client's wishes even though their professional judgment was that he was mentally incompetent and should plead not guilty by reason of insanity? The problem was averted when he agreed to a plea bargain of four life sentences (Barker and Cosentino, 2003). However, the case begs the question as to whether the attorneys should have bowed to his demands or insisted upon their right to use the insanity defense.

**QUOTE and QUERY**

About half the practice of a decent lawyer consists in telling would-be clients that they are damned fools and should stop.

Source: Reported in M. Glendon, *A Nation Under Lawyers* (New York: Farrar, Straus and Giroux, 1994): 76.

You're an attorney. It's your duty to lie, conceal and distort everything, and slander everybody.

Source: J. Giradeaux, *The Madwoman of Chaillot* (adapted by Maurice Valency) (New York: Random House, 1949): Act Two.

**Which of these statements represents a legal agent statement? Which represents a moral agent statement?**

Research indicates that the position taken by attorneys depends partially on whom they represent. Although public defenders take a more authoritarian role and seem to support the attorney as a "guru" who tells the client what to do, attorneys for corporations, on the other hand, indicate a more client-centered approach (Mather, 2003).

In an interesting application of Carol Gilligan's ethics of care approach, Vogelstein (2003) argues that attorneys' rules are concerned with rights, not care. Thus, attorneys must sacrifice third parties if they are to follow the rules and protect their clients' interests. This, she argues, contributes to the negative perception of attorneys. She proposes a type of moral agent approach where the attorney must take into consideration the needs of others, as well as of the clients. Of course, others, such as Memory and Rose, who argued against Cohen's propositions, would strongly disagree. It should be noted that there are glimmers of the moral agent idea in the rules—for instance, Rule 2.1 states that "a lawyer may refer not only to law but to other considerations such as moral, economic, social and political factors . . ." in making decisions. Again, though, the rules are not much help when there is a strong disagreement between the client and attorney over what is the right thing to do.

## A Higher Standard of Behavior?

In Chapter 7 we discussed the concept of police officers, as public servants, being held to a higher standard of conduct than those they serve. This same principle applies to attorneys. The Model Code of Professional Responsibility for lawyers dictates that they should be "temperate and dignified" and "refrain from all illegal and morally reprehensible conduct." The Model Rules expect that "a lawyer's conduct should conform to the requirements of the law, both in professional service to clients and in the lawyer's business and personal affairs." These are prescriptions similar to those found in the Law Enforcement Code of Ethics. Both groups of professionals are expected to uphold a higher standard of behavior than the general public. They provide protection and help enforce the rules and provide a model of behavior for the rest of us. Because both professions have a special place in society's attempt to control individual behavior, it is not unreasonable to expect a higher standard of behavior to apply.

However, some allege that instead of a *higher* standard, lawyers (like some police officers) allow themselves a *double* standard. Lying is lying unless it is done by a lawyer, and then it is just doing one's duty, or a "misstatement of fact." Glendon (1994), in a highly critical overview of the legal profession, proposes that the legal profession has changed in very dramatic ways, not all of which have been for the better. Although the practice of law was once governed by rules of ethics and etiquette and lawyers acted like gentlemen (literally, because the profession was for the most part closed to women, minorities, and the lower class), it has become open to those excluded groups in the last twenty-five years. However, it has also become a world of "no rules" or, more accurately, only one rule: "Winning is everything."

## Ethical Issues for Defense Attorneys

The role of the defense attorney is to protect the due-process rights of the defendant. Due process is supposed to minimize mistakes in judicial proceedings that might result in a deprivation of life, liberty, or property. Due-process rights, including notice, neutral fact finders, cross-examination, and presentation of evidence and witnesses, are supposed to minimize the risk of error. The defense attorney is there to ensure that these rights are protected—for instance, during interrogation to make sure no coercion is used, at lineup to make sure it is fair and unbiased, and during trial to ensure adequate cross-examination and presentation of evidence. This pure role of advocate is contradictory to the reality that the defense attorney must, if he or she is to work with the other actors in the court system, accommodate their needs as well as those of clients.

Defense attorneys are always in the position of balancing the rights of individual clients against overall effectiveness. Extreme attempts to protect one client's rights will reduce the defense attorney's effectiveness for all clients. Furthermore, defense attorneys must balance the needs and problems of the client against their ethical responsibilities to the system and profession. Individual rights are balanced by other considerations.

Except for a few high-powered "stars" across the country, defense attorneys have a fairly negative reputation in the legal community, as well as with the general public. They are seen as incompetent or unable to compete on the higher rungs of the status ladder of law (those higher rungs being corporate, tax, and international law). Alternatively or additionally, they are seen as "shady" or "money grubbers" who get the guilty off by sleazy tactics. In fiction, defense attorneys are presented as either fearless crusaders who always manage to defend innocent clients (usually against unethical prosecutors) or as sleazy deal makers who are either too burned out or selfish to care about their clients. The reality, of course, fits none of these portrayals. Kittel (1990) finds that the majority of defense attorneys would not change their career given an opportunity to do so, and that most chose their career because they were interested in the trial work it offered or for public policy reasons, as opposed to the common myth that criminal defense attorneys enter that field because they couldn't make it anywhere else.

Many defense attorneys started out as prosecutors. This sometimes causes problems when they have trouble making the transition from "good guy battling evil" to the more subtle role of defender of due process. Often, those whom one represents are not people whom one can feel proud to be helping. If the attorney cannot make the transition from prosecution to defense and feel comfortable in the role, then it is difficult to do a zealous defense (Cohen, 2001).

As mentioned earlier, the system tends to operate under a presumption of guilt. Indeed, defense attorneys are often in the position of defending clients they know are guilty. The rationale for defending a guilty person is that a person deserves due process before a finding of guilt and punishment. Before punishment can be morally imposed, a fair procedure must ensure that the punishment is appropriate. To ensure appropriate punishment, a set of fact-finding procedures is necessary, and the defense attorney's role is to make sure that the rules are followed. If defense attorneys are doing their job, then we can all be comfortable with a conviction. If they do not do their job, then we have no system of justice, and none of us is safe from wrongful prosecution and the awesome power of the state to investigate, prosecute, and punish. Due process protects us all by making the criminal justice system prove wrongdoing "beyond a reasonable doubt." The person who makes sure that no shortcuts are taken is the defense attorney.

In the early 1990s the ABA promulgated its Standards for Criminal Justice. "The Defense Function," Chapter 4, covers a multitude of issues, such as these:

- The function of defense counsel
- Punctuality
- Public statements
- Duty to the administration of justice
- Access and the lawyer–client relationship
- Duty to investigate
- Control and direction of litigation
- Plea bargaining
- Trial conduct
- Appeal

### IN THE NEWS  A Lack of Advocacy

I decided that Mr. Tucker deserved to die, and I would not do anything to prevent his execution.

This statement was made by defense attorney David Smith of Greensboro, North Carolina, who accepted a capital appeal case and then admitted he "sabotaged" the appeal of his client because he believed the man deserved execution. He went through a moral crisis afterward and confessed to the state bar what he did.

Source: S. Rimer, "Lawyer Sabotaged Case of a Client on Death Row," *New York Times,* November 24, 2000.

**You are on a state bar disciplinary committee. Would you vote to disbar Smith?**

These standards are much more specific than the Law Enforcement Code of Ethics. Instead of being aspirational, the standards are specific guidelines for behavior. We will explore only a few of the many different ethical issues that confront defense attorneys in their representation of clients.

## Responsibility to the Client

*The basic duty defense counsel owes to the administration of justice and as an officer of the court is to serve as the accused's counselor and advocate with courage and devotion and to render effective, quality representation (Standard 4-1.2(b)).*

Defense attorneys are always in the position of balancing the rights of the individual client against overall effectiveness. Extreme attempts to protect these rights will reduce the defense attorney's effectiveness for other clients. Furthermore, defense attorneys must balance the needs and problems of the client against their ethical responsibilities to the system and profession.

A lawyer is supposed to provide legal assistance to clients without regard for personal preference or interest. A lawyer is not allowed to withdraw from a case simply because he or she no longer wishes to represent the client. Only if the legal action is for harassment or malicious purposes, if continued employment will result in a violation of a disciplinary rule, if discharged by a client, or if a mental or physical condition renders effective counsel impossible can a lawyer be withdrawn. In other cases, a judge may grant permission to withdraw when the client insists upon illegal or unethical actions, is uncooperative and does not follow the attorney's advice, or otherwise makes effective counsel difficult. In general, judges are loathe to allow a defendant to proceed with a *pro se* defense (by oneself) because of the risk that the conviction will be overturned on appeal.

Legal ethics mandate that people with unpopular causes and individuals who are obviously guilty still deserve counsel and that it is the ethical duty of an attorney to provide such counsel. In fact, although many people condemn attorneys, and especially the American Civil Liberties Union's attorneys, for defending such groups as the American Nazi Party or the Ku Klux Klan or individuals such as Charles Manson or notorious drug dealers, clearly they could not do otherwise under the ethical principles of their profession.

Some lawyers have no problem at all with defending "unworthy" clients. Drug cases are well-known as lawyers' pork barrels. Many lawyers have made millions of dollars defending major drug smugglers and dealers. In effect, they share in the wealth generated by illegal drugs. Is it ethical to accept any client able to pay large and continuing bills? It is commonly believed that any time a criminal defendant can and will pay, a lawyer can always be found to take the case to trial and conduct innumerable appeals, no matter the likelihood of winning.

The Racketeer Influenced and Corrupt Organizations Statute (18 U.S.C. Sections 1961–68), usually referred to as RICO, has been used to confiscate drug money, including fees already paid to attorneys. Defense attorneys object strenuously to this practice, protesting that it endangers fair representation for drug defendants because attorneys may not be willing to defend these clients when there is a possibility that their fees will be confiscated. Some prosecutors, it should be noted, have gone a step further and are starting to prosecute attorneys themselves if there is evidence that an attorney is engaged in a continuing conspiracy to further a criminal enterprise by his or her association with the client. This use of the RICO statute is extremely controversial, as are other uses of it that will be discussed later.

Many people are firmly convinced that the quality of legal representation is directly related to how much money the defendant can pay. When people can make bail and hire private attorneys, do they receive better justice? Do defense attorneys exert more effort for clients who pay well than they do for court-appointed clients? Obviously, professional ethics would dictate equal consideration, but individual values also affect behavior. If an attorney felt confident that his or her court-appointed clients received at least adequate representation, then could one not justify a more zealous defense for a paying client? Where adequate representation is vaguely and poorly defined, this question is problematic.

## Confidentiality

*Defense counsel should not reveal information relating to representation of a client unless the client consents after consultation, except for disclosures that are impliedly authorized in order to carry out the representation and except that defense counsel may reveal such information to the extent he or she reasonably believes necessary to prevent the client from committing a criminal act that defense counsel believes is likely to result in imminent death or substantial bodily harm (Standard 4-3.7(d)).*

The **attorney–client privilege** refers to the inability of authorities to compel an attorney (through subpoena or threat of contempt) to disclose confidential information regarding his or her client. The ethical duty of confidentiality prohibits an attorney from disclosing to any person, or using for one's own gain, information about one's client obtained through the attorney–client relationship.

The confidentiality protection is said to be inherent in the fiduciary relationship between the client and the attorney, but more important is that the client must be able to expect and receive the full and complete assistance of his or her lawyer. If a client feels compelled to withhold negative and incriminatory information, he or she will not be able to receive such assistance; thus, the lawyer must be perceived as a completely confidential agent of the client. Parallels to the attorney–client relationship are relationships between husband and wife and between priest and penitent. In these cases the relationship creates a legal entity that approximates a single interest rather than two, so a break in confidentiality would violate the Fifth Amendment protection against self-incrimination (Schoeman, 1982: 260).

The only situations wherein a lawyer can ethically reveal confidences of a client are these:

(a) when the client consents
(b) when disclosure is required by law or court order
(c) when one needs to defend oneself or employees against an accusation of wrongful conduct
(d) to prevent reasonably certain death or substantial bodily harm

(e)  to prevent the client from committing a crime or fraud that is reasonably certain to result in substantial injury to the financial interests or property of another and the lawyer's services have been used to accomplish that end

(f)  to prevent, mitigate, or rectify substantial injury to the financial interest or property of another that is reasonably certain to result or has resulted from the client's commission of a crime or fraud when the lawyer's services have been used

One of the most debated portions has been the part of this rule that specifies what type of crime can be used to support divulging the confidences of a client. The Model Code (used before the Model Rules) allowed disclosure to prevent *any* crime. An earlier version of the Model Rules dictated that an attorney may violate a client's confidence only to prevent a future crime involving imminent death or grievous bodily harm. Many state bar associations refused to adopt the restrictive rule, or have enlarged it to include any crime. The current version allows for financial crimes if there is substantial injury, but it also protects a lawyer who divulges confidences to mitigate or rectify a financial crime. The Enron and WorldCom cases no doubt influenced the committee that updated this rule. Proponents of enlarging the scope of the rule argued that such a rule would have prevented Enron lawyers from participating in the scheme to defraud stockholders by hiding the true level of debt.

Neither the restricted nor the inclusive rule regarding disclosing a client's future crime applied to the Garrow incident (described in the "In the News" box), so the lawyers felt ethically bound to withhold the location of two bodies from the family of the victims.

---

**IN THE NEWS  Legal Agent with No Morals?**

In July 1973, Robert Garrow killed four people in the Adirondack Mountains of New York. In early August, he was captured by state police and indicted for the murder of a student from Schenectady. At the time of the arrest, no evidence connected Garrow to the other deaths. His two court-appointed attorneys, Francis R. Belge and Frank H. Armani, were told by Garrow about the murders, and they even located one of the bodies but did not tell police. The body was finally discovered four months later by two children playing in the mine. In September, the lawyers found the second body by following Garrow's directions. They didn't tell police of this body either, and it was found by others as well. Belge and Armani maintained their silence until Garrow made statements from the witness stand that implicated him in the other three murders. The local community was outraged, but the lawyers believed they had honored the letter and spirit of their professional duty.

Source: From C. Harris, *Applying Moral Theories* (Belmont, CA: Wadsworth, 1986): 114–115. Used by permission.

*Do you think the lawyers should have found some way to disclose the location of the bodies?*

Harris (1986) evaluated the actions of Garrow's two lawyers under the utilitarian ethical framework and decided that they did the right thing because it is ethically acceptable for lawyers to break client confidentiality only in cases in which a death or crime could be prevented by disclosure. This rule is justified by utilitarianism because it is believed that society benefits in the long run from the presence of the attorney–client confidence. Therefore, this confidence should be sacrificed only when it endangers a life.

Religious ethics might condemn the attorneys' actions because withholding the location of the bodies was a form of deception. On the other hand, in the Catholic religion, a similar ethical dilemma might arise if someone confessed to a priest. It would be impossible for the priest to betray that confession no matter what the circumstances.

Ethical formalism is difficult to reconcile with the lawyers' actions. First of all, under the categorical imperative, the lawyers' actions must be such that we would be willing for all others to engage in similar behavior under like circumstances. Could one will that it become universal law for attorneys to keep such information secret? What if you were the parents who did not know the whereabouts of their daughter, or even if she was alive or dead? It is hard to imagine that they would be willing to agree with this universal law. On the other hand, if one were the criminal, or one's son or daughter were the criminal, one would not want a lawyer to betray confidences that would hurt the case. If you were a lawyer, you would want a rule that encouraged a client to be truthful in order to provide an adequate defense. Ethical formalism is also concerned with duty; it is obvious that the duty of an attorney is always to protect the interests of his or her client. As with the utilitarian formulation, we might differentiate between circumstances of future crimes and circumstances of past crimes.

The ethics of care would be concerned with the needs of both the client and the parents in the case described. It would perhaps resolve the issue in a less absolutist fashion than the other rationales. For instance, when discussing this case in a college classroom, many students immediately decide that they would call in the location of the bodies anonymously, thereby relieving the parents' anxiety and also protecting, to some extent, the confidential communication. However, this compromise is unsupported by an absolute view of confidentiality because it endangers the client (perhaps he would not even be charged with the crimes if the bodies were never found). However, it does protect the relationship of the attorney and the client and still meets the needs of the parents.

It should be noted that the rule of confidentiality does not apply to physical evidence. Anything that is discoverable in the possession of a client is equally discoverable if in the possession of an attorney. Therefore, an attorney must hand over files or other incriminating evidence subject to a valid search warrant, motion, or subpoena. If the attorney is merely told where these items may be found, he or she is not obliged to tell the authorities where they are. For instance, if a client tells an attorney that a murder weapon is in a certain location, the attorney cannot divulge that information to authorities. However, if the client drops a murder weapon in the attorney's lap, the lawyer runs the risk of being charged with a felony if it is hidden or withheld from the police. If the attorney is told where a murder weapon is and goes to check, that information is still protected; however, if the attorney takes the weapon back to his or her office or moves it in any way, then the attorney may be subjected to felony charges of obstruction of justice or evidence tampering.

A defense attorney's ethics may also be compromised when a client insists on taking the stand to commit perjury. Disciplinary rules specifically forbid the lawyer from allowing perjury to take place; if it happens before the attorney realizes the intent of the client, the defense must not use or refer to the perjured testimony (Freedman, 1986; Kleinig, 1986). The quandary is that if the attorney shows his disbelief or discredits the client, then this behavior violates the ethical mandate of a zealous defense, and to inform the court of the perjury violates the ethical rule of confidentiality.

Pellicotti (1990) explains that an attorney should first try to dissuade the client from committing perjury. If the client persists in plans to lie, the attorney then has an ethical duty to withdraw from the case, and there is some authority that the attorney should disclose to the court that the client plans to lie. Withdrawal is problematic because it will usually jeopardize a case, and disclosure is even more problematic because, arguably, it affects the judgment of the hearing judge. An attorney may refuse to call witnesses who plan to lie, but if the defendant's testimony will be perjured, it is, arguably, a violation of his or her rights for the attorney not to allow the defendant to take the stand.

*Nix v. Whiteside* (475 U.S. 157, 89 L.Ed.2d 123 [1986]) held that it did not violate the defendant's Sixth Amendment right to counsel for the attorney to refuse to help the defendant commit perjury. In this murder case, the defendant told his lawyer that he had not seen a gun in the victim's hand. At a later point, he told his attorney that if he didn't testify that he saw a gun, he would be "dead" (lose the case). The attorney told him that if he testified falsely, he would have to impeach him and would seek to withdraw from the case. The defendant testified truthfully, was found guilty, and then appealed based on ineffective counsel. The court found that the right to counsel did not include the right to an attorney who would suborn perjury.

Pellicotti (1990) describes the *passive* role and the *active* role of an attorney with a client who commits perjury. In the passive role, the attorney asks no questions during direct examination that would elicit untruthful answers, and may make a statement that the client is taking the stand against the advice of an attorney. The attorney does not refer to perjured testimony during summation or any arguments. The active role allows for the attorney to disclose to the court the fact of the perjured testimony. There is no great weight of authority to commend either approach, leaving attorneys in a difficult ethical dilemma. The best defense of some attorneys is not to know about the lie in the first place.

If the attorney is not sure the client would be committing perjury, then there is no legal duty to disclose; in fact, the weight of authority indicates that the attorney with doubts should proceed with the testimony—any disclosure of such doubts is improper and unethical. Thus, some attorneys tell their client, "Before you say anything, I need to tell you that I cannot participate in perjury and if I know for a fact that you plan to lie, I cannot put you on the stand," or ask their client, "What do I need to know that is damaging to this case?" rather than if the client is guilty of the crime. Further, many attorneys argue that all defendants lie about everything and you can't believe them anyway. If this is true, then some attorneys may conclude that there are always doubts, and this allows an easy justification for allowing the defendant to say anything on the stand.

## Conflicts of Interest

*Defense counsel should not permit his or her professional judgment or obligations to be affected by his or her own political, business, property, or personal interests (Standard 4-3.5(a)).*

Attorneys are prohibited from engaging in representations that would compromise their loyalty to their clients. Specifically, attorneys must not represent clients who may have interests that conflict with those of the attorney—for instance, an attorney may not represent a client who owns a company that is a rival to one in which the attorney has an interest. The attorney also must not represent two clients who may have opposing interests—for instance, co-defendants in a criminal case, for very often one will testify against the other. The attorney would find it impossible in such a situation to represent each individual fairly. Disciplinary rules even prohibit two lawyers from a single firm from representing clients with conflicting interests. In some informal and formal decisions from ethics committees, this rule has even been used to prohibit legal aid or public defender offices from defending co-defendants, yet this is a fairly routine practice (American Bar Association, 1986).

Although attorneys may not ethically accept clients with conflicting interests, there is no guidance on the more abstract problem that all criminal clients in a caseload have conflicting interests if their cases are looked upon as part of a workload rather than considered separately. Many defense attorneys make a living by taking cases from people with very modest means or taking court-appointed cases with the fee set by the court. The defense attorney then becomes a "fast-food lawyer," depending on volume and speed to make a profit. What happens here, of course, is that quality may get sacrificed along the way. When lawyers pick up clients in the hallways of courtrooms and from bail company referrals, the goal is to arrange bail, get a plea bargain, and move on to the next case. Rarely do these cases even come to trial.

The vast majority of cases in the criminal justice system are settled by a **plea bargain,** an exchange of a guilty plea for a reduced charge or sentence. The defense attorney's goal in plea bargaining is to get the best possible deal for the client—probation or the shortest prison sentence that the prosecutor is willing to give for a guilty plea. The defense attorney is aware that he or she cannot aggressively push every case without endangering the ongoing relationship with the prosecutor. A courtroom appearance may be an isolated event for the client, but for the defense attorney and prosecutor, it is an ongoing, weekly ritual—only the names of the defendants change. Because of the nature of the continuing relationship, the defense attorney must weigh present needs against future gains. If the defense becomes known as unwilling to play ball, reduced effectiveness may hurt future clients.

Another conflict of interest may occur if the attorney desires to represent the client's interests in selling literary or media rights. Standard 4–3.4 specifically forbids entering into such an agreement before the case is complete. The temptations are obvious—if the attorney hopes to acquire financial rewards from a share of profits, his or her professional judgment on how best to defend the client may be clouded. Whether putting off signing such an agreement until the case is complete removes the possibility of unethical decisions is debatable. In the O. J. Simpson trial, it appears that every major player wrote a book about the trial. One wonders if trial tactics and speeches aren't evaluated, at least in passing, on how they will appear in a later first-person narrative or movie screenplay. The potential for biased judgments is obvious—for instance, if an attorney has a client who has committed a particularly spectacular crime, there is the potential for celebrity status only if the case comes to trial, so a plea bargain—even if it is in the best interest of the client—may be less carefully considered by the attorney.

## Zealous Defense

*Defense counsel, in common with all members of the bar, is subject to standards of conduct stated in statutes, rules, decisions of courts, and codes, canons, or other standards of professional conduct. Defense counsel has no duty to execute any directive of the accused which does not comport with law or such standards. Defense counsel is the professional representative of the accused, not the accused's alter ego (Standard 4-1.2(e)).*

Few would challenge the idea that all people deserve to have their due-process rights protected. However, what many people find unsettling is the zeal with which some defense attorneys approach the courtroom contest. How diligent should the defense be in protecting the defendant's rights? A conflict may arise between providing an effective defense and maintaining professional ethics and individual morality. Lawyers should represent clients zealously within the bounds of the law, but the law is sometimes vague and difficult to determine. Some actions are simply forbidden. The lawyer may not engage in motions or actions to intentionally and maliciously harm others, knowingly advance unwarranted claims or defenses, conceal or fail to disclose that which he or she is required by law to reveal, knowingly use perjured testimony or false evidence, knowingly make a false statement of law or fact, participate in the creation or preservation of evidence when he or she knows or it is obvious that the evidence is false, counsel the client in conduct that is illegal, or engage in other illegal conduct. The attorney is also expected to maintain a professional and courteous relationship with the opposing attorneys, litigants, and witnesses and to refrain from disparaging statements or badgering conduct. The defense attorney must not intimidate or otherwise influence the jury or trier of fact or use the media for these same purposes.

Despite these ethical rules, practices such as withholding evidence, manufacturing evidence, witness badgering, and defamation of victims' characters are sometimes used as tactics in the defense arsenal. For instance, the practice of bringing out the sexual history of rape victims is done purely to paint her as a victim who deserved or asked for her rape. Even though rape-shield laws exist that prohibit most exposés of sexual history, attorneys still attempt to bring in such evidence. Destroying the credibility of honest witnesses is considered good advocacy. For instance, if a witness accurately testifies to what he or she saw, a good attorney may still cast doubt in the jurors' minds by bringing out evidence of the use of glasses, mistakes of judgment, and other facts that tend to obfuscate and undercut the credibility of the witness. Attorneys will do this even when they know that the witness is telling the truth. A zealous defense demands the questioning of the credibility of a prosecution witness.

In some cases, defense attorneys go to extreme lengths to change the course of testimony, such as bribing witnesses, allowing their client to intimidate a witness, or instructing their client to destroy physical evidence or to manufacture an alibi and then commit perjury. Chapter 9 discusses noble-cause corruption on the part of law enforcement officers, and this type of motivation is also the case with blatantly criminal behavior on the part of attorneys. Most ethical conflicts occur over more subtle questions of how far one should go to provide a zealous defense. It is sometimes difficult to determine when a defense attorney's treatment of a witness is badgering as opposed to energetic cross-examination, or when exploring a witness's background is a character assassination as opposed to a careful examination of credibility. Some attorneys focus attacks on opposing counsel—female attorneys report that opposing male attorneys attempt to infantalize, patronize, or sexualize them in front of the judge and jury as a trial tactic to destroy their credibility. Young attorneys encounter treatment by opposing counsel—with such comments as "what my young colleague here has evidently not learned yet . . ."—designed to persuade the jury that the older attorney is more wise, honest, or mature than the younger attorney. Personal attacks on credibility and more subtle attempts to influence juries' perceptions of opposing counsel may also occur—such as talking during opposing counsel's opening or closing, rolling one's eyes in response to a statement or question, and making other verbal or physical gestures indicating disbelief, amusement, or disdain. These tactics are obviously not in the same category as bribing witnesses or manufacturing evidence, but are they ethical?

Defense attorneys may sacrifice integrity or friendships for the sake of a case. For instance, in one trial a defense attorney and a prosecutor were getting ready to argue a barroom murder case. The prosecutor was able to present only one eyewitness to the shooting—the bartender. No one else in the bar was willing to testify that they saw anything. The prosecutor had other circumstantial evidence of the defendant's guilt, but the eyewitness was crucial. Unfortunately, the bartender had a ten-year-old murder conviction—a fact that would reduce his credibility in the jury's eyes. This fact could be brought out by the defense under the rules of evidence; however, the prosecutor could petition the court to have the fact suppressed and have a good chance of succeeding because it bore no relevance to the case and would be prejudicial. In this instance, however, she had forgotten to file the appropriate motion. Just before the trial was about to start, the prosecutor asked the defense attorney if he was going to bring out this fact on his cross-examination of the bartender. If he planned to do so, the prosecutor would have asked for a continuance and filed a motion to have it suppressed, or at least brought it out on direct to reduce its impact. He told her specifically and clearly that he had no intention of using that information or questioning the witness about it because it was so long ago and irrelevant to the case. When the direct examination of this witness was over and the defense attorney started his cross-examination, his very first question was "Isn't it true that you were convicted of murder in 19--?" Although the prosecutor may have committed an error in judgment by trusting the defense attorney, the defense attorney deliberately misled the prosecutor as to his intentions—he lied.

When asked about his actions, the defense attorney explained that it "just slipped out" and complained that the prosecutor took these things "too seriously." This behavior is an example of a lie used for short-term gain, an egoistic rationalization, and a view of due process as a game, for when an opponent is offended by the lie, she is taking things "too seriously." In this case, the defense attorney may have lost more than he gained by the trick; a conviction was achieved in spite of the witness's background, and the attorney found that previously cooperative prosecutors were suddenly unwilling to agree to continuances, closed their files to him even though it was generally an "open file" office, and in other ways treated him as untrustworthy, which indeed he was, but was he unethical or just zealously defending his client?

### Jury Consultants

A recent innovation in trial tactics is the development of "scientific" jury selection. Attorneys often contend that a trial has already been won or lost once the jury has been selected. Whether or not this is true, attorneys are becoming increasingly sophisticated in their methods of choosing which members of a jury panel would make good jurors. However, a good juror is not someone who unbiased and fair but rather someone who is predisposed to be sympathetic to that attorney's case. Jury experts are psychologists, communication specialists, or other professionals who sit with the attorney and, through a combination of nonverbal and verbal clues, identify those jury panel members who are predisposed to believe the case presented by the attorney.

In the O. J. Simpson trial, candidates were asked to fill out a seventy-eight-page list of questions devised by Judge Ito, defense and prosecution attorneys, and the defense jury consultant. Actual questions included "What TV shows do you watch? Do you think police are trustworthy? Do you attend church?" This information was then used to screen jurors. Some allege that jury consultants can help to stack juries with the least sophisticated or most educated group, or any other type of group desired by the attorney.

Some lawyers, such as the famed "Racehorse" Haynes of Houston, have used methods such as surveying a large sample of the population in the community where the case is to be tried to discover how certain demographic groups feel about issues relevant to the case so that these findings can be used when the jury is selected. Another method uses a **shadow jury**—a panel of people selected by the defense attorney to represent the actual jury that sits through the trial and provides feedback to the attorney on the evidence being presented during the trial. This allows the attorney to adjust his or her trial tactics in response. Some of these methods were used in the William Kennedy Smith rape trial in Florida, which resulted in an acquittal. More recently, they were used by the defense "dream team" in the O. J. Simpson case.

Attorneys have always used intuition and less sophisticated means to decide which jury members to exclude, but the more modern tactics are questioned by some as too contrary to the basic idea that a trial is supposed to start with an unbiased jury (Smith and Meyer, 1987). Consultants provide such services as

- preparing witnesses
- assisting with mock trials
- developing desirable juror profiles
- conducting phone surveys on public attitudes about a case
- analyzing "shadow juries"
- giving advice on effective posture, clothing choice, and tone of voice

One powerful tactic is to use "focus groups," informal talk sessions, to find out opinions about a case. Consultants work on an estimated 6,000 trials a year, mostly civil cases. The American Society of Trial Consultants, a professional organization, has more than 400 members, who charge around $150 an hour (Gavzer, 1997).

### Ethical Analysis of Zealous Defense

Can our ethical systems help to determine what actions are ethically justified in defending a client zealously? Utilitarianism and egoism would probably allow a greater range of actions, depending on the particular interests or rewards represented by the case. Ethical formalism and religion might restrict the actions of a defense attorney to those allowed by a strict interpretation of the Model Rules.

Aronson (1977: 59–63) discusses two methods for resolving ethical dilemmas. The first is called the **situational model**, wherein lawyers weigh the priorities and decide each case on the particular factors present. This is similar to our explanation of situational ethics. For instance, client confidentiality may be sacrificed when others' interests are at stake but be paramount in other considerations. The **systems model**, on the other hand, would be a more absolute or legalistic model in that behavior would always be considered wrong or right depending on the ethical rule guiding the definition. Obviously, these two systems of decision making bear a great deal of resemblance to the situational ethics and absolutist models discussed in Chapter 2. As a pure advocate, the defense attorney's duty is to pursue a client's interest. As long as the attorney does not run afoul of the law or ethical mandates, the client's defense is the sole objective.

# Ethical Issues for Prosecutors

Prosecutors do not serve an individual client; rather, their client is the system or society itself. Pursuit of justice rather than pursuit of the best interest of the client characterizes the aims of prosecutors. As the second line of decision makers in the system, prosecutors have extremely broad powers of discretion. The prosecutor acts like a strainer—he or she collects some cases for formal prosecution while eliminating a great many others. Because of limited resources, the difficulty of enforcing outdated or unsupported laws, and weak cases, prosecuting every case is impossible. It might be inappropriate in some situations to impose criminal sanctions, even when laws have been broken, because these particular laws are trivial or lacking in public support. Early diversion of such cases saves taxpayers money and saves individuals trouble and expense.

To guide discretion, there are ethical standards relating specifically to the role of the prosecutor. Typically, a state's code of criminal procedure provides standards for prosecutors. In addition, the state may have a Code of Professional Responsibility that may specifically mention prosecutors' duties. There are also National Prosecution Standards promulgated by the National District Attorneys Association. Finally, Chapter 3 of the ABA Standards for Criminal Justice covers the prosecution function. These standards cover topics similar to those for defense attorneys, but they also make special note of the unique role of the prosecutor as a representative of the court system and the state (Douglass, 1981).

## *Use of Discretion*

*A prosecutor should not institute . . . criminal charges . . . not supported by probable cause (Standard 3–3.9(a)).*

The prosecutor must seek justice, not merely a conviction. Toward this end, prosecutors must share evidence, exercise restraint in the use of their power, represent the public interest, and give the accused the benefit of reasonable doubt. Disciplinary rules are more specific. They forbid the prosecutor from pursuing charges when there is no probable cause and mandate timely disclosure to defense counsel of evidence, especially exculpatory evidence or evidence that might mitigate guilt or reduce the punishment. Despite these ideals of prosecutorial duty, an unstated influence over prosecutorial discretion is that prosecutors want to and must (to be considered successful) win. Their choice of cases is influenced by this fact.

The decision to prosecute is influenced by political and public pressures, the chance for conviction, the severity of the crime, a "gut" feeling of guilt or innocence, prison overcrowding, and the weight of evidence. The prosecutorial role is to seek justice, but justice doesn't mean the same thing to everyone and certainly does not mean prosecuting everyone to the fullest extent of the law. Whether to charge is one of the most important decisions of the criminal justice process. The decision should be fair, neutral, and accomplished with due process, but this is an ideal that is sometimes supplanted by other considerations. Prosecutors don't usually use their charging power for intimidation or harassment, but other factors may be involved in the decision to charge. For instance, a prosecutor might have a particular interest in a type of crime such as child abuse or drugs that results in the prosecutor pursuing these cases more intensely.

Other considerations include pressure from law enforcement—for instance, when there is a bargain struck and a lesser charge will result in testimony or information that could lead to further convictions. There is also the pressure of public opinion. Prosecutors might pursue cases that they would otherwise have dropped if there is a great deal of public interest in the case. However, prosecutors might not pursue cases that have no stakeholders of importance. For instance, victims who have mental impairments may not make the best witnesses, and there may be less chance of getting a conviction. In one such case, five women with developmental disabilities had been raped and terrorized by the owner of a licensed home they lived in. The prosecutor declined to pursue charges under the rationale "that any woman with a developmental disability would have zero credibility in court." Only when the licensing authority secured additional testimony, revoked the license of the owner, and publicly exposed the situation did the prosecutor press charges (Hook, 2001).

Prosecutors in state capitals often have "public integrity" units that prosecute wrongdoing on the part of public officials. Prosecutors might charge at election time for political purposes; on the other hand, they might be falsely accused of such political considerations when they do charge politicians with public integrity violations. In September 2005, Tom DeLay, the powerful majority leader of the U.S. House of Representatives, was indicted by a grand jury in Austin, Texas. The Democratic prosecutor was accused of playing politics and using his office for political reasons. However, critics neglected the fact that the prosecutor and his public integrity unit had been involved in charging more Democrats during his tenure than Republicans, probably because there had been, until recently, more Democrats in office than Republicans (Blumenthal, 2005).

A special case of discretion and charging is the decision to pursue a capital homicide conviction. Prosecutors have the power to decide whether to seek the death penalty or a prison term. It is clear that the decision to seek the death penalty is not made uniformly across jurisdictions. In Texas, for instance, there is wide disparity in the number of cases in which the death penalty is sought. The Harris County (Houston) district attorney seeks the death penalty in a disproportionately greater number of cases than other jurisdictions. One of the biggest considerations is cost. Because capital trials are very expensive, counties that have bigger budgets are more likely to seek the death penalty. They have the resources and staff to handle the cases (Hall, 2002). Obviously, these considerations have nothing to do with justice, and it should cause concern that a criterion other than severity of the crime or future risk affects whether an offender ultimately receives the death penalty.

The decision not to charge is also open to ethical scrutiny. To give one defendant accused of brutal crime immunity to gain testimony against others is efficient, but is it consistent with justice? To not charge people because they contribute to judicial campaigns or are relatives of powerful politicians is obviously an unethical use of discretion. In some situations, prosecutors do not charge because of an outpouring of public sympathy or support for the accused, perhaps because of the type of crime or identity of the victim. Prosecutors who do not charge in these cases may attribute the reason to lack of evidence or the unlikelihood of obtaining a conviction, but their political popularity probably also has something to do with their decision.

Various studies have attempted to describe prosecutors' decision making; one cites office policy as an important influence:

1. *Legal sufficiency* is an office policy that weeds out those cases in which the evidence is not strong enough to support further action.
2. *System efficiency* is an office policy with goals of efficiency and accountability; all decisions are made with these goals in mind, so many cases result in dismissals.
3. *Defendant rehabilitation* emphasizes diversion and other rehabilitation tools rather than punitive goals.
4. *Trial sufficiency* is an office policy that encourages a charge that can be sustained through trial. (Jacoby, Mellon, and Smith, 1980)

Another study looked at the prosecutor as operating in an exchange system. The relationship between the prosecutor and the police was described as one of give and take. Prosecutors balance police needs or wishes against their own vulnerability. The prosecutor makes personal judgments about which police officers can be trusted. Exchange also takes place between the prosecutor's office and the courts. When the jails become overcrowded, more recommendations may be made for deferred adjudication and probation; when dockets back up, charges may be dropped. Finally, exchange takes place between defense attorneys and prosecutors, especially because many defense attorneys have previously served as prosecutors and may be personally familiar with the procedures and even personalities in the prosecutor's office (Cole, 1970).

On one hand, discretion is considered essential to the prosecutorial function of promoting individualized justice and softening the impersonal effects of the law. On the other hand, the presence of discretion is the reason that the legal system is considered unfair and biased toward certain groups of people or individuals. Even though we would not want to eliminate prosecutorial discretion, it could be guided by regulations or internal guidelines. For instance, an office policy might include a procedure for providing written reasons for dropping charges, and this procedure would respond to charges of unbridled discretion.

## Conflicts of Interest

*A prosecutor should avoid a conflict of interest with respect to his or her official duties (Standard 3.1-3(a)).*

Part-time prosecutors present a host of ethical issues. A Bureau of Justice Statistics bulletin (1992) reported that 47 percent of prosecutors held their jobs as a part-time occupation (Dawson, 1992: 1). Obviously, this poses the possibility of a conflict of interest. It may happen that a part-time prosecutor has a private practice, and situations may occur where the duty to a private client runs counter to the duty of the prosecutor's duty to the public. In some cases, it may be that a client becomes a defendant, necessitating the prosecutor to hire a special prosecutor. Even when there are no direct conflicts of interest, the pressure of time always poses a conflict. The division of time between the private practice, where income is correlated with hard work, and prosecuting cases, where income is fixed no matter how many hours are spent, may result in a less energetic prosecutorial function than one might wish.

It is well-known that the prosecutor's job is a good stepping-stone to politics, and many use it as such. In these cases, one has to wonder whether cases are taken on the basis of merit or on their ability to place the prosecutor in the public eye and help his or her career. Winning also becomes more important.

In populous counties, there are many assistant district attorneys (A.D.A.s); only the district attorney is elected. For instance, in Harris County, Texas, there are more than 200 A.D.A.s. Many work in the prosecutor's office for a number of years and then move into the private sector. The reason has largely to do with money. Assistant district attorneys make an average of $40,000 to $60,000, but in private practice they could make much more than that (Cohen, 2001). The question then becomes this: Does the career plan to work for a defense firm affect their prosecutorial decision making?

### Asset Forfeiture

The RICO statute has increasingly been used for its **asset forfeiture** provision, a tool to confiscate property and money associated with organized criminal activity. Once this tactic was approved by the courts, a veritable flood of prosecutions began that were designed, it seems, primarily to obtain cash, boats, houses, and other property of drug dealers. Making decisions based on the potential for what can be confiscated rather than culpability of offenders is a very real and dangerous development in this type of prosecution.

The origin of civil forfeiture was in the Comprehensive Drug Abuse and Control Act of 1970 and the Organized Crime Control Act of 1970. Both of these laws allowed mechanisms for the government to seize assets gained through illegal means. Eventually, the types of assets vulnerable to seizure were expanded, including those assets *intended* to be used as well as those gained by or used in illegal activities. All states have passed similar asset forfeiture laws. The "take" from asset forfeiture increased from

$27.2 million in 1985 to $874 million in 1992 (Jenson and Gerber, 1996). Since the early 1990s, the total amount of federal forfeiture proceeds shared with state and local law enforcement is $2.5 billion! (Hartman, 2001).

There are a number of problematic issues with asset forfeiture. The exclusionary rule does not apply to civil forfeiture proceedings, so some allege that police are now pursuing assets instead of criminals, because in a civil proceeding the defendant does not receive legal aid. A civil forfeiture hearing can take place without any criminal prosecution and without the presence of the alleged criminal. Unlike a criminal trial, in asset forfeiture it had been the case that the government needed only to show probable cause, and then the burden of proof shifted to the individual to prove his or her innocence. This changed when President Clinton signed into law the Civil Asset Forfeiture Reform Act, which shifted the burden of proof from the claimant to the government (Worral, 2001). Now at least the presumption of innocence has been put back into place.

Perhaps one of the most troubling aspects of civil forfeiture is that third parties are often those most hurt by the loss. For example, the spouse or parents of a suspected drug dealer may lose their home. In one of the most widely publicized forfeiture cases, a man solicited a prostitute; the state instituted proceedings and was successful in seizing the car he was driving when he solicited the prostitute—which was, in fact, his wife's car! This case received so much press because the Supreme Court ruled that no constitutional violation occurred with the forfeiture, even though his wife had nothing to do with the criminal activity. Another case that received a great deal of media attention was a man who lost his very expensive motorboat when one marijuana cigarette was found on it.

These and other uses of asset forfeiture have spurred reforms and court decisions that are curtailing its use to some extent. The Supreme Court has ruled that the Eighth Amendment prohibiting excessive fines did apply to civil forfeiture; therefore, the government must regulate its forfeiture to some standard of proportionality with the crime. Another case indicated that the accused must be provided notice and some type of adversarial hearing before assets can be seized unless there are "exigent" circumstances (Jensen and Gerber, 1996). However, it is very clear that asset forfeiture has become an almost indispensable source of revenue for law enforcement and the courts (Worral, 2001).

## Plea Bargaining

*A prosecutor should not knowingly make false statements or representations as to fact or law in the course of plea discussions with defense counsel or the accused (Standard 3–4.1(c)).*

As discussed earlier, there are serious ethical concerns over the practice of plea bargaining. Most conclude that plea bargaining, even if not exactly "right," is certainly efficient and probably inevitable. Even in those jurisdictions that have moved to determinate sentencing, what has happened is that plea bargaining has become charge bargaining instead of sentence bargaining. Should we measure the morality of an action by its efficiency? This efficiency argument is similar to that used to defend some deceptive investigative practices of police. If the goals of the system are crime control or bureaucratic efficiency, then plea bargaining makes sense. If the goals of the system are the protection of individual rights and the protection of due process, then plea bargaining is much harder to justify under a utilitarian argument, or any other. Obviously, plea bargaining would fail under the categorical imperative, for the individual is treated as a means in the argument that plea bargaining is good for the system. See the Policy Box for a critique of the policy.

Arguments given in defense of plea bargaining include the heavy caseloads, limited resources, legislative over-criminalization, individualized justice, and legal problems of cases (legal errors that would result in mistrials or dropped charges if the client didn't plead) (Knudten, 1978: 275). If we concede that plea bargaining can be justified, there are remaining ethical problems over specific practices relating to it. Only 36 percent of chief prosecutors reported that explicit criteria for plea bargains were in place in 1990 (Bureau of Justice Statistics, 1992). Guidelines providing a range of years for certain types of charges would help the individual prosecutors maintain some level of consistency in a particular jurisdiction.

---

**POLICY BOX 10-1  Plea Bargaining**

The practice of exchanging a reduced charge or reduced sentence for a guilty plea is widespread. Although some disagree with the practice and say it leads to innocent people pleading guilty and a reduction in the integrity of the system, most argue that the system couldn't work without the practice. Also, proponents argue that it is ethical to give the offender something in exchange for not putting the state to the expense of a trial.

**Law:** U.S. Supreme Court opinions have legitimated the use of plea bargaining. They have held that prosecutors and judges must abide by agreements made and that defendants cannot turn around and claim that the exchange was unfair afterward.

**Policy:** Different prosecutors' offices handle plea bargaining differently. Some have "books" that are basically guidelines that indicate what the individual prosecutor can offer for any given crime, and others leave it to the prosecutor's discretion. In general, there are informal office policies so that some offices may give more generous offers than other jurisdictions. Plea bargaining is something that is covered in the training of new prosecutors.

**Ethics:** Prosecutors' ethical issues with plea bargaining include whether or not to overcharge to get someone to plead or to lie about how much evidence there is. Defense attorneys' ethical issues include the extent to which they will try to convince an individual to plead who swears he or she is innocent. Judges have ethical issues as well in that they do not have to accept a plea in a case where they do not believe there is sufficient evidence to uphold the verdict.

Should prosecutors overcharge—that is, charge at a higher degree of severity or press more charges than could possibly be sustained by evidence—so that they can bargain down? Should prosecutors mislead defense attorneys about the amount of evidence or the kind of evidence they have or about the sentence they can offer to obtain a guilty plea? Gershman (1991) documents prosecutors engaged in false promises, fraud, misrepresentation of conditions, deals without benefit of counsel, package deals, and threats during plea bargaining. Critics contend that prosecutors hold all the cards in plea bargaining. Defense attorneys can take what is offered (perhaps without knowing the nature of the evidence against the client) or argue, but most of the time arguing with a plea-bargain offer does not do the client much good and does the attorney even less.

## *Media Relations*

The prosecutor has an important relationship with the press. The media can be enemy or friend, depending on how charismatic or forthcoming the prosecutor is in interviews. Sometimes cases are said to be "tried in the papers," with the defense attorney and the prosecutor staging verbal sparring matches for public consumption. Prosecutors may react to cases and judges' decisions in the paper, criticizing the decision or the sentence and, in the process, denigrating the dignity of the system. More often, the defense attempts to sway the press to a sympathetic view of the offense, which is easier to accomplish during prosecutorial silence.

ABA Model Rule 3.6(b) is a prohibition against out-of-court statements that a reasonable person should expect would have a substantial likelihood of materially prejudicing a proceeding. Prosecutors are probably not as inclined to use the media to try a case as defense attorneys, but when they do make statements, it is possible there is more damage done. Defense attorneys might be *expected* to make statements to exonerate their client and disparage the state's case, but prosecutors' statements have a greater ring of authority. The rule specifies that no statements should be given involving any of the following topics:

- The character, credibility, reputation, or criminal record of a party, suspect, or witness
- The identity of a witness
- The expected testimony of a party or witness
- The performance or results of any test or examination
- The refusal of any party to submit to such tests or examinations
- The identity or nature of physical evidence
- Inadmissible information
- The possibility of a guilty plea
- The existence or contents of a confession or admission
- The defendant's refusal to make a statement
- An opinion about the guilt or innocence of the defendant or suspect
- A statement that the defendant has been charged with a crime unless it is in the context that a charge does not mean the party is guilty

The following facts may be disclosed:

- The general nature of the claim or charge
- Any information in a public record
- The fact that the matter is being investigated and the scope of the investigation
- The schedule of litigation
- A request for assistance in obtaining information
- A warning of danger
- The identity, residence, occupation, and family status of the accused
- Information to enable the accused's capture (if at large)
- The fact, time, and place of arrest
- The identity of investigating and arresting officers

One wonders, when reading the papers and listening to television news reports, if prosecutors and defense attorneys have ever read these rules. Certainly in high-profile cases they seem to be ignored.

## Expert Witnesses

*A prosecutor who engages an expert for an opinion should respect the independence of the expert and should not seek to dictate the formation of the expert's opinion on the subject (Standard 3–3.3(a)).*

Expert witnesses, who can receive a fee, are often accused of compromising their integrity for money or notoriety. The use of expert witnesses has risen in recent years. Psychiatrists often testify as to the mental competency or legal insanity of an accused. Today, criminologists and other social scientists may be asked to testify on such topics as victimization in prison, statistical evidence of sentencing discrimination, the effectiveness of predictive instruments for prison riots and other disturbances, risk assessment for individual offenders, mental health services in prison, patterns of criminality, the battered-woman syndrome, and so on (see Anderson and Winfree, 1987). Expert testimony is allowed as evidence in trials when it is based on principles generally accepted in the scientific community. This standard is applied by judges, who can accept or bar such evidence from being offered to the jury.

When the expert is honest in his or her presentation as to the limitations and potential bias of the material, no ethical issues arise. However, expert witnesses may testify in a realm beyond fact or make testimony appear factual when some questions are not clearly answerable. Because of the **halo effect**—essentially, when a person with expertise or status in one area is given deference in all areas—an expert witness may endow a statement or conclusion with more legitimacy than it may warrant. When expert witnesses take the stand, they run the risk of having their credibility attacked by the opposing side.

Credibility is obviously much easier to attack when a witness has attempted to present theory or supposition as fact or conclusion, either for ideological reasons or because of pressure from zealous attorneys. Those who always appear on one side or the other may also lose their credibility. For instance, a doctor who is used often by prosecutors in one jurisdiction during capital sentencing hearings has become known as "Dr. Death" because he always determines that the defendant poses a future risk to society, which is one of the necessary elements for the death penalty. Although this doctor is well-known to both prosecutors and defense attorneys by reputation, juries would not be expected to know of his predilection for finding future risk and would take his testimony at face value unless the defense attorney brings this information out during cross-examination.

Competing expert witnesses who present entirely different "facts" to the jury create an atmosphere of cynicism and distrust. There is a tendency to believe that expert witnesses are neutral and "teach" the facts to the jury, but recent cases have brought to light that expert witnesses might be incompetent in their methodology or interpretation, might testify to certain facts for political or other reasons, or might simply enjoy the notoriety of testifying. Because much of expert testimony concerns scientific principles that are incomprehensible to laypeople, the potential for being misled by an expert witness is magnified.

### CSI and the Courts

For many years, forensic experts have testified regarding factual issues of evidence ranging from ballistics to blood spatter. Television shows such as *CSI* and *Crossing Jordan* contribute to the mystique of crime scene investigators as scientific Sherlock Holmes types who use physics, chemistry, and biology to catch criminals. However, the fact is that some of this kind of "expert" testimony has been called *junk science* (McRoberts, Mills, and Possley, 2004).

As mentioned in the last chapter, the FBI's and several police labs have come under fire for shoddy practices or biased analyses. The Houston police crime lab has been investigated and closed down and several defendants have been exonerated by retests of the DNA evidence that convicted them. Criticism of the lab included poorly trained technicians, lax procedures, shoddy records, overstated testimony, and the inability to do certain tasks such as separate DNA from mixed samples. Thousands of cases are being reviewed, but because Harris County has sent more defendants to death row than any other county in Texas, some of those convicted through tainted evidence may have already been executed (Liptak, 2003; Axtman, 2003).

The highly respected Virginia state crime lab has also been investigated after outside experts hired by the defense called into question the DNA analysis that sent a man to death row. In fact, this case is one of several dozen death row cases around the country that are being reviewed because of potentially faulty, biased, or perjured lab analyst testimony (Possley, Mills, and McRoberts, 2004). Two other lab scandals—in Oklahoma and in West Virginia—have led to millions of dollars in settlements for those falsely incarcerated and reviews of hundreds of cases. In Montana, there was a petition to the state supreme court to undertake independent testing of hundreds of cases handled by a lab examiner who was responsible for three false convictions based on faulty hair analysis (Possley, Mills, and McRoberts, 2004).

Even when mismanagement, shoddy practices, and untrained staff aren't the issue, many areas of the so-called science of **criminalistics** seem to be more in the nature of art than science. Criminalists have been defined as those professionals who are involved in the "scientific discipline directed to the recognition, identification, individualization, and evaluation of physical evidence by the application of the natural sciences to law—science matters" (Lindquist, 1994: 59). Questions have been raised in virtually all areas of this science about the reliability of methods:

1. *Hair analysis.* A Justice Department study of 240 crime labs found hair comparison error rates ranging from 28 percent to 68 percent. In fact, hair comparison testimony is so suspect that it is outlawed in Michigan and Illinois, but not in other states (Hall, 2002). In Montana a chief lab analyst collected over 5,000 hair samples and claimed a statistical analysis that could identify a person's hair from the sample with an error rate of 1 in 1,000. A panel of experts disagreed, and there have been convictions overturned because of his faulty hair analysis (Possley, Mills, and McRoberts, 2004).

2. *Arson investigation.* This is called an "inchoate science" because empirical testing shows that most of it may be guesswork and imagination. It has been said that arson investigators rely on a collection of beliefs and folk wisdom rather than science. Prosecutors are still convicting people on theories of arson that have been debunked by scientists (Possley, 2004). Arson "science" started when arson investigators used their experience with thousands of fires, confessions of suspects, and crude experiments to identify burn patterns and accelerants. "Facts" such as "fires started with accelerants burn hotter" have been disproved. So-called "pour" patterns that have been used as proof of arson have now been associated with a natural phenomenon called "flashover," which occurs when smoke and gas in a room build to a point where the entire room explodes in flames, consuming everything. The flashover effect also calls into question the traditional belief that if the floor showed burning, it was arson because heat rises and the floor shouldn't show burning unless an accelerant is used. Part of the reason why older theories of arson are not supported by current experimentation is that the presence of synthetics has changed the composition of fires, so what arson investigators observed thirty years ago no longer has any relevance to today's fires. Synthetics burn hotter and are very combustible; thus, fires are more likely to be mislabeled as arson (Possley, 2004).

3. *Ballistics testing.* Recently, there have been questions raised as to the accuracy of the chemical composition tests the FBI labs use to match bullets. This method has been used in thousands of cases to tie suspects to the bullet retrieved at the crime scene. The theory is that the chemical composition of bullets in a single production batch is similar and that bullets from a single batch are different from other batches. Bullets owned by the suspect are compared to the crime scene bullet, and the expert testifies on whether the crime scene bullet came from the suspect's box of remaining bullets. Emerging scientific evidence challenges the method because tests indicate that there is a large margin of error—chemical compositions between batches are more similar than believed, and the chemical composition within a batch can vary quite a bit depending on a number of factors. These findings are problematic because ballistics experts from the FBI lab and other labs have testified in a way that greatly overstates the importance of the chemical matches. It is possible that some people have been wrongly convicted because of this evidence (Piller and Mejia, 2003; Piller, 2003).

4. *DNA testing.* DNA testing has also been called into question (Anderson, 1989). The use of DNA evidence has risen dramatically in recent years. Based on the scientific principle that no two individuals possess the same DNA (deoxyribonucleic acid), a DNA "fingerprint" is analyzed from organic matter such as semen, blood, hair, or skin. Whereas a blood test can identify an individual only as being a member of a group (e.g., all those with blood type A positive), DNA testing can determine, with a small margin of error, whether two samples come from the same individual. It has been described as the greatest breakthrough in scientific evidence since fingerprinting, but there are problems with its use. Careless laboratory procedures render results useless, and there are no enforced guidelines or criteria for forensic laboratories conducting DNA tests.

Labs often only have a very small amount of organic matter to extract DNA. They use a procedure whereby the incomplete DNA strand is replicated using computer simulation models. This procedure allows a DNA analysis of the tiniest speck of blood or skin, but critics argue that it opens a door to a margin of error that is unacceptable. Without vigorous investigation and examination of lab results from the opposing counsel, incorrect DNA test results or poorly interpreted results may be entered as evidence and used to determine guilt or innocence.

5. *Fingerprint analysis.* Most citizens assume that fingerprint analysis is infallible, that all criminals' fingerprints are accessible through computer matching technology, and that fingerprint technicians can retrieve fingerprints from almost any surface and can use partials to make a match. Unfortunately, the reality is far from what is seen on television. In fact, there have been attempts to undertake a comprehensive analysis of how much of a partial print is necessary in order to have a reliable match, an objective that is resisted by professional fingerprint examiners. Most fingerprints are partials and smudged. Some studies show that about a quarter of matches are false positives. Three FBI fingerprint examiners recently mistakenly identified the fingerprint related to a terrorist bombing in Madrid, Spain. Standards do not exist for determining how many points of comparison are necessary in order to declare a match (Mills and McRoberts, 2004).

6. *Bite mark comparison.* There is no accurate way to measure the reliability of bite mark comparisons, yet forensic dentists are used to obtain convictions. Such testimony has resulted in the convictions of several innocent defendants. Evidently, the experts sometimes can't even agree if an injury is a bite mark at all. One study indicated that identifications were flawed in two-thirds of the cases. Even their own organization cautions that analysts should never use the term "match" because the technique is not exact enough, but many do. Contrary to popular belief, a bite mark is not just like a fingerprint. Teeth change over time, and the condition of the skin or other substance holding the bite mark changes the indentation patterns of teeth (McRoberts and Mills, 2004).

The use of expert witnesses can present ethical problems when the witness is used in a dishonest fashion. Obviously, to pay an expert for his or her time is not unethical, but to shop for experts until one is found who benefits the case may be unethical, for the credibility of the witness is suspect. Another difficulty is presented when either side obtains an expert who develops a conclusion or set of findings that would help the other side. Ethical rules do not prohibit an attorney in a civil matter or criminal defense attorneys from merely disregarding the information and not giving notice to their opponent that there is information that could benefit his or her case. However, prosecutors operate under a special set of ethics because their goal is justice, not pure advocacy. Any exculpatory information is supposed to be shared with the defense; this obviously includes test results and may also include expert witness findings.

Another problem is when prosecutors intentionally use scientific evidence that they know to be false. There are proven instances where prosecutors put on so-called experts that they knew were unqualified and/or their expertise without merit (Gershman, 2003). Prosecutors may bolster a witness's credentials or allow him or her to make gratuitous and unsupported claims on the witness stand, such as to state "unequivo-cally" that the fingerprint, or hair, or lip print was the defendant's.

In their closing arguments, prosecutors may overstate the expert's testimony so that "is consistent with" becomes "matched" (Gershman, 2003: 36). In some egregious cases, prosecutors have simply lied about physical evidence, such as stating that the red substance on a victim's underpants was blood when, in fact, it was paint (Gershman, 2003: 36).

## Zealous Prosecution

*The duty of the prosecutor is to seek justice, not merely to convict (Standard 3-1.2(c)).*
Just as the defense attorney is at times overly zealous in defense of clients, prosecu-tors may be overly ambitious in order to attain a conviction. The prosecutor, in preparing a case, is putting together a puzzle—each fact or bit of evidence is a piece of that puzzle. Any piece of evidence that doesn't fit the puzzle is sometimes conveniently ignored. The problem is that this type of evidence may be exculpatory, and the prosecutor has a duty to provide it to the defense.

Tactics such as using witnesses with less than credible reasons for testifying, preparing witnesses (both in appearance and testimony), and "shopping" for experts are prosecutorial tools as well as defense tools. Witnesses are not supposed to be paid, but their expenses can be reimbursed, and often this is incentive enough for witnesses to say what they think the prosecutor wants to hear. Further, one tool in the prose-cutor's arsenal that the defense attorney does not have is that prosecutors can make deals to reduce charges in return for favorable testimony. There are many offenders in prison because of co-defendant testimony against them that was "bought" by a reduced charge or sentence. These practices are not illegal, but whether they are ethical is a dif-ferent question.

Prosecutors want to win, and there are very few checks or monitors on their behavior. The result is that noble-cause corruption occurs when prosecutors do any-thing it takes to win a case. This can take the form of persistent references to illegal evidence, leading witnesses, nondisclosure of evidence to the defense, appeals to emotions, games and tricks, and so on. One prosecutor admitted that early in his career he sometimes made faces at the defendant while his back was to the jury and the defense attorney wasn't looking. The jury saw the defendant glowering and looking angry for no discernible reason, which led to a negative perception of his sanity, temper, or both. Of course, the defense attorney may be engaged in the same type of actions, so the contest becomes who has better "tricks" rather than who has the better case.

## *Prosecutorial Misconduct*

When prosecutors forget that their mission is to protect due process, not obtain a conviction at all costs, misconduct can occur. In an earlier chapter, the evidently false confession obtained by N.Y.P.D. detectives from the "Central Park rapists" was discussed. However, the fact is that in New York, prosecutors are involved at a very early stage of investigation; thus, there was a prosecutor who evaluated that confession knowing full well the circumstances, and used it to secure a conviction. If there is any blame to be distributed regarding coercive tactics leading to a miscarriage of justice, then the prosecutors involved also deserve some portion of it. The types of misconduct range from fairly nonserious lapses of ethical rules to commission of criminal acts (such as hiding evidence). The following paragraphs offer some of the possible rules that are violated when prosecutors forget their mission.

### Communications with Defendants

When a criminal defendant is represented by an attorney, the prosecutor should not attempt any communication with the defendant outside the presence of the defense attorney. The attorney's presence is designed to eliminate the possibility of improper or intimidating behavior, illegal deals, and improper interrogation or plea-bargain offers.

### Ex Parte Communications with the Judge

Prosecutors and judges work together on a daily basis. There is a prohibition on attorneys and judges discussing a case outside the presence of the other attorney, but because of working conditions, this is much more likely to apply to prosecutors than to defense attorneys. The reason for the rule is fairness. It is not fair for the judge to hear one side without the other side there to defend its point of view. This rule applies to casual conversations as well as more formal interchanges or offerings of information.

### Duty to Correct False Testimony

Similar to a defense attorney's quandary when a witness commits perjury, a prosecutor must also take steps to avoid allowing false testimony to stand. In point of fact, the prosecutor's role is the easier one because there are no conflicting duties to protect a client; therefore, when a prosecution witness perjures himself or herself, the prosecutor has an affirmative duty to bring it to the attention of the court. The prosecutor in the Tulia case, mentioned in a previous chapter, knew the police officer on the stand had lied about his past, yet he did not disclose that information and allowed the perjury to stand. He was sanctioned by the Texas bar and almost lost his law license. Many believe that he should have, considering his role in the convictions.

### Failure to Disclose Evidence

Perhaps the most common charge leveled against prosecutors, failure to disclose evidence, stems from a duty to reveal exculpatory evidence to the defense (if the defense files a "Brady motion" requesting such evidence). Because the rule indicates that only evidence that is "likely to lead to a different outcome" is subject to this discovery requirement, some prosecutors who withhold evidence argue that "It wasn't important" or "I didn't believe it." These rationalizations ignore a basic difference between their role and the role of the defense attorney. Whereas the defense attorney's only mission is the defense of his or her client, the prosecutor's role is to seek justice. This means that all evidence should be brought forward and shared so that "truth shall prevail."

### Examples

Examples of prosecutorial misconduct typically involve ignoring the procedural protections of due process. When prosecutors are too zealous in their attempts to obtain a conviction, their role as officer of the court is ignored and they become judge and jury. A *Chicago Tribune* investigation found that since 1963, 381 defendants across the country have had a homicide conviction thrown out because prosecutors concealed exculpatory evidence or presented evidence they knew to be false. Of the 381, 67 had been sentenced to death and were exonerated by DNA evidence or independent investigations. Nearly 30 of the 67 on death row were freed, but they served between 5 and 26 years before their convictions were reversed (Armstrong and Possley, 2002). The prosecutorial misconduct included the following:

- Concealed evidence that discredited their star witnesses, pointed to other suspects, or supported defendants' claim of self-defense
- Suppressed evidence that the murder occurred when the defendant had an alibi, or where the murder occurred
- Depicted red paint as blood
- Portrayed hog blood as human
- Suppressed statements of eyewitnesses that offenders were white when prosecuting two black men
- Received a knife from a crime scene from police but hid it, and when defendant argued that he killed after he had been stabbed with the knife, the prosecutor challenged the defense because of the absence of a knife
- Hid a victim's gun when the defendant argued self-defense
- Hid an iron pipe the victim had used to attack the defendant
- Hid blood-spatter expert's report that supported the defendant's version of events

- Withheld evidence suggesting that a police informant had framed the defendant
- Concealed evidence indicating their chief witness was the killer, not the defendant (Armstrong and Possley, 2002)

## Sanctions

There are very few controls on the behavior of prosecutors in the courtroom. Voters have some control over who becomes a prosecutor, but once in office most prosecutors stay in the good graces of a voting public unless there is a major scandal or an energetic competitor. In cities, most work is conducted by assistant prosecutors, who are hired rather than elected. Misconduct in the courtroom is sometimes orally sanctioned by trial judges. Perhaps an appellate decision may overturn a conviction, but prosecutors are rarely punished even when cases are overturned. In the "In the News" box, it seems clear that identifying misconduct by prosecutors does not automatically result in sanctions for them.

Gershman (1991) writes that prosecutors misbehave because it works and they can get away with it. Because misconduct is scrutinized only when the defense attorney makes an objection and then files an appeal (and even then the appellate court may rule that it was a harmless error), there is a great deal of incentive to use improper tactics in the courtroom. The main reason prosecutors engage in misconduct is that they want to win and there is very little chance of their being punished.

The Supreme Court has ruled that prosecutors cannot be subject to civil suits against them even in cases of egregious rule breaking. The most important fact uncovered in the *Chicago Tribune* investigation was that not one of the prosecutors was convicted of a crime, and none were even disbarred. Some became judges or district attorneys, and one became a congressman! (Armstrong and Possley, 2002).

---

**IN THE NEWS  Prosecutor Misconduct**

Serious errors or misconduct on the part of Bronx prosecutors has led to the false imprisonment of several defendants. Actions by prosecutors included inappropriate closing arguments and failing to disclose exculpatory evidence. None of the prosecutors involved in the cases were disciplined. In one case a man who spent 7 years in prison received a $5-million settlement because the prosecutor hid evidence that the accuser was not credible. It has been reported that since 1970 there have been more than 2,000 cases of prosecutorial misconduct that resulted in dismissed charges, reversed convictions, or reduced sentences.

Source: A. Elliott and B. Weiser, "When Prosecutors Err, Others Pay the Price," NYTimes.com, 2004. Retrieved on March 23, 2004, from http://www.nytimes.com/2004/03/21/nyregion/-21prosecute.html.

---

*What do you think should happen to a prosecutor who withholds evidence in a criminal case?*

# Conclusion

In this chapter we have examined the source of legal ethics and the reasons that the public seems to have such a poor opinion of the ethics of legal professionals. One might expect that the public's respect and trust for legal professionals, as guardians of the justice system, would be high, but that is not the case. Part of the reason is the ability to take "either side" in a controversy. Also, the advocacy role that attorneys embrace at times justifies "means" that appear to be and even may be ethically questionable.

In the practice of criminal law, one side is represented by the defense attorney, and the other is represented by the prosecutor. There are similar duties for both parties, but there are also crucial differences in the duties and ethical responsibilities of these professionals. The prosecutor's goal is justice, which should imply an objective pursuit of the truth; however, we know that in a few cases, the only goal seems to be winning.

# Key Terms

**asset forfeiture**  a legal tool to confiscate property and money associated with organized criminal activity

**attorney–client privilege**  the legal rule by which an attorney cannot (even through subpoena or threat of contempt) disclose confidential information regarding his or her client

**criminalistics**  the profession involved in the application of science to recognize, identify, and evaluate physical evidence

**halo effect**  the phenomenon in which a person with expertise or status in one area is given deference in all areas

**plea bargain**  an exchange of a guilty plea for a reduced charge or sentence

**shadow jury**  a panel of people selected by the defense attorney to represent the actual jury that sits through the trial and provides feedback to the attorney on the evidence being presented during the trial

**situational model**  a model in which lawyers weigh the priorities in each case and decide each case on the particular factors present

**systems model**  an absolute or legalistic model in that an attorney's behavior would always be considered wrong or right depending on the ethical rule guiding the definition

**tort reform**  legislation that limits the nature of personal injury lawsuits, either by restricting the type of suit, who can be sued, or the amount of damages

# Review Questions

1. What do polls show regarding the public's attitude toward attorneys?
2. Where do rules of behavior for attorneys come from, and how are they enforced?

3. Describe the moral agent, legal agent, and special relationship views of the attorney–client relationship.
4. What is Cohen's position regarding the lawyer's role? How do Memory and Rose criticize this position?
5. Explain the confidentiality rules of defense attorneys, and explain some situations where they may be able to disclose confidential information.
6. Compare the potential conflicts of interest of defense attorney and those of prosecutors.
7. Compare the potential zealous defense issues of defense attorneys and those of prosecutors.
8. Discuss what jury consultants do and why they have been criticized.
9. Discuss the various forms of forensic testimony and why they have been criticized.
10. List and describe the kinds of misconduct engaged in by prosecutors.

# Discussion Questions

1. Should attorneys pursue the wishes of their clients even if they think it is not in the clients' best interest? What if it would hurt a third party (but not be illegal)?
2. Would you be able to zealously defend Timothy McVeigh (convicted in the Oklahoma City bombing of a federal building)? Why or why not? Would you be able to defend a terrorist caught and tried for the World Trade Center bombing?
3. Do you think that attorneys should maintain confidentiality if their clients are involved in ongoing criminal activity that is not inherently dangerous?
4. A prosecutor was working with police in a standoff between a triple murderer and police. When the murderer demanded to talk to a public defender, the police did not want to have a public defender get involved, so the prosecutor pretended to be one. He spoke with the suspect on the telephone and lied about his name and being a public defender; the man then surrendered to police. The prosecutor was sanctioned by the state bar for misrepresentation and was put on probation and required to take twenty hours of continuing legal education in ethics, pass the Multistate Professional Responsibility Examination, and be supervised by another attorney (Tarnoff, 2001). Do you think he did the right thing? Why or why not?
5. Are the following actions of a prosecutor legal? Are they ethical?
   - Authorizing the arrest of one brother for drugs, even though the prosecutor knows the charge would be thrown out (but the young man would lose a scholarship to college), in order to have leverage so that he would give evidence against his brother
   - Announcing a suspect of a drive-by shooting to the media so that the offender is in danger from the rival gang members, and then offering protective custody only if the man will plead guilty
   - Authorizing the arrest of a ten-year-old boy who confessed to a crime, even though there was no serious possibility that he was guilty, in order to pressure a relative to confess

The nomination and ultimate confirmation of John Roberts in 2005 illustrated the
intense partisanship that accompanies the selection of Supreme Court justices.
Is this partisanship *despite* judicial objectivity or *because of* the fallacy of the concept?

# 11

# Justice and Judicial Ethics

*Perceptions of Judicial Processing*

*Ethical Issues for Judges*

*Justice on Trial?*

*Judicial Independence and the Constitution*

*Conclusion*

## Key Terms

bureaucratic justice
confirmatory bias
exclusionary rule
federal sentencing
  guidelines
innocence projects
interpretationist

natural rights
recuse
strict constructionist
wedding-cake
  illustration

# Chapter Objectives

1. Understand the various perceptions of judicial processing.

2. Understand the responsibilities and challenges of judges in the criminal justice system.

3. Become familiar with the criticisms of the justice system, including those that allege that it perpetuates racism and social inequities.

4. Understand the concept of natural law and the perception of the source of rights.

Many people refer to the criminal justice system as the criminal *injustice* system because of a perception that practices in this nation's courtrooms do not necessarily conform to the ideals of justice. As mentioned in previous chapters, justice is a goal that is not necessarily synonymous with law, and a legal system may not always be capable of achieving moral justice. The basic elements of a justice system are an impartial fact-finding process and a fair and equitable resolution. There is no person more important in this process than the person wearing the judicial robe. In this chapter we will examine the role of the judge in the judicial process. However, it is important to first identify the various perceptions of the judicial process.

# Perceptions of Judicial Processing

The ideal of the justice system is that two advocates of equal ability will engage in a pursuit of truth, guided by a neutral judge. The truth is supposed to emerge from the contest. Actual practices in our justice system are very different. Various descriptions profess to offer a more realistic picture of the system. One approach is to look at judicial processing as a game. "Hidden agendas" (covert motivations and goals) exist. The adversarial system pits the defense attorney against the prosecutor, and the judge may be considered the umpire in this contest. The judge sets down the rules and, unless there is a jury, decides who wins the contest.

Does the "best" opponent always win? If a powerful and rich defendant is able to hire the best criminal lawyer in the country, complete with several assistants and investigators, the prosecutor (who is typically overworked and understaffed) may be overwhelmed. Of course, this is the exception, and more commonly a defendant must rely on an overworked and probably inexperienced public defender or an attorney who can make criminal law profitable only by high caseloads and quick turnover. In these instances, the defense is outmatched by a prosecutor in a public office with greater access to evidence and investigative assistance. Heffernan and Kleinig (2000) discuss how poverty affects a wide range of judicial processing decisions. It is hard to refute the notion that one's socioeconomic status affects one's experience in the justice system.

A variation of game theory is offered by Blumberg (1969), who refers to the practice of law as a *confidence game* because both prosecutor and defense attorney conspire to appear as something they are not—adversaries in a do-or-die situation. What is more commonly the case is that the prosecutor and the defense attorney will still be working together when the client is gone; thus, their primary allegiance is not to the client, but to themselves. For defense attorneys, this may involve either making the case appear more difficult than it is in order to justify their fee or, if the client has no resources, arbitrarily concluding a case that has merit.

Attorneys and judges may conspire against the client, as in the following example cited by Blumberg (1969: 329):

> [Judges] . . . will adjourn the case of an accused in jail awaiting plea or sentence if the attorney requests such action. While explicitly this may be done for some innocuous and seemingly valid reason, the tacit purpose is that pressure is being applied by the attorney for the collection of his fee, which he knows will probably not be forthcoming if the case is concluded.

The game here is to make the client believe that the advocacy system is working for him or her whereas, in reality, it is being used against his or her interest. Other examples include attorneys asking for continuances because of a missing witness—"Mr. Green"—which, in reality, means simply that the attorney hasn't been paid yet and wants the court to exert pressure by keeping the client in jail or continuing the pending criminal case until payment is rendered.

For this charade to be successful, all players in the system must cooperate; evidently, in many situations they do. Great shows of anger and emotion in the courtroom help clients believe that they are getting something for their money, but such performances are belied by the jocular relationship sometimes apparent between the defense attorney and the prosecutor shortly after trial or between courtroom sessions. In fact, many defense attorneys are ex-prosecutors. In some respects, this is helpful to their clients because they know the way the prosecutor's office works and what a reasonable plea offer would be. But one must also assume that the prosecutorial experience of these attorneys has shaped their perceptions of clients and what would be considered fair punishment. Moreover, their continuing relationships with prosecutors overlap into their social and personal lives, so it is not surprising that allegiances are more often lawyers against civilians, rather than defense versus prosecution. Judges are also a part of this social network and often have close personal relationships with the attorneys who practice in front of them.

Other authors have also used the analogy of a confidence game to describe the interaction among prosecutors, defense attorneys, and clients. For example, Scheingold (1984: 155) writes the following:

> [T]he practice of defense law is all too often a "confidence game" in which the lawyers are "double agents" who give the appearance of assiduous defense of their clients but whose real loyalty is to the criminal courts. The defendant, from this

perspective, is only an episode in the attorney's enduring relationships with the prosecutors and judges whose goodwill is essential to a successful career in the defense bar.

Another perspective describes our courts as administering **bureaucratic justice**. Each case is seen as only one of many for the professionals who work in the system, and the actors merely follow the rules and walk through the steps. The goal of the system—namely, bureaucratic efficiency—becomes more important than the original goal of justice. Also, because each case is part of a workload, decision making takes on more complications. For instance, a defense lawyer may be less inclined to fight very hard for a "loser" client if he or she wants a favor for another client later in the week. The prosecutor may decide not to charge a guilty person in order to get him or her to testify against someone else. In this sense, each case is not separately tried and judged, but is linked to others and processed as part of a workload.

The bureaucratic system of justice is seen as developing procedures and policies that, although not intentionally discriminatory, may contribute to a perception of unfairness. For instance, a major element in bureaucratic justice is the presumption of guilt, whereas the ideal of our justice system is a presumption of innocence. District attorneys, judges, and even defense attorneys approach each case presuming guilt and place a priority on achieving the most expeditious resolution of the case. This is the basic rationale behind plea bargaining, whether it is recognized or not: The defendant is presumed to be guilty, and the negotiation is to achieve a guilty plea while bargaining for the best possible sentence—the lowest possible sentence is the goal of the defense whereas the highest possible sentence is the goal of the prosecutor. Plea bargaining is consistent with the bureaucratic justice system because it is the most efficient way of getting maximum punishment for minimum work.

Descriptions of bureaucratic justice such as the following (Scheingold, 1984: 158) allow for the fact that efficiency is tempered with other values and priorities:

> [T]he coercive thrust of the presumption of guilt is softened somewhat by the operational morality of fairness that leads the participants to make certain that defendants get neither more nor less than is coming to them—that defendants, in other words, get their due.

Scheingold is referring to the practices of judges, prosecutors, and defense attorneys who adapt the system to their personal standards of justice. This is exemplified by a judge who determines that an individual offender is a threat to society and so overlooks errors during trial to make sure that the individual ends up in prison. On the other hand, a person who is legally guilty might get a break because it is determined that he is a decent guy who made a mistake rather than a "crook." Moreover, in almost all cases there may be general consensus on both sides about what is fair punishment for any given offender. Defense attorneys who argue for unrealistically low sentences do so in a desultory and uncommitted fashion, knowing that the prosecutor would not and could not offer such a sentence. Prosecutors put up very little argument when defense attorneys ask for sentences that fit office guidelines.

Instead of describing the justice system as one that practices the presumption of innocence and takes careful steps to determine guilt, what may be more realistic is to view it as a system wherein all participants assume guilt, take superficial steps to arrive at the punishment phase, and operate under a value system that allocates punishment and mercy to offenders according to an informal consensus of fairness. It should be noted that there has been increased influence from victims in this process so that today what is "fair" may also be determined by the victim's wishes. Prosecutors may not agree to a plea bargain if the victim actively opposes it. Only in cases where the victim does not take an active part does the bureaucratic system operate unfettered (Stickels, 2003).

One other perception of the criminal justice system is that of Samuel Walker's (1985) **wedding-cake illustration,** based on a model proposed by Lawrence Friedman and Robert Percival. In this scheme, the largest portion of criminal cases form the bottom layers of the cake, and the few "serious" cases form the top layer. The top layer is most dramatically represented by cases such as the murder trial of O. J. Simpson. In this highly publicized case, the defendant had an extremely skilled (and highly paid) team of attorneys as well as trial consultants, investigators, and public relations specialists. Los Angeles County paid millions to keep up with its own team of attorneys, experts, and investigators. The criminal processing and trial proceeded with admirable speed. Each side worked incredibly hard and used an arsenal of tactics (that were then critiqued by armchair experts each evening). The case itself was used in law school evidence classes because of the wealth of material present in pretrial discovery, exclusionary motions, jury selection, and the like. The bottom of the cake is represented by the thousands of cases that are processed every year in which defendants may meet with an attorney only once or twice immediately before agreeing to a plea arrangement.

It is no wonder that many believe that justice is for sale in this country, with lawyers as the panderers. Because the public is exposed only to the top of the wedding cake, it develops a highly distorted perception of the system. The majority of the U.S. public is perhaps disgusted with the multitude of evidentiary rules and the Byzantine process of the trial itself. However, these concerns may be valid only for a very small portion of criminal cases. According to Walker's wedding-cake analysis, the courtroom work group is believed to share definitions of seriousness and operate as a unit to keep the dynamics of the courtroom static, despite changes that are forced upon it.

Changes such as the exclusionary rule, determinate sentencing, and other recent legislation have had surprisingly little impact on court outcomes because of a shared perception of serious crime and appropriate punishment. The vast majority of crime is considered trivial, and the processing of these cases involves very little energy or attention from system actors (Walker, 1985).

Dershowitz's view of the criminal justice system (see Box 11-1 on the next page) is probably, as Dershowitz admits himself, a bit overstated, but it is a slightly different illustration of the courtroom work group or bureaucratic justice system in operation. The major ethical problem with this (if it does represent reality) is that innocence, truth, and due process are perceived as inconvenient and expendable.

---

**BOX 11-1 Rules of the Justice Game**

Rule I: Almost all criminal defendants are, in fact, guilty.

Rule II: All criminal defense lawyers, prosecutors, and judges understand and believe Rule I.

Rule III: It is easier to convict guilty defendants by violating the Constitution than by complying with it, and in some cases it is impossible to convict guilty defendants without violating the Constitution.

Rule IV: Almost all police lie about whether they violated the Constitution in order to convict guilty defendants.

Rule V: All prosecutors, judges, and defense attorneys are aware of Rule IV.

Rule VI: Many prosecutors implicitly encourage police to lie about whether they violated the Constitution in order to convict guilty defendants.

Rule VII: All judges are aware of Rule VI.

Rule VIII: Most trial judges pretend to believe police officers who they know are lying.

Rule IX: All appellate judges are aware of Rule VIII, yet many pretend to believe the trial judges who pretend to believe the lying police officers.

Rule X: Most judges disbelieve defendants about whether their constitutional rights have been violated, even if they are telling the truth.

Rule XI: Most judges and prosecutors would not knowingly convict a defendant whom they believe to be innocent of the crime charged (or a closely related crime).

Rule XII: Rule XI does not apply to members of organized crime, drug dealers, career criminals, or potential informers.

Rule XIII: Nobody really wants justice.

SOURCE: Alan Dershowitz, *The Best Defense* (New York: Vintage, 1982): xxi.

---

# Ethical Issues for Judges

Perhaps the most well-known symbol of justice is the judge in his or her black robe. Judges are expected to be impartial, knowledgeable, and authoritative. They guide the prosecutor, defense attorney, and all the other actors in the trial process from beginning to end, helping to maintain the integrity of the proceeding. This is the ideal, but judges are human, with human failings.

## *Ethical Guidelines*

To help guide judges in their duties, the Model Code of Judicial Conduct was developed by the American Bar Association. The latest revision, undertaken in the summer of 2005, is still in a preliminary draft form. This code identifies the ethical considerations unique to judges. The primary theme of judicial ethics is impartiality. If we trust the judge to give objective rulings, then we must be confident that his or her objectivity isn't marred by any type of bias. The five canons of the code cover the following areas:

1. Impropriety and the appearance of impropriety
2. Impartiality and diligence
3. Personal affairs
4. Extra-judicial activities
5. Political activity

Judges should not let their personal prejudices influence their decisions. To avoid this possibility, the ABA's code specifies that each judge should try to avoid all appearance of bias as well as actual bias. Judges must be careful to avoid financial involvements or personal relationships that may threaten objectivity. We expect judges, like police officers and prosecutors, to conform to higher standards of behavior than the rest of us. Therefore, any hint of scandal in their private lives also calls into question their professional ethics. The obvious rationale is that judges who have less than admirable personal values cannot judge others objectively and that those judges who are less than honest in their financial dealings do not have a right to sit in judgment of others.

There are a number of problematic issues in the perceived objectivity of judges. For instance, in those states where judges are elected, the judges must solicit campaign contributions. These monies are most often obtained from attorneys, and it is not at all unusual for judges to accept money from attorneys who practice before them. In fact, quite often the judge's campaign manager is a practicing attorney. Does this not provide at least the appearance of impropriety? This situation is exacerbated in jurisdictions that use court appointments as the method for indigent representation. In these jurisdictions, judges hand out appointments to the same attorneys who give money back in the form of campaign contributions, or have other ties to the judge. In one jurisdiction, it was discovered that a female attorney in her first year out of law school received appointments totaling more than $100,000 from a family court judge with whom she had a personal relationship (Harper, 1992: A9). Obviously, the appearance, if not the actuality, of bias is present in such a situation.

The practice of awarding indigent cases to one's friends or for reasons other than qualifications may not only be unethical but may also have serious consequences for the defendant. A Texas Bar Report called "Muting Gideon's Trumpet: The Crisis in Indigent Defense" (2000) reported that many capital cases were appointed to friends of judges and to lawyers who were known for speeding cases through the system. Some lawyers who received appointments had been disciplined by the state bar. The 2001 Fair Defense Act of Texas requires counties to appoint qualified attorneys and pay fair fees, but the fact is that indigent defense, when run on the appointment system, creates a potential for abuse.

## Use of Discretion

Judges' discretion occurs in two major areas: interpretation of the law and sentencing. The first area is in the interpretation of the law in court cases. For instance, a judge might be called upon to assess the legality of evidence and make rulings on the various objections raised by both the prosecutors and the defense attorneys. A judge also writes the extremely important instructions to the jury. These are crucial because they set up the legal questions and definitions of the case. Judges must rule on the legality of evidence; they may make a decision to exclude a confession or a piece of evidence because of the way it was obtained and by so doing allow the guilty to go free.

The **exclusionary rule** has generated a storm of controversy because it can result in a guilty party avoiding punishment because of an error committed by the police. The basis for the exclusionary rule is that a fair society cannot accept a conviction based on tainted evidence. The ideals of justice reject such a conviction because accepting tainted evidence, even if obtained against a guilty party, is a short step away from accepting any type of evidence, no matter how illegal, and thus poses a threat to the whole concept of due process. The conviction is so violative of due process that it is ruled void. A more practical argument for the exclusionary rule is that if we want police officers to behave in a legal manner, then we must have heavy sanctions against illegalities. Arguably, if convictions are lost due to illegal evidence collection, police will reform their behavior. Actual practice provides little support for this argument, though. As can be seen below, police have learned how to get around the exclusionary rule, and in any event, cases lost on appeal are so far removed from the day-to-day decision making of the police that they have little effect on police behavior.

Court decisions have created several exceptions to the exclusionary rule. Judges can now rule that the evidence be allowed because of public safety, good faith, or inevitable-discovery exceptions. Those who decide to exclude evidence and set aside convictions do so by disregarding short-term effects for more abstract principles— specifically, the protection of due process. Do the ethical frameworks justify allowing a guilty person to go free because of "tainted" evidence?

- Religious ethics doesn't give us much help unless we decide that this ethical system would support vengeance and thus would permit the judge to ignore the exclusionary rule in order to punish a criminal. On the other hand, religious ethics might also support letting the criminal go free to answer to an ultimate higher authority, for human judgment was in this case imperfect.
- Egoism would support the decision to let a criminal go free or not, depending on the effect it would have on the judge's well-being.
- Ethical formalism's categorical imperative would support the exclusionary rule, on one hand, because one would not want a universal rule accepting tainted evidence. On the other hand, one would have to agree to retry all criminals, regardless of the severity of the crime, whenever the evidence was tainted, despite the possibility of further crime or harm to individuals.
- Act utilitarianism would support ignoring the exclusionary rule if the crime was especially serious or if there was a good chance the offender would not be retried successfully. The utility derived from ignoring the rule would outweigh the good. However, rule utilitarianism could be used to support the exclusionary rule, for the long-term effect of allowing illegal police behavior would be more serious than letting one criminal go free.

The judge is called upon to decide many and various questions throughout a trial. Of course, he or she is guided by the law and legal precedent, but in most cases each decision involves a substantial element of subjectivity. Judges have the power to make it difficult for either the prosecutor or the defense attorney through their pattern of rulings on objections, evidence admitted, and even personal attitude toward an attorney, which is always noted by the jury members and is influential in their decision.

Despite the belief that simply applying the rules will lead to the right conclusion or decision, the reality is that judges and justices are simply human and have very real biases influencing their decision making. The suspicion that some appellate court judges decide where they want to end up and make up the argument to get there is one that is hard to deny after analysis of certain cases. At times, appellate decision making seems to reflect a complete absence of "equity" thinking (basic fairness) in place of hyper-technical application of rules. Cases that are denied because a deadline was missed or appeals denied because they were not drawn up in the correct fashion are examples of this application of discretion.

**EXERCISE How Would You Rule?**

Assume you are a judge with the appropriate jurisdiction to decide the following:

1. You are a judge who must decide whether to allow the jury to consider a lower level of homicide for Andrea Yates. She drowned all five of her children in the bathtub and then called police. Although the jury makes the factual judgment, the judge decides if, as a matter of law, there is enough evidence to consider a lower charge.
2. You are an appellate judge and must decide whether to set aside a conviction of a woman who murdered an infant. The defense alleges that the sheriff violated attorney–client privilege by obtaining a warrant to seize a map drawn by the convicted woman showing where the baby was buried. She drew the map for her lawyer, and, as such, legal experts contend it should be protected under the attorney–client privilege. The trial judge granted the warrant because of testimony by the sheriff and his deputies that they believed the baby might still be alive and they needed the map to find him, but evidence presented to you indicates that all the law enforcement officials involved believed that the baby was dead and wanted the map only to help convict the offender. There is overwhelming evidence of guilt, and a new trial would subject the parents to continued reminders of their loss. What would you do?
3. You must decide whether a particular piece of artwork is obscene. The artist has painted a series of sex scenes, including bondage, sadomasochism, bestiality, and necrophilia, interspersed with paintings of nude children at play. She states that her art has redeeming social qualities because it is a statement of the many faces of humanity. The series of paintings is being displayed in a public gallery supported by city and federal funds. The district attorney has filed for an injunction to close the show due to obscenity. How would you rule? How did you make your decision?

For example, in the case of Delma Banks, lawyers were denied a clemency hearing from the State Board of Pardons and Paroles despite the fact that there was new forensic evidence that Banks was out of town when the murder he was convicted of occurred, one of the chief prosecution witnesses was coached, and the transcript of the coaching was deliberately withheld from the defense for close to nineteen years and finally surrendered only when ordered by a federal district judge. The reason the board denied the petition? It was filed one week late (Pasztor, 2003a, 2003b).

Judges may simply apply black-and-white rules, or they may attempt to enact the "spirit of justice." At times, however, even those who believe their job is simply to apply the rules find that there are no bright-line rules or that they are difficult to interpret in specific cases, such as in the exercise on page 365.

### Sentencing

The second area of judicial discretion is in sentencing. The following makes clear the small amount of training judges receive for this awesome responsibility (L. Johnson, 1982: 20):

> Few judges have the benefit of judicial training sessions prior to embarking upon the often bewildering and frequently frustrating task of pursuing that vague, if not indefinable, entity so commonly known as justice. . . . Thus, it is not uncommon for the new judge, relying upon a philosophy often formulated hastily, to be placed in the unenviable position of pronouncing a sentence upon another human being without any special preparation.

Judges' decisions are scrutinized by public watchdog groups and appellate-level courts. In fact, one wonders if judges aren't overly influenced in their sentencing by the current clamor for strict punishments. However, if judges are supposed to enact community sentiment, perhaps it is proper for them to reflect its influence. Is there one just punishment for a certain type of offender, or does the definition of what is just depend on community opinion of the crime, the criminal, and the time? After completing the exercise "How Would You Rule?" below, do you think your views on sentencing have changed any?

---

### EXERCISE   How Would You Rule?

Assume you are a judge who must sentence the following people:

1. A young woman who was led into drug use and sales by her stepfather, who had been sleeping with her since she was eleven
2. A father who killed the man who molested his child
3. An honors college student who drank at a fraternity rush party, drove back to the dorm, and, on the way, ran over a pedestrian and killed her
4. A poor single mother who embezzled money from her employer to pay for her child's needed surgery since the employer did not provide health insurance

Evidence indicates that the decision making of judges is actually based on personal standards, for no consistency seems to appear between the decisions of individual judges in the same community. One study found that two judges in Louisiana had remarkably different records on numbers of convictions. The two also differed in their patterns of sentencing (Pinkele and Louthan, 1985: 58). Hofer, Blackwell, and Ruback (1999) point out that most sentencing disparity in the federal system before sentencing guidelines came into effect occurred because of different patterns exhibited by individual judges. They cite studies that found, for instance, that judges' sentences were influenced by whether they had been prosecutors and by their religion.

The other extreme is when judges have no discretion in sentencing. **Federal sentencing guidelines** are written by Congress and require the judge to impose a specific sentence unless there is a proven mitigating or aggravating factor in the case. Hofer, Blackwell, and Ruback (1999) examined the effect of guidelines on federal sentencing disparity and concluded that they had a small but significant effect on reducing disparity. However, there were some areas that were resistant, including regional differences in drug sentencing.

The federal sentencing guidelines have received a great deal of criticism because of the draconian sentences applied to drug crimes. A racial bias is alleged since crack cocaine receives a sentence that is one hundred times longer than that given for powder cocaine. The argument supporting this disparity is that crack cocaine is more associated with other crimes and there are good reasons for distinguishing the two; however, there is a widespread belief that the disparity is simply racism in action, for African Americans are much more likely to be convicted of crack crimes and whites for powder cocaine (Hofer et al., 1999). Some federal judges, such as Lawrence Irving in 1991, have been so appalled by the sentences that they have refused to sentence or even quit, rather than impose the mandated sentences (Tonry, 2005: 43).

Recently, the U.S. Supreme Court has ruled on the constitutionality of sentencing guidelines. In January 2005, it ruled that the defendant's Sixth Amendment rights were violated if the judges used elements to increase the sentence without first proving such elements in a court of law. They ruled that if this occurred, the guidelines should be advisory rather than mandatory. However, they also ruled that this finding would not be retroactive, so all the thousands of individuals who have already been sentenced under what is now considered to be unconstitutional procedures cannot appeal their sentence on the basis of the ruling (*United States v. Booker,* 125 S.Ct. 1006 [2005]). See the Policy Box 11-1 for a discussion.

## Judicial Misconduct

Examples of judicial misconduct are fairly rare, perhaps because judges' behavior is more shielded than other actors in the system. Operation Greylord in Chicago is probably the most well-known exposé of widescale judicial corruption. This investigation resulted in convictions of thirty-one attorneys and eight judges for bribery. Judges accepted bribes to "fix" cases, meaning to rule in favor of the attorney offering the

---

**POLICY BOX 11-1** **Sentencing Guidelines**

There has been widespread controversy concerning the federal sentencing guidelines. The original use of sentencing guidelines was quite different. They emerged in the 1970s and early 1980s as a response to criticism that indeterminate sentencing created disparity. Guidelines were created by collecting the sentencing of all the judges in a jurisdiction and averaging their sentences, then presenting the average sentence to the judges, who would determine whether or not they could agree to that number. Then the guidelines would be available for all to use, but judges would not be required to do so if they felt that a particular individual deserved more or less of a sentence. Federal guidelines were mandatory, and they were set by Congress, not the judges themselves.

**Law:** Recent Supreme Court cases have ruled unconstitutional the use of guidelines except as advisory because to establish a sentence, these guidelines used evidence that had not been proven in court. Supreme Court justices were also troubled by the arbitrary nature of what are, in effect, mandatory sentences. Congress has vowed to rewrite the laws establishing guidelines in order to ensure their continued existence despite the rulings of the Supreme Court.

**Policy:** After the Supreme Court held that the federal guidelines were unconstitutional, some circuits stopped using them, some continued to use them on a voluntary basis, and some used them but allowed individual judges to follow their conscience in individual cases.

**Ethics:** The federal sentencing guidelines have always been controversial in that many federal judges believe the sentences are too harsh for drug offenders, and they have chafed at the lack of discretion allowed in sentencing. Several federal judges have, in fact, resigned over their objections to the guidelines. When a federal judge believes that justice is not served by the sentence given by the guideline, he or she has an ethical dilemma. Members of Congress also have an ethical issue in the disparity between crack cocaine and powder cocaine and their unwillingness to do anything about it, even if it is to explain the differential because of their belief that the two types of the same drug require different punishments.

---

bribe. Not unlike law enforcement's "blue curtain of secrecy," not one attorney came forward to expose this system of corruption, even though what was occurring was fairly well-known (Weber, 1987: 60).

Neutrality is questioned when judges voice strong opinions on issues or cases. Talking to the media used to be rare, but now many judges find a venue to express their views, take a stand, and act as advocate. Many question this role for judges, and judges have needed to **recuse** themselves—step down and allow another judge to take over the trial—when they have indicated to news media that they already had opinions on a case before it was concluded.

Some question judges' motives in allowing cameras in the courtroom—personal vanity rather than the interests of justice could be an issue. There seems to be real concern that judges and lawyers play to the camera, perhaps to the detriment of the swift resolution of the case. Judges' relationships with other actors in the courtroom always raise suspicion of bias. For instance, in the O. J. Simpson case the fact that Judge Ito was married to a homicide detective caused many to question whether he could be objective when the defense planned to attack the credibility of police procedure. However, because many of those who work in the justice system develop friendships, socialize, and sometimes marry others in the system, to recuse oneself from every case that involved some overlapping acquaintances or relations would be impossible for many judges.

Courtroom decorum is established by the judge, and if he or she displays an irreverent or self-aggrandizing attitude or flaunts the law, his or her behavior degrades the entire judicial process. Some judges seem to be overly influenced by their power—as was the case of one district court judge who instructed courtroom workers to address him as "God." Most courtroom gossip includes the idiosyncrasies of some judges, such as the judge who was reputed to keep a gun under his robes and point it at tardy attorneys, the judge who arrested citizens in the hall outside his courtroom for creating a public disturbance because they were talking during a court session, the judge who ordered a woman arrested for contempt when she wrote a scathing letter to a newspaper regarding his competence, the judge who sentenced a man to probation for killing his wife (excusing such behavior in open court with a statement indicating that the nagging victim deserved it), or the judge who signed an order of execution with a smiley face. These individuals illustrate that putting on a black robe doesn't necessarily give one the wisdom of Solomon. In the "In the News" box on page 370, the judges certainly seem to have forgotten their role.

Other forms of unethical behavior are less blatant. Judges have a duty to conclude judicial processing with reasonable punctuality. However, there are widespread delays in processing, and part of the reason is the lack of energy with which some judges pursue their dockets. In the same jurisdiction, and with a balanced assignment of cases, it is not unusual for one judge to have only a couple dozen pending cases and another judge to have literally hundreds. The reason is that some judges routinely allow numerous continuances, set trial dates far into the future, start the docket call at 10:00 A.M. and conclude the day's work at 3:00 P.M., and in other ways take a desultory approach to swift justice.

We must be careful not to paint with too broad a brush. The most egregious examples of unethical behavior, such as taking bribes or trampling the due-process rights of defendants, are performed by only a few judges, in the same way that extreme behaviors are committed by only a small percentage of police officers, defense attorneys, and prosecutors. Most judges are ethical and take great care to live up to the obligations of their role. However, as with the other criminal justice professionals, sometimes there are systemic biases and subtle ways in which the principles of justice and due process are subverted. It cannot be ignored that the justice system is assailed as violative of the rights of defendants, especially minorities.

**IN THE NEWS   Judicial Misconduct**

It was reported that 128 complaints were filed against Utah judges to the Judicial Conduct Commission in 2005. Two high-profile cases involved one judge who was arrested on drug charges and another who was charged with violating the law for not deciding juvenile cases by deadlines set by law. Members of the Utah Judicial Conduct Commission argue that Utah judges have fewer misconduct charges than other states, where judges have been disciplined for DUI, sexual harassment, and "using a sexual device while on the bench."

Source: G. Fattah, "Complaints Against Utah Judges Rise," 2005. Desertnews.com. Retrieved August 11, 2005, from http://desertnews.com/dn/print/1,1442,600154724,00.html.

A Texas judge earned the attention of the Texas Commission on Judicial Conduct when she held a party for a defendant who had jumped bail and was recaptured a year later. The defendant was brought into her court in handcuffs to be greeted by streamers, balloons, and a cake celebrating his return. He was not amused, especially when he found out that he had been sentenced to life in prison in *absentia*.

Source: Associated Press, 2004. CNN.com. Retrieved on October 26, 2004, from http://cnn.com/2004/LAW/10/26/prison.sendoff.ap/index.html.

*Do you think that the party was inappropriate? What sanctions, if any, should the judge receive?*

# Justice on Trial?

One of the reasons that many people distrust our justice system is that there seems to be a small—but steady—stream of cases in which prosecutors, along with police, deliberately ignore evidence, destroy exculpatory evidence, lie about evidence, or do not share exculpatory evidence with the defense. Radelet, Bedau, and Putnam (1992) gathered together dozens of capital cases where innocent defendants were convicted of crimes they did not commit. Some were sentenced to death. False convictions occurred because of incompetent defense counsel and unethical and illegal practices on the part of prosecutors and police. Scott Christianson (2004) has also gathered together forty-two recent cases where innocent people were convicted. The errors occurred largely through the actions of police, prosecutors, and judges who neglected their duty to be objective officers of the court and traded neutrality for an individual "ends"-based approach to their duties. Eyewitness perjury (sanctioned by the prosecutor), ineffective counsel, the use of false confessions, police misconduct, fabrication of evidence, and misuse of forensics were the reasons that these innocent people were convicted (Christianson, 2004). Their stories are chilling reminders that there are innocent people in prison.

The Delma Banks case illustrates the problem: Banks was convicted based on testimony of a police informant and a long-time drug offender who was promised a shorter sentence and coached to provide details of the crime scene. Neither of these facts was brought out at trial. Further, the jury pool was race-coded by prosecutors, and all African American jurors were excluded. Recent reanalysis of forensics indicates that the victim was killed possibly when Banks was out of town. Despite these new findings, the Texas Court of Criminal Appeals and the Board of Pardons and Paroles refused to stay the execution. The U.S. Supreme Court issued a writ of certiorari and granted a stay of execution, and, evidently refusing to ignore the very distinct possibility that an innocent man was to be executed, overturned the verdict and remanded the case for a new trial (Pasztor, 2003; *Banks v. Dretke*, 540 U.S. 668 [2004]).

Another case that illustrates the weakness of the system is the Clarence Brandley case. Brandley was a high school janitor in a small Texas town near Houston. In 1980 a young woman on a visiting girls' volleyball team disappeared while her team was practicing. The school was empty except for five janitors and the volleyball team. A search uncovered the girl's body in the school auditorium; it was later determined that she had been raped and strangled. Clarence Brandley and another janitor found the body and were the first to be interrogated by police. Brandley was black; the other janitor was white. The police officer who interrogated them reportedly said, "One of you two is going to hang for this." Then he said to Brandley, "Since you're the nigger, you're elected." Police and prosecutors then evidently began a concerted effort to get Brandley convicted:

- Evidence that might have been helpful to the defense was "lost" (such as Caucasian hairs near the girl's vagina that were never tested and compared to those of the other janitors).
- Witnesses were coerced into sticking to stories that inculpated Brandley (one of the janitors reported that he had been threatened with jail if he didn't promote the story supporting Brandley's guilt).
- Witnesses who came forward with contrary evidence were ignored and sent away (the father-in-law of one of the janitors who later became a prime suspect told the prosecutor that this man had told him where the girl's clothes would be found two days before police actually found them).
- Defense attorneys were not told of witnesses (such as a woman who came to the prosecutor after the second trial and stated that her common-law husband had confessed a murder to her and ran away the same night the girl's body had been found). This woman's husband had worked as a janitor at the school, had been fired a month previous to the murder, but had also been seen at the school the day of the murder.

What defense attorneys eventually discovered was that in all probability this man and another janitor had abducted and murdered the girl. The other janitors had seen the girl with these two men (not Brandley) but had lied during the two trials. Here are the words of an appellate judge who ruled on the motion for a new trial:

In the thirty years that this court has presided over matters in the judicial system, no case has presented a more shocking scenario of the effects of racial prejudice . . .

and public officials who for whatever motives lost sight of what is right and just. . . . The court unequivocally concludes that the color of Clarence Brandley's skin was a substantial factor which pervaded all aspects of the State's capital prosecution against him. (quoted in Radelet, Bedau, and Putnam, 1992: 134)

Yet, even after this finding, it took another *two years* for the Texas Court of Criminal Appeals to rule that Brandley deserved a new trial. Clarence Brandley served nine years on death row before his defense attorneys finally obtained his freedom. He was at one point six days away from execution.

Others have been executed, and only afterward did evidence or perpetrators' confessions exonerate the accused and expose the prosecution's misconduct that led to the miscarriage of justice (Radelet, Bedau, and Putnam, 1992). Whereas some of the cases described by Radelet, Bedau, and Putnam involved pure and extreme racial prejudice, probably a more common factor in misguided prosecution is a more subtle form of racism—one shared by many in the criminal justice system—a prejudgment of the guilt of the accused, especially if he is a black man. There is a pervasive stereotypical belief that all defendants are guilty, and most defendants are black. This thought pattern shapes and distorts decision making on the part of those prosecutors who sift and use evidence in a way to support their predetermined beliefs.

In Boston, Charles Stuart murdered his wife, threw her body into a river, and then faked a mugging. He described a fictional black assailant who robbed him and murdered his pregnant wife. In South Carolina, Susan Smith also described a fictional black assailant who abducted and killed her children, after she drowned them by driving her car into a lake with the children strapped in their car seats. Is it a coincidence that both chose African American men as their fictional criminals? Many argue that Stuart and Smith consciously or unconsciously relied on our common stereotype of blacks as criminals. Even though these cases did not result in a false finding of guilt for some innocent man, they could have. If Radelet, Bedau, and Putnam's facts are accurate, such miscarriages of justice have occurred and are probably continuing to occur.

When police or prosecutors allow their biases and prejudices to influence their decision making, evidence is lost or ignored, witnesses are discounted and disbelieved, tests aren't conducted, and true perpetrators literally "get away with murder" if there is a convenient suspect who looks guilty. When judges allow their biases to affect their rulings, the misconduct of the prosecutor and police is exacerbated. This is an ever-present and pervasive reality in our justice system and probably accounts for why there is such a divergence in the perceptions of blacks and whites regarding the fairness of the system. For instance, in a Gallup poll, 71 percent of whites said murder charges against O. J. Simpson were probably or definitely true, but only 28 percent of African Americans agreed (reported in Mitchell and Banks, 1996: B1). Is this a reflection of a different way of measuring evidence or a different perception of trust in law enforcement and legal professionals' ability to collect and interpret evidence? Is the lack of trust warranted? Unfortunately, the answer to that question is probably yes.

In a study conducted by the Columbia Law School, 68 percent of all death verdicts handed down between 1973 and 1995 were reversed due to serious errors.

**QUOTE and QUERY**

"Is it better for 100,000 guilty men to walk free rather than have one innocent man convicted? The cost–benefit policy answer is no" (prosecutor).

"No rate of preventable errors that destroy people's lives and destroy the lives of those close to them is acceptable" (law professor).

Source: Liptak (2004: 3).

*Which statement represents ethical formalism? Which statement represents utilitarian thinking?*

Since 1993, ninety death row inmates have been exonerated for the crimes of which they were accused. The errors involved defense lawyers' incompetence, but also police and prosecutors suppressing exculpatory evidence or engaging in other types of professional misconduct. Almost 10 percent of the cases sent back for retrial resulted in not-guilty verdicts. The study concluded that the high rate of errors occurred because of the indiscriminant use of the death penalty and factors such as race, politics, and poorly performing law enforcement systems (Columbia Law School, 2002). This study has led to a growing storm of controversy concerning the prevalence and causes of innocent defendants being convicted.

A law school study of 328 cases over the last 15 years in which the individuals were exonerated (usually by DNA) indicates that there may be thousands of innocent people in prison. Most of the cases that reach national attention are homicide and rape cases, so less serious cases, which may also suffer from the errors of mistaken eyewitness testimony, evidence withholding, and other misconduct, go undiscovered. Prosecutors have objected to the study's methodology, arguing that the study counted cases where the evidence was weak but the defendant might still be guilty. Further, they argue that the number of exonerations is quite small compared to the number of convictions. The study found 199 exonerations of murder suspects and 120 exonerations of rape suspects. It appeared that rape suspects who were mistakenly identified by victims were disproportionately black. There have also been 125 cases identified where the mistaken verdict depended upon false confessions, usually of the mentally ill, the mentally retarded, and juveniles (Liptak, 2004; Columbia Law School, 2002).

Another study reviewed different sources to estimate wrongful convictions and concluded that the range was 1 percent to 15 percent, depending on which sources were used (with inmate reports illustrating the higher figure) (Poveda, 2001). Even at the lower range, however, the number of innocent people imprisoned is quite substantial, given the fact that close to two million are incarcerated in prisons and jails.

It has been reported that the major cause of false convictions is mistaken eyewitness testimony. Although most people in the criminal justice system know that eyewitness testimony is notoriously unreliable, jurors don't, and prosecutors evidently rely on that misperception in order to gain convictions. Reasons for false conviction include the following:

- mistaken eyewitness testimony
- perjury by informants
- police and prosecutorial misconduct
- false confessions
- "junk science"
- ineffective assistance of counsel
- racial bias
- **"confirmatory bias"** (when a specific suspect has been fixated upon and other possibilities are ignored) (Schehr and Sears, 2005)

One of the most often cited reasons for false convictions (in addition to eyewitness testimony) is ineffective assistance of counsel. The legal standard for what constitutes ineffective counsel is set quite high—so high, in fact, that the "sleeping lawyer" case (discussed below) resulted in an appellate court finding that if a lawyer wasn't sleeping during a *crucial* part of the trial, it wasn't ineffective counsel. Other behaviors reported of lawyers in capital and other cases include the following:

- attorney use of heroin and cocaine during trial
- attorney letting defendant wear the same clothes described by victim
- attorney admitting that he didn't know the law or facts of the case
- attorney not being able to name a single death penalty case holding
- attorney drinking heavily each day of the trial and being arrested for a .27 blood alcohol level (Schehr and Sears, 2005)

What cannot be ignored is that for every case, there was a judge who did nothing to prevent the conviction even though these actions must have been obvious and harmful to the defendant's case.

Race seems to be a part of this phenomenon. As mentioned previously, wrongly accused rape suspects are disproportionately black. Further, race plays a part in the confirmatory bias mentioned above in that there is a stereotype that blacks are more likely to be criminals. Racial bias in wrongful convictions has been attributed to individual factors and structural factors. Structural factors include systemic bias against minorities in all institutions of society (political, economic, and social) that leads to different opportunities and treatment. Individual factors include these:

- racism
- higher error rate in cross-racial identification
- stereotyping
- lack of resources of defendant (Schehr and Sears, 2005)

**Innocence projects**, staffed by lawyers and law students, are springing up all around the country to reexamine and provide legal assistance to convicts when there is a probability that serious errors occurred in their prosecution. In 2004 it was reported that there were innocence projects in thirty-five states (Schehr and Weathered, 2004). Unfortunately, most of these projects are under-resourced and overwhelmed. Some argue that what is needed is a model such as Great Britain's Criminal Cases Review

Commission, which is a governmental agency rather than a volunteer and/or private organization. Others question the efficacy of Britain's model, arguing that

- It is subordinate to the Court of Appeal and thus deferential to it.
- It relies on untrained caseworkers to review cases.
- It relies on petitioners to raise claims.
- It is understaffed and pays too little attention to each case. (Schehr and Weathered, 2004)

Others argue that the innocence projects can serve an important purpose but that they must be better funded and not left to the vagaries of budget cuts (Schehr and Sears, 2005).

In Texas, between 1976 and 2002, 927 people were sentenced to death, 285 were executed, and 188 had sentences reduced—most for violations of procedure, but some because of fundamental errors or misconduct, such as withholding exculpatory evidence. Twelve were set free because their convictions were reversed and the state declined to retry, or they were acquitted on retrial (Hall, 2002: 124):

1. *Randall Dale Adams* was the subject of *The Thin Blue Line,* a documentary about his case. He was convicted in 1976 of killing a Dallas police officer who stopped a car driven by David Harris. Harris said Adams was the gunman; Adams said he wasn't even in the car. The state relied on an eyewitness who had picked someone else out of a lineup and Harris, a sixteen-year-old with a long juvenile record. Harris eventually confessed he killed the officer alone.
2. *Clarence Brandley,* discussed earlier, was the subject of a *60 Minutes* investigation that eventually led to his release. He was convicted of a 1980 rape and murder of a high school cheerleader. Police intimidated witnesses who had evidence that another had committed the crime, and the prosecutor lost evidence that could have proven his innocence. His conviction was overturned, and he was eventually freed.

## IN THE NEWS Innocence Project in Arizona

In Arizona, between 1974 and 2001, 7 of the 220 death-row inmates have been freed and 12 have had sentences reduced from death to time in prison ranging from 10 to 35 years. Some Arizona lawyers are now suggesting an innocence project to review all death-penalty cases, similar to the national projects. Arizona does have a law that sets no deadline for post-appeal DNA testing; thus, inmates like Larry Youngblood of Tucson, who spent over 10 years in prison for a conviction of sexual molestation, was freed when DNA tests proved he wasn't guilty.

Source: Sowers (2001).

*Do you think all states should review the cases of those on death row rather than depend on the volunteer services of attorneys working in innocence projects?*

3. *Ricardo Guerra* was convicted in 1982 of killing a police officer. Shots were fired from another's gun, and both the officer and the gun owner were killed. All evidence pointed to the dead man as the shooter, but prosecutors and police pursued a conviction against Guerra, hiding evidence pointing to the other suspect and bullying witnesses to lie. His conviction was overturned in 1997, and a federal court called the police misconduct outrageous.

4. *Kerry Max Cook* was convicted of sexually mutilating and killing a woman in 1977. His sentence was overturned in 1997 because the prosecution withheld evidence. DNA proved that semen stains on the victim's underwear belonged to her married boyfriend.

5. *Federico Macias* was convicted in 1984 of killing an El Paso couple. His defense attorney never called alibi witnesses. *Pro bono* appeal lawyers found witnesses and raised doubts, and the federal court overturned his conviction in 1992. The grand jury refused to re-indict. (Hall, 2002: 124–167)

Another case that might be added to the list of innocents is that of Cameron Todd Willingham. In what may be a tragic miscarriage of justice, he was put to death in February 2004. Willingham was convicted in the arson deaths of his three daughters. The arson evidence upon which he was convicted has since been repudiated, and four national arson experts claim that there was no evidence of arson, much less that Willingham used arson to kill his daughters. Despite their report and Willingham's pleadings of innocence, the State Board of Pardons and Paroles and the appellate courts did not stop the execution (Mills, 2005).

There are other cases where the Texas Court of Criminal Appeals failed to correct trial errors. For instance, the Calvin Burdine "sleeping lawyer" case received national attention when the Texas Court of Criminal Appeals held that Burdine did not deserve a new trial because there was no showing that the lawyer slept during *crucial* parts of the trial. Roy Criner challenged his conviction and ninety-nine-year sentence for rape because of a DNA test that showed the sperm in the victim was not Criner's. The trial judge ordered a new trial, the state appealed, and the Court of Criminal Appeals, in a five-to-three decision, denied the new evidence, arguing that it didn't establish innocence, for he could have used a condom or not ejaculated. In another case, a defendant who confessed because police threatened to have Mexican police harm his relatives was denied a new trial because the Court ruled it was "harmless error" (Hall, 2002).

The Texas Court of Criminal Appeals has been called the "worst court in Texas" for its seemingly irrational and mean-spirited holdings (Hall, 2004). The court was known as too liberal in the 1980s but swung completely toward the right in the Republican sweep of political offices that occurred in Texas when George W. Bush claimed the governor's mansion. It has since become even more conservative, and its holdings are attributed to the fact that seven of the nine members are former prosecutors who ran on a conservative law-and-order platform. Stung by criticism, in 2004 the Court of Criminal Appeals allocated $20 million to fund "innocence projects" in Texas law schools to investigate claims of wrongful convictions (Liptak and Blumenthal, 2004).

Ordinarily, state courts that lean too far in one direction would be adjusted by appellate decisions; however, the Fifth Circuit, the federal appellate court that

**QUOTE and QUERY**

A circuit that forty years ago was justly famous for implementing the mandates of the Bill of Rights and the Supreme Court respecting racial fairness is now justly notorious for its outright refusal to apply fundamental principles of due process to the criminal justice system.

Source: Eric Freedman, law professor at Hofstra University, quoted in Liptak and Blumenthal (2004: 4).

*Does it trouble you that the court's approach to rights seems to have something to do with who happens to be sitting on the bench?*

receives Texas cases, has been the target of criticism as well. It has been admonished by the U.S. Supreme Court because of what some call its "insolence" in not applying the holdings of the Supreme Court decisions to rehearings. In the case of Thomas Miller-El, the Supreme Court ruled in favor of the defendant's appeal based on systematic exclusion of black jurors in Dallas County and remanded the case to the Fifth Circuit. The judges on the Fifth Circuit then used (some say plagiarized) a dissent by Clarence Thomas to deny relief. The case was appealed to the Supreme Court again, and it once again granted relief and rebuked the court, ordering the Fifth Circuit to apply its legal reasoning (Liptak and Blumenthal, 2004; *Miller-El v. Dretke*, 125 St. Ct. 2317 [2005]). As the Quote and Query box indicates, the current position of the Fifth Circuit is unprecedented.

Legal scholars argue that the defiance displayed by the Fifth Circuit is extremely troubling because the U.S. Supreme Court takes only about eighty cases a year, and usually only those cases that illustrate a conflict between lower appellate courts. There is no room in the system to "fix" appellate decisions that defy precedent and Supreme Court rulings. One issue with the Fifth Circuit has been jury instructions that were ruled unconstitutional in 2001 and were still being used in cases that were upheld by the circuit court. In effect, the Fifth Circuit has been ignoring the Supreme Court ruling. Some of the individuals have already been executed (Liptak and Blumenthal, 2004).

The ideal, or vision, of our justice system is that it is fair, unbiased, and, through the application of due process, arrives at the truth before finding guilt and assessing punishment. The reality is that the law is administered by humans with human failings and that errors and misconduct result in innocent people being convicted, incarcerated, and sometimes executed. There is also a pervasive theme of racism in these miscarriages of justice. This indicates that something else is at work besides individuals not performing their duties and that what is wrong is more fundamental than simply bad or unethical decision making. In the last section, we continue to examine how judges' belief systems lead to judicial outcomes.

# Judicial Independence and the Constitution

Recall that discretion is the ability to make a decision and that discretion exists at each stage of the criminal justice system. Professionals at each stage have the opportunity to use their discretion wisely and ethically, or, alternatively, they may use their discretion unethically. In the courts, prosecutors have discretion to pursue prosecution or not, defense attorneys have discretion to accept or refuse cases and choose trial tactics, and judges have discretion to make rulings on evidence and other trial procedures, as well as decide on convictions and sentences.

One view of law is that it is neutral and objective and that formal rules of law are used in decision making (Pinkele and Louthan, 1985: 9). However, the reality is that lawmakers, law enforcers, and lawgivers are invested with a great deal of discretion in making and interpreting the law. Far from being absolute or objective, the law is a dynamic, ever-changing symbol of political will. Just as lawmaking and interpretation are influenced by political will and power groups, individual lawgivers and those who work in the system also have a great deal of discretion in interpreting and enforcing the law.

If we accept that discretion is an operating reality in the justice system, then we must ask in what ways legal professionals use this discretion. If individual value systems replace absolute rules or laws, then these value systems may be ethical or unethical. For instance, a judge may base a decision on fairness, or the judge may base the decision on prejudicial beliefs (e.g., that blacks are more criminal and deserve longer sentences, or that women are not dangerous and should get probation).

There may be many other situations where one's biases and prejudices are not so easily identified. Judges' rulings on evidentiary matters are supposed to be based on rules of evidence, but sometimes there is room for interpretation and individual discretion. Although most judges use this discretion appropriately and make decisions in a best effort to conform to the spirit of the evidentiary rule, other judges use arbitrary or unfair criteria, such as personal dislike of an attorney, disagreement with a rule, a desire for one side or the other to win the case, or, as in the case of at least one particular judge, awarding favorable rulings to each attorney by turns with no regard to the merit of each objection.

Defense attorneys and prosecutors have a great deal of discretion in the decisions they must make. Prosecutors must decide whether to charge and what to charge. They must decide trial strategy and what to offer in a plea bargain, but, arguably, it is the judge who shapes the system and protects or ignores its principles. Discretionary decisions at the trial level can be reexamined through the process of appeal. Appeals are part of due process in that they serve as a check on the decision making of trial judges. Supposedly, any gross errors will be corrected, and any extremely unethical actions will result in a new trial. However, appeals are not conducted in all cases, and even in cases that are appealed, many errors go unnoticed and uncorrected. For instance, courtroom behavior is seldom noticed or corrected unless it extremely and blatantly violates constitutional rights. Further, it is possible—and indeed, probable—that politics and other considerations affect appellate decisions.

In this text we address the ethical issues in the *implementation*, rather than the *creation*, of law. As you learned in political science or government classes, the creation of law is political. Laws are written by federal and state representations who supposedly enact the public will. One might think that once a law is created, its implementation would be fairly straightforward, but it should be clear by now that this is not the case.

The discussion concerning the Texas Court of Criminal Appeals and the Fifth Circuit illustrates how a court's decision making can change over time and be influenced by political shifts in power. Far from being static, the implementation of law reflects political realities, in a direct contrast to the ideal of judicial independence that is the cornerstone of our system of government. If the judiciary is not independent of political powers, this calls into question the very existence of the checks and balances upon which this country's government is constructed. For instance, many Democrats suspected that the composition of the Supreme Court had a great deal to do with its decision in the case challenging the Florida vote after the Bush–Gore election. Whether or not the allegations are true, it should be obvious that the strength of the justice system rests on the independence of its judiciary. If the investigation described in the "In the News" box below discovers political retaliation for a legitimate investigation, then that would be a serious assault on the independence of the justice system.

If the judiciary is a pawn or agent of political power, then due process is a sham and the very essence of democracy is threatened. The importance of due process is that even criminals and enemies of the state are given due-process rights that protect them from errors in the deprivation of life, liberty, and property. If due process is reserved only for those who are not enemies of the state, then all are threatened because anyone may become an "enemy." In fact, if for some reason state power became despotic, it would be very likely to label as enemies anyone who favored open government and democracy. What this illustrates is that the law (and the nature of its protections) is more important than the state and, indeed, is even more important than threats to the state. Those who are more influenced by political allegiance than allegiance to due process and civil liberties create a weak point in the mantle of protection against state power.

---

### IN THE NEWS  Political Retaliation?

A federal prosecutor who had begun a probe of Jack Abramoff, a powerful lobbyist and political friend of the Bush administration, was summarily demoted and barred from conducting any public corruption cases. A new FBI investigation is exploring whether the demotion might have been retaliatory.

Source: Associated Press, "Prosecutor's Demotion Is Investigated," *Austin American Statesman*, September 27, 2005, A6.

*Do you think that the White House (regardless of political party) puts pressure on the Justice Department and federal prosecutors to pursue certain cases and ignore other potential wrongdoing? If so, why has the investigation of Abramoff continued?*

This issue bubbled to the surface in 2005 when political figures, including Tom DeLay, became frustrated with the federal judiciary in the Terry Schiavo case, and a few threatened to begin impeachment proceedings against judges whom they accused of pushing "ideological positions." In other instances, members of Congress chastised judges who did not follow federal sentencing guidelines for drug offenders. These blatant public attempts to intimidate the judiciary led to criticism by the American Judicature Society as well as other legal analysts.

The U.S. Supreme Court, as the ultimate authority of law in this country, decides constitutionality, and these interpretations are far from neutral, despite the myth of objective decision making. This is the reason that the selection of Supreme Court justices (as well as all federal judges) is such a hard-fought political contest. Ideological positions do make a difference, and no one is fooled that a black robe removes bias. The recent confirmation of John Roberts as Chief Justice illustrates this fact. Opponents sought to obtain information about his belief systems concerning social and legal issues such as abortion and civil rights. Roberts took the stand that he could not comment on cases in advance and that he would be guided by legal precedent. This is a legitimate stand, but one that few are comforted by because precedent has not stopped the court from overturning decisions in the past.

Judges can strive to be objective, but their individual beliefs, background, politics, and even friendships no doubt influence, to a greater or lesser extent, their decision making. There are also more fundamental perceptions at work. Generally, judges are called conservative or liberal because of their perception of the source of rights. Conservatives are also called "**strict constructionists**" because they argue that an individual

## QUOTE and QUERY

"[T]he time will come for the men responsible for this to answer for their behavior. . . . [I want to] look at an arrogant, out-of-control, unaccountable judiciary that thumbed their nose at Congress and the president" (Tom DeLay, U.S. House of Representatives majority leader, speaking in response to the Schiavo case, May 2005).

Source: M. Allen, "DeLay Wants Panel to Review Role of Courts." April 2, 2005. Retrieved October 1, 2005, from http://www.washingtonpost.com/ac2/wp-dyn/A19793-2005Apr1?language=printer.

Attempts to intimidate judges into deciding pending cases in a particular way with threats of impeachment or investigation, as has been the recent practice of some members of Congress, have no place in a functioning democracy.

Source: *American Judicature*, "Judicial Independence," 2005. Retrieved on August 17, 2005, from http://www.ajs.org/include/story.asp?content_id=418.

*Do you think that members of Congress should be sanctioned for threatening impeachment when they don't like the decisions of federal judges? On the other hand, who does serve as oversight for judges who are appointed for life?*

has no rights unless these rights are specified in the Constitution or have been created by some other legal source. The extreme view of this position is that if a right isn't recognized and written down, it doesn't exist. An "**interpretationist**" (or liberal) uses a looser reading of the Constitution and reads into it rights that the Framers might have recognized or that should be recognized due to "evolving standards."

The Warren Court was called activist or liberal because it recognized a whole range of civil liberties and due-process rights for groups that had been historically disenfranchised. The source of such rights was found in an expansive reading of the Constitution and based on the idea of "fundamental liberties"—those freedoms and protections that the Framers would have recognized if they had been asked. Central to this view is the idea of **natural rights**. Recall that the natural law ethical system holds that there are natural laws of ethics that humans may or may not discover.

Several of the authors of the Bill of Rights were natural law theorists; thus, taken out of the context of their time, they would probably recognize that humans have the following rights:

- to be free
- to be treated equally to other groups
- to be able to make decisions over personal matters without governmental interference
- to be free from torture and punishments that degrade the human spirit
- to have some protections against state power (and so on)

In addition, there may be recognition that humans also have rights:

- to basic necessities to survive
- to avail themselves of opportunities to better themselves

The first set of rights leads to less government; the second set leads to more government. That is why the political terms of *conservative* and *liberal* are not strictly comparable to "strict constructionist" and "interpretationist" and why there is such confusion when such terms are being used to describe judicial and political appointees and elected officials. "Liberals" argue that if the Warren Court hadn't interpreted the Constitution to recognize civil rights, African Americans would still be eating at separate lunch counters. Constructionists argue that if interpretationists had their way, government and the courts would be involved in every decision from birth to death.

One thing is clear—a judge is human and carries baggage of personal, political, and social bias. Judges no doubt strive for objectivity, and we attempt to protect their independence, but very few are naïve enough to believe that the judiciary is as fair and balanced as the ideal of justice would have it be.

# Conclusion

The use of discretion in the criminal justice system is pervasive, and decision makers are often influenced by individual values and ethics that prompt them to stray from the parameters of structured laws and rules. This is also true for judges, who are the final arbiters and interpreters of the law. Thus, it is crucial that these professionals remember and believe in the basic tenets of due process and be ever vigilant against the influence of prejudice or bias in the application of law toward the pursuit of justice.

# Key Terms

**bureaucratic justice** the approach in which each case is treated as one of many, actors merely follow the rules and walk through the steps, and the goal is efficiency

**confirmatory bias** the situation in which a specific suspect has been fixated upon and other possibilities are ignored

**exclusionary rule** a judge-created rule that bars illegally obtained evidence except in certain instances, such as "good faith," "public safety," and "inevitable discovery"

**federal sentencing guidelines** guidelines written by Congress instructing the judge to impose a specific sentence unless there is a proven mitigating or aggravating factor in the case

**innocence projects** organizations staffed by lawyers and law students that reexamine cases and provide legal assistance to convicts when there is a probability that serious errors occurred in their prosecution

**interpretationist** an interpretive approach to the Constitution that uses a looser reading of the document and reads into it rights that the Framers might have recognized or that should be recognized due to "evolving standards"

**natural rights** the idea that certain rights and morals are "natural"—that is, not created by humans

**recuse** to excuse oneself from deciding a case because of real or apparent bias

**strict constructionist** the belief that an individual has no rights unless these rights are specified in the Constitution or have been created by some other legal source

**wedding-cake illustration** the model of justice in which the largest portion of criminal cases form the bottom layers of the cake and the few "serious" cases form the top layer; the bottom-layer cases get minimal due process

# Review Questions

1. Describe the models of court processing.
2. What are Alan Dershowitz's rules regarding the reality of the justice system?
3. What are the two areas of judicial discretion described? Give examples.
4. What are the areas covered by the Code of Judicial Conduct? Give examples of each.
5. Describe at least three issues related to a judge's ethical obligations.
6. Discuss the number of innocents who may be imprisoned. What are the sources for the estimates? What are the criticisms of the sources?
7. What factors have been identified as contributing to false convictions?
8. Why would people give false confessions? Which people are identified as highly vulnerable to false confessions?

9. What is the evidence to indicate a pervasive pattern of racial bias in the system?
10. Describe the importance of judicial independence, but also explain why judicial oversight is necessary.

# Discussion Questions

1. Give at least three instances where you feel the exclusionary rule is not appropriate.
2. Using ethical and moral criteria, evaluate recent courtroom practices: the use of videotaped testimony, allowing television cameras into the courtroom and jury room, and victim statements during sentencing.
3. Using moral and ethical criteria, analyze some recent innovations designed to improve crime prevention. Some possibilities to consider are such things as preventive detention, neighborhood justice centers that mediate rather than find guilt or innocence, the use of a waiver to adult court for violent juvenile offenders, increased sentences for gang-related or drug-related crimes, and criminalization of nonpayment of child support.
4. Watch a movie (outside of class!) that presents a legal dilemma (e.g., *Criminal Law, Penalty Phase, Presumed Innocent, The Witness*), and analyze the dilemmas by using one of the ethical frameworks described in this book.
5. Do you believe that cameras should be allowed to record jury deliberations?
6. Do you believe that congressional hearings should be able to investigate a judicial candidate's beliefs about abortion, affirmative action, and other issues, and use such findings to decide whether or not to confirm?
7. Do you believe a judge can ever be purely impartial in a case?

# Ethical Dilemmas

### *Situation 1*

You are a judge who must sentence two defendants. One insisted on a jury trial and, through his defense attorney, dragged the case on for months with delays and motions. He was finally convicted by a jury. The other individual was his co-defendant, and he pleaded guilty. Apparently, they were equally responsible for the burglary. How will you sentence them?

### *Situation 2*

You are a member of a jury. The jury is hearing a child molestation case in which the defendant is accused of a series of molestations in his neighborhood. You have been advised by the judge not to discuss the case with anyone outside the courtroom and especially not to anyone on either side of the case. Going down in the elevator after the fourth day of the trial, you overhear the prosecutor talking to one of the police officer witnesses. They are discussing the fact that the man has a previous arrest for child molestation but that it has not been allowed in by the judge as being too prejudicial to the jury. You were pretty sure the guy was guilty before, but now you definitely believe he is guilty. You also know that if you tell the judge what you have heard, it will probably result in a mistrial. What would you do?

### Situation 3

You are a court administrator and really like Judge Sonyer, your boss. He is pleasant, punctual, and hardworking. One day you hear him talking to the prosecutor in chambers. He is talking about the defendant in a trial that is about to start, and you hear him say that the son-of-a-b*tch is "as guilty as sin." You happen to be in law school and know that first, the prosecutor and judge should not be talking about the case without the presence of the defense attorney, and second, that the judge has expressed a preexisting bias. The judge's statement is even more problematic because this is a bench trial and he is the sole determiner of guilt or innocence. What would you do?

### Situation 4

You are a federal judge and are about to start a federal racketeering trial that is quite complicated. Prosecutors allege that certain lobbyists funneled money into political campaigns by "washing" it through individual employees of a couple of large corporations. On the other hand, the evidence seems equivocal, at least what you've seen so far. You get a call from one of your state's U.S. senators (who is not implicated in the case although members of his party are), and the conversation is innocuous and pleasant enough until he brings up the case and jocularly pressures you to agree with him that it is a "tempest in a teapot." Then he brings up the fact that a higher, appellate-level judgeship is coming open and that he is sure that you would like his support on it. The message is not subtle. What would you do?

### Situation 5

You are a federal judge and are faced with a drug defendant. The federal sentencing guidelines dictate that you sentence this individual to five years in prison. You believe that the sentence is arbitrary and not responsive to the individual circumstances of the defendant. You think that the individual deserves probation, community service, and drug counseling. What would you do?

## Suggested Readings

Christianson, S. 2004. *Innocent: Inside Wrongful Conviction Cases*. New York: New York University Press.

Dwyer, J., Neufeld, P., and Scheck, B. 2001. *Actual Innocence: When Justice Goes Wrong and How to Make It Right*. New York: Signet.

Hall, M. 2004. "The Worst Court in Texas." *Texas Monthly* (November): 155–263.

Liptak, A., and Blumenthal, R. 2004. "Death Sentences in Texas Cases Try Supreme Court's Patience." NYTimes.com. December 5, 2004. Retrieved on December 7, 2004, from http://www.nytimes.com/2004/12/05/national/05texas.html?oref=login&pagewanted=print.

Radelet, M., Bedau, H., and Putnam, C. 1992. *In Spite of Innocence*. Boston: Northeastern University Press.

Spence, G. 1989. *With Justice for None*. New York: Penguin.

The 13th Amendment prohibits slavery for all groups, except for convicted felons. Chain gangs are certainly not the most punitive example of what we do in the name of punishment.

# 12

# The Ethics of Punishment and Corrections

*Rationales for Punishment and Corrections*

*Ethical Frameworks for Corrections*

*Punishment*

*Private Corrections*

*Conclusion*

## Key Terms

cruel and unusual
   punishment
expiation
general deterrence
incapacitation
just deserts model
justice model
new rehabilitationists

prevention
punishment
reintegrative shaming
retribution
specific deterrence
stigmatizing shaming
three-strikes laws
treatment

## Chapter Objectives

1. Understand the definitions of punishment and treatment and their rationales.

2. Learn how the ethical frameworks justify punishment.

3. Become familiar with the arguments for and against capital punishment.

4. Understand the role that discretion, authority, and power play in corrections.

5. Explore the ethical issues involved with the privatization of corrections.

After someone has been found guilty of a criminal offense, an array of possible sanctions and treatments are possible. A suspended sentence or probation with restitution or community service as conditions may be required. If the crime is serious, the offender is dangerous, or both, incarceration for a period of time is a possibility. During incarceration, the wrongdoer may be required to participate in treatment programs ranging from self-help groups such as Alcoholics Anonymous to psychosurgery. The ultimate punishment the state can impose, of course, is death.

According to one author (Leiser, 1986: 198), five elements are essential to the definition of **punishment**:

1. There are at least two persons—one who inflicts the punishment and one who is punished.

2. The person who inflicts the punishment causes a certain harm to occur to the person who is being punished.

3. The person who inflicts the punishment has been authorized, under a system of rules or laws, to harm the person who is punished in this particular way.

4. The person who is being punished has been judged by a representative of that authority to have done what he or she is forbidden to do or to have failed to do what he or she is required to do by some relevant rule or law.

5. The harm that is inflicted upon the person who is being punished is specifically for the act or omission mentioned in Condition 4.

We also need to define **treatment**. According to correctional terminology, treatment may be anything used to induce behavioral change. The goal is to eliminate dysfunctional or deviant behavior and to encourage productive and normal behavior patterns. In prison, treatment includes diagnosis, classification, therapy, education, religious activity, vocational training, and self-help groups.

The infliction of punishment and even treatment is usually limited by some rationale or guideline. For instance, von Hirsch (1976: 5) presents the following restrictive guidelines:

1. The liberty of each individual is to be protected so long as it is consistent with the liberty of others.

2. The state is obligated to observe strict parsimony in intervening in criminals' lives.

3. The state must justify each intrusion.
4. The requirements of justice ought to constrain the pursuit of crime prevention (that is, deterrence and rehabilitation).

In this chapter we will first explore the various rationales for punishment, briefly discuss capital punishment in particular, and discuss private corrections. In the next chapter we will examine ethical issues related to institutional corrections. In Chapter 14 we will discuss ethical issues relevant to community corrections.

## Rationales for Punishment and Corrections

Does society have the right to punish or correct miscreants? If it does, where does that right come from? The rationale for punishment and corrections comes from the social contract. In the same way that the social contract forms the basis for police power, it also provides a rationale for further control in the form of punishment and corrections. Recall that according to this theory, we avoid social chaos by giving the state the power to control us. In this way we protect ourselves from being victimized by others by giving up our liberty to aggress against others. If we do step outside the bounds, the state has the right to control and punish us for our transgressions. Concurrently, the state is limited in the amount of control it can exert over individuals. To be consistent with the social contract, the state should exert its power only to accomplish the purpose of protection; any further interventions in civil liberties are unwarranted.

Corrections pursues a mixture of goals, including retribution, reform, incapacitation, deterrence, and rehabilitation. The long-standing argument between proponents of punishment and proponents of treatment reveals a system without a clear mandate or rationale for action. Garland (1990) writes that even the state's goal of punishment is problematic because it is marked with inconsistencies between the intent and the implementation. The moral contradictions are that it seeks to uphold freedom by means of its deprivation and it punishes private violence by inflicting state violence.

Can treatment and punishment occur at the same time? Or, as many critics argue, is the treatment ethic simply empty rhetoric? Since the emergence of penitentiaries in this country, we can see recurring cycles of emphasis—reform is replaced with retribution and then swings back again. In our current punitive cycle, we have virtually abandoned rehabilitation as a goal. Can a punishment system in which the definition of "just" punishment is relative and changes with time ever be considered an ethical or moral one? We simply do not seem to agree on what an individual offender deserves; therefore, specific punishments for similar crimes vary according to time, place, persons involved, and other factors.

An important question to ask is "Whom are we punishing?" Studies show that only a very small minority of individuals who commit crimes end up in prison; furthermore, we may assume that those numbers are not representative of the larger population. Those in our jails and prisons are there not only because they committed crimes, but also because they are poor, members of a minority group, or powerless. Certain types of criminals tend to avoid the more punitive sanctions of the corrections system. For instance, businesses routinely bilk consumers out of billions of dollars annually and chalk up the punitive fines incurred to operating expenses, yet it would not be uncommon in some jurisdictions for a shoplifter to be sent to prison. Streams and land are routinely polluted by industrial waste, but again, punitive fines are the typical sanctions, and these cannot begin to restore what has been taken away in the flagrant pursuit of financial profit. In fact, such costs are typically passed on to the consumers, so taxpayers suffer the crime and then also pay the fine.

Very seldom do we see executives responsible for company policy go to prison. White-collar criminals routinely receive fines, probation, or short stays in halfway houses, whereas so-called street criminals receive prison sentences. In the Enron and WorldCom scandals, there were some very public arrests and promises of prosecutions, but in the subsequent years, we have seen very few of the initial actors actually prosecuted. By the time the legal system finally completes the process, it is doubtful that many will see the inside of a prison, and if they do, it will probably be a short stay in a minimum-security federal prison. Recently, the imprisonment of Martha Stewart was hailed by some as an example that the justice system was neutral and that even rich and powerful people could not escape punishment. Other, more cynical, observations noted that Stewart may be rich, but she is not a part of the network of power holders who control business and politics. She could be considered a type of sacrificial token, and the reality is that most white-collar offenders do not even see the minor months-long prison sentence that she received.

Long ago, criminals were viewed as sinners with no ability to change their behavior, so punishment and incapacitation were seen as the only logical ways to respond to crime. Bentham (1748–1833) and Beccaria (1738–1794) viewed the criminal as rational and as having free will, and therefore saw the threat of punishment as a deterrent. Neoclassicists such as Quetelet (1796–1894) and Guerry (1802–1866) recognized that the insane and juveniles could not be held entirely responsible for their actions and therefore believed that they should not be punished. The insane and the young were treated differently because they were considered moral infants, not possessing the sense to refrain from wrongdoing. Then the positivist school influenced thinking to the extent that all criminal acts were believed to be merely symptoms of an underlying pathology.

The treatment programs created in the last hundred years or so operate under the assumption that we can do something to offenders to reduce their criminal activity. That "something" may involve

- treating a psychological problem, such as a sociopathic or paranoid personality
- addressing social problems, such as alcoholism or addiction
- resolving more pragmatic problems, such as chronic unemployment, with vocational training and job placement

Obviously, the perception of the criminal influences the rationale for correction and punishment.

The two major justifications for punishment and treatment are **retribution** and **prevention**. The retributive rationale postulates that punishment is an end in itself, whereas the prevention approach views punishment as a means rather than an end and embraces other responses to crime. The retributive rationale is probably more consistent with a view of the criminal as rational, and the prevention rationale, with certain exceptions, is more consistent with the view of the criminal as somehow less responsible for his or her behavior.

## *Retribution*

As mentioned before, the social contract provides the rationale for punishment. Members of society implicitly agree to society's rules and right to punish. One criticism of the social contract theory is that it is completely contingent on a consensus perspective of society. That is, the members of society are assumed to share the same goals, beliefs, and power. All people benefit from the social contract because they get to keep what they've got, with the assumption that what they've got is fairly equally distributed.

The conflict perspective views society as made up of a number of conflicting groups: When one wins, the other loses, because their interests can never be the same. Under contract theory, there is less reason for people to agree to the social contract. For some people, no advantages are received from the sacrifice of liberties. If someone perceives himself or herself as disenfranchised from society, does the right to punish still exist? Can we still use the social contract as the rationale for punishment?

The retributive rationale for punishment is consistent with the social contract theory. Simply stated, the retributive rationale is that the individual offender must be punished because he or she deserves it. Mackie (1982: 4) describes three specific types of retribution:

1. *Negative retribution* dictates that one who is not guilty must not be punished for a crime.
2. *Positive retribution* demands that one who is guilty ought to be punished.
3. *Permissive retribution* allows that one who is guilty may be punished.

This formulation states that retribution may support punishment but may also limit it. There are limits as to who may be punished (only those who commit crimes) and restrictions on the amount of punishment (only that sufficient to balance the wrong). Further, this formulation implies that punishment need not be administered in all cases. The exceptions, although not discussed by Mackie, may involve the concepts of mercy or diminished responsibility.

Our system of justice was created to take the place of private vengeance. We do not allow victims to seek their own revenge but rather replace *hot vengeance* with *cool justice,* dispassionate in its determination and distribution. The social contract supports the notion that it is intrinsically right for the state, rather than the victim's family, to execute a killer. The state has taken over the necessary task of punishment to ensure the survival of society by preventing private vengeance. Intentionally inflicting pain on another is an evil, but not if it meets the definitional elements of punishment.

Another retributivist justification for punishment is that it is the only way the individual can achieve salvation. In fact, we owe the offender punishment because only through suffering can atonement occur, and only through atonement or **expiation** can the offender achieve a state of grace. Some would strongly object to this interpretation of religious ethics and argue that Christianity, while supportive of just punishment, does not necessarily support suffering as the only way to achieve a state of grace: There must be repentance, and there is also room for forgiveness. One other view consistent with retribution is that punishment balances the advantage gained by a wrongdoer. The criminal act distorts the balance and parity of social relationships, and only a punishment or similar deprivation can restore the natural balance that existed before the criminal act.

**IN THE NEWS  No Mercy!**

Carla Faye Tucker was executed by the state of Texas in 1998. Her crime was a gruesome double murder. Many people across the world, including the Pope, argued that she should be spared the death penalty because (a) she was a born-again Christian, (b) she was truly repentant, (c) she committed her crime in a drug- and alcohol-induced haze, and (d) she was an abused child whose mother introduced her to prostitution at the age of twelve.

*Do you believe that the Board of Pardons and Paroles and Governor George W. Bush should have commuted her sentence to life in prison? If not, for what sort of person should the power of commutation be reserved?*

As discussed in an earlier chapter, there is always the possibility of mercy in any justice and punishment system. On the other hand, mercy is not automatic, as the "In the News" box above illustrates.

The question of whether to punish the crime or the criminal is long-standing and important in any discussion of retributive punishment. Jeremy Bentham believed that each criminal offense deserves a measure of punishment calculated to balance the potential pleasure or profit of the criminal offense. However, the neoclassicists allowed some characteristics of the offender to influence the punishment decision. This debate continues today with those who argue for determinate sentencing over indeterminate sentencing.

Determinate sentencing punishes the offense, with the length of the sentence determined by the seriousness of the crime. Indeterminate sentencing, in contrast, allows judges a great deal of discretion so that they can tailor the punishment to fit the individual offender. A young offender might get a second chance because he has the potential to change; a woman might receive probation instead of prison because she has an infant to take care of; a habitual criminal might be the unhappy recipient of an increased sentence because he is considered unsalvageable. This type of individualized justice is inconsistent with a retributive rationale because punishment is based on *who* the criminal is rather than on *what* the crime was.

What is an appropriate amount of punishment? This is a difficult question even for the retributivist. The difference between a year in prison and two years in prison is measurable only by the number of days on the calendar, not by how it is experienced by different people. Should this be considered during sentencing? Punishment of any kind affects individuals differently. For instance, a whipping may be worse than death for someone with a low tolerance for pain, better than prison for someone with a great need for freedom, and perhaps even pleasurable for someone who enjoys physical pain. Prison may be experienced as an inconvenience for some and such a traumatic experience for others that it may induce suicide. Our current system of justice seldom recognizes these individual vulnerabilities or sensitivities to various punishments.

Sentencing studies routinely show that little or no agreement exists regarding the type or amount of punishment appropriate for a wrongdoer. Disparity in sentencing is such a problem that many reforms are aimed at reducing or even eliminating judges' discretion. Yet when legislators take on the task themselves by setting determinate sentences, their decisions are arrived at by obscure methods, probably more influenced by political pressure and compromise than by the need for the application of fair and equitable standards. The basic premise of retribution is that offenders deserve punishment. If we are retributivists, we feel the balance is restored when offenders have suffered as much as their victims.

The **justice model** and the **just deserts model** are both retributive rationales for punishment (Fogel, 1975; Fogel and Hudson, 1981). Early advocates of the *justice model* describe the perspective as including concepts relating to the nature of humankind, the function of law, and the right of society to punish. This model, described more fully in the accompanying box, may be seen as part of a backlash against the abuse of discretion that characterized the rehabilitative era of the 1970s; it promotes a degree of predictability and equality in sentencing by reverting to earlier retributive goals of punishment and restricting the state's right to use treatment as a criterion for release. See Box 12-1 for more detail concerning the justice model.

---

**BOX 12-1  The Justice Model**

1. The criminal law is the "command of the sovereign."
2. The threat of punishment is necessary to implement the law.
3. The powerful manipulate the chief motivators of human behavior—fear and hope—through rewards and punishments to retain power.
4. Socialization of individuals, however imperfect, occurs in response to the commands and expectations of the ruling social–political power.
5. The criminal law protects the dominant prescribed morality (a system of rules said to be in the common and best interest of all), reflecting the enforcement aspect of the failure of socialization.
6. In an absence of any absolute system of justice or "Natural Law," no accurate etiologic theory of crime is possible, nor is the definition of crime itself historically stable.
7. Although free will may not exist perfectly, the criminal law is largely based upon its presumed vitality and forms the only foundation for penal sanctions.
8. A prison sentence represents a punishment sanctioned by a legislative body and meted out through the official legal system against a person adjudged responsible for his behavior. Although a purpose of such punishment may be deterrence or rehabilitation, more specifically, such punishment is the deprivation of liberty for a fixed period of time.
9. When corrections becomes mired in the dismal swamp of preaching, exhorting, and treating it becomes dysfunctional as an agency of justice.
10. Correctional agencies should engage prisoners as the law otherwise dictates; as responsible, volitional, and aspiring human beings, and not conceive of them as patients.

The *just deserts model* is also retributive and bases punishment on "commensurate deserts" (von Hirsch, 1976: xxvi). As the spokesperson for this view, von Hirsch (1985: 138) disagrees with deterrence and punishment theorists who feel that retributive and deterrent or incapacitative goals can be combined. However, von Hirsch does approve of a system of punishment that incorporates incapacitative features in judging the weight of a crime by its recidivism potential. Offenders who commit similar crimes are punished equally, but the rank ordering of crimes is determined by recidivistic potential. This system, categorical incapacitation, combines deserts and prevention but in a way that, according to von Hirsch, is not unjust to the individual offender (von Hirsch, 1985: 150).

Von Hirsch continues to disagree with the **new rehabilitationists,** who he feels are trying to resurrect a rehabilitative ethic with the rationale that humane conditions during incapacitation require some treatment options. Von Hirsch believes that although treatment options may be offered within the same categories of punishments, they should never be substituted for punishment itself or be part of the equation (von Hirsch and Maher, 1992).

Garland (1990) offers a different view. He believes that if social control is what is desired, then the emphasis should be placed on ways of accomplishing that purpose other than punishment after the fact. If we had a system that was better at socializing and integrating its citizens—he calls this a system of social justice and moral education—then we would not have to worry so much about punishing them. The punishment that was still necessary would be viewed as morally expressive rather than instrumental, and would be retributive rather than attempt prevention goals. Feeney (2005) continues this idea that sentencing should be purely retributive. He argues that one of the problems of the federal sentencing guidelines is that judges are not allowed to determine the morally appropriate amount of retribution and that the sentencing exercise loses its attributes of moral significance and moral condemnation.

No one doubts that we have become more punitive in sentencing and that offenders are serving more time in prison. The *New York Times* analyzed sentences of life (which usually meant that the offender would be paroled at some point) and found that although the number of murderers sentenced to life increased (totaling 132,000 in 2005), the number who were ever paroled drastically declined over the last 24 years to about 7 percent (Liptak, 2005). Up until 2005, jurors in Texas had two choices— death or life with parole. Legislators periodically attempted to create a "life without parole" option, but opponents resisted, perhaps because it was felt that the option would reduce the number of people Texas jurors sentenced to death. Finally, in the 2004 legislative term, the measure passed, but only because the bill's sponsors agreed to an amendment that swapped the life with parole option for it, so now jurors still have only two options: death or life without parole (Liptak, 2005). Some argue that it ignores the possibility of redemption. The next "In the News" box makes the same argument.

## Prevention

Three common justifications or rationales for punishment can all be subsumed under a general heading of prevention. Prevention assumes that something should

---

**IN THE NEWS  No Mercy!, Part 2**

Jackie Lee Thompson killed his girlfriend in 1969, when they were both fifteen. He was sentenced to life in prison. During the next thirty-five years he learned carpentry, masonry, plumbing, welding, mechanics, and electric wiring. He earned a high school diploma and an associate's degree. He had exemplary behavior. He earned the support of a prison official who offered him a job and place to stay. Even the victim's father asked the parole board to release him. They refused. "We can forgive him . . . why can't you?" said the victim's father.

Source: A. Liptak, "No, Life in Prison Means Exactly That," *Austin American Statesman*, October 2, 2005, A7.

*What factors should be considered in deciding when someone should be paroled? If the facts that the offender was fifteen, the victim's family wanted the release, and exemplary prison behavior aren't the criteria, what is?*

---

be done to the offender to prevent future criminal activity. There are three possible methods of prevention:

deterrence
incapacitation
treatment

Each of these goals is based on certain assumptions that must be considered in addition to the relevant moral questions—for instance, it is a factual question as to whether people can be deterred from crime, but it is a moral question as to what we should do to an individual to ensure deterrence.

## Deterrence

There are two types of deterrence. **Specific deterrence** is what is done to offenders to prevent them from deciding to commit another offense. **General deterrence** is what is done to an offender to prevent others from deciding to engage in wrongful behavior. The first teaches through punishment; the second teaches by example.

Our right to deter an individual offender is rooted in the same rationale used to support retribution. By virtue of membership in society, individuals submit themselves to society's controls. If we feel that someone's actions are damaging, we will try various means to persuade him or her to cease that activity. The implicit assumption of a deterrence philosophy is that in the absence of controls, society would revert back to a jungle-like, dangerous "war of all against all"; we need the police and official punishments to keep us in line. Under this rationale, the true nature of humankind is perceived to be predatory and held in check only by external controls. Deterrence advocates support deterrence as a justification of punishment. In recent years, general deterrence has given way to specific deterrence because empirical support for the efficacy of general deterrence is lacking (von Hirsch, 1985).

### QUOTE and QUERY

1. Those who violate others' rights deserve punishment.
2. However, there is a countervailing moral obligation to not deliberately add to the amount of human suffering, and punishment creates suffering.
3. Deterrence results in preventing more misery than it creates, thus justifying punishment.

Source: Adapted from von Hirsch (1976: 54).

*Is this utilitarian thinking or ethical formalism? Explain your answer.*

The rationale of specific deterrence depends on the effectiveness of punishment in deterring future behavior. Unfortunately, it is very difficult to find any studies that show that anything we do to the offender, whether under the heading of punishment or treatment, has any predictable effect on subsequent behavior. Arguments are made that this ineffectiveness is due to implementation problems; in other words, punishment doesn't deter because it is inconsistent, uncertain, and slow. If punishment was applied more consistently and with more swiftness, the argument goes, then we would see a deterrent effect.

The amount of punishment needed for deterrence is even more problematic if we seek to deter others. First, it becomes much harder to justify. If we know that a term of imprisonment will not deter an offender, can it be justified? If the prison term is much more than what would be needed to deter the individual but is the amount needed to deter others, can this further punishment be justified? A clear example of this situation is the so-called passion murderer who probably does not need specific deterrence because the chance of killing again is slim. However, he or she is usually given a long sentence to make it clear that killing will not be tolerated. (There is, of course, also a good retributive rationale for the long sentence.) Under deterrence theory, the offender is only a tool to teach a lesson to the rest of us. The sociologist Emile Durkheim believed that the value of criminals is in establishing the parameters of acceptable behavior. By their punishments, we can define ourselves as good and resolve to stay that way.

If one's goal is purely general deterrence, there does not necessarily need to be an original crime. Consider a futuristic society wherein the evening news routinely shows or describes the punishments received by a variety of criminals. The crime—or the punishment, for that matter—does not have to be real to be effective. If punishing innocent people for crimes they *might* do were just as effective as punishing criminal offenders, this action might satisfy the ends of deterrence but would obviously not be acceptable under any system of ethics, except perhaps act utilitarianism.

Actually, what the public hears about sentences bears little resemblance to what the individual offender actually serves, except perhaps in states that have determinate sentencing laws. Although the public is becoming more sophisticated in this regard, many do not know that when the judge sentences an offender to fifteen years in prison, with good time, time served, and parole, the actual prison time may be much less. Actual time served seems to be an inconsistent phenomenon having more to do with prison overcrowding, politics, and the availability of prison cells rather than some standard of justice. On the other hand, many members of the public often *underestimate* how much time is served by offenders because states have drastically reduced their use of parole and other forms of discretionary release.

## Incapacitation

Another purpose of punishment is to prevent further crime through **incapacitation.** Strictly speaking, incapacitation does not fit the classical definition of punishment, for the purpose is not to inflict pain but only to hold an offender until there is no risk of further crime. The major issue concerning incapacitation is prediction. Unfortunately, our ability to predict is no better for incapacitative purposes than it is for deterrence purposes. Two possible mistakes may be made: releasing an offender who commits further crimes and *not* releasing an offender who would not commit further crimes.

Carrying the goal of incapacitation to its logical conclusion, one would not have to commit a crime at all to be declared potentially dangerous and subject to incapacitation. We now incarcerate career criminals, not for their last offense but for what they might do in the future. We justify habitual-felon laws by the prediction that these criminals will continue to commit crime. Some argue that a small group of offenders commit a disproportionate share of crime and that those individuals can be identified by predictive elements such as the following: prior conviction for the crime they are in prison for, having been incarcerated for more than 50 percent of the last two years, a conviction before the age of sixteen, time in juvenile detention, heroin or barbiturate use in the preceding two years, heroin or barbiturate use as a juvenile, and having been employed less than 50 percent of the last two years (Greenwood, 1982).

Selective incapacitation is a policy of incarcerating these individuals for longer periods of time than other criminals. More recent studies indicate that our ability to predict who would commit further crime is actually very poor. Auerhahn (1999) points out that the original study by Peter Greenwood had a 48-percent error rate. Replications have error rates as high as 55 percent. This means that more than half of the time a prediction is made that the offender would re-offend, that prediction is wrong. Auerhahn concludes that until our prediction methods appreciably improve, there are grave ethical issues in using the selective incapacitation concept to lengthen sentences.

**Three-strikes laws** are a type of selective incapacitation. These laws are defended under an incapacitative rationale because it is argued that these individuals are more likely to commit future crime, so they should be held for long periods of time. More than half of all states now have some type of three-strikes or habitual-offender laws, but only a few states have used their laws to any great extent (King and Mauer, 2001). California has the dubious honor of incarcerating the most offenders under its three-strikes law (40,511 as of 2001).

Critics argue that for both practical and ethical reasons, the California three-strikes sentence is bad policy. It incarcerates those past their crime-prone-age years, it incarcerates nonviolent offenders for very long periods of time, and it is so expensive that it draws resources away from other social needs, such as schools. Further, it is unfairly

**IN THE NEWS  Three-Strikes Law**

*Ewing v. California* challenged Ewing's twenty-five-to-life sentence for stealing golf clubs worth a couple hundred dollars. Those who opposed three-strikes legislation argued that it was not fair when used with nonviolent offenders. They also noted that the application of three-strikes laws seemed to be differentially applied by race. To many people's surprise, the U.S. Supreme Court in March 2003 upheld California's right to impose the sentence under the state's three-strikes law, even though Justice Breyer's dissent argued that it was two to three times longer than any other jurisdiction would impose for a similar crime. The court was following precedent in that it had previously upheld habitual-felon laws.

*Do you agree or disagree with habitual-offender laws? What should a three-time nonviolent offender receive as punishment?*

disproportionate to the crime. Some offenders committed fairly minor third felonies and then received twenty-five years to life (King and Mauer, 2001; Zimring, Hawkins, and Kamin, 2001). Another troubling aspect of three-strikes laws is that African Americans tend to be disproportionately affected (Cole, 1999). The U.S. Supreme Court considered two challenges to California's three-strikes law in its 2002 term after the Ninth Circuit in California ruled that the law violated the Eighth Amendment. The Ninth Circuit ruled that it was grossly disproportional to sentence nonviolent, fairly minor third felons to twenty-five years to life. However, the Supreme Court ruled in March 2003 that it was not grossly disproportionate and deferred to the state's authority in setting punishments (*Lockyer v. Andrade*, 538 U.S. 63 [2003] and *Ewing v. California*, 538 U.S. 11 [2003]). It is clear that if three-strikes laws are overturned, it will have to be through state constitutional rights, not federal.

In 2004, California had the opportunity to reduce the number of felonies available for three-strikes sanctions in order to bring state law in line with all other states that had such laws. The bill also required the crimes to be violent rather than nonviolent. Public surveys indicated that the bill was going to pass. Grass-root supporters were led by Joe Klaas, the grandfather of Polly Klaas, the child-murder victim who was the face and spirit behind the passage of the first three-strikes bill. The proposed bill toughened penalties for child molesters but removed nonviolent felons from those who could receive longer sentences. In an eleventh-hour campaign by Governor Schwarzenegger and Marc Klaas, the victim's father, public opinion turned, and the bill was narrowly defeated. In Policy Box 12-1, the law, policy, and ethics of the three-strikes movement are untangled.

## Treatment

If we can find justification for the right to punish, can we also find justification for treatment? Treatment is considered to be beneficial to the individual offender as well as to society. It is a very different approach from the moral rejection implicit in retributive

---

**POLICY BOX 12-1** **Three Strikes**

Many states have three-strikes legislation, yet the majority of the public is probably not aware that it is not a new type of sentencing but has been around for a long time. The basic assumption is that the second or third felony is more serious than the first and/or that punishment must be made harsher because it did not deter the first time. The first is a deontological rationale; the second is a utilitarian rationale. Opponents argue that it is contrary to our justice system in that it sentences two individuals differently for a similar crime.

**Law:** With the recent rulings by the Supreme Court, it is clear that there is no constitutional right that is violated by a state habitual-criminal sentencing law.

**Policy:** There is great disparity between jurisdictions in how prosecutors apply habitual sentence laws. Some jurisdictions account for the majority of three-strikes offenders in the system, but others use it hardly at all. Thus, whether or not an offender receives a life sentence may depend, partially, on the county or state in which the crime was committed. As long as prosecutors have discretion in whether or not to charge under three-strikes statutes, such disparity will continue. Some argue also that three-strikes and habitual-offender laws are used disproportionately against minorities.

**Ethics:** Although prosecutors have discretion in whether or not to charge offenders under three-strikes statutes, there are ethical and unethical criteria for such decisions. Ethical criteria would be the danger posed to the public based on the felonies the offender has committed, whereas unethical criteria would include political pressure or the race of the offender.

---

punishment. Treatment implies acceptance rather than rejection, support rather than hatred. However, the control over the individual is just as great as with punishment; some people, in fact, would say it is greater.

What is treatment? We sometimes consider anything experienced after the point of sentencing to be treatment, including education, prison discipline, and religious services. Can treatment be experimental? Must it be effective to be considered treatment? A court was obliged to define treatment in *Knecht v. Gillman*, 488 F.2d 1136 (1973). Inmates challenged the state's right to use apomorphine, a drug that induces extreme nausea and a feeling of imminent death, as a form of aversive conditioning. In its holding the court stated that calling something treatment did not remove it from Eighth Amendment scrutiny. In other words, merely labeling some infliction of pain as treatment would not necessarily justify it. *Treatment* was further defined as that which constitutes accepted and standard practice and which could reasonably result in a "cure." More recently, the court had occasion to consider whether prison officials could administer antipsychotic drugs against the will of the prisoner.

Despite arguments that even prisoners had an inherent right to be free from such intrusive control, the court held in *Washington v. Harper*, 494 U.S. 210 (1990), that an inmate's right to refuse such medication did not outweigh the state's need to administer it if there was a showing that the inmate posed a security risk.

What we think needs to be cured is another issue. Recall the discussion of whether our society could be characterized by consensus or conflict. Treating a deviant may be justifiable if one believes that society is basically homogeneous in its values and beliefs, but viewed from a conflict perspective, treatment may look more like brainwashing and a coercive use of power. Civil libertarians would point out that it is no accident that political dissidents in totalitarian states are often handled as if they have mental problems and are treated with mind-altering drugs and other brainwashing regimens. The greater intrusiveness inherent in treating the mind is sometimes considered worse than punishment.

According to some experts, treatment can be effective only if it is voluntary—others disagree. It is true that much of the treatment that inmates and other correctional clients participate in is either implicitly or directly coerced. Providing treatment for those who want it is one thing; requiring those who are resistant to participate in psychotherapy, group therapy, religious activities, or chemotherapy is quite another. It is not justifiable under a retributivist ethical system; is it consistent with a prevention perspective? The answer is yes, as long as the results support the intervention.

The evaluation literature on rehabilitative treatment programs could fill a room. We now have over forty years of evaluations, as well as dozens of meta-analyses, and a number of sources that reviewed the research (see, for instance, Pollock, 2004; Palmer, 1994). The answers are not that "nothing works," as was widely believed through the 1980s and 1990s. But what works is more complicated than one program for all offenders (Toch, 1997). Further, sometimes a program works because of the staff characteristics, not the modality of the program. Thus, we can see again that the individual ethics and performance of public servants (treatment professionals in corrections) have a great deal to do with how well the system (in this case, treatment) works.

# Ethical Frameworks for Corrections

The various rationales for punishment just described are well established, and most can be found in many texts. The ethical systems that were introduced in Chapter 2 are less commonly discussed in corrections texts, but they form the underlying philosophical rationale for the goals or missions of retribution and prevention (including deterrence, incapacitation, and treatment). Ethical formalism and utilitarianism receive a disproportional amount of attention here, but the reader is urged to apply the other ethical systems as well.

## *Utilitarianism*

Utilitarianism is often used to support the last three rationales of punishment: deterrence, incapacitation, and treatment. According to utilitarianism, punishing or treating the criminal offender benefits society, and this benefit outweighs the negative effect on the individual offender. It is a teleological argument because the morality of the punishment is determined by the consequences derived—reduced crime.

Jeremy Bentham was the major proponent of the utilitarian theory of punishment and established basic guidelines for its use.

Bentham believed that punishment works when it is applied rationally to rational people, but is not acceptable when the person did not make a rational decision to commit the crime, such as when the law forbidding the action was passed after the act occurred, the law was unknown, the person was acting under compulsion, or the person was an infant, insane, or intoxicated (Bentham, 1970; also see Beccaria, 1977). The utility of the punishment would be lost in these cases; therefore, punishment could not be justified (Borchert and Stewart, 1986: 317). "Bentham's Rules of Punishment" are described in Box 12-2.

---

### BOX 12-2 **Bentham's Rules of Punishment**

1. The value of the punishment must not be less, in any case, than what is sufficient to outweigh that of the profit of the offense.
2. The greater the mischief of the offense, the greater is the expense it may be worth while to be at, in the way of punishment.
3. When two offenses come in competition, the punishment for the greater offense must be sufficient to induce a man to prefer the less.
4. The punishment should be adjusted in such manner to each particular offense, that for every part of the mischief there may be a motive to restrain the offender from giving birth to it.
5. The punishment ought in no case to be more than what is necessary to bring it into conformity with the rules here given.
6. That the quantity of punishment actually inflicted on each individual offender may correspond to the quantity intended for similar offenders in general, the several circumstances influencing sensibility ought always to be taken into the account.
7. That the value of the punishment may outweigh the profit of the offense, it must be increased in point of magnitude, in proportion as it falls short in point of certainty.
8. Punishment must be further increased in point of magnitude, in proportion as it falls short of proximity.
9. When the act is conclusively indicative of a habit, such an increase must be given to the punishment as may enable it to outweigh the profit, not only of the individual offense, but of such other like offenses as are likely to have been committed with impunity by the same offender.
10. When a punishment, which in point of quality is particularly well calculated to answer its intention, cannot exist in less than a certain quantity, it may sometimes be of issue, for the sake of employing it, to stretch a little beyond that quantity which, on other accounts, would be strictly necessary.

*continued*

---

**BOX 12-2 Continued**

11. In particular, this may be the case where the punishment proposed is of such a nature as to be particularly well calculated to answer the purpose of a moral lesson.

12. In adjusting the quantum of punishment, the circumstances by which all punishment may be rendered unprofitable ought to be attended to.

13. Among provisions designated to perfect the proportion between punishments and offenses, if any occur which by their own particular good effects would not make up for the harm they would do by adding to the intricacy of the code, they should be omitted.

SOURCE: Bentham (1843/1970).

---

All of Bentham's rules ensure that punishments are acceptable to the utilitarian framework. The basic formula provides that the utility of punishment to society outweighs the negative of the punishment itself. Utilitarian theory also supports treatment and incapacitation if they can be shown to benefit society. If, for instance, treatment and punishment had equal amounts of utility for society, treatment would be the more ethical choice because it has a less negative effect on the individual. Likewise, if incapacitation and punishment are equally effective in protecting and providing utility to society, then the choice with the least negative utility would be the ethical one.

## Ethical Formalism

Contrast the utilitarian views toward punishment discussed in the previous section with Kant's views (see the Quote and Query box on the next page). Ethical formalism clearly supports a retributive view of punishment. It is deontological because it is not concerned with the consequences of the punishment or treatment, only its inherent morality. It would support the idea that a criminal is owed punishment because to do otherwise would not be according him or her equal respect as a human. However, the punishment should not be used as a means to any other end but retribution. Treatment is not supported by ethical formalism because it uses the offender as a means to protect society.

Several arguments support this retributive rationale. First, Mackie (1982) discusses the universal aspects of punishment: The urge to react in a hostile manner to harm is an element inherent in human nature; therefore, one might say that punishment is a natural law. Another supporting argument is found in the principle of forfeiture, which postulates that when one intrudes on an innocent person's rights, one forfeits a proportional amount of one's own rights. By restraining or hurting a victim in some way, the aggressor forfeits his or her own liberty; in other words, he or she forfeits the right to be free from punishment (Bedau, 1982).

## QUOTE and QUERY

Juridical punishment . . . can be inflicted on a criminal, never just as instrumental to the achievement of some other good for the criminal himself or for the civil society, but only because he has committed a crime; for a man may never be used just as a means to the end of another person. . . . Penal law is a categorical imperative, and woe to him who crawls through the serpentine maze of utilitarian theory in order to find an excuse, in some advantage to someone, for releasing the criminal from punishment or any degree of it, in line with the pharisaical proverb "it is better that one man die than that a whole people perish"; for if justice perishes, there is no more value in man living on the earth. . . . What mode and degree of punishment, then, is the principle and standard of public justice? Nothing but the principle of equality. . . . Thus, whatever undeserved evil you inflict on another person, you inflict on yourself. . . .

Source: Kant, quoted in Borchert and Stewart (1986: 322).

*Do you understand what Kant was trying to say? Rephrase the passage to make it more simple and current.*

## Ethics of Care

The ethics of care would probably not support punishment unless it was essential to help the offender become a better person. This ethical system defines good as that which meets everyone's needs—victim and offender alike. The rationale that most closely approximates the ethics of care is an entirely different one from retribution or prevention—it is restorative justice, which we will discuss more fully in Chapter 14.

Several authors have discussed the ethics of care in relation to the justice and corrections system. For instance, Heidensohn (1986) and Daly (1989) discuss differences in the perception of justice from a care perspective versus a retributive perspective. They discuss these as female and male perceptions, respectively. The female care perspective emphasizes needs, motives, and relationships.

The corrections system, ideally, should be supported by a caring ethic because it takes into account offender needs. Community corrections, especially, emphasize the relationship of the offender to the community. In this perspective, one should help the offender to become a better person because that is what a caring and committed relationship would entail. Retributive punishment and deterrence are not consistent with the ethics of care. However, some say that retribution and a care ethic are not, nor should they be considered, dichotomous. Restorative justice might be considered the merger of the two in that this approach views the offender as responsible for the wrong committed but the responsibility is satisfied by reparation to the victim rather than by punishment and pain.

## *Rawlsian Ethics*

John Rawls presents an alternative to utilitarianism and retributivism. Rawls's defense of punishment starts with Kant's proposition that no one should be treated as a means, and with the idea that each should have an "equal right to the most extensive basic liberty compatible with a similar liberty to others." According to Rawls, a loss of rights should take place only when it is consistent with the best interests of the least advantaged. Rules regarding punishment would be as follows (cited in Hickey and Scharf, 1980: 169):

1. We must punish only to the extent that the loss of liberty would be agreeable were one not to know whether one were to be the criminal, the victim, or a member of the general public [the veil of ignorance].
2. The loss of liberty must be justified as the minimum loss consistent with the maintenance of the same liberty among others.

Furthermore, when the advantage shifts—when the offender instead of the victim or society becomes the one with the least advantage—then punishment must cease. This theory leaves a lot of unanswered questions. For instance, if victims were chosen carefully (i.e., only those who would not suffer financially or emotionally) and the criminal came from an impoverished background, then the criminal would still be at a disadvantage and, thus, not morally accountable for his or her actions. On the other hand, Rawls's system does seem to be consistent with the idea that the criminal act creates an imbalance between offender and victim, and that punishment should be concerned with regaining that balance. The utilitarian thread in this proposition is that by having this check-and-balance system in the determination of punishment, all of society is benefited.

# Punishment

We have discarded many punishments that were acceptable in earlier times, such as flogging, hanging, banishment, branding, cutting off limbs, drawing and quartering, and pillories and stocks. Although we still believe society has the right to punish, what we do in the name of punishment has changed substantially. As a society, we became gradually uncomfortable with inflicting physically painful punishments on offenders, and as these punishments were discarded, imprisonment was used as the substitute. Inside prison, we have only relatively recently abandoned physical punishments as a method of control (at least formally), but that is not to say that prisons are not injurious. In addition to the informal corporal punishments that are inflicted by offices and fellow inmates, prison is painful because it is banishment and condemnation; it is separation from loved ones and deprivation of freedom. More subtly, it is an assault on one's self-esteem in that it incapacitates the person from almost all the ways an individual has to create self-esteem. About the only self-definition left is as a prison "tough guy"—a stance that destroys the spirit and reduces the individual to a baser form of humanity.

The rate of imprisonment has tripled in the last twenty-five years. The United States pays about $167 billion in court- and justice-related expenses. These expenditures have also tripled in the last twenty-five years. This represents a tax burden of $586 per resident, compared to $158 in 1982. In most states the amount of money directed to justice and corrections has gone up while the amount of the budget directed to education and social services has decreased. Some argue that the costs are justified and have resulted in the reduction in crime that we have seen in the last decade, but others argue that there does not seem to be a relationship between correctional spending and decreased crime rates, or that the effect is modest and the crime rate has been affected by other social factors (Austin and Fabelo, 2004; Pollock, 2004). Note that it is a utilitarian question as to whether we are now paying "too much" to keep people locked up (comparing the cost to the benefit of reduced crime or incapacitation). Whether all of the two million people in jails and prisons "deserve" to be locked up is a retributive, deontological question (West and Morris, 2000).

## *Humane Punishment*

The Eighth Amendment protects all Americans from **cruel and unusual punishment.** Although what is "cruel and unusual" is vague, several tests have been used to define the terms, such as the following, discussed in *Furman v. Georgia*, 408 U.S. 238, 92 S.Ct. 2726, 33 L.Ed.2d 346 (1972):

1. *Unusual* (by frequency): Those punishments that are rarely, if ever, used thus become unusual if used against one individual or a group. They become arbitrary punishments because the decision to use them is so infrequent.
2. *Evolving standards of decency:* Civilization is evolving, and punishments considered acceptable in the nineteenth century are no longer acceptable in the twentieth century.
3. *Shock the conscience:* A yardstick for all punishment is to test it against the public conscience. If people are naturally repelled by the punishment, then it must be cruel and unusual by definition.
4. *Excessive or disproportionate:* Any punishment that is excessive to its purpose or disproportionately administered is considered wrong.
5. *Unnecessary:* Again, we are looking at the purpose of the punishment in relation to what is done. If the purpose of punishment to deter crime, then we should administer only an amount necessary to do so. If the purpose is to protect and the offender presents no danger, then prison should not be used.

These tests have eliminated the use of the whip and the branding iron, yet some say that we may have done nothing to move toward humane punishment and that, in fact, we may have moved away from it. Graeme Newman points out the possibility that corporal punishment, at least the less drastic kinds such as whipping, is actually less harmful than a prison sentence. In fact, physical punishment may be more of a deterrent and yet less damaging to a person's future. After all, a whipping takes perhaps days or weeks to get over, but a prison sentence may last years and affect all future earnings (Newman, 1978: 270).

A criminal offender may be sentenced to probation, with a fine or other conditions of probation attached. For instance, a probationer may be required to perform community service, pay court costs, pay restitution to the victim, find employment, submit to drug tests and complete drug counseling, or conform to any number of other conditions. Some recent examples of conditions include those convicted of driving while intoxicated (DWI) being required to have an instrument attached to their car that measures their blood alcohol level, the use of electronic monitoring instruments, and, in one case, being forced to donate blood to a blood bank. So-called "shaming" conditions include DWI offenders having special license plates that indicate to other drivers that the driver has been convicted of DWI, probation officers putting signs up in the yard or nailing them to the door of convicted sex offenders warning people that a sex offender lives there, announcing to one's church congregation one's criminal conviction and asking for forgiveness, and taking out an advertisement in the town newspaper for the same purpose. These conditions are rarely challenged in court because the offender would usually prefer them to a prison sentence. However, there is some question as to the legal authority for such conditions (Book, 1999).

We could also examine them in light of the ethical systems above. One real question concerning the "shaming" conditions is the effect such conditions have on family members of offenders and whether these conditions constitute a type of extralegal punishment for them without any due-process procedures of trial and conviction. Braithwaite (2000), Karp (1998), and others distinguish between **stigmatizing shaming** and **reintegrative shaming**. Although the first is a rejection of the individual and has negative effects, the second is only a rejection of the person's behavior and creates a healthier relationship between the individual and his or her community. We will revisit these concepts in Chapter 14 when we discuss restorative justice.

## Capital Punishment

What sets capital punishment apart from all other punishments is its quality of irrevocability. This type of punishment leaves no way to correct a mistake. For this reason, some believe that no mortal should have the power to inflict capital punishment because there is no way to guarantee that mistakes won't be made. Certainly, Radelet, Bedau, and Putnam's (1992) collection of cases concerning innocent people who were executed in error, and the other investigations that have also documented errors in the prosecutions in capital cases, support this viewpoint.

The Bureau of Justice Statistics (2005) reports that in 2004, 59 inmates were executed. In 2001, 66 were executed, and in 2000, 85 were executed. In 2003, 3,374 prisoners were on death row. This compares to the 3,581 who were on death row in 2001. There are only 47 women and almost equal numbers of whites (1,878) and blacks (1,418). About a third had no prior felony conviction. Our rate of sentencing offenders to death was at a 20-year low in the early 2000s and continues to go down (BJS, 2005; *Corrections Digest,* 2002).

The major ethical positions that can support the death penalty are utilitarianism and retribution. Because of controversy over the factual issues involved, utilitarian arguments are used both to defend and condemn capital punishment. If we believe, as do retentionists, that capital punishment is just because it deters people, then we must show proof that it does indeed deter. The abolitionists present evidence that it does not.

Arguments for the retention of the death penalty include considerations of justice and considerations of social utility. Considerations of justice involve the retributivist, deontological view that the moral order is upset by the commission of an offense, and the disorder can be rectified only by punishment equal in intensity to the seriousness of the offense. Utilitarians view the evil of capital punishment as far outweighed by the future benefits that will accrue to society. However, Walker (1985: 79) summarizes the evidence marshaled on both sides of the deterrence question and finds very little support for the proposition that executions are useful deterrents. Further explorations of the issue also conclude that there is little reason to believe that capital punishment has any deterrent effect (Kronenwerter, 1993).

Abolitionists emphasize the "inherent worth and dignity of each individual." The taking of a human life is judged a morally unacceptable practice and is believed to be nothing more than vengeance (Mappes, 1982: 83–87). In fact, executions may even create a net negative effect for society because although criminals may receive what they deserve, society is negatively affected by the brutalizing image of execution. This view would be one consistent with the idea that "violence begets violence," and, far from showing societal intolerance toward murder, capital punishment is seen as actually cheapening human life and encouraging bloodlust (Bedau, 1991).

Religious ethics have been used both to support and condemn capital punishment. The Old Testament law supporting the taking of "an eye for an eye" is used by retentionists whereas the commandment "Thou shalt not kill" is used by the abolitionists. Kania (1999) presents a comprehensive religious justification for capital punishment, along with a social contract justification. The ethical justification of capital punishment presents serious and probably irresolvable problems. It is a telling commentary that for as long as society has used capital punishment to punish wrongdoing, critics have defined it as immoral (Johnson, 1991).

Questions also arise about the methods and procedures of capital punishment. Should all murderers be subject to capital punishment, or are some murders less serious than others? Should we allow defenses of age, mental state, or reason? If we do apply capital punishment differentially, doesn't this open the door to bias and misuse? Evidence indicates that capital punishment has been used arbitrarily and discriminatorily in this country. Minorities are more likely to be executed when their victims are white; in Georgia, black offenders charged with killing a white were 4.3 times more likely to be sentenced to death than those charged with killing a black. Yet the U.S. Supreme Court has stated that evidence of statistically disproportional administration is not enough to invalidate the death penalty (*McClesky v. Kemp*, 481 U.S. 279 [1987]).

Because our justice system is based on rationality, executions of the mentally ill and the mentally retarded have been vehemently criticized. The Supreme Court has ruled that executing the mentally ill is cruel and unusual (*Ford v. Wainwright,* 477 U.S. 399 [1986]). Miller and Radelet (1993) present a detailed account of the *Ford* case, describing the mental deterioration of Ford and the long ordeal of appeals before the Supreme Court finally ruled. They also point out the ethical issues involved when psychiatrists, other medical professionals, and psychologists participate in procedures that involve certifying someone as *death ready* and then assist in the administration of the chosen method of execution. There are deep and divisive views in these professions regarding the seeming inconsistency between identifying oneself as a helping professional and then helping someone be put to death.

In *Penry v. Lynaugh,* 107 S.Ct. 2934 (1989), the Supreme Court ruled that evidence of mental retardation should be presented to the jury to consider mitigation of the sentence. The *Penry* case involved a man who had committed a brutal rape and murder but who had an IQ that was just barely above the level that would ordinarily result in institutionalization. After the Supreme Court ruled that the state of Texas could execute someone who was mentally retarded, but that the trial judge must allow evidence of mental retardation to be provided to the jury in consideration of mitigation, a retrial resulted in a second death sentence from the new jury.

In June 2002 the Supreme Court finally decided that it was cruel and unusual to execute a retarded person. In *Atkins v. Virginia,* 536 U.S. 304 (2002), the court held that a man with an IQ of 59 could not be put to death, finding that the evolution of decency and public opinion supported such a decision. The dissent, comprising the most conservative of the Justices (Rehnquist, Scalia, and Thomas), argued that there was no common consensus regarding executing the mentally retarded and that it was not violative of the Eighth Amendment.

Another issue is whether capital punishment should be used for juveniles. Up until very recently, this country was one of a very few that had laws allowing the execution of juveniles, and some argued that it put the United States in violation of international human rights treaties (*Criminal Justice Newsletter,* 2002). In the 2004 term the Court held that it was unconstitutional to execute those who had committed their murder when under the age of eighteen. In *Roper v. Simmons,* 125 S.Ct. 1183 (2005), the Court, in a narrow ruling (5–4), held that juvenile offenders could not be classified as the "worst" offenders; therefore, it violated the Eighth Amendment to allow death sentences of juveniles. The dissent argued that there was no national consensus on the matter. A number of outside groups filed *amicus curiae* briefs in the case and/or urged the Court to abolish the practice, including the U.S. Conference of Catholic Bishops, the American Medical Association, sixteen Nobel Peace Prize winners, former U.S. President Jimmy Carter, the European Community, and the Pope. The ruling affected the sentences of seventy-two people on death row who had committed their crimes before the age of eighteen. Note that the question of culpability and whether or not the death sentence is just for mentally ill, retarded, or juvenile offenders is both a legal and a moral question.

Although one would assume that the offender must have had to kill someone to receive a death sentence, that is not the case. In *Tison v. Arizona,* 481 U.S. 137 (1987), the Court ruled that crime partners in a felony that resulted in a death could be executed even if they did not kill the victim and they did not intend a death to occur. The Tison brothers had no criminal records, but they helped their father escape from an Arizona prison. During the escape, their father and a fellow escaped convict killed a family after kidnapping them for their car. The brothers did not participate but by this point were felons themselves because of their role in the escape. A massive search ensued, and they were separated from their father, who eventually ended up dying of exposure in the desert. (One wonders if the fact that he escaped his punishment was the reason that the brothers were then tried for capital murder.) Responding to their appeal, the Supreme Court affirmed the state's right to execute for felony murder because crime partners become responsible for any murder that occurs in the course of a felony they participate in, regardless of their role in the killing.

Unless the Supreme Court revises its current position, which seems unlikely, the legality of executions is not in question, even though the procedures used to arrive at the decision to execute may continue to be challenged. However, the morality of capital punishment is still very much a topic of debate, and it elicits strong feelings on the part of many people. As discussed earlier, Governor Ryan of Illinois, deeply disgusted with the number of errors in the legal process leading to a death sentence, commuted all death sentences in his state as one of his last acts as governor. Whether his act is a portent of things to come remains to be seen.

## Private Corrections

In much of the foregoing discussion, we described punishment as a state function. However, the state may delegate the authority to punish. Private prisons are built and then leased to the state or, in some cases, actually run by the private corporation, which bills the state for the service. Many have objected to the profit motive being introduced into corrections and point to a number of ethical issues raised by private "profiteers" (Pollock, 2004). First, there are potential abuses of the bidding process, as in any situation where the government contracts with a company for services or products. Money may change hands to ensure that one organization receives the contract, companies may make informal agreements to "rig" the bids, and other potentially corrupt practices may go on. Legal as well as ethical issues abound when private and public motives are mixed.

In the building phase, private corporations may cut corners and construct buildings without meeting proper standards for safety. Managing the institution also raises the possibility that a private contractor will attempt to maximize profits by ignoring minimum standards of health and safety and will, if necessary, bribe inspectors or monitors to overlook the deficiencies. It has certainly happened in other areas, such as nursing homes, that those who contract with the state government and receive state monies reap large profits by subjecting clients to inhumane conditions.

King, Mauer, and Huling (2003) analyzed the effect of prison building on rural communities. In the last twenty years, the majority of new prisons were built in rural counties, and many of those prisons were private correctional institutions. The new prison was "sold" to the county as an economic boon, and counties that were experiencing economic downturns and anemic economies sometimes competed to have the prison built in their county. Actually, an economic analysis showed that the county received a very minimal economic benefit when the prison was built. The construction contracts were not directed to local companies but rather went to companies that had the experience, qualifications, and history with building institutions, and correctional workers were often imported from outside the county. What happened in some cases was that in return for tax breaks and sometimes even free land, counties got very little. One might argue that it is unethical for the planners of these prisons to promise benefits that have never emerged from the building of a prison.

In a more general sense, some feel that punishment and profit are never compatible and that linking the two has led to a variety of historical abuses (such as the contract labor system in the South). Although the decision to use private corporations is made by legislators, correctional administrators are faced with a variety of ethical dilemmas because of it, such as whether to support the idea, whether to accept a part-time position as a consultant to a private corporation when one has decision-making authority over issues that concern the corporation, whether to take anything of value from the corporation (from a free lunch to a "grant" for personal study), and whether to allow one corporation to have insider information in order to prepare a more favorable bid.

On the other hand, private corporations report that some state systems subject them to endless and picayune rules and continually audit them to the point that it appears that state prison officials are trying to find noncompliance in order to return the "action" to state actors. There is probably some truth that some corrections department officials are not happy to have legislators approve the use of private contractors and would like to see them fail.

Private prisons hold about 5 percent of all prison beds in the country (Parenti, 1999: 218). Correctional corporations such as Corrections Corporation of America and Wackenhut have their stock traded on the New York Stock Exchange. Corrections Corporation of America is the largest player in the private prison industry, holding a little more than half of all private prison beds (over 60,000 beds in the United States alone). In late 1998 it merged into the Prison Realty Trust (PRT), an accounting move that allowed the entity to be exempt from tax liability as long as it distributed 95 percent of its earnings to its stockholders (Geis, Mobley, and Shichor, 1999). There are troubling connections between C.C.A. executives and Tennessee politicians. Researchers have tracked campaign contributions from C.C.A. in states where the company received lucrative contracts (Mobley and Geis, 2002).

In 2001, C.C.A.'s stock lost 93 percent of its 2000 value (Greene, 2001: 26). This financial meltdown was partly caused by a decline of crime and prisoners, and partly fueled by a rash of scandals that plagued C.C.A.'s prison facilities. Account after account of escapes, violence, undertrained officers, and understaffing had plagued C.C.A. for several years (Parenti, 1999: 219). C.C.A. was also the target of a loosely organized, global organization of students and reformers that sought to persuade college campuses to drop their contracts with Sodexho Marriott Services, a corporation

**QUOTE and QUERY**

Sorry to be late clueing you to this great new money-making opportunity, but there may still be time to get in on the seminar that will show you how to imprison people for fun and profit. . . . If you're looking for something really reliable, what better to invest in than human misbehavior? It has been a sure thing since Cain and Abel.

Source: columnist Tom Teepen (1996).

*Teepen's "pitch" is sarcasm, but the question remains: Is there something unseemly about making a profit out of imprisonment?*

that owned about 48 percent of C.C.A. stock. Students, upset that their money was being used to fund a corporation that "violat[ed] the human rights of prisoners and prison employees by sacrificing health and safety to improve the corporate bottom-line," were successful in getting several large campuses to drop their contracts with Sodexho (Pranis, 2001). The giant corporation bowed to their threat and sold its shares in C.C.A. (Ward, 2001).

Wackenhut has more than 25,000 beds at several dozen facilities across the country and is considered number two among the private prison providers. It holds 11,000 prison beds internationally (57 percent of the international market of private prisons) (Austin and Irwin, 2001: 66; Perez, 2001). It also runs mental health facilities and addiction treatment centers. Since going public in 1994, Wackenhut's stock price has increased by 800 percent. Wackenhut has also had a series of incidents reported in its facilities that have affected its reputation and financial standing (Greene, 2001). Lawsuits and investigations in states concern the use of tear gas (Louisiana), failing to prevent sexual abuse (Texas), paying $3 million to a member of the state's prison policy panel (Florida), and a murder rate that is much higher than that of the state-run institutions (New Mexico) (Solomon, 1999; Fecteau, 1999).

In addition to the big two, there are more than a dozen smaller companies across the nation that compete for the private prison bids put out by the states. In a process replete with allegations of bribes, sweetheart deals, and other forms of corruption, some critics contend that the private prison industry seems to be characterized by crooks on both sides of the bars. A New York scandal concerned allegations that a private corrections company paid money to several New York politicians in return for favors in seeking state contracts. Some of the campaign contributions evidently came in the name of workers who said they were not responsible for the contribution. The lead whistleblower in the case was fired when he refused to work on a politician's campaign (Levy, 2003a, 2003b).

In one unusual case, a jury in Arizona acquitted an inmate of escape based on the self-defense of "necessity." He testified that he had to get out of the C.C.A. prison in

Arizona that housed him and other prisoners from Alaska because correctional staff refused to give him his heart medication. He also stated that they gave him the wrong medicine and that he had a stroke. C.C.A. staff argue that his charges are untrue (Toomey, 2000).

Proponents argue that private corrections can save the state money. Arguments include the idea that private corporations are more efficient, they can build faster with less cost and less red tape, and they have economies of scale (i.e., they can obtain savings because of their size). It may be true that private prisons can be built faster because private corporations are not bound by restrictions placed on government. For instance, a state would most likely have to go to voters to pass a bond in order to build new prisons; however, it can contract with a private provider without voter approval. States and local governments are bound by a myriad of bidding and siting restrictions, unlike private corporations. However, a General Accounting Office meta-analysis concluded that private and public institutions cost about the same (GAO, 1996). Any profits realized by a private entity being "leaner and meaner" are offset by the profit margin that private companies maintain and a regulatory system that the state must put in place to make sure contract specifications are adhered to.

Some studies have concluded that private prisons produce results equal to those of state institutions for less cost. Bourge (2002) describes Segal and Moore's study that examined twenty-eight governmental and institutional studies comparing public and private facilities, and found that twenty-two of the private prisons showed cost savings of 5 to 15 percent. They concluded that there is "significant evidence" that private facilities can provide quality comparable to that of state institutions. However, critics argue that studies that look only at costs and ignore higher assault rates in private prisons and other indices of quality of service are flawed.

One of the emerging problems is that low wages prevent the hiring of qualified staff. In one situation a private corrections company, Capital Correctional Resources, was forced to defend the actions of its officers who were videotaped using stun guns and dogs to brutalize inmates. It was later discovered that two of the officers had been fired from the state system for brutality (Langford, 1997). Generally, private corrections pay officers a lower salary than the state, so officers often transfer to state departments after they are trained. Turnover is high in both private corrections and state corrections.

There have been issues concerning the evaluators, as well. The evaluation by Segal and Moore, for instance, was funded by a libertarian think tank that arguably would be inclined to promote private enterprise over government involvement (Bourge, 2002). The biggest scandal in private prison evaluation research concerned Charles Thomas, a University of Florida professor who published many articles and books as "objective" evaluations of private prisons.

Thomas testified before Congress and state legislatures considering private prison contracts. He consistently promoted the effectiveness and efficiency of private prisons, arguably as an independent, objective evaluator. However, his objectivity was called into question when it was discovered that he was a highly paid consultant of C.C.A.

and owned over \$500,000 in C.C.A. stock. He was sanctioned by the state of Florida in 1999 for violating its conflict of interest laws, yet he continues to write articles on private prisons and to provide evaluations that tout their effectiveness (Geis, Mobley, and Shichor, 1999; Mobley and Geis, 2002).

Ogle (1999) argues that private correctional facilities operate in a Catch 22, where organizational imperatives are contradictory. On the one hand is the corporate imperative of profit; on the other is the public service imperative of legitimacy. The two conflict when the most profitable way to run a prison conflicts with the perceived "just" or "humane" way to run a prison. When the private corporation is pursuing profit, it uses adaptations such as compromise and avoidance techniques or defiance and manipulation techniques to circumvent governmental mandates for services and contract fulfillment.

A more abstract and subtle criticism of private corrections is that if people are making money from incarcerating offenders, where is the incentive to correct them? If recidivism were to somehow mysteriously plummet, corporations would show reduced profits and stockholders would lose money. The financial incentive to incarcerate more people for longer periods of time arguably ensures that we will never see a reduction of imprisonment as long as privatization continues to grow. Of course, private corrections officials scoff at the above scenario. They point out that their piece of the "corrections pie" is quite small in comparison to that of the states, that they are closely monitored by staff officials who are unhappy with sharing any amount of resources with them, and that there is plenty of opportunity to expand in other states and even in other countries without somehow conspiring to keep offenders in prison solely for some profit motive.

## Conclusion

In this chapter we have looked at some of the ethical rationales for punishment. What we do to offenders is influenced by our views on such things as free will and determinism, the capacity for individual change, and the basic nature of humankind. Punishment has always been used against those who hurt other members of society and thus might be considered consistent with natural law. However, the limits of punishment have been more changeable and have been subject to the laws and mores of each historical era. Today, our punishments primarily consist of imprisonment or some form of restricted liberty, such as probation or parole. The death penalty continues to be used; however, the controversy surrounding it continues as well.

We have seen a trend where the state delegates its authority to punish. Serious questions have arisen over this practice. Some argue that the profit motive is incompatible with the awesome power of the state to deprive individuals of liberty in the name of punishment.

# Key Terms

**cruel and unusual punishment** punishment proscribed by the Eighth Amendment because it is disproportional and/or gratuitous

**expiation** atonement for a wrong to achieve a state of grace

**general deterrence** what is done to one person discourage future crime by anyone

**incapacitation** holding an offender until there is no risk of further crime

**just deserts model** Fogel's idea that the punishment of an individual should be limited by the seriousness of the crime although treatment could be offered

**justice model** von Hirsch's idea that the punishment of the individual should be purely retributive and balanced to the seriousness of the crime

**new rehabilitationists** current theorists and researchers who believe there is evidence that rehabilitative programs do result in lower recidivism

**prevention** a rationale for punishment that views it as a means rather than an end and embraces any method that can prevent crime, painful or not

**punishment** pain or unpleasantness administered by one in lawful authority in response to a transgression of law or rules

**reintegrative shaming** Braithwaite's idea that certain types of punishment can lead to a reduction of recidivism as long as they do not involve banishment and they induce healthy shame in the individual

**retribution** a rationale for punishment that states that punishment is an end in itself and should be balanced to the harm caused

**specific deterrence** what is done to one person to discourage him or her from committing more crime

**stigmatizing shaming** the effect of punishment whereby the offender feels cast aside and abandoned by the community

**three-strikes laws** habitual-offender laws

**treatment** anything used to induce behavioral change with the goal of eliminating dysfunctional or deviant behavior and encouraging productive and normal behavior patterns

# Review Questions

1. Define punishment, and then discuss the major rationales of punishment.
2. Now defend the rationales of punishment through the use of the ethical systems.
3. What are the three different objectives or approaches to prevention? Explain some issues with each.
4. How would Bentham defend punishment? Contrast that position with Kant's position.
5. What are Mackie's three types of retribution?
6. Support three-strike laws through a retributive rationale and then through a utilitarian rationale.
7. What are some ethical problems with treatment?
8. What are the ways in which prison is harmful?

9. Support or criticize the use of private corrections, and give your reasons.
10. Discuss imprisonment rates, and defend them using utilitarian and retributive philosophies.

# Discussion Questions

1. Would you rather spend a year in prison or receive a severe whipping?
2. Would you rather spend a year in prison or receive five years of probation with very stringent restrictions?
3. Would you rather spend a year in prison or pay a $30,000 fine?
4. If you knew for certain that prison did not deter, would you still be in favor of its use? Why?
5. If we could predict future criminals, would you be willing to incapacitate them before they commit a crime in order to protect society?
6. Should we have guidelines for what we do in the name of treatment? What should they be?
7. State your belief on the use of capital punishment and the reasons for your position. Now take the opposite side, and give the reasons for this view.

# Ethical Dilemmas

## Situation 1

A legislator has proposed a sweeping new crime and punishment bill with the following provisions for punishment. Decide each issue as if you were being asked to vote on it:

- Mandatory life term with no parole for any crime involving a weapon
- Corporal punishment (using an electrical apparatus that inflicts a shock) for all personal violent crimes
- Mandatory five-year prison sentences for those convicted of DWI
- Public executions
- Abolition of probation, to be replaced with fines and prison sentences for those who are not able to pay or are unwilling to do so

## Situation 2

Another legislator has suggested an alternate plan with the following provisions. Vote on these:

- Decriminalization of all drug crimes
- Mandated treatment programs for all offenders who were intoxicated by alcohol or other drugs at the time of the crime

- Restructuring the sentencing statutes to make no sentence longer than five years, except for homicide, attempted homicide, robbery, and rape
- Implementation of a restitution program for all victims whereby offenders stay in the community, work, and pay the victims back for the losses and/or injuries they received

### Situation 3

Your state is one of the few that allows relatives of homicide victims to witness the execution of the perpetrator. Your brother was killed in a robbery, and the murderer is about to be executed. You receive a letter advising you of the execution date and your right to be present. Would you go? Would you volunteer to be the executioner?

### Situation 4

Your house has been burglarized. Your community has a circle sentencing program, and the program's directors have asked you to participate along with the offender who burglarized your house. As you understand it, this means that you would be sitting down with representatives from the police department and court system and the offender and his family. The group would discuss and come to an agreement on the appropriate punishment for the crime. Would you do it?

### Situation 5

You are a legislator who is part of a committee that is revamping the sentencing system. You are contemplating a return back to indeterminate sentencing from the determinate sentencing structure that your state passed in the early 1980s. How would you vote?

## Suggested Readings

Austin, J., and Fabelo, T. 2004. *The Diminishing Returns of Increased Incarceration.* Austin, TX: JFA Institute.

Bedau, H. 1991. "How to Argue About the Death Penalty." *Israel Law Review* 25, 466–480.

Bureau of Justice Statistics, 2005. "Capital Punishment Statistics." Retrieved on October 4, 2005, from http://www.ojp.usdoj.gov/bjs/cp.htm.

Feeney, J. 2005. "The Wisdom and Morality of Present-Day Criminal Sentencing." *Akron Law Review* 38: 853–867.

Kania, R. 1999. "The Ethics of the Death Penalty." *The Justice Professional* 12: 145–157.

Kronenwerter, M. 1993. *Capital Punishment: A Reference Handbook.* Santa Barbara, CA: ABC-CLIO.

Palmer, T. 1994. *A Profile of Correctional Effectiveness and New Directions for Research.* Albany, NY: SUNY Press.

Pollock, J. 2004. *Prisons and Prison Life: Costs and Consequences.* Los Angeles: Roxbury.

Sheldon, R. 2001. *Controlling the Dangerous Classes.* Boston: Allyn and Bacon.

Toch, H. 1997. *Humanistic Corrections.* Guilderland, NY: Harrow and Heston.

West, W., and Morris, R. (Eds.). 2000. *The Case for Penal Abolition.* Toronto, ON: Canadian Scholars Press.

Folsom prison is more than just a line in the song by Johnny Cash.
It has been home to countless inmates.

# 13

# Ethics and Institutional Corrections

*Correctional Professionals*

*Correctional Officers*

*Treatment Staff*

*Management Issues*

*Conclusion*

## Key Terms

correctional officer
hostile work
environment

human service officer
pluralistic ignorance
reciprocity

# Chapter Objectives

1. Become familiar with the role conflict and subculture of correctional officers.

2. Become familiar with the ethical issues for correctional officers.

3. Become familiar with the ethical issues for treatment professionals.

4. Understand some of the unique ethical issues for correctional managers and administrators.

In the last chapter, we examined the rationales for punishment and corrections. In this and the next chapter, we turn our attention to the ethical issues of correctional professionals. As with law enforcement officers and court professionals, discretion is an important topic when discussing the ethics of working in corrections.

# Correctional Professionals

Institutional correctional personnel can be divided into two groups: (1) correctional officers and their supervisors, and (2) treatment professionals, a group that includes educators, counselors, psychologists, and all others connected with programming. These groups have different jobs and different ethical questions. In this book we devote a disproportionate amount of attention to correctional officers, primarily because most of the available information concerns prison personnel. A number of ethical issues that treatment personnel may be faced with are similar to those experienced in a more general way by all treatment professionals, so available sources dealing with ethics in the helping professions would also be applicable to those who work in the corrections field (see, for instance, Corey, Corey, and Callanan, 1988).

We have previously discussed how discretion plays a role in each phase of the criminal justice system. In corrections, discretion is involved when a correctional officer decides to write a disciplinary ticket or merely delivers a verbal reprimand; this is similar to the discretion police have that allows them the decision to arrest. Discretion is also involved when the disciplinary committee makes a decision to punish an inmate for an infraction: The punishment can be as serious as increasing sentence length through loss of good time or as minor as a temporary loss of privileges. What punishment may be administered depends on state law and U.S. Supreme Court decisions related to prisoners' rights, but also largely on the discretion of disciplinary committees. This type of discretion is similar to the discretion of the prosecutor and judge in a criminal trial.

Correctional psychiatrists, psychologists, and counselors have a responsibility to the correctional client. Like the defense attorney, they must use discretion to balance the client's needs against the larger needs of the system or institution. Their role may actually involve more ambiguity than the defense lawyer's because there is some question as to whether they owe their primary allegiance to the offender or to society. Hence, we see that similarities exist between correctional personnel and the other professionals in the criminal justice system. As always, when the power of discretion is present, the potential for abuse is also present. Professional ethics should guide individual decision makers in their use of discretion, but, as with law enforcement and legal professionals, adherence to a code of ethics is influenced by the occupational subculture and institutional values. Formal ethics for correctional personnel will be discussed in more detail shortly.

Correctional officers (C.O.s) are similar to police officers in that their uniform represents the authority of the institution quite apart from any personal power of the person wearing it. Some C.O.s are uncomfortable with this authority and do not know how to handle it. Some C.O.s revel in it and misperceive the bounds of authority given to them as a representative of the state. The following statement is a perceptive observation of how some C.O.s misuse the authority they have (Kauffman, 1988: 50):

> [Some officers] don't understand what authority is and what bounds you have within that authority. . . . I think everyone interprets it to meet their own image of themself. "I'm a corrections officer [slams table]! You sit here! [Slam!] You sit there!" Rather than "I'm a person who has limited authority. So, you know, I'm sorry gentlemen, but you can't sit there. You are going to have to sit over there. That's just the rules," and explaining or something like that the reason why.

This observer obviously recognizes that the uniform bestows the authority of rational and reasonable control, not unbridled domination. The power of the C.O. is limited. In actuality, it is impossible to depend on the authority of the uniform to get tasks accomplished, and one must find personal resources—respect and authority stemming from one's personal reputation—in order to gain cooperation from inmates. Some officers who perceive themselves as powerless in relation to the administration, the courts, and society in general may react to this perceived powerlessness by misusing their little bit of power over inmates. They may abuse their position by humiliating or abusing those in their control.

Thus, in ways somewhat similar to those of police officers, correctional officers have power over offenders. They have the full range of coercive control, including loss of liberty through physical force if necessary. Their power may be misused; a blatant example would be an officer who beats an inmate or a psychologist who coerces sex from an inmate. These are abuses of power, and the possibility for them exists because of the powerlessness of the offender relative to the correctional professional. Sensitivity to ethical issues involves the recognition and respect that one has for this element of the profession.

# Correctional Officers

During the rehabilitative era of the 1970s, professional security staff in corrections exchanged their old label of *guard* for a new one—**correctional officer**. However, the slang terms used to describe these individuals, such as *hack, screw,* and *turnkey,*

have been more resistant to change. Although increasing professionalism and greater knowledge acquisition now characterize the individuals in this occupation, correctional officers, by any name, are still perceived as operating under punitive goals. Crouch (1986/1995) examined how changing goals in the 1970s and 1980s created role conflict and ambiguity for the correctional officer. Along with greater rights for inmates, this era brought danger, loss of control, stress, racial and sexual integration, and deviant behavior among officers. Other factors that have changed the role of the guard include unionization, professionalism, and bureaucratization (Crouch, 1986/1995; Silberman, 1995; and Johnson, 1987/1996/2002).

The American Correctional Association's Code of Ethics outlines formal ethics for correctional professionals (see Box 13-1). The original code was adopted in 1975 and was revised in 1990. The changes between the 1975 version and the 1990 version included changing male pronouns to gender-neutral language. The other consistent change was all references to the offender as *client* were deleted in favor of the use of the term *individual* or *person*. This change may be interpreted as moderating the influence of the treatment ethic and medical model in corrections. The changes made in 1994 were fairly minor.

---

### BOX 13-1 American Correctional Association Code of Ethics

**Preamble**

The American Correctional Association expects of its members unfailing honesty, respect for the dignity and individuality of human beings and a commitment to professional and compassionate service. To this end, we subscribe to the following principles.

Members shall respect and protect the civil and legal rights of all individuals.

Members shall treat every professional situation with concern for the welfare of the individuals involved and with no intent to personal gain.

Members shall maintain relationships with colleagues to promote mutual respect within the profession and improve the quality of service.

Members shall make public criticism of their colleagues or their agencies only when warranted, verifiable, and constructive.

Members shall respect the importance of all disciplines within the criminal justice system and work to improve cooperation with each segment.

Members shall honor the public's right to information and share information with the public to the extent permitted by law subject to individual's right to privacy.

Members shall respect and protect the right of the public to be safeguarded from criminal activity.

Members shall refrain from using their positions to secure personal privileges or advantages.

Members shall refrain from allowing personal interest to impair objectivity in the performance of duty while acting in an official capacity.

---

Members shall refrain from entering into any formal or informal activity or agreement which presents a conflict of interest or is inconsistent with the conscientious performance of duties.

Members shall refrain from accepting any gifts, service, or favor that is or appears to be improper or implies an obligation inconsistent with the free and objective exercise of professional duties.

Members shall clearly differentiate between personal views/statements and views/statements/positions made on behalf of the agency or Association.

Members shall report to appropriate authorities any corrupt or unethical behaviors in which there is sufficient evidence to justify review.

Members shall refrain from discriminating against any individual because of race, gender, creed, national origin, religious affiliation, age, disability, or any other type of prohibited discrimination.

Members shall preserve the integrity of private information; they shall refrain from seeking information on individuals beyond that which is necessary to implement responsibilities and perform their duties; members shall refrain from revealing nonpublic information unless expressly authorized to do so.

Members shall make all appointments, promotions, and dismissals in accordance with established civil service rules, applicable contract agreements, and individual merit, rather than furtherance of personal interests.

Members shall respect, promote, and contribute to a work place that is safe, healthy, and free of harassment in any form.

SOURCE: Adopted August 1975 at the 105th Congress of Correction. Revised August 1990 at the 120th Congress of Correction. Revised August 1994 at the 124th Congress of Correction. Reprinted with permission of the American Correctional Association, Lanham, MD.

There exist many similarities between this code and the Law Enforcement Code presented in Chapter 7. For instance, integrity, respect for and protection of individual rights, and service to the public are emphasized in both codes, as are the importance and sanctity of the law. Also, the prohibition against exploiting professional authority for personal gain is stressed in both codes.

Another similarity between this code and the Law Enforcement Code is the disparity that sometimes exists between the ideal behavior it describes and what actually occurs. The A.C.A. Code of Ethics describes the ideal behavior of correctional staff; however, as was discussed in Chapter 7, subcultural values may be inconsistent with and subvert formal ethical codes. This is also the case with correctional personnel. Although the ethical code clearly calls for fair and objective treatment, integrity, and high standards of performance, the actual practices of some correctional staff may be quite different.

In an interesting discussion of implementing an ethics program for correctional officers, Barrier and associates (1999) described how officers presented the elements of what they felt were important in an ethics code:

- Acting professionally
- Showing respect for inmates and workers

- Maintaining honesty and integrity
- Being consistent
- Acting impartially
- Being assertive but not aggressive
- Confronting bad behavior but reinforcing good behavior
- Standardizing rule enforcement
- Respecting others
- Practicing the golden rule
- Encouraging teamwork
- Using professional language
- Not abusing sick leave
- Telling inmates the truth
- Admitting mistakes

These elements are similar to those expressed in the Law Enforcement Code of Ethics and are consistent with the ethical frameworks.

## The Correctional Officer Subculture

The correctional officer subculture has never been as extensively described as the police subculture, but some elements are similar. First of all, the inmate may be considered the enemy, along with superiors and society in general. Moreover, the acceptance of the use of force, the preference toward redefining job roles to meet only minimum requirements, and the willingness to use deceit to cover up wrongdoing are evident in both subcultures (Johnson, 1996; Crouch, 1980; Grossi and Berg, 1991).

Kauffman (1988: 85–112), in an excellent study of the officers' world, notes the following norms of the correctional officer subculture:

1. *Always go to the aid of another officer.* Similar to law enforcement, the necessity of interdependence ensures that this is a strong and pervasive norm in the correctional officer subculture. Kauffman describes a "slam" in Walpole Prison as when the officer slams a heavy cell door, which reverberates throughout the prison building, bringing a dozen officers to his or her aid in minutes—an obvious parallel to the "officer down" call in law enforcement.

2. *Don't lug drugs.* This prohibition is to ensure the safety of other officers, as is the even stronger prohibition against bringing in weapons for inmates. The following norm against "ratting" on a fellow officer may except informing on an officer who is a known offender of this lugging norm.

3. *Don't rat.* In similar ways to the law enforcement subcultural code and, ironically, the inmate code, correctional officers also hate those who inform on their peers. Kauffman notes two subordinate norms: Never rat out an officer to an inmate, and never cooperate in an investigation or, worse yet, testify against a fellow officer in regard to that officer's treatment of inmates.

4. *Never make a fellow officer look bad in front of inmates.* This applies regardless of what the officer did, for it jeopardizes the officer's effectiveness and undercuts the appearance of officer solidarity.

5. *Always support an officer in a dispute with an inmate.* Similar to the previous provision, this prescribes behavior—not only should one not criticize a fellow officer, but one should support him or her against any inmate.

6. *Always support officer sanctions against inmates.* This is a specific version of the previous provision. This includes the use of illegal physical force as well as legal sanctions.

7. *Don't be a white hat.* This prohibition is directed at any behavior, attitude, or expressed opinion that could be interpreted as sympathetic toward inmates. Kauffman also notes that it is often violated and does not have the strong subcultural sanctions that accompany some of the other norms.

8. *Maintain officer solidarity against all outside groups.* Similar to police officers, correctional officers feel denigrated and despised by society at large. This norm reinforces officer solidarity by making any other group, including the media, administration, or the public, the out-group.

9. *Show positive concern for fellow officers.* This norm promotes goodwill toward other officers. Two examples are: never leave another officer a problem, which means don't leave unfinished business at the end of your shift for the next officer to handle; and help your fellow officers with problems outside the institution, meaning lending money to injured or sick officers or helping out in other ways.

Kauffman notes that this code may vary from institution to institution, depending on such factors as permeability, the administration, the level of violence from inmates, architecture, and the demographic profile of officers. Distrust of outsiders, dissatisfaction, and alienation are elements of both the police and the correctional officer subcultures. In both professions, the individuals must work with sometimes-unpleasant people who make it clear that the practitioner is not liked or appreciated. Further, there is public antipathy (either real or perceived) toward the profession, which increases the social distance between criminal justice professionals and all others outside the profession. In addition, the working hours, the nature of the job, and the unwillingness to talk about the job to others outside the profession intensify the isolation that workers feel. One additional point to be made about the occupational subculture is that both law enforcement and corrections have experienced an influx of minorities, the college educated, and women. This demographic change has, no doubt, altered the dynamics of the subculture in both fields.

It should also be pointed out that some researchers feel that some of the values embedded in the correctional officer subculture may not be shared by most officers—a concept referred to as **pluralistic ignorance**. This refers to the idea that a few outspoken and visible members shape the perception that all group members have toward the characteristics of the majority. In a prison, this may mean that a few officers endorse and publicize subcultural values, whereas the majority of officers, who are silent, privately believe in different values (Johnson, 1996: 130). Kauffman found this to be true in attitudes toward the use of force and toward the value of treatment. Individually, officers expressed more positive attitudes than they believed to be typical of the subculture (1988: 179). This situation is probably true of the police subculture as well.

## Relationships with Inmates

One would assume that the general relationship between officers and inmates is one of hatred. That is not necessarily the case. As Martin (1993), a prisoner writer, points out, the posturing and vocalization from either side come from a small number, with the majority of inmates and officers living in an uneasy state of truce, hoping that no one goes over the line on either side. Those officers who engage in unethical activities can go in one direction or another—there are officers who become too friendly with inmates, and there are officers who conduct campaigns of harassment or terror against inmates. The Quote and Query box illustrates this idea.

The majority of both guards and inmates prefer to live in peace and understand that they need to treat each other with some modicum of respect to get along. Unfortunately, both feel they must take sides when conflict occurs. Even though prisoners have come to the aid of officers in physical confrontations, in general, inmates must support their fellow inmates and guards must support their fellow guards, regardless of how little support the individual deserves. Thus, a brutal guard may be protected by his fellows, and a racist guard will not be informally or formally sanctioned. Likewise, an assaultive inmate will not be kept in check by his peer group unless his actions are perceived to hurt their interests.

One serious threat to an officer's ethics and professionalism occurs when relationships with inmates become personal. Gresham Sykes (1980) discussed the issue of **reciprocity** in supervision: Officers become dependent on inmates for important task completion and the smooth management of the tier; in return, C.O.s may overlook inmate infractions and allow a certain degree of favoritism to enter their supervision style (cited in Crouch, 1980: 239). One example of a type of reciprocal relationship that may lead to unethical actions is that between an officer and an informant. Hassine (1996: 119) relates that the widespread use of informants created several negative elements in the prison where he was housed, including pervasive tension and distrust within the inmate population, particularly between parole violators and long-termers,

---

### QUOTE and QUERY

Some convicts hate all prison guards. They perceive them as the physical manifestation of their own misery and misfortune. The uniform becomes the man, and they no longer see an individual behind it. . . . Many guards react in kind. The hatred is returned with the full force of authority. These two factions become the real movers and shakers in the prison world. They aren't a majority in either camp, but the strength of their hatred makes its presence known to all.

Source: D. Martin, *Committing Journalism: The Prison Writings of Red Hog* (New York: Norton, 1993): 94–95.

*How would one reduce the level of hate between these small numbers of prisoners toward guards and guards toward prisoners?*

because parole violators were more likely to snitch to obtain favorable treatment in their short stay. Officers elevated snitches to higher-status positions through granting favored jobs and privileges. The practice did not reduce the prevalence of drugs in prison, according to Hassine, because informers informed only on some drug dealers and not others. Marquart and Roebuck (1986) also discuss the practice of giving special privileges in return for informing. According to these officers, prison management, for the most part, depended on information supplied by snitches.

C.O.s who become personally involved with inmates compromise their professional judgment. Involvement is possible because of proximity and close contact over a period of time, combined with shared feelings of victimization by the administration. Officers may start to feel they have more in common with inmates than with the administration, especially now that officers are more likely to come from urban areas, come from minority groups, and be more demographically similar to the inmates they supervise. Identification and friendship may lead to unethical conduct, such as ignoring infractions or doing illegal favors for an inmate. McCarthy (1991) writes of this exchange relationship as an incentive for further corruption. He also points out that lack of training, low visibility, and unfettered discretion contribute to a variety of corrupt behaviors.

The subcultural norms against sympathizing with or becoming too friendly with inmates, as described by Kauffman (1988), may be seen as a preventative to avoid this identification with inmates. An officer who is too close to inmates is not to be trusted. The subculture minimizes this possibility by a view of inmates as animalistic and not worth human sympathy. Kauffman also notes that inmates themselves make it difficult for C.O.s to continue to hold sympathetic or friendly views. In her study, new officers were continually harassed by inmates until the neutral or positive views they held at entry were replaced with negative views. She described Walpole in the 1970s as overrun with rats and roaches, with excrement smeared on the walls and garbage ankle-deep on the floors—inmates wouldn't clean up, and officers could not. Extreme inmate-on-inmate violence, including mutilations and torture, was commonplace, and officers feared being thrown from the tiers, being knifed in the back, or being hit in the head by soup cans or other heavy objects thrown from the tiers above. This description obviously is not representative of most prisons, then or now, but the elements of inmate hostility, fear, and hopelessness are characteristic of all prisons to some degree.

Just as officers may act in unethical ways when they like an inmate, officers have the power to make life difficult for the inmate they do not like. These extralegal harassments and punishments may include "forgetting" to send an inmate to an appointment, making an inmate stay in "keeplock" longer than necessary, or pretending not to hear someone locked in a cell asking for toilet paper or other necessary items. Lombardo (1981/1989) noted the practice of putting an inmate in "keeplock" on a Friday even without a supportable charge because the disciplinary committee would not meet until the following Monday to release the inmate, the use of profanity toward inmates even in front of families, not notifying an inmate of a visitor, and losing passes.

Kauffman (1988) notes that during the time period she studied, officers sometimes flushed cell toilets to aggravate inmates, dumped good food into the garbage, withheld toilet paper or matches, made up "tips" reporting contraband in a cell that resulted in a shakedown, scratched artwork, and in other innumerable informal ways made the targeted inmate's life miserable. Because prisoners are in a position of need, having to ask for things as simple as permission to go to the bathroom, officers have the power to make inmates feel even more dependent than necessary and humiliated because of their dependency. The relative powerlessness of the officers in relation to their superiors, the administration, and society in general creates a situation where some take advantage of their only power—that over the inmate.

Even more so than police, C.O.s work every day with large numbers of men or women who simply do not like—indeed, sometimes hate—the correctional officer for no other reason than the uniform he or she is wearing. There is always the potential of injury from an unprovoked attack, while subduing an inmate, while breaking up a fight, or from being taken hostage. Officers will say this last possibility is never far from their minds and may affect to a certain extent their supervision of inmates, for it is potentially dangerous to be personally disliked. On the other hand, on a day-to-day basis inmates are not that much different from anyone else; some are friendly, some are funny, and some are good conversationalists. A comfortable alliance is sometimes formed between the guards and the guarded, especially in work settings, that is not unlike a foreman–employee relationship. This strange combination of familiarity and fear results in a pervasive feeling of distrust. Officers insist that "you can be friendly with inmates, but you can never trust them."

Mature officers learn to live with this basic inconsistency and are able to differentiate situations in which rules must be followed from those in which rules can be relaxed. Younger and less perceptive officers either take on a defensive attitude of

## QUOTE and QUERY

I never shake hands with an inmate. . . . They neither are nor ought to be viewed as equals.

Source: George Beto, administrator of Texas prison system, 1962–1972, quoted in Dilulio (1987: 177).

[T]he Sergeant had succeeded in making me feel even more isolated from the world that existed outside the prison walls. I was no longer so proud to be an American. I was just a convict without rights. . . .

Source: Victor Hassine, inmate (1996: 52).

Because legitimate power is so unevenly distributed between the keepers and the kept, left to its own inertia abuses of that power will inevitably creep into any prison without diligent and sensitive oversight.

Source: Patrick McManus, state correctional official, reported in Martin (1993: 333).

*Should the attitude of correctional professionals be that inmates are not worthy of a handshake, or does that isolation from the "community of man" create the potential for abuse?*

extreme distrust or are manipulated by inmates because they are not able to tell the difference between goodwill and gaming. In the Quote and Query box on page 428, the concept of the gulf between the status of guard and guarded is the theme.

## *General Conduct and the "Good Officer"*

Historically, correctional officers have been described as role models for inmates. In reference to an early and idealistic view of who should be hired and for what reasons, one author writes that this was a "pursuit of men with 'special gifts of personality and character' capable of achieving the moral transformation of their fellow men merely by the exercise of 'personal influence'" (Hawkins, cited in Crouch, 1980: 55). This was, by and large, probably a false dream, but it has always been true that no one else in corrections has more day-to-day contact with inmates. For this reason, it is important to look at the types of individuals hired to fill correctional officer positions and how they respond to the environment of the prison.

Officers, of course, are individuals, and they respond differently to the demands and job pressures of corrections. Officers fall into various types:

1. *The violence-prone,* who use the role of correctional officer to act out an authoritarian role.
2. *Time-servers,* who serve time in prison much the same way as the inmates do, avoiding trouble and hoping that nothing goes wrong on their shift.
3. *Counselors,* who seek to enlarge their job description and perceive their role as including counseling and helping the inmate rather than merely locking doors and signing passes. This type of officer has been called the **human service officer** and incorporates the tasks of providing goods and services, acting as a referral agent or advocate, and helping with institutional adjustment problems. (Johnson, 1987/1996/2002)

Not surprisingly, C.O.s and inmates tend to agree on a description of a good officer:

1. A good officer is described as one who treats all inmates fairly with no favoritism, but who does not always follow rules to the letter. Discretion is used judicially; when a good officer makes a decision to bypass rules, all involved tend to agree that it is the right decision.
2. A good officer is not quick to use force, nor afraid of force if it becomes necessary.
3. A good officer treats inmates in a professional manner and gives them the respect they deserve as human beings.
4. A good officer will treat the inmate in the way anyone would like to be treated; if the inmate abuses the officer, then that inmate earns different treatment, but it is through formal channels, not informal. In some cases such an officer will go far outside regular duties to aid an inmate who is sincerely in need; however, he or she can detect game playing and cannot be manipulated.

These traits—consistency, fairness, and flexibility—are confirmed as valuable by research (Johnson, 1987: 139). Although many officers in prisons reach this ideal, the trend today seems to be a less honorable approach to the position because of some new pressures (Conover, 2000). Recent changes have taken away much of the service functions that C.O.s used to perform. Lombardo (1997), in his update of an older study, found that in the ten years that ensued since his first study, much of the ability of C.O.s to grant favors had been taken away. For instance, telephones in the yard eliminated the need for C.O.s to run interference for inmates and get them a pass to make a phone call. This situation increased the autonomy of inmates, but it reduced the ability of the C.O.s to develop helping relationships with inmates, or, to put a more negative interpretation on their loss, it reduced their ability to create debts from the inmate—favors owed in return for favors given. C.O.s have much less discretion today, and practically every decision that in the past had been made by a C.O. is now made by sergeants and specialized officers. C.O.s feel less responsible and, one might argue, act less responsibly because of this feeling.

Like police, correctional officers feel that court decisions and administrative goals have not supported their needs and have sacrificed their safety to meet inmates' demands. One result of this feeling that superiors and society do not protect their interests is an individualistic response to the ethical issues that may come up in the course of the job. The following presents a fairly negative view of the correctional officer's ethical position (Carroll, cited in Crouch, 1980: 318):

> [T]he officers are not working for the inmates, they are working for themselves. Unable to secure compliance with their directives by the enforcement of a set of impersonal rules, they seek to secure compliance by means of friendships, overlooking infractions, and providing highly desired information to inmates. Their behavior is not so much a repudiation of the goal of custodial control as it is an attempt to maintain order, and at the same time to protect themselves, in the face of institutional changes that have made order more difficult to maintain and their position more vulnerable.

Correctional officers report much stress, and stress-related illnesses such as hypertension are common, as well as social problems such as alcoholism and divorce. Some reports indicate that these problems exist in higher numbers with correctional officers than with police officers. Correctional officers feel criticized and even scorned by many, and it is little wonder that they adapt to their role by such means, yet it is important to understand the consequences of such a position. Kauffman (1988: 222) talked to officers who reported that they had lost their morality in the prison:

> These officers experienced anguish at the change that was wrought in them by the prison environment: Initially, many attempted to avoid engaging in behavior injurious to inmates. . . . As their involvement in the prison world grew and their ability to abstain from morally questionable actions within the prison declined, they attempted to neutralize their own feelings of guilt by regarding prisons as separate moral realms with their own distinct set of moral standards or by viewing inmates as individuals outside the protection of moral laws. When such efforts failed, they shut their minds to what others were doing and to what they were doing themselves.

Without a strong moral and ethical code, correctional officers may find themselves drifting into relativistic egoism: What benefits the individual is considered acceptable, despite long-term effects or inconsistencies with their role and their personal value system. The result is feelings of disillusionment and anomie, and the side effects can be serious dissatisfaction and depression. To maintain a sense of morality in an inherently coercive environment is no easy task, yet a strong set of individual ethics is probably the best defense against being changed by the negative environment of the prison.

## *Use of Force*

The use of force is a legal and sometimes necessary element of correctional supervision, and most observers say that the serious abuse that occurred in prisons in the past simply does not occur today. For instance, "tune-ups" in the Texas prisons involved "verbal humiliation, profanity, shoves, kicks, and head and body slaps"; "ass-whipping"; and using blackjacks and batons to inflict injury. Severe beatings were reserved for those few inmates who attacked staff members (Crouch and Marquart, 1989: 78). Murton (1976) described a litany of abuses that occurred in Arkansas prison farms, including the "Tucker telephone," an electrical device that was attached to the genitals of inmates and used to deliver severe shocks as a form of torture (see the Quote and Query box). These uses of force are not pervasive today; however, there are still reports that force is used as an extralegal punishment against unruly or aggressive inmates.

Ironically, the reduction of official oppression in the late 1970s and 1980s opened the door to gangs and inmate cliques who filled the power vacuum and used violence to get what they wanted. Inmates in the 1980s had less to fear from guards but more to fear from one another as racial gangs and other powerful cliques or individuals solidified their control over prison black markets. There was a time in the 1970s and 1980s when officers described some prisons as "out of control." There were prisons where guards were afraid to walk into living units, and inmates literally controlled some parts of the prison. In Rhode Island, for instance, officers who felt betrayed by the courts and management, in effect, gave up guarding. Carroll tracked the changes that occurred during the 1970s in Rhode Island and described how the events there were quite similar to those of Texas in the 1980s and those of other states when court decisions upset the balance of power (Carroll, 1998). Taylor (1993) documented similar changes in the Mississippi system.

---

**QUOTE and QUERY**

. . . lashing an inmate ten times a day with the "hide," a five-foot leather strap capable of maiming. This official method of discipline was augmented by such illegal but customary techniques as inserting needles under the fingernails, crushing knuckles and testicles with pliers, hitting the inmate with a club, blackjack, or "anything you can lay your hands on," kicking inmates in the groin, mouth, or testicles—and, of course, use of the infamous "Tucker Telephone."

Source: T. Murton, *The Dilemma of Prison Reform* (New York: Irvington, 1976): 147.

*Explain how individual guards could justify to themselves the use of such devices of torture.*

The "golden years" of prison depend on one's perspective. Glenn (2001), a retired prison warden, described the Texas prison system in the early 1960s as "fair" and "just," arguing that the allegations of abuse by guards and building tenders were slander (2001: 24). He then describes the forms of punishment used. The "rail" was a two-by-four turned on its side. An inmate found guilty of a minor offense was required to stand on the rail for a period of four hours; if he fell off, the time would start again. If an inmate didn't pick enough cotton, he would be made to stand on a barrel for four or five hours. Up to four inmates might be placed on a single barrel, and if one fell off, the time would start again for them all. Other inmates would have their hands raised above their head and handcuffed to the bars in the inmate mess hall; their feet would be cuffed as well. They might be hanging all night (2001: 25–26).

Glenn also described a situation where an inmate tried to escape, was shot, and then was hung on the front gate, bleeding, for the field hoe squads to see as they came back in from the fields. This was described by Glenn as an "effective . . . object lesson" rather than brutality (2001: 44). Glenn also described a prison captain who played a "game" with inmates who he believed weren't working hard enough on the hoe squad. He would have them tied and stripped, and then he would lower his pants and threaten to sodomize them (2001: 69).

According to observers, this type of official violence has been drastically reduced or even eliminated entirely. However, less pervasive violence continues. As with the use of force in law enforcement, policy definitions of *necessary force* are vague. This may mean that the resort to violence is the absolute last alternative available, or it may mean that force is used when it is the most convenient way to get something accomplished (Morris and Morris, cited in Crouch, 1980: 253). During the course of a fistfight or a struggle with an inmate, officers react to violence instinctively—that is, without much rational thought as to whether a blow is necessary or gratuitous.

Evidence that beatings still exist can be found in court cases. For instance, in *Hudson v. McMillian* (503 U.S. 1 [1992]) the U.S. Supreme Court dealt with a case involving an inmate who had been forced to sit in a chair while two officers hit him in the head and chest area, with a lieutenant looking on. The state argued that because there was no "serious injury," there was no constitutional violation, because cruel and unusual punishment had to involve serious injury. Although some justices agreed with this logic, the majority held that injuries need not be serious for a constitutional violation to occur if the injury was gratuitous.

Some uses of force may result in death. Nine Florida guards were indicted in 1999 for the murder of an inmate. The inmate died from injuries including broken ribs, swollen testicles, and innumerable cuts and bruises. He was on death row for killing a prison guard in a botched escape attempt in 1983. Prosecutors alleged he was killed because he was planning to go to the media with allegations of widespread abuse in the prison. Accused guards insisted he killed himself by flinging himself against the concrete wall of his cell or, alternatively, that he was killed by other inmates (Cox, 2000). The first three officers who were tried were acquitted in February 2002 ("Three Guards," 2002).

C.O.s may view such beatings as utilitarian in that they serve as warnings to all inmates that they will receive similar treatment if they attack C.O.s; thus, the action protects all officers to some extent from inmate aggression. Officers might also defend the action on retributive grounds because the inmate would probably not be punished for the attack through legal channels. However, these retaliations always represent the most brutal and inhumane aspects of incarceration and damage the integrity of all correctional professionals.

Bowker (1980) and other authors describe the victimization of inmates by correctional officers, including psychological torture, racial discrimination, and severe physical abuse. The explanations for why this type of behavior on the part of officers exists include the officers' pervasive sense of fear and the C.O. subculture that tolerates if not encourages such victimization. Crouch and Marquart (1989) and Crouch (1986/1995) also discuss the use of violence as a rite of passage for the correctional officer, a way to prove oneself as competent. Baro (1995) describes a more systemic brutality in the Hawaii prison system that eventually led to an investigation by the U.S. Attorney General's office.

The use in federal prisons of special operations and response teams (SORT)—the prison version of special weapons and tactical teams (SWAT)—is a new wrinkle in the use of force in prison. These officers respond to incidents in full riot gear, making them look like a mixture of a professional football team, astronauts, and toxic waste disposal experts. They epitomize depersonalized violence—they are so fully padded, helmeted, and hooded that they can hardly feel pain, and they come in such numbers that the individual inmate is immediately overwhelmed. This approach is touted as actually preventing official brutality and minimizing the injuries that can occur to inmates and officers alike when there is an altercation. The highly trained team members subdue an inmate before he can strike any blows; they are so swift that the inmate is stripped, handcuffed, and picked up and carried away in a matter of minutes. These teams also exist in state prisons. The very depersonalization of such teams leads to worries about abuse. In the same way an inmate can be subdued, stripped, and moved by the team, they can also take him down a flight of stairs, with his head hanging and hitting every step. Their masks give them the anonymity that was not available to officers in the "old days," when inmates were just called into the captain's office for a "tune-up." In fact, in some prisons it is a practice not to let it be known which officers are on the team—because of the hatred that prisoners feel for team members.

It should be noted that prison brutality is not a uniquely American phenomenon. The United Kingdom, Australia, and other countries have had their own scandals concerning abuse of prisoners. For instance, the Bathurst riots in New South Wales (Australia) in the 1970s prompted a commission inquiry and report. The report included a scathing commentary on the prison management's efforts to cover up the widespread practice of "bashing intractables" upon entry to the prison and for the most trivial of rule infractions (Findlay, 1982).

## Corruption

McCarthy (1991, 1995) and Souryal (1999a) discuss the major types of corruption engaged in by correctional officers and other officials in institutional corrections. Categories include theft, trafficking, embezzlement, and misuse of authority. Under misuse of authority McCarthy details the following:

- Accepting gratuities for special consideration for legitimate purposes
- Accepting gratuities for protection of illicit activities

- Mistreatment/harassment or extortion of inmates
- Mismanagement (e.g., prison industries)
- Miscellaneous abuses

Souryal (1999a), in another typology, describes the types of corruption as falling into the following categories:

- Arbitrary use of power (treating workers or inmates preferentially or in a biased fashion)
- Oppression and failure to demonstrate compassion/caring
- Abusing authority for personal gain (extortion, smuggling, theft)

Periodically, news stories will describe officers who committed illegal and/or unethical acts. For instance, four state prison guards faced felony bribery charges after they agreed to launder money for inmates. One received $60,000 with the understanding that he would get $10,000 for his services (A.P., 2000: B3). In 1990, wide-scale corruption involving smuggling drugs into Florida's Martin Correctional Institution resulted in fifteen arrests of corrections officers (Houston, 1999: 360). Carroll (1998) presents other examples where investigations uncovered abuses including sexual abuse of inmates, brutality, and bribery at the highest levels of corrections departments.

As discussed earlier, Tom Murton uncovered a web of corrupt practices in Arkansas in the early 1970s. His experience was fictionalized to some extent in the movie *Brubaker,* but the worst aspects of prisoner abuse shown in the movie were real. An associate superintendent from a prison in Pennsylvania testified before an investigative committee of the state legislature after a four-day riot in which inmates and officers were savagely beaten (cited in Hassine, 1996: 149–152; also see Murton and Hyams, 1969). His testimony detailed the widespread corrupt practices of many of the officers and supervisors in the prison, including the following:

- An officer was beaten up by other officers in the prison.
- An officer was caught smuggling in contraband (sneakers, coffee, chewing gum, letters, etc.) for inmates.
- An officer was caught attempting to deliver methamphetamine.
- An officer allowed an inmate into restricted housing, where he beat another inmate for two hours.
- An officer raped an inmate.
- A female officer sent inmate money and personal items, visited an inmate at another institution, and wrote letters to inmates.
- A staff member appeared at work under the influence of cocaine.
- An instructor was found with a box of ammunition and alcoholic beverages in his van at the rear gate of the prison.
- An activities director embezzled funds from the inmates' Jaycees and Lifers association.
- An officer engaged an inmate in a fistfight in the dayroom over losing a bet with the inmate.
- An instructor smeared peanut butter into a black inmate's hair, put flour and jelly in other inmates' hair, rubbed an onion in the face of another, conducted

a mock hanging off a steam pipe dressed as a Ku Klux Klan member, and abused others verbally—his actions were directed only to African American inmates.

- A labor foreman purposely slammed on his brakes and flipped an inmate over the hood of his truck.
- A food service supervisor allowed a food fight in the kitchen.
- An officer engaged in horseplay—punching and wrestling an inmate.
- An officer was investigated for shoplifting.

More recently, Corcoran prison guards in California were accused of setting up gladiator-type fights between inmates and encouraging or allowing prisoner rapes. One former guard testified that a "loudmouth" prisoner was placed with a prison rapist known as the "Booty Bandit" (Arax, 1999: A3). Other guards were accused of an unlawful use of force by shooting an inmate during one of the gladiator fights. Eventually, several guards received federal indictments and were tried for the killing, as well as the other acts of oppression. Some argue that the officer union "tainted" the jury pool by running television ads before the jury selection that showed officers as tough, brave, and underappreciated. The television ads, with the tagline of "Corcoran officers: They walk the toughest beat in the state," aired only in the Fresno area where the trial was held (Lewis, 1999). The accused guards were acquitted even though former guards and other experts supported the inmates' allegations ("Three Guards," 2000).

California's Department of Corrections has been described as corrupt from "the top down" because investigations of wrongdoing seem to be thwarted by powerful union leaders. There have been allegations that members of the independent Office of Inspector General were fired at the behest of the correctional officer union (Thompson, 2004). Subsequently, the office was to have been subsumed under the management of the Department of Corrections, a condition that was described as the "fox guarding the chickens," and there was enough public criticism that the governor's office withdrew the plan.

Legislative hearings about events in the corrections system, including a Folsom riot that was said by some to have originated through guards conspiring with one of the gangs, were provided heavy security. One legislator received death threats, and witnesses were under protective custody (Thompson, 2004). The riot and its cover-up evidently led directly to the suicide of an officer who attempted to thwart the riot but was stopped by a supervisor. He left a message that said "My job killed me" (Warren, 2004).

One whistleblower, Donald Vodicka, a fifteen-year correctional officer veteran, testified that the code of silence was pervasive, especially at the Corcoran and Pelican Bay prisons, and that a whistleblower would not be protected by the Department of Corrections against fellow guards. In response to a request by an Internal Affairs lieutenant, he provided memorandums about the activities of a group of officers at Salinas Valley Prison called "The Green Wall." The group was formed when inmates who had injured officers in a disturbance were beaten by the officers in turn. Even officers in Internal Affairs were affiliated with the group, using such markers as green armbands, green ink, and lapel pins. One officer was given an engraved green-handled knife upon a promotion. The Internal Affairs lieutenant transferred in frustration when nothing was done about the "officer gang," and Vodicka learned that his memos had been leaked when he was challenged, berated, and threatened by other officers. He transferred to another prison, but his supervisors there continued the harassment. He eventually took a stress-related leave (Arax, 2004).

Since the hearings, the new director has circulated memos promising zero tolerance for any code-of-silence sanctions. He has incurred the ire of the correctional union for his seeming condemnation of all officers, not just wrongdoers. Several wardens and assistant wardens have resigned, have taken early retirement, or were fired over the Folsom Prison riot scandal, and dozens of correctional officers have been fired for wrongdoing in 2004 and 2005. Observers note that it may be that the department is finally serious about reducing the level of corruption and ensuring that whistleblowers are not sanctioned by the code of silence (Warren, 2004).

Questionable practices are engaged in by individuals in every level of the prison structure. In Texas, Andy "James" Collins, an ex-director of the Department of Corrections, was investigated for his business association with a Canadian company that made VitaPro—a vegetable-based protein substance that evidently tasted bad and created digestive problems for some people. It was discovered that

(a) The state prison system had warehouses full of this product because inmates wouldn't eat it and the state was locked into a contract that mandated a certain number of pounds of it had to be bought every month.

(b) The contract, which was worth millions, had not been approved by the Board of Criminal Justice, an overseer body, because of a loophole that allowed products for prison industry to avoid the bidding and approval process, yet the only relationship this product had to prison industry was that prisoners repackaged the stuff for attempted sale to other prisons, but the planned sales never materialized because no other prison system would buy it.

(c) The director, immediately upon leaving his job in 1996, started as a thousand-dollar-per-day consultant with the same company. In 2001 he and the director of that company were finally convicted by a federal jury on charges of bribery, conspiracy, and money laundering. The case is on appeal.

A Florida news article reported that prison guards were more than twice as likely as police officers to violate state standards of conduct. An analysis of the state records for disciplinary actions showed that from January 1998 to June 1999, 769 corrections officers (29.6 per 1,000) were brought up on disciplinary charges, including sexual assault, shoplifting, and excessive force. During the same period 559 law enforcement officers from city, county, and state police forces were sanctioned (14.0 per 1,000) (Kleindienst, 1999). What can be made of this statistic? Perhaps nothing, but if it is true that correctional officers have a higher pattern of misconduct, then it would be important to identify the cause and remedy the situation. Possible reasons are the following:

1. There is less of a culture of professionalism.
2. There is a lack of hiring incentives and standards.
3. Training may lack the component of ethics.

One would expect that state corrections departments would want to know and understand the reasons that officers misbehave. Corruption exists in prisons today, and it will probably continue to exist, but there are measures that can be used to address the existence of corruption.

Correctional managers should generate a strong anti-corruption policy (obviously, managers should not be engaging in corrupt practices themselves). Such a policy would include

1. proactive measures such as mechanisms to investigate and detect wrongdoing
2. reduced opportunities for corruption
3. screening of employees using state-of-the-art psychological tools
4. improved working conditions
5. providing good role models in the form of supervisors and administrators who follow the Code of Ethics presented earlier in this chapter (McCarthy, 1991)

By most accounts, law enforcement seems to be ahead of corrections in ethics training for its officers. The "trickle down" theory of ethical management is that officers will treat inmates the way they perceive they are being treated—with fairness, compassion, and respect. Or with less than fairness, respect, and compassion if that is the way they felt they are treated by management. It becomes easier to justify unethical actions if one feels victimized (Houston, 1999; Souryal, 1999a). Furthermore, staff who are coerced to do unethical or illegal actions by management are more likely to behave in unethical and illegal ways by their own initiative.

## Loyalty and Whistleblowing

There are many similarities between police and correctional staff in use-of-force abuses, the code of silence, and feelings of isolation. There are also differences. The most striking difference between the two jobs is that C.O.s must deal with the same people daily in a closed, oppressive environment. Police officers have freedom of movement and can avoid peers or citizen troublemakers to a certain extent, but C.O.s have no such luxury. If a C.O. fears an inmate, he or she must still face him or her every day. If a C.O. violates the correctional subcultural code, the sanctions are felt perhaps even more acutely than by police officers, because one must work closely with other C.O.s all day long. Whereas police officers cite the importance of being able to trust other officers as backups in violent situations, one could make the argument that C.O.s need to trust one another more completely, more implicitly, and more frequently, given that violence in some institutions is pervasive and unprovoked, and the C.O. carries no weapon. An officer described to Kauffman (1988: 207) the result of violating peer trust:

> If an incident went down, there was no one to cover my back. That's a very important lesson to learn. You need your back covered and my back wasn't covered there at all. And at one point I was in fear of being set up by guards. I was put in dangerous situations purposely. That really happened to me.

Fear of violating the code of silence is one reason that officers do not report wrongdoing. Loyalty is another. C.O.s feel a strong *esprit de corps* that is similar to the previously discussed loyalty among police. This positive loyalty also results in covering for other officers and not testifying or reporting offenses. McCarthy (1991) discusses types of corrupt behaviors in a prison, including theft, trafficking in contraband, embezzlement, and misuse of authority. These offenses are known yet unreported by other correctional officers because of loyalty and subcultural prohibitions against "ratting." A pattern of complicity also prevents reporting. New officers cannot possibly follow all the many rules and regulations that exist in a prison and still adequately deal with inmates on a day-to-day basis. Before long, they find themselves involved in activity that could result in disciplinary action. Because others are usually aware of this activity and do not inform supervisors, an implicit conspiracy of silence develops so that no one is turned in for anything because each of the others who might witness this wrongdoing has engaged in behavior that could also be sanctioned (Lombardo, 1981: 79).

Hamm (1989) discusses whistleblowing in corrections. He presents examples where correctional professionals did come forward. The examples included instances of norm violations including injustice, inefficiency, ineffectiveness, fairness, and incompetence. It may be a person or a policy that was the object of whistleblowing. He also points out that whistleblowers are sometimes pursuing self-interest or personal goals by informing. At times, there are minimal costs; however, in instances where the individual goes against the subculture, there may be serious consequences. See the "In the News" box for one example.

A rabble-rouser or whistleblower can be defined as someone who finds it impossible to live with knowledge of corruption without doing something about it—usually creating a scandal that exposes the corruption. The term has negative connotations, but it actually describes someone who is typically responding to a higher ethical code than those whose behavior is exposed. Tom Murton found his career dramatically altered when he was hired by the Arkansas Department of Correction as its director of corrections. Upon arriving in the Arkansas system, he discovered abuses and inhumane

---

**IN THE NEWS "I Should Have Kept Quiet"**

One correctional employee wished he hadn't been a whistleblower in an incident in New Jersey. Frank Preston, an education supervisor, filed a formal complaint and also wrote a letter to the governor when he saw two C.O.'s use what he considered to be excessive force against an inmate. He was fired three weeks later. He also alleged that correctional officers in the prison somehow received a copy of his confidential complaint and copied and distributed it to other officers, necessitating a transfer for his own safety. The allegations are counter to the policy advocated by the department of corrections which encourages officers to come forward to expose wrongdoing.

Source: R. Hepp, "Corrections Worker: I Should Have Kept Quiet," NJ.com, May 16, 2005. Retrieved on May 18, 2005, from http://www.nj.com/printer/printer.ssf?/base/news-0/1116293400232240.xml.

*How can you tell when someone is fired for whistleblowing as opposed to legitimate reasons?*

conditions, described later in several writings and immortalized in the movie *Brubaker*. The U.S. Supreme Court case of *Holt v. Sarver*, 442 F.2d 304 (8th Cir. 1971), also documented the abuses. In addition to extreme physical treatment, including the "Tucker telephone"—an electrical apparatus used to shock inmates—Murton had information that there were hundred of inmates listed as escapees who had evidently disappeared. Acting on the information of one informant, he dug up (on the grounds of the prison) two bodies that had injuries exactly as the inmate described—one had been decapitated, and one had a crushed skull. Opposing testimony at the legislative hearing called in response to his investigation proposed that the bodies were from an old church cemetery. Instead of pursuing the matter further and digging up more bodies or testing them in any way for age and other identifying marks, state officials fired Murton and threatened him with prosecution as a grave robber (Murton, 1976).

## Jail Officers

Very little has been written about jail officers. Jail officers may be sheriff deputies who must complete their assignment at the jail before they can "promote" to street patrol. Sometimes jail officers are street deputies who are transferred back to the jail for punishment. In other situations, jail officers are not deputies and have a separate title and pay scale (usually lower). In all these situations, the tasks and skills associated with managing jail inmates are discounted or ignored. There is a need for greater recognition of the profession of jail officer; the position should not merely be a dreaded rite-of-passage assignment, a punishment, or a stepping-stone to deputy status, because the body of knowledge required to do the job well is different from that which a street deputy needs. Recently, there has been an attempt to professionalize the image of jail officers, starting again with a code of ethics. See the "American Jail Association Code of Ethics for Jail Officers" in Box 13-2.

---

**BOX 13-2  American Jail Association Code of Ethics for Jail Officers**

As an officer employed in a detention/correctional capacity, I swear (or affirm) to be a good citizen and a credit to my community, state, and nation at all times. I will abstain from all questionable behavior which might bring disrepute to the agency for which I work, my family, my community, and my associates.

My lifestyle will be above and beyond reproach and I will constantly strive to set an example of a professional who performs his/her duties according to the laws of our country, state, and community and the policies, procedures, written and verbal orders, and regulations of the agency for which I work.

On the job I promise to:

**Keep** the institution secure so as to safeguard my community and the lives of the staff, inmates, and visitors on the premises.

*continued*

---

---

**BOX 13-2 Continued**

**Work** with each individual firmly and fairly without regard to rank, status, or condition.

**Maintain** a positive demeanor when confronted with stressful situations of scorn, ridicule, danger, and/or chaos.

**Report** either in writing or by word of mouth to the proper authorities those things which should be reported, and keep silent about matters which are to remain confidential according to the laws and rules of the agency and government.

**Manage** and supervise the inmates in an evenhanded and courteous manner.

**Refrain** at all times from becoming personally involved in the lives of the inmates and their families.

**Treat** all visitors to the jail with politeness and respect and do my utmost to ensure that they observe the jail regulations.

**Take** advantage of all education and training opportunities designed to assist me to become a more competent officer.

**Communicate** with people in or outside of the jail, whether by phone, written word, or word of mouth, in such a way so as not to reflect in a negative manner upon my agency.

**Contribute** to a jail environment which will keep the inmate involved in activities designed to improve his/her attitude and character.

**Support** all activities of a professional nature through membership and participation that will continue to elevate the status of those who operate our nation's jails.

**Do my best** through word and deed to present an image to the public at large of a jail professional, committed to progress for an improved and enlightened criminal justice system.

SOURCE: Reprinted with permission of the American Jail Association.

---

Arguably, the job of jail officer is even more difficult than that of correctional officer because jail officers must deal with a transitory population rather than a fairly stable one. Offenders come into jail intoxicated, suffer from undiagnosed epilepsy or other diseases, may suffer overdoses, and may be suicidal. Visitation is more frequent, and family issues are more problematic in jails than prisons. The constant activity and chaotic environment of a jail often create unique ethical dilemmas. One can also find the same type of unethical behavior that one finds with police and correctional officers—jail officers can be uncaring and insensitive to human needs. Then again, some jail officers' behavior could be considered that of a human service officer described earlier. In the "In the News" box on the next page, the jail officers present a chilling example of what can happen when officers forget their ethical duties.

Farkas (1999), in a study of 125 county correctional officers, found that many officers expressed support for rehabilitation. For instance, more than 70 percent disagreed with the statement "rehabilitative programs are a waste of time and money."

---

**IN THE NEWS** **Jail Guards Taunt Prisoner Dying of Cocaine Overdose**

FORT PIERCE, FLA.—A man who swallowed cocaine when he was arrested died after jailers ignored his pleas for help and taunted him in a three-hour ordeal captured on video by a jail surveillance camera. Two sheriff's deputies were later fired, and five others disciplined.

Anderson Tate moaned, thrashed and chanted prayers for more than three hours while bound to a chair Dec. 3 at the St. Lucie County Jail. Jail employees and deputies walked past him, and one made fun of him. "I don't want to die. I'm burning up," he said on the footage released Wednesday. "I'm 300 degrees. I've got too much cocaine in my system." State prosecutors are investigating and will decide whether to bring criminal charges against the officers. . . . Tate is black; six of the officers are white, and the other is Hispanic. . . . Tate had been pulled over for not having a license plate and driving without a valid license. He apparently swallowed some cocaine he was carrying when he was arrested but initially refused medical treatment, said St. Lucie County Undersheriff Dennis Williams. One of the fired deputies taunted Tate, clapping and stomping his feet to the beat of Tate's chants and fanning him with a clipboard when he said he was burning up, Williams said. Jail officials didn't become alarmed until the 22-year-old man went into convulsions and stopped breathing. Tate died about 11 hours later at a hospital.

Rubin said a jail nurse checked on Tate three times. Williams called the officers' behavior unacceptable. Deputies told investigators that they knew something wasn't right but that everyone assumed someone else was taking charge, the undersheriff said.

Source: Associated Press, *Austin American-Statesman*, February, 8, 1997, A16. Reprinted with permission of the Associated Press.

*Why didn't at least one of the jail officers call for medical assistance?*

---

These officers were not naïve; they also overwhelmingly agreed that you couldn't trust an inmate (84 percent) and that a personal relationship with an inmate invited corruption (95 percent). Furthermore, Farkas found that older officers expressed greater support for a counseling orientation, consistent with earlier research by Toch and Klofas (1982). Female officers were more likely to express both high agreement with counseling principles and a punitive approach. However, work variables were more influential than individual characteristics (e.g., shift, contact hours, job satisfaction, role conflict), although some of the relationships are a bit puzzling. For instance, high job satisfaction correlated with less support for a counseling role and less agreement with harsher conditions. High job satisfaction correlated with a desire for greater social distance from inmates. Whether these findings can be applied to a prison guard sample is debatable, but it does seem clear that there are differences between officers and that these differences aren't always simply limited to age, race, and sex. These differences have obvious relevance to whether unethical behaviors are likely.

# Treatment Staff

Treatment specialists have their own ethical dilemmas. Although hired by the state, many feel their loyalties lie with the offender. Prison psychologists may be privy to information or confessions that they feel bound to hold in confidence, even though the security of the prison may be jeopardized. The professional goal of all treatment specialists is to help the client. This may be fundamentally inconsistent with the prison (or jail) environment, which emphasizes punishment. Making the decision as to whether the individual is cured also involves mixed loyalties. Any treatment necessarily involves risk. How much risk one is willing to take depends on whether the public should be protected at all costs, in which case few people would be released, or whether one feels that the public must risk possible victimization in order to give offenders a chance to prove themselves.

Another dilemma is the administration of treatment programs. If a program has potential, someone must make decisions on who gets into it. Ideally, one would want similar people in the treatment program and in a control group. However, it is sometimes hard to justify withholding the program from some people who may sincerely wish to participate. Laypersons have difficulty understanding the concepts of random sampling and control groups. Pressure sometimes exists to admit anyone who sincerely wants a chance to participate, despite what this might do to experimental design.

Another, more basic issue is the ethics of providing treatment to people who do not want it. In particular, psychiatrists and psychologists have to reconcile their professional ethics in two fields, corrections and psychiatry, and at times this is hard to do. Psychiatrists in corrections, for instance, feel at times that they are being used for social control rather than treatment. Disruptive inmates, although needing treatment, pose security risks to prison officials, so intervention, especially chemotherapy, often takes the form of control rather than treatment, as the Quote and Query box illustrates.

---

**QUOTE and QUERY**

[discussing an inmate who was not violent, but was extremely talkative, loud, and inclined to discuss his delusions] As it was, John's illness needed to be controlled, not because he was unhappy with it, but because those around him found it objectionable. What can the psychiatrist do in cases like this?

Source: Arboleda-Florez (1983: 52).

*Should psychiatrists use drugs to quiet an inmate who is not violent?*

The practice of using antipsychotic drugs is especially problematic for treatment professionals. Although the Supreme Court has determined that the administration of such drugs to unwilling inmates is not unconstitutional, the practice must be scrutinized and held to due-process protections in order to uphold professional ethical standards. Some allege that psychotropic drugs are used to control inmates, rather than for legitimate treatment purposes. There are pervasive stories from ex-inmates of inmates being maintained on high dosages of drugs during their prison stay. The problem is that once released, they may experience withdrawal and have no assistance from community mental health facilities because of governmental cutbacks in services (Martin, 1993).

Psychologists have their own ethical code, and some principles seem especially relevant to corrections. For instance, under the principle of responsibility, psychologists are instructed to prevent the distortion, misuse, or suppression of their psychological findings by the institution or agency by which they are employed. This obviously affects institutional psychologists, who may feel that their findings are compromised by custody concerns. For instance, something confessed to in a counseling session may be used in parole reports to prevent release, findings may be used to block transfer, behavior brought out in psychological testing may be punished, and so on ("Ethical Principles," 1981: 633). Other principles involve the treatment of clients: "In their professional roles, psychologists avoid any action that will violate or diminish the legal and civil rights of clients or of others who may be affected by their actions" ("Ethical Principles," 1981: 634). This principle may be applicable to certain treatment programs in prison that restrict inmates' liberty or choice—for instance, some of the behavior modification programs have been questioned legally and ethically.

Many treatment professionals think that behavior modification has been subverted by the prison environment. Although it may be effective in inducing behavioral change, some professionals feel uneasy participating in a punishment-oriented program in an environment that is already one of deprivation. The coercive power inherent in the prison setting creates the potential for unethical practices by treatment personnel. The fact that prisoners are captive audiences makes them attractive subjects for experimentation of all kinds. Most programs ask for volunteers rather than force participation, but in a prison environment the assumption is always there that release is tied to compliance, so what may appear as voluntary action may be the result of no choice at all.

Lichtenberg, Lune, and McManimon (2004) use the movie *Clockwork Orange* (1971) to discuss issues of voluntariness and morality in treatment. The movie is a critical treatment of behavior modification and illustrates the fear that manipulating people's minds through aversive conditioning takes away, in some respects, the essence of what it means to be a free individual. Although the film is a satire, and obviously an extremely drawn portrait of the power of aversive conditioning, the idea that when people have been conditioned they are not rationally choosing good because they cannot freely choose evil is relevant and important to our discussions of moral culpability.

What is the ethical responsibility of a counselor when an offender threatens future violence toward a particular victim? As in the legal profession, confidentiality is an issue for psychologists. As their ethical principles state,

> Psychologists have a primary obligation to respect the confidentiality of information obtained from persons in the course of their work as psychologists. They reveal such information to others only with the consent of the person or the

person's legal representative, except in those unusual circumstances in which not to do so would result in clear danger to the person or to others. Where appropriate, psychologists inform their clients of the legal limits of confidentiality. ("Ethical Principles," 1981: 636)

Some psychiatrists find it hard to be associated with something as damaging as prison and feel a moral resistance to involvement with prison treatment efforts, given the negative effects that are inevitable. As Thomas (quoted in Tanay, 1982: 386) writes,

The length of sentences and the nature of maximum-security prisons combine to damage the personalities of the prisoners to such a degree as to make it especially difficult for them to function as autonomous and independent individuals in a free society following their release. I believe that whenever a man serves three or more years in a maximum security prison, the experience will usually have a lasting deleterious effect on his personality.

Even for those who feel comfortable working in prison, treatment and security concerns clash in many instances. The treatment professional must choose between two value systems. To emphasize security concerns puts the psychiatrist or counselor in a role of a custodian with professional training used only to better control inmate behavior. To emphasize treatment concerns puts the professional in an antagonistic role vis-à-vis the security staff, and he or she may be in situations where these concerns directly conflict. For instance, if the superintendent demands to see a client's file to support a disciplinary committee's decision, should the psychiatrist surrender the information that was given in confidence? In answer to this dilemma, the psychiatrist or psychologist should probably have never allowed the inmate to assume that information regarding rule infractions or potential wrongdoing could ever be confidential. However, if inmates believe that counselors and psychologists can offer no confidentiality protections, then is there any possibility of a trusting relationship? The issues that confront treatment personnel in prison seem to always involve the conflicting goals of punishment and treatment.

Although religion has always had a role in corrections, the separation of church and state has relegated religion to a separate element, unsanctioned while not necessarily unsupported by prison officials. This may change now that faith-based programs have been supported and encouraged by the White House. Prison Fellowship Ministries, Inc., a Washington, D.C., group headed by Watergate figure Charles Colson, is one such prison program. The program is Christ centered, biblically rooted, and values based, and it emphasizes family, community, and Jesus Christ. Inmates volunteer for the program (Ward, 1996).

A recent evaluation by the state of Texas Criminal Justice Policy Council showed that prison inmates who completed a religion-based program were less likely to commit new crimes. The program was the Innerchange Freedom Initiative, introduced in 1997. The study tracked 177 offenders who were released from the program and compared them to a control group that met the selection criteria but did not participate. Only 8 percent of program participants returned to prison, compared to 20 percent for the control group during the two-year study period (Criminal Justice Policy Council, 2003).

The existence of such programs in prison raises several issues. Some argue that such programs violate the separation of church and state and are an unconstitutional violation of freedom of religion. If a Christian program offers hope for early release or other advantages, Muslims or those following other religions may participate only if they also compromise their faith.

# Management Issues

Administrators are removed from day-to-day contact with inmates, but their power over decision making may actually be greater than that of line staff. Administrators emphasize the goal of control—that is, keeping the organization out of the newspapers and minimizing negative publicity. Because of this emphasis, administrators may be faced with difficult choices. For instance, in prisons or jails all treatment programs using outside people are potential security risks. An easy solution would be to prohibit all outsiders from entering the prison. Obviously, few prison administrators are this stringent in their control, but the choice may be made in specific instances to limit entry based on convenience and security. The decision to limit entry could probably be justified under a utilitarian framework, but other ethical systems may not support it.

Another dilemma that decision makers face is the balance between needs and costs. If inmates' programming is sparse, clothing is minimal, or medical care is inadequate, or if officers' safety and efficiency are compromised because too few are employed or too much overtime is required, a decision maker must, at some point, determine priorities. Obviously, administrators often have no choice because they can work only within the budget given. However, situations do arise in governmental agencies where workers are told there is no money in the budget for needed items such as office supplies and equipment or overtime pay, yet at the same time administrators manage to find the money to order expensive new office furniture or go on expensive training weekends. This discrepancy between what administrators say and what workers see is demoralizing to those who try to make do with increasingly smaller budgets. Moral leadership is exhibited by those administrators who share the sacrifices. Ethical decisions for administrators arise when budget allocations are made, when program futures are decided, and when rules and procedures are developed.

Barrier and colleagues (1999) discussed an ethics training program with correctional officers, and part of the training involved having the officers identify important elements of an ethics code. Many of the elements involved had to do with practices of management rather than officers:

- Treating all staff fairly and impartially
- Promoting based on true merit
- Showing no prejudice
- Leading by example
- Developing a mission statement that is clear in every way

- Reducing the negative tone of a code of ethics and making a list of dos, not don'ts
- Creating a culture that promotes performance, not seniority
- Soliciting staff input on new policies
- Being respectful
- Letting the word out that upper management cares about ethics

## Correctional Management and the Courts

Administrators have found themselves forced to change after prisoners' rights suits have resulted in court mandates to change. The implementation of court-ordered changes has often been halting and superficial, showing that compliance to the letter of a court ruling may be different from compliance to the spirit of one. Is this response to court-ordered change an ethical one? *Cruz v. Beto* (Civil No. 71-H-1371 [S.D.Tex. 1976]) was a case dealing with the actions of administrators in the Texas system in response to a particularly active prisoners' rights attorney who was taking on cases *pro bono* that challenged the practices of the Texas Department of Corrections. First, the director barred her from all prisons in the state, and then, when forced to allow her back into the prison because the ban was an unconstitutional infringement on the inmates' right to legal assistance, transferred all inmates who were her clients to one unit, deprived them of good behavior points that were necessary for higher security classifications and favorable parole decisions, and evidently subjected the inmates to a barrage of pressure, indicating that if they dropped her as their lawyer they would have all privileges reinstated. Not surprisingly, the court took a dim view of these actions. What ethical system would justify such behavior?

Administrators have also found themselves in the position of testifying in court about conditions or the actions of their employees. Their testimony may be perjured to protect themselves or others; in this situation, their ethical dilemma is similar to that of police officers testifying about undercover activities. However, an issue more specific to administrators is pleading ignorance of activities for which they arguably should be held responsible.

Individuals are often forced to make a choice between their career and challenging unethical or illegal practices. For administrators, this dilemma may appear more often because their scope of knowledge is broader than that of line staff. The career path of an administrator, with its investment of time and energy and the mandate to be a "company man," often creates an immersion in bureaucratic thinking to the point that an individual loses sight of ethical issues. For instance, protecting the department or the director from scandal or litigation becomes more important than analyzing the behavior that created the potential for scandal in the first place. If decision making becomes influenced solely by short-term gains or avoidance of scandal, then decisions may be unsupported by the ethical systems discussed previously.

Another issue for correctional managers is what to do when faced with a worker alleging sexual harassment. The type of behavior defined as constituting a **hostile work environment** was common when women first entered as officers in prisons for males. Female officers reported behavior such as C.O.s making sexual references and disparaging comments to them in front of inmates, "setting them up" by having inmates masturbate when they were sent down the tier, putting up posters with naked women and sexual messages, and even more serious behaviors such as assaults and attempted rapes. Today, the behavior that women experience is usually not so blatant, but some workers still experience problems.

When a correctional manager is approached by a female subordinate who is being subjected to a work environment where other officers or workers conduct themselves in a manner that makes her uncomfortable, there is a tendency to encourage her to handle it herself and not rock the boat. All administrators fear negative publicity and lawsuits, and if a problem such as sexual harassment can be swept under the rug, there is a great temptation to do so. Even ethical administrators face conflicting duties. They have a duty to the organization (to keep from having to defend it against a lawsuit) but also to the employee (to help the employee undertake the best course of action), and that might be to pursue charges.

Possible ethical resolutions to the problem might be to talk to the individuals involved, punish the wrongdoers, or encourage the complainant to pursue internal or external sanctions. Obviously, administrators and managers themselves should take pains to avoid behavior that may be misconstrued as sexual coercion or be perceived by their employees as offensive. Managers have a higher duty than co-workers to set a tone for an office free from sexual innuendo that may lead to a description of the workplace as a hostile work environment. They have an ethical and legal affirmative duty to stop sexual humor, inappropriate touching, and inappropriate behavior before there is a complaint.

Administrators are in a difficult position when officers under their command have been accused of (and are guilty of) wrongs against inmates or probationers or parolees, such as brutality or harassment. If the administrator supports the officer (publicly or privately), he or she is in effect condoning that behavior and allowing it to continue. If the administrator exposes the officer and subjects him or her to punishment, then there is a possibility that the administrator will lose the trust and allegiance of other officers who feel betrayed. Of course, the ideal situation would be one where everyone involved would not condone such behavior and would resolve it satisfactorily. Realistically, this is usually not the case. Probably the best an administrator can do is to make clear to all what will not be tolerated and to serve as a role model; when wrongdoing is exposed, to treat the individuals involved fairly, with due process and offering them an opportunity to change; and if sanctions are deemed necessary, to administer them fairly and without favoritism.

It should be noted that in cases where there is a pattern of corruption, whether it be brutality or types of graft, it is hard to make the argument of ignorance. Prisons are smaller than small towns, and like a small town, there are no secrets unless one is willfully ignorant of them. Top administrators often have an outward orientation because their role is to communicate with legislators, the central office, and the community; however, a good administrator never ignores his or her own backyard. Management by walking around, or MBWA, and having a good sense of what is happening in the institution have always been the mark of a good administrator and are also the best defense against having the institution end up on the front page of the newspaper.

## Correctional Management and Unions

Unions have so far been seen by researchers as a resistant force to rehabilitation, and only concerned with individual benefits for members rather than the mission or goal of corrections. Unions provide legal assistance to officers in personnel and legal attacks, and often support officers who, many would argue, have no business working in corrections. In California, for instance, unions have provided legal assistance to officers who have been accused of assaulting inmates, having sex with inmates, giving drugs to inmates, and setting up gladiator fights between inmates (Josi and Sechrest, 1998: 161). In the late 1990s, Governor Davis attempted to direct $4 million to the correctional officer union for the officers' defense fund. In effect, the public would have ended up paying for the prosecution of errant officers *and* their defense costs, as well as their salary. When senators discovered the plan, criticism was so strong that the administration canceled the funding, although the officers' union still received the money to be used for other things, and officers obtained the pay raise and other concessions demanded in contract negotiations (Salladay, 1999).

Governor Schwarzenegger has also had trouble with the correctional officers' union while attempting to balance an out-of-control budget; the contract with union members promised that they would be the only state employees receiving raises for several years in a row. In the latest budget cuts in California, only corrections has so far escaped proposed cuts, and some observers contend that this has more to do with the strength of the correctional officers' union than Californians' desire to take money away from health services and education and give it to prisons. Unions have been very successful in protecting and improving the position of the correctional officer. There is no doubt that states where unions are active are those states where correctional officers receive better pay and working conditions. Whether unions create a more professional and ethical work force is a different question.

## Cross-Sex Supervision

Cross-sex supervision is emerging as a volatile issue in the management of prisons. In the seventeenth and eighteenth centuries, female prisoners were housed together with men in jails, with predictable results. Women were raped and sexually exploited, and they sold themselves for food and other goods. With the development of the Walnut Street Jail and penitentiaries, women were separated from male inmates, but still guarded by men, and sexual exploitation continued. Various scandals and exposés of prostitution rings led to women's reform groups pressuring legislatures to build completely separate institutions for women in the late 1800s and early 1900s. Finally, women were guarded by women, although men often held the highest administrative positions in these institutions.

This pattern continued until the mid-1970s, when female officers challenged state prison systems' hiring patterns that barred them from working in institutions for men. Female officers had a very constricted career path in corrections when they were allowed only in institutions for women. Few could get promoted, and they often had to move great distances to the only facility in the state for women even if a prison for men was in their hometown. States resisted assigning women to prisons for men because of a fear that they would be victimized, that they would have less control over the inmates, and that they would "sexually excite" the inmates, leading to disruption in the institution.

In *Dothard v. Rawlinson,* 433 U.S. 321 (1977), the U.S. Supreme Court agreed with these fears, but only because the Alabama prison where Diane Rawlinson wanted to work had such high levels of violence that it was already under a federal monitor. The dictum of this case convinced many state systems that despite the holding that Rawlinson could be prohibited from the Alabama prison, in most situations, women would have to be allowed in. They were allowed to work in men's prisons, and early evaluations showed that they did their job about as well as male officers (Zimmer, 1986; Zupan, 1992). Inmates tended to appreciate the presence of women, although evaluations indicated that inmates had concerns over privacy and the ability of female officers to protect them. Male officers were much more antagonistic toward their presence.

Today, women make up about 20 percent of the state correctional officer force and 30 percent of the federal correctional officer force. Women work in prisons for men in forty-six states (Reichel, 1997: 379). However, there is great variability in how many women work in prisons for men. In some states only about 1 percent of the work force in prisons for men are women, but in others the percentage is closer to 10 percent (Reichel, 1997: 379). Criticism of female officers in prisons for men has centered on the fact that they tend to be weaker and less able to protect themselves, that they may be subject to intimidation or seduction from inmates, and that they create sexual tension in the prison. Male inmates express mixed views regarding female officers. Understandably, they object to having women watch them take showers or go to the bathroom. Some also complain that women engender desire and fantasies. However, male inmates also report appreciating the presence of women, who, some inmates say, will listen to them and be less confrontational than male officers.

Another type of problem occurs when the actions of female C.O.s may be misinterpreted by male inmates. Even if the female C.O. is merely expressing a professional interest in the inmate, or when she performs her job in a manner that is more interactive than that of male C.O.s, a male inmate may see the female C.O. as desiring a personal relationship. Female C.O.s must learn to interact with male inmates in such ways as to make it clear that they do not desire personal involvement. Of course, there are also situations where romantic relationships do develop—between female C.O.s and male inmates, between male C.O.s and female inmates, and between C.O.s and inmates of the same sex (Marquart, Barnhill, and Balshaw-Biddle, 2001). These are always against institutional rules, unethical, and illegal in many states.

The ironic effect of these court cases and the entry of women into prisons for men was that male officers were no longer barred from working in prisons for women. In the early 1980s, fairly small percentages of male officers could be found in prisons for women, and they were restricted to public places. Today, male officers are assigned to all posts inside prisons for women, including sleeping and shower areas. In some states, over half of the officers in women's prisons are men. Thus, male officers again are in positions of power over women, and again, abuses are occurring. An increasing number of incidents have been substantiated where male officers have coerced female prisoners to have sex or, in some cases, sexually assaulted them.

it as a fundamental liberty interest guaranteed by the Constitution. Earlier Supreme Court cases had established the right of prison officials to transfer prisoners to more-secure custodial institutions without due process. In *Meachum v. Fano*, 427 U.S. 215 (1976), the Supreme Court held that prison officials could transfer for good reason, bad reason, or no reason to more-secure facilities. Later cases indicated that prison rules and regulations could create liberty interests. Then in *Sandin*, the Court abandoned the approach and held that only when the challenged condition was "atypical" of a prison sentence and induced a "significant hardship" could a liberty interest be found and ruled, in this case, that punitive segregation did not pose such an atypical condition. In *Wilkinson*, the Court did find a liberty interest when an inmate was transferred to the supermax prison and noted its extremely severe conditions, but came short of finding the right in the Constitution and seemed to say that the right must exist in the state's policies and that *Sandin* acts as a limit when such rights are recognized.

## *Abu Ghraib: A Prison by Any Other Name*

When the abuse in Iraq's Abu Ghraib prison was exposed, there were many who made comparisons between the behaviors of military prison guards and those of correctional officers in U.S. prisons. The comparisons were hard to ignore because several of the worst abusers were correctional officers in civilian life and the person who helped set up the Abu Ghraib prison was Lane McCotter, an ex-head of the Texas, New Mexico, and Utah prison systems. There were scandals during his tenure in all states, and he was forced to resign in Utah when a mentally ill inmate died after being strapped to a chair for sixteen hours. McCotter responded that he had left Abu Ghraib shortly after it opened and was not responsible for any of the events that transpired after his departure. It is also true that there are scandals in all prison systems and that the executive in charge cannot be expected to prevent all cases of abuse. The more important point is whether the very environment of an incarcerative facility brings out the worst in people.

The Zimbardo experiment of the 1970s was one of the experiments that spurred the creation of human-subjects review boards in colleges and universities. In this experiment, college men were arbitrarily assigned to be guards or inmates, and a mock prison was set up in the basement of a building on the grounds of Stanford University. The changes in both groups were so profound that the experiment was canceled after six days. Zimbardo noted that about one-third of the guards became brutal and author-itarian, and prisoners became manipulative and exhibited signs of emotional distress and mental breakdown (Zimbardo, 1982). If college men who know the experiment is artificial succumb to the temptation to inflict their will on those who are in their power, is it possible that the environment itself causes people to act in ways that they would not otherwise?

This history of prisons is replete with extreme brutality on the part of guards:

- Gladiator fights in Corcoran Prison
- The "Tucker telephone" in Arkansas
- Using "dog boys" as live quarry for Texas dog handlers
- Beatings and the use of dogs on prisoners (most recently videotaped in Brazoria County, Texas)
- Looking the other way while inmates beat and raped a victim

In recent accounts, allegations of abuse in prisons and jails in the United States include abuses that are very similar to what took place in Abu Ghraib:

- Inmates being forced to wear pink underwear as punishment (Phoenix jail)
- Inmates being stripped as punishment (Pennsylvania)
- Inmates being made to wear black hoods (Virginia) (Butterfield, 2004)

In all cases of abuse in prison, the reasons are listed as leadership failure and lack of discipline, training, and supervision (Ward, 2004).

## Conclusion

In this chapter we have touched on some of the ethical issues that correctional personnel face in institutional corrections. These individuals have much in common with other criminal justice practitioners, especially in the area of discretion, but they are also in a unique position in that they hold power over the most basic aspects of life for confined inmates. This position allows correctional officers either to intensify the humiliation that incarcerated offenders feel or to make the prison experience more tolerable for those who serve time. The difficult decisions for correctional officers arise from the personal relationships that develop with inmates, the trust that is sometimes betrayed, the favors that seem harmless, and the coercive environment that makes violence normal and caring abnormal. Correctional treatment personnel have their own problems in resolving conflicts between loyalty toward clients and toward the system.

To be in a helping profession in a system geared for punishment is a difficult challenge for anyone, and the temptation to retreat into bureaucratic compliance is always present. Although this chapter has discussed officers mistreating inmates and correctional professionals engaging in other unethical conduct, we do not mean to imply that criminal justice workers are blatantly or pervasively unethical. Arguably, the criminal justice system operates as well as it does only because of the caring, committed, honest people who choose it as a career.

## Key Terms

**correctional officer** the term that replaced the old label of *guard*, indicating a new role

**hostile work environment** one type of sexual harassment whereby sexual innuendo or joking makes the workplace so uncomfortable that the employee perceives it as hostile and has difficulty coming to work

**human service officer** the corrections officer who perceives the role to include influencing and interacting with the offender

**pluralistic ignorance** the idea that the majority misperceive the prevalence of a belief because of a vocal minority

**reciprocity** Sykes's term for the situation that occurs when officers become indebted to inmates and return favors

# Review Questions

1. Describe how C.O.s have discretion similar to police officers and court personnel.
2. Describe the role ambiguity that C.O.s faced in the 1970s and 1980s.
3. Describe the formal ethical code for correctional personnel, and compare it to the law enforcement code.
4. Describe the C.O. subculture.
5. Describe pluralistic ignorance. Describe the "good" officer.
6. List and describe some forms of corruption committed by C.O.s.
7. What are some ways to reduce corruption?
8. What are the two interests that members of the treatment staff have to balance? Give examples of some ethical concerns of treatment personnel.
9. Explain the issues involved in cross-sex supervision.
10. Choose and discuss three ethical issues of managers.

# Discussion Questions

1. Discuss whether or not you would like to be a correctional officer. What would be the hardest thing about the job?
2. Discuss whether or not you would like to be a counselor in a prison. What would be the hardest thing about the job?
3. If you were a new warden and you knew that there was corruption in the prison, how would you go about doing something about it?
4. If you were a correctional professional and an inmate held out his hand to shake it, would you be inclined to shake it or not, and why?
5. Do you think correctional officer unions should be able to contribute to political campaigns? Why or why not?

# Ethical Dilemmas

### *Situation 1*

You are a prison guard supervising a tier. One of the inmates comes to you and asks a favor. Because he is a troublemaker, his mail privileges have been taken away. He wants you to mail a letter for him. You figure it's not such a big deal; besides, you know he could make your job easier by keeping the other inmates on the tier in line. What would you tell him?

### *Situation 2*

As a new C.O., you soon realize that there is a great deal of corruption and graft taking place in the prison. Guards routinely bring in contraband for inmates in return for money, food bought for the inmates' mess hall finds its way into the trunks of staff cars, and money is being siphoned from inmate accounts. You are not sure how far up the corruption goes. Would you keep your mouth shut? They're just inmates, anyway.

Would you go to your supervisors? What if, in exposing the corruption, you implicated yourself? What if you implicated a friend?

### Situation 3

You are a prison psychologist, and during the course of your counseling session with one drug offender, he confessed he has been using drugs. Obviously, this is a serious violation of prison rules. Should you report him? What if he told you of an impending escape plan?

### Situation 4

You are a prison warden, and a new C.O. comes to you and says she has been sexually harassed by the captain. You know that the captain has been with the prison for twenty years and has not had any negative reports in his record. You like him and think that he is an excellent captain. On the other hand, she seems very earnest and believable and is quite upset, so you think something must have happened. What is the ethical course of action? What is the legal course of action?

### Situation 5

You are a prison counselor and have a good relationship with all the other counselors. You all go out drinking after work sometimes, and in general you like and respect everyone. Recently, you've noticed that something seems to be going on with one of the other counselors. Stella is usually quite outgoing and cheerful, but lately she seems distracted and upset. You see her in the parking lot one evening and ask her what's the matter, and she confides to you that she is in love with an inmate. She knows it is wrong, but she says that they had an instant chemistry and that he is like no man she has ever known. She has been slipping him love notes, and he has also been writing her. You tell her that she has to stop it or else quit her job. She tearfully tells you that she can't let him go, she needs her job, and you've got to keep quiet or you'll get her fired. What would you do?

## Suggested Readings

Conover, T. 2000. *New Jack: Guarding Sing Sing*. New York: Random House.

Crouch, B. 1995. "Guard Work in Transition." In K. Haas and G. Alpert (Eds.), *The Dilemmas of Corrections*, 3rd ed., pp. 183–203. Prospect Heights, IL: Waveland.

Crouch, B. (Ed.). 1980. *Keepers: Prison Guards and Contemporary Corrections*. Springfield, IL: Charles C. Thomas.

Johnson, R. 2002. *Hard Time: Understanding and Reforming the Prison*. Pacific Grove, CA: Brooks/Cole.

Kauffman, K. 1988. *Prison Officers and Their World*. Cambridge, MA: Harvard University Press.

Lerner, J. 2002. *You've Got Nothing Coming: Notes from a Prison Fish*. New York: Broadway.

Lombardo, L. 1989. *Guards Imprisoned: Correctional Officers at Work*. Cincinnati: Anderson.

Martin, D. 1993. *Committing Journalism: The Prison Writings of Red Hog*. New York: Norton.

Pollock, J. 2003. *Prisons and Prison Life: Costs and Consequences*. Los Angeles, CA: Roxbury.

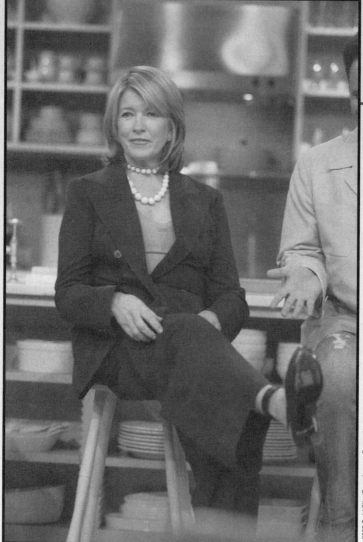

Martha Stewart may not have given fashion points to the electronic
ankle monitor she had to wear, but many offenders appreciate the fact
that it allows them to be released to community supervision.

# 14

# Ethics and Community Corrections

## Key Terms

# Chapter Objectives

1. Understand the concept of community corrections.

2. Understand the ethical issues that might face probation and parole officers.

3. Understand the concept of peacemaking corrections and restorative justice.

4. Understand the ethical issues inherent in the restorative justice approach.

In the last chapter we focused on institutional corrections; however, the majority of offenders are under some form of community supervision—either probation or parole. The correctional professionals who supervise offenders in the community have different ethical issues than do those who work in an institution.

# The Concept of Community Corrections

Community corrections has a more positive and helpful image than does institutional corrections. However, even in this subsystem of the criminal justice system, the ideals of justice and care become diluted by bureaucratic mismanagement and personal agendas. Professionals in community corrections do not have the same power as police or correctional officers to use physical force, but they do have a great deal of nonphysical power over the clients they control. Their authority and power can be used wisely and ethically or can become subverted to personal ends.

The concept of community corrections is supported by the ethics of care. It promotes meeting the needs of the offender and the victim (through restitution). A prison sentence is basically a rejection or banishment; however, community supervision represents the concepts of acceptance and integration with the community. Even parole, coming after a prison sentence, originally operated with the philosophy of reintegration.

Utilitarianism also supports community corrections because the benefit to the community by not banishing the offender to prison is both financial and emotional. Even a retributive philosophy can support community corrections because some crimes are simply not serious enough to justify a prison sentence.

Souryal (1996a) also discussed the "mystique" of probation. He described John Augustus, the so-called grandfather of probation, as personifying the concepts of probation, including the belief in redemption. Other principles that are consistent with the mystique include honesty, fidelity and obligation, justice, public service, and self-control.

Typically, **community corrections** is a term that encompasses halfway houses, work release centers, probation, parole, and any other intermediate sanctions, such as electronic monitoring—either as a condition of probation or as a sentence in itself.

> ## QUOTE and QUERY
>
> [Community corrections] signifies moral concern for the individual, one that is consistent with the natural law ethics of "dignity of man," the constitutional ethics of individualized treatment and perhaps the religious ethics of redemption.
>
> Source: Souryal (1992: 356).
>
> ***Explain how community corrections is either consistent or inconsistent with the various ethical systems.***

Jails are somewhat of a hybrid. They are located in the community but also share many characteristics of institutional corrections. We considered jail officers in the last chapter because the dilemmas that they face *vis-à-vis* whistleblowing, the officer subculture, and the use of coercive force against inmates are more similar to the issues faced by correctional officers than the issues faced by probation and parole officers.

Probation and parole sentences involve supervision but also usually require meeting some other conditions. Some of these conditions pose special issues of privacy, liberty, and impact on others. For instance, should conditions specify whom the offender can associate with? Mandate that the offender go to church? Dictate to the offender where he can live or what type of job he can have? Require the use of contraception?

Electronic monitoring programs, usually using ankle bracelets and a telephone, raise issues of privacy. Such sanctions are said to blur the line between the offender and his or her family. Electronic monitoring sometimes involves a camera connected to the telephone. When the offender calls into a monitoring station, the monitor can see past the offender into the home. Is this a violation of family members' privacy, or do we consider it a consent entry? In general, probation and parole entail consent for warrantless searches, but is it really consent when the option is prison? And if the offender is said to give consent, how does that affect family members?

Some contend that we are needlessly "widening the net" of corrections and putting more and more people on some form of correctional supervision. Further, the use of surveillance techniques against offender populations is spilling over into other contexts. For instance, drug testing started with probationers and now seems to be common in the workplace. Other forms of surveillance started with correctional populations but then became accepted practices in other applications. For instance, metal detectors are used now in a number of settings, and some workplaces use a polygraph, monitor employees' calls, use video cameras, track e-mails, and in other ways apply the surveillance practices created for lawbreakers to the rest of us (Staples, 1997).

The use of alcohol programs and the threat of punitive sanctions raise issues of personal liberty and freedom. Because alcohol is a legal substance, should we punish convicted felons for drinking while on probation? The argument is that convicted felons do not have to accept conditions of probation that prohibit alcohol—they could choose prison—but is that a legitimate choice? Further, although such conditions may make sense for those convicted of driving while intoxicated, do the technical conditions of "no alcohol" make sense for a burglar who did not attempt to explain or defend his actions by claiming to be drunk at the moment of the crime?

The danger of intermediate sanctions is that because they are typically so innocuous, they are used more frequently for offenders who may not have received any formal system response in years past. Unfortunately, what sometimes happens is that the offender, once in the system, fails because of technical violations and becomes more and more immersed in the system. This problem of **net widening** is not only problematic from an ethical stand but also for purely pragmatic reasons of cost. Can we foresee a time when a large portion of the population is on some type of governmental monitoring status? Some say it is already here. We may be happy to note that tax monies may not be burdened by such monitoring because the trend to charge offenders supervision fees is growing. Still, other than providing employment for the legions of criminal justice students who are graduating from colleges and universities, are there good reasons for the dramatic expansion of the net of corrections?

# Probation and Parole Officers

Formal ethical guidelines for probation and parole officers are provided by the A.C.A. code as well as by their own ethics codes (see Box 14-1). Probation and parole officers are considered more professional than correctional officers:

- They typically have at least a bachelor's degree if not a graduate degree.
- They are subject to fewer organizational controls in the form of rule books and policies.
- They have a great deal of discretion.

The formal ethics of the profession is summarized by the ideal of service—to the community and to the offender. In fact, whether to emphasize offenders' needs over community needs, or vice versa, is at the heart of a number of different ethical dilemmas for the probation and parole officer. Other ethical issues are more similar to those encountered in the other subsystems discussed—they primarily revolve around decisions to substitute personal values and goals for organizational values. In the next several sections we will touch on some of the themes of previous chapters—the use of discretion, officer subcultures, and relationships with clients.

## *The Use of Discretion*

Discretion in probation exists at the point of sentencing: Probation officers make recommendations to judges concerning sentences. Discretion also exists during supervision:

- Probation officers decide when to file violation reports.
- They decide what recommendation to make to the judge during revocation hearings.
- They make numerous decisions along the way regarding the people on their caseload.

---

**BOX 14-1   Federal Probation Officers' Association Code of Ethics**

As a Federal Probation Officer, I am dedicated to rendering professional service to the courts, the parole authorities, and the community at large in effecting the social adjustment of the offender.

I will conduct my personal life with decorum, will neither accept nor grant favors in connection with my office, and will put loyalty to moral principles above personal consideration.

I will uphold the law with dignity and with complete awareness of the prestige and stature of the judicial system of which I am a part. I will be ever cognizant of my responsibility to the community which I serve.

I will strive to be objective in the performance of my duties, respect the inalienable rights of all persons, appreciate the inherent worth of the individual, and hold inviolate those confidences which can be reposed in me.

I will cooperate with my fellow workers and related agencies and will continually attempt to improve my professional standards through the seeking of knowledge and understanding.

I recognize my office as a symbol of public faith and I accept it as a public trust to be held as long as I am true to the ethics of the Federal Probation Service. I will constantly strive to achieve these objectives and ideals, dedicating myself to my chosen profession.

SOURCE: Adopted September 1960. Federal Probation Officers' Association, Washington, D.C. Revised March 1993. Reprinted with permission. All rights reserved.

---

Parole board members or their designees make decisions regarding release, and parole officers have the same discretion in managing their caseload that probation officers do. What are the criteria used for these decisions? Usually, the risk to the public is the primary factor, but other considerations also intrude. Some of these other considerations are ethical; some might not be. How would one evaluate the ethics of the following criteria?

- race
- crime
- family ties
- crowding in institutions
- status of the victim
- judge's preference
- publicity generated by the crime

Probation officers write pre-sentence reports to help judges decide sentences, but research has found that there may be errors in the information presented and that some officers are not as thorough as others in gathering information. This may not make much difference if it is true, as some have found, that probation officers' recommendations and judges' decisions are almost completely determined by the current offense and prior record (Whitehead, 1991).

Probation and parole officers have the authority and power to recommend revocation. This power is also limited because probation and parole officers' recommendations can be ignored by the judge or parole hearing officer. Yet the implicit power an officer has over the individuals on his or her caseload must be recognized as an important element of the role, not to be taken lightly or misused.

Some practices in decision making are clearly unethical and illegal. Peter Maas's (1983) book *Marie* details a scheme in Tennessee that involved "selling" paroles to convicts. However, other situations are perhaps more difficult to judge as unethical or not. In a controversy in Texas, ex-parole board members were found to have sold their services as "parole consultants" to inmates and inmates' families in order to help them obtain a favorable release decision. Although the practice evidently was not against any state law at the time and those who participated described their help as simply explaining the process and helping the inmate prepare a presentation to the board, many viewed it as unethical. Rules now exist that restrict such practices.

There is at least the possibility that what the inmate was buying was a former parole board member's influence. The situation was brought to light when a serial killer was arrested for yet another murder while out on parole. When how he obtained parole was investigated, it was discovered that one of these former parole board members/"parole consultants" had been hired by the inmate. Whether that had anything to do with a favorable parole decision will never be known, but many allege there is at least the appearance of impropriety in the arrangement, and steps were taken to eliminate the practice.

Any time that government officials go into the private sector and trade on their status as ex-officials, we feel uncomfortable. There are specific laws against influence peddling at some levels of government, reflecting this discomfort. In some situations, the possibility of private gain may influence how the official performs his or her job while in office, as in the case of military officers who make decisions on contracts with private vendors and then end up in highly paid, visible positions with the company immediately upon retirement. In other instances, the ability to provide an open door, inside information, or a favorable decision is considered unfair when used only for those who are willing to pay, as in the case of ex–White House staff members who sell their services as consultants to foreign countries or corporations, or those with family connections to the White House who are paid by those seeking presidential pardons.

## The Probation/Parole Officer Subculture

The subculture of probation and parole officers has never been as extensively documented as that of police and correctional officers. Due to differences between these professions, the subculture of the former is not as pervasive or strong as that of the latter. On the one hand, probation and parole officers do not feel as isolated as police or correctional officers do. They experience no stigmatization, they have normal working hours, they do not wear a depersonalizing uniform, and they have a less obviously coercive relationship with their clients. These factors reduce the need for a subculture.

On the other hand, one can probably identify some norms that might be found in any probation or parole office:

1. *Cynicism.* There is a norm of **cynicism** toward clients. The subculture promotes the idea that clients are inept, deviant, and irredeemable. Probation and parole professionals who express positive attitudes toward clients' capacity for change are seen as naïve and guileless.
2. *Lethargy.* There is a pervasive subcultural norm of lethargy or minimal work output. This norm is supported by the view that officers are underpaid and overworked.
3. *Individualism.* A norm of individualism can be identified. This relates to the idea that although parole and probation officers may seek opinions from other professionals in the office, there is an unspoken rule that each runs his or her own caseload; to offer unsolicited opinions about decisions another person makes regarding his or her client violates this norm of autonomy.

Although there does not seem to be the "blue curtain of secrecy" to the same extent as found in policing, there is no doubt a norm against informing on colleagues for unethical or illegal behaviors. This relates somewhat to the norm of individualism but is also part of the pervasive occupational subculture against informing on colleagues. Probation and parole officers may see and hear unethical behaviors and not feel comfortable in coming forward with such information. If they work in an office where the norm against exposing such wrongdoing is strong, they may indeed suffer similar sanctions as police and correctional officers for exposing others' wrongdoing.

There also seems to be the same management tendency that is seen in law enforcement to hide or ignore wrongdoing on the part of individual officers. This may be a misguided utilitarianism in managers who are attempting to protect the organization from public scandal, or it may be simply self-interested egoism from managers who fear that the blame will be directed at them. For whatever reason, there seems to be a tendency to ignore officers who are obviously unable or unwilling to do the job. Some officers even point out that those who are arrested for DWI or other crimes continue to work as probation and parole officers. If this is true, it seems ironic that some probation and parole officers seem to have no better morals than do the clients they supervise.

Probation and parole officers have been described as adopting different roles on the job. Recall that police have been described by the watchman, caretaker, and law enforcer typology. In the same way, probation and parole officers have been described by their orientation to the job and individual adaptation to organizational goals. For instance, Souryal (1992) summarizes other literature in his description of the following types:

1. the punitive law enforcer
2. the welfare/therapeutic practitioner
3. the passive time server
4. the combined model

Different ethical issues can be discussed in relation to each of these types. For instance, the **punitive law enforcer** may need to examine his or her use of authority. This officer may have a tendency to use illegal threats and violate the due-process protections that each client deserves. The **welfare/therapeutic worker** may need to think about natural law rights of privacy and autonomy. These officers have a tendency to infringe on clients' privacy because of their mindset that they are helping the client (and indeed, they might be), but the client may prefer less help and more privacy. The **passive time server** needs to be aware of ethical formalism and concerns of duty.

All of us may have some tendency to be a time server in our respective professions. It is important to continue to take personal inventories and ask whether we are still putting in a "day's work for a day's pay." As is the case for many of the other criminal justice professionals we have discussed in this book, parole and probation officers often have a great deal of flexibility in their day. They leave the office to make field contacts; they often "trade" weekdays for weekend days because weekends are more conducive to home visits. This flexibility is necessary if they are to do the job, but some abuse it and use the freedom to accomplish personal tasks or spend time at home. Some offices have attempted to prevent this behavior by instituting measures such as time clocks and strict controls on movements, but these controls are inconsistent with professionalism and not conducive to the nature of the task.

Other offices develop norms that accept unethical practices and lethargy. Once this occurs, it becomes a difficult pattern to change. If it is already present, a single officer will have a hard time not falling into the pattern. If all officers feel overwhelmed by their caseloads and the relative lack of power they have to do anything about failure, then the result may be that they throw up their hands and adopt a "who cares?" attitude. If the supervisor does not exhibit a commitment to the goal of the organization, does not encourage workers, treats certain officers with favoritism, or seems more concerned with his or her personal career than with the needs of the office, then there is an inevitable deterioration of morale.

Whitehead (1991) discusses workers' frustration over incompetents being promoted, low wages, and high caseloads that lead to burnout. Souryal (1992) notes that low pay, a public view that probation and parole are ineffective, and the politicization of parole and probation are factors in professionals' feeling that their role is ambiguous, contradictory, and politically vulnerable. Disillusionment becomes almost inevitable. Although these issues exist in many organizations, they are especially problematic in a profession that requires a great deal of emotional investment on the part of the practitioner. If the organization does not encourage and support good workers, then it is no wonder that what develops is an informal subculture that encourages minimum effort and treats organizational goals with sarcasm and cynicism.

## *Caseload Supervision*

Discretion exists not only at the recommendation to release stage, but also throughout supervision. Officers do not make the decision to revoke, but they do make the decision to file a violation report and make a recommendation to the judge or the parole hearing examiner as to whether to continue on supervision status with perhaps new conditions, or revocation and a prison sentence. Many do not submit violation reports automatically upon discovery of every offender infraction. In this way they are like police officers, who practice selective enforcement of the laws. Like police officers, some of their criteria for decision making are ethical, and some are not. Also like police officers, the individual officer may experience ethical dilemmas when the law doesn't seem to be able to take into account social realities, such as poverty.

The discretion to decide when to write a violation report is a powerful element in the control that the officer has over the offender, but this can obviously be a difficult decision to make sometimes. If the officer excuses serious violations (e.g., possessing a firearm or continuing drug use), and the decision to do so is based on personal favoritism, fear, or bribery, then that officer is putting the community at risk and is unethical in the decision to do so. Those situations in which the officer sincerely believes the offender made a mistake, has extraordinary excuses for such misbehavior, and is a good risk still present a danger to the community. Is the decision any more ethical because of the officer's belief in the offender? Would it be more ethical to conduct oneself "by the book" and always submit violation reports when the offender committed any violation, including a purely technical one?

Probation and parole officers are presented with other dilemmas in their supervision of offenders. For instance, the offender often acquires a job without the employer's knowledge of his or her previous criminality. Is it the duty of the officer to inform the employer and thereby imperil the continued employment of the offender? What about when offenders become personally involved with others and refuse to tell them about their past history? Does the probation or parole officer have a duty to the unwary party? Recently, the issue of confidentiality vis-à-vis AIDS has emerged. If the probation or parole officer knows or suspects that the offender is HIV-positive and the offender begins an intimate relationship with someone, does the officer have a duty to warn the other party? Most states protect the confidentiality of victims of AIDS, and in these cases the officer has a legal duty *not* to disclose.

This issue is extremely problematic: The rights of the offender, the rights of unwary innocents, and the responsibilities of society are not well sorted out at this point. What is the probation or parole officer's responsibility to the offender's family? If family members are unwilling to help the offender and perhaps fear his or her presence, should the officer find a reason for revocation? Again, these questions revolve around competing loyalties to public and client. The correctional professional must balance these interests in every decision, and the decisions are often not easy to make.

Very similar to the police officer, at times the probation officer's role as a family member or friend conflicts with the professional role. Family members and/or friends may expect special treatment or expect that the officer will use his or her powers for unethical purposes. These are always difficult dilemmas because family and friends may not be sympathetic to the individual's ethical responsibilities to the organization and to society at large. Probation and parole officers are likely to have overlapping circles of acquaintances and family connections with those on their caseloads, especially in small towns. Confidentiality and favoritism are issues that come up frequently.

The officer also has to contend with the issue of gratuities. Again, similar to the police officer, probation or parole officers may be offered special treatment, material goods, or other items of value because of their profession. In most cases the situation is even more clearly unethical for probation and parole officers because the gift is offered by a client over whom decisions are made, as opposed to police officers who may or may not ever be in a position to make a decision regarding a restaurant or convenience store manager. Probation departments have clear rules against any "business relationships" with probationers, and this makes sense, but probation officers in very small towns ask, "How can I avoid a business relationship with a client when the only coffee shop in town is run by one of my clients? Am I never to go there during the years he is on probation?" In the same manner as police, some probation and parole officers feel that the gifts offered are given in the spirit of gratitude or generosity and not to influence decision making.

Some probation or parole officers encounter ethical conflicts when they seek part-time employment at counseling centers. They may have counseling or drug treatment licenses that allow them to run groups and engage in individual counseling to earn extra income. This becomes an ethical issue when their part-time employment may involve working with correctional clients. Because their role as private counselor would conflict with their role as professional correctional supervisor, ethics boards have ruled that such employment is acceptable only when they do not interact with clients.

Because probationers may appear to be similar to the probation or parole officer in socioeconomic status, family background, lifestyle, or personal value systems, there is a greater tendency to feel affinity and friendship for some clients. Some probation officers have been known to have clients baby-sit for them, to rent a room in their house, or to socialize with them and their families. Obviously, these personal relationships hinder the ability to perform one's official function as a protector of the community and enforcer for the legal system. Personal relationships of any type—romantic, platonic, or financial—are simply not appropriate or ethical for the probation and parole professional.

## Corruption

No doubt there are some probation recommendations based on bribery or favoritism, or decisions not to violate based on unethical criteria. Sexual coercion of clients may exist. Urinalysis testing may be subverted by a corrupt scheme to switch test results. One should not be surprised if these practices exist, although they are not widespread and many people will complete their careers and retire without having heard about or being involved in any of them. However, it would be a wise approach to consider what one would do in a situation similar to the dilemmas described in this section or similar to any of the others in this book. Corrupt practices exist because honest people allow them to. For instance, in the followng "In the News" box, is it possible that others knew of this probation officer's misconduct before the formal investigation began?

Organizations experience corruption partly because they do not support and nurture ethical workers. Hopefully, the increasing professionalism of each of the subsystems of the criminal justice system will create a situation in which "rabble-rousers" don't have to lose careers and suffer subcultural sanctions because of standing up for what is ethical.

**IN THE NEWS Probation Officer Sentenced**

A Florida state probation officer was sentenced in federal court to four months imprisonment and three years of supervised release for accepting bribes from a probationer in exchange for allowing the probationer to avoid mandatory drug testing and other restrictions. The officer was tried in federal court under Title 18, United States Code, Section 1951 (Hobbs Act).

Source: News Release, U.S. Department of Justice, July 28, 2005. Retrieved on October 7, 2005, from http://www.usdoj.gov/usao/fls/050728-02.html.

*How often do you think probation officers accept bribes from clients to avoid conditions? Why do we hear about probation officer corruption so much less often than police officer corruption?*

# Parole

We have been discussing probation and parole officers simultaneously in the sections above, but there are some important distinctions between the two. First, parolees are perceived to be more of a threat to the community, so the supervision role of parole officers is emphasized much more strongly than in probation, where supervision has been balanced with a service/counseling emphasis. Further, the offenders are usually older and have a longer criminal record, so the relationship between supervisor and client might be different. It is certainly true that the problems faced by parolees are quite different than those probationers face.

It is estimated that roughly 600,000 prisoners are reentering our communities each year (King and Mauer, 2002: 3). In fact, the number of releasees has increased in recent years. There was an increase of 8.4 percent in the number of individuals released from 1998 and 2000 (B.J.S., 2002a: 7). This is probably due to the drastic increase in the number of those incarcerated during the 1980s. Even if the use of parole decreases, the sheer number of those eligible for parole will be swelling the ranks of parole caseloads for decades to come. Most of them have the same low levels of education and vocational skills that they had going into prison and have not had access to many, if any, rehabilitative programs in prison. Further, many of the new releasees will be those who *maxed out*—meaning they completed their entire sentence with no requirements to be supervised (Talbot, 2003).

Many of those released from prison return—in fact, according to a recent Justice Department study, 67 percent of released inmates were charged with at least one serious crime within three years. The study tracked 272,111 released inmates in 15 states. Other study findings indicated that the recidivism rate of offenders is worse than 20 years ago, not better, despite longer sentences imposed. Men were more likely to recidivate than women (68 percent compared to 57 percent), African Americans were more likely to recidivate than whites (73 percent compared to 63 percent), and young people (under 18) were more likely to recidivate than older offenders (45 and above) (80 percent compared to 45 percent). Offenders with the highest recidivism rates included car thieves, those convicted of receipt of stolen property, burglars, and those convicted of robbery (K. Murphy, 2002).

The fact is that our incarceration rates, currently some of the highest in the world, have had a tremendously negative impact on communities. Whole neighborhoods are affected when a large percentage of their population is sent away for years at a time. Generational effects are obvious; we know that children of inmates are six times as likely to be delinquent. More subtle effects exist as well. The economy and the social fabric of a community are also affected when large numbers of young people are removed (Mauer, Chesney-Lind, and Clear, 2002). Community corrections professionals have some amount of power in this scenario—they can make release recommendations and affect revocation rates. They can help offenders with reentry problems, or they can blindly enforce every bureaucratic rule.

Recall that under ethical formalism, to be an ethical professional one must do one's duty. What is the parole officer's duty? Some officers feel that they have met their ethical duty by explaining the rules to a parolee and then catching the person if he or she "messes up." Others see a more expanded role wherein the officer has some duty to help the offender readjust to society. This may involve taking some responsibility for counseling the offender, referring him or her to services, acting as a troubleshooter or mediator in conflict with family or others, and acting as an advocate in obtaining help. In other words, this officer takes a proactive approach to the parolee's success. Is filing a violation report a success (because the offender was caught) or a failure (because the offender did not succeed)?

# A New Paradigm of Corrections?

The high incarceration rate of this country has made a few people rich and others economically comfortable because of strong unions and/or white-collar jobs in corrections. Many more people have found poorly paid jobs as correctional officers. A huge network of profitable enterprise has sprung up because of the corrections industry. At the American Correctional Association meeting, delegates are enticed to a huge ballroom or conference hall filled from front to back with vendors. Participants pick up freebies of pens, water bottles, candy, and other items while they look at prison wares—everything from riot batons to stainless-steel stools is displayed. The fact is that the field of corrections is big business, and it supports a huge number of ancillary businesses. We have become so inured to the concept of deprivation of liberty that it is hard to think of a different approach—but there might be one.

A relatively recent philosophical approach to crime and punishment has been called *restorative justice* or **peacemaking corrections**. Reichel (1997) briefly describes the origins of the movement during the development of restitution and community service sentences in the 1970s. Although these innovative sentences were originally touted as rehabilitative, as rehabilitative goals lost favor with public sentiment, rationales and justifications were redefined, and, instead of rehabilitation, restoration

POLICY BOX 14-1  **Restorative Justice**

Restorative justice programs are primarily used for juvenile and nonviolent offenders. These programs have been financially supported by the federal government, and they have been widely hailed as a progressive advancement in the justice system. However, there are critics who argue that they take away the victim's right to seek retribution, that they create a net-widening effect, and that there are problems when the formal due process of the justice system is bypassed.

**Law:** Typically, programs that use different sentences or different sentencing structures must have enabling legislation before they can be put into practice. In some cases, judges promote such programs and use their discretion by allowing some offenders to be diverted from the system into the programs.

**Policy:** Policies must be established regarding who is eligible for such programs and who will make the decision on whether an offender is referred or not. Ordinarily, the offender and the victim must give consent for the case to be shifted to an alternative sentencing procedure. Policies must also be established for when an offender "fails" and what happens when he or she does not complete the program successfully. Typically, the case is then sent back for official processing. These policies do not carry the force of law, and they are often changed after the program has been in operation for some period of time. Inevitably, there may arise cases where the policies do not seem to result in a fair outcome; then informal policies are often applied that do not carry the force of law or the sanction of formally approved policies.

**Ethics:** The individual decision makers (judge, probation officer, restorative justice staff, attorneys) must apply the law, policy, and their own individual ethics in the decision as to who goes into the program, what the offender is required to do, and what sanctions are given, keeping in mind the needs of the victim, the system, and the offender.

or reparation (for the victim) became the philosophical rationale behind such programs (Bazemore and Maloney, 1994). See Policy Box 14-1 for a discussion of the law, policy, and ethics of the concept.

Whether restitution is to the individual (with compensation paid directly to the victim) or symbolic (where the community benefits from the offender's labor or payments), the idea of alternative justice is to restore the victim to his or her condition before the victimization event, or if the victim is not easily identifiable, to produce a measurable positive effect for the community. For instance, Bazemore and Maloney (1994) discuss one program where community service offenders helped rebuild a town ravaged by a tornado. There are five goals of the approach:

1. The service should meet a clearly defined and obvious need.
2. Service should symbolically link offender and victim, or offender and his or her community.

3. Offenders should be viewed as resources, and outcome measures should be directed to the work itself (rather than the offender's behavior).
4. Offenders should be involved in planning and executing the projects.
5. Included should be a sense of accomplishment, closure, and community recognition. (adapted from Bazemore and Maloney, 1994: 27)

The historical origins of and analogies to restorative justice can be found throughout recorded history; early laws demanded victim compensation, and reparation has a much longer history than does penal servitude. Many advocates (see Umbreit, 1994; Umbreit and Carey, 1995; van Ness and Heetderks Strong, 1997; Perry, 2002) now believe that restorative justice quite appropriately places the emphasis back onto the victims, but can be life affirming and positive for the offender as well. The key is in finding a method of restoration that is meaningful and somehow related to the offense instead of merely punitive labor—such as the infamous rock pile—which is devoid of worth to the victim, the offender, or society.

There are strong similarities and overlap between restorative justice and the peacekeeping model of corrections. Peacemaking corrections offers a similar approach of care and of *wholesight,* or looking at what needs to be done with both the heart and the head (Braswell and Gold, 2002). Both approaches are consistent with the ethics of care and might be considered a "feminine" model of justice because of the emphasis on needs rather than retribution.

It is said that a retributive, punitive orientation results in an offender's perception of unfairness (through denial of victim, denial of injury, or a belief that a more serious victimization was visited upon the offender). A different model may reduce those feelings and force the offender to squarely face his or her own responsibility. Arguably, a restorative justice program that focuses attention on the injuries of the victim and does not involve stigma, banishment, or exclusion for the offender would not create the opportunity to generate rationalizations and excuses for the offender's behavior.

- *Peacemaking (or sentencing) circles* or *healing circles* are one model of this type of correctional approach. In these circles, adapted from interventions used in Native American and other indigenous cultures, the offender meets with the victims, his or her family, and other interested parties. The goal is to find some resolution to the problem, but the problem may not be simply the offender's wrongdoing; it could be the victim's behavior or the family's failings. The orientation is acceptance of the person and rejection of the behavior (Umbreit, Coates, and Vos, 2002). Similar programs involve only the family (family group conferencing).
- *Victim–offender mediation* is another type of program where offenders meet with their victims so that they can tell the offender face-to-face how the offense affected them—both monetarily and emotionally. There is usually an element of restitution in these programs, with the offender and victim agreeing on the amount of restitution that the offender will pay.
- *Community reparative boards* present another form of restorative justice. The board members are individuals who are representatives of the community and who determine the sentence in a way that attempts to meet the needs of both parties.

- *Victim education programs* are somewhat similar in motive to the victim–offender mediation programs, but they do not match the victim with their particular offender. Instead, volunteer victims meet with offenders either in prison or community settings and explain to offenders what the effect of victimization has been on them. There is also more general education on victim rights and general victimization research. The goal is to create empathy toward victims, and the programs show moderate success (Monahan, Monahan, Gaboury, and Niesyn, 2004).

## Reintegrative Shaming Versus Stigmatizing Shaming

As mentioned in Chapter 12, there are a number of punishments inflicted on offenders today that incorporate the concept of shame. Judges have made those convicted of DWI use special license plates, sex offenders have had to put signs on their house, and offenders have had to confess and seek the forgiveness of their community by publishing an advertisement or making a public appearance of some kind.

These types of shaming punishments hark back to the days of the stocks and pillory, when punishment was effective arguably more because of community scorn rather than the physical pain involved. Some believe that it is not a useful or helpful trend; for instance, one A.C.L.U. spokesperson called such punishments "gratuitous humiliation that serves no social purpose" (cited in Book, 1999: 653). Whitman (1998) argues that the use of such penalties is contrary to a sense of dignity and creates an "ugly complicity" between the state and the community by setting the scene for "lynch justice." There is even some question as to whether such punishments are legal because some state laws demand that probation conditions have a "rehabilitative function." In general, however, judges have imposed these punishments without much serious challenge. Legally, they seem to be acceptable, but what about ethically?

The major issue seems to be whether such shaming conditions are reintegrative or stigmatizing. Braithwaite (2000) is the most well-known spokesperson for reintegrative shaming. He argues that shame is different from guilt because it comes from one's beliefs about how one's community feels about the crime. He argues that societies that don't have shame attached to certain crimes have a lot of that type of crime. Thus, what is necessary to reduce crime is a return to the concept of shame.

According to Braithwaite (2000), **stigmatization** is disrespectful shaming. In punishments where the offender is treated as a bad person rather than someone who has done a bad act, the society is rejecting the individual, which leads the individual to reject society. Braithwaite points out that some African societies that use reintegrative shaming have low crime rates, as does Japan, which uses techniques of reintegrative shaming for delinquents. The difference is that these cultures do not reject the individual; rather, they reject only the behavior. Individuals continue to feel a part of their family, school, neighborhood, and community. Stigmatizing punishments lead to oppositional subcultures; reintegrative interventions do not. It is not a coincidence that communities that are more integrated and have stronger social ties have less crime. These communities are much more likely to be able to employ the concept of reintegrative shaming and, thereby, control their members. The corollary to this, of course, is that if one feels disenfranchised from society, then shaming will not work at all (Karp, 1998).

## QUOTE and QUERY

Key values of restorative justice are healing rather than hurting, respectful dialogue, making amends, caring and participatory community, taking responsibility, remorse, apology, and forgiveness.

Source: Braithwaite (2000: 300).

*Do you think that restorative justice principles will ever be widely adopted by the criminal justice system? Why or why not?*

Karp (1998) provides an interesting perspective on why restorative justice and reintegrative shaming interventions have received positive responses. The public may not feel that probation or other forms of alternative sanctions have the same moral condemnation that prison does; therefore, they cheapen or lessen the moral blame of the offender. However, shaming penalties emphasize the individual's responsibility to the victim and society. There is a strong dose of morality and redemption in such programs, and the public seems to respond to that.

Karp also emphasizes the difference between stigmatizing and reintegrative shaming. He points out that most of the shaming punishments that have been reported, such as sex offenders being required to post signs on their doors, are stigmatizing shaming punishments. They may lead to unintended results, such as the offender being victimized by the community through vigilante justice. This is what Whitman (1998) finds problematic and distasteful about such punishments.

Recall that Whitman saw the state as setting the scene for "lynch justice," and, in fact, such punishments have led to the community victimizing offenders. **Megan's laws**—laws that require registration of sex offenders and allow the publication of such lists—are questioned by some who point out that such laws have led to cases where an offender or his family have been attacked and, in some cases, actually driven from the community. Although one's response might be "So what, he is a sex offender!" it should be noted that in some states, all sex crimes are covered, and this may include a man who was convicted of statutory rape when he was eighteen because his girlfriend was sixteen. Further, the family members are also stigmatized, and, arguably, they are innocent of wrongdoing.

Stigmatizing shaming punishments are ineffective with those who are already "on the margins" of society anyway. Reintegrative shaming uses whatever "community" the offender has, whether that be a family, workplace, neighbors, or school, to instill the shame that can lead to changing behavior. However, it may work only with those types of offenders who feel that they are a part of a community. These interventions are most common with juveniles and less serious offenders.

Dzur and Wertheimer (2002) discuss how restorative justice can further forgiveness and ask a question: Is forgiveness a social good? They also question whether the justice system should be pursuing restoration and forgiveness. They summarize the philosophy of restorative justice and note that it gives the victim a chance to voice his

**IN THE NEWS  Sexual Predator or Thought Police?**

A defense attorney characterized the arrest of a cyber-sexual predator as an example of punishing someone for their thoughts. He was arrested for the crime of attempted sexual performance from a child when he arrived at a meeting place he had arranged with a detective who was posing as a thirteen-year-old in an Internet chat room. He had to register as a sex offender and will be on probation and have to attend sex offender treatment. His attorney said he thought he would meet an adult who was posing as a child and that he was just engaging in fantasy and fantasy is not a crime. Sexual offender registration is public information. Some argue that cyber-sex investigations where offenders do not ever come into contact with a child-victim are pushing the law too far, especially considering the dramatic effect of sex offender registration on someone's life.

Source: A. Miller, "Predator Gets Probation," *San Marcos Daily Record*, August 18, 2005, A1, A10.

***Do you think someone should be arrested and convicted for an attempted sex crime when he engages in cyber-discussions with someone who says she is thirteen?***

or her emotions. In this public discourse, there is a presence of the victim that is not felt in the professional and objective traditional justice procedures. It is believed that the dialogue and the opportunity to be heard aid forgiveness and that forgiveness is good for the victim. The authors then argue against the idea that what is good for the individual victim is also good for everyone else. Using a utilitarian approach, they argue that there may be a greater good in incarcerating offenders who may re-offend. Note that this is an empirical question because it is a question about consequences: Does restorative justice deter fewer people than traditional punishment? Also, the authors point out that forgiving offenders may be good for the individual victim but may not be good for the "class of victims" who might have yet to be victimized. There are other issues as well, such as determining who the victim is in attempted crimes. Should the burden of proof be lowered in restorative justice programs because there is no punishment when finding a person guilty? The basic point is that restorative justice may be good for the individual victim but not result in a greater good for society. In the next section we will discuss other ethical issues in restorative justice.

## *Ethical Issues in Restorative Justice*

Restorative justice seems to be a healthy alternative to prison. However, certain issues merit discussion. First, because such interventions are seen as benign, they have the potential to create "net widening," further enlarging the scope of corrections over the citizenry (Roach, 2000). There are also questions of due process and whether restorative justice meets the traditional goals of crime prevention (Dzur and Wertheimer, 2002).

Another issue is the potential privacy issues of both the offender and other members who are involved. One of the strengths of restorative justice interventions is the inclusion of a number of parties, including the offender's family, co-workers, and friends, as well as the victim and the victim's support group. But what if some individuals important to the process choose not to participate? In fact, even schools have trouble getting some parents to involve themselves in their children's progress. It is entirely possible that a juvenile, otherwise qualified for a program, would not be able to participate because of the unwillingness of family members. Does this mean that the juvenile would be punished for having uncaring or unwilling parents? It may be that parents are caring but choose not to allow the state to intervene in what is considered "private" family business. Parents and relatives may point out that they have not broken any laws and that the state cannot tell them what to do. Even when the process is seen as a positive intervention, whenever state actors are involved, there is a potential for coercion, and some people react strongly to that idea.

Restorative justice programs are looked upon with favor by victims' rights groups because of the idea of restoration and restitution for victims. However, what happens when victims do not suffer much and offenders have great needs? The approach is oriented to meeting the needs of victims and offenders, and in some cases, it may be that the offender is needier. Would a victim reject such an approach? Should the victim be able to veto this approach and demand traditional punishment? Is it possible for a victim to be too vindictive?

One example of an interesting program that can be labeled restorative is the Texas mediation program. This program allows the family members of homicide victims to meet with the killer, even if the killer is on death row. Such meetings are preceded by months of counseling by trained volunteers for both the offender and the victims. The counselors decide when both parties are ready to meet, and the meeting doesn't take place if the victim is seen as too emotionally fragile or too retaliatory, or if the offender is seen as too manipulative or doesn't admit culpability.

In one mediation session, a woman and her teenage granddaughter met with the killer of the woman's daughter and young girl's mother. The father and brothers refused to participate, but the mother and daughter wanted to see and talk to their loved one's killer. The daughter was only five years old when the killing took place, and she wanted to learn more about how her mother died and to see the man who did it. The offender turned out to be a man who had killed the victim when he was fifteen. His childhood was marked by sexual abuse, physical abuse, and abandonment. He and another teenager were high on "speedballs" (cocaine and methamphetamine) when they were picked up by the young mother after their car broke down. They raped and killed her.

In prison, he got to know the family of a cellmate, who eventually adopted him. The family evidently had been instrumental in changing his life and outlook. His goal for participating in the program was to tell the victim's family how sorry he was for the crime and ask forgiveness. The mediation between the women and young man continued for most of one day. The counselor guided the discussion. The offender told them what he remembered from the crime, and they told him about the dead woman. At the end of the day, the two women hugged the murderer and had a picture taken with his arms around their shoulders (Nowell, 2001).

While not all, or even most, mediations end with the victims and offenders hugging, this story is amazing in the illustration of the power of humans to move beyond anger, hate, and grief to some type of solace and forgiveness. The women experienced a good deal of negative reaction from their family members for participating and, especially, for having their picture taken with the murderer. From their point of view, the experience left them with something more than they had before—they had some glimpse of their loved one in her final hours, and some reassurance that the offender was not a monster.

It should be noted that victims' rights groups tend to be cautious about restorative justice programs in general because of the focus on offenders. The anger that victims feel at the offender and the system that ignores their needs leaves little room for forgiveness. Most groups advocate harsher punishments, not restorative justice; they discuss "rights" rather than "needs" and thus draw their moral legitimacy from retribution rather than the ethics of care. However, there are other sources that also argue that forgiveness and restorative justice are just as beneficial to the victim as the offender (Morris, 2000).

There is an emerging perspective that indicates the pendulum has swung too far in making the victim feel a part of the process. The **victim satisfaction model** (Stickels, 2003) proposes that Packer's models of due process or crime control have given way to victim satisfaction. That is, the system and its actors (specifically, prosecutors) attempt to appease the victim in all decisions from charging to plea bargaining. This creates a situation wherein the criminal justice system becomes, in effect, a civil system with the victim as plaintiff and the prosecutor a plaintiff's attorney. The implications are diverse and include cost–benefit issues (is it worth prosecuting some cases?) and also justice (does the victim's perspective of just resolution always equal an objective view of a just resolution?). This emerging perspective is contrary to the more established perspective that the system "forgets" the crime victim and is solely focused on the offender.

Does a murderer ever deserve forgiveness? Did the women in the mediation program forgive the offender or simply recognize his humanity? We can't say that the family members who can't forgive are wrong, so is there ever a good in forgiveness? These questions are at the heart of restorative justice and probably explain why it has, thus far, been limited largely to nonserious property crimes and to juvenile offenders. However, the questions posed are at the very heart of any discussion of justice and are ones that we've asked in prior chapters. Specifically, do criminals ever deserve forgiveness?

# Conclusion

In this chapter we looked at two approaches to community corrections. The first approach includes the traditional forms of community corrections: probation and parole. We looked at the ethical issues of these professionals in the same way that other criminal justice professionals were considered in previous chapters. The second approach is a new paradigm of justice called restorative justice. In this model, rights are replaced with needs, and punishment is replaced with restoration. It is a fairly new idea in corrections, and the concepts are still being formed. However, it presents important questions about how best to meet the ends of justice.

# Key Terms

**community corrections** a term that encompasses halfway houses, work release centers, probation, parole, and any other intermediate sanctions, such as electronic monitoring—either as a condition of probation or as a sentence in itself that takes place in the community rather than prison

**cynicism** a trait of those in corrections characterized by a pessimistic view of offenders and their ability to change

**Megan's laws** laws requiring sex offenders to register in order to alert law enforcement about their presence in the community

**net widening** the concept that some intermediate sanctions are used for those who would not have received any formal correctional sanction before, so instead of diverting those who would have been sentenced to harsher sanctions, the program increases the total number under correctional supervision

**passive time server** the type of officer who does the bare minimum on the job to stay out of trouble

**peacemaking corrections** an approach to corrections that depends on care and *wholesight,* or looking at what needs to be done with both the heart and the head

**punitive law enforcer** the type of officer who perceives the role as one of enforcer, enforces every rule, and goes "by the book"

**stigmatization** disrespectful shaming

**victim satisfaction model** Stickels's concept that the system has shifted too far in the direction of satisfying the victim's need for revenge and retribution

**welfare/therapeutic worker** the type of officer who perceives the role as one of counselor to the offender and who helps to effect rehabilitative change

# Review Questions

1. Explain the concept and ideology of community corrections.
2. Explain the concept of "net widening."
3. Describe the discretion of probation and parole officers, and provide examples of ethical and unethical applications of discretion.
4. Describe the probation officer subculture.
5. Describe the types of probation officers and ethical issues for each.
6. Discuss ethical issues for probation and parole officers, and differentiate these issues.
7. Describe the principles of restorative justice, and contrast them with traditional models of justice.
8. Provide some examples of programs that use the restorative justice approach.
9. Distinguish between reintegrative shaming and stigmatizing shaming.
10. Explain whether the ethical systems would support restorative justice programs, and discuss some ethical issues that arise in restorative justice programs.

# Discussion Questions

1. Assume that you are a probation officer, and resolve the following dilemmas. Share your answers with others. Now apply ethical formalism to the situation, and see if doing so results in different answers. What about utilitarianism?
   a. A judge directed me to change my negative recommendation for probation to a favorable recommendation.
   b. I found out that my supervisor changed a negative recommendation I had given to a positive recommendation.
   c. A judge instructed us that if we can convince female defendants to get Norplant (a birth-control device), he will waive court costs and fines.
2. What would you do if you were the probation officer in the following cases?
   a. One morning a fellow officer was meeting with a probationer. This officer was yelling profanities and was very rude to this probationer, for whatever reasons.
   b. A close colleague at work was dating a probationer, and they were planning to move in together. The close colleague told me about it.
   c. I took a supervisor's job, and one of the officers I supervised didn't do anything—all day. Read magazines at her desk. The thing was, I was told I couldn't fire her. She had already been transferred around, and now I was stuck with her.
   d. In one office I worked, there was an officer who took naps in the afternoon. It was well-known. He would close his door and lie down on the floor. After a couple hours he would open his door again and go on.
3. Here are additional probation officers' dilemmas—what would you do?
   a. I had a cousin on probation for his second DWI. No one in the family knows he is on probation. At a family gathering I see the probationer drinking (more than one drink).
   b. A friend from high school had a boyfriend on probation. The boyfriend had violated his conditions of probation, and an M.T.R.P. (Motion to Revoke Probation) was filed in his case. The girlfriend wanted me to give her confidential information out of his file.
   c. I was having dinner at a nice restaurant, and the manager on duty happened to be on my caseload and offered me a free dinner and gave me basketball tickets to five games.
   d. I discovered that the applicant was an illegal alien but had a family of four with a baby who was born with a defect. His wife did not work, and he was the sole provider for the family. The dilemma was that if INS was contacted, the individual would be deported while his family stayed with no support.
   e. Do I not collect fees from a client who is a single mother with three children because it would come out of her budget and mean she must neglect the needs of her children, or do I collect the fees and disregard the problems the client is struggling with and alienate the client more?
4. Would you want to meet with the murderer of a loved one? What would you want to ask him or her? Would you be able to forgive?
5. You are a legislator asked to sponsor legislation that would enable the creation of restorative justice sentencing. Would you agree to sponsor such legislation? Why or why not?

# Ethical Dilemmas

### Situation 1

You are a probation officer and have a specialized sex-offender caseload. The judge disagrees with a recommendation for a prison sentence and places an offender on probation. This man was convicted of molesting his four-year-old niece. One of the conditions of his probation is that he notify you whenever he is around children. He becomes engaged and moves in with a woman who has three children under the age of twelve. You believe that the man is not repentant and that there is a good chance he will molest these children. Although the woman knows his criminal history, she does not seem to care and, in fact, allows him to baby-sit the young girls. The judge has indicated that he will not entertain new conditions or a revocation unless there is evidence of a crime, but you understand from the offender's counselor that he continues to be sexually aroused by children. What can you do? What should you do?

### Situation 2

You are a probation officer with a DWI probationer who has not been reporting for any of the court-sanctioned programs, and a motion to revoke was supposed to be filed. However, a very-high-ranking administrator in your office tells you not to file the M.T.R. or take any other negative actions because this person is a personal friend and, anyway, he isn't a "serious criminal." What would you do?

### Situation 3

You are a parole officer who has a single mother with three hyperactive, attention-deficit-disordered young children on your caseload. She receives no support from her ex-husband. Her own mother wants nothing to do with her or the children, believing that "God is punishing her." The mother works as a topless dancer but hates it. She continues dancing because it pays the bills so well. You know that she smokes marijuana on a fairly regular basis in an effort to deal with stress. Obviously, this is a violation of probation. However, if you file a violation report on her, she will go back to prison. You know she is doing the best she can with her kids, she is very involved with their school, and they are strongly bonded to her. You worry about what will happen to the kids. What would you do?

### Situation 4

You are the director of a restorative justice program in your community. It is set up for juvenile offenders and involves "circle sentencing," whereby the offender meets with family members, school officials, and the victim and the victim's relatives and friends. The circle comes up with what should be done, and often there is no punishment *per se*, but rather the juvenile is connected to programs that can help him or her get back in school, get a job, or receive vocational training. In the case you are reviewing, you suspect that there are real questions as to whether or not the juvenile actually committed the burglary he is accused of. There is no evidence to link the juvenile with the crime, and he and his court-appointed attorney have claimed innocence. They then changed their plea and agreed to the restorative justice program, perhaps because if it is successfully completed, the juvenile will have no criminal record. Should you care whether the juvenile is innocent or not, given that the program is restorative, not punitive?

### Situation 5

You have some real concerns about your co-worker's treatment of offenders. You hear him screaming obscenities at them in his office, and one time you saw him pat a female probationer on the rear end and say, "Be sweet to me and I'll keep you out of jail." On the other hand, no one else seems to notice anything is wrong, and the exchange with the client might have been misinterpreted and be simply in bad taste rather than sexual harassment. Should you do anything?

## Suggested Readings

Braithwaite, J. 2000. "Shame and Criminal Justice." *Canadian Journal of Criminology* 42(3): 281–301.

Braswell, M., McCarthy, B., and McCarthy, B. 2002. *Justice, Crime, and Ethics*. Cincinnati: Anderson.

Dzur. A., and Wertheimer, A. 2002. "Forgiveness and Public Deliberation: The Practice of Restorative Justice." *Criminal Justice Ethics* 21(1): 3–21.

Mauer, M., Chesney-Lind, M., and Clear, T. 2002. *Invisible Punishment: The Collateral Consequences of Mass Imprisonment*. New York: The Sentencing Project.

Perry, J. (Ed.). 2002. *Repairing Communities Through Restorative Justice*. Lanham, MD: American Correctional Association.

Van Ness, D., and Heetderks Strong, K. 1997. *Restoring Justice*. Cincinnati: Anderson.

The Abu Ghraib prison was the site of horrendous abuse by United States soldiers against Iraqi citizens. The pictures, smuggled out by a soldier using a camera phone, shocked the world and tarnished the United States' reputation as an advocate for human rights.

# 15

# Ethical Choices
# and the "War on Terror"

*The Threat of Terrorism*

*Crime Control and "Means–End" Thinking*

*Crime Control, Human Rights, and the War on Terror*

*Conclusion*

## Key Terms

crime control
  approach
"front page test"
"just war" debate
principle of double
  effect

public service
  approach
rights-based model
terrorism

# Chapter Objectives

1. Become familiar with the connection between the war on terror and traditional law enforcement.

2. Understand the connection between crime control and means–end thinking.

3. Understand the human rights model of policing.

4. Understand the consequences of means–end thinking.

In this book we have explored ethical issues in each of the subsystems of the criminal justice system. We have discovered certain themes that run through each of the subsystems:

- The use of authority, power, force, and discretion
- Subcultural barriers to ethical decision making
- The importance of ethical leadership
- The tension between deontological ethical systems and teleological or "means–end" ethical analysis

In this final chapter we will reiterate some of these themes and discuss more specifically some of the current challenges facing public servants today.

# The Threat of Terrorism

On September 11, 2001, the United States was changed forever. The terrorist attack on the World Trade Center was the single most devastating terrorist attack in this country and, indeed, the world, with over 3,000 deaths and the complete destruction of two buildings that stood as icons of Western capitalism. Although we had experienced earlier incidents—the 1993 bombing of the World Trade buildings, the Oklahoma City bombing, and numerous attacks on U.S. targets worldwide—nothing prepared the country for the severity of the attack. The event traumatized a city, affected the American psyche, led to U.S. military engagement on foreign soil in two countries, and spurred the dramatic restructuring of federal law enforcement. The long-term effects of this event are still unfolding, with pervasive changes occurring in law enforcement on both the federal and local level.

We conclude this book with the unique challenges that terrorism presents for our public safety and for justice professionals. Terrorists are not garden-variety criminals. Therefore, our analyses of the activities of police, court, and correctional professionals thus far may or may not be applicable. One thing is clear: In the "war on terror," it is not just the military or even federal agents who are affected. Every law enforcement and justice agency in the land may have occasion to be involved. Targets of terrorist activity include not only buildings and bridges in big cities but also dams, power plants, schools, government buildings, and farms in the most remote areas.

**Terrorism** has been defined as the "deliberate, negligent, or reckless use of force against noncombatants, by state or non-state actors for ideological ends and in the absence of a substantively just legal process" (Rodin, 2004: 755). Modern terrorism has included acts by the Irish Republican Army, which attacked civilian targets in England to protest continued British presence in northern Ireland; the Palestinians who have targeted Israelis and others across the world in their continued protest over Israeli occupation of what they believe to be the Palestinian homeland; and, obviously, Al Qaeda, a fundamentalist Islamic group that is opposed to all Western secular power and is responsible for the attack on the World Trade Center as well as numerous other attacks all over the world. Terrorists also include groups that are separatists (Tamil Tigers in Indonesia), racial hegemonic groups (Ku Klux Klan), or even environmentalists (Earth Liberation Front) (Rodin, 2004). Terrorism has led to new questions being asked about what is appropriate or ethical in law enforcement investigative techniques, individual rights *vis-à-vis* the government, and what is legal and ethical in the detention and treatment of prisoners.

## The "Just War" Debate

The question of what is acceptable and not acceptable in fighting terrorism is not a new dilemma. Philosophers have been engaged in the **"just war" debate** since Cicero, who asked, specifically, when war is justified and what is justified in times of war (McMahan, 2004). The justification of war is condensed by Crank and Gregor (2005: 230) and Hicks (2004) to include the following:

1. The threat must be grave, lasting, and certain.
2. There are no other means to avert the threat.
3. There must be a good probability of success.
4. The means must not create a greater evil than the threat responded to.

These justifications seem to be consistent with a utilitarian system of ethics. They are not inconsistent with ethical formalism either, for ethical formalism includes the principle of forfeiture, which states that someone who impinges on others' rights forfeits his or her rights to the same degree.

The means that are ethically acceptable in furtherance of a just war have also been analyzed, and, again, utilitarian ethics and ethical formalism tend to agree in general upon the restrictions and guidelines for means. In determining just means, the extent of the harm is weighed against the end or injury averted, just as when one asks if the war itself is justified. Ethical formalism may be less accepting of harming innocents or noncombatants. However, the **principle of double effect** states that if one undertakes an action that is a good but that also results in a negative end, as long as the negative end was not the intent of the actor, then the good action and the good end can be considered a good. So, for instance, if one bombs a military target and innocents are harmed during the bombing, then the act, if otherwise considered ethical, does not become unethical because of the death of civilians.

"Just war" rationales have been applied to the war in Iraq. Crank and Gregor (2005) summarize the conflicting views regarding the Iraq war:

1. The war effort effectively targeted a center of terrorism and is engaging the enemy in a place far away from the shores and civilians of the United States.
2. The war effort deposed an evil tyrant and opened the door to democracy for the Iraqi people.
3. There was no connection between Iraq and Al Qaeda, and, in fact, Iraq, as a secular state, was an enemy of Al Qaeda.
4. The use of terrorism is a smoke screen, and the occupation of Iraq is simply a military effort to secure Iraq's oil.
5. Whether it was or wasn't a center of terrorism before the war, it is now because Al Qaeda and other insurgents have flocked to the area to engage U.S. soldiers.
6. Whatever is the motivation of occupying Iraq, the effect has been that Afghanistan is being ignored, the Taliban is regrouping, and Al Qaeda is growing stronger; thus, the effect of the war has been exactly the opposite of the expressed goal.

Although questions concerning the ethics and morals of the Iraq war are outside the scope of this text, the means acceptable to combat terrorism in this country are not. There has been a good degree of argument and analysis over whether traditional "just war" arguments can be applied to the fight against terrorists (Crank and Gregor, 2005; Zohar, 2004). Smilansky (2004) points out that terrorists have no moral justification and attack democracies partially because the ethos and values of such countries prohibit taking an "any means necessary" response. However, more often than not, when faced with terrorist threats, such governments do resort to means that cannot be justified by law or morals. The "Dirty Harry" problem discussed in reference to law enforcement is whether police officers should use any means necessary to obtain information from a criminal suspect in order to save a life. The "Dirty Harry" problem can be applied to terrorism. Are any means acceptable when dealing with terrorists?

## The Response to 9/11

Since 9/11, we have seen a fundamental shift in the goals and mission of law enforcement and public safety. This shift includes more law enforcement, a nationalization of law enforcement, and a reduction of civil liberties. We have seen federal money directed to training law enforcement officers to act as "first responders" to critical events such as terrorist attacks. There has also been more federal money available for hardware purchases. The trend of community or neighborhood policing that sought to forge links between law enforcement and the community it served has now slowed, and indications are that federal support for such programs has been withdrawn. In the place of community policing, one sees troubling tendencies to engage in zero-tolerance policies that capture many more in the net of crime control. Further, there are increasing links between local law enforcement and immigration services and federal law enforcement.

Many observers note that the creation of Homeland Security indicates a move toward the nationalization of our police force. Historically, a national police force has been resisted because of the origins of this country and the legacy of distrust of centralized power, yet it seems more of a possibility today (Stuntz, 2002). Although communication between different levels and agencies of law enforcement is long overdue, some critics argue that centralized communication has the potential to endanger privacy. For instance, a centralized DNA data bank is proposed by law enforcement as an important and effective step in the discovery and apprehension of criminals, and we are heading in that direction; however, the use of DNA may also have potential privacy risks. Some point out that once DNA is in a data bank, it may be misused to refuse health insurance or deny jobs to individuals based on their health risks.

There is no doubt that the response to the threat of terrorism has led to greater law enforcement powers in investigation. The immediate federal response to the World Trade Center was the passage of the Patriot Act. This legislation includes the following elements:

1. It allows federal agencies to spy on Americans without probable cause or even reasonable suspicion.
2. It also allows authorities to share with prosecutors information obtained via search warrants obtained through the Foreign Intelligence Surveillance Act, which does not require probable cause.
3. It allows deportation for anyone who financially supports a "terrorist organization," but the definition is so ambiguous that it might be used if a person contributed humanitarian aid.
4. It requires all Arab-born citizens to report to immigration offices around the country to be interviewed and registered under the National Security Entry–Exit Registration system. There was enough anxiety in the Arab community that volunteers took information from registrants as they went into the federal buildings—in case they didn't come back out again. (Wood, 2003)

The Patriot Act was passed swiftly, with little debate. Later proposals have been more closely scrutinized, but debate is still framed to portray those who are against such "protections" as unpatriotic (Etzioni and Marsh, 2003).

The Total Information Awareness pilot program was an initiative proposed by the government to collect voluminous amounts of information about citizens through the Internet. Although some were not concerned about this privacy invasion, others were very concerned about growing legal surveillance and the potential invasion of privacy (Kravets, 2003; Moss and Fessenden, 2002). Another proposal—"Operation TIPS"—encouraged citizens to spy on one another and proposed an official identity card. These programs, at least initially, have been rejected by legislators (Cole, 2002).

---

### QUOTE and QUERY

We're protecting freedom and democracy, but unfortunately freedom and democracy have to be sacrificed.

Source: Jethro Eisenstein—a New York lawyer quoted in Moss and Fessenden (2002: A18).

***Is this claim overstating the issue?***

Since 9/11, we have detained thousands of noncitizens for months without charging them. Some argued that those held in Guantanamo Bay without charging or trials were "enemy combatants" and not deserving of liberties ensured by the Constitution, but citizens have been held as well (Cole, 2002; Crank and Gregor, 2005). There are disturbing analogies to the World War II detainment of 110,000 Americans of Japanese ancestry. We now have secret detentions and secret proceedings—concepts that have been an anathema to the concepts of democracy and liberty. It is indeed ironic that those who came to this country seeking the freedoms that are held to be the essence of its strength and tradition have found that these freedoms and liberties do not apply to them because of the color of their skin or their national heritage (Cole, 2002; Etzioni and Marsh, 2003).

Others, suspected of being Al Qaeda members, have been held in the United States at undisclosed locations. Their legal status was not clarified, and they were not given rights under international law and treaties. At least two U.S. nationals have also been held in similar conditions (Crank and Gregor, 2005: 212). Recently, the U.S. Supreme Court has ruled on some detention practices and held that they violate individual rights. In *Hamdi v. Rumsfeld,* 542 U.S. 507 (2004), the Court held that U.S. citizens could not be held indefinitely without charges even if they were labeled "enemy combatants." In *Rasul v. Bush,* 542 U.S. 466 (2004), the Court held that detainees in Guantanamo could challenge their detention in U.S. federal courts. In *Clark v. Martinez,* 125 S.Ct. 716 (2005), the Court held that the government may not indefinitely detain even illegal immigrants, undercutting the administration's policy of using immigrant status to detain suspects. The case concerned Cubans who had been held in federal prisons since the 1980 Mariel boatlift. Legal or illegal immigrants may be held for a "reasonable" period of time, said the Court, but then must be deported or released. Legal analysts note that these decisions have directly contradicted the administration's position on its authority over what it calls illegal combatants.

Perhaps as a response to 9/11, there has been a shift in policy so that there is less openness in governmental activities. Specific elements of this include admonitions by the government to be careful of what is printed, fewer White House briefings, secrecy about who was held and where they were held in the detainment of thousands after 9/11, and punishing government employees for giving unclassified information to the press (Crank and Gregor, 2005: 223).

According to Cole (2001), secret proceedings encourage distrust and hatred of the government. Cole (2001) points out that in the secret detainments after 9/11 and when government held individuals based on secret evidence, it was discovered later that the evidence was merely innuendo and rumor, and most individuals were released. The reason for openness is so that governmental actions and decision making can be vetted by a fair and balanced debate. Although certain information essential to national security should never be subject to public dissemination, the question is what secrets protect the country, and what secrets protect the government?

The Patriot Act reached its sunset provision in December 2005, and Congress extended it by only five months. The effort to get the Patriot Act renewed was made difficult by the news that President Bush had authorized secret wiretapping of U.S. citizens, bypassing the secret court created to ensure due process and oversight.

**IN THE NEWS  Unprecedented Government Secrecy?**

More than thirty nonprofit groups have banded together to fight what they call "unprecedented" governmental secrecy. Their website, www.openthegovernment.org, seeks to raise awareness of a growing number of sealed court cases, classified documents, and hidden reports that hinder the people's ability to determine whether governmental officials are truly serving the public good. The media are also involved in this coalition as several recent cases, such as a reporter having his recording of a speech by Justice Scalia confiscated, have raised serious questions as to whether federal officials are engaging in oversight that may cross the line into intimidation. Government officials say that the government is as open as it has ever been.

Source: R. Carr, "Coalition Fights Unprecedented Government Secrecy," *Austin American Statesman,* May 13, 2004, A10.

***Do you feel that the government is hiding more information than it used to? How would we know?***

Ironically, government secrecy prevents an open discussion of whether or not the act has prevented terrorism. As Hamm (2005) points out, it is an impossible task to evaluate the act in any case because a series of executive orders have changed various rules within it.

Other actions that the United States has taken in response to 9/11 have occurred overseas. The CIA has been accused of ignoring the sovereign rights of other countries and engaging in criminal acts. For instance, Italy has alleged that CIA operatives kidnapped a radical Egyptian cleric in February of 2003 and smuggled him out on a U.S. military airplane. Officials in Sweden and Germany have also alleged that the CIA has kidnapped individuals in those countries and subjected them to torture in interrogations to discover what they knew about terrorist activities. The practice called "rendition" is usually done with the host country's knowledge, but in these cases there was no notice given or permission granted; thus, the country's leaders object to the U.S. practice of ignoring the sovereign right of the country and its laws. U.S. officials argue that the practice is necessary in the fight against terrorism (Whitlock, 2005). As this book goes to press, there are news reports that the U.S. government may be operating "secret" prisons in Eastern European countries. The idea that the United States places secret prisons in formerly Soviet countries is ironic indeed because one of the criticisms directed at the Soviets during the Cold War was their use of secret detentions. If it is true, perhaps the secret nature of such detention facilities is so pictures cannot be taken and publicized showing the treatment of prisoners. It was Dostoyevsky, a Russian, who said that a country's civilization can be measured by its treatment of prisoners. If that is true, then what can one say about the United States?

The abuses at Abu Ghraib have been discussed in earlier chapters of this text. They have been attributed to either a few "sick" soldiers or, alternatively, to a lack of standards concerning what were legal and officially approved methods of interrogation. Such abuses included the following:

- Forcing naked prisoners to pose in humiliating, sexually oriented poses
- Forcing hooded prisoners to stand on a box and be attached to electric wires
- Beating prisoners to death
- Threatening male detainees with rape
- Sodomizing a male detainee with a broomstick
- Threatening detainees with attack dogs
- Pouring chemicals from broken lightbulbs onto detainees (Massimino, 2004)

In other military prisons, practices included the following:

- Interrogators stepping on the neck of a detainee and kicking him in the genitals
- Being forced to roll back and forth on the floor of a cell kissing the feet of the interrogators
- Being made to pick plastic bottle caps out of a drum mixed with excrement and water (Golden, 2005)
- Being stuffed in a sleeping bag, wrapped in electrical cord, and beaten to death (White, 2005)

Although some characterize such acts as the result of "bad apples" (similar to the argument as to why there are corrupt cops), the question remains: Why did soldiers pose for photographs if they thought their activities would be punished by those in authority? The other explanation is that these abuses occurred because of a widespread belief that there was official approval of torture.

In fact, similar abuses occurred at another military prison in Afghanistan. At the Bagram prison a young taxi driver was literally killed by interrogators who suspended him from the ceiling and beat his legs so badly that an autopsy revealed his leg bones were pulverized (see the Quote and Query box). It was discovered that

---

### QUOTE and QUERY

"It became a kind of running joke, and people kept showing up to give this detainee a common peroneal strike just to hear him scream out 'Allah.' . . . It went on over a 24-hour period, and I would think that it was over 100 strikes." (Statement by one of the soldiers assigned as a military guard at the prison. The prisoner subsequently died.)

Source: T. Golden, "Cruel and Unusual Punishment," *Austin American Statesman*, May 21, 2005, A16.

*How does utilitarian ethics justify this treatment? Does any ethical system justify it? Why would soldiers continue such treatment if it was not associated with interrogation?*

Dilawar, the taxi driver, had no association at all with insurgents and that his taxi and the passengers in it had been picked at random by an Afghan guerrilla commander who told the Americans that they were responsible for bombing a U.S. camp. Later it was discovered that the commander himself was responsible for the bombing. The interrogators at the Bagram prison were redeployed to Iraq to interrogate prisoners at Abu Ghraib after there had been documented deaths because of their methods in Afghanistan (Golden, 2005).

Evidently, White House counsel Alberto Gonzales circulated a memorandum that opined that forms of interrogation that had been banned by the Geneva Convention did not apply to detainees from Afghanistan and Iraq. Practices that have been characterized as "not quite torture" include the following:

- being beaten
- thrown into walls
- subjected to loud noises and extreme heat and cold
- deprived of sleep, light, food, and water
- bound or forced to stand in painful positions for long periods of time
- kept naked and hooded
- shackled to the ceiling (Massimino, 2004: 74)

Amnesty International and the Red Cross were concerned about conditions in detention facilities, and there were indications that abusive practices were fairly routine long before the pictures of Abu Ghraib hit the national airwaves. As the following indicates, the Abu Ghraib abuses were only the latest and most extreme actions in a pattern of brutality that started when U.S. interrogators orchestrated kidnappings of suspects and sent the prisoners to countries that practiced torture, and also engaged in questionable practices in Guantanamo Bay, as the "In the News" box illustrates.

Military investigations and prosecutions now expose the fact that paramilitary units called Scorpions, which included CIA operatives, special forces, and civilians, used tactics in Afghanistan and Iraq that included beating prisoners. In the case of

---

**IN THE NEWS** Guantanamo Bay

An anonymous source gave information to reporters that a military investigation recommended a reprimand for the former commander of the Guantanamo Bay prison, finding that he failed to oversee interrogations that led to abusive treatment, but the report stopped short of defining the abuses as torture. The commander was not reprimanded and was sent to Iraq to supervise interrogations there. The investigation was begun when FBI agents generated internal memorandums complaining about the abusive treatment they witnessed at Guantanamo.

Source: D. Cloud, "Guantanamo Bay Inquiry Finds Violations," *Austin American Statesman,* July 13, 2005, A12.

*Should we believe anonymous sources?*

**QUOTE and QUERY**

"We take this moral high ground to make sure that if our people fall into enemy hands, we'll have the moral force to say, 'You have got to treat them right.' If you don't practice what you preach, nobody listens" (Senator Lindsey Graham, in support of an amendment banning torture of military prisoners).

Source: J. Galloway and J. Kuhnhenn, "Senators Add Anti-Torture Words to Bill," *Austin American Statesman,* October 6, 2005, A4.

***Is this argument against torture a utilitarian argument or an ethical formalist argument?***

the prisoner being stuffed in a sleeping bag, such practices led to death. However, what is important to understanding the practices is that the soldiers involved defended their actions as legal and continue to argue that they did nothing wrong (White, 2005).

Kleinig (2001) and others, even before the worst abuses were revealed, examined the weak justification for torture and abusive practices during interrogation, but also pointed out that it has been used in Northern Ireland, Israel, South Africa, and South America, among many other countries. The so-called "doctrine of necessity" is purely utilitarian, as is the argument of some that there must be secrecy concerning interrogation tactics so that they are more effective. To the contrary, Kleinig points out that torture dehumanizes both victim and oppressor: "There is a loss of the moral high ground, a compromising of values that supposedly distinguish a society as civilized and worth belonging to" (2001: 116).

The Senate, in a clear attempt to illustrate its views concerning U.S. participation in acts of torture, attached an amendment to the military funding bill in October 2005 that added language banning the use of "cruel, inhuman or degrading" treatment of military prisoners. Even though the White House threatened to veto the bill if the amendment was added, it passed by a resounding majority (90–9) and was backed by Republicans such as John McCain (a former prisoner of war) and Lindsey Graham (see the Quote and Query box above) (Galloway and Kuhnhenn, 2005). Evidently, the White House wanted exemptions to the language for the CIA. It seems to be literally the case that the White House pressured the Congress for permission to torture. The argument was that the "end" of finding out information is more important than the "means" of how to obtain it. Finally, the White House capitulated, and the funding bill with the anti-torture amendment was passed.

## Crime Control and "Means–End" Thinking

The response to terrorism has been justified as necessary in order to investigate and deter terrorist activity. Utilitarianism is the ethical justification for the Patriot Act and other governmental actions. The argument is framed in this manner: The "end" of deterring or preventing terrorist attacks outweighs all of the following:

- The privacy rights of individuals (so that government agents can search and not notify the individual of their search)
- Due-process rights (when immigrants are held without charges and without deportation for extended periods in investigative detentions)
- The First Amendment right to associate (when individuals are deported or, if they are citizens, investigated simply for associating with groups that have been defined by the State Department as terroristic)
- Even the right not to be tortured (when one is considered an insurgent or a terrorist who may have information)

This justification is simply a restatement of the crime control approach discussed in an earlier chapter. Instead of police and court practices being justified because of their role in deterring or preventing crime (most specifically, drug-related activity), the new practices are justified as preventing or deterring terrorism.

Our theme in the chapters concerning law enforcement is that the police role in society is either that of crime fighter or public servant. This discussion can be expanded to examine the whole system of public safety and justice, and the shift from the war on drugs to the war on terror. The **crime control approach** is associated with means–end or utilitarian thinking that determines good by the result (crime control). Utilitarian reasoning is employed to analyze tactics. For instance, Cohen (1987: 53) uses a utilitarian approach in the following justification for police action:

1. The end must itself be good.
2. The means must be a plausible way to achieve the end.
3. There must be no alternative, better means to achieve the same end.
4. The means must not undermine some other equal or greater end.

Crank and Caldero (2005) also use utilitarian thinking in their examination of noble-cause corruption. However, they state that those who employ such tactics do not weigh the utility of the acts correctly, arguing that in today's multicultural reality, police will have to negotiate an "end" that takes into account the needs of all groups in society. It cannot be denied that a crime control model may subvert law, policy, or human rights if utilitarian reasoning justifies it. In other words, the end, if important enough, will justify any means.

In the **public service approach**, the values and ethos of law enforcement and justice professionals focus on human rights, including the right to due process, and the fundamental duty of all public servants is to protect those rights. In this approach, the protection of rights is more important than the end of crime control. Kappeler, Sluder, and Alpert (1994: 243) present the U.S. Department of Justice recommendations for the values of a police department as the following:

1. Preserve and advance the principles of democracy
2. Place the highest value on preserving human life
3. Prevent crime as the number-one operational priority

4. Involve the community in delivering police services
5. Believe in accountability to the community served
6. Commit to professionalism in all aspects of operations
7. Maintain the highest standards of integrity

A **rights-based model** of policing recognizes the police as servants of the public good. Although crime control is important, protection of civil liberties is the fundamental mission. Note that in the Department of Justice's list, there is an inherent conflict between the third goal, which states that preventing crime is the number-one operational priority, and the seventh goal, which states that officers should maintain the highest standards of integrity. What if lying is the best way to catch a criminal and prevent crime? What if lying is the only way? Further, preserving and advancing the principles of democracy is not exactly a clear mandate—which principles, exactly, is this item referring to? Upholding human life is an important goal that no one would disagree with, but what if it conflicts with preserving democracy?

A crime control approach is utilitarian, and a rights-based approach is not. Under the rights-based approach, which is deontological, there is no end that would justify taking away human rights. This discussion has become incredibly more pressing in the face of terrorist threats. It is interesting to note that for many who have argued that the "end" of catching criminals does not justify certain means, such as racial profiling, the answer seems to be different when the end is preventing terrorist attacks. Thus, although racial profiling has been legally and ethically condemned as a violation of rights when used to catch drug dealers, it has been resurrected as an appropriate and justified response to catching terrorists. Our Supreme Court has held that privacy is more important than catching criminals, so wiretaps have been used sparingly and with judicial oversight. However, the prevention of terrorist attacks has changed this balance, and many are willing to give up their privacy rights in order for the government to protect them from terrorism.

The United States has belatedly condemned and apologized for the detainment without due process of Japanese Americans during World War II but has justified the recent detainment of those of Middle Eastern descent (not all of whom had visa violations). Forty years from now, will the United States apologize again?

Some argue that it is a false argument to weigh privacy or any civil liberty against security. Alderson (1998: 23), writing before the attack on the World Trade Center, presents a prescient argument against the "end" of security as a justification for taking away liberties:

I acknowledge that liberty is diminished when people feel afraid to exercise it, but to stress security to unnecessary extremes at the price of fundamental freedoms plays into the hands of would-be high police despots. Such despots are quick to exploit fear in order to secure unlimited power.

Alderson also addressed terrorism directly: "It is important for police to maintain their high ethical standards when facing terrorism, and for their leaders to inspire resistance to any degeneration into counter-terrorism terror" (1998: 71).

**QUOTE and QUERY**

A police devoid of a sense and a spirit of justice is inimical to the healthy progress of democracy.

Source: Alderson (1998: 67).

*Why does Alderson believe that it is so important to democracy that the police hold sound ethical values?*

The major problem of the utilitarian ethical system or "means–end thinking" is that we are unable to know the outcome of our actions. Justifying otherwise unethical means by arguing they will lead to a good end depends on the ability to know that the means will result in the desired outcome. Unfortunately, this is impossible. In our haste to protect ourselves from terrorists, it is at least conceivable that we may create more terrorists (Bender, 2005). The current generation of Middle Eastern children may identify the United States only as an aggressor. Our actions, misunderstood, could create many times more terrorists than the number we are trying to control today. In this country, those of Arab descent who came here for freedom now find that their heritage denies them that precious gift. In detaining Arab American men without the due process that protects most citizens, we may germinate the seeds of future destruction in the children who watch their fathers being taken away. In engaging in "renditions," operating secret prisons, and defending the right to torture, we lose allies across the world and, in the process, threaten our future security. We also, by parceling out human rights for some and not for others, weaken civil liberties for all citizens. The point is that utilitarian justifications always depend on predicting the future. One's predictions regarding the outcome of actions are sometimes woefully inadequate and tragically wrong.

# Crime Control, Human Rights, and the War on Terror

The premise of rights-based law enforcement is that some acts are never justified. No end is so important that governments can stoop to slavery, genocide, or torture. No situation ever justifies sexism, racism, murder, rape, or intimidation (Paul and Elder, 2003). There is a suspicion of state power in rights-based law enforcement and a fear that police will be used to oppress the powerless. The way to avoid this is to place protection of rights as the central theme of policing, rather than crime control, because the definition of crime and the identification of who is a criminal may be subverted for political ends. Further, the suspicion of state power leads to a "stacking" of rights on the side of the individual in any actions (such as criminal prosecution) taken by the government against the individual. Arguably, the individual needs these due-process rights because of the awesome power of the state against the weakness of one individual. So the individual is protected against state power by the Bill of Rights and by case law that identifies even the right to be informed of such rights (e.g., the Miranda ruling). Yes, it is usually criminals who get to exercise these rights. But they are there to protect all of us, and if they were not there, arguably, more innocents would be arrested, prosecuted, and imprisoned.

Rights-based law enforcement may be more prevalent in Europe. The United Nations Code of Conduct for Law Enforcement Officials illustrates the values and premise of the rights-based approach: "In the performance of their duty, law enforcement officials shall respect and protect human dignity and maintain and uphold the human rights of all persons" (Article 2, reported in Kleinig, 1999).

Neyroud and Beckley (2001: 62) describe the police standards of the United Kingdom as reflecting an emphasis on human rights. Standards include the following provisions:

1. To fulfill the duties imposed on them by the law
2. To respect human dignity and uphold human rights
3. To act with integrity, dignity, and impartiality
4. To use force only when strictly necessary and then proportionately
5. To maintain confidentiality
6. Not to use torture or ill-treatment
7. To protect the health of those in their custody
8. Not to commit any act of corruption
9. To respect the law and the code of conduct and oppose violations of them
10. To be personally liable for their acts

Because European police have had a longer history of dealing with terrorism, it is interesting that the trend there evidently has been to move toward a rights-based model of policing. For instance, British police have had their share of noble-cause corruption in dealing with Irish terrorists, Spain has dealt with Basque terrorists, Germany dealt with the Baeder–Meinhoff gang in the 1970s and more recently with neo-Nazi groups, and so on. It might be argued that "the end justifies the means" thinking by law enforcers who have dealt with terrorists inevitably led to violations of civil liberties and to fear. Arguably, there has been a recognition that official oppression always leads to more bitterness and disenfranchisement among certain groups of people and, ultimately, more unrest and terror. Thus, those who have been through the cycle realize that rights are more important than the "end" if the "end" requires the deterioration of rights. That may be why British and European countries are more attuned to human rights and limits on state power than the United States is.

On the other hand, we have seen recent examples where British police, faced with the subway bombings in July 2005, have resorted to questionable means, so the idea that British and European police subscribe wholeheartedly to rights-based policing may be overstated. In recent events, British police have been criticized for shooting an unarmed Brazilian who was a suspect in a subway bombing. It has never been made clear why police were following him or why they felt that the threat was so imminent that they had to shoot him (Buchholz, 2005). They have also been criticized for engaging in racial profiling of Muslim men. Such practices have led to the Muslim community becoming less cooperative. Observers note that one of the reasons the police were able to identify the subway bombers so quickly was cooperation by the Muslim community but that recent police actions have enraged community members and hardened opinion against police (Emling, 2005).

The Universal Declaration of Human Rights mandates thirty articles. They include the following:

- All humans are born free and equal in dignity and rights.
- Everyone has the right to life, liberty, and security of person.
- No one shall be held in slavery or servitude.
- No one shall be subjected to torture or to cruel, inhuman, or degrading treatment or punishment.
- Everyone has the right to a standard of living adequate for the health and well being of himself and of his family.
- Everyone has the right to education.
- Everyone has the right to freedom of peaceful assembly and association.
- Everyone is entitled to all the rights and freedoms set forth in this Declaration, without distinction of any kinds, such as race, color, sex, language, religion, political or other opinion, national or social origin, property, birth, or status.
- All are equal before the law and are entitled, without any discrimination, to equal protection of the law.

Even though more than 130 countries have adopted the declaration, virtually every country in the world violates one or several of these principles. The United States hasn't even ratified the treaty. It did, on the other hand, ratify the United Nations Convention Against Torture and Other Cruel, Inhumane or Degrading Treatment or Punishment in 1994, and passed a law (Title 18, Section 2340 of the United States Code) that makes torture illegal. This is why, arguably, some detainees have been sent to countries that have not ratified the treaty, such as Egypt and Syria, so that they can be tortured.

In an earlier chapter we discussed the importance of an independent judiciary. This concept is an essential element of this discussion as well. There is no coincidence that the United Nations and the European Union both mandate that a country have an independent judiciary in order for that nation to be considered protective of human rights and thus eligible to join the European Union. The way to freedom and democracy is through the recognition of human rights, and the way to protect human rights is through an independent judiciary (Keith, 2002). Some of the elements of an independent judiciary have been identified as the following:

- guaranteed terms of office
- finality of decisions
- exclusive authority
- ban against exceptional or military courts
- fiscal autonomy
- separation of powers
- enumerated qualifications (Keith, 2002: 196–197)

Some of the elements are problematic, even in the United States. Certainly the secret military courts that have been increasingly used since 9/11 to try "combatants" are questionable, considering the prohibition against exceptional or military courts. The element of finality of decisions is problematic as well because there seems to be more overturning of older Supreme Court decisions and, as we discussed in an earlier chapter, lower courts ignoring Supreme Court decisions. The exclusive authority provision, fiscal autonomy, and separation of powers could also be questionable, considering recent events in the United States. Despite these issues, there is no doubt that an independent judiciary is vitally important to safeguarding human rights and protecting due process.

As this book went to press, to the country was engaged in a great debate over Judge Samuel Alito. The confirmation of Judge Alito as a Supreme Court Justice was not focused on his qualifications. Even his staunchest critics agreed that he was well-qualified for the role. What was at issue was his "conservativeness"—that is, his views on the source of rights, individual rights versus governmental power, and the power of courts versus legislatures. His views were the determiner as to whether a legislator (or common citizen) supported or objected to his confirmation. Thus, there is never the reality of an independent judiciary; however, it is important to at least strive toward the ideal of one.

## A License to Commit Crime?

We have established that means–end thinking comes into conflict with a human rights approach of public service. A recent news article (highlighted in the Quote and Query box on the next page) pointed out that soldiers who have committed crimes against Iraqi civilians typically receive less punishment than soldiers who commit much less serious crimes against other soldiers. In one case, for instance, two soldiers robbed an Iraqi shop owner and his family at gunpoint. Both were found guilty of armed robbery. One was sentenced to five months, but the other was sentenced to only one month of confinement. This contrasts with another punishment case where a soldier was also imprisoned for six months—but for adultery! In an investigation of a soldier who shot a teenager for stealing a box of food, an investigator noted that the soldier seemed surprised that anyone would care that an Iraqi civilian was shot (Carollo and Kaplow, 2005: A9).

There are instances of soldiers who have shot, robbed, and raped Iraqi citizens. The investigation shows that, typically, these soldiers receive very minor punishments. The ex-military judge and prosecutor highlighted in the next Quote and Query box points out that all Iraqis are associated with insurgents and that insurgents are not considered to be deserving of the same "justice" as others; thus, soldiers feel free to treat them in any way they like. Only a few soldiers are inclined to abuse and victimize Iraqis, but they feel free to do so because of the deterioration of rights and the belief that Iraqis don't deserve the same rights as Americans.

The Iraq situation seems to be parallel to the case of rogue officers who robbed and, in a few instances, killed drug dealers for their money. It is also similar to prosecutors who feel that they can lie about or hide evidence because they are prosecuting

## QUOTE and QUERY

"I think it's an attitude that starts at the very top that these people (insurgents) somehow are beyond the law, and if they are beyond the law, they are essentially fair game" (ex-military judge and prosecutor).

Source: R. Carollo and L. Kaplow, "In Iraq, Military Justice in Doubt," *Austin American Statesman,* October 2, 2005, A1, A9.

*Is it possible that the tendency to believe that our enemies (insurgents) don't deserve justice leads to a deterioration of justice for innocent groups as well (Iraqi victims of criminal soldiers)?*

a "guilty" defendant, or correctional officers who believe that they can steal from the inmate fund or coerce sex from inmates because they are, after all, "just inmates." These cases are also similar to the situation in Abu Ghraib, where the soldiers felt they could do anything to prisoners with impunity. Rogue cops target drug dealers and rogue soldiers target Iraqi civilians or civilian detainees perhaps because they feel that these individuals are outside the protection offered by systems of justice. Once we start parceling out human rights and justice differentially, it opens the door to those who look for an excuse to abuse and victimize. Once the door is open, however, everyone is less safe, such as the innocent taxi driver who was killed by U.S. soldiers in Afghanistan during an interrogation that involved torture.

Why are we discussing terrorism and the Iraq war in a book on the criminal justice system? The answer is that the war on terror has replaced the drug war, and the crime control perspective has morphed into a much broader government mandate. In response to that mandate, government's powers of investigation and control were expanded in order to address terrorism. However, we see that the powers given to government in the "war against terror" have also been used against "garden-variety criminals." Crank and Gregor (2005) note cases where the arsenal of responses against terror have been used for ordinary criminals, such as a federal law against terroristic threats applied to a lovesick woman who wanted the cruise ship she was on to turn around, the use of a law against weapons of mass destruction against a methamphetamine "cook," and the use of federal subpoena power to investigate members of an antiwar group that sponsored a rally with signs that said "Bring the Iowa Guard Home."

Thus, extreme measures that were rationalized because of extreme threats have been used against common criminals and citizens engaging in constitutionally protected activities. The U.S. public, in response to fear, submits to ever-increasing predations on liberties. The investigative powers given by the Patriot Act have led to routine partnerships between law enforcement and national security in investigations against U.S. citizens suspected of criminal activity. The preceding chapters have pointed out how noble-cause corruption can pollute due process, and there is no reason to believe that the same tendency will not occur when public servants think they are protecting society from terrorists.

Bayley (2002) argues that in order to reduce the means–end thinking that leads police to violate rights and engage in corruption, police must be shown that such behaviors do not result in effective crime control. The same argument can be made against certain practices in the war on terror. Bayley argues that noble-cause corruption

1. Contributes marginally to deterrence (e.g., searches through racial profiling are less successful than through other methods)
2. Reduces enforcement effectiveness (because it alienates the public and reduces cooperation)
3. Weakens the authority of law (because the majority of people follow the law because they believe in it; thus, justice professionals must never lose their moral authority)
4. Makes scapegoats of police (if the law can't respond, then we shouldn't expect police to)
5. Depresses morale and makes police work less satisfying (because it conflicts with individual belief systems)
6. Wastes community resources (through overturned convictions and retrials)
7. Puts police officers at risk (through illegal activities)

These elements can also be applied to the practices and tactics used in the war on terror:

1. Torture contributes marginally to deterrence because it often creates more extreme views among those who are tortured.
2. Torture, illegal detainments, and governmental violation of individual liberties alienate both the target group (terrorists) as well as ordinary citizens who are caught in the net of investigation and enforcement.
3. These practices definitely weaken the authority of law because public servants are violating such laws as the law against torture and the Geneva Convention.
4. The practices make scapegoats of state and federal law enforcers as well as soldiers who are caught and then punished as public scapegoats for enacting practices that were informally approved.
5. These practices depress morale because of individual moral crises such as the soldier who sent the Abu Ghraib pictures home and encountered both praise and condemnation for doing so; furthermore, many soldiers believe they are fighting for freedom and democratic ideals and so are appalled that they are associated with just the opposite.
6. The practices waste incredible resources in legal defense and reparative costs to victims.
7. They create a situation where we have no moral authority when our soldiers or agents are caught and imprisoned because we have been publicly exposed as engaging in the worst practices of torture against Iraqis, Afghans, and others.

In short, whenever our soldiers or our police officers sacrifice their moral authority in a utilitarian means-oriented campaign against crime or terror, they have lost more than they could ever hope to gain by such means.

# Conclusion

Cynicism and burnout have been identified as factors leading to unethical practices in the criminal justice system. However, there is a third—fear. The World Trade Center attack and other assaults on U.S. targets around the world have created a sense of vulnerability and fear (Hamm, 2005). The response to this fear has been to reduce civil liberties by using law, policy, and individual practices. In earlier editions, we discussed the "means–end" thinking that was used to justify skirting due-process requirements and laws in order to catch criminals and protect the public. Noble-cause corruption describes

- *Testilying* as acceptable if it puts a criminal behind bars
- Intimidation as justified as long as it results in a confession
- Beating a prisoner or defendant as justified by the fact that he must be taught a lesson so that he doesn't attack other guards or police officers
- Racial profiling as unfortunate for young black men, but justified because it results in the capture of drug dealers

This "end justifies the means" thinking is insidious—even more so now that that threat is so much greater. Fear, unfortunately, leads to bad decisions. Fear causes police officers and correctional officers to use illegal force. During World War II, fear caused this country to incarcerate tens of thousands of citizens whose only crime was being of Asian descent. Fear causes a country's leaders to trample the rights of the very individuals they are sworn to protect and defend.

In this chapter we took a last look at ethical decision making. Many readers may heartily disagree with many of the statements made in this chapter. That is understandable—such debate is, and should be, taking place all across this country.

## QUOTE and QUERY

Political liberty, which is one of the greatest gifts a people can acquire for themselves, is threatened when social order is threatened. It is dismaying to see how ready many people are to turn to strong leaders in hopes that they will end, by adopting strong measures, the disorder that has been the product of failed or fragile commitments. Drug abuse, street crime, and political corruption are the expression of unfettered choices. To end them, rulers, with the warm support of the people, will often adopt measures that threaten true political freedom. The kind of culture that can maintain reasonable human commitments takes centuries to create but only a few generations to destroy.

Source: James Q. Wilson, cited in Cole (2002: 234).

*Although Wilson's statement is discussing the sacrifice of due process in the drug war and crime control, it has incredible relevance to the issues of terrorism. Interestingly, it was made by a noted conservative. How do we meet the threat of terrorists?*

However, it is important to clearly identify what ethical system might support any contested practice, act, or government policy. If it is utilitarianism, the idea that "the end justifies the means," then one must also show what facts exist to prove that the desired end will be brought about and that negative side effects do not outweigh any good that may come about. On the other hand, it may be the case that even a good end cannot justify certain acts; there may be certain human rights that belong to everyone—even terrorists. In the crime war, drug war, or war on terror, the most important element of making ethical decisions is to apply ethical reasoning and not succumb to fear.

# Key Terms

**crime control approach**  the law enforcement approach that uses means–end or utilitarian thinking to determine good by the result, which is crime control

**"front page test"**  a test that asks whether an individual would be comfortable if his or her action was reported on the front page of the newspaper

**"just war" debate**  philosophical argument about when war is ethically justified and what methods are ethical

**principle of double effect**  the idea that if one undertakes an action that is a good but that also results in a negative end, as long as the negative end was not the intent of the actor, then the action and the end can be considered a good

**public service approach**  the law enforcement approach whereby the values and ethos of law enforcement and justice professionals focus on human rights, including the right to due process, and the fundamental duty of all public servants is to protect those rights

**rights-based model**  the policing approach that recognizes the police as servants of the public good; although crime control is important, protection of civil liberties is the fundamental mission

**terrorism**  the "deliberate, negligent, or reckless use of force against noncombatants, by state or non-state actors for ideological ends and in the absence of a substantively just legal process" (Rodin, 2004: 755)

# Review Questions

1. Explain one way to resolve an ethical dilemma.
2. What are the elements Cohen identifies as justifying police action?
3. What are the most problematic elements of the Patriot Act?
4. What are the holdings of *Hamdi v. Rumsfeld*, *Rasul v. Bush*, and *Clark v. Martinez*?
5. What are some responses that the federal government has taken in response to terrorism?
6. What is the argument in support of torture? What is the argument against it?
7. What are some rights recognized by the United Nations and the European Union?
8. What is the relationship between an independent judiciary and human rights? What are the elements of an independent judiciary?
9. Explain why "means–end" thinking leads to criminal actions.
10. What is the "just war" argument?

# Discussion Questions

1. Select the most difficult ethical dilemma in the previous chapters, and try to answer it again by considering it in terms of law, policy, and ethics. Also, use the **"front page test."** This is a quick ethics test that asks if you would feel comfortable if your action was published on the front page of the newspaper. If you would not want it to be, there may be an ethical problem with your action.
2. Now select an ethical or moral dilemma from your own life, and try to solve it by using any guidelines derived from this book. Be explicit about the procedure that you used to arrive at a decision and about the decision itself.
3. Write a code of ethics for yourself.
4. What are your views on torture?
5. What are your views on the Patriot Act?

# Ethical Dilemmas

### *Situation 1*

You are a member of Congress, and the Patriot Act is coming up for a vote to renew its provisions. What would you do, and why?

### *Situation 2*

You are a soldier in Iraq and have taken pictures of fellow soldiers engaging in various acts of abuse and torture. What, if anything, would you do with the pictures?

### *Situation 3*

You are a new police officer and are talking with other officers before roll call. The group is loudly and energetically proposing various gruesome torture techniques to get Al Qaeda operatives to talk. There is some amount of hyperbole in the discussion, but also the sincere belief that torture is justified by the circumstances. How do you feel about this position? If you object to torture, would you make your position known?

### *Situation 4*

You live next door to an Arab family, and you hear the husband talking negatively about the United States. Your friends at work tell you that you should report him to the police because he might be a terrorist. What would you do? Why?

### *Situation 5*

You have been sitting in a criminal justice ethics class all semester and disagree with virtually everything the teacher has said. You want to get a good grade, so you think maybe you shouldn't disagree although the professor has never indicated that she takes disagreement personally or would punish someone for expressing any opinion. However, very few people in the class seem to share your opinions, or if they do, they are also keeping quiet. Would you ever express your opinion? Why or why not?

## Suggested Readings

Albanese, J. 2006. *Professional Ethics in Criminal Justice: Being Ethical When No One Is Looking.* Boston: Allyn & Bacon.

Alderson, J. 1998. *Principled Policing: Protecting the Public with Integrity.* Winchester, MA: Waterside.

Braswell, M., McCarthy, B., and McCarthy, B. 2002. *Justice, Crime and Ethics.* Cincinnati: Anderson.

Crank, J., and Gregor, P. 2005. *Counter Terrorism After 9/11: Justice, Security and Ethics Reconsidered.* Cincinnati: Lexis/Nexis Publishing.

Etzioni, A., and Marsh, J. (Eds.). 2003. *Rights Vs. Public Safety After 9/11: America in the Age of Terrorism.* Lanham, MD: Rowman & Littlefield.

# Bibliography

Adams, V. 1981. "How to Keep 'Em Honest." *Psychology Today,* November: 52–53.

Alain, M. 2004. "An Exploratory Study of Quebec's Police Officers' Attitudes Toward Ethical Dilemmas." In *The Contours of Police Integrity,* eds. C. Klockars, S. Ivković, and M. Haberfeld, 40–55. Thousand Oaks, CA: Sage.

Albanese, J. 2006. *Professional Ethics in Criminal Justice: Being Ethical When No One Is Looking.* Boston: Allyn & Bacon.

Albert, E., T. Denise, and S. Peterfreund. 1984. *Great Traditions in Ethics.* Belmont, CA: Wadsworth.

Alderson, J. 1998. *Principled Policing: Protecting the Public with Integrity.* Winchester, MA: Waterside.

Allen, H., and C. Simonsen. 1986. *Corrections in America: An Introduction.* New York: Macmillan.

Allen, M. 2005. "DeLay Wants Panel to Review Role of Courts." April 2, 2005. Retrieved October 1, 2005, from http://www.washingtonpost.com/ac2/wp-dyn/A19793–2005Apr1?language= printer.

Alpert, G., and J. MacDonald. 2001. "Police Use of Force: An Analysis of Organizational Characteristics." *Justice Quarterly* 18(2): 393–409.

American Bar Association. 1986. *Informal Opinions, Committee on Ethics and Professional Responsibility.* Chicago: American Bar Association.

"American Digest." 2005. *Austin American-Statesman,* September 18: H1.

*American Judicature.* 2005. "Judicial Independence." Retrieved on August 17, 2005, from http://www.ajs.org/include/story.asp?content_id=418.

American Society for Public Administration. 1979. *Professional Standards and Ethics: A Workbook for Public Administrators.* Washington, DC: American Society for Public Administration.

Amnesty International. 1999. *"Not Part of My Sentence": Violations of the Human Rights of Women in Custody.* London: Amnesty International.

Anderson, C. 1989. "DNA Evidence Questioned." *American Bar Association Journal,* October: 18–19.

Anderson, P., and L. T. Winfree. 1987. *Expert Witnesses: Criminologists in the Courtroom.* Albany, NY: SUNY Press.

Arafat, I., and K. McCahery. 1978. "The Relationship Between Lawyers and Their Clients." In *Essays on the Theory and Practice of Criminal Justice,* ed. R. Rich, 193–219. Washington, DC: University Press.

Arax, M. 1999. "Ex-Guard Says 4 Men Set Up Rape of Inmate." *Los Angeles Times,* October 14: A3.

Arax, M. 2004. "Guard Challenges Code of Silence." LATimes.com, January 20, 2004. Retrieved on January 21, 2004, from http://www.lattimes.com/news/printededition/california/la-me-guard20jan20,1,5834171.story?coll=la-headlines-pe-california.

Arboleda-Florez, J. 1983. "The Ethics of Psychiatry in Prison Society." *Canadian Journal of Criminology* 25(1): 47–54.

Arbuthnot, J. 1984. "Moral Reasoning Development Programmes in Prison: Cognitive– Developmental and Critical Reasoning Approaches." *Journal of Moral Education* 13(2): 112–113.

Arbuthnot, J., and D. Gordon. 1988. "Crime and Cognition: Community Applications of Sociomoral Reasoning Development." *Criminal Justice and Behavior* 15(3): 379–393.

Armstrong, K., and M. Possley. 2002. "The Verdict: Dishonor." *Chicago Tribune* Reports, November 11, 2002. Retrieved November 11, 2002, from http://www.ishipress.com/ dishonor.htm.

Aronson, R. 1977. "Toward a Rational Resolution of Ethical Dilemmas in the Criminal Justice System." In *Criminal Justice Planning and Development,* ed. A. Cohn, 57–71. Beverly Hills, CA: Sage.

Associated Press. 1997. "After Cash Rains Down in Miami, Finders Remain Quiet Keepers." *Austin American-Statesman,* January 10: A7.

Associated Press. 1997. "Jail Guards Taunt Prisoner Dying of Cocaine Overdose." *Austin American-Statesman,* February 8: A16.

Associated Press. 2000. "Prison Guards Suspected of Money Laundering." *Austin American-Statesman,* January 27: B3.

Associated Press. 2004. CNN.com. Retrieved on October 26, 2004, from http://cnn.com /2004/LAW/10/26/prison.sendoff.ap/index.html.

Associated Press. 2005. "Houston Crime Lab Inquiry on Hold Until City OK's Funding." *Austin American-Statesman,* August 5: B5.

Associated Press. 2005. "La. Governor Takes Blame for Response." *Washington Post.* Retrieved on September 22, 2005, from www.washingtonpost.com/wpdyn/content/ article/2005/09/14/AR2005091402254.html.

Associated Press. 2005. "Prosecutor's Demotion Is Investigated." *Austin American-Statesman,* September 27: A6.

Attorney General's Commission on Pornography. 1986. *Final Report.* Washington, DC: U.S. Government Printing Office.

Aubert, V. 1969. *Sociology of Law.* London: Penguin.

Auerhahn, K. 1999. "Selective Incapacitation and the Problem of Prediction." *Criminology* 37(4): 705–734.

Austin, J., and T. Fabelo. 2004. *The Diminishing Returns of Increased Incarceration.* Austin, TX: JFA Institute.

Austin, J., and J. Irwin. 2001. *It's About Time: America's Imprisonment Binge.* Belmont, CA: Wadsworth.

Axtman, K. 2003. "Bungles in Texas Crime Lab Stir Doubt Over DNA." *Christian Science Monitor,* April 18, 2003. Retrieved April 21, 2003, from http://www.csmonitor. com/2003/0418/p03s01-usgn.html.

Babwin, D. 2001. "In Chicago, Allegations Plague Police Department." *Austin American-Statesman,* April 22: A26.

Baelz, P. 1977. *Ethics and Beliefs.* New York: Seabury.

Baker, M. 1985. *Cops.* New York: Pocket.

Bannister, A., and D. Carter. 2004. "Racial Profiling." In *Controversies in Policing,* eds. Q. Thurman and A. Giacomazzi, 93–100. Cincinnati: Anderson.

Barker, J., and M. Cosentino. 2003. "Current Development 2002–2003: Who's in Charge Here? The Ethics 2000 Approach to Resolving Lawyer–Client Conflicts." *Georgetown Journal of Legal Ethics* 16: 505–519.

Barker, T. 1983. "Rookie Police Officers' Perceptions of Police Occupational Deviance." *Police Studies* 6: 30–40.

Barker, T. 2002. "Ethical Police Behavior." In *Policing and Misconduct,* ed. K. Lersch, 1–25. Upper Saddle River, NJ: Prentice-Hall.

Barker, T., and D. Carter. 1991. "Police Lies and Perjury: A Motivation-Based Taxonomy." In *Police Deviance,* 2d ed., eds. T. Barker and D. Carter. Cincinnati: Anderson.

Barker, T. and D. Carter (Eds.), 1994. *Police Deviance,* 3rd ed. Cincinnati: Anderson.

Barker, T., and D. Carter. 1999. "Fluffing Up the Evidence and Covering Your Ass: Some Conceptual Notes on Police Lying." In *Policing Perspectives,* eds. L. Gaines and G. Cordner, 342–351. Los Angeles: Roxbury.

Baro, A. 1995. "Tolerating Illegal Use of Force Against Inmates." In *Morality in Criminal Justice,* eds. D. Close and N. Meier, 380–396. Belmont, CA: Wadsworth.

Barrier, G., M. Stohr, C. Hemmons, and R. Marsh. 1999. "A Practical User's Guide: Idaho's Method for Implementing Ethical Behavior in a Correctional Setting." *Corrections Compendium* 24(4) (April): 1–3.

Barry, V. 1985. *Applying Ethics: A Text with Readings.* Belmont, CA: Wadsworth.

Bartollas, C., and S. Miller. 2001. *Juvenile Justice in America.* Upper Saddle River, NJ: Prentice-Hall.

Bayley, D. 2002. "Law Enforcement and the Rule of Law: Is There a Tradeoff?" *Criminology and Public Policy* 2(1): 133–154.

Bazemore, G., and D. Maloney. 1994. "Rehabilitating Community Service: Toward Restorative Service Sanctions in a Balanced Justice System." *Federal Probation* 58(1): 24–35.

Beauchamp, T. 1982. *Philosophical Ethics.* New York: McGraw-Hill.

Beccaria, C. 1977. *On Crimes and Punishment,* 6th ed. Trans. Henry Paolucci. Indianapolis: Bobbs-Merrill.

Bedau, H. 1982. "Prisoners' Rights." *Criminal Justice Ethics* 1(1): 26–41.

Bedau, H. 1991. "How to Argue About the Death Penalty." *Israel Law Review* 25: 466–480.

Bender, B. 2005. "War Turning Young Arabs into Terrorists, Studies Say." *Austin American-Statesman,* July 23: A21, A24.

Bennett, R. K. 1995. "How Honest Are We?" *Reader's Digest,* December: 49–56.

Bentham, J. 1970. "The Rationale of Punishment." In *Ethical Choice: A Case Study Approach,* eds. R. Beck and J. Orr. New York: Free Press (original work published 1843).

Blumberg, A. 1969. "The Practice of Law as a Confidence Game." In *Sociology of Law,* ed. V. Aubert, 321–331. London: Penguin.

Blumenthal, R. 2005. "The DeLay Inquiry." *New York Times,* September 29: A26.

Bohm, R. 1996. "Crime, Criminal, and Crime Control Policy Myths." In *Justice, Crime, and Ethics,* eds. M. Braswell, B. McCarthy, and B. McCarthy, 341–363. Cincinnati: Anderson.

Book, A. 1999. "Shame on You: An Analysis of Modern Shame Punishment as an Alternative to Incarceration." *William and Mary Law Review* 40, 2: 653–683.

Borchert, D., and D. Stewart. 1986. *Exploring Ethics.* New York: Macmillan.

Bossard, A. 1981. "Police Ethics and International Police Cooperation." In *The Social Basis of Criminal Justice: Ethical Issues for the 80's,* eds. F. Schamalleger and R. Gustafson, 23–38. Washington, DC: University Press.

Bourge, C. 2002. "Sparks Fly Over Private v. Public Prisons." UPI. Retrieved February 21, 2002, from www.upi./com/view.cfm?storyID=20022002–064851–41221.

Bouza, A. 2001. *Police Unbound: Corruption, Abuse, and Heroism by the Boys in Blue.* Amherst, NY: Prometheus.

Bowie, N. 1985. *Making Ethical Decisions.* New York: McGraw-Hill.

Bowker, L. 1980. *Prison Victimization.* New York: Elsevier.

Boyce, W., and L. Jensen. 1978. *Moral Reasoning: A Psychological–Philosophical Integration.* Lincoln: University of Nebraska Press.

Boyer, P. 2001. "Bad Cops." *The New Yorker,* May 21, 2001. Retrieved on January 17, 2003, from http://www/newyorker.com/printable/?fact/010521fa_FACT.

Braithwaite, J. 2000. "Shame and Criminal Justice." *Canadian Journal of Criminology* 42(3): 281–301.

Braithwaite, J. 2002. "Linking Crime Prevention to Restorative Justice." In *Repairing Communities Through Restorative Justice,* ed. J. Perry, 67–83. Lanham, MD: American Correctional Association.

Braswell, M. 1996/2002. "Ethics, Crime, and Justice: An Introductory Note to Students." In *Justice, Crime, and Ethics*, eds. M. Braswell, B. McCarthy, and B. McCarthy, 3–9. Cincinnati: Anderson.

Braswell, M., and J. Gold. 2002. "Peacemaking, Justice, and Ethics." In *Justice, Crime, and Ethics*, eds. M. Braswell, B. McCarthy, and B. McCarthy, 25–43. Cincinnati: Anderson.

Braswell, M., B. McCarthy, and B. McCarthy. 2002. *Justice, Crime and Ethics*, 3rd ed. Cincinnati: Anderson.

Braswell, M., and J. Whitehead. 1999. "Seeking the Truth: An Alternative to Conservative and Liberal Thinking in Criminology." *Criminal Justice Review* 24(3): 50–63.

Brown, M. 1981. *Working the Street*. New York: Russell Sage Foundation.

Buchholz, B. 2005. "Innocents Are Dying, in the Name of Security." *Austin American-Statesman*, September 4: H1.

Bureau of Justice Statistics. 1992. *Prosecutors in State Courts, 1990*. Washington, DC: U.S. Department of Justice.

Bureau of Justice Statistics. 2002a. *Prisoners in 2001*. Washington, DC: U.S. Department of Justice.

Bureau of Justice Statistics. 2002b. *Capital Punishment, 2001*. Washington, DC: U.S. Department of Justice.

Bureau of Justice Statistics. 2005. "Capital Punishment Statistics." Retrieved on October 4, 2005, from http://www.ojp.usdoj.gov/bjs/cp.htm.

Buttell, F. 2002. "Exploring Levels of Moral Development Among Sex Offenders Participating in Community-Based Treatment." *Journal of Offender Rehabilitation* 34(4): 85–95.

Butterfield, F. 2004. "Mistreatment of Prisoners Is Called Routine in U.S." NYTimes.com, May 8, 2004. Retrieved May 12, 2004, from http://www.nytimes.com/2004/05/08/ national/08PRIS. html?.

Callahan, Daniel. 1982. "Applied Ethics in Criminal Justice." *Criminal Justice Ethics* 1(1): 1, 64.

Cane, P. 2002. *Responsibility in Law and Morality*. Portland, OR: Oxford Press.

Cao, L., J. Frank, and F. Cullen. 1996. "Race, Community Context and Confidence in the Police." *American Journal of Police* 15(1): 3–22.

Carey, M. 2005. "Social Learning, Social Capital, and Correctional Theories: Seeking an Integrated Model." In *What Works and Why: Effective Approaches to Reentry*, ed. American Correctional Association, 1–33. Lanham, MD: American Correctional Association.

Carollo, R., and L. Kaplow. 2005. "In Iraq, Military Justice in Doubt," *Austin American-Statesman*, October 2: A1, A9.

Carr, R. 2004. "Coalition Fights Unprecedented Government Secrecy." *Austin American-Statesman*, May 13: A10.

Carroll, L. 1998. *Lawful Order: A Case Study of Correctional Crisis and Reform*. New York: Garland.

Carter, D. 1999. "Drug Use and Drug-Related Corruption of Police Officers." In *Policing Perspectives*, eds. L. Gaines and G. Cordner, 311–324. Los Angeles: Roxbury.

Casey, R. 1996. "Cop Wins One Million in Whistleblower Appeal." *Ethics Roll Call* 4(6) (Fall): 1.

Chattha, Z., and S. Ivković. 2004. "Police Misconduct: The Pakistani Paradigm." In *The Contours of Police Integrity*, eds. C. Klockars, S. Ivković, and M. Haberfeld, 175–194. Thousand Oaks, CA: Sage.

Chevigny, P. 1995 *The Edge of the Knife: Police Violence in the Americas*. New York: New Press.

Christianson, S. 2004. *Innocent: Inside Wrongful Conviction Cases*. New York: New York University Press.

Clinard, M. 1985. "Illegal Corporate Behavior." In *Exploring Crime*, ed. J. Sheley, 205–218. Belmont, CA: Wadsworth.

Close, D., and N. Meier. 1995. *Morality in Criminal Justice*. Belmont, CA: Wadsworth.

Cloud, D. 2005. "Guantanamo Bay Inquiry Finds Violations." *Austin American-Statesman*, July 13: A12.

Cloud, D. 2005. "Lynndie England Guilty of Abuses." *Austin American-Statesman,* September 27: A1, A4.

CNN.com. 2001. "Florida Judge Hears Motions in Child Murder Case." CNN.com Law Center, February 23, 2001. Retrieved on February 6, 2003, from http://www.cnn.com/ 2001/law/02/23/child.killer. hearing.

Cohen, E. 1991. "Pure Legal Advocates and Moral Agents: Two Concepts of a Lawyer in an Adversary System." In *Justice, Crime, and Ethics,* eds. M. Braswell, B. McCarthy, and B. McCarthy, 123–163. Cincinnati: Anderson.

Cohen, E. 2002. "Pure Legal Advocates and Moral Agents Revisited: A Reply to Memory and Rose." *Criminal Justice Ethics* 21(1): 39–55.

Cohen, H. 1983. "Searching Police Ethics." *Teaching Philosophy* 6(3): 231–242.

Cohen, H. 1985. "A Dilemma for Discretion." In *Police Ethics: Hard Choices in Law Enforcement,* eds. W. Heffernan and T. Stroup, 69–83. New York: John Jay Press.

Cohen, H. 1986. "Exploiting Police Authority." *Criminal Justice Ethics* 5(2): 23–31.

Cohen, H. 1987. "Overstepping Police Authority." *Criminal Justice Ethics* 6(2): 52–60.

Cohen, H, and M. Feldberg. 1991. *Power and Restraint: The Moral Dimension of Police Work.* New York: Praeger.

Cohen, R. 2001. "How They Sleep at Night: DAs Turned Defenders Talk About Their Work." *American Lawyer: The Legal Intelligencer* (April 9, 2001).

Cole, D. 1999. *No Equal Justice.* New York: Free Press.

Cole, D. 2001. "Secret Evidence." In *Policing, Security and Democracy: Special Aspects of Democratic Policing,* eds. S. Einstein and M. Amir, 281–295. Huntsville, TX: Office of International Criminal Justice (OICJ), Sam Houston State University.

Cole, D. 2002. "Trading Liberty for Security After September 11." *Foreign Policy in Focus Policy Report.* Retrieved August 29, 2002, from http://www.foreignpolicy-infocus. org/papers/post9–11_body.html.

Cole, D., and J. Lamberth. 2001. "The Fallacy of Racial Profiling." *New York Times,* May 13: A19.

Cole, G. 1970. "The Decision to Prosecute." *Law and Society Review* 4 (February): 313–343.

Coleman, S. 2004a. "Police, Gratuities, and Professionalism: A Response to Kania." *Criminal Justice Ethics* 23(1): 63–65.

Coleman, S. 2004b. "When Police Should Say 'No!' to Gratuities." *Criminal Justice Ethics* 23(1): 33–44.

Columbia Law School. 2002. "A Broken System, Part II: Why There Is so Much Error in Capital Cases, and What Can Be Done About it." Columbia Law School Publications. Retrieved February 11, 2002, from http://www.law.columbia.edu/brokensystem2/ exe_summary.html.

Commission on Accreditation for Law Enforcement Agencies (CALEA). 1994. *Standards for Law Enforcement Agencies.* Fairfax, VA: CALEA.

Conlon, E. 2004. *Blue Blood.* New York: Riverhead.

Conover, T. 2000. *New Jack: Guarding Sing Sing.* New York: Random House.

Corey, G., M. Corey, and P. Callanan. 1988. *Issues and Ethics in Helping Professions.* Pacific Grove, CA: Brooks/Cole.

*Corrections Digest.* 2002. "Capital Sentences Dip 21% to 20-Year Low." *Corrections Digest* 33(1): 4–5.

Cox, D. 2000. "Grand Jury Inquiry Into Death of Inmate Extended." *Sun-Sentinel* (Ft. Lauderdale), January 5.

Craig, G. 2003. "Suit Alleges Rampant Female-Inmate Abuse." *Rochester Democrat and Chronicle.* Retrieved January 30, 2003, from http://www.rochesterdandc.com/news/forprint/ 0129story2_news.shtml.

Crank, J. 1998. *Understanding Police Culture.* Cincinnati: Anderson.

Crank, J. 2003. *Imagining Justice.* Cincinnati: Anderson.

Crank, J., and M. Caldero. 2000/2005. *Police Ethics: The Corruption of Noble Cause.* Cincinnati: Anderson.

Crank, J., and P. Gregor. 2005. *Counter Terrorism After 9/11: Justice, Security and Ethics Reconsidered.* Cincinnati: Lexis/Nexis Publishing.

*Criminal Justice Newsletter.* 2002. "Supreme Court Declines Case on Juvenile Death Penalty." *Criminal Justice Newsletter* 32(19): 2–4.

Criminal Justice Policy Council. 2003. "Initial Process and Outcome Evaluation of the Inner Change Freedom Initiative." Available from www.cjpc.state.tx.us.

Crouch, B. 1980. *Keepers: Prison Guards and Contemporary Corrections.* Springfield, IL: Charles C. Thomas.

Crouch, B. 1986/1995. "Guard Work in Transition." In *The Dilemmas of Corrections,* 3d ed., eds. K. Haas and G. Alpert, 183–203. Prospect Heights, IL: Waveland.

Crouch, B., and J. Marquart. 1989. *An Appeal to Justice: Litigated Reform in Texas Prisons.* Austin: University of Texas Press.

Curry, M. 2002. "Faulty Drug Cases Draw Police Inquiry." *Dallas Morning News,* February 21: 25A.

Daley, R. 1984. *Prince of the City.* New York: Berkley.

Daly, K. 1989. "Criminal Justice Ideologies and Practices in Different Voices: Some Feminist Questions About Justice." *International Journal of the Sociology of Law* (17): 1–18.

Dart, B. 2004. "Police Use Taser Guns 'Excessively,' Rights Group Asserts." *Austin American-Statesman,* November 30: A14.

Davis, M. 1991. "Do Cops Really Need a Code of Ethics?" *Criminal Justice Ethics* 10(2): 14–28.

Davis, M., and F. Elliston. 1986. *Ethics and the Legal Profession.* Buffalo, NY: Prometheus.

Dawson, J. 1992. "Prosecutors in State Courts." *Bureau of Justice Statistics Bulletin.* Washington, DC: U.S. Department of Justice.

Delaney, H. 1990. "Toward a Police Professional Ethic." In *Ethics in Criminal Justice,* ed. F. Schmalleger, 78–95. Bristol, IN: Wyndham Hall.

Delattre, E. 1989a. *Character and Cops: Ethics in Policing.* Washington, DC: American Enterprise Institute for Public Policy Research.

Delattre, E. 1989b. "Ethics in Public Service: Higher Standards and Double Standards." *Criminal Justice Ethics* 8(2): 79–83.

Dershowitz, A. 1982. *The Best Defense.* New York: Vintage.

Dershowitz, A. 1994. *The Abuse Excuse and Other Cop-Outs, Sob Stories, and Evasions of Responsibility.* Boston: Little, Brown.

Deutsch, L. 2001. "L.A. Police Corruption Probe Set to Wrap Up." *San Jose Mercury News.* Retrieved November 12, 2001, from http://www.mercurycenter.com/premium/local/docs/rampart08.htm.

Dilulio, J. 1987. *Governing Prisons: A Comparative Study of Correctional Management.* New York: Free Press.

Dix, G. 1991. "When Government Deception Goes Too Far." *Texas Lawyer* 7(31): 12–13.

Donn, J. 2003. "Ex-Agents Say FBI Overlooked Informants' Violent Crimes." *Austin American-Statesman,* March 2: A16.

Dorschner, J. 1989. "The Dark Side of the Force." In *Critical Issues in Policing,* 2d ed., 254–274. Prospect Heights, IL: Waveland.

Douglass, J. 1981. "Prosecutorial Ethics." In *The Social Basis of Criminal Justice: Ethical Issues for the 80's,* eds. F. Schmalleger and R. Gustafson, 109–171. Washington, DC: University Press.

Dror, Y. 1969. "Law and Social Change." In *Sociology of Law,* ed. V. Aubert, 90–100. London: Penguin.

Dunningham, C., and C. Norris. 1999. "The Detective, the Snout, and the Audit Commission: The Real Costs in Using Informants." *Howard Journal of Criminal Justice* 38(1): 67–87.

Durkheim, E. 1969. "Types of Law in Relation to Types of Social Solidarity." In *Sociology of Law,* ed. V. Aubert, 17–29. London: Penguin.

Dzur, A., and A. Wertheimer. 2002. "Forgiveness and Public Deliberation: The Practice of Restorative Justice." *Criminal Justice Ethics* 21(1): 3–20.

Edelbacher, M., and S. Ivković. 2004. "Ethics and the Police: Studying Police Integrity in Austria." In *The Contours of Police Integrity,* eds. C. Klockars, S. Ivković, and M. Haberfeld, 19–39. Thousand Oaks, CA: Sage.

Einstein, S., and M. Amir. 2001. *Policing, Security and Democracy: Special Aspects of Democratic Policing.* Huntsville, TX: Office of International Criminal Justice (OICJ), Sam Houston State University.

Einstein, S., and M. Amir. 2003. *Police Corruption: Paradigms, Models and Concepts: Challenges for Developing Countries.* Huntsville, TX: Office of International Criminal Justice (OICJ), Sam Houston State University.

Einstein, S., and M. Amir. 2004. *Police Corruption: Challenges for Developed Countries: Comparative Issues and Commissions of Inquiry.* Huntsville, TX: Office of International Criminal Justice (OICJ), Sam Houston State University.

Elias, R. 1986. *The Politics of Victimization.* New York: Oxford University Press.

Ellington, K. 2003. "Justice Tempered with Mercy." *Houston Chronicle,* January 30: 10A.

Elliott, A., and B. Weiser. 2004. "When Prosecutors Err, Others Pay the Price." NYTimes.com. Retrieved on March 23, 2004, from http://www.nytimes.com/2004/ 03/21/nyregion/ 21prosecute.html.

Ellis, L., and A. Pontius. 1989. *The Frontal–Limbic–Reticular Network and Variations in Pro-antisociality: A Neurological Based Model of Moral Reasoning and Criminality.* Paper presented at the 1989 ASC conference, Reno, NV.

Elliston, F. 1986. "The Ethics of Ethics Tests for Lawyers." In *Ethics and the Legal Profession,* eds. M. Davis and F. Elliston, 50–61. Buffalo, NY: Prometheus.

Elliston, F., and M. Feldberg. 1985. *Moral Issues in Police Work.* Totawa, NJ: Rowman & Allanheld.

Emling, S. 2005. "Terror Crackdown Upsets British Race Relations." *Austin American-Statesman,* August 6: A18.

Engel, R. S., J. Calnon, and T. Bernard. 2002. "Theory and Racial Profiling: Shortcomings and Future Directions in Research." *Justice Quarterly* 19(2): 249–273.

"Ethical Principles for Psychologists." 1981. *American Psychologist* 36 (June): 633–638.

Etzioni, A., and J. Marsh. 2003. *Rights v. Public Safety After 9/11: America in the Age of Terrorism.* Lanham, MD: Rowman & Littlefield.

Ewin, R. 1990. "Loyalty and the Police." *Criminal Justice Ethics* 9(2): 3–15.

Farkas, M. 1999. "Correctional Officer Attitudes Toward Inmates and Working with Inmates in a 'Get Tough' Era." *Journal of Criminal Justice* 27(6): 495–506.

Farrell, G. 2005. "Sentence's Message: Crime Doesn't Pay." *USA Today,* July 14: B1–B2.

Fattah, G. 2005. "Complaints Against Utah Judges Rise." Desertnews.com. Retrieved August 11, 2005, from http://desertnews.com/dn/print/1,1442,600154724,00.html.

"FBI, Media Could Face Lawsuit in Jewell Case." *Austin American-Statesman,* October 27: A1, A8.

Fecteau, L. 1999. "Private Prisons Warned." *Albuquerque Journal,* August 27, 1999. Retrieved from http://www.albqjournal.com/news/2news08–27–99.html.

Feeney, J. 2005. "The Wisdom and Morality of Present-Day Criminal Sentencing." *Akron Law Review* 38: 853–867.

Feibleman, J. 1985. *Justice, Law and Culture.* Boston: Martinus Nijhoff.

Feinberg, J., and H. Gross. 1977. *Justice: Selected Readings.* Princeton, NJ: Princeton University Press.

Felkenes, G. 1984. "Attitudes of Police Officers Towards Their Professional Ethics." *Journal of Criminal Justice* (12): 211–220.

Felkenes, G. 1987. "Ethics in the Graduate Criminal Justice Curriculum." *Teaching Philosophy* 10(1): 23–36.

Feurer, A., and W. Rashbaum. 2005. "Blood Ties: Two Officers' Long Path to Mob Murder Indictments." *New York Times Online.* Retrieved September 29, 2005, from http://www.ipsn.org/indictments/caracappa_indictment/blodd_ties_2_officers.htm.

Fielding, N. 2003. "Integrity Is Non-Negotiable: Cultural, Legal and Organizational Responses to Police Corruption in the United Kingdom." In *Police Corruption: Challenges for Developed Countries,* eds. M. Amir and S. Einstein, 53–74. Huntsville, TX: Office of International Criminal Justice (OICJ), Sam Houston State University.

Findlay, M. 1982. "Bathurst—Riots, Bashings and Cover Up." In *The State of the Prison,* ed. M. Findlay, 21–41. Australia: Mitchell College Printery.

Fink, P. 1977. *Moral Philosophy.* Encino, CA: Dickinson.

Fishbein, D. 2000. *Biobehavioral Perspectives on Criminology.* Belmont, CA: Wadsmorth.

Fishman, E. 1994. "'Falling Back' on Natural Law and Prudence; A Reply to Souryal and Potts." *Journal of Criminal Justice Education* 5(2): 189–203.

Fitzgerald, G. 1989. *Report of a Commission of Inquiry Pursuant to Orders in Council.* Brisbane, Australia: Goprint Publishers (cited in T. Prenzler and C. Ronken, 2001).

Flanagan, D., and K. Jackson. 1987. "Justice, Care, and Gender: The Kohlberg–Gilligan Debate Revisited." *Ethics* (97): 622–637.

Fletcher, G. 1993. *Loyalty: An Essay on the Morality of Relationships.* New York: Oxford University Press.

"Florida Opens Faith-Based Prison for Women." 2004. *L.A. Times,* April 15: A27.

Fogel, D., 1975. *We Are the Living Proof.* Cincinnati: Anderson.

Fogel, D, and J. Hudson. 1981. *Justice as Fairness.* Cincinnati: Anderson.

Fogelson, R. 1977. *Big City Police.* Cambridge, MA: Harvard University Press.

Foot, P. 1982. "Moral Relativism." In *Relativism: Cognitive and Moral,* eds. J. Meiland and M. Krausz, 152–167. Notre Dame, IN: University of Notre Dame Press.

Fountain, J. 2001. "Former Top Chicago Detective Admits to Leading Theft Ring." *New York Times,* October 26: A16.

Freedman, M. 1986. "Professional Responsibility of the Criminal Defense Lawyer: The Three Hardest Questions." In *Ethics and the Legal Profession,* eds. M. Davis and F. Elliston, 328–339. Buffalo, NY: Prometheus.

Fulghum, R. 1986. *All I Really Needed to Know I Learned in Kindergarten.* New York: Villard.

Fuller, L. 1969. *The Morality of Law.* New Haven, CT: Yale University Press.

Galloway, J. and J. Kuhnhenn, 2005. "Senators Add Anti-Torture Words to Bill." *Austin American-Statesman,* October 6: A4.

Gallup Poll (2001). *Gallup Poll Online,* January 4, 2002. Retrieved February 20, 2003, from http://www.gallup.com/polltopics/hnsty_ethcs.asp.Jan4,2002.

Galston, W. 1980. *Justice and the Human Good.* Chicago: University of Chicago Press.

Garland, D. 1990. *Punishment and Modern Society.* Chicago: University of Chicago Press.

Garner, J., C. Maxwell, and C. Heraux. 2002. "Characteristics Associated with the Prevalence and Severity of Force Used by the Police." *Justice Quarterly* 19(4): 705–745.

Gavaghan, M., K. Arnold, and J. Gibbs. 1983. "Moral Judgment in Delinquents and Nondelinquents: Recognition Versus Production Measures." *Journal of Psychology* (114): 267–274.

Gavzer, B. 1997. "Are Jury Consultants Good for Justice?" *Parade,* January 5: 20.

Geis, G., A. Mobley, and D. Shichor. 1999. "Private Prisons, Criminological Research and Conflict of Interest." *Crime and Delinquency* 45(3): 372–388.

General Accounting Office (G.A.O.). 1996. *Private and Public Prisons—Studies Comparing Operational Costs and/or Quality of Service.* Washington, DC: U.S. Government Printing Office.

General Accounting Office (G.A.O.). 1998. *Law Enforcement Information on Drug-Related Police Corruption.* Report to the Honorable Charles B. Rangel, House of Representatives. Washington, DC: U.S. General Accounting Office.

Gershman, B. 1991. "Why Prosecutors Misbehave." In *Justice, Crime, and Ethics,* eds. M. Braswell, B. McCarthy, and B. McCarthy, 163–177. Cincinnati: Anderson.

Gershman, B. 2003. "The Use and Misuse of Forensic Evidence." *Oklahoma City University Law Review* 28: 17–45.

Getlin, J. 2002a. "Officer Refuses to Arrest Homeless." *Austin American-Statesman,* November 30: A8.

Getlin, J. 2002b. "DA Suggests Overturning Convictions in Jogger Case." *Austin American-Statesman,* December 6: A16.

Gibbs, J., K. Arnold, H. Ahlborn, and F. Cheesman. 1984. "Facilitation of Sociomoral Reasoning in Delinquents." *Journal of Consulting and Clinical Psychology* 52(1): 37–45.

Gibbs, J., L. Kohlberg, A. Colby, and B. Speicher-Dubin. 1976. "The Domain and Development of Moral Judgment: A Theory and Method of Assessment." In *Reflections on Values Education,* ed. J. Meyer, 19–20. Waterloo, Ontario: Wilfrid Laurier University Press.

Gilligan, C. 1982. *In a Different Voice: Psychological Theory and Women's Development.* Cambridge, MA: Harvard University Press.

Gilligan, C. 1987. "Moral Orientation and Moral Development." In *Women and Moral Theory,* eds. E. F. Kittay and D. Meyers, 19–37. Totawa, NJ: Rowman and Littlefield.

Giradeaux, J. 1949. *The Madwoman of Chaillot,* adapted by Maurice Valency. New York: Random House.

Glendon, M. 1994. *A Nation Under Lawyers.* New York: Farrar, Straus and Giroux.

Glenn, L. 2001. *Texas Prisons: The Largest Hotel Chain in Texas.* Austin, TX: Eakin.

Glover, S., and M. Lait. 2000. "71 More Cases May Be Voided Due to Rampart." *Los Angeles Times.* Retrieved on April, 20, 2000, from www.latimes.rampart/lat_ rampart000418.html.

Golab, J. 2000. "L.A. Confidential." Salon.com. Retrieved on January 17, 2003, from http://dir.salon.com/news/feature/2000/24/rampart/index.http.

Gold, J., M. Braswell, and B. McCarthy. 1991. "Criminal Justice Ethics: A Survey of Philosophical Theories." In *Justice, Crime, and Ethics,* eds. M. Braswell, B. McCarthy, and B. McCarthy, 3–25. Cincinnati: Anderson.

Golden, T. 2005. "Cruel and Unusual Punishment." *Austin American-Statesman,* May 21: A16.

Greene, J. 1999. "Zero Tolerance: A Case Study of Police Policies and Practices in New York City." *Crime and Delinquency* 45(2): 171–187.

Greene, J. 2001. "Bailing Out Private Jails." *American Prospect* 12(16): 23–27.

Greenwood, P. 1982. *Selective Incapacitation.* Santa Monica, CA: Rand Institute.

Grossi, E., and B. Berg. 1991. "Stress and Job Dissatisfaction Among Correctional Officers: An Unexpected Finding." *International Journal of Offender Therapy and Comparative Criminology* 35(1): 79–110.

"Guards Acquitted of Staging Gladiator Fights." 2002. *New York Times,* June 10: A16.

Haberfeld, M. 2006. *Police Leadership.* Upper Saddle River, NJ: Prentice-Hall.

Hafetz, D. 2002. "Their Innocence Proved, Men Sue." *Austin American-Statesman,* November 8: B1.

Hall, M. 2002. "Death Isn't Fair." *Texas Monthly,* December: 124–167.

Hall, M. 2004. "The Worst Court in Texas." *Texas Monthly,* November: 155–263.

Hamm, M. 1989. "Whistleblowing in Corrections." *Sociological Viewpoints* 5(1): 35–45.

Hamm, M. 1995. *The Abandoned Ones.* Boston: Northeastern Press.

Hamm, M. 2005. "The USA Patriot Act and the Politics of Fear." In *Cultural Criminology Unleashed,* ed. J. Ferrell, 287–299. London: Glasshouse.

Harper, J. 1992. "Local Judge on Hot Seat Over Conduct." *Houston Post,* July 6: A9.

Harris, C. 1986. *Applying Moral Theories.* Belmont, CA: Wadsworth.

Harris, D. 2004. "Review Essay/Profiling: Theory and Practice." *Criminal Justice Ethics* 23(2): 51–57.

Hart, H. L. 1961. *The Concept of Law.* London: Oxford.

Hartman, V. 2001. "Implementing an Asset Forfeiture Program." *FBI Law Enforcement Bulletin,* 70(1): 1–7.

Hassine, V. 1996. *Life Without Parole: Living in Prison Today.* Los Angeles: Roxbury.

Hays, K. 2005. "Report: Houston Crime Lab Was Long Neglected." *Austin American-Statesman,* July 1: B7.

Heffernan, W., and J. Kleinig. 2000. *From Social Justice to Criminal Justice: Poverty and the Administration of Criminal Law.* New York: Oxford University Press.

Heffernan, W., and T. Stroup. 1985. *Police Ethics: Hard Choices in Law Enforcement.* New York: John Jay Press.

Heidensohn, F. 1986. "Models of Justice: Portia or Persephone? Some Thoughts on Equality, Fairness and Gender in the Field of Criminal Justice." *International Journal of the Sociology of Law* (14): 287–298.

Hentoff, N. 1999. "Serpico: Nothing Has Changed." VillageVoice.com. Retrieved November 4, 1999, from http://www.villagevoice.com/issues/9944/hentoff.shtml.

Hepp, R. 2005. "Corrections Worker: I Should Have Kept Quiet." NJ.com, May 16, 2005. Retrieved on May 18, 2005, from http://www.nj.com/printer/printer.ssf?/ base/news-0/1116293400232240.xml.

Herbert, B. 2002. "In Tulia, Justice Has Gone into Hiding," *Austin American-Statesman,* August 13: A9.

Herbert, B. 2003. "Truth Has Been Told About Tulia, But Story Isn't Over Yet." *Austin American-Statesman,* April 29: A9.

Herbert, S. 1996. "Morality in Law Enforcement: Chasing 'Bad Guys' with the Los Angeles Police Department." *Law and Society Review* 30(4): 799–818.

Hersh, F. 1979. *Developing Moral Growth: From Piaget to Kohlberg.* New York: Longman.

Hickey, J., and P. Scharf. 1980. *Toward a Just Correctional System.* San Francisco: Jossey-Bass.

Hicks, W. 2004. "Constraints in the Police Use of Force: Implications of the Just War Tradition." *American Journal of Criminal Justice* 28(2): 254–270.

Hight, B. 2005. "In Atoning for Tragedy, a Former Navy Captain Finds His Voice." *Austin American-Statesman,* March 11: A11.

Hinman, L. 1998. *Ethics: A Pluralistic Approach to Moral Theory,* 2d ed. Ft. Worth, TX: Harcourt Brace.

Hockstader, L. 2003. "Texas to Toss Drug Convictions Against 38 People." *Washington Post,* April 2: A3.

Hofer, P., K. Blackwell, and R. B. Ruback. 1999. "The Effect of Federal Sentencing Guidelines on Inter-Judge Sentencing Disparity." *Journal of Criminal Law and Criminology* 90(1): 239–321.

Holmes, M. 2000. "Minority Threat and Police Brutality: Determinants of Civil Rights Criminal Complaints in U.S. Municipalities." *Criminology* 38(2): 343–336.

Hook, M. 2001. "How and Why the System Is Failing Victims with Mental Impairments." *Crime Victims Report* 4(6): 81–82.

Hook, S. 1977. "Social Protest and Civil Disobedience." In *Moral Philosophy,* ed. P. Fink, 122–130. Encino, CA: Dickinson.

Hopfe, L. 1983. *Religions of the World.* New York: Macmillan.

Hornum, F., and F. Stavish. 1978. "Criminology Theory and Ideology: Four Analytical Perspectives in the Study of Crime and the Criminal Justice System." In *Essays on the Theory and Practice of Criminal Justice,* ed. R. Rich, 143–161. Washington, DC: University Press.

Houston, J. 1999. *Correctional Management: Functions, Skills, and Systems.* Chicago: Nelson-Hall.

Human Rights Watch. 1998. *Shielded from Justice: Police Brutality and Accountability in the U.S.* New York: Human Rights Watch.

Hunter, R. 1999. "Officer Opinions on Police Misconduct." *Journal of Contemporary Criminal Justice* 15(2): 155–170.

Huspek, M., R. Martinez, and L. Jiminez. 2001. "Violations of Human Civil Rights on the U.S.–Mexico Border, 1997–1997: A Report." In *Notable Selections in Criminal Criminology and Criminal Justice,* eds. D. Baker and R. Davin, 183–202. Guilford, CT: McGraw-Hill/Dushkin.

"Informant Killed." 1993. *Houston Post,* January 24: A20.

Ivković, S., and C. Klockars. 2004. "Police Integrity in Croatia." In *The Contours of Police Integrity,* eds. C. Klockars, S. Ivković, and M. Haberfeld, 56–74. Thousand Oaks, CA: Sage.

Jablon, R. 2000. "L.A. Confronts Police Scandal That May Cost Tens of Millions." *Austin American-Statesman,* February 19: A18.

Jaccoby, J., L. Mellon, and W. Smith. 1980. *Policy and Prosecution.* Washington, DC: Bureau of Social Science Research.

Jenson, E., and J. Gerber, 1996. "The Civil Forfeiture of Assets and the War on Drugs: Expanding Criminal Sanctions While Reducing Due Process Protection." *Crime and Delinquency* 42(3): 421–434.

Johnson, C., and G. Copus. 1981. "Law Enforcement Ethics: A Theoretical Analysis." In *The Social Basis of Criminal Justice: Ethical Issues for the 80's,* eds. F. Schmalleger and R. Gustafson, 39–83. Washington, DC: University Press.

Johnson, D. 2004. "Police Integrity in Japan." In *The Contours of Police Integrity,* eds. C. Klockars, S. Ivković, and M. Haberfeld, 130–160. Thousand Oaks, CA: Sage.

Johnson, L. 1982. "Frustration: The Mold of Judicial Philosophy." *Criminal Justice Ethics* 1(1): 20–26.

Johnson, R. 1987/1996/2002. *Hard Time: Understanding and Reforming the Prison.* Belmont, CA: Wadsworth.

Johnson, R. 1991. "A Life for a Life? Opinion and Debate." In *Justice, Crime, and Ethics,* eds. M. Braswell, B. McCarthy, and B. McCarthy, 199–210. Cincinnati: Anderson.

Johnston, M. 1995. "Police Corruption." In *Morality in Criminal Justice,* eds. D. Close and N. Meier. Belmont, CA: Wadsworth.

Josephson Institute of Ethics. 2005. *Preserving the Public Trust.* Available through www.josephsoninstitute.org.

Josi, D., and D. Sechrest. 1998. *The Changing Career of the Correctional Officer: Policy Implications for the 21st Century.* Boston: Butterworth-Heinemann.

Kamisar, Y., W. LeFave, and J. Israel. 1980. *Modern Criminal Procedure: Cases, Comments, and Questions.* St. Paul, MN: West.

Kane, R. 2002. "The Social Ecology of Police Misconduct." *Criminology* 40(4): 867–896.

Kania, R. 1988. "Police Acceptance of Gratuities." *Criminal Justice Ethics* 7(2): 37–49.

Kania, R. 1999. "The Ethics of the Death Penalty." *The Justice Professional* 12: 145–157.

Kania, R. 2004. "The Ethical Acceptability of Gratuities: Still Saying 'Yes' After All These Years." *Criminal Justice Ethics* 23(1): 54–63.

Kant, I. 1949. *Critique of Practical Reason,* trans. Lewis White Beck. Chicago: University of Chicago Press.

Kant, I. 1981. "Ethical Duties to Others: Truthfulness." In *Lectures on Ethics,* ed. L. Infield, 224–232. Indianapolis: Hackett.

Kaplan, M. 1976. *Justice, Human Nature and Political Obligation.* New York: Free Press.

Kappeler, V., M. Blumberg, and Potter, G. 2000/2005. *The Mythology of Crime and Justice.* Prospect Heights, IL: Waveland.

Kappeler, V., R. Sluder, and G. Alpert. 1984/1994. *Forces of Deviance: Understanding the Dark Side of Policing.* Prospect Heights, IL: Waveland.

Karmen, A. 1984. *Crime Victims: An Introduction to Victimology.* Pacific Grove, CA: Brooks/Cole.

Karp, D. 1998. "The Judicial and Judicious Use of Shame Penalties." *Crime and Delinquency* 44(2): 277–295.

Kauffman, K. 1988. *Prison Officers and Their World.* Cambridge, MA: Harvard University Press.

Keith, L. 2002. "Judicial Independence and Human Rights Protection Around the World." *Judicature* 84(4): 195–200.

Kessler, G. 1992. *Voices of Wisdom: A Multicultural Philosophy Reader.* Belmont, CA: Wadsworth.

King, R., and M. Mauer. 2001. *Aging Behind Bars: Three Strikes Seven Years Later.* Washington, DC: The Sentencing Project.

King, R., and M. Mauer. 2002. *State Sentencing and Corrections Policy in an Era of Fiscal Restraint.* Washington, DC: The Sentencing Project.

King, R., M. Mauer, and T. Huling. 2003. *Big Prisons, Small Towns: Prison Economics in Rural America.* Washington, DC: The Sentencing Project.

Kittel, N. 1990. "Criminal Defense Attorneys: Bottom of the Legal Profession's Class." In *Ethics in Criminal Justice,* ed. F. Schmalleger, 42–62. Bristol, IN: Wyndam Hall.

Kleindienst, L. 1999. "Florida Prison Guards Twice as Likely as Police to Commit Violations." *Sun-Sentinel* (Ft. Lauderdale), August 25: A1.

Kleinig, J. 1986. "The Conscientious Advocate and Client Perjury." *Criminal Justice Ethics* 5(2): 3–15.

Kleinig, J. 1999. "Human Dignity and Human Rights: An Emerging Concern in Police Practice." In *Human Dignity and Police: Ethics and Integrity in Police Work,* ed. G. Lynch, 8–40. Springfield, IL: Charles C. Thomas.

Kleinig, J. 2001. "National Security and Police Interrogations: Some Ethical Considerations." In *Policing, Security and Democracy: Special Aspects of Democratic Policing,* eds. S. Einstein and M. Amir, 105–127. Huntsville, TX: Office of International Criminal Justice (OICJ), Sam Houston State University.

Klockars, C. 1983. "The Dirty Harry Problem." In *Thinking About Police: Contemporary Readings,* ed. C. Klockars and S. Mastrofski, 428–438. New York: McGraw-Hill.

Klockars, C. 1984. "Blue Lies and Police Placebos." *American Behavioral Scientist* 27(4): 529–544.

Klockars, C., S. Ivković, and M. Haberfeld. 2004. *The Contours of Police Integrity.* Thousand Oaks, CA: Sage.

Klockars, C., S. Ivković, W. Harver, and M. Haberfeld. 2000. *The Measurement of Police Integrity? NIJ Research in Brief.* Washington, DC: U.S. Department of Justice.

Knudten, M. 1978. "The Prosecutor's Role in Plea Bargaining: Reasons Related to Actions." In *Essays on the Theory and Practice of Criminal Justice,* ed. R. Rich, 275–295. Washington, DC: University Press.

Kohlberg, L. 1976. "Moral Stages and Moralization." In *Moral Development and Behavior: Theory, Research and Social Issues,* ed. T. Lickona, 31–53. New York: Holt, Rinehart and Winston.

Kohlberg, L. 1983. *Essays in Moral Development,* Vol. 2. *The Psychology of Moral Development.* New York: Harper & Row.

Kohlberg, L. 1984. *The Psychology of Moral Development.* San Francisco: Harper & Row.

Kohlberg, L., and D. Candel, 1984. "The Relationship of Moral Judgment to Moral Action." In *The Psychology of Moral Development,* ed. L. Kohlberg, 498–582. San Francisco: Harper & Row.

Kottak, C. 1974. *Anthropology: The Exploration of Human Diversity.* New York: Random House.

Kramer, R. 1982. "The Debate Over the Definition of Crime: Paradigms, Value Judgments, and Criminological Work." In *Ethics, Public Policy and Criminal Justice,* eds. F. Elliston and N. Bowie, 33–59. Cambridge, MA: Oelgeschlager, Gunn and Hain.

Kraska, P., and V. Kappeler. 1995. "To Serve and Pursue: Exploring Police Sexual Violence Against Women." *Justice Quarterly* 12(1): 85–111.

Kraus, C. 1994. "Poll Finds a Lack of Faith in the Police." *New York Times,* June 19: A1.

Kravets, D. 2003. "ACLU: Privacy Rights Diminished." Salon.com. Retrieved January 16, 2003, from http://www.salon.com/tech/wire/2003/01/16/aclu/index.http.

Krisberg, B. 1975. *Crime and Privilege: Toward a New Criminology.* Englewood Cliffs, NJ: Prentice-Hall.

Krogstand, J., and J. Robertson. 1979. "Moral Principles for Ethical Conduct." *Management Horizons* 10(1): 13–24.

Kronenwerter, M. 1993. *Capital Punishment: A Reference Handbook.* Santa Barbara, CA: ABC–CLIO.

Lait, M., and S. Glover. 2000. "LAPD Chief Calls for Mass Dismissal of Tainted Cases." LATimes.com. Retrieved February, 1, 2000, from http://www.latimes.com/news/state/200000127/t000008518.http.

Laitinen, A. 2002. *Corruption of the Police: Is It Not at All a Problem in Finland?* Paper presented at ACJS, Anaheim, CA, March 2002.

Laitinen, A. 2004. "Corruption and Policing in Finland." In *Police Corruption: Challenges for Developed Countries,* eds. M. Amir and S. Einstein, 383–413. Huntsville, TX: Office of International Criminal Justice (OICJ), Sam Houston State University.

Lane, C. 2005. "5–4 Supreme Court Abolishes Juvenile Executions." *Washington Post,* March 2: A1.

Langford, T. 1997. "Company Defends Its Jailers' Conduct." *Austin American-Statesman,* August 22: B3.

Leahy, R. 1981. "Parental Practices and the Development of Moral Judgment and Self Image Disparity During Adolescence." *Developmental Psychology* 17(5): 580–594.

LeDuff, C. 2002. "Los Angeles Police Chief Faces a Huge Challenge." *New York Times.* Retrieved October, 25, 2002, from http://www.nytimes.com/2002/10/24/national/ 24GANG.html.

Leff, L. 2005. "Girl, 11, Avoids Jail for Assault." *Austin American-Statesman,* August 4: A18.

Leiser, B. 1986. *Liberty, Justice and Morals.* New York: Macmillan.

Lersch, K. (Ed.). 2002. *Policing and Misconduct.* Upper Saddle River, NJ: Prentice-Hall.

Lersch, K. 2002. "All Is Fair in Love and War." In *Policing and Misconduct,* ed. K. Lersch, 55–85. Upper Saddle River, NJ: Prentice-Hall.

Levine, C., L. Kohlberg, and A. Hewer. 1985. "The Current Formulation of Kohlberg's Theory and Response to Critics." *Human Development* (28): 94–100.

Levy, C. 2003a. "Prison Company's Courtship Provokes New York's Scrutiny." NYTimes.com. Retrieved on February, 20, 2003, from http://www.nytimes.com/2003/ 02/17/nyregion/17PRIS.http.

Levy, C. 2003b. "Prison Company Faces Fine on Gaps in Lobbying Records." NYTimes.com. Retrieved on February, 10, 2003, from http://www.nytimes.com/ 2003/02/06/nyregion/06LEGI.html.

Lewis, D. 1998. *Guilty by Reason of Insanity.* New York: Ivy.

Lewis, M. 1999. "Corcoran Guards Launch Ads." *Fresno Bee,* September 17: A1.

Lichtenberg, I., H. Lune, and P. McManimon. 2004. "'Darker Than Any Prison, Hotter Than Any Human Flame': Punishment, Choice, and Culpability in *A Clockwork Orange.*" *Journal of Criminal Justice Education* 15(2): 429–449.

Lickona, T. 1976. *Moral Development and Behavior: Theory, Research and Social Issues.* New York: Holt, Rinehart and Winston.

Lindquist, C. 1994. "Criminalistics in the Curriculum: Some Views from the Forensic Science Community." *Journal of Criminal Justice Education* 5(1): 59–68.

Liptak, A. 2003. "Houston DNA Lab Worst in Country, Experts Say." *Austin American-Statesman,* March 11: B1.

Liptak, A. 2004. "Study Suspects Thousands of False Convictions." NYTimes.com, April 19, 2004. Retrieved on April 20, 2004, from http://www.nytimes.com/2004/ 04/19/national/19DNA.html?pagewanted=print.

Liptak, A. 2005. "No, Life in Prison Means Exactly That." *Austin American-Statesman,* October 2: A7.

Liptak, A., and R. Blumenthal. 2004. "Death Sentences in Texas Cases Try Supreme Court's Patience." NYTimes.com, December 5, 2004. Retrieved on December 7, 2004, from http://www.nytimes.com/2004/12/05/national/05texas.html?oref=login&pagewanted=print.

Lombardo, L. 1981. *Guards Imprisoned: Correctional Officers at Work.* New York: Elsevier.

Lombardo, L. 1989. *Guards Imprisoned: Correctional Officers at Work.* Cincinnati: Anderson.

Lombardo, L. 1997. "Guards Imprisoned: Correctional Officers at Work." In *Correctional Contexts,* eds. J. Marquart and J. Sorensen, 189–203. Los Angeles: Roxbury.

Longmire, D. 1983. "Ethical Dilemmas in the Research Setting." *Criminology* 21(3): 333–348.

Lord, V., and B. Bjerregaard. 2003. "Ethics Courses: Their Impact on the Values and Ethical Decisions of Criminal Justice Students." *Journal of Criminal Justice Education* 14(2): 191–211.

Lucas, J. 1980. *On Justice.* Oxford, England: Oxford University Press.

Lundman, R., and R. Kaufman. 2003. "Driving While Black: Effects of Race, Ethnicity, and Gender on Citizen Self-Reports of Traffic Stops and Police Actions." *Criminology* 41(1): 195–220.

Lutwak, N., and J. Hennessy. 1985. "Interpreting Measures of Moral Development to Individuals." *Measurement and Evaluation in Counseling and Development* 18(1): 26–31.

Lynch, G. (Ed.). 1999. *Human Dignity and the Police: Ethics and Integrity in Police Work.* Springfield, IL: Charles C. Thomas.

Maas, P. 1973. *Serpico.* New York: Viking.

Maas, P. 1983. *Marie.* New York: Random House.

MacIntyre, A. 1991. *After Virtue.* South Bend, IN: University of Notre Dame Press.

MacIntyre, A. 1999. *Dependent Rational Animals: Why Human Beings Need the Virtues.* Chicago: Open Ct.

Macintyre, S., and T. Prenzler. 1999. "The Influence of Gratuities and Personal Relationships on Police Use of Discretion." *Policing and Society* 9: 181–201.

Mackie, J. L. 1977. *Ethics: Inventing Right and Wrong.* New York: Penguin.

Mackie, J. L. 1982. "Morality and the Retributive Emotions." *Criminal Justice Ethics* 1(1): 3–10.

Maestri, W. 1982. *Basic Ethics for the Health Care Professional.* Washington, DC: University Press.

Malloy, E. 1982. *The Ethics of Law Enforcement and Criminal Punishment.* Lanham, NY: University Press.

Mankiewicz, J. 2005. "Why Do We Care About Natalee, Laci, Jennifer?" MSNBC, *Dateline NBC.* Retrieved on September 5, 2005, from www.msnbc.msn.com/id/ 8667821.

Manning, P. 1997. *Policework,* 2d ed. Prospect Heights, IL: Waveland.

Manning, P., and L. Redlinger. 1991. "Invitational Edges." In *Thinking About Police: Contemporary Readings,* eds. C. Klockars and S. Mastrofski, 398–413. New York: McGraw-Hill.

Mappes, T. 1982. *Social Ethics.* New York: McGraw-Hill.

Margolis, J. 1971. *Values and Conduct.* New York: Oxford University Press.

Marks, F., F. Raymond, and D. Cathcart. 1986. "Discipline Within the Legal Profession." In *Ethics and the Legal Profession,* eds. M. Davis and F. Elliston, 62–105. Buffalo, NY: Prometheus.

Marquart, J., M. Barnhill, and K. Balshaw-Biddle. 2001. "Fatal Attraction: An Analysis of Employee Boundary Violations in a Southern Prison System, 1995–1998." *Justice Quarterly* 18(4): 877–911.

Marquart, J., and J. Roebuck. 1986. "Prison Guards and Snitches." In *The Dilemmas of Corrections: Contemporary Readings,* eds. K. Haus and G. Alpert, 158–176. Prospect Heights, IL: Waveland.

Marquez, J. 2005. "In Los Angeles, Computers Sniff Out Rogue Cops." *Austin-American-Statesman,* July 24: A15.

Martin, D. 1993. *Committing Journalism: The Writings of Red Hog.* New York: Norton.

Martinelli, T. 2000. *Combating the Charge of Deliberate Indifference Through Police Ethics Training and a Comprehensive Risk Management Policy.* Paper presented at the 2000 Annual Meeting of the Academy of Criminal Justice Sciences, New Orleans, LA.

Marx, G. 1985a. "Police Undercover Work: Ethical Deception or Deceptive Ethics?" In *Police Ethics: Hard Choices in Law Enforcement,* eds. W. Heffernan and T. Stroup, 83–117. New York: John Jay Press.

Marx, G. 1985b. "Who Really Gets Stung? Some Issues Raised by the New Police Undercover Work." In *Moral Issues in Police Work,* eds. F. Elliston and M. Feldberg, 99–129. Totawa, NJ: Rowman and Allanheld.

Marx, G. 1991. "The New Police Undercover Work." In *Thinking About Police: Contemporary Readings,* ed. C. Klockars and S. Mastrofski, 240–258. New York: McGraw-Hill.

Marx, G. 1992. "Under-the-Covers Undercover Investigations: Some Reflections on the State's Use of Deception." *Criminal Justice Ethics* 11(1): 13–25.

Massimino, E. 2004. "Leading by Example? U.S. Interrogation of Prisoners in the War on Terror." *Criminal Justice Ethics* 23(1): 2, 74–76.

Mastrofski, S., M. Reisig, and J. McCluskey. 2002. "Police Disrespect Toward the Public: An Encounter-Based Analysis." *Criminology* 40(3): 519–551.

Mather, L. 2003. "Ethics Symposium: What Do Clients Want? What Do Lawyers Do?" *Emory Law Journal* 52: 1065–1088.

Matthews, J., and R. Marshall. 1981. "Some Constraints on Ethical Behavior in Criminal Justice Organizations." In *The Social Basis of Criminal Justice: Ethical Issues for the 80's,* eds. F. Schmalleger and R. Gustafson, 9–22. Washington, DC: University Press.

Mauer, M., M. Chesney-Lind, and T. Clear. 2002. *Invisible Punishment: The Collateral Consequences of Mass Imprisonment.* New York: The Sentencing Project.

McAnany, P. 1981. "Justice in Search of Fairness." In *Justice as Fairness,* eds. D. Fogel and J. Hudson, 22–51. Cincinnati: Anderson.

McCarthy, B. 1991. "Keeping an Eye on the Keeper: Prison Corruption and Its Control." In *Justice, Crime, and Ethics,* eds. M. Braswell, B. McCarthy, and B. McCarthy, 239–253. Cincinnati: Anderson.

McCarthy, B. 1995. "Patterns of Prison Corruption." In *Morality in Criminal Justice,* eds. D. Close and N. Meier, 280–285. Belmont, CA: Wadsworth.

McGurrin, D., and V. Kappeler. 2002. "Media Accounts of Police Sexual Violence." In *Policing and Misconduct,* ed. K. Lersch, 121–142. Upper Saddle River, NJ: Prentice-Hall.

McMahan, J. 2004. "The Ethics of Killing in War." *Ethics* 114: 693–733.

McRoberts, F., and S. Mills. 2004. "From the Start, a Faulty Science." *Chicago Tribune—Online Edition.* Retrieved October 19, 2004, from http://www.chicagotribune.com/news/specials/chi-0410190150oct19,1,2959538,print.story.

McRoberts, F., S. Mills, and M. Possley. 2004. "Forensics Under the Microscope." *Chicago Tribune—Online Edition.* Retrieved October 19, 2004, from http://www. chicagotribune.com/news/specials/chi-0410170393oct17,1,7219383,print.story.

Meehan, A., and M. Ponder. 2002. "Race and Place: The Ecology of Racial Profiling African American Motorists." *Justice Quarterly* 19(3): 399–430.

Memory, J., and C. Rose. 2002. "The Attorney as Moral Agent: A Critique of Cohen." *Criminal Justice Ethics* 21(1): 28–39.

Messner, S., and R. Rosenfeld. 1994. *Crime and the American Dream.* Belmont, CA: Wadsworth.

Metz, H. 1990. "An Ethical Model for Law Enforcement Administrators." In *Ethics in Criminal Justice,* ed. F. Schmalleger, 95–103. Bristol, IN: Wyndam Hall.

Mieczkowski, T. 2002. "Drug Abuse, Corruption, and Officer Drug Testing." In *Policing and Misconduct,* ed. K. Lersch, 157–192. Upper Saddle River, NJ: Prentice-Hall.

Milgram, S. 1963. "Behavioral Study of Obedience." *Journal of Abnormal and Social Psychology* 67: 371–378.

Miller, A. 2005. "Predator Gets Probation." *San Marcos Daily Record,* August 18: A1, A10.

Miller, K., and M. Radelet. 1993. *Executing the Mentally Ill.* Newbury Park, CA: Sage.

Mills, S. 2005. "Texas May Have Put Innocent Man to Death." *Chicago Tribune,* April 20: A7.

Mills, S., and F. McRoberts. 2004. "Critics Tell Experts: Show Us the Science." *Chicago Tribune,* October 17: A18.

Mitchell, J., and S. Banks. 1996. "Once Again, Americans Fall into Racial Rut." *Austin American-Statesman,* February 9: B1.

Mobley, A., and G. Geis. 2002. "The Corrections Corporation of America a.k.a. The Prison Realty Trust, Inc." In *Justice, Crime and Ethics,* eds. M. Braswell, B. McCarthy, and B. McCarthy, 329–349. Cincinnati: Anderson.

Monahan, L., J. Monahan, M. Gaboury, and P. Niesyn. 2004. "Victims' Voices in the Correctional Setting: Cognitive Gains in an Offender Education Program." *Journal of Offender Rehabilitation* 39(3): 21–34.

Moore, M. 1997. *Police Integrity: Public Service Without Honor.* Washington, DC: U.S. Department of Justice.

Mores, T. 2002. "Police Misconduct: A Global Problem." *Crime and Justice Inter-national,* January: 9–10, 24–26.

Morris, R. 2000. *Stories of Transformative Justice.* Toronto: Canadian Scholars Press.

Moss, M., and F. Fessenden, 2002. "War Against Terrorism Stirs a Battle Over Privacy." *Austin American-Statesman,* December 11: A17–A19.

Muir, W. 1977. *Police: Streetcorner Politicians.* Chicago: University of Chicago Press.

Murphy, C. 2002. "Monitor Gives DC Police Mixed Review." *Washington Post.* Retrieved on August 8, 2002, from www.washingtonpost.com/wp-dyn/articles/A52807– 2002Aug6.http.

Murphy, J. 1985/1995. *Punishment and Rehabilitation.* Belmont, CA: Wadsworth.

Murphy, J. 1988. "Forgiveness, Mercy, and the Retributive Emotions." *Criminal Justice Ethics,* 7, 2: 3–15.

Murphy, K. 2002. "States Get Grants to Help Ex-Offenders." Stateline.org. Retrieved July 17, 2002, from www.stateline.org/story.do?storyID=248888.

Murphy, P., and D. Caplan. 1989. "Conditions That Breed Corruption." In *Critical Issues in Policing,* eds. R. Dunham and G. Alpert, 304–324. Prospect Heights, IL: Waveland.

Murphy, P., and K. Moran. 1981. "The Continuing Cycle of Systemic Police Corruption." In *The Social Basis of Criminal Justice: Ethical Issues for the 80's,* eds. F. Schmalleger and R. Gustafson, 87–101. Washington, DC: University Press.

Murton, T. 1976. *The Dilemma of Prison Reform.* New York: Irvington.

Murton, T., and Hyams, J. 1969. *Accomplices to the Crime: The Arkansas Prison Scandal.* New York: Grove.

"Muting Gideon's Trumpet: The Crisis in Indigent Defense." (2000). Report by the Committee on Legal Services to the Poor in Criminal Matters, Texas State Bar. Retrieved on January 2, 2005, from http://www.uta.edu/pols/moore/indigent.

Nash, L. 1981. "Ethics Without the Sermon." *Harvard Business Review,* November– December: 81.

National Institute of Justice. 1992. "Community Policing in the 1990s." *National Institute of Justice Research Bulletin,* August: 2–9.

Nelson, J. 2000. *Police Brutality.* New York: Norton.

Nettler, G. 1978. *Explaining Crime.* New York: McGraw-Hill.

Newman, G. 1978. *The Punishment Response.* New York: Lippincott.

Neyroud, P., and A. Beckley. 2001. *Policing, Ethics and Human Rights.* Devon, England: Willan.

Noddings, N. 1986. *Caring: A Feminine Approach to Ethics and Moral Education.* Berkeley: University of California Press.

Nowell, S. 2001. "Face to Face." *Houston Press,* September 27 to October 3.

Office of Juvenile Justice and Delinquency Prevention (OJJDP). 2001. *National Report Series Bulletin: Law Enforcement and Juvenile Crime,* December 2001. Washington, DC: U.S. Department of Justice.

Ogle, R. 1999. "Prison Privatization: An Environmental Catch 22." *Justice Quarterly* 14(3): 579–600.

O'Hagan, M. 2000. "Putting Police to Honesty Test." *Washington Post,* October 6: B1.

Packer, H. 1968. *The Limits of the Criminal Sanction.* Stanford, CA: Stanford University Press.

Palmer, T. 1994. *A Profile of Correctional Effectiveness and New Directions for Research.* Albany, NY: SUNY Press.

Paoline, E., S. Myers, and R. Worden. 2000. "Police Culture, Individualism, and Community Policing: Evidence from Two Police Departments." *Justice Quarterly* 17(3): 575–605.

Papke, D. 1986. "The Legal Profession and Its Ethical Responsibilities: A History." In *Ethics and the Legal Profession,* eds. M. Davis and F. Elliston, 29–49. Buffalo, NY: Prometheus.

Parenti, C. 1999. *Lockdown America: Police and Prisons in the Age of Crisis.* New York City: Verso (New Left Books).

Pasztor, D. 2003a. "Lawyer, Ex-Judges Fear Texas About to Kill an Innocent Man." *Austin American-Statesman,* March 6: A1, A11.

Pasztor, D. 2003b. "Rejected Appeals Leave Inmate with Execution Date a Day Away." *Austin American-Statesman,* March 11, 2003: A1.

Paul, R., and L. Elder. 2003. "Ethical Reasoning: The Foundation for Critical Thinking." Retrieved February 11, 2003, from www.criticalthinking.com.

Payne, D. 2002. *Police Liability: Lawsuits Against the Police.* Durham, NC: Carolina Academic Press.

Pearson, F. 2002. "The Effects of Behavioral/Cognitive–Behavioral Programs on Recidivism." *Crime and Delinquency* 48(3): 476–497.

Pellicotti, Joseph. 1990. "Ethics and the Criminal Defense: A Client's Desire to Testify Untruthfully." In *Ethics and Criminal Justice,* ed. F. Schmalleger, 67–78. Bristol, IN: Wyndam Hall.

Pepinsky, H. 1999. "Peacemaking Criminology and Social Justice." In *Social Justice/Criminal Justice,* ed. B. Arrigo, 51–69. Belmont, CA: Wadsworth.

Perez, E. 2001. "For Profit Prison Firm Wackenhut Tries to Break Shackles to Growth." *Wall Street Journal.* Retrieved May 15, 2001, from www.msnbc.com/news/ 570728.asp?cpi=1.

Perry, J. (Ed.). 2002. *Repairing Communities Through Restorative Justice.* Lanham, MD: American Correctional Association.

Piller, C. 2003. "FBI's Crime Scene Bullet Analysis Test Flawed." *Austin American-Statesman,* November 21, A28.

Piller, C., and R. Mejia. 2003. "FBI's Bullet Analysis Method Is Flawed, Studies Suggest." *Austin American-Statesman,* February 4: A8.

Pinkele, C., and W. Louthan. 1985. *Discretion, Justice and Democracy: A Public Policy Perspective.* Ames: Iowa State University Press.

Platt, A. 1977. *The Child Savers.* Chicago: University of Chicago Press.

Plohetski, T. 2002. "Hearing Resumes Today for Fired Austin Officer." *Austin American-Statesman,* November 18: B3.

Pollock, J. 2004. *Prisons and Prison Life: Costs and Consequences.* Los Angeles: Roxbury.

Possley, S. 2004. "Arson Myths Fuel Errors." *Chicago Tribune—Online Edition.* Retrieved October 19, 2004, from http://www.chicagotribune.com/news/specials/ chi0410180222oct18,1, 1517744,print.story.

Possley, S., S. Mills, and F. McRoberts. 2004. "Scandal Touches Even Elite Labs." *Chicago Tribune—Online Edition.* Retrieved October 25, 2004, from http://www.chicagotribune. com/technology/ chi-0410210285oct21,1,2398403,print.story.

Postema, G. 1986. "Moral Responsibility in Professional Ethics." In *Ethics and the Legal Profession,* eds. M. Davis and F. Elliston, 158–179. Buffalo, NY: Prometheus.

Poveda, T. 2001. "Estimating Wrongful Convictions." *Justice Quarterly* 18(3): 689–708.

Power, C., and L. Kohlberg. 1980. "Faith, Morality, and Ego Development." In *Toward Moral and Religious Maturity,* eds. J. Fowler and C. Bursselmans, 311–372. Morristown, NJ: Silver Burdett.

Pranis, K. 2001. "Sodexho to End Support for Right Wing Lobby." News Release. Retrieved April 20, 2001, from www.nomoreprisons.org.

Prenzler, T. 1995. "Police Gratuities: What the Public Thinks." *Criminal Justice Ethics* 14(1): 15–26.

Prenzler, T. 2000. "Civilian Oversight of Police: A Test of Capture Theory." *British Journal of Criminology* 40: 659–674.

Prenzler, T., A. Harrison, and A. Ede. 1996. "The Royal Commission into the NSW Police Service." *Current Affairs Bulletin,* April/May: 4–13.

Prenzler, T., and J. Ransley. 2002. *Police Reform: Building Integrity.* Sydney, Australia: Hawkins.

Prenzler, T., and C. Ronken. 2001a. "Police Integrity Testing in Australia." *Criminal Justice* 1(2): 319–342.

Prenzler, T., and C. Ronken. 2001b. "Models of Police Oversight: A Critique." *Policing and Society* 11: 151–180.

Price, A. 2005. "Soldier's Path Winds from Front Lines to Protest Line." *Austin American-Statesman,* September 19: A1, B9.

Prior, W. 1991. "Aristotle's Nicomanchean Ethics." In *From Virtue and Knowledge: An Introduction to Ancient Greek Ethics,* ed. W. Prior, 144–193. New York: Routledge, Kegan Paul.

Puonti, A., S. Vuorinen, and S. Ivković, 2004. "Sustaining Police Integrity in Finland." In *The Contours of Police Integrity,* eds. C. Klockars, S. Ivković, and M. Haberfeld, 95–115. Thousand Oaks, CA: Sage.

Quinney, R. 1974. *Critique of the Legal Order.* New York: Little, Brown.

Radelet, M., H. Bedau, and C. Putnam. 1992. *In Spite of Innocence: Erroneous Convictions in Capital Cases.* Boston: Northeastern University Press.

Raphael, D. 1980. *Justice and Liberty.* London: Athlone.

Rawls, J. 1957. "Outline of a Decision Procedure for Ethics." *Philosophical Review* 66: 177–197.

Rawls, J. 1971. *A Theory of Justice.* Cambridge, MA: Belknap.

Reasons, C. 1973. "The Politicalization of Crime, the Criminal and the Criminologist." *Journal of Criminal Law, Criminology and Police Science* 64 (March): 471–477.

Reichel, P. 1997. *Corrections.* Minneapolis: West.

Reiman, J. 1990/2004. *Justice and Modern Moral Philosophy.* New Haven, CT: Yale University Press.

Reiman, J. 2005. *The Rich Get Richer and the Poor Get Prison: Ideology, Class, and Criminal Justice.* Boston: Allyn & Bacon.

Reisig, M., J. McCluskey, S. Mastrofski, and W. Terrill. 2004. "Suspect Disrespect Toward the Police." *Justice Quarterly* 21(2): 241–268.

Reisig, M., and R. Parks. 2000. "Experience, Quality of Life, and Neighborhood Context: A Hierarchical Analysis of Satisfaction with Police." *Justice Quarterly* 17(3): 607–630.

Report of the Commission on Obscenity and Pornography. 1970. *Final Report.* New York: Random House.

Reuss-Ianni, E. 1983. *Two Cultures of Policing: Street Cops and Management Cops.* New Brunswick, NJ: Transaction.

Rich, R. 1978. *Essays on the Theory and Practice of Criminal Justice.* Washington, DC: University Press.

Riddle, A. 2001. "Recent Murder Trial Sparks Debate." *ABC News.* Retrieved on May 21, 2001, from http://dailynews.yahoo.com/h/ap/20010518/vs/young_killers/.http.

Rimer, S. 2000. "Lawyer Sabotaged Case of a Client on Death Row." *New York Times,* November 24, 2000. Retrieved on November, 11, 2002, from http://www.againstdp. org/sabotage.http.

Roach, K. 2000. "Changing Punishment at the Turn of the Century: Restorative Justice on the Rise." *Canadian Journal of Criminology* 42(3): 249–269.

Roberg, K. 1981. "Management Research in Criminal Justice: Exploring Ethical Issues." *Journal of Criminal Justice* 9: 41–49.

Robinson, C. 2003. "Perry Wants Review of Convictions in 1999 Sting." *Houston Chronicle,* May 14: A02.

Rodin, D. 2004. "Terrorism Without Intention." *Ethics* 114: 752–771.

Roser, M. A. 1996. "Business Study Finds Women More Ethical." *Austin American-Statesman,* December 26: A1, A11.

Roth, A., and J. Roth. 1989. *Devil's Advocates: The Unnatural History of Lawyers.* Berkeley, CA: Nolo.

Rothbart, M., D. Hanley, and M. Albert. 1986. "Differences in Moral Reasoning." *Sex Roles* 15(11/12): 645–653.

Rothlein, S. 1999. "Policy Agency Efforts to Prevent Abuses." In *Human Dignity and the Police: Ethics and Integrity in Police Work,* ed. G. Lynch, 15–27. Springfield, IL: Charles C. Thomas.

Ruiz, J., and C. Bono. 2004. "At What Price a 'Freebie'? The Real Cost of Police Gratuities." *Criminal Justice Ethics* 23(1): 44–54.

Ryan, J. 2002. "The Appearance of Ethics." *Austin American-Statesman,* November 16: A11.

Salladay, R. 1999. "Prison Guard Union, Davis Cozy Pairing," *San Francisco Examiner,* September 14: B3.

*San Antonio Express News.* 2002. "Lawyers Should Not Aid, Abet Wrongdoers." *San Antonio Express News,* December 29: 2H.

Sapp, A. 1994. "Sexual Misconduct by Police Officers." In *Police Deviance,* 3rd ed., eds. T. Barker and D. Carter, 187–200. Cincinnati: Anderson.

Schafer, J. 2002. "Community Policing and Police Corruption." In *Policing and Misconduct,* ed. K. Lersch, 193–217. Upper Saddle River, NJ: Prentice-Hall.

Schanberg, S. 2002. "A Journey Through the Tangled Case of the Central Park Jogger." *Village Voice.* Retrieved on September 5, 2005, from www.villagevoice.com/generic/ show_print. php?id=39999&page=schanberg&issue=O.

Schehr, R., and J. Sears. 2005. "Innocence Commissions: Due Process Remedies and Protection for the Innocent." *Critical Criminology* 13(2): 181–209.

Schehr, R., and L. Weathered. 2004. "Should the United States Establish a Criminal Cases Review Commission." *Judicature* 88(3): 122–145.

Scheingold, S. 1984. *The Politics of Law and Order.* New York: Longman.

Schoeman, F. 1982. "Friendship and Testimonial Privileges." In *Ethics, Public Policy and Criminal Justice,* eds. F. Elliston and N. Bowie, 257–272. Cambridge, MA: Oelgeschlager, Gunn and Hain.

Schoeman, F. 1985. "Privacy and Police Undercover Work." In *Police Ethics: Hard Choices in Law Enforcement,* eds. W. Heffernan and T. Stroup, 133–153. New York: John Jay Press.

Schoeman, F. 1986. "Undercover Operations: Some Moral Questions About S. 804." *Criminal Justice Ethics* 5(2): 16–22.

Schweigert, F. 2002. "Moral and Philosophical Foundations of Restorative Justice," In *Repairing Communities Through Restorative Justice,* ed. J. Perry, 19–37. Lanham, MD: American Correctional Association.

Sellin, T. 1970. "The Conflict of Conduct Norms." In *The Sociology of Crime and Delinquency,* eds. M. Wolfgang, L. Savitz, and N. Johnston, 186–189. New York: Wiley.

Serrano, R., and R. Ostrow. 2000. "Probe of FBI Lab Reviews 3,000 Cases—Affects None." LATimes.com. Retrieved August 21, 2000, from http://www.latimes.com/ news/front/ 20000817/t0000077169.http.

Shakespeare, W. 1969. *The Merchant of Venice,* Act IV, Scene i, *William Shakespeare: The Complete Works.* Baltimore: Penguin.

Shea, C. 2005. "Disaster Experts Rebut Tales of Looting." *Austin American-Statesman,* September 18: H1, H4.

Sheley, J. 1985. *Exploring Crime.* Belmont, CA: Wadsworth.

Sherman, L. 1981. *The Teaching of Ethics in Criminology and Criminal Justice.* Washington, DC: Joint Commission on Criminology and Criminal Justice Education and Standards, LEAA.

Sherman, L. 1982. "Learning Police Ethics." *Criminal Justice Ethics* 1(1): 10–19.

Sherman, L. 1985a. "Becoming Bent: Moral Careers of Corrupt Policemen." In *Moral Issues in Police Work,* eds. F. Elliston and M. Feldberg, 253–273. Totawa, NJ: Rowman and Allanheld.

Sherman, L. 1985b. "Equity Against Truth: Value Choices in Deceptive Investigations." In *Police Ethics: Hard Choices in Law Enforcement,* eds. W. Heffernan and T. Stroup, 117–133. New York: John Jay Press.

Silberman, M. 1995. *A World of Violence: Corrections in America.* Belmont, CA: Wadsworth.

Simerman, J., D. Ott, and T. Mellnik. 2005. "Early Data Challenge Assumptions About Katrina Victims." *Austin American-Statesman,* December 30: A1, A8.

Skolnick, J. 1982. "Deception by Police." *Criminal Justice Ethics* 1(2): 40–54.

Skolnick, J., and J. Fyfe. 1993. *Above the Law: Police and the Excessive Use of Force.* New York: Free Press.

Skolnick, J., and R. Leo. 1992. "Ideology and the Ethics of Crime Control." *Criminal Justice Ethics* 11(1): 3–13.

Smilansky, S. 2004. "Terrorism, Justification and Illusion." *Ethics* 114: 790–805.

Smith, B., and M. Holmes. 2003. "Community Accountability, Minority Threat, and Police Brutality: An Examination of Civil Rights Criminal Complaints." *Criminology* 41(4): 1035–1063.

Smith, D. 1982. "Ideology and the Ethics of Economic Crime Control." In *Ethics, Public Policy and Criminal Justice,* eds. F. Elliston and N. Bowie, 133–156. Cambridge, MA: Oelgeschlager, Gunn and Hain.

Smith, M., and G. Alpert. 2002. "Searching for Direction: Courts, Social Science, and the Adjudication of Racial Profiling Claims." *Justice Quarterly* 19(4): 673–703.

Smith, S., and R. Meyer. 1987. *Law, Behavior, and Mental Health.* New York: New York University Press.

Sniffen, M. 1997. "FBI Suspends Agent Whose Charges Led to Critical Report." *Austin American-Statesman,* January 28: A5.

Snyder, H. 2004. *Juvenile Arrests—2002.* Washington, DC: U.S. Department of Justice/ OJJDP.

Solomon, A. 1999. "Wackenhut Detention Ordeal." *Village Voice.* Retrieved on March 5, 1999, from http://www.villagevoice.com/features/9935/solomon.html.

"Sorry, No Breaks!" 1996. *Ethics Roll Call* 3(1): 2.

Souryal, S. 1992. *Ethics in Criminal Justice: In Search of the Truth.* Cincinnati: Anderson.

Souryal, S. 1996a. "Probation as Good Faith." *Texas Probation* 11(3): 1–6.

Souryal, S. 1996b. "Personal Loyalty to Superiors in Public Service." *Criminal Justice Ethics,* Summer/Fall: 44–62.

Souryal, S. 1999a. "Corruption of Prison Personnel." In *Prison and Jail Administration: Practice and Theory,* eds. P. Carlson and J. Garrett, 171–177. Gaithersburg, MD: Aspen.

Souryal, S. 1999b. "Personal Loyalty to Superiors in Criminal Justice Agencies." *Justice Quarterly* 16(4): 871–906.

Souryal, S., and Potts, D. 1996. "What Am I Supposed to Fall Back On? Cultural Literacy in Criminal Justice Ethics." *Journal of Criminal Justice Education* 4: 15–41.

South, N. 2001. "Police, Security and Information: The Use of Informants and Agents in a Liberal Democracy." In *Policing, Security and Democracy: Special Aspects of Democratic Policing,* eds. S. Einstein and M. Amir, 87–105. Huntsville, TX: Office of International Criminal Justice (OICJ), Sam Houston State University.

Sowers, C. 2001. "Lawyers Seek Panel to Investigate When Innocents Sent to Prison." *Arizona Republic.* Retrieved on November 12, 2001, from http://www.arizonarepublic.com/arizona/articles/1112innocence12.html.

Spader, D. 1984. "Rule of Law v. Rule of Man: The Search for the Golden Zigzag Between Conflicting Fundamental Values." *Journal of Criminal Justice* 12: 379–394.

Spence, G. 1989. *With Justice for None.* New York: Penguin.

Stace, W. 1995. "Ethical Relativity and Ethical Absolutism." In *Morality and Criminal Justice,* eds. D. Close and N. Meier, 25–32. Belmont, CA: Wadsworth.

Staples, W. 1997. *The Culture of Surveillance.* New York: St. Martin's.

Stefanic, M. 1981. "Police Ethics in a Changing Society." *The Police Chief,* May: 62–64.

Sterba, J. 1980. *The Demands of Justice.* Notre Dame, IN: University of Notre Dame Press.

Sterngold, J. 2000. "Los Angeles Police Admit a Vast Management Lapse." *New York Times,* March 2: A14.

Stewart, D., and M. Totman. 2005. *Don't Mind If I Take a Look, Do Ya? An Examination of Consent Searches and Contraband Hit Rates at Texas Traffic Stops.* Austin, TX: Texas Criminal Justice Coalition.

Stickels, J. 2003. *The Victim Satisfaction Model in Criminal Justice.* Ph.D. dissertation, University of Texas.

Stitt, B., and G. James. 1985. "Entrapment: An Ethical Analysis." In *Moral Issues in Police Work,* eds. F. Elliston and M. Feldberg, 129–147. Totawa, NJ: Rowman and Allanheld.

Stover, R. 1989. *Making It and Breaking It: The Fate of Public Interest Commitment During Law School,* ed. H. Erlanger. Urbana: University of Illinois Press.

Stuntz, W. 2002. "Terrorism, Federalism, and Police Misconduct." *Harvard Journal of Law and Public Policy* 25(2): 665–680.

Sutton, L. 1991. "Getting Around the Fourth Amendment." In *Thinking About Police: Contemporary Readings,* ed. C. Klockars and S. Mastrofski, 433–446. New York: McGraw-Hill.

Sykes, G. 1980. "The Defects of Total Power." In *Keepers: Prison Guards and Contemporary Corrections,* ed. B. Crouch. Springfield, IL: Charles C. Thomas.

Sykes, G. 1989. "The Functional Nature of Police Reform: The Myth of Controlling the Police." In *Critical Issues in Policing,* eds. R. Dunham and G. Alpert, 292–304. Prospect Heights, IL: Waveland.

Sykes, G. 1996. "How Much Is Our Credibility Worth?" *Ethics Roll Call* 3(1): 5.

Talbot, M. 2003. "Catch and Release." *The Atlantic online.* Retrieved January 23, 2003, from http://www.thatlantic.com/cgi-bin/send.cgi?page=http%2A//www.theatlantic. com/ issues.

Talvi, S. 2002. "The Other War." *The Nation,* December 24.

Tanay, E. 1982. "Psychiatry and the Prison System." *Journal of Forensic Sciences* 27(2): 385–392.

Tanner, R. 2002. "Central Park Case Puts Focus on Confessions." *Austin American-Statesman,* December 7: A9.

Tarnoff, S. 2001. "Hard Line on a White Lie." *ABA Journal* 87: 32–33.

Taylor, W. 1993. *Brokered Justice: Race Politics and Mississippi Prisons 1798–1992.* Columbus: Ohio State University Press.

Teepen, T. 1996. "For Private Prisons, Crime Does Pay." *Austin American-Statesman,* December 12: A15.

Terrill, W. 2001. *Police Coercion: Application of the Force Continuum.* New York: LFB Scholarly Publishing.

Terrill, W., and S. Mastrofsky. 2002. "Situational and Officer-Based Determinants of Police Coercion." *Justice Quarterly* 19(2): 216–248.

Terrill, W., E. Paoline, and P. Manning. 2003. "Police Culture and Coercion." *Criminology* 41(4): 1003–1034.

Thevenot, B., and G. Russell. 2005. "No Evidence Supports Tales of Murder, Rape." *Austin American-Statesman,* September 28: A1, A7.

Thoma, S. 1986. "Estimating Gender Differences in the Comprehension and Preference of Moral Issues." *Developmental Review* 6: 165–180.

Thompson, D. 1980. "Paternalism in Medicine, Law and Public Policy." In *Ethics Teaching in Higher Education,* eds. D. Callahan and S. Bok, 3–20. Hastings, NY: Hastings Center.

Thompson, D. 2004. "Prison System Blasted by Lawmakers, New Administration." Sandiego.com, January 20, 2004. Retrieved on January 22, 2004, from http://signonsandiego.com/news/state/20040120–1658-ca-prisonhearings.html.

"Three Guards Acquitted." 2002. *New York Times,* February 16: A13.

Timerman, J. 1981. *Prisoner Without a Name, Cell Without a Number,* trans. Toby Talbot. New York: Knopf.

Toch, H. 1977. *Living in Prison.* New York: Free Press.

Toch, H. 1997. *Humanistic Corrections.* Guilderland, NY: Harrow and Heston.

Toch, H., and J. Klofas. 1982. "Alienation and Desire for Job Enrichment Among C.O.s." *Federal Probation* 46: 35–47.

Tonry, M. 2005. "The Functions of Sentencing and Sentencing Reform." *Stanford Law Review* 58: 37–67.

Tonry, M., L. Ohlin, and D. Farrington. 1991. *Human Development and Criminal Behavior.* New York: Springer Verlag.

Toohey, M. 2005. "Soldier a Willing Participant, Prosecutors Say." 2005. *Austin American-Statesman,* September 23: B1, B3.

Toomey, S. 2000. "Unusual Defenses Work for Alaskans Charged with Prison Escape." *Anchorage Daily News,* March 1, 2000. Retrieved March 7, 2000, from http:// www.adn.com/stories/T00030167.html.

Transparency International. 2003. "Annual Report." Retrieved on December 30, 2005, from www.transparency.org/publications.

Tyler, T. 1990. *Why People Obey the Law.* New Haven, CT: Yale University Press.

Umbreit, M. 1994. *Victim Meets Offender: The Impact of Restorative Justice and Mediation.* Monsey, NY: Criminal Justice Press.

Umbreit, M., and M. Carey. 1995. "Restorative Justice Implications for Organizational Change." *Federal Probation* 59(1): 47–54.

Umbreit, M., R. Coates, and B. Vos. 2002. "Peacemaking Circles in Minnesota: An Exploratory Study." *Crime Victims Report* 5(6): 81–82.

Uniform Crime Reports (U.C.R.). 1998. *Crime in the United States.* Washington, DC: U.S. Department of Justice.

Van Maanen, J. 1978. "The Asshole." In *Policing: A View From the Street,* eds. P. Manning and J. van Maanen, 221–240. Santa Monica, CA: Goodyear.

Van Natta, D. 2003. "Blurry Line Marks Banned, Acceptable in Interrogations." *Austin American-Statesman,* March 2: A13.

Van Ness, D., and K. Heetderks Strong. 1997. *Restoring Justice.* Cincinnati: Anderson.

Vogelstein, R. 2003. "Confidentiality vs. Care: Re-evaluating the Duty to Self, Client, and Others." *Georgetown Law Journal* 92: 153–171.

von Hirsch, A. 1976. *Doing Justice.* New York: Hill and Wang.

von Hirsch, A. 1985. *Past or Future Crimes.* New Brunswick, NJ: Rutgers University Press.

von Hirsch, A., and L. Maher. 1992. "Can Penal Rehabilitation Be Revived?" *Criminal Justice Ethics* 11(1): 25–31.

Walker, L. 1986. "Sex Difference in the Development of Moral Reasoning." *Child Development* 57: 522–526.

Walker, S. 1985/2000. *Sense and Nonsense About Crime.* Monterey, CA: Brooks/Cole.

Walker, S. 2001. *Police Accountability: The Role of Citizen Oversight.* Belmont, CA: Wadsworth.

Walker, S., and G. Alpert. 2002. "Early Warning Systems as Risk Management for Police." In *Policing and Misconduct,* ed. K. Lersch, 219–230. Upper Saddle River, NJ: Prentice-Hall.

Walker, S., C. Spohn, and M. DeLone. 2000. *The Color of Justice.* Belmont, CA: Wadsworth.

Walsh, A. 1995. *Biosociology: An Emerging Paradigm.* Trenton, NY: Praeger.

Walsh, A. 2000. "Evolutionary Psychology and the Origins of Justice." *Justice Quarterly* 17(4): 841–864.

Walsh, A. 2001. *Biosocial Criminology: Introduction and Integration.* Cincinnati: Anderson.

Ward, G. 2001. "C.C.A. Majority Shareholder to Sell Stocks." *Tennessean.* Retrieved May 23, 2001, from www.tennessean.com/business/archives/01/04/05094888.shtml?Element_ ID=50948.

Ward, M. 1996. "State Approves Faith-Based Pre-Release Program for Texas Inmates." *Austin American-Statesman,* November 16: B12.

Ward, M. 2004. "Echoes of Texas' Sordid Past in Iraq Prison Abuse." *Austin American-Statesman,* May 12: B4.

Warren, J. 2004. "Guards Tell of Retaliation for Informing." LATimes.com, January 21, 2004. Retrieved Janaury 22, 2004, from http://www.latimes.com/news/local/la-me-prison?1jan21,1, 1780985.story?coll=la-headlines-california.

Warren, J. 2004. "State Penal System Is Hammered in Report." LATimes.com. Retrieved September 19, 2004, from http://www.latimes.com/news/local/la-me-prisons16Jan16,1, 6085723.story?coll=la-home-headlines.

Weber, D. 1987. "Still in Good Standing. The Crisis in Attorney Discipline." *American Bar Association Journal,* November: 58–63.

Weisburd, D., and R. Greenspan. 2000. *Police Attitudes Toward Abuse of Authority: Findings from a National Study (Research In Brief).* Washington, DC: U.S. Department of Justice.

Weitzer, R. 1999. "Citizens' Perceptions of Police Misconduct: Race and Neighborhood Context." *Justice Quarterly* 16(4): 819–846.

Weitzer, R., and S. Tuch. 2000. "Reforming the Police: Racial Differences in Public Support for Change." *Criminology* 38(2): 391–416.

Weitzer, R., and S. Tuch. 2002. "Perceptions of Racial Profiling: Race, Class, and Personal Experience." *Criminology* 40(2): 435–456.

West, W., and R. Morris (Eds.). 2000. *The Case for Penal Abolition.* Toronto, ON: Canadian Scholars Press.

Westmarland, L. 2004. "Policing Integrity: Britain's Thin Blue Line." In *The Contours of Police Integrity,* eds. C. Klockars, S. Ivković, and M. Haberfeld, 75–94. Thousand Oaks, CA: Sage.

White, J. 2005. "Documents Tell of Brutal Improvisation by GIs." *Washington Post,* August 3: A1.

Whitehead, J. 1991. "Ethical Issues in Probation and Parole." In *Justice, Crime, and Ethics,* eds. M. Braswell, B. McCarthy, and B. McCarthy, 253–273. Cincinnati: Anderson.

Whitlock, C. 2005. "CIA Role in Abductions Investigated." *Austin American-Statesman,* March 13: A5.

Whitman, J. 1998. "What Is Wrong with Inflicting Shame Sanctions?" *Yale Law Journal* 197(4): 1055–1092.

Wiley, L. 1988. "Moral Education in a Correctional Setting: Reaching the Goal by a Different Road." *Journal of Offender Services and Rehabilitation* 12(2): 161–174.

Williams, G. 1984. *The Law and Politics of Police Discretion.* Westport, CT: Greenwood.

Wilson, J. Q. 1976. *Varieties of Police Behavior.* New York: Atheneum.

Wilson, J. Q. 1993. *The Moral Sense.* New York: Free Press.

Wilson, M., and R. Barry Ruback. 2003. "Hate Crimes in Pennsylvania, 1984–1999: Case Characteristics and Police Responses." *Justice Quarterly* 20(2): 373–398.

Wood, D. 2003. "Registration for Arabs Draws Fire." FindLaw.com. Retrieved February 10, 2003, from http://news.findlaw.com/csmonitor/s/20030206/ 06feb2003104706.http.

Wood, J. 1997. *Royal Commission into the New South Wales Police Service, Final Report.* Sydney: Government of the State of N.S.W. (cited in T. Prenzler and C. Ronken, 2001).

Worden, R., and S. Catlin. 2002. "The Use and Abuse of Force by Police." In *Policing and Misconduct,* ed. K. Lersch, 85–120. Upper Saddle River, NJ: Prentice-Hall.

Worrall, J. 2001. "Addicted to Drug War: The Role of Civil Asset Forfeiture as a Budgetary Necessity in Contemporary Law Enforcement." *Journal of Criminal Justice* 29(3): 171–187.

Worrall, J. 2002. "If You Build It They Will Come: Consequences of Improved Citizen Complaint Review Procedures." *Crime and Delinquency* 48(3): 355–379.

Wozencraft, Kim. 1990. *Rush*. New York: Random House.

Wren, T. 1985. "Whistle-blowing and Loyalty to One's Friends." In *Police Ethics: Hard Choices in Law Enforcement*, eds. W. Heffernan and T. Stroup, 25–47. New York: John Jay Press.

Zernike, K. 2001. "Crackdown on Threats in Schools Fails a Test." *New York Times*. Retrieved on May 17, 2001, from www.nytimes.com/2001/05/17/nyregion/ 17THRE.html.

Zhao, J., N. He, and N. Lovrich. 1998. "Individual Value Preferences Among American Police Officers." *Policing: An International Journal of Police Strategies and Management* 21(1): 22–37.

Zimbardo, P. 1982. "The Prison Game." In *Legal Process and Corrections,* eds. N. Johnston and L. Savitz, 195–198. New York: Wiley.

Zimmer, L. 1986. *Women Guarding Men*. Chicago: University of Chicago Press.

Zimring, F., G. Hawkins, and S. Kamin. 2001. *Punishment and Democracy: Three Strikes and You're Out in California*. Oxford, England: Oxford University Press.

Zohar, N. 2004. "Innocence and Complex Threats: Upholding the War Ethic and the Condemnation of Terrorism." *Ethics* 114: 734–751.

Zupan, L. 1992. "The Progress of Women Correctional Officers in All-Male Prisons." In *The Changing Roles of Women in the Criminal Justice System*, ed. I. Moyer, 323–343. Prospect Heights, IL: Waveland.

# Name Index

# Subject Index

# Table of Cases